Maps. 502. 81. 1

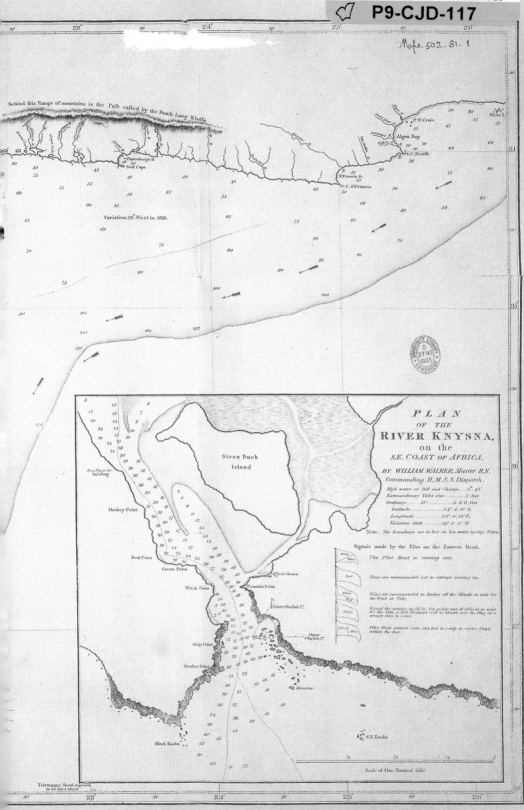

PLAN
OF THE
RIVER KNYSNA,
on the
S.E. COAST of AFRICA.

BY WILLIAM WALKER, Master R.N.
Commanding H.M.S.S. Dispatch.

High water at Full and Change ___ 5ʰ.45ᵐ
Extraordinary Tides rise ___ 7 feet
Ordinary ___ Dᵒ ___ 5 · 8 · 6 feet
Latitude ___ 34°. 4 .0" S.
Longitude ___ 23°. 6. 15" E.
Variation 1818 ___ 29°. 6 . 0" W.

Note, The Soundings are in feet at low water spring Tides.

Signals made by the Pilot on the Eastern Head.

The Pilot Boat is coming out.

Ships are recommended not to attempt coming in.

Ships are recommended to Anchor off the Mouth, to wait for the Wind or Tide.

Signal for coming in, if in for going out, if obliged to wait for the Tide, a Red Pendant will be shown over the Flag at a proper time to come.

Pilot Boat cannot come out, but is ready to receive Ships within the Bar.

Behind this Range of mountains is the Pass called by the Dutch Lang Kloff.

Plattenbergs B.
Seal Cape

Variation 29° West in 1818.

Lt. St. Croix
Algoa Bay
Cn. C. Recliffe
St. Francis B.
C. St. Francis

Steen Buck Island

Best Place for Building

Monkey Point

Best Cove

Green Point

Black Point

Ship Point

Needles Point

Black Rocks

Pilots House

Fountain Point

Inner Obelisk Pt.

Outer Obelisk Pt.

Minstone

S.E. Rocks

Scale of One Nautical Mile

Telemaque Shoal supposed to be here about

Dec.ʳ 1.1818. according to Act of Parliament.

RICA

A NARRATIVE HISTORY

BY THE SAME AUTHOR

The Profit of the State
The Afflicted State
Uneasy City
Building the Trireme
First Blood
The Companion Guide to the Lake District
A Borrowed Place: The History of Hong Kong

SOUTH AFRICA

A NARRATIVE
HISTORY

FRANK WELSH

Kodansha International
NEW YORK · TOKYO · LONDON

Kodansha America, Inc.
114 Fifth Avenue, New York, New York 10011, U.S.A

Kodansha International Ltd.
17–14 Otowa 1-chome, Bunkyo-ku, Tokyo 112, Japan

Published in 1999 by Kodansha America, Inc.

Library of Congress Cataloging-in-Publication Data

Welsh, Frank.
        South Africa : a narrative history / Frank Welsh.
              p.   cm.
        Includes bibliographical references and index.
        ISBN 1-56836-258-7 (alk. paper)
        1. South Africa--History.   I. Title.
DT1787.W45   1998
968--dc21

Book design by Vera Brice

Manufactured in The United States of America

99   00   01   02   10 9 8 7 6 5 4 3 2 1

CONTENTS

LIST OF ILLUSTRATIONS ix

LIST OF MAPS xiii

ACKNOWLEDGEMENTS xvii

INTRODUCTION xix

1 The Fairest Cape
in the Whole Circumference
of the Earth 1

The dogs bark just as they do in Portugal 1
The other Honorable Company 12
Coree's people 15

2 An Inn on the Road to the Indies 21

A dry and barren waste 21
Dull, stupid, lazy, stinking people 28
The anticipated profits disappear in smoke 33

3 Victualling Station to Colony 40

The first Afrikaners 50
Dangers, expense, and troubles 55
Khoikhoi to Hottentot 61
Towards the end of the Honorable Company 65

4 The Last Days of the Honorable Company 68

Among the finest specimens of the human race 68
The Hundred Years War begins 79

5 Kaapstad to Cape Town   88

The Redcoats' first arrival   88
Efficient protection and occasional acts of kindness   92
An idealistic interlude   96
Revolutionaries in black coats   105

6 Alarms and Excursions   116

Baneful radical influences   116
Washing the spears   136

7 The Myth of the Great Trek   146

Nerves and bowels in agitation   146
A more formidable enemy   158
The camp at Thaba Nchu   164
The Republic of Natalia   169
As a body they are ignorant and wicked   175

8 Ruthless Worthless Savages   184

If the savages retaliate no one can blame them   190
We want no more church-going niggers   195
Representative government   198
Transorangia: the Empire draws back   203
Natal: the peace and security which
*   a good government affords*   209

9 First Steps to Self-Government   216

The emergent republics   221

10 Uncertain Imperialists   234

The rock on which South Africa will be built   234
Griqualand West   240
Responsible government   243

Contents

Kaffir justice: guilty until proved innocent   247

Twitters at the helm   250

Zululand delenda est   262

Majuba   267

11   Picking up the Pieces   274

Westminster   275

A mistake as well as a crime   277

This Bechuana business   280

The Cape Parliament   286

The wretched little colony   296

The Orange Free State   298

12   War   300

The City of Gold   300

We have got the Maxim gun, and they have not   307

A fiasco would be most disastrous   315

All for a people whom we despise   321

13   Peace   338

A shameful peace   338

You have only to sacrifice the 'nigger'   348

The return of the Liberals   357

14   The Union of South Africa   364

Flabby friends   364

Chiefs of royal blood and gentlemen of our race   374

'You cannot govern South Africa
   by trampling on the Dutch'   379

15   Pact and Fusion   390

Post-war traumas   390

Afrikaner resurgence   399

The purified politicians   405

16 The Shadows of Apartheid   414

   Homespun fascists   414
   Afrikaner apotheosis   427
   The protectorates   435

17 The Era of Show Trials   444

   Only temporary residents   444
   Wind of change   453
   A nation mourns   461

18 Disintegration   474

   We hate the language and we hate the owners of it   474
   The Great Crocodile   479
   The beginning of the end   493

19 Such a Tumultuous Land   500

   NOTES   515
   BIBLIOGRAPHY   549
   INDEX   575

ILLUSTRATIONS

Between pages 132 and 133

Martellus' world map. c.1490. (*British Library, Add.15760.Fol.68v–69*)

Seventeenth-century sketch of Khoikhoi women dancing. (*South African Library, Cape Town*)

Engraving of 1742, showing Kaapstad as a modest settlement. (*South African Library, Cape Town*)

Lady Anne Barnard's sketch of a Coloured wetnurse suckling a white baby. (*South African Library, Cape Town*)

Rosina, a Khoi-San girl photographed in 1860. (*South African Library, Cape Town*)

A horrific crossing of the Outeniekwaberge, near the town of George. (*National Archives of South Africa, Cape Town*)

Zulu warrior in parade dress. (*South African Library, Cape Town*)

Sotho warrior. (*South African Library, Cape Town*)

Meeting of the Anti-Slavery Convention in Exeter Hall, London, in 1840 (*National Portrait Gallery, London*)

Anti-Stockenström propaganda: cartoon by Frederick l'Ons, 1838. (*Brenthurst Library, Cape Town*)

Sarili (1815–92), paramount chief of the Xhosa. (*National Archives of South Africa, Cape Town*)

Moshoeshoe (c.1787–1870), founder of the Basuto nation. (*South African Library, Cape Town*)

Adam Kok III (1811–75), Griqua chief. (*National Archives of South Africa, Cape Town*)

Langalibalele (1818–89), leader of the Natalian Hlubi people. (*National Archives of South Africa, Cape Town*)

Thomas Baines sketch of 1870, showing slave traders. (*Natural History Museum*)

Sir Harry Smith. (*National Portrait Gallery, London*)

Sir George Grey (1812–98). (*National Portrait Gallery, London*)

Between pages 260 and 261

The Xhosa warrior Macomo (1798–1873). (*South African Library, Cape Town*)

Kgama (c.1830–1923), founderof the independent country of Botswana. (*South African Library, Cape Town*)

Tause Soga. (*South African Library, Cape Town*)

The Xhosa girls Nongqawuse and Nonkosi, whose visions led to the tragic cattle-killings. (*South African Library, Cape Town*)

Kimberley mines, 1875. (*South African Library, Cape Town*)

Zulu king Cetshwayo (1826–84). (*South African Library, Cape Town*)

Bishop Colenso (1814–83). (*National Portrait Gallery, London*)

Cetshwayo's brother Dabulamanzi, who led the disastrous Zulu attack on Rorke's Drift in January 1879. (*Local History Museum, Durban*)

John Dunn's Scouts, many of them Zulu warriors. (*Killie Campbell Africana Library, University of Natal, Durban*)

The Raad (council) of the Rehoboth Bastaard community. (*South African Library, Cape Town*)

The emergence of a Coloured middle class: Minnie Adonis and her young man. (*South African Library, Cape Town*)

Boer leaders in the First War of Independence, 1880–81. (*National Archives of South Africa, Cape Town*)

Jan Smuts' Boer War commando. (*National Archives of South Africa, Cape Town*)

Bondelswarts chief Morenga's officers (1905). (*National Archives of South Africa, Cape Town*)

The Cape Colony Cabinet in 1884. (*University of Cape Town, South Africa*)

Between pages 356 and 357

Punch, an accurate barometer of British public opinion, marks the progress of South African events in 1899.

Foreign attitudes to the Boer War: New York's *Punch*; *Le Rire* of Paris; *Simplicissimus* of Munich; Vienna's *Humoristiche Blätter*.

Jingoist propaganda for Britain's 'khaki' election of October 1900. (*Author's collection*)

Boer photograph of British dead on Spion Kop. (*National Archives of South Africa, Cape Town*)

Gunners of the Staatsartillerie at the siege of Mafeking. (*National Archives of South Africa, Cape Town*)

Emily Hobhouse, who attacked the administration of Kitchener's 'concentration' camps. (*National Portrait Gallery, London*)

Sir Alfred, later Lord, Milner. (*National Portrait Gallery, London*)

Jan Christiaan Smuts. (*Camera Press. Photograph by Karsh of Ottawa*)

The first Nationalist Cabinet, in 1948. (*National Archives of South Africa, Cape Town*)

The Sharpeville massacre of March 1960. (*Popperfoto*)

Private Eye's comment on Verwoerd's assassination. (*Private Eye*)

Illustrations

Between pages 484 and 485

Balthazar Johannes Vorster, Prime Minister 1966–78, State President 1978–79. (*Popperfoto*)

Steve Biko. (*Rex Features*)

Nobel Peace Prize-winner Albert Lutuli. (*Associated Press*)

'Bantu rehousing'. (*Topham Picturepoint*)

Black Sash members demonstrate. (*Killie Campbell Africana Library, University of Natal, Durban*)

Black protesters take over whites-only railway carriages in September 1982. (*Topham Picturepoint*)

Alleged SWAPO guerrillas killed by the Koevoet (irregular South African police) in Namibian fighting. (*Photograph © John Liebenberg*)

The last Afrikaner Presidents: P.W. Botha and F.W. de Klerk. (*Link Picture Library*)

Nelson Mandela voting in the April 1994 election. (*Frank Spooner Pictures*)

April 1994: the first election for sixty years in which the franchise was not restricted to whiles, and the first non-racial election ever. (*Rex Features*)

Zulu Inkatha leader Chief Mangosuthu Buthelezi. (*Link Picture Library*)

Winnie Mandela. (*Rex Features*)

Archbishop Desmond Tutu. (*Link Picture Library*)

Thabo Mbeki, South African Deputy President and President of the ANC in succession to Nelson Mandela. (*PA News*)

President Nelson Mandela and F.W. de Klerk, 10 May 1994. (*Popperfoto*)

MAPS

Physical map of South Africa   xiv–xv

Early exploration   3

Cape Colony 1800 borders   98–99

Basutoland   141

Mfecane incursions   142–144

Xhosa land losses   154–155

Cape Colony: pre-1848 and post-1854 borders   204–205

Natal region, 1846   211

The Boer War   332–333

Livestock distribution   381

Present-day South Africa   510–511

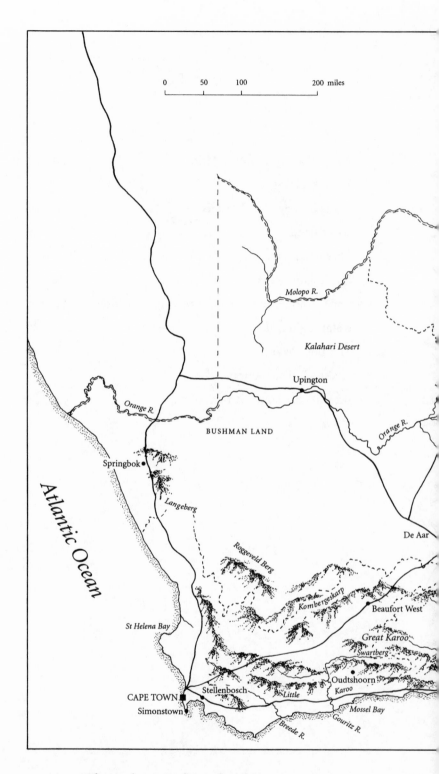

MAP 1 *Physical map of South Africa*

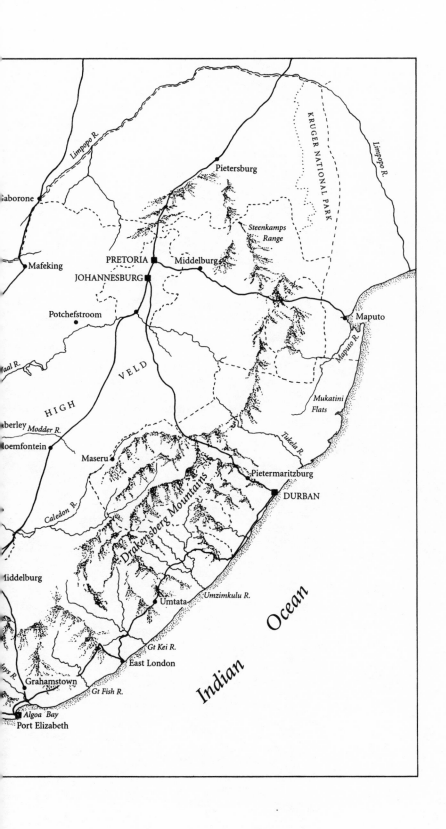

ACKNOWLEDGEMENTS

One of the most pleasurable parts of writing this book has been the privilege of working in some very attractive South African libraries, with the help of able and obliging staff. The Brenthurst Library in Johannesburg must have the most beautiful setting of any, and a building which combines elegance and efficiency; the Johannesburg Public Library by contrast is cramped and unattractive; but the help proffered in both is professional, kindly, and unstinted. I owe much to the thoughtful guidance of Karol Schoeman of the South African Library in Cape Town, again an outstanding building and a cultural resource of which any country would be proud. Much valuable help was given by the staff of the Cape Archives, the Bloemfontein Afrikaner Museum and Library, the Orange Free State University collections, the Killie Cambell Africana Library, the Local History Museum Durban, the University of Natal Durban, and the Witwatersrand University Library.

In Britain I express my obligation to the staff of the British Library, Cambridge University Library, the Hove Public Library, Rhodes House, the Bodleian Library, the Commonwealth Institute, the South African High Commission London, Public Records Offices, Kew, Belfast and Edinburgh, the National Library of Scotland and the School of Oriental & African Studies. In particular, I would single out Jackie Loos, Mrs M. J. Eldrege, Nellie Soamers, Mr and Mrs Sanders, Storm Reilly, Nat Kirschner, Dr and Mrs Tony Woodward, Dr and Mrs Brookes Hayward, Trish Downing, Sue Smith, Robert Maxtone Graham, who presented me with two valuable volumes, Angus Trimble, Laurent de Villepreux and Michael Graham-Jones. Dr Priscilla Roberts found copies of the John Buchan and Isie Smuts correspondence and Jim Bailey's experienced wisdom has been much appreciated.

The patient cooperation of HarperCollins, especially the editorial skills of Robert Lacey, and the encouragement of Stuart Proffitt, whose absence will continue to be deplored by many authors, is gratefully acknowledged. Finally, without the patient deciphering of my handwriting, driving, finding illustrations and general shepherding by my wife this book would never have been finished.

INTRODUCTION

Anyone rash enough to attempt, in a single volume, to sketch the history of so complex a society as that of South Africa should tread delicately. More than three hundred years of dissension, wars, debates, clashes – and fusions – between cultures and traditions have produced a complex society often at odds with itself, harbouring mutual resentments sometimes amounting to hatred, an emotion frequently justifiable. At the same time the people of South Africa continue to show a creative ebullience, a spirit of enterprise, and a patient forbearance that has helped to make their country the most advanced, economically and institutionally, in that tumultuous continent. The same complexity of cultures – the original Khoi-San (Bushman-Hottentot), living alongside the advancing Bantu-speaking black peoples; the Dutch merchants and colonists first accommodating and then supplanting them, transmuting over time into a distinctive Afrikaner people; English-speaking immigrants, enterprising Indians and that other great, individual South African people, the Coloureds, who in themselves unite most of the others – has resulted in a nation rich in potential. That the country is also rich in having a considerable percentage of the world's most valuable minerals contributes more than a little to its future prospects.

Occupying an area similar in size to France, Germany, Belgium, Holland and Great Britain combined, South Africa is by some way the most powerful and prosperous country on the continent. Its gross domestic product per capita is exceeded by only the oil-rich Libyan state, and far excels that of such potentially rich countries as Nigeria, the Congo and Zambia, endowed with plentiful natural resources but hampered by corrupt and ineffective governments. Half of the electricity generated in the whole of Africa comes from South Africa; the country has the continent's most modern and productive agriculture – more than one-third of all African tractors are found there; South Africa also possesses the most advanced manufacturing industry, with an important export trade, including sophisticated armaments (South Africa has developed and tested nuclear weapons); its stock exchange, the only such market of any significance in Africa, is the world's tenth largest, ranking just below that of Hong Kong. What happens in this regional superpower will affect not only its forty-two million people, but all sub-Saharan Africa.

This powerful infrastructure has been developed by two centuries of colonization, and by the inclusion of South Africa in the industrialized capitalist economy. Colonial history, which has resulted in substantial material benefits as well as manifest injustices, is reflected in the region's ethnic mix. Alone among black African countries South Africa has a population with a substantial minority of other races. The aboriginal inhabitants have almost vanished, only a few Bushmen communities remaining in desert regions, the rest, together with the other brown-skinned people, the Khoikhoi or Hottentots, having merged with black and white races. Some physical characteristics and traces of their language survive among those Bantu-speaking black peoples who moved south over the last two millennia; among these, Nelson Mandela's Thembu combine the genes of both races. Taken together the three main black linguistic groups, the Xhosa of the old Cape Colony, the Zulu, and the Sotho/Tswana/Pedi of the north, all with approximately similar numbers, constitute some three-quarters of the population; a powerful, but not overwhelming majority. While there have been disputes and divisions between the black nations, especially between Xhosa and Zulu, encouraged by the apartheid governments, the oppressive character of white '*baaskap*' (domination) has done much to unite those blacks whom traditions, language and history have separated. Of the remaining nine million South Africans, 1.8 million of the whites and most of the one million Indians are English-speaking; 2.7 million white Afrikaners and a majority of the 3.2 million Coloureds have Afrikaans as their first language; and almost all the blacks active in politics and business are fluent in English. The complexity of such a society defies easy generalities.

This evolution of a South African nation occurred under conditions of sometimes extreme pressure. Change has been rapid, often violent, and always bringing considerable stress. Take, for example, some family histories. 'Old' Soga, a man of substance, a Xhosa aristocrat, principal counsellor to the powerful chief Sandile, was born in about 1800, and helped lead his people through the difficult adjustments to colonial rule and the devastating consequences of the 1857 cattle-killing. His son became the Reverend Tiyo Soga, translator of *Pilgrim's Progress* into Xhosa, the first black South African clergyman, educated in Scotland and married to a Scots girl; their children included Sotello Festiri, the first South African veterinary surgeon; John Henderson, who wrote the first history of the Xhosa; and Allen Kirkland, one of the founders of the African National Congress.

At the same time that Old Soga, wrapped in his fine skin caross, was bitterly criticizing the folly of his people in slaughtering all their cattle in the delusion that they would be replaced by supernatural agencies, Tiyo, in black frock-coat, was beginning his clerical career. Fifty years later Allen Kirkland Soga, a leader and shaper of opinion, assisted in establishing the ANC, which went on eventually to win the first democratic South African election in 1994. It might be noted that all Tiyo's sons were themselves voters in the Cape Colony, along with those of other races who met the franchise qualifications. Yet by the time John Henderson died, killed by a Luftwaffe bomb in an air raid on Southampton, his grandfather's people were impoverished, subjected and disenfranchised.

Or the Jabavu family, no aristocrats but Mfengu refugees, driven from their lands by the disturbances of the 1820s and thirties which devastated all Southern African black nations, eventually settling in the Cape Colony. Ntwamambi Jabavu was a poor labourer who, with his wife Mary and like almost all his people, had accepted Christianity and cooperated with the British colonial administration. Their son, John Tengu Jabavu, a teacher and a Methodist local preacher, became editor of the first newspaper to voice the views of his people, and a powerful political figure. John Davidson Don Jabavu, his eldest son, a man of immense charm and accomplishment, was the inspiration behind Fort Hare University, where so many African leaders were educated.

From the Tswana peoples, hundreds of miles away north of the Drakensberg Mountains, one might select a contemporary of Tiyo Soga. Kgama, chief of the Ngwato tribe and founder of the Botswana state, was born in about 1830, eldest son of the great chief Sekgoma, a staunch traditionalist. Becoming a Christian in 1860, Kgama succeeded as chief in 1872. In his reign of half a century he united the other Tswana tribes, secured British protection against the predatory Transvaalers and the even more threatening emissaries of Cecil Rhodes, and confirmed his people's independent status in a visit to London in 1895. Seventy years later his grandson, Sir Seretse Khama, became the first President of the Republic of Botswana, one of the most prosperous of African states.

While there are a number of such examples of speedy mastery of new languages and concepts, many more blacks were less fortunate. Loyal to militant leaders reacting forcefully against colonial encroachments, hundreds of thousands of black Africans perished in the nineteenth-century wars, and millions more were sucked into the shifting urban labour market while their old cultures atrophied around them. The pressures were immense. In the three generations between Mary and John Davidson Don Jabavu, or between Old Soga and his talented grandsons, the black communities of South Africa had faced the challenges of new languages and new laws, the imposition of a social order in which they occupied a subordinate place, a shockingly quick transition from a pastoral and agricultural economy to an industrial and urban society, and, most disturbing of all, the shattering revelations of a confident Christianity. The emergence of an assured and cultivated elite, more than capable of holding its own in an unequal society, is a tribute to black energy and adaptability; and the eventual transition, after the cruel disappointment of earlier hopes and the loss of hard-won influence, to a fully democratic society is a demonstration of astonishing patience.

The first white community has undergone not dissimilar vicissitudes. A century and a half of usually quiet Dutch settlement begun in 1652 was supplanted by the integration of the Cape into the expanding British Empire, which brought its own language and culture, including many concepts of freedom and equality, to threaten the existing order. Some Dutch-speakers accepted the new rule: Sir Christoffel Brand, a fourth-generation African whose forebears came to the Cape shortly after Peter Stuyvesant arrived in America, a godson of the famous botanist and explorer Joseph Banks, became the first Speaker of the Cape Parliament. His son, Sir John Brand, five times President of the Orange Free State, 'everyone's favourite republic', was succeeded by the lively Francis Reitz, translator of Burns into the new language of Afrikaans, whose father, also Francis, had learned his farming skills in Scotland. In time the Free Staters rebelled against later encroachments of British imperialism, and joined with other Dutch-speakers who had earlier found English ideas abhorrent, trekking off into the interior to establish '*voortrekker*' communities of their own. In these an 'Afrikaner' identity emerged, with its own language, religious fervour and republican idealism, having to fight for survival through military defeat and perceived humiliation. Grossly perverted by the exercise of power, Afrikaner society is now struggling to regain its true character.

Introduction

Although the recognition of a South African nation can be traced back three hundred years, and in 1852 a parliamentarian of Dutch ancestry could speak of 'Africanders of Dutch, French, German, English, Danish, Portuguese, Mozambiquean, Malay and Hottentot extractions', South Africans have always been conscious of their own racial and linguistic identities. Since these have been linked with power and privilege, great sensitivity has been aroused by markers and descriptions seen as denoting inferiority. 'Kaffir' (Caffre or Kafir), once a usual description among whites and Zulu of Xhosa-speakers, has become so pejorative that at least one contemporary writer, in misquoting historical documents, has replaced the offensive word with 'Xhosa'. For a time 'San' was considered more acceptable than 'Bushman', until it was discovered that it was originally a pejorative; 'Bushman' is now preferred. Such idiosyncrasies are not of great importance, and have on the whole been subordinated here to the need for clarity, but much more damaging is the rewriting of history either to accord with current prejudices or to cultivate a myth which can be used for political advantage. Thus the *voortrekker* myth of British persecution and a divinely authorized mission was developed to encourage Afrikaner self-assertion, and a celebration of martial qualities is today being exploited to encourage Zulu-speakers to behave aggressively. Myths need some foundation in reality, and these myths have some respectable validity, but their very potency demands a critical analysis and some plain speaking. It is inadvisable to tread too delicately if the crude belligerence of many colonists, who objected to 'church-going niggers' and celebrated the killing of paramount chief Hintsa, the venerated head of the Xhosa people, by cutting off the dead man's ears, is to be clearly understood for what it was.

For clarity's sake an axe has been taken to the correct rendering of proper names. Strictly speaking the Xhosa should be referred to as the AmaXhosa, the Pedi as the BaPedi, the BaSotho as a people speaking SeSotho and living in Lesotho; the usage common in the contemporary documents has been preferred, and such neologisms as AmaFengu for Mfengu or Fingoes avoided. Any other policy threatens the reader with sentences such as 'The Rozvi themselves adopted the local tjiKalanga dialect and no longer spoke their original chiZezuru dialect of chiShona.'

Although a history written by a non-African may start with the advantage of a more detached view (which might to some extent conceal mere ignorance), there should be no necessity either to adopt or to explain away any Eurocentric cultural superiority: a continent that has seen the holocausts in Nazi Germany and Stalinist Russia, and the recent sadistic violence in Bosnia, has few grounds for condescending to Africans; nor can a country which has shuffled off responsibility for at least one massacre in Ulster afford to be superior about Sharpeville or Soweto.

On the other hand, in view of recent assertions, particularly in the United States (and usually advanced without any historical justification) of a peculiarly African culture, in which the Egyptian pyramids are conflated with Benin bronzes, it is important to stress the peculiar isolation of Southern Africa. It is certainly true that Africa has been no strange continent to the rest of the world. Egyptian Pharaohs extended their rule four thousand miles, from the equatorial Nile north to Palestine, and Egyptian culture a great deal further. Indian and Chinese navigators followed Egyptians and Phoenicians down Africa's east coast, and were succeeded by the enterprising Arabs, who for centuries colonized the seaboard as far south as Zanzibar. Some evidence also suggests that Western African societies, first visited by modern Europeans in the fifteenth century, may have been linked in an Atlantic/Mediterranean trading zone as early as 7000 B.C.[1]

But most of the lands now forming the Republic of South Africa were left to themselves, isolated from the rest of the world. There seemed little to attract intruders: extensive gold deposits lay towards the north, producing a trade which encouraged the massive medieval walls of Great Zimbabwe, but the southern tip of Africa was inhabited by communities with little to offer except skins and ivory, which were more accessible elsewhere, and who had a determination not to allow any of their people to be sold as slaves. When, at the turn of the fifteenth century, the Portuguese made some tentative landings near the Cape of Good Hope, they were given such a murderous reception as to discourage any further adventures.

Oddly enough, historians of the Atlantic slave trade seem never to have asked themselves why slaves came only from the west and east coasts of Africa, where victims were provided with the consistent support of the local rulers, and never from the south.[2] Southern Africans were, it is true, extremely difficult to get at. For thousands of miles along the western and eastern coasts of Africa there are few practicable harbours except for those around the Cape of Good Hope. Once having left São Paolo de Luanda in Angola, ships had no other refuge along those dangerous shores until they reached either India or the southern coast of Mozambique; and since the coast was swept by dangerous currents the whole region was best avoided. For an even greater distance, from the mouth of the Congo to the Zambezi, no river was navigable for more than a few miles, a grave disincentive to exploration at a time when water transport was often the only method of penetrating the interior. Access by land was rendered difficult by the great swathe of desert that stretched from the Atlantic to the Vaal, and by the unhealthy swamps of Mozambique. As a result of this geographical isolation, while other regions of Africa were, for better or worse, part of the world economy, trading with Europe and Asia, southern Africa was left to develop at its own pace, without access to the technologies that produced the magnificent art of the west coast. Abdullah al Bekri, writing in the year after the Norman conquest of England, described King Tenkaminen of Ghana, 'master of a large empire', who possessed an army of two hundred thousand warriors, sitting 'in a pavilion around which stand ten pages holding shields and gold-mounted swords'.[3] Nothing of this glory was to be found among the herdsmen of what is now South Africa, but its people were developing a less tangible, but perhaps ultimately more powerful heritage, that of a peaceful and adaptable society in which disputes could be settled by a patient consideration of recognized laws.

Within South Africa the land's physical features have had an often decisive effect on history. The most striking feature, the great escarpment that curves round from coast to coast, rising sharply on the southern side to the peaks of the Drakensberg and sloping gently through the fertile highveld into the desert on the north and west, divided first the black communities, the Sotho/Tswana from the Nguni, and later the Boer republics from the British colonies. The mountains have provided security for two of the independent states, Lesotho and Swaziland, and the semi-desert a refuge for the third, Botswana.

The mountains also govern the rainfall, a matter of prime importance. It is not so much that South Africa is permanently short of rain as that a great deal of it comes at the wrong time and so unreliably. Devastating floods can be followed by disastrous droughts. The general weather system is one of moisture-laden clouds from the Indian Ocean providing precipitation on the seaward side of the escarpment, a good deal of it in the north, decreasing nearer the Cape, and feeding dozens of short, fast-flowing rivers that divide the coastal plain. On the western side of the mountains the extensive plateau of the highveld has a reasonable rainfall of between twenty and thirty inches annually, which declines through arid areas into absolute desert. This area is served by two major river systems. The Orange, with its tributaries the Vaal/Gariep and Caledon, rises in the Drakensberg to flow through the desert to the Atlantic, losing much of its water in the process. Its counterpart, the Limpopo and its tributary the Olifants, has a different character, flowing from the mountains in a great curve eastwards through the highveld and tropical north to the Indian Ocean.

The Cape of Good Hope has its own, near-Mediterranean climate and some individual features that affected early European settlement there. A reasonable anchorage and reliable fresh water dictated the position of the initial Dutch settlement at Kaapstad, now Cape Town, but expansion was limited first by the sandy Cape flats and the menacing Hottentots Holland mountains to the east, and the arid lands of the Namib in the north. When, after two generations, stock farmers moved across the mountains, they found one stretch of reasonably good land, the Little Karoo, paralleling the coast, and a much more extensive tract of semi-desert, the Great Karoo, drawing the newcomers ever further into the interior in search of better land. And there, after more than a century, during which the indigenous Khoi-San had either been dispersed or absorbed into the colonial society, the Dutch farmers came across their black counterparts, and the troubled history of modern South Africa began, falling neatly enough into two centuries.

Beginning with the British occupation of the former Dutch colony at the Cape of Good Hope and the shattering experience of the '*mfecane*', the period of devastation that disrupted and then re-formed many black societies, the nineteenth century was a time of conquest, expansion and compromise. It ended with two systems in conflict: the colonial British ideal of progress towards a multiracial democracy, slowing but still powerful, facing the Dutch republicans' unflinching assertion of white dominance and denial of political rights to all others. The British victory in the Anglo–Boer war of 1899–1902 proved illusory. Within seven years the former Dutch republicans had come to power in a united South Africa and new restrictions on black political rights were gradually enforced, inspiring in turn new black political organizations. After 1948, when the policies of apartheid – separate development – and *baaskap* – frank white domination – were introduced, the fabric of decent society began to disintegrate.

Many white South Africans were angrily surprised at the detestation with which their state was regarded as a pariah by the rest of the world. There were, they argued with some reason, many more violent, corrupt and undemocratic nations which continued to enjoy the tolerance, and even approbation, of the international community (Argentina, for example, contrived to allow its forces to murder at least fifteen thousand people in the six years after 1976, while retaining the support of the United Nations). The non-white majority in South Africa may have had few political rights and been subject to perpetual harassment, but they were better housed, fed and educated than most other black Africans, and ingenious solutions were sought to allow them something more than the shadow of political power without infringing the essential principle of *baaskap*. Bolstered by the support of the United States, for many years ready to welcome the most atrocious regimes as allies in their crusade against communism, South African apartheid was allowed nearly forty years to develop its own rationale and to crush opposition without much international interference. Only in the 1980s, with the internal contradictions of the system becoming ever more obvious, the inescapable fact that a modern economy could not be run with the violent opposition of three-quarters of the population forced South African governments into retreat. The end of the Cold War completed the process by negating whatever value the country had been thought to have as a bulwark against communism, and at the same time depriving the black opposition of a powerful support. Compromise was essential, and four painful years eventually produced this in the first elections held under a democratic franchise in April 1994.

Paradoxically, South Africa can be regarded either as the first African state to gain independence from colonizing powers, or the last. In 1910, when Britain relinquished her imperial role, the rest of the continent was, formally or informally, more or less effectively, controlled by European powers. By 1994, when the first South African government to be elected on a fully democratic franchise came to power, all other African countries were independent self-governing states (although European and American influence remained often strong, and internal chaos not uncommon).

This book does not claim to be anything but a colonial history, an account, drastically curtailed, of many races and cultures contending and cooperating to arrive at the unique society that is South Africa at the end of the twentieth century.

Frank Welsh
February 1998

ONE

The Fairest Cape in
the Whole Circumference of the Earth

The dogs bark just as they do in Portugal

On the third day of February 1488 herdsmen on the shore of what is now Mossel Bay underwent an extraordinary, unprecedented experience. The sea, that unpredictable and dangerous element, had produced huge objects, bigger by far than any man-made structure, from which human-like figures were emerging. Prudently, the herdsmen retired, driving their cattle away from the shore, but when it was seen that the strangers attempted nothing more threatening than filling containers with water, they advanced, beginning to throw stones. Some of these struck home, whereupon one of the sea-people snatched up a crossbow. It was the first encounter between Europeans and the people of what is now South Africa.[1]

The Africans on the shore were slight, yellow-skinned Khoikhoi – men of men, later known as Hottentots to the Europeans – who for centuries had inhabited the south-west corner of Africa, following the seasonal growth of pasture and becoming skilled in the management of their flocks. The sailors were the crews of Bartolomeu Dias, who had just doubled Cape Aguilas and crossed from the Atlantic to the Pacific Ocean, the first men to do so. Unlike the western and eastern coasts of the continent, which had been in contact with the rest of the world, from China to Peru, the south-west had been isolated – from the sea by its lack of harbours, and from the north by the Namibian desert. Only along the eastern coast, many miles from Mossel Bay, were Khoikhoi in touch with other peoples, the bigger, darker, Bantu-speaking communities, themselves a long way south of the Limpopo and Great Zimbabwe, centres of trade and commerce with connections to Arabia, India and China. Europeans were latecomers on the African scene, but for the south theirs are the only written records; local African languages were given their written form by Europeans in the nineteenth century, and until recently even oral testimonies were recorded in European languages. Before such written evidence becomes available, South African history has to be based on archaeology, in the same way that the history of Celtic Britain depends on the records left by the Roman occupiers.

After anchoring in Mossel Bay, which they named Bahia dos Vaqueros because of the herds of cattle, Dias' ships made their way some three hundred miles up the coast as far as Cape Padrone, on the eastern tip of Algoa Bay. There they landed and erected a stone pillar to commemorate their achievement before turning for home, satisfied that the way to the Indies was open. On the return passage Dias did at least sight the Cape of Good Hope, to which he gave the less attractive name of Cabo de Todos los Tormentos, the Cape of all Storms.

Portuguese sailors had been nosing their way down the west coast of Africa for most of the century before they reached the southern extremity, initially encouraged by Dom Henrique, Iffante of Portugal, grandson of Edward III of England and known to the English as Prince Henry the Navigator. Both the Canary Islands and the Azores had already been discovered – in the sense of being shown on charts, although Arab geographers had earlier at least known of their existence – by about 1350, but the first Portuguese expedition was to Madeira, in 1420. Five years later the port of Ceuta, on the African coast opposite Gibraltar, was captured by the Portuguese. Gibraltar itself remained in Muslim hands, but the Moorish hold on southern Spain was slipping, and by the end of the century the passage from the Mediterranean to the Atlantic would be in Christian control. This was of particular importance since the rapid expansion of Turkish power threatened to disturb the land communications with the East. In 1396 the Turks had – with, it might be noted, the enthusiastic assistance of the Serbs – massacred a crusading army at Nicopolis on the Danube. Only Constantinople itself was holding out, and that precariously. Even if the Ottoman empire allowed the precious spices and silks from India and China to pass through to Western Europe, high duties were likely to be added to the already considerable costs of caravan transport. Since a small caravel with a twenty-man crew could carry the loads of a thousand camels, a sea route to India was an objective worth much effort.

There was general acceptance that such a route existed. The maps of the period, which had not changed much since those of the Greek geographer

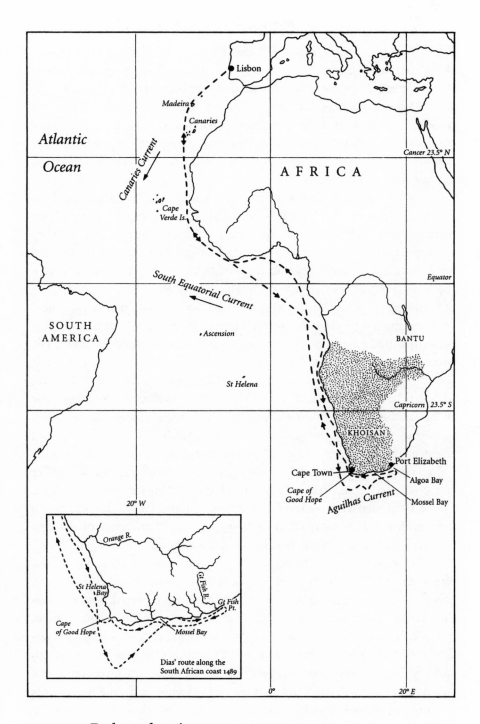

MAP 2 *Early exploration*

Ptolemy of the second century AD, showed the East African coast in reasonable detail as far as the island of Zanzibar; the slightly earlier 'Periplus of the Erythrean Sea' gave sailing instructions for that section of the coast, as well as for the coasts of Arabia and western India; later Arab and Chinese traders regularly visited this area.[2] The western and central regions of the continent were much less well described, and maps were largely theoretical – entirely so south of the Bight of Benin – but a narrow and difficult strait around the southern coast was indicated.

Other reasons than that of discovering a sea route to India existed for Prince Henry's endeavours. It was known that the barren coast of the Sahara, which stretched for a thousand miles south of the Pillars of Hercules, ended in a rich and populous land from which the Arabs exported gold and slaves to their cities on the North African coast. 'Bilad Ghana' – the Land of Wealth – was watered by the Senegal River, which flowed into the Atlantic. If access to this country from the sea could be established, avoiding the long treks through the desert during which many slaves perished, this trade could be diverted at a stroke into Portuguese hands. For some years the explorers' efforts met with little success – the desert is not a propitious place for slave-raiders – and they had to content themselves with sealskins and oil, but by 1441 Prince Henry's ships had rounded Cape Blanco and reached a populous country. Under the banners of the Order of Christ, the Portuguese slave-hunters slaughtered all who resisted, and shipped the remainder, some 230 on the first expedition, back to Lisbon.

In 1445 a fleet of twenty-six ships left Lagos to search for a steadier supply of slaves, and succeeded in reaching the Senegal River and Bilad Ghana itself, henceforward to be known as Guinea. Ivory, and an African lion, captured with some effort, joined the slaves as evidence of the new country's riches; the Iffante became Duke of Guinea, which together with the other discoveries, of the Azores, the Cape Verde islands and Madeira, was recruited into the recognized pattern of Christendom. While these acquisitions were being consolidated exploration progressed slowly. It was discovered more efficient, the market for slaves in Europe being limited, to trade those captured survivors of Portuguese expeditions with the established Arab slavers. The ivory and gold offered in exchange were easier to stow, while the Arabs were happy to avoid the often dangerous labour of catching the slaves. It was a pity that the blacks would be denied the benefits of Christianity, and forced to become followers of Mahomet; but business was business.

After Prince Henry's death in 1460 his nephew, King Affonso V, subcontracted the task of exploring the African coast to Fernando Gomes, who covenanted to cover a hundred leagues of it each year. By the time of Affonso's death in 1481 Gomes' captains had made their way right round the Bight of Benin to prove that the coast then took a southerly direction.

Confidence in the existence of the sea route to the Indies quickly developed, but it was left to King João II, one of the ablest and most personable of Renaissance monarchs, to establish its practicability. He began by commissioning Diego Cam, who reached the desolate coast of Namibia in 1485, recording his passage by placing padrones – stone pillars, two of which are preserved in the Lisbon museum – at his landing places. The following year Bartolemeu Dias, who had already made some voyages to Guinea, with fleets in which the young Genoese Cristofero Colombo also sailed, was given instructions that, come what may, he was to get around the extremity of the continent. Following in Cam's wake, his three small ships reached the latitude of twenty-six degrees twenty-eight minutes south, the present Luderitz Bay. There, impatient with contrary winds and the adverse currents found close inshore, Dias struck out due south into the open sea. After a fortnight the ships changed course to make for where the coast was expected to be. When after four hundred miles' sailing no land was sighted, Dias headed back north to make the landfall in Mossel Bay. It was clear that he had succeeded in sailing around the tip of Africa, and that the route to the Indies was open. On the expedition's return King João, delighted with the news, and with an eye to public relations, tactfully renamed the Cabo de Todos los Tormentos 'Cabo de Boa Esperanza' – the Cape of Good Hope.

Dias' discovery was not hailed elsewhere with particular enthusiasm, more interest being attracted by Colombo's proposals for an alternative route to the Indies, across the Atlantic. Much to his later chagrin King João rejected these ideas – as did Henry VII of England – and so had to accept Spanish dominance of the New World. Making the best of a bad business, the King deployed his considerable diplomatic skill to ensure that Portugal got her fair share of whatever new lands remained to be discovered. Pope Alexander VI Borgia attempted to settle things between Spain and Portugal in 1493, but King João was not satisfied with the adjudication; the Pope, being a keen family man, with the interests of his daughter Lucrezia and his son Cesare much at heart, had allowed himself to be too openly bribed by Spain. Eventually, in the Treaty of Tordesillas, King João got what he wanted: a boundary between Spain and Portugal running north to south at a distance of 370 leagues (about 1175 miles) west of the Azores, an arrangement that gave to Portugal all Africa, India and China, as well as the yet-to-be-identified country of Brazil. No other country was considered, the future imperial nations of Britain, Holland and France being too much occupied with their internal affairs at the time to consider risky explorations that would be likely to bring them into conflict with the Iberian countries.

As a first step in exploiting Portugal's still theoretical new empire an expedition, under Vasco da Gama, was despatched to secure the new route round Africa and to arrange matters in India. Da Gama was instructed to sail direct for the Cape of Good Hope, rather than creeping around the coast as had his predecessors, and then to cross the Indian Ocean for the Malabar coast, a voyage far exceeding in distance and danger those of Colombo. That historic passage across the Atlantic had been some 2,600 miles, accomplished in thirty-six days, but when, on 4 November 1497, da Gama made his landfall in St Helena Bay, seventy miles north of the future Cape Town, it was after ninety-three days and a distance of 3,770 miles out of sight of land. There he found more Khoikhoi, 'swarthy' men who 'eat only sea-wolves and whales', whose 'arms are staff of wild olives tipped with fire-hardened horns', and whose dogs barked exactly as did those in Portugal. Eight days were spent there, tolerably pleasantly, with tentative efforts made to establish contact with the inhabitants, before da Gama and his men rounded the Cape to Mossel Bay, where they, unlike Dias' company, and the first Europeans to do so, fraternized with the natives of South Africa. First impressions were favourable, and led to the Portuguese being supplied with sheep and cattle, and to an impromptu concert, the Africans performing on flutes, 'harmonizing together very well for blacks from whom music is not to be expected', the Portuguese on trumpets. Even da Gama himself joined in the dancing. A fat ox was bought and all appeared tranquil, but before the Europeans left there were disagreements. A cannon was discharged and in retaliation the padrone that had been erected was knocked down.[3]

Da Gama's ships continued their voyage, having doubled the Cape and noting a 'very large bay' – False Bay – just to the east. Six months later they arrived off Calicut, on the western coast of India; they had succeeded where Colombo had failed, in proving that a veritable sea route from Europe to the Indies existed.

Such unprecedented voyages were made possible by a combination of new and revived technologies. By the beginning of the fifteenth century two distinct European ship types had emerged – the Atlantic coast cog, or round ship, and the Mediterranean galley. Neither of these was well suited to ocean voyages. The Mediterranean carrying trade, which had flourished for two thousand years, together with its more recent overspill into the Indian Ocean via the Red Sea, had remained an affair of short coastal stages. The shallow-draught galleys, lightly built and sparred, rendered highly manoeuvrable by powerful oar systems, could rapidly make port when the weather demanded, but could never cope with foul weather far from any safe haven.

Foul weather was a continuous hazard for North Sea, English Channel and Biscay mariners, who carried wines from Bordeaux, wool from East Anglia, building materials from Normandy, herrings from the Netherlands, and pilgrims from everywhere in their sturdy ships. Cogs were simply rigged with single square sails on one or more masts, deep-hulled and solidly built, well able to withstand rough seas, but unhandy and restricted in their ability to sail against contrary winds. This was a weighty disadvantage to those setting off into unknown waters; the fine favourable breezes that wafted the sailor on his outward voyage would, unless he could make some headway against them, effectively prevent him from reaching home again.

Some time about the end of the fourteenth century a ship type emerged that enabled this to be done. The caravel, which served all the early Iberian explorers, was a small vessel, with the deep hull, short masts and transom stern of the North Sea ships, but with a modified Mediterranean lateen rig. This combination, as well as being eminently seaworthy, allowed some modest progression into the direction from which the wind blew, and gave mariners the comfort of knowing that a safe passage home might be achieved.

Added to this, for the first time navigators were able to be tolerably sure of where they were at any given time, and to produce reliable maps of their journeys. Medieval Arab and Jewish scientists had already produced navigational instruments, the astrolabe and cross-staff being the most important. With these, adapted for use at sea, together with the magnetic compass, in use since the beginning of the fourteenth century, long ocean voyages, and the accurate delineation of newly discovered territories, became feasible.

These techniques were little different from those which had been employed by Chinese mariners for many centuries. The Chinese who visited East Africa at the same time that the Portuguese were feeling their way down the west coast did so in ships at least as well equipped and much larger than those of the Europeans; and the Arab dhows that made the passages to India and even as far as the South China Sea were able, sea-worthy vessels.[4] But the caravels and their successors, the carracks, had one decisive advantage, which goes far to explain how Europeans were able to establish extensive empires. The strong and deep hulls of their ships were able to accommodate powerful batteries of cannon: the *Regent*, built for Henry VII of England in 1495, mounted 225 guns. Against the forces of the great Ottoman, Moghul and Chinese empires European nations could deploy only handfuls of soldiers, but with the naval power at their disposal they could defend any trading posts they might be able to establish in the Indies, and control all maritime trade routes.

It was to secure such bases, and to develop the trade that might flow through them, that was the object of da Gama's voyage, and all subsequent expeditions for a century and a half. There seemed nothing on the coast of southern Africa, beyond the most basic of supplies, to warrant much interest, whereas within twenty years of da Gama's first voyage a Portuguese commercial empire, governed from Goa by a succession of viceroys, the first of whom was da Gama himself, had established trading stations from Mozambique to Macao, whence the caravels freighted pepper, spices, silks, gold and precious stones home to Lisbon. The stream of wealth coming across the Atlantic to Spain was matched, for the time being, by a similar flow around the Cape of Good Hope to Portugal.

Lines of communication were secured by new fortified posts on the Angolan coast, centred on São Paolo de Luanda; on the eastern coast of Mozambique the existing Arab settlements were taken over by the Portu-guese. In this way more than two thousand miles of African coast, together with a vast expanse of hinterland, was claimed for Portuguese colonies, and so remained for nearly five centuries, although Portugal was never in a position to control more than a few trading stations and some routes to the interior. Only the possibility of picking up a few slaves attracted the venturers to southern Africa. The development of the sugar industry in Madeira, and later the need for labour in Iberian America, where the natives were proving unsatisfactory workers and dying off in embarrassing quantities – fifteen million of them in the first twenty years, the missionary

Father las Casas estimated – had given a new stimulus to the trade. Slaves in quantity were available through the well-established markets on the West Coast, where Arab traders had for centuries cooperated with local rulers to supply North African demand, but prices were high. If it were possible to capture enough of the southern Africans undamaged, the middlemen could be cut out and profit margins multiplied.

But the southern coast of Africa proved both a disappointing source of slaves and a highly dangerous region, a fact emphasized when, in 1510, a strong raiding party under the leadership of Bernardo d'Almeida, on his way to assume the viceroyship of the Indies at Goa, landed at the Cape. Trouble had been experienced there seven years previously, when one Antonio de Saldanha having landed – by mistake – in the bay, for many years after known as Saldanha Bay, found a good supply of fresh water, only to be ambushed by some two hundred men. His party escaped with only minor injuries, but d'Almeida was less fortunate, encountering fierce resistance in an unexpected form. One of the crew described their reception. The natives,

> having called their cattle, which are accustomed to this form of warfare, began to whistle to them and to make signs by which to guide them, so that forming into a squadron, and sheltered by the cattle, they attacked our men with wooden darts hardened by fire. Some fell wounded and were trodden down by the cattle, and as most were without shields, their only weapons being lances and swords, in this kind of warfare they could not do much damage to the negroes, who from among their cattle hurled their weapons against our men, which had immediate effect.[5]

Viceroy d'Almeida and no fewer than fifty of his men were killed in this battle, which was enough to discourage others from exploiting the inhabitants of the Cape. The English abstained, being more attracted by the possibility of a north-west passage around the coasts of Newfoundland and Canada, as had first been suggested by one Robert Thorne, a merchant living in Seville, where he had been in a position to receive first-hand accounts of d'Almeida's fate. Francis Drake passed the Cape in 1580, during his circumnavigation, describing it as 'a most stately thing, and the fairest Cape we saw in the whole circumference of the earth'.[6] But it was not until 1591, nearly a century after the first Portuguese landings, that the British arrived at Table Bay. They were more successful, and perhaps more diplomatic, than their Portuguese predecessors. Under the command of George

Raymond and James Lancaster, *Penelope*, *Merchant Royal* and *Edward Bonaventure* first called at Saldanha, where they found 'certaine Blacke Savages very brutish, whiche would not stay'. They managed to lay hands on one such, 'a Negro, whom we compelled to march into the country with us' in search of cattle. Finding none, the sailors 'let the Negro go with some trifles. Within eight dayes after, he, with some thirty or forty other Negros, brought us downe some forty bullocks and oxen . . . very large and well-fleshed, but not fat,' which were duly paid for.[7]

Four years later the first Dutch squadron appeared, under Cornelis de Houtman, doubling the Cape and landing a couple of days' sail further along the coast. There they found no difficulty in persuading the natives to sell 'fine oxen like those of Spain; large, fine and tasty sheep such as I have never eaten elsewhere' in exchange for iron and copper; 'each wanted to be the first to trade, giving two fine oxen and three sheep for a 75 pound iron rod broken into five parts' – but the Khoikhoi spurned such trinkets as mirrors and bells in favour of metal and strong drink.[8]

Thereafter the Cape became a favourite calling place for northern European ships, mainly British and Dutch, but also French and Danish, intent on breaking into the Portuguese monopoly of trade with the Far East. In 1601, on a second voyage to the Indies, but this time with the authority of the newly formed Honorable East India Company (HEIC) behind him, James Lancaster called once more at Table Bay. Again he was able to buy fresh meat, conversing with the 'Countrey people' in the 'Cattels Language (which was never changed at the confusion of Babell), which was Moath for Oxen and Kine, and Baa for Sheepe'.[9] Sir Thomas Roe, a great explorer, stopped at the Cape in 1615 on his way to the court of the Emperor Jehangir; he was also conveying several 'Japanzas' back to their native land. In 1619 another East India Company commander, Andrew Shilling, formally took possession of the Table Bay, building 'King James His Mount' and leaving a small flag with 'the natives, which they carefully kept'. Shilling was killed later in the voyage and the title, such as it was, allowed to lapse.[10]

At that time the English and Dutch were officially allies, and the Admiral of the Dutch fleet then lying in the bay, 'Nicolas van Baccum a gentleman by report that lived 7 yeares in Oxford', was able to agree Shilling's annexation.[11] It would have been a meaningless acquisition, since Britain was at that time unable to assert much power in the Indies, where in 1623 the Dutch had underlined their hegemony there by executing a number of English merchants who had set up a competitive enterprise at Amboina;

the English government agreed a truce, but popular feeling ran high and was waiting for the moment of revenge. This was many years coming – only in the 1650s did Cromwell's navy begin to make English sea-power felt – and in the meantime the newly established United Provinces of the Netherlands was unchallenged as the principal heir to the Portuguese trading empire in the East.

This collection of fiercely independent and particularist towns and provinces had been subjected to twenty years of oppression by their nominal overlord, the King of Spain. Philip II, who would have made a competent office manager had it not been for his shiftiness, but was a miserable failure as a monarch, had attempted to force his northern possessions back into the fold of Roman Catholicism. Although it was to be another sixty years before the attempt was finally abandoned, by 1585 Spanish persecution had forged an unruly and precarious alliance of seven of the fifteen provinces into a nation. The remaining southern states, approximating to the present-day Belgium, Luxembourg and French Flanders, remained Catholic and subjected, but the northern provinces – those now forming the Kingdom of the Netherlands, popularly known, then as now, by the name of its largest constituent, Holland – developed into an enthusiastically Protestant and mercantile nation.

The war of independence on land was protracted and costly, but from the outset the Dutch seized the initiative at sea. That dubious collection of patriots and pirates the 'Sea Beggars' defied the mighty Spanish forces, and after the defeat of the Spanish Armada in 1588 the Dutch were able to build a battle fleet. While the land war against Spain continued its damaging course the new Dutch squadrons, with astonishing rapidity, became capable of carrying the war into Spain itself; the battle of Gibraltar in 1607 left the Spanish fleet annihilated in its own harbour by the Dutch Admiral Heemskerk.

Behind such a shield Dutch commerce expanded even under the constraints imposed by war. The previous centre of trade, Antwerp, had been left impoverished in the rump of the Spanish Netherlands. From the new commercial capital, Amsterdam, the largest carrying trade in the world developed. Initially this was to the Baltic – as early as 1601 over eight hundred vessels left Amsterdam within the space of three days – with Russian corn and Scandinavian timber, hemp and tar being carried south, but it was soon extended to the Mediterranean, previously dominated by the Genoese and Venetians; a Dutch consulate was established in Constantinople, and a Directorate of Mediterranean Trade regulated the merchants. Commercial organization on an unprecedented scale was initiated; Amsterdam merchants not only made a market in all these commodities, but perfected banking and exchange services that served not only Dutch trade, and soon replaced the Hanseatic and Lombard cities as bankers to Europe.

The other Honorable Company

Merging the existing provincial companies which had pioneered the first voyages to the East Indies into an effective single unit was a complicated financial exercise. Amsterdam, Zeeland and Delft had formed locally financed corporations in the 1590s, and it was only after many months of patient negotiation under the auspices of the most influential architect of Dutch independence, the great Jan van Oldebarnveldt, that these were persuaded to unite, and offer shares to the other provinces. When the Dutch East India Company, the Vereenigde Oost-Indische Compagnie (VOC) was formed in 1601 the lion's share naturally fell to Amsterdam – 3,675,00 guilders of the starting capital of 6,440,200 guilders; Zeeland, always the second most important province, subscribed just under half as much.[12] Seats on the board of directors were allotted proportionately; the 'Heeren *majores in patria*,' commonly known as the Heeren XVII, divided themselves as to eight from Amsterdam and four from Zeeland, the remaining five members being shared by the smaller provinces. As a sweetener these retained their original company structure by the creation of provincial chambers within the VOC, each with some independent powers, which were able to mount their own ventures to the East.[13]

Day-to-day control was entrusted to a staff headed by a senior official, the First Advocate, but final power remained firmly in the hands of the Heeren XVII, a self-perpetuating oligarchy, nominated from the richest merchants of the community, who were inevitably also influential in the direction of national politics. Since the objects of directors and shareholders were identical – to maximize profitability and to secure dividends – there was rarely any conflict between them. The shareholders were drawn, for the most part, from the prosperous burghers, and displayed a keen interest in the dividends and capital growth of their holdings, which were dealt on the new Amsterdam bourse.

Within three years of its foundation the VOC had despatched fleets to the Indian Ocean, turfing out the Portuguese – much enfeebled since the annexation of Portugal by Spain in 1580 – where this was feasible, negotiating where necessary, and establishing the infrastructure of a trade that more than matched the Iberian commerce with the Americas. European appetites were stimulated by new products: coffee, from the Dutch factory at Mocha, on the tip of the Arabian peninsula; tea, from Formosa, where a fort was built in 1624. An inter-Indies trade between the Dutch stations in Arabia, India, Ceylon, the Indonesian archipelago, China and even Japan developed to rival that between the East and Europe, quickly superseding the previous Portuguese monopoly.

The direction of such an enterprise, whose activities were separated from the head office by thousands of miles and many months of difficult voyaging, inevitably had to be delegated. From 1609 a capital, appropriately named Batavia (the Batavi being the inhabitants of Holland in Roman times), was established on the site of the present Djakarta, and a Governor General of the VOC appointed there. This official, nominated for five years by the Heeren XVII, was accorded the widest powers: to make alliances and treaties, erect forts and establish trading posts, and to appoint subordinate governors.

Competition from the English East India company, established a few months before the VOC, was restricted to the mainland of India after the 1623 'massacre' of the English at Amboina, but for the moment British and Dutch companies managed an ungracious cohabitation in the Indian Ocean, sharing at least some of the facilities. Of these one, of minor importance, was access to Table Bay.

Many ships chose not to stop there, finding St Helena or Mauritius, both Dutch since the second decade of the century, more convenient. There were considerable disadvantages to the Cape. Outward-bound fleets preferred to steer clear of Africa, keeping well out in the Atlantic and avoiding the adverse offshore currents. For several months of the year the harbour at Table Bay was exposed to dangerous storms, and losses of ships at anchor were not infrequent. Nevertheless the bay had its uses, for the English in particular, as a watering place and a post office, where mail was left to be picked up by ships sailing in the opposite direction.[14]

Patching up relations after Amboina, the Dutch agreed that access to Table Bay should be shared between ships of both nations. This arrangement was not without dissension: the English claimed that the Dutch abused the natives, making them reluctant to supply visitors; the Dutch retorted by flying English colours, ensuring that any recriminations were transferred. As the trade developed the terse logs of sea captains were supplemented by descriptions of more erudite travellers. Young Thomas Herbert was only twenty-one when he visited the Cape in 1627, but had already attended both Oxford and Cambridge universities, and left an account copiously annotated and with many quotations from the classics; Peter Mundy, one of the best-travelled men of his time – he reckoned that he had covered more than a hundred thousand miles by sea and land, and had become the first Englishman to sight what was to be the British Crown Colony of Hong Kong – made sketches of the bay, and calculated with tolerable accuracy the height of Table Mountain.

Travellers such as these began to take a more informed interest in the people they encountered, and to the offhand descriptions afforded by the seafarers added their own observations. It was agreed that the Cape men were short, agile, well-formed and active; civil enough when treated fairly, although expert at picking and stealing. All newcomers admired their ability as cattlemen, in breeding fine animals, maintaining them in condition, and controlling their movements by whistling – a skill that had helped in the defeat of d'Almeida's men. Their personal habits were, however, deplored; a fashion of covering themselves so thickly in animal fat that it was possible to engrave patterns in the grease, and garlanding their limbs with entrails, rendered them unpleasant close companions.[15]

Sir Thomas Smythe (or Smith), first Governor of the Honorable East India Company, was responsible for the appearance of the first indigenous South African in historical records. In the year 1613 one 'Coree' was kidnapped from the Cape by a homeward-bound Indiaman (*Hector*, Captain Towerson) and carried back to London. There, although lodged in Sir Thomas's own house, cherished and adorned with a suit of brazen armour, he was unhappy: 'for when he had learned a little of our language he would daily lie upon the ground and cry very often thus in broken English, "Coree go home, Souldania go, home go." '[16]

Coree was duly returned, laden with 'tinkerlie treasure'; 'he had no sooner set footing on his own shore, but presently he threw away his cloathes, his linen, with all other covering, and got his sheepskins upon his back.' Once home Coree took some pride in his adventure, and taught his people to chant 'Sir Thomas Smithe English Shippes,' which they did 'with great glorye'. Later visitors found Coree usually helpful, willing to provide cattle and sheep, but his residence in England had taught him something of European values, and he insisted on proper prices for his beasts, which particularly annoyed the Dutch. Misunderstandings sometimes occurred, usually because the seamen, knowing nothing of African society, assumed that Coree had greater powers than he in fact possessed.

With Coree's help communications were established, in a sort of English, Europeans finding it impossible to master the native language, a complex affair of grunts and palatal clicks often likened to turkeys gobbling or, according to one French observer, as though 'they fart with their tongues in their mouths'. In an attempt to describe it the traders lit on the onomatopoeic 'Hottentot', which thereafter served as a name for the native herdspeople. Watching each other with wary reserve, the visitors and inhabitants contrived, on the whole, to profit from their intercourse; as long, that is, as the visitors remained only transient.

Coree's people

The London to which Coree was taken was the city of Rebecca Rolfe, better known as the Princess Pocahontas, and Shakespeare's Caliban. Savages, especially well-mannered ones, were fashionable objects of friendly curiosity. Seafarers visiting the Cape, being dependent upon the goodwill of the inhabitants, continued friendly relations, but without showing much curiosity as to how the people there lived. No one strayed far from the beach, and it was not until the first settlers arrived that much discord arose. Even then relations remained superficial, as were the travellers' descriptions of the natives. Not until the end of the eighteenth century, when methodical anthropological studies began, did the Cape people begin to be understood; and by then their society had been damaged beyond repair.[17]

Coree's people were one of the many small Khoikhoi communities. They possessed little more than stone-age technology, but were most skilful cattle-breeders, cherishing the beasts which formed the centre of their social activities. Their command over cattle was extraordinary: riding them was commonplace, the beasts could be trained for warfare, and at night they would lay themselves down in the centre of the camp. Probably originating further north, the Khoikhoi had over the centuries drifted south-west to what is now Namibia and the Western Cape in search of pasture, moving in regular patterns within specific territories. Like most nomadic peoples the Khoikhoi were self-limiting in numbers: in Coree's time probably fewer than 100,000 spread over a territory the size of France or Texas. Of this region they were the undisputed masters, the nearest similar communities being the Bantu-speaking blacks five hundred miles east of Table Bay.

On the fringes of Khoikhoi territory, by the coast and in the arid semi-desert the Bushmen – 'San' to the Khoikhoi, and to many later writers – led an even more scattered existence. The distinction between the two peoples is possibly artificial, relating more to their modes of life than to any more fundamental difference. Khoikhoi were essentially pastoralists, cultivating nothing except the narcotic *dagga*, while Bushmen were hunter-gatherers, possessing an intimate knowledge of the land, the location of water and the edible plants – *veldkos* – found even in the desert. Using carefully constructed poisoned arrows, the heads of which detached themselves in the animals' flesh, Bushmen were expert in the pursuit of game, even the largest. Since under the head of game the Bushmen sometimes classed Khoikhoi cattle, relations between the two groups were cool. Both used similar languages, and individuals could pass reasonably easily between groups: Khoikhoi who had lost their cattle might revert to the life of hunter-gatherers.

Neither Khoikhoi nor San were adept at the arts of metal working, pottery or weaving, relying wherever possible on trading with more technically advanced black communities, but they contrived an existence much less unpleasant than that imagined by Thomas Hobbes as being the life of primitive man – 'solitary, poor, nasty, brutish and short'. Both frequently appeared to attain a healthy old age, in comparison to European contemporaries; game, fruit, edible plants and roots were plentiful, and Khoikhoi had a good supply of milk and occasional meat. Strife, usually arising from disputes over cattle, was in the nature of an angry confrontation rather than a battle, and was rarely dangerous. Khoikhoi shelters were simple – those of the Bushmen being nothing more than windbreaks – but adequate for the climate, as was their simple clothing. Bushman rock paintings, forming a chronicle of that people's life from the Stone Age to the coming of the white man with his ships and guns, are magnificent artistic achievements by any standards.[18] Internal strife was rare, and external enemies unknown. All who came across Khoikhoi were impressed by their good nature and high spirits, and by their social life. Olfert Dapper, who never visited Africa but whose sources were reliable, commented: 'Dull-witted, dirty and coarse as these people are, they yet seem to preserve the law of nations as inviolate . . . as it is among the most polished nations of Europe

. . . in generosity and loyalty to those nearest them, they appear to shame the Dutch.' Above all, both groups had a vital and rich spiritual existence, with regular ceremonies and festivals.[19] But it was a fragile existence, in that each band had to be able to range freely over a territory extensive enough to provide grazing, game and foodstuffs, and to have access to the vital supplies of water. Conditions near the Cape were good, and the Cape Khoikhoi were numerous and cohesive, but in less favoured areas natural catastrophes or raids could have more serious consequences.

Early travellers were struck by the dissimilarities between Khoi-San and the Negroes they had met further up the coast. Khoi-San were 'yellowish in colour, like mulattos or yellowish Javanese', or 'not darker than an ordinarily white Mestiso'.[20] Laurens van der Post, who in the early years of the twentieth century had a San nurse, described her as 'apricot' complexioned. Bushmen-San were generally slighter than Khoikhoi, well under five feet tall on average, with very small hands and feet. But their most interesting peculiarities, which all travellers noted with excited curiosity, were that not only were Khoikhoi and San possessed of remarkably protruding buttocks, but the female genitalia were particularly interesting. The first Englishman to record his impressions of South Africa was the Revd. Patrick Copland, in 1611. He found the people 'loving, afraid at first by reason of the unkindnesse of the Dutch' (who plundered their cattle), but later 'more kind'. The women 'were shame-faced at first; but at our returne homewards they would lift up their Rat-skinnes and shew their privities'. Hottentot anatomy continued to captivate travellers; examining the extraordinary elongated labia of Khoi-San women – a small fee payable in tobacco was exacted – became a recognized diversion, but the modest Francis Galton, two and a half centuries after Copland, had resort to measuring Khoikhoi ladies with a sextant.[21]

As in other primitive pastoral communities – the highlands of Scotland, for example – units were those of the extended family. Patrilineal clans were grouped into tribes, the chief of which held a real but uncertain authority, dependent upon his own abilities and character. Within a group justice was administered by communal decisions, under the presidency of the accepted headman, but with the permanent possibility of a disgruntled individual being able to pick up his weapons and walk off elsewhere, into the unlimited spaces of Africa, where he would somewhere find a welcome. On the eastern borders this might well be among the black communities, who accepted individual Khoikhoi on equal terms, intermarrying freely.

This liberty of movement, unequalled in the more crowded conditions of Europe, has continued to influence African history. The voortrekkers who later moved off hundreds of miles into the veld to escape the annoying effects of a methodical British liberalism were following an ancient African tradition, and in fact were guided and protected on their journey by many of the descendants of the Khoikhoi and San.

This loosely organized, sparse and open Khoi-San society was open to assimilation much more readily than would have been the black communities found elsewhere in Africa. Had the first European settlers in the south been faced with powerful tribes, with a sense of specific identity amounting to something like nationalism, and under strong leadership, the most likely outcome would have been conquest, as in Ashante, or a system of treaties backed by the threat of coercion, as in Nigeria. As it was, the Dutch at the Cape were able to settle into a form of symbiosis with the Khoikhoi and even, for a century or so, with the annoyingly independent Bushmen.[22]

Early European settlers, finding themselves in a strange and sometimes terrifying country, and often possessing few essential survival skills, learned much from the San hunters, and the Khoikhoi skills in managing oxen were transmitted to the Trekboers, those nineteenth-century heroes of Afrikanerdom. This Khoi-San heritage was not much acknowledged, nor was their intermarriage with the Europeans, contributing to the energetic people variously called Bastaards, Griquas or Oorlams, who later fought alongside their Boer cousins in wresting the land from the black nations, and got little credit for so doing.

European attitudes to African and other non-European societies have undergone a number of changes in the last five centuries. The first, Portuguese, explorers of Africa viewed the natives they discovered either as potential merchandise or – often indeed as well as – benighted souls to be saved. They displayed little of the anthropological curiosity that was manifested by the second wave, those Dutch and Germans who settled in the Cape after 1652. Protestant enthusiasm for soul-saving was at the time not great, and more skilled slaves were available from the Dutch possessions in the East Indies; but a new interest in scientific matters, the 'Great Instauration' of new learning, brought with it more methodical observers, whose accounts form the first reliable historical evidence. A century later another shift in European perceptions of other cultures emerged, inspired by Rousseau and popularized by such romantic writers as Chateaubriand, with his idealized portrait of American Indians; the idea of the 'noble savage', unspoilt by corrupt civilizations, was widespread. Such illusions were not shared by the first British-based missionaries, who arrived in South Africa at the end of the eighteenth century; these tough-minded and realistic apostles accepted their black brothers with all their weaknesses, real and apparent, and set about improving their material as well as their spiritual lives. And in the latest shift, a combination of general distaste at twentieth-century South African policies and a more informed appreciation of different cultures has led to the present atmosphere of embarrassed diffidence or angry recrimination in which any discussion of race is difficult.

Parallel to these changes in sensibility were alterations in the balance of power between colonists and natives. For many years different communities contrived to co-exist a good deal more comfortably than did their contemporaries in North America or Europe. Only after the absorption of the Cape into the British Empire at the beginning of the nineteenth century did the deployment of power decisively shift the advantage to the white man. A century of increasingly violent struggles ended with white supremacy being accepted, with greater or lesser – generally much lesser – enthusiasm. Another century of exploitation and increasing repression, tempered by some efforts towards black political advancement and education, was accompanied by the conflict between British and Boer traditions and the emergence of an effective opposition to white domination.

It was some time after the first use of Table Bay as a watering place and post office before Europeans thought of actually living in South Africa. For more than half a century the pattern of seasonal visits by a few ships, resting the crews, watering, bartering for livestock, and then continuing their voyage, continued. No European attempted a settlement there; at least not voluntarily. A Portuguese crew was wrecked in 1630, and contrived to pass some months in Table Bay without undue suffering, maintaining friendly relations with the natives, but left no detailed account of their experiences. 'Imprudent bumptiousness' by the skipper was blamed for the wreck of the VOC ship *Mauritius Eiland* in 1644, but the crew were speedily relieved by the rest of the outward-bound Dutch fleet. It was therefore not until 1647, after the wreck of the East Indiaman *Haarlem*, whose crew were obliged to spend a year on shore, that Europeans became aware of the potentialities of the Cape.[23]

Thomas Aldworth, the HEIC factor at Surat, made the first suggestion of establishing a European settlement in South Africa. Writing to Sir Thomas Smythe in 1611, Aldworth described the Cape with enthusiasm; he had never in his life seen a better country, with 'very courteous and tractable folk'. Just the place, he considered, to receive a hundred convicts each year, to be allowed to prosper or perish. After due consideration Smythe agreed, but only ten convicts were placed at the Cape, provided with 'half a pecke of turnopp seedes with others & a spade to digg the grounde' under the leadership of one James Crosse, an unsuccessful highwayman. The venture was a complete failure. The terrified convicts sought shelter from the alarming natives on the stony and waterless Robben Island, where they eked out a miserable existence until visiting ships took pity on them. Three made their way back to England, where, directly on landing, they stole a purse. Incompetents that they were, their crime was immediately discovered, and within hours they found themselves on the gallows.[24]

Smythe tried once more, but the second batch of prisoners, once arrived in Table Bay, begged the captain of their ship to hang them then and there, rather than abandoning them to the same fate as their predecessors. Unable to oblige, the captain left them on shore, whence, however, they were rescued only a few days later by another English ship.

It fell rather to the Dutch to establish the first European settlement, although as a victualling station and trading post rather than a colony, and so to begin the methodical recording of South African history.

TWO

An Inn on the Road to the Indies

A dry and barren waste

It may sound crass to identify Jan van Riebeeck as the founder of modern South Africa. A face said to be his, but more probably that of an obscure infantry officer, was until recently imprinted on banknotes; a ten-foot-high statue still overlooks Table Bay; but he and his mixed European community were late arrivals on the continent, intruders into established societies, who brought with them the forebears of those Afrikaners who became, in the eyes of most South Africans, *the* enemy. But if today's South Africa is truly a unique heterogeneous 'rainbow community', in which many cultures and races have their place, van Riebeeck's landing was a critical starting point, and an exceptionally well-documented one.[1] Certainly that short, fiery and energetic pragmatist, who endured ten years' service in a place he detested, among people he disliked, always yearning to return to the East Indies, ensured that the settlement at the Cape of Good Hope was solidly established as a victualling station. In justice, however, the distinction of founding modern South Africa should be shared with such later men as Simon van der Stel and Hendryk van Rheede. Not until 1687, twenty-five years after van Riebeeck arrived, could the Cape settlement be described as much more than a fortified camp, with few amenities and still reliant on the goodwill of neighbouring Khoikhoi.

Starting his career with the VOC in 1639 as a surgeon's mate, the lowest of grades, van Riebeeck had quickly worked his way up to the rank of *onderkoopman* (junior merchant) at the age of twenty-three. Two years later he was in charge of the Company's establishment at Tonkin (North Vietnam), and he made his first appearance in the Company's records when in 1645 he reported an '*extraordinarien tuffon ende hoge watervloeden*'.[2] Shortly afterwards van Riebeeck found himself accused of private trading, by no means unusual but regarded as a serious offence, and was sent home to await formal sentence, which was to be dismissed from the Company's service. Back in Amsterdam he immersed himself in business, made voyages as far afield as Greenland and the West Indies, but hankered after re-employment by the VOC and the chance to make his fortune in the East.

The opportunity came when in 1650 the directors considered an enthusi-astic memorandum from Junior Merchant Leendert Janzoon, who had been left in charge of the shipwrecked crew of the Indiaman *Haarlem*, advocating an establishment at the Cape. His 'Remonstrance' fairly bubbles with enthusiasm.[3] The bay was extensive, but sheltered, with good holding ground; a freshwater spring was adjacent to the beach; in the admirable climate almost any crop could flourish; a 'multitude of sick' could be restored to health, with an abundance of pumpkins, watermelons, cabbages, carrots, radishes, turnips, onions, leeks, orange, lemon, citron, shaddock, apple, pear, plum, cherry, currant and gooseberry grown on the spot; meat, cheese, butter and milk could be procured from the inhabitants. Under the guidance of experienced men from Holland, Chinese convicts from Batavia could till the land: 'they are an industrious people, most of them understand gardening, and there are always enough of them in irons.' Some claimed the locals were aggressive, and cannibals to boot – this last a foul slander – but if so it was only as a result of bad treatment: 'the farmers in this country [Holland], were we to shoot their cattle or take them away without payment, if they had no justice to fear, would not be one hair better than these natives.' If, on the contrary, 'these natives' were treated properly and entertained 'with stomach-fulls of peas and beans, which they are greatly partial to', quantities of cattle would doubtless be forthcoming.

Moreover they were ripe for conversion, 'whereby not only would God's holy name be magnified', but 'by so doing beyond all doubt, your Honour's trade all over India will be more and more blessed'. All that would be necessary, Leendert insisted, was to build a small fort, and to establish a garden, for which a community of sixty or seventy soldiers and sailors who could turn their hands to manual labour should prove sufficient. The annual cost would not be more than fourteen thousand guilders, which sum would quickly be covered by savings; ships would need to carry fewer provisions, with a consequent gain in profitable cargo space; the sick could recover while ships were watered and provisioned; and profitable local industries could be established.

For some months the directors pondered Leendert's recommendations. There was little enthusiasm for another cost-centre, which could never be expected to generate much in the way of income, but it was true that economies might be made. Casualties on the Company's voyages to the East were considerable – in the 1652 season, by no means particularly bad, 611 crew and passengers died on the outward passage.[4] Scurvy was widespread and debilitating but could be quickly relieved by fresh vegetables (and by lemon-juice, as James Lancaster, but apparently not subsequent captains, well knew). The space taken up by these useless bodies, together with that occupied by their provisions – water was particularly troublesome – could be put to good use for extra stowage on the return passage. An opinion was sought from the newly-forgiven van Riebeeck, as one who had called at the Cape.

'Further considerations and reflections upon some points of the Remonstrance', the document he submitted in June 1651, is very much what one might expect, 350 years later, from a middle-ranking manager to the directors of a large corporation. It is respectful – he invokes their 'greater experience', proffers his opinion 'in correction of persons of place of a better', but points out that he has all the necessary qualifications to superintend such an enterprise – experience of China and Japan, similar in climate, and of Greenland, where he has observed the whalers at work (surely another possible industry?); and he offers his own suggestions on the establishment of hide- and skin-processing plants. When passing the Cape on his way from India he had taken the opportunity of looking round. The land that could be seen from the Cape hills – 'a good ten miles wide' – was 'so fertile and rich that neither Formosa, which I have seen, nor the New Netherlands [the present-day states of New York and New Jersey], which I have heard of, can be compared with it'. Even thousands of those Chinese convicts could not 'take up or cultivate a quarter part of this land'. At the end came the earnest hope that the directors, 'being satisfied in every respect, may find an opportunity of thinking about our further promotion'.

Van Riebeeck's review was absurdly optimistic, and a source of later embarrassment. The Cape flats, the nearly-twenty-mile stretch of land between the mountains of the Cape Peninsula and the precipitous crags of Hottentots Holland, which he had clearly seen only from a distance, was in reality nothing more than a sandy waste, nor were there thousands of industrious Chinese available. But the directors were sufficiently impressed, and, Leendert being no longer available, gave van Riebeeck the task of establishing a settlement. Although hardly a plum job – there was no specific increase in rank, and although styled 'Commander', van Riebeeck's substantive status remained that of 'Merchant', at the not-too-generous salary of seventy-five, rising to a hundred guilders a month – it was at least a step towards resuming his career in the East Indies. He was not, nor were his immediate successors, given the title of 'Governor', underlining that there was no intention in the directors' minds of founding a settlement colony.

Dutch experience with settlement colonies had been disappointing. The West India Company had made a serious effort to plant Dutch farmers in the fertile Hudson Valley, but after forty years only a thousand or so had settled, in spite of the Company subcontracting its work to '*patroons*'. Kiliaen van Rensselaer, the greatest of these absentee landlords, who held three quarters of a million acres, complained: 'We seek to populate the country and at the same time to propagate the doctrine of Holy Writ by settling a multitude of people there; they [the West India Company directors] on the contrary, want but a few people only to gorge themselves on the profits of the pelts.'[5] The results formed a sad contrast to conditions in the neighbouring New England states, which had shaken off their original Company backers and become largely self-governing communities; but the Dutch East India Company adopted the same policies in Africa, and invariably put cash-flow and profits first, not seeking to populate the country with demanding and obstreperous settlers. At the forefront of the directors' minds must have been the unhappy experience of their sister company in Brazil. Many investors held shares in both West and East India Companies, and in 1652 the West Indians' prize colony, Brazil, had collapsed. Tremendous effort, much expense, and the appointment of the Most Eminent Count John Maurice of Nassau as Governor, had failed in the face of Portuguese opposition. Losses, both in prestige and cash, had been heavy, and once having been badly burned Dutch entrepreneurs remained shy of attempting more large-scale commitments. The Cape had to remain an 'inn on the road to the Indies', staffed by whoever might be persuaded to go there, and run on the proverbial shoestring.

All that his directors required van Riebeeck to do was build a primitive fort, an earthwork on which cannon salvaged from the *Haarlem* could be mounted to cover the watering-place. Given the limited range of contemporary guns, the fact that the site was overlooked by higher ground, and that easy landing places in the neighbourhood abounded, such a fort could never be an adequate defence against invasion, but it would serve against any attacks by the Khoikhoi. Vegetables and fruit enough to provision visiting Company ships were to be grown, while for meat the commander could, according to Leendert, rely on the Khoikhoi being willing to sell their animals. These tasks could be carried out by a few score soldiers, as cheaply as possible, and without other assistance. No money was available to support clashes with the natives, nor need too much trouble be taken about 'propagating the doctrine of Holy Writ'. Each community should keep itself to itself, and cattle must be obtained by friendly barter: fighting was not cost-effective. Once this work was complete, and it might take a couple of years, van Riebeeck believed that he would be posted on to a more attractive post in the Indies.

Government at the Cape station began in the simplest form, adapted from the method used by the VOC on its ships, and evolved into that of other Company '*comptoirs*' or offices. A Council of Policy headed by the Commander or Governor and his Secunde (Deputy) was responsible for administering the station in much the same way that a local board might oversee the affairs of a subsidiary company. The senior military officer and, later, the Independent Fiscal, a legal officer, together with ranking senior and junior merchants, completed the Council; except that when ships were in the harbour their captains were co-opted onto it. Also, which was to become a cause of annoyance to the station administrators, any senior Company official passing by the Cape could bring the powers of a Commissioner, enabling him after only a few days' stay to make criticisms and issue orders which permanent staff thought ill-judged – a corporate practice not unknown today; 'Chatterers' (*sy praters*) who see things only 'cursorily and superficially', growled van Riebeeck. In the early days, however, the composition of the Council was fluid, with the highest rank under the commander being that of the sergeant in command of troops. It was not until August 1655 that a secunde, Onderkoopman Jacob Reynierz, was appointed.

In so small a station Council members were in almost permanent touch with each other, but formal meetings took place once a week. The proceedings of these, together with the daily log, were recorded with meticulous care and despatched both to the Governor General's office at Batavia and to the Company directors in Amsterdam. Officially the Cape station was a sub-office of Batavia, but in practice, since it was many weeks' sail closer to the Netherlands, orders often came straight from the directors; the situation was that of a department with line responsibility to the head office (Batavia), but with frequent interference from the shareholders (Amsterdam). Within the limits set down by the Statutes of India, under which the Dutch Eastern empire was governed, the Cape Council of Policy had full powers, both executive and legislative, although subject to the Commander's final decision. Directives were issued in the form of '*placaaten*', which had the force of law.

It was confusing enough to have a single body acting as executive and legislature, but the members also formed the Court of Justice, pronouncing the penalties for infractions of their own statutes. Batavia and the visiting Commissioners did their best to tidy up the resultant muddle and unfairness, but in spite of reforms the system, acceptable for a garrison, became increasingly unworkable as a colonial society developed. Since in the early years all those at the Cape were co-employees, the directives were simply announcements of management decisions; later, as the number of private citizens grew, the accumulation of these frequent summary pronouncements often made the law incomprehensible, especially when Company officers appeared to be using their powers to feather their own nests. Much later, in the nineteenth century, when Dutch settlers in the newly-established republics set up their own constitutions, this arbitrary form of legislation was sometimes adopted, with much ensuing dissension.

On 6 April 1652, when van Riebeeck's ships *Drommedaris*, *Reijger* and *Goede Hoop* anchored in Table Bay, the methodically recorded history of South Africa began. From then, for 150 years, the VOC officers kept a detailed journal, which gives an almost day-by-day account of events; together with the judicial records and official despatches between the Cape, Amsterdam and Batavia, life at the Cape can be described with uncommon precision.[6]

Van Riebeeck set about his task with great energy. Some years later, when he was bitterly recounting his achievements to what seemed an ungrateful board of directors, he wrote that he had 'been landed on a dry and barren waste, without a place to live in, and with only a parcel of light materials, the largest piece of timber being only some trumpery beams, planks, and spars, in order, under your instructions, to erect such a fort as would suffice for your purpose, without a single man possessed of any kind of skill – but with sick in abundance – without a single herb for our

refreshment – and thus with some 90 weak, unskilful, sea-worn and scor-
butic men, we had to commence the work, at which ... they were so raw
that the Commander was obliged to set to work himself as engineer, exca-
vator, gardener, farmer, carpenter, mason, blacksmith & etc.' He might
have added that, even had they been fit, his men were often bad bargains,
idle, deceitful and quarrelsome. Most were soldiers of fortune – Dutch,
German, English and Danish – who had joined for the sole reason of
making as much money as they could, and often thereafter spending it in
the shortest possible time; none had come with any intention of settling
in that wild and distant land.[7]

Fortunately, some of the company were more admirable characters. The
krankbesoeker (literally 'sick visitor', or perhaps lay reader, the station being
too insignificant to warrant a chaplain), Willem Wylant, was dedicated to
his work – somewhat unusually, for krankbesoekers had a poor reputation:
'drink-visitors' and 'clownish idiots' were among the epithets applied to
them. Hendrik Boom, the master gardener, and Pieter van Mierhoff, assistant surgeon, both distinguished themselves. Boom and Wylant had brought
their families out with them, as had van Riebeeck himself, so that from
the beginning the settlement had some civilizing female influence, much
needed, and led by the Commander's wife, Maria de la Quellière, described
as 'one of the most perfect women I have ever seen', and liked by everyone.

Van Riebeeck's determination was tested, but within eight months earth-
works had indeed been built, gardens laid and seeds sown, and even some
vegetables harvested. Nevertheless, far from being able to provision the first,
homeward-bound, fleet adequately when it arrived the following March, the
ships themselves were obliged to contribute several tons of rice, together
with salt meat and biscuit, to the hungry garrison; some fresh vegetables
and sufficient fresh meat for their crews in harbour were however made
available. Even this was a considerable achievement, for life at the Cape
had been hard. Landing at the approach of winter, the expedition discovered
that the Khoikhoi herder bands had moved off for the season, and the only
inhabitants were some San '*strandloopers*' who led a precarious beachcomb-
ing existence. Without fresh meat, rations were reduced to fish, seals,
seagulls, penguins and even cormorants, an unappetizing fowl. Volunteer
Vogelaer, furious at being served penguin instead of Christian beef or pork,
'desired the Devil to take the Purser',[8] and received a hundred blows with
a musket butt for his offence. On 24 September 1652, the day that an
optimistic despatch was sent claiming that the initial work had gone so

well 'it therefore begins to be time to look about for some profits to
our masters, towards solace for the costs already incurred', four Dutchmen deserted, with 'four biscuits and fish ... four swords, two pistols
and the dog'. They lasted less than a week, persecuted by rhinoceroses and
a porcupine, before deciding to return and take their punishment – 150
lashes, and two years' slavery – as being preferable to the perils of the
hinterland.

Soon thereafter things improved; moving in their customary annual
pattern, the Khoikhoi bands reached the Cape with 'thousands of cattle
and sheep'. By the beginning of December some cattle were forthcoming,
traded for tobacco, and copper, all in the greatest amity: 'the Saldanhars
seek to show us all the friendship they can' wrote van Riebeeck on 8
December. They did not stay long, and only five days later van Riebeeck
was considering an uncomplicated way of ensuring future supplies – simply
commandeering the cattle, seizing the unsuspecting owners who 'always
come to us unarmed', and packing them off to the Indies in irons. Since
this was completely contrary to the Company's policy he regretfully concluded that he would take no such action, at least not until further instructions. What trouble there was came from within. An apparently deranged
soldier, Martinus de Hase, stole the carpenters' tools and food; when discovered he pleaded earnestly to be shot. And the Dutch herdsmen were
proving careless, allowing cattle to be stolen: they were duly punished,
again with a hundred blows with the butt-end of a musket.

Dull, stupid, lazy, stinking people

This comparatively happy state of affairs did not last for long, since the
Khoikhoi and their herds moved inexorably with the seasons, burning the
grass after them to ensure a fresh new growth. Suspicions that they were holding back, waiting for the English ships to arrive, were voiced. None of the
newcomers could grasp the native language, and in fact were forbidden by
the VOC to make the attempt, since Dutch must be the only language used
on the station. Absolute reliance was therefore placed on those very few
Africans who had learnt some Dutch or English, and of these one Hadah,
known as Herry or Harry,[9] was the most prominent. The leader of a small
band of *strandloopers*, he had picked up some English together with some
knowledge of European oddities on a voyage to Batavia. Henceforward, for

some years, the Dutch had to accept, although with increasing suspicion, Harry's version of Khoikhoi affairs.

Van Riebeeck was in something of a dilemma when he drafted his first annual report to the board on 14 April 1653. After his enthusiastic comments back in Amsterdam he was obliged to proffer some delicately phrased excuses: the outward-bound fleet had not touched as promised, only two small vessels arriving; much of the tobacco, that essential item, which had been provided was of inferior quality and rejected by the Khoikhoi connoisseurs. His apologia ended with a passionate plea to be moved on:

> I will now, to conclude, most humbly, respectfully, and earnestly pray, that your Honours will think of removing me hence to India, and to some better and higher employment, in order that in due time, and in consideration of better services than I can render here, I may earn promotion; for, among these dull, stupid, lazy, stinking people, little address [*subtylteyt*] is required as among the Japanese, Tonquinese and other precise nations thereabouts, who, as I have sufficiently experienced in my ten years' service, give enough to do to the brains of the cleverest Dutchman;

and, since he was accorded the title of Commander, could he please be paid accordingly? Three weeks later, on 4 May, van Riebeeck tried another tack. He had heard from a German priest that sea communication could easily be established up the east coast, where at a distance of some 750 miles 'much gold, ivory, ebony and naked Caffers or slaves, are to be had at a very cheap rate'. Might he be allowed to visit this place, 'which many maintain is the true Ophir . . . before my departure for Batavia'. The answer was negative, van Riebeeck's hopes were dashed; he was destined to spend another nine years with this 'dull, stupid, lazy, stinking people'.

Not only did no further supplies come, but little trading was possible before disaster struck. On 19 October 1653, while the garrison was at Sunday service, the boy in charge of the herd was killed and all the Company cattle stolen. Harry, it appeared, was responsible, with his *strandloopers*; the ungrateful Harry, whom 'we always acknowledged as the chief of his little tribe . . . fed him from our table as a great friend in our house, clothed him in Dutch attire'.

Forbidden by the Company's original instructions to attempt any retaliation, the garrison were wild with frustration; there was not a single Council member, van Riebeeck reported, who would not have voted for a punitive expedition to seize the cattle and enslave the predators, sending them off in chains to work in the silver mines which would doubtless soon be discovered. At least the supply ships arrived in March 1654, a year after they were expected; but the *Breda*, *Lam*, *Kalf* and *Draak* anchored with many sick of scurvy and with a disappointing contribution to provisions: 'not a tenth of the groats or peas to fill mens' bellies . . . an essential for Dutchmen if you want them to do any work'.

A despatch was sent off to the victualling station at St Helena, then in Dutch hands, in an effort to augment supplies, but the garrison was reduced to penguins and cabbage, varied with the flesh of a dead baboon. Cattle continued in short supply, and demand looked likely to rise, since English ships began to put in after 1655. War between England and the United Provinces had broken out in 1652, the outcome of which, in the following year, had been damaging for the Dutch. Their fleets decisively defeated by Cromwell's admirals Blake and Monck, the United Provinces were made to pay compensation of £80,000 for the Amboina massacre and other losses.

For the next ten years of uneasy peace English crews calling at the Cape were treated cautiously, provisioned but fobbed off whenever feasible with the carcasses of animals already deceased from natural causes. The crew of the first English East Indiaman to visit the Cape were therefore supplied only with vegetables, although festive dinners were exchanged and a present of beer, spirits, good cheese and six smoked tongues made by the English captain. With the peace came increased traffic as the VOC trade recovered, twenty-one vessels calling in that first season and consolidating the importance of the Cape station.

On 15 February 1655 van Riebeeck received the directors' answer to his letter telling them of Harry's theft, which authorized limited punitive measures. For the first time a hint was given that the Cape's function as a victualling station might be expanded. A VOC captain, David Claes, had reported that Hout Bay,[10] a few miles to the south, which he claimed to be a better anchorage than Table Bay, was eminently suitable for agriculture and stock farming, and suggested that 'a few families from this country would be very useful'.

The Commander replied in his third annual report in April 1655, sounding rather hurt. Captain Claes' remarks were all very well (although he was mistaken about the safety of Hout Bay), but van Riebeeck professed himself 'not aware that your Honours would be inclined to establish any colony here, otherwise we should have communicated to you our ideas on the subject; but we always supposed it to be your sole object to raise here sufficient refreshments for the shipping, and if possible to find out something to meet the expenses'. Now that the board had decided otherwise, he was happy to offer suggestions based on a more intimate knowledge than that of Captain Claes: colonists were a doubtful proposition – as soon as they had made some money they would want to be off back home; they would be more inclined to fill their pockets quickly by setting up taverns than to undertake the arduous and uncertain business of pioneering; and they would need the help of a good many slaves. These difficulties could be avoided if the Company remained in sole control, and colonists need not be sought since there were already at the Cape some Company employees who had been released from their contractual obligations and allowed to set up business on their own. As a preliminary step married men were allowed as much land as they could manage for their own gardens; Mevrouw Boom, already renting cows from the Company, was permitted to open an inn, as was Sergeant Haewarden's wife; but all the menfolk remained full-time Company employees.

While this despatch was on its way to Amsterdam, on 23 June 1655, 'entirely unexpectedly', Harry turned up again with a band of 'fifty ... strange armed natives and a herd of about 40 head of fine cattle'. There had been, he explained, a regrettable misunderstanding: the herd-boy had been killed and the cattle carried off by another group of villainous Khoikhoi, known to the Dutch as *Caepmen*, led by the Fat Captain, upon which the innocent Harry had fled, fearful that he might be blamed. But now all would be well, and cattle would be made plentifully available and at a fair rate if Harry's people were allowed to return to 'the place of their birth and their own country with its abundance of fresh water that their hearts continually hankered after'. With this brighter prospect a tentative start was made in relaxing the Company's monopoly, and also thereby reducing costs. Accordingly nine Company employees were discharged in February 1657 to become 'free burghers' (*vrijburgheren*), who were to be given as much land as they could cultivate within three years. It was a very restricted freedom: they might trade only with the Company and at fixed prices, and had to make over annually one tenth of their stock; if they failed to give satisfaction they could be returned to the Company to work out the balance of their contracts; they had no political rights, and remained subject to Company discipline. These were altogether very unenticing conditions, and in no way comparable to the status of a domestic Dutch burgher, who was entitled to civic privileges and licensed to follow otherwise closed trades. The term was used in a different sense in the East India Company: all non-native people, Europeans or Asiatics, who were neither employees nor slaves were *vrijburgheren*, or simply burghers. The Cape nine – six Netherlanders and three Germans – formed themselves into two groups, under Harman Remagen, an arquebusier, and Steven Botma, a seaman 'well-versed in tobacco-growing', and took up their holdings on the eastern slopes of the Cape hills close to the fort and the settlement.

Although the more optimistic forecasts failed to materialize at least the perils of starvation were avoided. The vegetable garden, once the seasonal variations had been taken into consideration, did well, and visiting ships could in future at least expect a supply of fresh greenstuffs, but meat continued a problem. Supplies from the various Khoikhoi communities were available only in the summer, when the Cape grass flourished, and even then a reluctance to trade continued. The 'Hottentots', becoming more sophisticated traders, raised their prices, and took every opportunity to pilfer from the garrison; the Commander would be entirely justified, he argued, in seizing the cattle of the worst offenders and banishing the ring-leaders to Robben Island, already identified as a convenient place of detention.

Both newcomers and original inhabitants, in spite of what clearly were considerable efforts, experienced difficulties in getting the measure of each other. Confined by their orders to the immediate environs of Table Bay, the Dutch had little opportunity of analysing the social structure of the Khoikhoi. It was understood that a number of communities existed, often at odds with each other, and that power struggles between individuals were as likely to be expected as in more civilized societies. Harry was strongly suspected of having used his contacts with the Dutch to claw his way up, a suspicion reinforced by reports from a young Khoikhoi girl, Eva, his niece, who was living in the Commander's house, adopted by Mevrouw van Riebeeck. Eva settled happily to Dutch customs, although she found Indian dress more becoming, and engaged the affections of Pieter van Mierhoff, the young Danish surgeon. The couple were formally married with some ceremony and Eva, speaking fluent Dutch, became the most reliable interpreter between the two communities. Another Hottentot girl, Cornelia, who lived in the same house, was found fifty years later speaking excellent Dutch and able to recall all the commanders from van Riebeeck on.

The anticipated profits disappear in smoke

Back in Amsterdam, although it was acknowledged that satisfactory progress had been made in some respects, it was felt that many deficiencies remained, and it was made clear to van Riebeeck that he had much to do before he could hope to be allowed to return to the Indies. In October 1656 his salary was raised to 130 guilders a month, and a three-year contract was offered; but he was not to be given the transfer he so much wanted. An inspector from head office, in the person of Rykloff van Goens, a very senior official, later Governor General, was sent to report. Van Goens had already visited the Cape in April 1655, when he had discussed the colonization project with the Commander. His report was submitted after a month's stay in April 1657. It was not uncritical: 'very little skill is required to point out your faults, and to call you to account for them'. Van Riebeeck had been tediously prolix in his own reporting to Amsterdam; his station was over-manned, with too many Company employees being retained on the payroll; too much building was being done, to the neglect of farming; 'above all attend to the support of grain cultivation; we shall never become noblemen here, until we shall first have been good farmers'. And there should be more active exploration: 'I see little difficulty in penetrating from this quarter to . . . Spirito Santu and the City of Monomatapa,' where the gold that found its way to Zimbabwe and the coast originated. To achieve these ends free burghers must be encouraged, and their interests safeguarded by having a burgher sit with the Council when it exercised its judicial function; Steven Botma was accordingly appointed, and Hendrik Boom, the gardener, now also a free burgher, joined him the following year. Boom's name had been selected from a list submitted by the burghers, a compromise between election and appointment which was to remain popular well after Company rule had ended.

Van Riebeeck was annoyed by the Commissioner's criticisms, and made sulky explanatory marginal notes. He had already attempted many explorations, with loss of men and health and without finding anything; far from cutting down on staff he must have more labour if adequate supplies were to be provided – if only, he lamented, he had Formosans and Chinese workers, agriculture would flourish. Nor was he pleased to have, yet again, the directors' policy towards the Cape inhabitants emphasized. Van Riebeeck's exasperation had led him to recommend aggressive action which was now condemned as 'barbarous and un-Christian, and would therefore be abhorred and punished by God'. Fortifications, his superiors insisted, in spite of the cost, and continued wariness were the only policies. Far too expensive, van Riebeeck complained, and wrote briskly that he would need at least 1,500 spades and shovels to do all that was required.

But the Council of India agreed with van Goens' 'well-digested instructions'. 'Speculations of remote advantages . . . should be thrown aside,' and van Riebeeck's grand ideas must be abandoned. Expenses were certain, and continuous, but 'the anticipated profits . . . come in very slowly, and, indeed, sometimes totally disappear in smoke'. Cutting down the overpaid establishment must be offset by increasing the number of unpaid free burghers. Company employees should be encouraged on their discharge to settle with their families 'with every assistance in your power'. Certainly no shortage of Company employees wishing to be discharged was noticeable: twenty asked to leave in September 1657, but only five were accepted as burghers. Others absconded without asking permission, abandoning any prospects of back-pay; in 1658 no fewer than twenty-one stowed away on the homeward-bound fleet. Gradually, however, the number of free burghers grew, and by the end of 1658 another forty or so had elected to try their chance at farming or such trades as carpentry, fishing or tailoring.

They soon became disillusioned. On 23 December 1658 Botma and Boom, on behalf of all the burghers, submitted a formal protest to the Council against the conditions imposed upon them, which they claimed made it impossible to work their holdings economically. This document, interspersed with van Riebeeck's indignant comments, demonstrates the complaints which, often justified and sometimes rectified, were to be constant for the next century: trading with the Khoikhoi was restricted or forbidden; the beasts provided by the company (on payment) were tiny – the size of a big dog; the fixed price for wheat was uneconomically low; Company officials feathered their own nests and neglected the farmers' interests.

The Commander was furious (the last accusation was a little near the bone, for the van Riebeeck farm was already notably the richest in the whole settlement), and angrily marginalized: 'With what a seditious spirit, and what pertinacity, they strove'; but the petitioners were placated with 'a rummer or two of wine', accompanied by promises to intercede with the directors for better prices. For their part the farmers shuffled their feet and acknowledged that they had blundered, and that the Commander had always done his best for them. When the petition reached the directors they were inclined to sympathize with the farmers' complaints: in September 1659 van Riebeeck was once more instructed to encourage the freemen, some of the restrictions on trade were relaxed, and prices were raised; but by this time other troubles were in the forefront of men's minds.

If Europeans could not be persuaded to produce the Company's food, and forcing the Khoikhoi to labour was forbidden, the obvious solution, van Riebeeck insisted, was to import slaves. Slave labour had seemed to serve the Company well in the East, where its brutal suppression of resistance had, as Leendert indicated, produced an ample supply of captives. Batavia, however, when consulted, disapproved; they had found slavery encouraged colonists to be idle and unwilling to labour for themselves; the Cape would do well to avoid importing slaves.

But Amsterdam eventually gave its permission, and sources of slaves were investigated. Nearer to the Cape, well-established markets existed in Angola and Mozambique, where the Portuguese and Arabs cooperated with African chiefs to export slaves to the Levant, the Indies and, increasingly, the West Indies and North America. Little feeling of moral obloquy then attached to the trade; slavery was almost unknown in Europe, but was fundamental to the economy of many European colonies – all Hispanic America and the Dutch East Indies, for example – and although unknown to English common law had an accepted place in all Roman-law countries, of which the Netherlands was one.[11] Van Riebeeck had accordingly been pestering the directors for three years, but they being reluctant to add even more to the expenses of the station it was not until 1657 that the first consignment from Angola arrived.

The decision to rely upon imported slave labour was a turning point in African history, the start both of the 'Cape Coloured' population, that talented and spirited combination of Khoikhoi, European, East Asian and black races, and of some deeply harmful attitudes of mind in the white, and especially the Dutch white, population. In April 1657 there were 144 people on the station: a hundred company employees, ten free burghers, six married women, twelve children, ten slaves and six convicts. The number of slaves increased sharply in March the next year, when a Portuguese slaver was captured and 250 head of her cargo taken to the Cape. Many of these were too young for work, and were sent to school under the chaplain, under the eye of the Commandant himself for the first few days; they were stimulated to industry by the promise of a tot of brandy and tobacco when their lessons were satisfactorily learnt. Some of the others who were fit for employment – relatively few – were transferred, on credit, to the free burghers to help on the farms. A further consignment came two months later, when 228 Guinea slaves (there had been a wastage of forty-three on the relatively short voyage) were landed. Those who survived looked more promising than their predecessors, and were sold for one hundred guilders a head to the free burghers on 9 May. They did not stay long: on 18 June 'Casper Brickman, *vry borger*, came with tears in his eyes to complain that all four of his Guinea slaves – male and female – had deserted.' Three days later all Jan Reynier's stock of slaves vanished in a single night, while the Company had already lost seven of theirs.

The loss was serious – the better part of two thousand guilders, the financial equivalent of four hundred times that number of good cattle. Two more slaves took off on 17 August, no fewer than fourteen on the night of the twenty-fifth, and yet another fourteen on 4 September. In an attempt to prevent further losses a proclamation allowing all slaves to be kept in irons was emitted; but the farmers felt that this was more bother than profit – even though they were 'treated well' the slaves showed an insatiable thirst for liberty, and if fettered merely ran with their valuable chains. On 8 September the free burghers handed back half of their slave stock to the Company. Fortunately the Khoikhoi were more than ready to hunt down the runaways, both for reward and since some of the fugitives, being cannibals, subsisted by eating Khoikhoi, and most of the slaves were recaptured; but reliance upon so uncertain a source of labour remained dangerous.

All this irritated the directors: 'the expenses of our Cape establishment have reached a large sum, and are daily increasing,' they grumbled in September 1658, yet returning crews had complained that 'they received a very small supply of vegetables' while at the Cape; nor was the quantity of meat satisfactory, and the Commander was reminded once more that since the directors would not sanction the use of force to obtain this, he must improve his stock-breeding methods. Harry was given much of the blame, and banished to Robben Island, solaced by a little tobacco and not made to work because of his advanced age. His place as interpreter was taken by one Doman, who was to prove even more exasperating.

At least the freemen and slaves managed to complete the ploughing, and some initiative was shown by a group who constructed a boat and contracted to fetch sealskins and eggs from Dassen Island, but many remained idle and even criminally inclined. Pieter Jacobsen, a fisherman, and his companion, 'a lazy lout', were deprived of their burgher rights and returned to the garrison until they had learnt discipline and paid off their debts. Hendrick Schayk was sentenced to a flogging and sixteen years' labour in chains for his participation in a sheep-stealing gang. But the Company's stocks increased to over 1,300 sheep and nearly four hundred cattle, a matter for some satisfaction. Contact was also made, through Eva, with her brother-in-law, the chief of the 'true Saldanhas', reputed to be more plentifully supplied with cattle than the Capemen, and more reliable. Chief Oedasoa was reported to be 'a middle-aged man, without any beard, small and lean, and much respected by his people'.

After seven years the teething troubles of the settlement appeared to be over; the homeward-bound ship *Naerden* was amply provisioned with a ton of bread and ample supplies of gunpowder, wine, oil, brandy etc. But just as some congratulations appeared to be in order, protracted violence, the first in the station's history, erupted in May 1659, when thefts of cattle became bolder and more frequent, culminating on the nineteenth of that month in a raid during which a burgher was killed. Indignation increased when it appeared that that incursion had been led by the very Doman who had been the Company's main interpreter and who had now succeeded in uniting the neighbouring tribes against the intruders. Half a century of reasonably friendly association came to an end with this first serious manifestation of Khoikhoi resistance to the intruding Europeans. Their new-found friend Oedasoa declining to become involved, recourse was had once more to Harry, and a punitive expedition prepared. This party of 150 armed men, eighty from the VOC ship *Honingen* and seventy from the garrison and the freemen, was divided into three companies, each headed by a 'commandant', and may be called the first 'commando', an *ad hoc* militia force assembled for a specific purpose that was to play so large a part in South African history.

Although a hundred guilders were offered for the capture of Doman and forty for that of a 'common Hottentot' (half that sum for a head, although an upper lip was an acceptable substitute), the commando met with limited success. Cattle thefts continued, but on 19 July a skirmish took place in which Doman was wounded and another, Eykamma, brought in mortally wounded. Asked why the raids had been made, the dying man replied 'in tolerable Dutch . . . that it was for no other reason than that they saw we were breaking up the best land and grass, where their cattle were accustomed to graze, trying to establish ourselves everywhere, with houses and farms, as if we were never more to remove'. It was an accurate forecast of later Dutch intentions, which would, when implemented, lead to the destruction of the Khoikhoi as a people.

It became clear to the Council that better defence works were needed, since although the time for spring sowing was approaching, almost all the grain lands had been abandoned. A cattle-proof hedge was therefore constructed, much as Peter Stuyvesant had built his stockade along Wall Street, linking two tiny blockhouses, Keert de Koe (Turn-the-cow) and Kijckuijt (Lookout). This was soon supplemented by fences enclosing the freemen's farm land. When completed the settlement covered an area about six miles by two, the eastern boundary running from Bosheuvel along the Liesbeeck, with an extension into Table Valley, where the town stood, all protected by a thick hedge. Behind these defences garrison life could continue relatively undisturbed: one shocking case of attempted buggery – but he claimed to have been drunk at the time – by one Lucas Caspersen, a Prussian, had to be referred to Batavia; more pleasantly two cooks, one being Louis Richart, 'an excellent pastry-cook', were released from their contracts to set up a bakery. In December a dangerous conspiracy was uncovered by the chief surgeon, Master William Robertson of Dundee, who found that a plot had been hatched among some discontented English and Scots Company soldiers in conjunction with two shepherds, Hendrick Hendrickse van Cloppenburg and Jacob Born of Glasgow. Peter Barber of Hampstead appeared to be one of the ringleaders, but Patrick the Jock of Glasgow was included among the troublemakers, who were apparently ready to murder the entire settlement in a bid to escape. Hearing of this dreadful affair, the directors decided that no more recruits from such disreputable nations should be engaged, although the 'honest, virtuous' Master Robertson was rewarded with fifty pieces of eight.

Commissioner Peter Sterthemius, admiral of the homeward-bound fleet which called at the Cape in March 1660, was told that the English had occupied St Helena the previous year, and that in view of the 'tottering condition' of the English government it was likely that another conflict might follow, which in fact it did, in 1663. With St Helena banned to Dutch fleets the possession of the Cape became almost vital, and henceforward the station occupied a greater importance in the Company's policy. Sterthemius congratulated van Riebeeck on 'duly and zealously' complying with orders, but went on to underline the need to 'encourage and assist' the freemen, to 'allow them to build their houses, and buy, sell and exchange sheep and cattle among each other without hindrance, and also, in as far as may be without detriment to the raising of corn, to cultivate and sell to the shipping as much tobacco and other herbs as will meet the consumption – for they cannot well produce too much of these articles' (but this was already 'liberally permitted', the Commander grumbled in the margin). And once more the Cape Councillors' desire to revenge themselves on the Khoikhoi was discouraged; it would be neither Christian nor dignified, and 'such a course these savages could not reconcile with justice'.

Van Riebeeck put an optimistic gloss on events in his report to the directors sent back with the fleet, concluding: 'In short, gentlemen, all our troubles and difficulties are, thank God, past and gone, and pleasing prospects are fully restored.' At the time of writing the Commander was not to know that no fewer than forty-one discontented men had stowed away on the homeward-bound ships – twenty Company employees and three convicts, the remainder being freemen. This badly damaged his credibility, and the directors wrote sternly back in August 1660, listing the Commander's misdemeanours: far from the settlement being self-sufficient in grain, as had been claimed, rice was still having to be sent from Batavia; 'exaction and extortion' were practised on the freemen; and Amsterdam was continuously receiving reports of 'hunger and hardships'; all much at variance with van Riebeeck's story. He was therefore, quite bluntly, sacked; instructed to hand over to Gerrit van Harn, on his way out from Amsterdam, on whose arrival the former Commander was to take himself off to Batavia, reverting to his former rank, to await instructions.

Since van Harn died before taking post van Riebeeck had the better part of two years' grace before Zacharaias Wagenaar arrived to take over on 2 April 1662. In that time the supply of food to the visiting fleets had materially improved, and van Riebeeck thought it worthwhile, with Wagenaar's agreement, to make a final plea to the directors; he was entering his eleventh year of service, during which he had 'converted this Cape from a barren waste – by the labour of his hands – to a desirable place of refreshment'. Could not therefore that most dutiful and obedient servant be favoured 'with augmentation, especially in rank and salary . . .'? But it was not to be. On 6 May 1662, after more than ten years of vigorous endeavour, the ex-Commander and his family left for Batavia, solaced by the thought that he had left behind at the Cape a flourishing farm, which a year later was sold for 1,600 guilders, a useful retirement bonus. Eventually van Riebeeck finished his career as Secretary to the Council of India, still only a middle-management post, dying in the East at the age of fifty-eight.

THREE

Victualling Station
to Colony

By comparison with van Riebeeck's brisk ten-year rule, that of his immediate successors did little to alter the character of the settlement which he had founded. Not that they had much chance to do so: Zacharias Wagenaar (originally Wagner, and from Saxony) was old and in poor health, frequently afflicted by gout and sciatica, anxious only to do nothing that would prejudice a comfortable retirement. The new Commander prudently followed his predecessor's advice to 'keep your attention constantly fixed – steadfast as a wall, to this point – to live without the slightest estrangement from your neighbours here,' and not to allow the farmers to stray beyond the Company's pale, for unrestricted intercourse with the natives was bound to lead to trouble.

Wagenaar was however particularly diligent in obeying the directors' instruction to explore the regions surrounding the settlement, a task which van Riebeeck had neglected during the early years of his commission, not despatching the first party until February 1659. Returning after a month's wanderings in the north they had found nothing but a 'dry and barren country', peopled by 'banditti, a very wild people, without horses or cattle, but well-armed'.[1] These were bands of San – Bushmen – who had given the Khoikhoi lands nearer the Cape a wide berth, restricting themselves to the semi-deserts and mountains where they could contrive to live off the land.

Only in November of the following year did the first official expedition leave. Van Riebeeck may have been dilatory in beginning the work, but once decided upon he approached the project with habitual energy. The explorers were given a long list of instructions: they were to stay away for at least three months, and return only when they had found 'permanent dwellings and tribes that are not of the Hottentot nation'; should these men not understand the two Khoikhoi members of the expedition – one was Doman – communication could be effected in Dutch, Italian, or Latin. Precise directions were given for reaching the city of Dagavul, on the great river Vigiti Magna, where the Emperor of Monomatapa kept his gold. On their way the party were to note the geography, mineralogy, habits and dress of the people, their agricultural practices and military strength, and to examine the possibility of trade.[2]

European knowledge of the African hinterland was still very limited. The nearest Portuguese coastal settlements to the Cape were over a thousand miles off, and any trade routes from the east coast, developed over the centuries to the commercial centre of Great Zimbabwe, were completely inaccessible. Surrounded by deserts and mountains, the Cape was the wrong place for beginning exploration. Hampered as they were by 'a few lazy and recalcitrant fellows', the explorers got little further than the Olifants River, some 150 miles north of what was now the large village of Kaapstad, where they were able to descry the distant fires of a Khoikhoi encampment. This so encouraged van Riebeeck that almost immediately on their return he commissioned another party, under the command of Corporal Pieter Cruijthoff, with the Danish surgeon Pieter van Mierhoff, who had distinguished himself on the first expedition and who was to become the husband of the Khoikhoi girl Eva, as lieutenant.

Cruijthoff's men did better by reaching, not realms of gold, but at least the Namaqua (Nama) people. Latin was not needed, for these were Khoikhoi, although differing in many ways from those found near the Cape. They had no pottery, but wore elegant ivory and copper decoration and carried oxhide shields; their chief, Akembie, was 'a gigantic man, much bigger than Cattibou, our tallest slave'. Akembie received the explorers civilly – they taught him how to smoke a pipe – but declined an invitation to visit the Cape, since he would have trouble with the Khoikhoi already there. As well as reaching the Namaquas, Cruijthoff's men also found an abundance of wild life – elephants, lion, hartebeest, ostriches and a 'living water monster with three heads, like cats' heads, and three long tails'.

So welcome was the success of this expedition that another was quickly despatched, with Mierhoff in charge, provided with many presents to encourage the various Khoikhoi bands to reach an amicable settlement of their differences. Yet another party, once more with Cruijthoff and Mierhoff, set off that November, but in spite of a hazardous three months' journey got no further; the difficulty was that the sandy wastes of the Namaquas, north of the Olifants River, were a distinct barrier, and that the fabled town of Monomatapa was only a fable, although the river Vigiti Magna, later known as the Orange, really did exist where the maps claimed it to be.

Wagenaar was happy to oblige the directors by continuing exploration, and sent an expedition off in October 1663, under the command of Sergeant de la Guerre 'an active man, and an unusually good shot', with, once more, Pieter Mierhoff, and fourteen of 'the strongest and most active fellows, accustomed to hardships'. This effort too petered out ten days into the waterless wastes, after a three-month journey of over six hundred nautical miles. Not surprisingly, after this 'the inclination of the greater part of the amateurs seems to be on the wane', and Commander Wagenaar concluded that further overland journeys to the north were likely to be too dangerous.[3]

The settlement remained concentrated on the Cape Peninsula, with an outstation at Saldanha Bay – which name was now given to the bay twenty miles north of Table Bay – staffed by some enterprising freemen who had acquired the 'small old sloop *Penguijn*'. Living in huts, the Saldanha men procured dried fish, seal meat and seabird eggs, all valuable supplements to the restricted diet, and train oil (from whales) for lighting. The *Penguijn* was also able to provide support to ships unable to make Table Bay, and to service the garrison on Robben Island, which served as a sheep-run and prison. Robben Island and Dassen Island, further to the north, both had sheltered anchorages which could be used as alternatives to Table Bay. The free farmers had not yet moved from the eastern slopes of the Cape hills across the sandy flats beyond which lay the menacing hills of Hottentots Holland.

Wagenaar remained unhappily at the Cape for over four years (May 1662 to September 1666), adding little to the work begun by his predecessor. Accustomed to the taxing discipline of the Company factories in Japan and the Indies, he was horrified by the Cape burghers: apart from not more than four or five prosperous and industrious farmers, and some who were active enough, 'grubbing in the ground like moles', but who could not get enough help to make a success of their endeavours, all were 'vagabonds or abandoned shameful drunkards'; moreover, living conditions were primitive, with no window glass, 'ugly, bare ... desolate', a sad contrast to the comforts of the East.

His superiors sympathized: 'twenty-five good Chinamen', they agreed, would be better than the 'lazy and unwilling' farmers at the Cape; they too had been deceived by van Riebeeck's highly coloured representations, which were 'mere rodomontade', and contrasted his optimistic projections with 'how ill it had turned out at last'. Visiting Commissioner van Odessen 'trusted that the freemen could have better hopes of success under your governorship than that which preceded it'. Could not the directors, pleaded Wagenaar in November 1663, replace some of these 'indolent, reckless and debauched' characters with more suitable and industrious people who would prosecute agriculture with more zeal?

Much regret, the directors responded; two wives, and some 'young girls, for the advancement of the population' would be sent out, but industrious farmers were not to be had; if the war with China continued there would be no want of useful slaves, but in the meantime Wagenaar must be satisfied with what he could get from established sources such as Madagascar; and he could always pack off undesirables to Mauritius, where a small station was maintained.

Wagenaar had not been in post two years before he was begging to be relieved, but it was another two years before his successor, Cornelis van Quaelberg, arrived. He lasted less than two years before being sent home in disgrace, having given too kind a reception and 'bestowed caresses' on visiting French squadrons – 'inexcusable offences'. Another decrepit Governor, Jacob Borghorst, succeeded in June 1668 to find the freemen no better behaved. If only, he complained in March 1669, they were as zealous in the culture and establishment of the colony as they were solicitous about keeping taverns, and other insufferable practices. But Borghorst kept expenses down, and was congratulated. The Company's livestock had been increased, 'and everything here is, thank God, well and in a very prosperous state'.

Commissioner van der Bronke (Broecke) met the next Commander, Pieter Hackius, in March 1670, when it was decided that the boundaries of the colony should be extended, crossing the bitter-almond barrier that Riebeeck had erected. It was a momentous decision, the first extension of the boundary outside the Cape Peninsula, the first step from station to colony, when an outstation was established across the Cape flats at Hottentots Holland, a place thought highly suitable for cereals, although the mountains, well-known to be the habitation of dragons, were much feared. Hackius, already an old man, was in an even worse state of health than his predecessor, and died in November of the following year after being confined to his bed for many months. At least he had the satisfaction of learning that, at long last, some promising colonists were setting out from Holland, with the option of proceeding to the Cape, Mauritius, Batavia and Ceylon, as they might prefer. Of the emigrants nine chose to stay at the Cape, among them one bearing a name that was to become famous – Herman Potgieter.

If the directors had been willing to treat the Cape station as a convalescent home, or even a hospice for moribund officials, their attitude changed when a serious international crisis loomed in 1671. The loss of St Helena to the English in 1659 had made the Cape the only convenient stop for homeward-bound convoys, and increasingly a welcome place of refreshment, in spite of the navigational disadvantages, for ships sailing to the Indies. Moreover, the campaigns against the Portuguese in Ceylon, which had been waged for a generation, had finally been successful in 1658, when the whole of that island passed under the rule of the VOC; the increase in trade, and still more the need to maintain a new colonial infrastructure, accentuated the Cape's value to the Company.

With the restoration of Charles II in 1660, more trouble with the English looked likely. At least Cromwell's Commonwealth had been sympathetic to the Dutch in religious matters, but King Charles was no friend to Calvinism – his brother and heir James, Duke of York, was a Catholic – and was to marry a Portuguese princess, Catherine of Braganaza, strengthening even more the Anglo–Portuguese treaty of 1654, which had given many privileges to English traders. Commercial rivalry with the Dutch intensified, and in 1665, without the formality of a declaration of war the English fleet began attacking Dutch possessions, the most significant result of these raids being the surrender of the New Netherlands to three ships and a few hundred men. In a furious naval campaign English and Dutch successes alternated, but the decisive factor was van Tromp's magnificent raid up the Medway, when he carried off the eighty-gun *Royal Charles*, the finest ship in the Royal Navy. At the Treaty of Breda in 1667 nothing fundamental was changed, with the exception of the New Netherlands becoming the states of New York and New Jersey, and New Amsterdam also changing its name to honour the Duke of York.

One lesson from this war should have been that colonial possessions were difficult, if not impossible, to defend against naval attack; in the course of the war the New Netherlands changed hands three times, and St Helena, recaptured by the Dutch, was re-retaken almost without a shot being fired. If the English had been unable to defend Tangier – part of Queen Catherine's dowry – with three thousand men, it must be irrelevant whether the Cape garrison was one hundred or three hundred, which level the directors authorized in 1671 when a third war threatened, not only with England, but this time with France as well. It was a worrying time for the Netherlands, as a deep division had developed between the supporters of the House of Orange and those of the brothers de Witt, in control of the administration; a problem solved by the Hague mob literally tearing the de Witts to pieces. In such troublesome circumstances the Cape station needed to be in capable hands, and Isbrande Goske was appointed, at a salary three times that of van Riebeeck, with the rank of Member of the Council of India, and the title of Governor. He was given instructions to build a new defensive work, in stone, and to a modern design, which remains today as the Castle.

Goske arrived in September 1672 to find that the legal position of the colony, as it now began to be called in official documents, had been changed. A visiting Commissioner, Arnout van Overbeke, had decided that it would be tidier, and would square better with Christian and commercial principles, for the Company to have a legal title to the land. Accordingly the *Caepman* Fat Captain's son was given the title of 'Prince Schacher', and assumed, for the purposes of the VOC's conscience, to have title to the whole of the Cape lands. This fictitious title was then ceded to the Company in April 1672 for goods to the paper value of four thousand pieces of eight, although in fact the cost of the merchandise in the Company's books was some 0.3 per cent of that sum; but the Prince and his people were granted the protection of the Company and the peaceful possession of his remaining territory, whatever that may have been. More realistically, the chief Dorha (or 'Captain Klaas') was appointed as a company agent to trade with the further-off Khoikhoi bands; and prospered considerably thereby.

The Hottentots Holland station had proved disappointing: the pasture, it was true, was excellent, but a garrison of fifteen, later rising to twenty-four, was needed to secure the place. The directors complained of the cost and ordered that the land should be made over to free farmers to spare expense; they would, however, despatch a quantity of large dogs, which would doubtless help. Since only ten-year leases were offered on the farms, the freemen were reluctant to avail themselves of the opportunity.

Even this modest geographical expansion of the colony would have been impossible without what was probably van Riebeeck's most important achievement – securing a small cavalry force. In the wide spaces of South Africa, as the British Army learned painfully two centuries later, the mounted man is the decisive factor. Without cavalry the Dutch could never hope to catch the elusive and nimble Bushmen, and it was many years before this was provided. Some horses had been left to await the expedition's arrival in 1652, and two more arrived the following year. 'I wish we had a dozen,' complained van Riebeeck, and wrote to Batavia asking for them, together with 'light English saddles, bridles, and light pistols', for the Batavian horses were small, 'more like English ponies'. Twenty serviceable mounts were needed, but by 1659 no more than four could be mustered, the remainder of the fourteen beasts 'being young foals, and some mares, which are quite knocked up by ploughing, and only fit to breed from'.

However it was managed, three years later van Riebeeck was able to record that the settlement was well supplied with horses, having forty-three in all, of which eighteen were fit for the saddle. When the next violence broke out, with the killing in 1672 (after a good deal of provocation from the garrison, who had been allowed to have things more their own way under the moribund rule of Hackius) of several burghers by Khoikhoi followers of Gonnema, the 'Black Captain', a troop of horse under the command of Lieutenant Elbert Dirksen Diemer, free burgher and tailor, accompanied the punitive expedition. Even with this help the trouble would never have been concluded had not Gonnema's rivals assisted in the pursuit; when some of the enemy were captured they were turned over to the allied Khoikhoi, who beat them to death with every appearance of pleasure.[4] This pattern of retaliatory actions, with colonial forces containing an increasingly high proportion of burgher cavalry, assisted by Khoikhoi auxiliaries, became the usual method of suppressing resistance, whether from other Khoikhoi, Bushmen, or, a century later, from those black nations who in the 1670s were a great distance from the Cape settlements.

Twenty years after van Riebeeck's landing, in 1672, Cape society had developed a long way from its inception as a VOC victualling station. Dr William Ten Rhyne left a pompous Latin account of a visit there in 1673, where he was entertained by Governor Goske, 'a man without equal'. As a keen botanist Ten Rhyne was particularly impressed by the Company's gardens, 'a lovely sight with its plantations of lemons, citrons and oranges, its close hedges of rosemary, and its laurels, equal in height to a tall tree, all fragrant in the sun. It is the very essence of greenness set in the midst of thorns and barren thickets.'[5] There was not, in truth, much more that could be admired at the time. The castle and the church were still building, and there was little else apart from small houses and inns. Dr Ten Rhyne had little to say about the European residents, being much more interested in the customs of the Khoikhoi, but by then the original Company hierarchy of officers and employees had become considerably more complex. Within a fluctuating total of some six hundred people a series of classes had emerged, the boundaries between them sometimes fluid, but each possessing an understood place in the community.

Company employees were still the majority – about 370 of them, although the number fluctuated as the fleets deposited their sick and criminal, contracts began or terminated, and international crises developed and dissolved. But there were now also sixty-four freemen, thirty-nine women, including widows, and sixty-five children. The free burghers employed fifty-three European servants – those working on the lands were '*knechts*', or wage labourers. Between Company and burghers sixty-three slaves, including women and children, were owned.

Even within the limited burgher population gradations had established themselves. At the top of the social order were established burgher councillors such as Steven Botma, head of one of the first 'colonies' in 1657, member of the Council the same year, and one of the sponsors of the petition which had so infuriated van Riebeeck in the following year. Unofficially, as a matter of grace, the burgher representatives on the Council of Policy were allowed to form a 'Burgher Council', responsible for the domestic affairs of Cape Town, and permitted to raise taxes for those purposes. Selected burghers also ran the Orphan Council, a trust fund, and the Matrimonial Chamber; but these concessions to self-administration were strictly limited by the virtually absolute power of the Governor-in-Council.

By 1660 Botma had established himself as the biggest free farmer, with thirty-four acres of land under cultivation, second only to the Governor himself, who had seventy-seven acres.[6] Another prominent burgher was Wouter Cornelis Moustert, council member, innkeeper and miller, who rose to be Burgher Lieutenant in charge of the newly formed commando. Not that either Moustert or Botma had unblemished records: both had been fined for illegally trading with Hottentots, and Botma was in trouble in 1680 for allowing his slave girl to beat another slave's wife. One interesting facet of this was that the plaintiff was a Negro freeman, for by no means all the burghers were Dutch. Antony of Bengal and Louis of Bengal were from the Dutch East Indies possessions, and eligible for burgher status. Both owned Negro slaves, with whom they had considerable trouble. Tuko de Chinees, otherwise Abraham de Vyf, was received into the Dutch Church, and another Chinese burgher, Oquanko, owned six slaves.[7] The population also included 'free Kaffers', one of whom, Jackie of Angola, was able to enforce payment of money due from Antony.

Burghers' wives were also capable of bad behaviour. Marikye van der Bergh, wife of Thilman Hendricks, was banished 'over the river' for buying unofficial sheep in 1671; her husband, a councillor and farmer, later killed by the Khoikhoi, was fined and dismissed from the Council. Two years later, convicted of cattle stealing, she was flogged and banished to Robben Island for twelve years. In spite of this, she was found guilty four years later of receiving stolen rice, flogged again, branded, and packed off to Mauritius. Tryntje Theumissen slaughtered two stray cows, and was also 'severely' flogged.

Among the free population was Eva van Mierhoff, whose husband Pieter had been killed while leading an expedition to Madagascar. After twenty years living with the Dutch Eva was still torn between two cultures, and found it difficult to adapt to life as a widow with two young children, but when she died in 1674 she was buried with pomp and circumstance within the church itself, a place reserved for persons of standing. Counted among the free children, but with an inferior status, were those of mixed race, with European fathers and usually Indian or Khoikhoi mothers. They were to be brought up as Christians, and were accorded their father's status when they came of age.

Bad characters continued to flourish among the free population. P. Bartolemi, carpenter, threatened to shoot Governor Goske 'like a dog'. J. Jans, freeman, got drunk, intoxicated some pigs and dogs with sugar and eggs mixed with wine, and picked the pockets of another drunk. He was flogged, given three years in chains, and all his property confiscated. Burgert Claas of Bremen ran off from his employer and survived for six weeks in the bush, returning sadder if not wiser.

A rung below the freemen, white or black, were the slaves. Under Dutch law, based on Roman practice, slaves had a recognized legal status; in English common law this did not exist, the institution of slavery having disappeared in the late Middle Ages (although in Scotland it remained officially until 1799, and the status of indentured servants, while in force, was little better). Dutch and English both were passionately attached to the ideal of the rule of law, but the differences between their ideals were the source of much misunderstanding. Since slaves, having no property, could not be fined, the only possible punishments were of the person. In a society where sodomy was punishable by death – a captain and two seamen were executed by drowning in July 1664 – and Marikye and Tryntje were flogged and branded for stealing, the sentence of flogging, branding, cropping of ears, and labour in chains for life levied on two slaves for stealing cabbages is more comprehensible.

Lowest of all, with no protection from the law, were the common convicts who had been sent from Batavia; such as Ytchio Wanckochuuse, accused of repeated violence and sentenced to be flogged and 'for the period of his banishment to perform all such vile offices as the council shall deem proper'.

But even convicts, their terms of punishment completed, were officially freemen. Also unfree, but enjoying a much higher status and often living in some comfort, were the political prisoners, leaders of resistance to the Company in the Indies, banished to the Cape. The best-known of these was Sheikh Yussuf, a renowned mystic who had led the resistance to the VOC in Java. Yussuf was allowed a large retinue, some fifty in all, maintained at the Company's expense, and his tomb is now a shrine for Muslim pilgrims.[8]

In all these gradations there was none specifically of colour. Indians, Chinese, Malays and black Africans could live as free burghers alongside the Dutch, subject to the same laws; the Khoikhoi girl Eva took her place among the respectable matrons, who could deplore the unruliness of such low creatures as Marikye van der Bergh. But there was a strong correlation between colour and status. Although at the very bottom convicts could be of any race, a cross-traffic of malefactors resulted in Europeans being despatched to serve their sentences in Mauritius or Batavia, and Chinese or Malays to the Cape; and although Governors and even Governors General could be of mixed race, no slaves were white.

The expected war that had brought Goske to the Cape as the first Governor duly began in March 1672 and ended, as far as England was concerned, two years later. Apart from an indemnity payment by the Dutch of two million florins and the concession, which had been the cause of so much previous hostility, of English hegemony at sea, the provisions of the peace treaty differed little from those signed at Breda. Thereafter Anglo–Dutch relations took a turn for the better, and in 1677 William of Orange, Stadtholder of Holland, nephew of Charles II, married Mary, daughter of James, Duke of York, thereby becoming heir presumptive to the thrones of England and of Scotland. From that time on, with a brief interlude at the end of the eighteenth century, English and Dutch became political allies while remaining commercial rivals.

This lessened tension was reflected at the Cape. Goske's replacement was a more junior man, Johann Bax van Herentals, previously second in command in Ceylon before arriving at the Cape in March 1676. Bax, a decent and conscientious man, who quickly made peace with Gonnema,[9] followed the instructions given to him by Commissioner Nicolas Verburg, who accompanied him to the Cape; apart fiom the usual strictures on unnecessary expense, Verburg confirmed that the Company intended the Cape to become a true colony, something more than a victualling station; it was 'highly necessary ... and a matter of course, that a good Dutch colony shall be planted and reared here'. To do this, the colonists, who 'bore the name of free men', should be liberated from the mass of petty and oppressive legislation that had poured out from the Council, and provision should be made to improve the lamentable standard of education. Modernizing the castle was still considered necessary, and this, a much easier task, Bax duly completed, setting a good example by participating in the work himself, together with his family. Bax only spent two years in office before dying of pneumonia in June 1678, but a start was made on transforming the Cape early that year when four enterprising farmers took over from Company staff the grazing at Hottentots Holland, twenty miles away across the Cape flats. The process was completed by his successor, Simon van der Stel, who arrived in October 1679 and stayed for the rest of his life, another thirty-two years.

The first Afrikaners

Van der Stel should certainly be regarded as one of the founding fathers of Afrikanerdom, the first famous 'Afrikaner' (the word came into use during his lifetime).[10] Unlike all previous commanders, who had been given the Cape either as a pre-retirement gratification or as a step in a Company career, the new Governor – who was also given a promotion to the rank of Councillor of India – came with his six children (but not his wife, with whom he had fallen out) to found a South African dynasty, casting off all links with the mother country. Holland was not, as it happened, van der Stel's homeland. He had been born in Mauritius, of Dutch and Indian stock (his maternal grandmother was one Monica, of Coramandel, and van der Stel was therefore what would later have been classified as 'Coloured', and as such banned from any office and even denied the vote), and was twenty-one before he went to Holland for the first time.

At the time of his arrival in Africa, the colony was still confined to the Cape peninsula, with outstations at Dassen Island, Saldanha Bay and, more recently, Hottentots Holland. Twenty-six years later, when his son Governor Willem van der Stel was recalled, it covered many hundreds of square miles, with the new towns of Stellenbosch and Drakenstein – the former with its own magistrate and council, the latter populated by industrious French refugees, already adopting the Dutch language and manners – serving the new farms along the Eerste and Berg Rivers; and Simon was the richest man in the colony, living in state on his handsome farm of Constantia, already famous for its fine wines.

Given such an extended period of control – he only retired in 1699 – a man with Simon van der Stel's relentless energy and talents could hardly fail to make an impression, even with restraints on expenditure continuing, for the Company wanted its colony on the cheap; its cost, as old Rykloff van Goens complained when on a final visit there with his nineteen-year-old wife after retiring as Governor General in 1681, was over a million guilders, 'a sum which almost exceeds the bounds of credibility'.[11]

Within a month of the new Governor's arrival he was off surveying his command, had identified a site for the new town of Stellenbosch, and laid out holdings for which, being all good fertile plots of up to 160 acres, watered by the Eerste River, there were no lack of takers. Farming and horticulture, subjects of which he was a master, were Simon's main enthusiasms. Oak trees, identified as likely to do well, and to provide dockyard materials, were planted in profusion; the Company gardens became horticultural treasure houses, tended by famous botanists; wine-making techniques, hitherto productive only of dubious beverages, improved until the wine from Simon's own farm, Constantia, was recognized as the equal of any European product; and above all an agricultural industry was established capable not only of supplying all the Cape's needs, but with considerable potential for exports.

The metamorphosis of station into colony that took place during the van der Stel era was materially assisted by the arrival, after 1688, of some two hundred French Protestant refugees, people of ability and character much superior to the discharged soldiers and adventurers who formed so large a proportion of the first free burghers. The emigration was the result of the misguided policies of King Louis XIV who, influenced by his religiously-inclined mistress Françoise de Maintenon, had embarked upon a campaign of persecution designed to extirpate Protestantism, a campaign which led to a veritable haemorrhage of wealth and talent as Protestants, often substantial and enterprising citizens, fled to Holland, England or America, founding such great houses as those of Du Pont and Courtauld.

Those who selected Holland as a home were Huguenots, rigid Calvinists who found the strict Dutch religion more sympathetic than the formal Anglican rite, which appealed more to the Lutherans. They were therefore well formed to fit into Cape society, and were, almost without exception, reliable and upright people who had been prepared to sacrifice their careers and possessions for the sake of conscience. Many had been prosperous and of some standing in France, and brought their skills and energy with them.[12] Van der Stel appreciated that this influx would bring with it a risk that the newcomers might form a distinct society, cleaving to their own language and traditions, and therefore insisted that Dutch must remain the only language permitted for instruction and worship, and that the use of French be phased out as quickly as possible. Accepting these restrictions – they had after all been rejected by their own country and were committed to making a success in Africa – by the second generation the emigrants had integrated into the Dutch community, although they were concentrated in the new villages of Franschhoek – 'the French Place' – and Drakenstein. Altogether more serious and educated a community than the common run of ex-Company soldiers and employees-turned-burghers, the French added a powerful dose of dour Calvinism to the previously relaxed moral order of the Cape.

Drakenstein was named after another man with a claim to be recognized among the founding fathers, Hendrik Adriaan van Reede van Oudshorn tot Drakenstein, Lord of Mijdrecht. Van Riebeeck is commemorated on banknotes, and no likeness of Simon van der Stel is available, but van Reede (or Rheede) has at least achieved the immortality of a cigarette advertisement.[13] From one of the most distinguished families in the Netherlands (his cousin Godert van Reede was a close friend of the Prince of Orange, later William III of England, and became the first Earl of Athlone),

Hendrik van Reede had already made a name for himself in learned European society by publishing the majestic *Hortus Indicus Malabaricus*, eventually a twelve-volume work of great magnificence. Altogether van Reede was a progressive, with advanced views on freedom of trade and the desirability of allowing colonial societies a measure of freedom from Company interference; views which made him unpopular with many of his contemporaries.

He came to the Cape in April 1685 as his first stop on a tour as Commissioner General, armed with the widest powers to reform the entire VOC administration in the East Indies. In his three-month stay he placed himself squarely behind van der Stel's expansionist policies. Stellenbosch, named in honour of the Governor, was to be 'a typical Dutch river town like Deventer, Zaandam or Dordrecht', with a council chamber, a church, a *drosdty* to accommodate the Landdrost (the equivalent perhaps of a stipendiary magistrate-cum-factor), and houses for the minister, the schoolmaster and the sexton taking priority. It was to have a local government of its own, with a Landdrost 'of good character, and having a knowledge of accounts and farming . . . to be allowed a Company's horse, and one slave, and two Dutch men to assist him' – the Veldwachtmaesters. In addition to controlling Company business in the district the Landdrost would preside over a court of Heemraden – district councillors, selected from the local burghers. The court's powers were limited to relatively minor civil and some criminal offences, ultimate jurisdiction being reserved for the Cape Council of Justice. While not too inconvenient, as Stellenbosch was only a day's ride away, these limitations made administration more difficult as the colony expanded, especially since the Landdrost was given little in the way of a police force, relying on part-time constables – '*ordonnantie ruyters*'. Not much resistance to the court was however likely, since in view of its composition it could normally be relied upon to put colonists' interests first, especially when they conflicted with those of slaves or Khoikhoi.

Constitutionally, van Reede formalized the Council of Policy, and added to it the new post of Independent Fiscal, responsible only to the Company directors. To that extent independent of the Governor and with considerable authority of his own as the senior legal official, the Fiscal had great potential power; but in practice Governors and Fiscals found collusion more rewarding than collision. The beginning of a judiciary was initiated by van Reede, with a Council of Justice distinct from the Council of

53

Policy, although with a considerable overlap of membership modifying the influence of the burgher representatives. Emphasis was placed on ensuring that burgher status was granted only to those of good character, and certainly not to Roman Catholics; any who had proved 'dissolute or irregular' should be shipped off back to Holland. Councillor van Reede made the point that many 'free burghers' were far from maintaining the status that this would imply in the Netherlands; it would be better, he suggested, if poor settlers should be classed as *'boeren en bouwlieden'* (peasants and farmhands).

Even at this early period of South African history a division had developed between the views of the European or Batavia-based officials accustomed to their more organized and less threatened societies and the colonists, permanently conscious of the fragility and dangers of their position on the tip of a strange and frightening continent. Van Reede felt himself obliged to read the unregenerate colonists the by-now usual lecture on the absolute need for fair treatment of the native population. In this he had the support of organized religion, which had come to the Cape in 1665 with the arrival of Dominus Johan van Arckel, when local presbyteries were established at every new settlement and the more picturesque irregularities suppressed. A great deal was said by van Reede about the treatment of slaves, 'these poor men ... who are bound, not only for all their lives, but for those of their children'. Children born to slave mothers by European fathers – and this was about three-quarters of the total – should be baptized, educated, and emancipated on reaching maturity, a policy which did not commend itself to the slave-owners (supported in this by the Dutch Cape Church). In time, van Reede went so far as to suggest, the whole country should be handed over to this mixed race, which was eminently fitted, he considered, to develop it. Equally ironically, in view of later events, the Commissioner continued: 'what will foreign nations say to our shame, if we allow them to live together by hundreds, like brutes, in utter licentiousness, and do not provide herein as for our own countrymen?'; which is, given the passage of time, as good a summary of the world's attitude to the twentieth-century South African government policy of 'apartheid' as might be imagined.

Impressed by van der Stel's ability and enthusiasm, van Reede made generous land grants both to the Governor and his senior officers, who were able to live in considerable comfort. Foreign visitors appreciated van der Stel's hospitality; in 1691 Captain William Dampier, an intrepid English circumnavigator, found him 'a very kind and knowing person, maintained in Grandeur . . . His Publick Table wants no plenty either of European or African wines.' Two years later the Revd. John Ovington wrote: 'The Governor of the Cape, Min Heer Simon Vanderstel . . . labours much in Improvements and Accommodations for the Inhabitants and Seamen.'[14] The Khoikhoi had less reason to be pleased, for van der Stel put an end to the mutually advantageous arrangement that had existed for nearly twenty years with Dorha (Captain Klaas), who had acted as an agent trading with more distant tribes. By arresting Dorha, without any good reason, and confiscating his people's stock, the Governor signalled the end of the previous policy of maintaining good relations with the natives.[15]

After Simon's retirement to his now-splendid estate of Constantia in 1699, the dynasty continued with the installation of his son Willem Adriaan as Governor. Inheriting all his father's zest for money-making and prickliness with subordinates (van Reede had felt obliged to advise Simon to mend his ways in this respect), but little of his administrative talents, Willem quickly overreached himself, attempting with the connivance of a thoroughly corrupt team of officials – the Fiscal, Chaplain, Secunde, Captain, and even the Cellar-Master all received generous land grants – to make himself as rich as his father; the younger van der Stel's estate at Vergelegen rivalled Constantia. Simon had looked after his own interests blatantly enough, and had set up his third son Frans as a prosperous farmer, without encountering more than grumbles from the other burghers. But Cape society had changed – by Simon's own efforts – and the farmers he had himself established were not prepared to accede to Willem's exactions.[16]

Dangers, expense, and troubles

Adam Tas of Stellenbosch was a very different burgher from those who had been browbeaten by van Riebeeck forty years previously. He kept a journal – most of the first settlers were near or wholly illiterate – which described the relaxed life on his prosperous farm (fittingly named 'Libertas', in one of the few recorded jokes of the time), visiting friends, sharing their own wine and 'sundry pipes of tobacco' while the ladies drank 'a dish of tea'; one Mr Greef overindulged, 'singing loudly several times, but he was full of sweet wine'[17] – probably not the van der Stels' expensive Constantia, 'a very racy and delicate sweet wine'. What the farmers could not grow themselves was readily available from the Cape, and in considerable quantities – 260 pounds of powdered sugar at one order, and Tas left in his will over a hundred silk handkerchiefs. 'The Cape,' Willem van der Stel's successor as Governor, van Assenburgh, was heard to say, 'hangs together by gorging and guzzling.' It was a life not unlike that of a contemporary English squire, and Tas had similar strongly independent views.

A protest against the exactions of Willem and his cronies was led by Tas's uncle, Henning Huising, whose butchery monopoly had been cancelled in 1705. A complaint was sent to Batavia, but the Governor blatantly rigged the subsequent inquiry, imprisoned and threatened the petitioners, and falsified the records. Nevertheless their action was successful. After a war of pamphlets – a valuable source of information about the contemporary Cape, including a perspective of the Governor's 'palatial residence' at Vergelegen, Willem was recalled in disgrace in 1706. Some of his henchmen were dismissed, and action against private trading by officials, so often denounced with so little effect, was finally enforced. Commissioner Cornelis Johan Simons assured the burghers that they need no longer fear the exactions of grasping officials. To some extent this was so, for future complaints – and there were many to come – concentrated on what was seen as interference combined with a lack of protection; but the old objections to low fixed prices continued.

This triumph of the settlers against Company officials might have been a turning point, at which the Cape was thrown open to colonization, enabling its development into a society capable of comparison with those in North America. Serious consideration was given to this a few years later, when events in Europe had settled down. The Treaty of Utrecht, although signed in 1713, remains a live issue in one respect, since it gave Gibraltar to Britain (no longer known as England after the union with Scotland in 1707) – a cession still disputed by Spain. It marked the end of the long-continued wars by Britain, the Austrian Empire and its German allies, together with the Netherlands, against the aggressive policies of Louis XIV of France. As well as Gibraltar and Minorca, Britain gained substantial territory in Canada, but for Holland the results were mixed. While the maintenance of a border barrier of fortresses against France was acknowledged, the end of Dutch supremacy in maritime trade and the emergence of Britain as the leading sea power were at least tacitly recognized as the Netherlands entered a slow period of economic decline, certainly relative to Britain and France, and in some measure absolute. Rather like Britain after the Second World War, Holland found herself no longer a major power; the Golden Age of the seventeenth century had given place to the 'Periwig Period' of comfortable stagnation.[18]

Considering future policy, the VOC directors now accepted that the Cape fortifications, in themselves, were of little utility, and that the expense of a sufficient regular garrison was unacceptable; probably the best, and certainly the cheapest, solution was a trained militia. Well-armed and mounted colonists were therefore essential. Between five and six hundred burghers, with Khoikhoi auxiliaries, were already available (including free blacks – in 1722 they formed their own militia company, which gave a good account of itself against the British in 1806), and in 1716 the Cape Council of Policy was asked to advise the directors whether more immigration should be encouraged.[19] The debate that followed was a re-enactment of that recorded in Brazil eighty years previously, and the results were similar; reflecting both the reluctance of officials to add to their own responsibilities, and distrust of the burghers' willingness to undertake military duties, the Council almost unanimously advised against further immigration. Governor Mauritius de Chavonnes, who assumed office in 1714, insisted 'all workmen, drivers, and the lower classes generally are addicted to drink', and 'farm labourers were more troublesome than slaves', and that, since recession was already beginning to bite, no immigrants were needed. Secunde Cranendonk agreed. There were not thirty families in Table Bay, Stellenbosch and Drakenstein combined that could be termed wealthy. For the rest, 'there was not one who has sufficient to support himself'. Much better, the Council felt, to import slaves, at an annual cost of only forty guilders each, against 175 for European workers.

Only one dissenting voice was raised, that of the Governor's brother, Captain Dominique de Chavonnes. His intervention is particularly interesting as an early attack on the principles of slavery. Only with free labourers, he said, could farmers enjoy a real sense of security, for slave labour brought 'only dangers, expense, and troubles': they frequently deserted, and 'then they have to be punished, as our sentence books, with their many sad examples, bear witness'. Moreover, the costs had to be viewed in the light of the acknowledged fact that two Europeans could do the work of three slaves.

But opinion was against the Captain, since the burgher representatives, the Landdrosts and Heemraden of the three districts were all ardent for slaves. They were accordingly obliged. In 1711 1,781 slaves were owned by burghers, and 440 by the Company; by 1778 there were probably over fourteen thousand, outnumbering the free population of 9,721. There was also an unspecified but substantial number of Khoikhoi, much exploited, but theoretically free, and increasingly integrating with white society. Clinging to their traditional way of life, Khoikhoi were often willing to work with pastoralists, but showed little inclination to provide a pool of agricultural wage labour. They were however usually ready to assist in suppressing any slave unrest, although as it turned out little serious resistance was ever offered by the slave population during the Company period.

The question remains whether, if immigration had been encouraged as Captain de Chavonnes had recommended, the Cape might have emulated the success of the British and French North American colonies. Apart from its greater distance from Europe, to some degree compensated by its lying on a frequented trade route, the Cape had disadvantages. The American Atlantic seaboard offered many safe havens, protected offshore passages, navigable rivers leading to the interior, and a fertile coastal plain uninterrupted for 1,500 miles. In South Africa no good natural harbours exist anywhere, north or east, away from the Cape itself, and there is no navigable river. On the other hand the Cape climate was admirable, and economic conditions in Holland were beginning to favour emigration. James Boswell, who studied, if that is not too strong a word, at Utrecht university in 1763, wrote: 'all the principal towns are sadly decayed, and instead of finding every mortal employed you meet with multitudes of poor creatures who are starving in idleness'.[20] Such a degeneration did not take place overnight.

But even in these straits the Dutch showed little inclination to leave their country. The majority of the immigrants who made their way to the Cape were of German origin (806 men and forty-eight women, compared with 494 Dutch men and 322 women in the period to 1795). Without a positive immigration policy, and with a reliance instead on the import of slaves, Cape society remained that of a seaport, the extraction of money from seafarers constituting its main object. This task progressively shifted into private hands, with the Company restricting itself to collecting taxes, trading profits on imports and the sale to individuals of monopolies on various trades, of which the most important were liquor licences, slaughterhouses, taxes on grain and duties on land transfers and rents. Unofficially the increasing number of underpaid and underemployed company staff (who outnumbered burghers as late as 1750, quadrupling their numbers by the end of the century at a time when the workload was rapidly declining), occupied themselves in feathering their own nests, considering their stay at the Cape as merely a temporary phase in their own careers or as a means of gaining enough wealth to be able to return to the fatherland.[21] The contrast between the Cape, without newspapers, universities or high schools, and the lively intellectual life of British America was striking. Without such stimuli Cape society remained stodgy, bucolic and provincial.

Once the decision to rely on slave labour had been taken, the number of slaves rapidly increased; over sixty-three thousand were imported in the following 150 years, their numbers reflecting the community's increasing prosperity, and increasing at very much the same rate as did the total population, to maintain similar numbers of free and servile. Most were owned by burghers, the Company having no reason to need more labour, and held in Cape Town and its neighbourhood. By 1773 over 90 per cent of all slaves were to be found at the Cape, or in Stellenbosch and Drakenstein. There were few large slave-owners, and ownership was widely spread among the reasonably prosperous, who included at least some free blacks.[22]

Slaves came from many regions, in approximately equal proportions of East Africans, Malagasies, Indians and colonial East Indians. During the first half of the eighteenth century most were Orientals, but thereafter the majority were brought from Mozambique. A distinct scale of desirability emerged, those from Delagoa Bay – 'a foul evil-smelling race' – being the least popular, much less satisfactory than Angolans. Oriental slaves were often highly skilled, although the Buginese were feared for their violent tendencies, and their importation was restricted after several violent crimes in 1767.[23] Nervous apprehension of a possible slave revolt seemed reasonable enough. Although total numbers of slave and free were not dissimilar, female and child slaves were comparatively few, there being many more adult men among the slaves than among the burghers. At the Cape the ratio was almost 3:1, but the only serious rising broke out in 1808, after the British had taken over and rumours of imminent emancipation had been encouraged by the abolition of the trade in slaves the previous year.

Isolated incidents of theft and murder by slaves did take place, and attempted escapes were common. A black slave could hope to find a welcome among the hospitable black communities still separated, although by a rapidly decreasing margin, from much contact with the colonists, provided he contrived to escape pursuit, usually entrusted to the enthusiastic Khoikhoi. Nearer at hand the Hantam and Bokkesberg mountains offered a refuge where escapers might hold out indefinitely. Large-scale attempts were organized, sometimes in conjunction with Company deserters and Khoikhoi. One such was led by Adam, a slave, and the Meij brothers, Bastaard-Hottentot farmworkers, during 1773–4. Some of this collection of runaways, who murdered a Khoikhoi family in the course of their escape, were eventually rounded up, but others, including two slaves, Cupido and Africa, made good their escape.

Cape whites accepted slavery as a natural institution. Slave-owners were as heterogeneous as any other group: rich and poor, brutal and kindly, exploitative and generous. No Cape record exists of some of the more hideous brutalities uncovered in Jamaica – one white owner was accused of boiling a slave alive; but he was tried and hanged for it – but beatings were frequent, and more ingenious methods of torment, such as curry-combing and thereby part-flaying a slave's back, not unknown. Being valuable property, actual murder of slaves was less common and was sometimes severely punished. More usually, even when an inquiry was made, murderous masters were discharged, or only fined. Other owners were humane and even generous, or perhaps more calculating. A useful slave could be controlled by rewards as well as punishments, and some were allowed to accumulate and 'to dispose of property as they pleased'. Some sold the produce of allotments, while others were given stock. Jephtha of Graaff-Reinet acquired ten cattle, eighty-two goats and sheep and even four horses, while skilled slaves at the Cape were permitted to live almost as free men, fending for themselves and paying part of their income to their owner.[24]

But such prosperity was rare, and the most common method of reward to both slaves and Khoikhoi was alcohol. Cape wine was cheap, and distilled into a brandy rendered even more disreputable by adulteration with tobacco and sugar, when it was known as Cape Smoke. Offering as it did a temporary escape from the unpleasantness of life and fuelling conviviality, alcohol remained, and remains, a vital instrument of social control, used without any regard to its horrifying consequences in addiction and violence.

Viewed as an economic institution, slavery has limited advantages. In an urban society such as that of classical Rome, where many unpleasant menial tasks exist and where control is tightly organized, or such labour-intensive agrarian economies as Roman latifundia, West Indian sugar- or Virginian cotton-plantations, slavery can prosper. By contrast, sparsely populated pastoral societies, especially when near a fluid frontier, find the problems of controlling slaves outweigh any economic advantages. Slaves are too valuable and apt to abscond to be used as herdsmen, especially when conditions make it necessary to mount and arm them. Willing Khoikhoi, easily rewarded by payment of sheep and cattle, controlled by doles of tobacco and closely rationed ammunition, were preferred: and if they did take themselves off, at least there was no capital loss.

Khoikhoi to Hottentot

After the first few minor clashes the whites had little difficulty in imposing their will on the Khoikhoi.[25] Although sporadic, and not ineffective, resistance was offered – the worried Stellenbosch Landdrost reported in 1759 that a hundred Khoikhoi armed with muskets had raided two hundred cattle and 2,400 sheep from the Piketberg, only eighty miles from Kaapstad – organized violent opposition to colonial encroachment was nullified by the absence of any strong unified chiefdom which might have formed a centre. Tobacco and brandy, those powerful agents, were enough to entice many Khoikhoi to sell their cattle and to accept service with white farmers. In that society they found a subordinate, but recognized place, sharing the primitive frontier life, receiving rations and a few beasts in exchange for their labour, and adopting those values and concepts they found relevant. In place of their own language such Khoikhoi took to using the pidgin that had emerged from the Cape's racial mix, which later evolved into Afrikaans. From their masters they learned to ride and to handle firearms, skills in which they soon became highly proficient, and therefore much valued by the authorities as 'good and faithful Hottentots' available to be called out on commando service, in which they often outnumbered the European burghers. Those who attached themselves to religious households were exposed to a form of Christianity which they accepted, although rarely with overmuch enthusiasm.

As far as Company writ ran, Khoikhoi were protected and farmers convicted of ill-treatment were sometimes punished.[26] Khoikhoi could not be forcibly enslaved, but their children might be 'apprenticed' until the age of twenty-five to the farm on which they had been raised; such apprenticeship became a favourite device for securing cheap labour. François Valentyn, a pastor in the VOC service who visited the Cape on four occasions between 1685 and 1714, criticized the 'barbarous' treatment of the Khoikhoi by these

'so-called Christians, who have not scrupled to rob them of all their animals
... and also very foully and scandalously ill-treat their innocent wives and
children'. Any chance of the Khoikhoi's survival as a people was dealt a
heavy blow by the smallpox epidemic which swept through the Cape
between 1710 and 1713, and which proved much more deadly to the native
people than to Europeans, many of whom had developed immunity to the
disease, while the Khoikhoi 'died by hundreds, so that they lay everywhere
along the roads as if massacred'. Some Khoikhoi prospered modestly
although pushed into marginal land on the fringes of white settlement in the
mountainous regions. Others, more adventurous, moved north in search of
new territories, and had crossed the Orange River by 1750. The communities
furthest removed from the centres of Dutch settlement survived more or
less intact, but many impoverished individuals reverted to a hunter-gatherer
existence, raiding for subsistence when the opportunity offered.

By that time, a century after the colonists' arrival, Khoikhoi society had
been disrupted, and the offspring of Khoikhoi slaves and settlers, variously
known as Bastaards (later Basters) 'such Hottentots, particularly of the
mixed race, who possessed some property, were more civilized: and Oorlams, who are born and lived with the farmers' had begun to form new
communities. One of the first to become prominent was Adam Kok, a
former slave who in about 1750 trekked north with his followers and cattle,
received burgher rights, and developed what became a recognizable state
under the leadership of his successors. Another dynasty, that of the
Afrikaner family, less respectable and more given to violence, raided extensively among the sparsely scattered black communities north of the
Drakensberg and back into the colony. The Khoikhoi were disintegrating,
changing and evolving into 'Hottentots'; gradually abandoning their traditional habits for European customs.[27]

For the first century of Company rule little economic or social progress
was made in the region of the Cape itself. A degree of independence was
allowed in 1747 when control was removed from Batavia, enabling the
Governor and Council to report directly to Amsterdam, where the VOC
directors, with more pressing troubles of their own (Company troops were
defeated by the Raja of Travancore in 1741, and a protracted revolt of
the Batavian Chinese was only suppressed with much bloodshed), were
increasingly disinclined to interfere with the men on the spot. European
events influenced the Cape only indirectly; after the Treaty of Utrecht
shipping arrivals increased – eighty-seven in 1720, a record not surpassed

until the 1770s. The great majority of these – typically three quarters – continued to be Dutch for the same period.[28]

Intellectual commerce was less thriving. Prosperous burghers sent their children back to Europe for their education, or imported tutors. One of these, the German O.F. Mentzel, left a comprehensive description of Cape life in the 1720s. He was not overly impressed. The VOC employees were not of the highest quality: 'the dregs of European Society, ingested by the great maw of the Dutch East India company with its insatiable appetite for manpower . . . uneducated louts from the heart of Germany'. Young soldiers spent all their money on drink and girls, passing their evenings in the Company's slave lodge (later the Supreme Court and now the South Africa Museum, next to the Anglican cathedral, a rare eighteenth-century survival), which served as a brothel. Three quarters of children born to slave mothers were of European parentage. Almost incredibly, in view of the potential richness of the Cape – and an indication of the colonists' lack of enterprise – food was mostly salt fish and beef; there was little point, Mentzel lamented, in giving dinner parties only to eat the same food in someone else's house. But he approved of the Chinese community, who were 'scrupulously clean', and led a 'humble, quiet and orderly life'.[29]

In spite of an increasing slave population (from 1,771 in 1711 to 5,361 in 1743), labour shortages continued. Every ordinary European, Governor General Baron van Imhoff complained, 'thought himself a gentleman'. Mere carpenters and labourers would not work for less than eight shillings a day, plus their food, yet produced less than a half-trained artisan in Europe.[30] Farmers were not real farmers, but 'plantation owners'. Imhoff's two-month visit of inspection to the Cape in 1743 also marked official acknowledgement that the colony's geographical limits had expanded, when a new church was established to serve the communities in the north of the colony at Roodezand, followed two years later by another at Zwartland. This area, the Land of Waveren, had been settled in the 1690s, but previously its inhabitants had been obliged to make the three-day journey to Cape Town, sixty miles away, for all official purposes and for the religious services that formed so important a focus of community life.

From the Company's point of view this extension was quite far enough, and attempts were constantly made to restrict expansion. The Cape's function as a victualling station was amply fulfilled by existing farms, which produced more than enough produce to satisfy all Company traffic; foreign vessels were not encouraged. Simon van der Stel, who had little respect for a farmer who did not know how to handle a plough, had warned his son not to let the farmers stray, or South Africa would be too small to hold them. In 1705 only those holding property in Stellenbosch and Drakenstein were permitted to own livestock, but there was no holding back the stock farmers, or *'veeboers'*. Within five years the number of cattle and sheep nearly doubled (from twelve thousand to over twenty thousand, and from seventy-six thousand to 132,000 respectively – and these were official figures, so doubtless underestimates[31]).

By 1714 attempts at control were abandoned, and land grants in the region known as 'Overberge', beyond the mountains to the east, were made. The nature of the land, which was best suited for grazing, and the ability of the western farms to supply most agricultural produce, led to them becoming ranches, requiring larger areas of land. To avoid dissension, farms had to be not less than an hour's walk from one another, which led to a typical grazing holding of some seven square miles. Land was made available by the Council of Policy on a 'loan farm' tenure, theoretically an annual lease, but in practice renewal was automatic, as long as a modest rent was paid; and often even when this was not forthcoming. By the end of the century there were farmers who had not paid any rent for forty years.

By the 1740s such farms had been established two hundred miles from the Cape, and well beyond any effective control; the *'veeboers'* were becoming *'trekboers'*, migrant or wandering farmers. Even further afield others ranged as they pleased, supplementing their resources by hunting and by trading with their black counterparts for hides and ivory. This was in spite of a 1739 ordinance strictly forbidding any private dealings with natives and banning travel further than the Baviaans/Gamtoos River, where the black communities were to be found – but even this boundary was four hundred miles from the Cape. Imhoff began plans for a new administrative division, to be based on the Breede River, some 150 miles distant from Cape Town, in a good position to control movement along the coastal route. This was to be the new *drosdty* and village of Swellendam, after Governor Swellengrebel, whose appointment in 1739 had marked another stage in the colony's development, for he was the first Afrikaner to become Governor. Afrikaner on both sides, since his mother was the daughter of Ensign Hieronymus Cruse, the explorer.

For a century the Overbergers – *veeboers* and *trekboers* – were left much to their own devices, concerning themselves with officials only when it suited. Marriages had to be solemnized, baptisms and deaths recorded and lawsuits settled, but such visits to the nearest *drosdty* and church might be at long intervals. Those living within a reasonable distance would make an effort to attend *nagmaal*, communion, every six months or so, but the most pressing requirements were for powder and shot. Less self-sufficient than their black counterparts, but equally dependent on hunting, the *vee-boers* cultivated little land, and were dependent on flour bought from the grain farms near the Cape. One of the few sanctions available to government was to cut off supplies of ammunition, without which frontier existence was impossible. Families were large, with ten or more surviving children common, and each son or daughter regarded a farm of their own as a birthright. Added to the tendency to change residences every few years, this could lead to a single family occupying an area the size of an English county in three generations. Possession of a farm was the only social distinction recognized among the independent-minded *veeboers*; every farmer was as good as his neighbour, a state of affairs very different from that at the hierarchical Cape. Living as they did a life similar to that of the Khoikhoi (and later the Xhosa) around them – 'the majority here now live not much better than the Hottentots'[32] – the most important distinction was that of colour. Free burghers on the frontier were white, and servants were brown or black. An inevitable result was that paid labour became unthinkable; a white would lose his only claim to social equality if he became employed for wages. Such attitudes encouraged a rapid expansion of territory, both to the east and the north, and also imprinted attitudes of mind that lingered on, with damaging results, until the late twentieth century.

Towards the end of the Honorable Company

In 1751 Governor Swellengrebel was succeeded by his brother-in-law Ryk Tulbagh, also an old Cape hand, having been employed there by the Company since the age of seventeen. Very popular in the colony, which he administered for the unprecedented period of twenty years, 'Father' Tulbagh belonged to the seventeenth century, in which he was born, and had little use for the liberal ideas then gaining ground in Europe. In his day social distinctions were strictly observed. The Governor had a lady, the officials, consorts; substantial burghers, wives; socially speaking, other females did not exist. Such differentiations were reinforced by Tulbagh's decrees, which ordained that umbrellas might only be carried by persons of appropriate rank; armorial bearings might only be placed on carriages of senior officers; silk gowns worn only by wives of solid citizens; and those seductive slave girls banned from flaunting themselves in brightly-coloured clothes. Even 'free black' women, legally equal to other burgher wives, were forbidden to wear coloured silks, fine lace or hooped skirts.

And slaves were, Tulbagh insisted, to be kept severely suppressed; so many had been mutilated by branding and the severance of their noses and ears that European susceptibilities were offended, and this salutary practice had to be stopped. When flogged, however, which was the usual punishment, awarded without trial, it was to be with a split rattan, and salt rubbed into the cuts. The death sentence for men was usually to be broken on the wheel, or impaled on a sharpened stake, which gradually sank into the body; death might take three days. Anders Sparrman, a Swedish companion of Captain Cook's who called at the Cape in 1772, was horrified by the sight of seven bodies rotting in chains, and found the place 'disgraced' by its 'horrid implements of torture'. Women were strangled, slowly, with burning reeds being held before the face; but it should be recollected that as late as 1762, in civilized Toulouse, the prosperous merchant Jean Calas was broken at the wheel for no other crime than being a Protestant.[33]

Earlier attempts, never vigorously sustained, to convert slaves and Khoikhoi had by now subsided. The Dutch Reformed Church had begun that process of adapting theology to suit the interests of its members, which was to culminate in its blessing apartheid, by discouraging conversions which would bring the obligation of receiving non-Europeans as full members of the community. Anders Sparrman doubted that anyone would 'trouble themselves with the conversion of these plain honest people [the Hottentots]' unless some political advantage could be gained.[34] When, in 1737, the Moravian Brethren despatched the saintly Georg Schmidt to minister to the Khoikhoi, this heretical sect, which allowed the possibility that others than the predestined elect might receive the Grace of God, was rejected by scandalized Dutch ministers as having 'sneaked into another house'.[35] As a matter of law, 'free blacks' were confirmed to possess equal rights with whites, but the restricted nature of these rights was causing increased frustration among the whole burgher community, which by 1770 included those much less conservative than Father Tulbagh and his cronies.

Swellendam's jurisdiction ended at the hills of the Zwartberge, leaving the plains of the Great Karoo the responsibility of the much-troubled

Stellenbosch Landdrost. The first trouble there had occurred after the illegal incursion in 1702, when a party of young Boers and Khoikhoi in search of game and cattle – which they were prepared to buy, if other methods failed – penetrated far to the east. For hundreds of miles they came across only some Khoikhoi and Bushmen, until three or four days west of the Gamtoos River they met, and clashed with, a formidable community of black men, the first to be encountered inland. Their enterprise had been severely condemned by the tranquillity-loving VOC directors, and led to the dismissal of the Governor. Subsequent expeditions were more discreet, but farmers moving north of the Zwartberge began to take up loan farms legally, at first near the borders of the existing colony. Without irrigation, the Karoo offered only sparse grazing, driving the herds on in search of something better, while the stockmen depleted the game to the point of extinction as they continued their inexorable advance towards the interior – with the Company officials attempting, usually ineffectually, to exercise some form of control – convinced that 'the farmer had the right to migrate to where the rain fell'.[36]

FOUR

The Last Days of
the Honorable Company

Among the finest specimens of the human race

It has sometimes been claimed, perhaps pointlessly, that whites were in
South Africa before the blacks, and there is just enough truth in the allega-
tion to make it worthwhile qualifying. Certainly when van Riebeeck landed
in 1652 there were no black communities for many hundreds of miles; the
Cape inhabitants were Khoikhoi and Bushmen. But further east, beyond
the Fish River, black societies had been established for centuries. To that
extent, the settlement of what is now South Africa was a joint enterprise,
but one in which the blacks had precedence over the whites; and, it might
be added in passing, there seems to be no logical reason why intruders
coming by sea should be any more blameworthy than those arriving by
land. We do not consider Huns more virtuous than Vikings, and the
persecuted Bushmen did not distinguish between their black and white
oppressors.

The Baviaan/Gamtoos River, which the Company had fixed as the colony's
boundary in 1739, is the most westerly of a series flowing from the
Sneeuwberg and Stormberg ranges, in a generally south-easterly direction.
From west to east the most significant are the Gamtoos, Sunday's, Bushman's, Fish, Keiskamma and Kei, debouching into a coastline of some 250
miles, of which the most notable feature is Algoa Bay. At different times
all these natural barriers were considered as a potential eastern frontier of
the colony, the definition of which was a principal concern of all succeeding
Cape governments until the late nineteenth century.

The men encountered west of the Gamtoos by the illicit expedition in 1702 were Xhosa, the outliers of a great migration that had been taking place for over a thousand years as Bantu-speakers moved south from the lakes of central Africa, in much the same way and at much the same pace as Indo-Europeans had previously drifted westwards from central Asia to the Atlantic. In the course of this slow movement the southern Bantu had become further removed from external influences than their neighbours to the north, as they found themselves in a territory without an accessible seaboard or navigable rivers to tempt Arab or European traders. At a time when such West Coast kingdoms as Benin and Ashante, and eastern states from Sofala north, were flourishing (the slave trade being the most important source of income) and developing large centralized states with advanced technologies, southern Bantu communities were dispersed into relatively loose political entities, with considerably more primitive techniques at their disposal. Trade routes ran along the great rivers of central Africa to Portuguese, Spanish, Danish and English ports established since the sixteenth century, and to Arab centres for nearly a thousand years before that, but it was only in the nineteenth century that southern black communities had to face a serious European intrusion.

So protracted a dispersion had been accompanied by the development of communities with distinctive traditions, customs and languages which played their individual parts in African history, and which have been exaggerated and exacerbated for political ends. But the common South African black characteristics are much more significant than the variances: strikingly well-formed and fit; able stockmen, devoted to their cattle, with agriculture very much a woman's task; a strong sense of moral order, a partiality for tranquillity and a preference for settling disputes according to law and custom allied to a vigorous martial ability; a settled framework of family and group relationships with accompanying duties loyally accepted.[1]

There were similarities between eighteenth-century Bantu societies and those of Bronze-Age Celtic regions: the same bardic traditions, where great men were praised and genealogies recalled in epic poetry; similar reverence for royal bloodlines combined with assertion of individual rights; a complex code of customary law administered with the assistance of elders; and a readiness to resist fiercely any external aggression. '*Ubuntu*', a word of majestic meaning, embracing humanity, decency, temperance, justice – every quality that dignifies the human race – was the measure of all judgements.

The unit of society was the homestead:[2] one man together with his wife or wives and other relatives or dependants. Local collections of homesteads grouped themselves under a chief, a member (or someone who could colourably claim to be a member) of a pre-eminent family lineage. All those claiming a common ancestor constituted a clan, often dispersed among several chiefdoms, although usually a chief's own clan was locally predominant. The chief's authority was bolstered by his quasi-magical powers; the chief had direct communication with the communities' ancestors, the guardians of the people and intercessors with the Supreme Being. He was in some measure a figure of dread, with 'the quality of *isithunzi* – shadow – an aura of fearsomeness and malevolent charisma',[3] and worked with the tribal shamans, dismissed as 'witch-doctors' by Europeans, but in reality providing a spiritual arm to reinforce the temporal powers of the chief. All misfortunes or untoward events – and South Africa's uncertain climate and lively fauna could produce plenty of them – were attributed to malevolence on the part of disruptive 'witches'. Identifying these, or protecting against their influence, was the business of the witch-doctor. Unpopular or disruptive men could be disposed of when identified as 'witches' by the shaman and their possessions confiscated by the chief. Warriors were encouraged by being blessed with sacred objects – the whole a close parallel of European practice, with the difference that the shaman, unlike the priest, was usually also an experienced healer. Many thaumaturgic specialities were recognized, from diviners through herbalists – still with many followers – to 'heaven-herds', protectors against storms; rainmaking, so important in a country perennially threatened by drought, was a chiefly prerogative.[4] Society was not stratified, in striking contrast to contemporary European communities. Very much as in the pre-Union Scottish highlands, every clansman was as good as the next, allowing only the chief and his kin any more elevated status. Chiefly authority was limited by the obligation to consult with the people, sometimes in general assembly – the Sotho-Tswana *'pitso'* could number thousands of men – and always by the need to exercise sound judgement. If this failed him, the chief's followers – realism being a consistent characteristic of the Bantu peoples – could melt away and seek another representative of the royal lineage, who polygamy ensured would be readily to hand. The British, in particular, were to experience difficulty in understanding both the limitations of chiefly power and the reverence in which a chief might – but not invariably – be held by his people.

Ethnographic classifications are usually academic and arbitrary (any system which groups white inhabitants of Maine and Alabama, or Yorkshire and Berkshire, together is open to suspicion), and those in Southern Africa before the nineteenth century more than most. In the absence of written records, and especially after the shattering disruptions in the 1820s, which produced three new black nations – Lesotho, Botswana, Swaziland – and the powerful Zulu people, any detailed analysis of previous black history is conjectural and only peripherally relevant to an understanding of current events; what is vital is the transmission of black culture and its influence on black communities' reactions to the challenges imposed upon them.[5]

In the broadest of terms southern black societies could be divided into the coastal and inland, each group with different languages and customs. Along the coast and south of the Drakensberg mountains lived the Nguni peoples, with a separate branch, the Tsonga, occupying the land which is now southern Mozambique. On the high plains north of the mountains, Sotho-Tswana- (whence Lesotho and Botswana) speakers had displaced or subjected earlier inhabitants. The Nguni may be divided into the northern and southern tribes; among those to the north, in what is now KwaZulu-Natal, was numbered a small clan later to become better known – the Zulu. Of those living further south and west the Xhosa were the most numerous, perhaps some hundred thousand of them at the end of the eighteenth century,[6] acknowledging one paramount chief. Behind the Xhosa, up the coast and towards the mountains lived other peoples, speaking a mutually intelligible language but with well-marked individual traditions; of these the most important were the Thembu and Mpondo.[7] All Nguni life centred around cattle, the source of wealth, 'practically the only subject of his care and occupation, in the possession of which he finds complete happiness'. Quiet contemplation of his animals formed one of the greatest pleasures of a Nguni farmer – as indeed it does of any dedicated stock breeder. Many taboos ensured that cattle remained strictly men's business. Women were not allowed in the cattle *kraal*, permitted to milk the cows, or even to touch the milk containers, being restricted to cultivating the corn and vegetable plots. Treaties were sealed by the transfer of cattle, and formal sacrifices made of the finest beasts. Since the number of cattle determined status, beef was rarely eaten; game, milk and porridge formed the staple diet.

Aristocratic women could exercise considerable power; queenly rule was not uncommon, and since the cultivation and preparation of the staple foods, and of the beer which formed as vital a part of both diet and social life as it did in medieval England, was entirely in female hands, all women shared in what was probably a considerable, if unacknowledged, influence. Cattle may have been a male preoccupation, but the vital business of life was the responsibility of women. Each wife had her own hut, and the status of women as producers as well as mothers was protected in a polygamous society by payments of '*lobola*', the sum due to the bride's family on marriage. Often misunderstood as bride-price, *lobola* had to be paid in cattle, and the disposal of property was defined in the marriage contracts. Present-giving was mutual, those given by the bride's family often equalling the *lobola*, underlining the compact between the two families by which the bridegroom entered into 'a lifelong bond' with his wife's parents. If a husband mistreated his wife she was allowed to return to her family, a right that was insisted on into modern times, even to the point of an aggrieved wife killing her husband when this was denied.[8] Chiefs had numerous wives according to their status; marriages were often political, cementing inter-community alliances, and favoured commoners could be rewarded with royal brides.

The transition into adult life, with the acceptance of the individual into full membership of the community, was marked with complex solemnities for both boys and girls. Masculine circumcision rites (the truly barbaric custom of female circumcision was never prevalent in South African black societies) were extended, and treated with the utmost seriousness. The groups of young men that underwent the ritual ordeals spent months together, segregated from the rest of the community, and in future life formed a brotherhood with the strongest mutual links.

Much traditional black law later proved not incompatible with British ideas. Chiefly powers could be transferred to a Governor and his representatives; great respect for law existed, and a popular activity was arguing points of law (often very ably, which impressed and exasperated European magistrates). Some chiefs displayed great patience in hearing cases brought before them; a wondering missionary once watched the powerful chief Sarili spend two days listening to a dispute of no particular moment – and that not a complaint brought by one of his own people, but by a Fingo, one of the dispossessed. Polygamy caused some difficulties to proselytizing Christians, but the sticking point came with the almost universal African practices of 'smelling witches' and ritual murders for 'magic' concoctions.

Like Thuggee in India, witchcraft was fiercely attacked by colonial governments. Thuggee was suppressed, but witchcraft survived.[9]

Moving north from the Mpondo lands, which extended to the
Mzimkhulu River, a cluster of other related tribes spoke a variant of the
Nguni language, which has since developed into Zulu. The most northerly
of the coastal peoples, the Tsonga, lived in a region subject to tsetse fly
infestation, and were restricted to small-animal farming, fishing and agriculture; a mark of the difference from the other cattle cultures is that hoes,
rather than cattle, were given in marriage settlements. Again, unlike the
southern Nguni and Sotho, the great majority of whom had never seen a
white face (none at all among the Sotho before the beginning of the nineteenth century), the Tsonga had been in contact with the Portuguese,
trading with da Gama and controlling the land approaches to the port of
Lourenço Marques, established in the sixteenth century.

Over the Drakensberg, well to the north of the Xhosa, on the high
plateau, the high veld, in much of what was later the Transvaal, the Orange
Free State and Bechuanaland/Botswana, the Sotho-Tswana and Pedi were
able craftsmen, smelting copper and iron, dealing extensively in their products, and living a more settled existence in large communities of up to
twenty thousand, often in stone-walled huts[10] – considerably larger versions
of the Celtic villages found in the higher regions of Britain. A less cattle-
centred economy was paralleled in Sotho rituals: while those of the Nguni
all honoured the ox as the source of wealth and prestige, those of the Sotho
were dedicated to the tribal totem – a wild beast or bird (or, in one
informative instance, that of the Rolong, iron and the hammer). Within
their own range of products, mostly implements of agriculture or war, the
Sotho were accomplished metal workers, but nowhere in southern Africa
is to be found anything similar to the marvellous bronze castings of western
Africa, or the magnificent long spears of the eastern Masai; the southerners'
isolation, which had preserved them from slavers' violence, had limited
their technology.[11]

Just as the Indo-European migrations left pockets of unabsorbed previous
populations – the persistent Basques in Europe and the Egyptians in North
Africa among them – Bantu-speakers lived alongside Khoikhoi communities, and at least one other racially distinct people, the Venda, shorter,
darker and stockier than the Sotho, survived to the south of the Limpopo
River. The Venda people are probably mostly autochthonous, subjected at
some stage by others coming from the north, who brought with them a

magic drum which caused the enemy to 'lay down in a deep sleep'. The different strains combined to form a distinctive new language and culture, more stratified than their neighbours' (even the chief's dogs had distinguishing collars) and, unlike all other communities, not circumcising.[12]

Living in so much larger communities, Sotho-Tswana society was at once more centralized and more stratified than that of the Nguni. Gradations of rank, often based on lineage, were observed, and the chief played a more active part in initiating activities and leading ritual. All Bantu societies displayed considerable powers of assimilation; moving into new territory did not necessarily imply ejecting those already in possession. Being as it were the advance guard – the *voortrekkers* – of the Nguni people, the Xhosa had absorbed some Khoikhoi customs and language, including some of the distinctive 'clicks', which to some extent differentiated them from tribes settled further north and along the coast. 'Settled' implies a misleading degree of permanence; although not strictly nomadic, moving as the seasons brought better pasture, and growing crops as occasion offered, the Xhosa had no permanent villages, and nothing in the way of such towns as were found in central and northern parts. While a strong attachment to a region might be maintained, a Xhosa group could move with all its belongings almost overnight, and it was the custom for chiefs on their accession to move to a new 'great place'. With so vast a territory and generally agreeable a climate, and a consequent high standard of nutrition, relaxed social behaviour developed. Strangers, even foreigners, prepared to accept clan customs, could be welcomed, as shipwrecked mariners testified; even today two groups in the Transkei (the Lungu – i.e. the 'whites' – and the Mholo) count their descent from such men. The Xhosa had no inhibitions about inter-racial marriages, having mingled with Khoikhoi for generations, to the extent that the westernmost groups had more Khoikhoi than Xhosa blood, the proportion decreasing further to the east.[13]

Such an ability to absorb strangers – a capacity vividly demonstrated later by the Zulu – was matched by a tendency to fission. Polygamy ensured a plentiful supply of heirs, all potential contenders for chiefly power. In the absence of more drastic solutions, not uncommon in West Africa, royal siblings tended to split off and form units of their own. Among the Nguni, divisions were encouraged by the practice of the chiefly families differentiating between the first-born son, whose offspring and followers formed the 'right-hand house', and those of the heir-apparent, son of the 'great wife', who formed the 'great house'. 'Great wives' were chosen later in life, with the result that the heir often succeeded as an infant. As long as no great pressure on natural resources was experienced, this led to regular division and expansion, but when competition for land became a factor the existence of separate factions could lead to fratricidal strife. By the end of the eighteenth century this had gone so far among the Nguni of the south that there were dozens of clans, each clustered in the neighbourhood of their own chief's 'great place' (usually nothing more than a few score huts and a cattle pound – the *kraal*, centre of social activity), but all owing a tenuous allegiance to a paramount chief.

All pretenders to chiefly power had to be able to claim 'royal' blood, which in the Xhosa was descent from Tshawe, who probably lived in the early seventeenth century. Descent was (and to some extent remains, since President Nelson Mandela is a descendant of Tshawe) a matter of as much import to Xhosa pastoralists as it was to Scots or Irish; Sir Harry Smith, a nineteenth-century British High Commissioner with elevated ideas of his own importance, was to find his undistinguished ancestry a drawback in negotiating with Xhosa aristocrats.

So fluid a society permitted much individual freedom; as with the Khoikhoi, if an individual family felt they could do better elsewhere, they were free to go, and being hunters as well as farmers could make their way without difficulty. A poor man could ask a chief for cattle to enable him to make a fresh start, and establish himself in due course as a member in full standing. Nor was there a tradition of slavery; even prisoners of war were not enslaved, but adopted into the lower ranks and allowed to work their way up the ladder of the new society (although the northern Tswana were markedly less open to the Khoi-San who, far from being welcomed as in Xhosa communities, were reduced to near-servile status). Slavery was common enough along the north coast beyond Lourenço Marques, but potential slave-traders operating to the south would have been discouraged by the lack of good harbours along the coast (although one English captain, Robert Drury, contrived to pick up a cargo in 1719). The idea of selling off members of the group themselves, as was not uncommon in Central Africa, was anathema to all Southern African black societies.

The first Europeans to describe Xhosa life in detail were the crew of the shipwrecked Dutch East Indiaman *Stavenisse* wrecked on the coast of Natal in 1687. The many members of her crew who were recovered spoke highly of the reception they had been given by the people, who were quite different from the Cape Khoikhoi, taller and more powerfully built, dark-brown and black rather than tawny yellow: 'among the finest specimens of the human race', as a later observer quite properly put it. Their habits were admirable: 'they are very civil, polite and talkative . . . revenge has little or no sway among them, as they are obliged to submit their disputes to the king . . . one may travel 200 or 300 miles through the country, without any cause of fear from men, provided you go naked, and without any iron or copper' (since the Xhosa were, it had to be said, also 'thievish and lying, and might murder for metal'), but 'Neither need one be in any apprehension about meat or drink, as they have in every village a craal or house of entertainment for travellers.' Moreover, their country was 'exceedingly fertile and incredibly populous, and full of cattle'. Moreover, 'it would be impossible to buy any slaves there, for they would not part with their children, or any of their connexions for anything in the world, loving each other with a most remarkable strength of affection.'[14]

After the first encounter it was some years before the Xhosa, moving slowly west, were much troubled by colonial expansion, driving east. These movements took place at different rates, for the Xhosa had reached the pleasant and fertile areas of Natal and the eastern Cape, while dissatisfied *veeboers* were advancing rapidly across the dusty Karoo in search of better grazing. When parties of hunters pushed well ahead of the main movement into Xhosa territory clashes occurred, but it was the Bushmen who were perceived as the main threat to expansion, with the Khoikhoi caught between them and the whites. Hunting grounds and watering-places had always been treated with great respect among the Bushmen bands, and any encroachments fiercely resisted; quite correctly, the white man's cattle were appreciated as the most threatening of these, for his occupation was intended to be permanent. The '*Bosjemans*' were a formidable enemy, since the small San bands had been reinforced by Khoikhoi, impoverished by the colonial advance, and were able to muster as many as a thousand men for their raids. On the other side, Khoikhoi who had thrown in their lot with the whites acquired guns and horses and joined in the burgher commandos. These were absolutely ruthless in their war of extermination. Colonel Collins, making a tour in 1809, met two commando leaders who claimed 'bags' of 3,200 and 2,700 Bushmen each.

Since the first Company employees had attempted to understand the social structure of the Khoikhoi, and the relationships between the various chiefs, Khoikhoi society had radically changed, disintegrating under pressure from the colonists and the attraction of Western habits – alcohol, tobacco, guns and horses – accelerated by devastating smallpox epidemics. Within two generations the Khoikhoi had either integrated into colonial society, formed communities of their own – often of mixed race – beyond colonial boundaries, or slipped back into a hunter-gatherer existence. Integration was rendered easier by the facility with which Khoikhoi became expert riders and marksmen – sometimes excelling the colonists in these arts, as they usually had in their roles of stockmen and hunters. Their position was usually inferior, as herdsmen or servants, but miscegenation was widespread, producing both the enterprising people proudly calling themselves 'Bastaards' and contributing a significant proportion of Khoikhoi genes to the white Afrikaners.[15] In later years, when it became necessary to justify the Afrikanervolk myth, the contributions of the Khoikhoi were written out of the record; but they and their descendants rode on commando and shared the perils of the Voortrekkers. Nearer the Cape, Khoikhoi were mustered in the Corps of Pandours, which in time developed into the distinguished Cape Mounted Rifles.

The savage campaigns against the Bushmen began in 1714 when, driven by the white man's cattle from their traditional hunting grounds, where all that was necessary to their life was available, the Bushmen fought back, raiding homesteads, carrying off and maiming cattle.[16] As the colonists moved deeper into areas hitherto occupied only by the hunter-gatherers, the struggle increased in ferocity, and defence against Bushman retaliation became the main preoccupation of the colonists. Whole districts were depopulated, while one commando alone, led by Gotlieb Opperman, appointed field commandant for the northern districts, killed 503 Bushmen. Khoikhoi often played the major part in these operations, acting both as scouts and in taking the brunt of the fighting. Little help could be expected from Cape Town or the Landdrosts of Stellenbosch, responsible in theory for the lands north of the Zwartberge, or from the newly-founded Swellendam, whose territory ran from the hills to the coast. The *trekboer*, the pioneering stock farmer, led a very different existence from his comfortable cousins at the Cape, managing their estates with the help of slaves, and living in elegant Cape Dutch farmhouses. Once beyond the mountains life became hard and uncertain. Families lived around their ox-wagons, the only wheeled transport possible in these roadless areas, or in the simplest of wattle-and-daub huts, their only valuables being their stock, horses and guns; always moving westward in search of better grazing and game.

The further they moved from the Cape, the more primitive the *trekboers'* existence became. Without schoolmasters, ministers, books other than the Bible – and many were in any case illiterate – life was centred around cattle and conflict. Towards the end of the eighteenth century many of the frontier farmers represented the third generation of those who had lived on the very edge of subsistence. During a journey to the interior in 1776, Hendrik Swellengrebel, son of the former Governor, described a *trekboer* hut, with clay walls three to four feet high, a single room, no chimney, holes serving as door and windows, a 'floor of clay mixed with cow dung on which is placed . . . butter, milk, freshly slaughtered meat, bread, etc., while hens, ducks, piglets wander around'. Swellengrebel worried that in time such people 'might become completely barbarous'.[17] Some improvement might have been possible had skilled slave labour been available, but very few slaves were found east of Stellenbosch. Even by 1806, when conditions had somewhat improved, less than two thousand of the thirty thousand slave population lived in the western districts, a high proportion of these in the townships. Labour was provided by the Khoikhoi and their offspring, provided by God to serve and service the white man without payment other than their food and a small share of the cattle.

In 1752 the Cape government sent off an expedition, under the command of Ensign Friedrich Beutler – another German – to report on the furthest parts of their territory, and on the surrounding country. It was the most extensive exploration to that date, and reached well into Xhosa country east of the Kei River, a long way past any colonial settlements, the most distant of these being then some 250 miles from Cape Town; but the party was able to follow all the way a track beaten by previous, illegal, hunting and trading expeditions. So little attention had been paid to the official frontier that Governor Tulbagh was obliged to issue dire warnings to any attempting to cross east of the Gamtoos, threatening corporal punishment, imprisonment and even death to transgressors. There was no perceptible effect. By 1772 settlers, led by Willem Prinsloo, had crossed the Great Karoo and found land that suited them behind the Bruintjes Heights, nearly 150 miles beyond the legal boundaries, in the secluded valley of Agter Bruintjes Hoogte, bringing them to the edge of the Suurveld, the coastal plain between the Bushman and Fish Rivers, territory already settled by the Xhosa; and the Xhosa were about to undergo something of an upheaval.

The Hundred Years War begins

The last paramount chief of the undivided Xhosa nation, Phalo, died in 1775, some two hundred years after his forebear Tshawe, regarded as the originator of the people. Even during Phalo's lifetime Xhosa unity had begun to dissolve as two of the chief's sons by different wives, Gcaleka and Rharhabe, disputed the succession.[18] After Rharhabe, the offspring of the 'right-hand house', was killed in attempting to extend his authority his heir, Ngqika, was a minor, and his uncle, Ndlambe, acted as regent; after Ngqika came of age the two quarrelled, and their followers divided. Gcaleka and his heirs held on to the eastern Xhosa lands beyond the Kei River, causing the other competing groups to look for opportunities further west, towards the colonial border. There they came up against a number of independent Xhosa and Xhosa/Khoikhoi clans, who in turn were pushed nearer the European farmers. However bitterly the Ngqikas and Ndlambes disputed, they continued to maintain allegiance to the original royal line, that of Gcaleka and his successors Hintsa (d.1835), Sarili (d.1892) and Sigcawu (d.1902).

Until they met the *trekboers*, the Xhosa's only contact with Europeans had been with shipwrecked mariners, who presented no threat. Nor can the *veeboers* have seemed very different from any other competitive cattle-men: the Xhosa had lived alongside the Khoikhoi for centuries, often amicably enough, absorbing much Khoikhoi culture and intermarrying freely, although doubtless with some armed clashes. Boers and Xhosa had mutual enemies in the hunter-gatherer Bushmen, who were attacked viciously by both peoples when they resisted the forward movement of the cattlemen. Nor were black and white farmers unevenly matched: the Xhosa had the advantage of numbers, and belonged to a warrior culture, while European firearms and horses, devastating in some circumstances, were of limited use in bush fighting. Without external support, the white farmers must have been obliged to come to some accommodation with the blacks, as indeed they contrived to do for most of the eighteenth century without more than a handful of serious raids and counter-raids in the intervals of mutually profitable intercourse. 'Kaffirs', as the Xhosa were commonly known to the Europeans, traded cattle with Boers and worked on their farms; only when the Cape became British were the Xhosa faced with unprecedented problems.[19]

In 1778 Governor Joachim van Plettenberg set off to investigate for himself the further limits of his colony, accompanied by the talented officer Colonel Robert Gordon, Dutch-born but of Scottish ancestry. In a three-month journey the enterprising van Plettenberg travelled as far as the Fish River, where he had conversations with the Gqunukhwebe Xhosa, a mixed Xhosa-Khoikhoi people, during which, the Governor believed, an agreement was reached to establish the colonial boundary on the river line. In the north, after receiving petitions from the scattered farmers in the Sneeuwberg for a Landdrost to be sent among them, the Governor placed a beacon demarcating the north/eastern boundary near present-day Colesberg. But whatever van Plettenberg's understanding, since the coastal region between the Sunday's and Fish Rivers, the Suurveld, was already inhabited by Xhosa and Khoikhoi, any attempt to exercise colonial authority there was bound to be resisted.[20] Rather pretentiously, van Plettenberg wrote on 7 March 1780: 'I thought about the treaties made by Wm. Pitt with the inhabitants of America ... I flattered myself that since I wished to emulate the Quaker in sincerity the Kaffers would follow the example of the American Indians.'[21]

It was an independent tribe, the Mdange, driven by Ndlambe across the Fish River, who first clashed with the Europeans, in Agter Bruintjes Hoogte. Adriaan van Jaarsveld, a prosperous farmer, had been appointed commandant on the frontier. A tough and unscrupulous fighter who had proved himself in warfare against the Bushmen, he nevertheless found his fellow colonists difficult: 'a band of rebels ... full of discords and disputes ... licentious and disobedient'. The worst of them were the Prinsloo family and the Bezuidenhouts, all from Agter Bruintjes Hoogte. The first trouble in 1780, which marked the start of a resistance struggle that continued intermittently over the next century, was 'chiefly caused', the Stellenbosch Landdrost, responsible for events five hundred miles off, reported, 'by the violence and annoyance committed against the Kaffirs by inhabitants' – notably Willem Prinsloo. The offended Xhosa retaliated by theft and raiding, reciprocated by a commando of 130 Boers and Khoikhoi headed by van Jaarsveld. Although his expedition was successful in 'recovering' five thousand cattle and driving the Xhosa behind the Fish River, the recalcitrant Boers persisted in raiding on their own account. Only a permanent magistracy could hope to keep them in order, argued van Jaarsveld, heading a petition for a Landdrost to control those 'who have departed from the ways of God, and, to our great injury, have become disobedient to Him, and to those who, by His will, are established in authority'.

their taxes and who had certainly suffered heavy losses, did not take kindly to the combination of feeble support and hectoring that was all their Landdrost seemed to offer. In February 1795 a public meeting was called, at which a paper was read accusing Maynier of not resisting the Xhosa vigorously enough, and not allowing the settlers to take action on their own. This '*Tesamenstemming*' advanced the concept of the '*volkstem*', the 'voice of the people', in opposition to the 'degenerate cabal' that the Heemrad had become. At that stage (and not infrequently in the future) the voice was only that of a minority of the noisiest, but it became an idea of great power; the Nationalist anthem which displaced 'God Save the King' in 1938 was '*Die Stem van Afrika*'. The other concept, that of the '*volk*', is fundamental to South African history. Neither the word nor the concept fits English language or thought. The obvious 'people' is too weak, indeed pejorative; we have seen too many 'people's republics' and 'people's courts' to be comfortable with the word. '*Volk*' has powerful connotations of racial and cultural identity, and developed in Afrikaner history almost mystical overtones.[24]

Van Jaarsveld stood somewhat aloof from the agitation, preferring to act as an intermediary when Cape Town sent an envoy to arrange matters after the expulsion of the Landdrost and two of the Heemraden. Olof de Wet, one of the Company's most senior officials, who arrived in Graaff-Reinet a few weeks later, fared no better and was also forced to leave. The argument was one of both methods and morality, exacerbated by Maynier's aloofly superior attitude to the 'peasantry'. The farmers, who had suffered considerable loss, were itching to attack the Xhosa and loot their cattle. Maynier was cynical about the Boers' martial ability (unless 'a considerable number of Hottentots' were there to be 'the first exposed to danger', commandos never succeeded), and was possessed of 'the most perfect conviction' that peace could be preserved by 'fair means' and with 'little trouble' if vigilance was preserved; 'attacking women and children' was both wrong and counter-productive.[25]

Nothing could be done by Cape Town to force the Graaff-Reinet rebels back to obedience, for not only was the Company in terminal decline, but the Netherlands itself was in grave difficulty. The period of Swellengrebel and Tulbagh, who were in office between 1739 and 1771, was one of stagnation. The adult free population had doubled, but the growth was not reflected in prosperity. Wheat production stayed constant, and cattle were said to have increased only from thirty-four to thirty-seven thousand, although sheep did better as the poorer grazing of the Karoo was used, increasing from 150,000 to 250,000. Shipping movements were also static, at between sixty and eighty annually; and fewer of these were Dutch, who seemed to be deserting the sea for a more comfortable existence on shore.

In the heyday of Dutch sea-power something like a tenth of the nation's whole population were seafarers; half the men in the small town of Graft had been sailors in 1635, but a century later only one in twelve followed the sea, and by 1811 only eight sailors were to be found. At the beginning of the eighteenth century the Zaan yards built over three hundred vessels a year; by 1770 only a tenth of that number were on the stocks, and in 1793 only one vessel left the yards; by the end of the decade the VOC did not own a single ship. The Dutch ships themselves were out of date, superseded by the bigger, faster English East Indiamen, who now had by far the largest share of that trade. Cornelius de Jong, captain of a Dutch frigate, refused a passage home in a Dutch ship, preferring to wait for a more up-to-date and reliable English vessel.[26] 'The going will be good as long as I live, and what happens after my death won't worry me then!' was the attitude of the once-haughty officials of the VOC.

Holland had not been immune from the revolutionary changes taking place in Europe. Reformist ideas, predominantly British – the Welsh minister Robert Price's 'Observations on Civil Liberty' was particularly successful – inspired the eccentric Baron Johan van der Capellen and young Pieter Paulus, who later became the first President of the Batavian Republic's National Assembly, to press for liberal advances.[27] Such disturbing ideas began to reach the provincial and insular society at the Cape only after 1780, in which year the pro-French and anti-English elements in Holland, encouraged by the success of the American colonists, made an attempt to recover lost ground by joining in the 'Armed Neutrality', a coalition of seafaring powers united against Britain. War was then declared, much to the distress of Lloyds of London, whose members had to pay up for seizures of Dutch goods by Lord Rodney. A French squadron under Admiral de Suffren de St Tropez, one of that rare breed, a successful French sea-fighter, contrived to avoid an English fleet and peacefully occupy the Cape in 1781. Himself representing the traditions of the *ancien régime*, being a Bailie of the Order of Malta, Suffren's young officers 'entirely corrupted the standard of living at the Cape' by their 'extravagance and indulgence in an unbroken round of amusements'. They also brought with them the works of Voltaire and Rousseau, thereby stimulating the intellectual as well as the social life of the colony.

Although this was the least serious of the Anglo–Dutch wars, one effect was to exacerbate the differences between the conservative supporters of the House of Orange, who were in favour of the British alliance, and the young enthusiasts, the 'Patriots', who supported the rising French reformers; another was to leave the country nearly bankrupt, and the VOC entirely so.

Further disturbing influences were felt as ships from the new United States began to touch at the Cape. The appropriate morals were drawn by Cape residents, who were becoming increasingly impatient of the restrictive Company rule: Barend Jacob Artoys wrote: 'The English have found to their detriment how impolitic it is to oppress their subjects.' While not enduring the hardships of the frontier settlers, the Cape men had reason for discontent. The Swedish botanist Carl Thunberg, visiting the Cape in the early 1770s, found the Europeans, both sailors and soldiers, treated worse and with less compassion than the slaves, while he thought Governor van Plettenberg nothing more than 'an unfeeling bon vivant'.[28] As in the past, however, the greater part of the grievances were economic: not only did the Company restrict trade to the disadvantage of the burghers – an ancient source of complaint – but officials had now formed trading firms on their own account which creamed off any other profits.

As in Boston, it took one incident to spark the discontent into rebellion, if the respectful protest of the burghers can be so described. Independent Fiscal Willem Cornelis Boers was high-handed, dictatorial, a doctor of law of the University of Utrecht and contemptuous of the burghers, whom he regarded (not entirely without justification) as 'little better than illiterate peasants'. Appointed at the age of thirty, Boers used the judicial system to line his own pockets, and had particularly vociferous opponents deported; eighteen in eight years, a record – so much for 'freedom'. Hendrik Swellengrebel attempted to intervene, since Governor van Plettenberg had no official control over the Fiscal's activites, but had to report failure.[29] Much muttering, many secret meetings and anonymous leaflets preceded the explosion of indignation which took place in 1779 when Boers ordered the deportation of one Carel Buijtendag, which was duly carried out by a patrol of 'Kaffirs', grey-uniformed slaves or Khoikhoi appointed as jailers' and executioners' attendants, entitled to carry swords. Buijtendag was known as a bad character, having a suspended sentence of deportation hanging over him as a result of his atrocities towards two Khoikhoi servants, and had indeed been arrested on a charge of domestic violence. Nevertheless, his arrest was considered a shocking humiliation, compounded by the fact that he was packed off to Company-controlled Batavia, rather than to the far more agreeable Netherlands.

Barend Artoys and three other burghers were chosen to lead a deputation to the directors, backed by over four hundred signatories to a petition. It was a revolutionary document only by the standards of the Glorious Revolution of 1668, or even Magna Carta, 'humbly submitted . . . under the respectful correction of Your Honours' wiser and more enlightened judgements', requesting that the Company's rules be applied impartially, and that authority should not be abused. Fiscal Boers had claimed that the 'so-called' burghers were free only insofar as they were not employed by the Company, and were therefore 'graciously permitted to live in the land'; but surely, the Cape men argued, all citizens, 'even the poorest farmer in the smallest country village', were accounted free men.[30] Even more directly looking back to 1215 rather than forward to 1789 were the pleas that the directors should make it clear to all, citizens and officials alike, exactly what laws were in force; regulations should be printed and circulated to ensure that officials could no longer invent off-the-cuff laws with no object other than that of extorting money.

The 'Cape Patriots' differed among themselves in many of their views. Such extremists as J.H. Redelinghuys accused his fellow-delegates of moderation, and attacked even so respected a person as Pieter Paulus, President of the National Assembly, for his 'treason' in giving up the Cape; but like later revolutionaries, Redelinghuys preferred the comfort of Holland, where he stayed.

The board prevaricated; Artoys and the deputation arrived in Holland with his petition in 1779, but a reply was only sent four years later, after consultation with van Plettenberg and his staff. Little was offered beyond the traditional reiteration of the ban on officials trading on their own account and the equally traditional despatch of a Commissioner to make sure they did so. Remaining dissatisfied, the Cape burghers elected a Representative Committee, which had Hendrik Swellengrebel, himself a third-generation Afrikaner, draft an appeal over the heads of the board of directors to the States-General. This was an altogether more sophisticated and radical document, claiming that the whole constitution of the colony was now completely out of date, and must be altered to reflect the fact that the Cape was no longer a mere 'refreshment station', but an entity in its own right.[31] By this time – 1784 – the discontented burghers had adopted the name of 'Patriots', in emulation of the reform movement jolted into life in Holland by van der Capellen in September 1781, which led to the Patriot revolt, precursor of the revolution eight years later in neighbouring France. From neither board nor States-General was much relief gained; both agreed that the existing order must be maintained and the monopoly preserved, although burghers were granted equal representation with officials on the Council of Justice, and it was agreed that deportations should no longer be made to Batavia, but back to the Netherlands; too late for Buijtendag, who had died on the voyage.

In terminal decline, kept afloat only by transfusions of public money, the VOC attempted to spend its way out of trouble at the Cape. Governor Cornelius van de Graaff, an engineer officer, built extensive and expensive fortifications which pushed up spending fivefold, resulting in the Cape costing more than all the other East Indian stations combined. Commemorated in the new settlement of Graaff-Reinet, the last of the Cape Governors was replaced by two Commissioners General in 1792, who on their arrival reported 'a spirit of confusion and insubordination towards all authority without exception'. By that time it was too late to do more than impose some new taxes and ban non-Dutch imports, neither of which did much to placate the unhappy colonists. It was hardly surprising that when a foreign force landed at the Cape resistance was less than dogged.

FIVE

Kaapstad to Cape Town

The Redcoats' first arrival

The desultory war of the Armed Neutrality ended in 1784, leaving the Netherlands deeply divided. Traditional support for the House of Orange remained, but had been eroded by the growing Patriot radical movement. In what was almost a dress rehearsal for the French Revolution the Patriots' Free Corps began an armed revolt, succeeded by a relatively mild-mannered civil war. This was brought to an end in 1787 by Prussian intervention, assisted by the British Secret Service, who spent heavily in supporting the Prince of Orange. But William V was not a man to inspire or retain loyalty. When the French Revolution led to an invasion of the Netherlands in 1794 the Patriots came to power, forcing William to seek refuge in England. In a situation similar to that of France in 1940, two Dutch governments claimed allegiance, one of refugees in London, the other remaining in The Hague, forced to toe the French occupiers' line. Again as in the Second World War, the question of what should happen to Dutch colonies arose.

Britain had been worried about the Cape of Good Hope since the defection of the Netherlands in 1780, and efforts had been made to gain possession of that strategic spot, either by negotiations or more robust methods. A London banker, Sir Francis Baring, added his weight to the argument, writing to Henry Dundas, Secretary at War, in January 1795.[1] Formerly chairman of the East India Company, Baring was acutely conscious of the importance of maintaining the route to India, now threatened by a second French intervention, and the possibility of another sailor of Suffren's quality cutting the sea lines. It was indeed only logical that since the English had supplanted the Dutch in the East Indies, they should take over its way-station, still the only strategic purpose served by the Cape of Good Hope. Dundas acted quickly, and within a few weeks of Baring's note an expedition was authorized by the exiled Prince of Orange, on the understanding that any Dutch territory taken by the British would be handed back when a general peace was signed. Sir James Craig was accordingly despatched to take over the Cape, with or without the consent of the Dutch Governor.

Commissioner General Sluysken found himself in a quandary when, on 11 June 1795, a British fleet anchored in False Bay, bearing a letter from the Prince of Orange requiring him to hand over the government of the colony. The community at the Cape was as divided as that in Holland. Sluysken's military commander Colonel Robert Gordon, who had spent his life in the Company's service and accompanied Governor van Plettenberg on his momentous journey, was a loyal Orangeman who had characterized the revolutionaries as 'barbarous ... [they] do not even believe in God any more and ... want to turn everything upside down in the apparent beautiful name of freedom and equality ... I will destroy them if they come.'[2] If the British represented the Prince of Orange, Gordon wanted to wish them 'heartily welcome', and deplored 'designing people' and 'indoctrinated dupes' who suggested resistance. Sluysken was less obliging, lacking any independent confirmation of affairs in Europe, and was conscious of much likely opposition, as well as the possible drastic personal consequences if he jumped the wrong way.

Discussions, growing progressively less friendly, and punctuated by a fight at Muizenberg in August, as the British battled their way from their base at Simonstown to Cape Town, went on for three months. The reluctant Commissioner finally decided on 12 September that he could not accept the British conditions. Defiance did not last long, and within forty-eight hours the Dutch proposed an armistice. This not being forthcoming, the prudent Craig, who had been wounded at Bunker Hill, and who like Wellington was cautious and methodical, took his time about marching on the town. The colony surrendered on 16 September, with few casualties having been incurred by either side, the promise of maintaining the value of Cape money being a powerful incentive. During the protracted preliminary manoeuvres the burgher militia had proved more effective than the Dutch regulars; but even so, the British lost only four killed in the entire operation. When he realized that the British had been less than frank, and that he was regarded as a traitor by his own people, Gordon, his illusions shattered, shot himself.

Two days after the takeover the British commanders addressed the populace, promising no new taxes, a review of those imposed by the

Commissioners, an end to the 'monopolies and oppressions of the VOC', and stating that the new regime's 'first wish' was 'to adopt every measure which may appear proper to promote the prosperity of the Settlement and the happiness of the inhabitants'. In spite of these well-meant sentiments, the British were not at first greeted cordially. Taking over temporarily as General Officer Commanding and Military Governor, Craig grumbled at 'the ignorance, the credulity, and the stupid pride of the people, particularly the Boers. The most absurd ideas as to their strength and importance are prevalent among them, nor indeed is there any opinion on any subject too ridiculous . . . not to be adopted by them.'[3] Given that the eventual restitution of the colony was probable, there was not too much a temporary administration could do, but Craig, in a typically British reaction, immediately outlawed all judicial torture, which had previously been freely applied, especially to slaves, and the more bizarre forms of execution. A protest was entered at such rash action by the Cape Court of Justice, complaining that 'cold and rude' slaves 'would hardly consider the privation of life as a punishment, unless accompanied by such cruel circumstances as greatly aggravate their bodily suffering'.[4]

Craig himself was reasonably well-fitted to be a colonial Governor. Although a man of sharp temper – and described as a 'pocket Hercules' – he was capable of great kindness, and had as open a mind as could be expected from a professional soldier. His administration was a scratch affair, with those Dutch supporting the Prince of Orange, and therefore sympathetic to British rule, continuing to run day-to-day affairs. Of these the most prominent, and one who was to continue at the centre of affairs for another sixteen years, was the Fiscal, Willem van Ryneveld, a good-natured man of solid ability. Olof de Wet continued in his post, and the former Deputy Governor, Johan Rhenius, became treasurer, but in general the foreign occupation was viewed suspiciously, with the stockmen in the outback continuing to protest angrily against any form of control from the Cape.[5]

The British made little alteration to the administrative system, contenting themselves with diminishing the extensive corruption of the VOC by paying proper salaries to officials. Dundas's instructions were to govern 'in conformity to the Laws and Instructions that subsisted under the antient [sic] Government of the said Settlement'.[6] Existing laws therefore remained in force, with local affairs left to the burgher councillors in Cape Town, now dignified as the Burgher Senate, and to Landdrosts and Heemraden in the districts. These were reinforced by a subordinate rank of officials, the Veldkornets, the old Veldwachmeesters, elected from among the burgher community to act as magistrates of sub-districts. All new appointments were made from the ranks of the burghers themselves, and – at the Cape, at least – accepted without overt opposition.

For some time the Cape was administered as a front-line military post; a Dutch relief expedition arrived in the following August, but quickly surrendered.[7] A more stable form of government was initiated in May 1797 with the appointment of the first Civil Governor. George, Earl Macartney, was an experienced diplomat, who had negotiated with the Emperor of China, Empress Catherine of Russia and Louis XVIII of France, been Governor of Madras, and turned down the offer of the Governor Generalship of India. But at sixty, suffering from gout and a gunshot wound sustained in a duel, Macartney was ill and tired, and took little active part in the government, much of his work being done by Craig's successor, General Francis Dundas, and by Colonial Secretary Andrew Barnard.

Dundas, a prickly and arrogant officer, had however the considerable advantage of being Henry Dundas's nephew. Fortunately another relation of the Secretary at War, Lady Anne Barnard, accompanied her husband, and reported regularly to Henry Dundas back in London. Lady Anne was a natural charmer, witty and affectionate, and during her five years at the Cape did much to mollify the prickly burghers and their wives. Fiscal van Ryneveld was among those charmed, and amused her by the bucolic present of a piece of salt beef, prepared *'par mes propres mains'*.[8] Balls, to which all the colonists who had paid visits to Government House were invited, proliferated, and an amateur dramatic society, that inevitable accompaniment of British colonization, was formed. Lord Wellesley, stopping en route for India, did not approve. In a 'most secret and private' communication to Barnard he wrote that theatricals would 'render the younger branches of the Public Service indolent, dissipated and intractable . . . broken Players, deranged Spouters'.[9] Others were more relaxed: even the 'Boers from the country' fell into the habit of dropping in to Government House at seven in the morning to drink a glass of gin with Lady Anne while she breakfasted; a far cry from the stiff formality and status-sensitivity of the VOC.

Roger Curtis, a young naval officer who visited the Cape between 1799 and 1802, found it still a dull, but not a disagreeable spot. There were individuals of taste and education, but most of the colonists led a placid existence:

The Dutch Colonists are in general tall and robust in Stature, and inclined to Corpulency. An unvaried Regularity prevails throughout their Lives, and the History of a day is that of the whole Period of their Existence. They rise early, breakfast at eight, dine at Twelve, and sup at Nine. In the country they are still earlier in the Meals. Immediately after they rise they drink Coffee: and between meals fortify their Stomachs with a Soapie, a Glass of strong Spirits. After Dinner they smoke a Couple of Pipes, and then retire to enjoy a nap for two or three Hours during the Heat of the day. The pipe fills up all the intermediate Intervals. Their Cookery is gross, and dishes fat and greasy.

The course of Life followed by the Ladies, with the Exception of the Pipe, and (I believe) the Soapie, is much the same.

The Ufrow, or Mistress of the Family, when not employed in Household affairs, sits supinely in a large Chair in the Hall, watching the Slaves, or takes the Air in sauntering or lounging on the Stoop. It is not to be wondered that these Sedentary habits generally occasion great Corpulency; and they account for the Magnitude of some of the Ladies up the Country. The ruling Passion of the Dutchman is Avarice. Of Literature they know nothing, and they are seldom seen with a book.[10]

Life had changed little in the twenty-five years since Sergeant Morgenstern had found life at the Cape 'very monotonous', and conversation 'too forced and awkward'.[11]

Efficient protection and occasional acts of kindness

At Swellendam General Craig inherited the previous 'rebellion', in which the inhabitants – all eight hundred of them – had gone so far as to elect a National Assembly (Nasionale Vergardering), with Hermanus Steyn, a respectable farmer, as president in an enormous cockaded hat. Among the fraternal demands of what had been claimed to be the first Afrikaner republic was one requiring that any captured Khoikhoi women should 'henceforth be the property of the farmer employing them, and serve him for life'. In spite of a solemn vow to 'hold out to the last man', these doubtful Swellendam republicans submitted quietly within a month. Graaff-Reinet, so much further off, took longer. Following the policy of appointing local men, and in response to a request from the leaders of the settlers themselves, Craig sent F.R. Bresler, previously a VOC official. He was not welcomed; the rebels, sporting tricolour cockades, inspired by 'Freedom's Child' Gert Rautenbach and the tenacious Adriaan van Jaarsveld, protesting against the 'Mameluks', expostulated that they would 'far rather . . . a born Englishman than a secretly partial, prying Africaander'.[12] Sensibly, since he had more important things to do, Craig simply assured the rebels that their previous sins would be forgiven them, and cut off their supplies. After some attempted negotiations the rebellion subsided, and by 1797 all the frontiersmen had formally submitted, with only five Stellenbosch burghers – 'stout, sulky, democratic fellows' – declining to accept British rule. One Hendrick Eckstein of Bergvliet restricted his expression of republican principles to despatching wedding invitations to 'Citizen So-and-so'. Lord Macartney was annoyed, and despatched the Mayor with a piquet of twenty dragoons to remonstrate, which, as Lady Anne reported, put the wedding 'into a glorious fright. Mynheer instantly began stroking down the whiskers of the Town Mayor, and noble ones has that pussie, frizzled out on each side of his face. He was invited to dance, and the whole thing treated as a jest.' But Eckstein proffered many apologies, and produced a bond of £1,000 against future misbehaviour.

Lord Macartney's Private Secretary John Barrow had accompanied Bresler to Graaff-Reinet. The indefatigable Barrow had been with Macartney in China, and had established something of a reputation as a geographer; in his later career as Secretary to the Admiralty he was to become very well-known indeed. Barrow was no polished product of the universities and court, but a man from a humble background brought up in one of the poorest parts of England, the Lancashire fringe of the Lake District. Well used to unpleasant conditions, he nevertheless found the frontier Boers primitive to the point of squalor, and an unhappy contrast to the pleasant society at the Cape – where he married a local girl, Miss Truter, planning to spend the rest of his life there. Barrow's *An Account of Travels into the Interior of Southern Africa* (1801), in which he gave free rein to his views, was received as gospel for many years by the home government, and had a considerable effect on the general unfavourable perception of the frontiersmen.

After visiting Graaff-Reinet, described by Barrow as nothing more an assemblage of mud huts, inhabited by grubby, idle and cruel Boers, Barrow and Bresler moved east to meet Ngqika, whom they considered to be the most powerful Xhosa chief. While this was for the moment true, Ngqika resting in undisturbed possession of the traditional Xhosa country east of the Fish River, it was his uncle and rival Ndlambe, together with dozens of minor chieftains, who were causing the trouble, having been ejected into what the Europeans regarded as their own territory, the Suurveld, west of the Fish. The most difficult was Chungwa, head of a group of mixed Xhosa and Khoikhoi, the Gqunukhwebe, who had met van Plettenberg twenty years previously; and stirring up this explosive mix was the renegade Coenraad de Buys, married to both Chungwa's sister and Ngqika's mother. However willing Ngqika might be to cooperate with the British, he had no control over these, or any Xhosa outside his own eastern territory.

Barrow was speedily as much taken with the Xhosa as he had been disgusted by the Boers – 'There is perhaps no nation on earth ... that produces so fine a race of men as the Kaffers'[13] – and attempted to reach an agreement with Ngqika. British requirements were exactly those of the VOC; only the Cape station was of importance, and its appendages nothing more than an embarrassment. A considerable embarrassment, since Plettenberg's accepted, but mainly arbitrary, boundary ran over a thousand miles from the Buffalo River to the Atlantic coast, along the mountains north of the Karoo to Algoa Bay. Much of this could safely be neglected, an area where isolated stockmen, European or Khoikhoi, managed to co-exist with the Bushmen as best they could. It was in the last 150 miles or so, where the parallel rivers Gamtoos, Sunday's, Bushman's, Kowie and Fish all joined the Indian Ocean, that the real potential for trouble lay. Here, it was agreed, a firm line of demarcation between colonists and Xhosa must be established and all communication between them forbidden, as certain to lead to trouble. Ngqika must therefore exercise his influence to ensure that those Xhosa already in the colony returned across the Fish River, and despatch any colonists found in his territories back to Graaff-Reinet.

Ngqika's views are conjectural, but were not likely to be favourable. Barrow had come with no impressive force, and his father-in-law de Buys was strongly anti-British. For his part Barrow had little idea of the structure of Xhosa society, and did not appreciate how limited a chief's power was, even over his own followers; the whole notion of fixed land frontiers had no meaning to the freely-moving Xhosa – and very little to the Boers.

Two years later it was painfully clear that this was so. Graaff-Reinet settled down to some extent after the return of Landdrost Bresler with an escort of twelve dragoons, reinforced by his predecessor Honoratus Maynier, promoted to Commissioner, and still correctly difficult. Some farmers began to return to their abandoned homesteads, encouraged by the promise of remission of past rents, extended six years into the future. Henry Dundas, a blunt and uncouth politician, possessed good common sense, and wrote with sensible advice on how the frontiersmen should be treated. They were to be regarded 'rather as distant tribes dependent upon His Majesty's Government, than as subjects necessarily answerable to all the laws and regulations established within the immediate precincts of that Government'. In time, by demonstrating the benefits of British rule, and showing them 'efficient protection and occasional acts of kindness', the whole tribe might be civilized.[14]

On the northern frontier the 'acts of kindness' worked well enough. Starving Bushmen, who had been driven to raiding colonial farms, were given stock by the colonists, who also arranged shoots to provide game. What trouble there was came from bands of predatory Khoikhoi-Bastaard raiders, equipped with horses and guns, under the leadership of one – 'a monster, known by the name of THE AFRICAN'[15] – Jager Afrikaner, and other members of that notorious family, who plundered indiscriminately from their lairs in the Orange Valley.

In the east, conditions were less satisfactory. The 'efficient protection' proved unhappily lacking. Co-existence with the Xhosa remained precarious, and reports of cattle thefts continued, but when trouble broke out there once more, in 1799, it was sparked off not by demands for a more aggressive policy, revolutionary sentiments, or even disgust at foreign rule (although all these existed), but through a banal attempt to avoid payment of mortgage interest. Adriaan van Jaarsveld, the veteran commandant, was arrested for forgery (quite justly, as it turned out), and while being taken to Cape Town was forcibly liberated by an armed party under Martinus Prinsloo. The British reaction was swifter than anything the VOC might have managed; a squadron of cavalry was despatched, reinforced by two infantry companies sent by sea. On their arrival the burghers quickly surrendered, and the ringleaders were sent to Cape Town for trial. Some Afrikaner historians have seen the insurrection as being significant in the development of an Afrikaner nation; others, including the most industrious, J.S. Marais, disagreed, as does Hermann Giliomee. Considering the Graaff-Reineters were equally hot against the VOC, the rapidity of the collapse, and the subsequent cooperation of the most influential inhabitants, the sceptics have it.[16]

The episode did not endear their new rulers to the frontiersmen, but they would have accepted the British more willingly if their forces had been more effective in quelling the growing unrest among the Khoikhoi and Xhosa. Sensing a division between the settlers and the British, who had again cut off supplies of ammunition after the van Jaarsveld affair, in 1799 many Khoikhoi took to plundering their late employers, and joining forces with the Xhosa. By now experienced horsemen and riflemen, the Khoikhoi terrified the 'completely unmanned' and 'panic struck' Boers whom previously 'they regarded not as their masters but their executioners'.[17] Seven hundred Khoikhoi, helped by Xhosa, defeated a commando and forced the colonists back a considerable distance.

Back at the Cape Lord Macartney, who would have authorized retaliation, had been replaced by the strikingly ineffective Sir George Yonge. The new Governor had nothing to recommend him but his friendship with King George III; he was old, nearly seventy, inexperienced, and corrupt to an extent shocking even to a society well accustomed to corruption, and so gross as to procure his recall within months. During the interregnums, and even when the incompetent Yonge was in office, General Dundas was left very much in charge. In spite of his dragoons being badly mauled in a Xhosa attack, he had no intention of starting the full-scale war that would have been necessary to re-establish British prestige. The Xhosa and the Khoikhoi together had got the better, in no uncertain terms, of both colonists and British, and a peace was accordingly patched up through the good offices of Maynier; but the whole frontier remained disturbed, with a third of the farms destroyed and their inhabitants dispossessed, bitterly looking for revenge. Their discontent focused on the innocent Maynier, who once again had to suffer the humiliation of being barricaded inside the *drosdty*, and being forced to resign, although a subsequent inquiry reinstated him.

An idealistic interlude

The first withdrawal of the British from the Cape of Good Hope began far away, in Ireland. As part of the price for Irish assent to parliamentary union with Britain in 1800, Prime Minister William Pitt had promised to liberate Roman Catholics from the restrictions on their civil liberties imposed since the sixteenth century. So revolutionary a suggestion led to the fall of his ministry and its replacement by one headed by Henry Addington, later Lord Sidmouth. Addington, with a government composed of notorious nonentities, was anxious to make a quick end to the expensive war with France, and speedily accepted an unlikely peace with Napoleon.

The future of the Cape had been much argued; many influential voices, including that of Lord Nelson, claimed it to be of no real use. Addington therefore had no qualms about giving up a colony whose expense 'had been enormous', and accordingly, by the Treaty of Amiens signed in March 1802, the Cape was restored to Holland. Not, as had been envisaged in 1795, to a Holland ruled by the House of Orange, but to the newly-formed Batavian Republic, the independence of which was, according to the Treaty of Luneville, guaranteed by the French.

Composed for the most part of well-intentioned reformers, believing in the benevolence of their French allies – they were soon to learn the errors of their ways – the Batavian National Assembly welcomed the idea of a territory of their own where they might create an ideal polity, according to the most approved doctrines of the French Revolution. The establishment of the new order at the Cape was entrusted to one of their members, Jacob Abraham Uitenhage de Mist. By no means himself an extremist – 'No one,' he once wrote, 'can have a greater horror of all so-called revolutionary measures'[18] – de Mist had indeed spent six months in prison on account of his loyalty to traditional political systems. A serious-minded and articulate – often tediously so – figure, he arrived at the Cape in January 1803 as Commissioner General, to take over from the British and to install a new constitution embodying all the favourite ideas of the republicans. These were not adulterated by any inconvenient practical experience; at the age of fifty-four de Mist had spent all his life in the closed society of urban Holland. Nor had the new Governor, General Willem Janssens, liberal in principle but authoritarian in practice, a patriotic nationalist, suspicious of the British and all their works, seen much of the world beyond the Dutch frontiers. Both were, however, quick studies, and adapted themselves to the realities of Africa.

No guillotines were erected in front of the Castle at Cape Town, the transfer of power being accomplished in a civil, even friendly manner. Van Ryneveld lost his official post, but remained trusted and influential, asked to recommend both economic and political policies. Even the amateur dramatic society continued, with the improving title Tot Nut en Vermaak (For Instruction and Amusement). The British administration had, de Mist believed, set 'an excellent example' in its modest reforms of justice, and in conciliating the Cape population, but much remained to be done if the

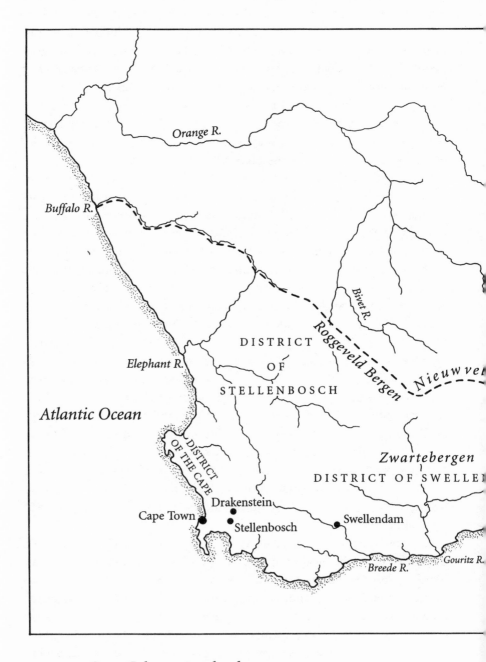

MAP 3 *Cape Colony: 1800 borders*

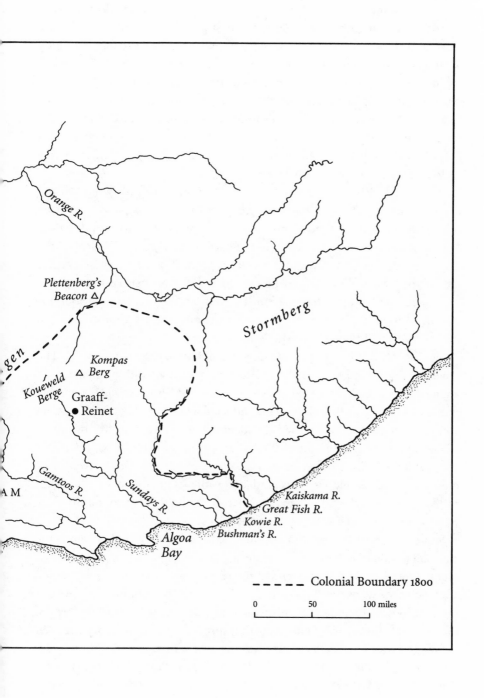

Orange R.

Plettenberg's
Beacon △

Stormberg

...gen

Kompas
△ Berg

Kouéweld
Berge

Graaff-
● Reinet

A M

Gamtoos R.

Sundays R.

Kaiskama R.
Great Fish R.
Kowie R.
Bushman's R.

Algoa
Bay

– – – – Colonial Boundary 1800

0   50   100 miles

system of 'unheard of Asiatic despotism' established by the VOC was to be replaced by a government along the best philosophic principles. Before leaving Holland the new Commissioner had prepared a paper outlining what he considered had been the mistakes that led to the Cape being racked by 'quarrels, divisions, disorders and disturbances of all kinds' (de Mist never believed in using one word when four would do), and to the lack there of all civilized amenities. This unhappy state the benevolent Batavians were determined to remedy, finding themselves in the enviable position of Sarastro-like philosopher-dictators, empowered to bring enlightened rule to their new subjects; at least in theory.

Slavery, de Mist insisted, was an abomination, and must be ended; but a short time at the Cape, together with van Ryneveld's advice, convinced him that unfortunate economic necessity demanded its continuance. Macartney had come to the same conclusion in 1797, and 'allowed the importation of Negroes, without a certain proportion of whom, extensive cultivation of a Colony cannot be carried out'.[19] An unsuccessful attempt was made to introduce Dutch colonists,[20] but far from ending the abominable institution, fresh imports of slaves at the rate of three to four hundred a year continued throughout the Batavian period.

On the condition of the unhappy Khoikhoi, Janssens reported: 'The cruelties committed against the Hottentots exceed everything that is said about it in Cape Town or what can be imagined.' Justice was lamentably skewed in favour of the white man, and the blacks were kept in subjection and ignorance. De Mist warned the 'debased and inhuman' frontiersmen, whose 'complete corruption of their moral sense was doubtless' due, *inter alia*, to their 'continual diet of meat', to beware 'lest the Great Avenger of innocent blood should visit this land, and smite its inhabitants'.[21] But again reality asserted itself and obliged both Janssens and de Mist to modify their views after seeing the frontier for themselves.

Some at least of the good intentions succeeded. Governor Janssens actually had a colonist hanged for shooting a Bushman, an unprecedented event; central control was extended by new *drosdties* at Uitenhage (named after de Mist, whose last name had unfortunate connotations[22]), between the Gamtoos and Sunday's Rivers which included the most difficult areas of the eastern frontier, and Tulbagh, with improved communications between them and Cape Town. An attempt was made to reorganize education, sadly neglected in Company days, in the *Schoolorde* of 1805, which envisaged a comprehensive lay system. Passionately opposed by the conservative inhabitants, the reform was never realized. Missionary education was frowned upon, but the admirable Maatschappij Tot Nut van t'Algemeen, commonly known as the 'Nut' and founded in Holland during the heady days of 1784 as an educational association, set up a 'department' in Cape Town in the same year of 1805 – for whites only.

The provision of other 'civilized amenities' was another matter. No subvention from Holland was forthcoming, and de Mist was obliged to issue paper money in order to provide public buildings and to further improved farming methods; inevitably the value of the rixdollar fell. It was cheaper, and almost as satisfactory, new names being fashionable, simply to change old titles: 'Landdrost' became 'Baillow', and 'Fiscaal' – 'a name they have learned to loathe' – 'Procureur Generaal'. There would have been a 'Chief Scholarch' too, had there been enough time to reorganize education. Religious freedom was guaranteed, and the first Islamic congregation, under Imam Achmed, officially recognized (although Craig had already licensed the Imam to minister to his people).

The Cape had become an integral part of the Batavian Republic, with its own new corpus of laws; there being no colonists acquainted with these, it was necessary to import expatriates to staff the new Council of Justice and to fill senior posts. Bringing with it these new concepts, and being run by Europeans, the Batavian administration was as much a foreign government, albeit one at least speaking the same language, as the British had been.

But it was willing to learn. Janssens, supported by Captains Ludwig Alberti, of the Waldeck regiment, the new Landdrost of Uitenhage, and Willem Paravicini di Capelli, an elegant ADC, with the scholarly young tutor of the general's son, Dr Henry Lichenstein, went off up-country to treat with the Xhosas. These – all newly-arrived foreigners – were accompanied by a native of the Cape, Dirk van Reenen, one of the colony's richest landowners.[23] Their first meeting, with Ndlambe, was hurried and unsatisfactory, after which the party moved on to meet Ngqika at the Kat River, and to be as much impressed by the Xhosa chief as had been Barrow ten years earlier. Rousseau himself could not have imagined a nobler savage than Ngqika, 'one of the handsomest men that can be seen, even among the Caffres uncommonly tall, with strong limbs and very fine features'.[24] It was a symbolic moment as the Batavians, full of the milk of human kindness, and acknowledging (in the abstract) the equality of man, were approached by the imposing Xhosa, surrounded by his wives. The idealist Janssens was overcome by the smell, turned aside, and was sick.[25]

Ngqika's personal dignity, which so struck all European observers, disguised the fact that his power was limited. He might exercise authority over his own immediate followers, but not over those Xhosa in the Suurveld, and certainly not over the subjects of his uncle Ndlambe, with whom he was continually at war. Neither British nor Batavians understood the mechanics of Xhosa society, in which a chief could command the sometimes passionate loyalty of his people, but could not order free Xhosa, accustomed as they were to wandering the wide spaces of Africa, to abstain from crossing a river, or to refrain from profitable trading or enjoyable raids. Powers of punishment were reserved for internal crimes, and the chief could not realistically be held responsible for the misdeeds of his followers. The whole concept of ownership of land was as incomprehensible to the Xhosa as it was to the North American Indians, which later led to the same tale of 'treaties' consistently broken, or native rights infringed; although it must be acknowledged that the imperial authorities made much greater efforts to be just and even-handed than ever did those of the United States.

Janssens and de Mist had also to concern themselves with the Europeans on the frontier. Both men – and de Mist's lively daughter Augusta – visited the village of Graaff-Reinet, where they discovered only some twenty houses and shabby public buildings, with a vindictively quarrelsome and litigious population who were making much the same complaints as they had to the British.[26] De Mist, finding the local commandants at odds, appointed a new Landdrost, the industrious and dedicated Swede Anders Stockenström, who had previously been selected by Craig as Secretary to the Swellendam Landdrost.

The Batavians at the Cape were not given much opportunity either of accustoming themselves to Xhosa customs or of implementing many of their own admirable plans. By May 1803, only a couple of months after the British garrison had finally left Cape Town, the peace was over. Napoleon, at his most Hitlerian, was determined to crush the British, and for his invasion plans the cooperation of the Dutch was essential. The Batavian government was given no choice in the matter; the French army simply marched in, and the unfortunate Dutch delegates at Paris were told sharply that they must do as they were ordered, or the Batavian Republic would become a French department. All the fine revolutionary ideals of liberty and human rights were swept away, and Holland joined the ranks of French satellites. In such circumstances even the most anti-British of Cape colonists would be reluctant to fight too patriotically when the British made their inevitable move. This was not for some time, since during the brief period of Addington's ministry the armed forces had been so drastically pruned – the Royal Navy lost half its effectives – that no geographical extension of hostilities was possible. It was well over two years, in January 1806, before an occupying force arrived.

The resistance was short-lived, since Janssens' European troops, who included a battalion of Dutch regulars, turned and ran at the first shots, any real fighting being done by the burgher militia – six hundred or so, of whom two thirds were free black gunners and the Khoikhoi Corps of Pandours, together with some French sailors from the National frigate *Atlante* who held out for another few days before, once again, a moderately amicable arrangement was reached.[27] Burghers in arms were not to be made prisoner, but allowed to remain in the colony or, if they wished, to be given free passage on full pay to Europe; all private property and existing constitutional rights were secured and freedom of work was guaranteed. General David Baird, a tough old soldier who had served at the Cape under Macartney, took over from General Janssens, and without a day's interruption the Burgher Senate continued to cooperate with the authorities, reporting to the Batavians on Tuesday and the British on Wednesday. The two generals discussed between them who might best serve in the new administration; Gerard van Blokland, the Batavian attorney general, slipped easily into the position of Secretary to the High Court, while Willem van Ryneveld again took up his old post of Fiscal.

The Civil Governor who arrived in May 1807 was an ambitious and well-intentioned young Irish peer, Du Pré Alexander, Earl of Caledon. Not, like most colonial Governors of the time, anxiously in need of money, Caledon was a rich man, concerned only 'to serve my country and to raise my character'.[28] In furtherance of these laudable objectives he had bought, at great expense, two seats in Parliament, which more or less assured him of any post he might want. Caledon's instinctive idealism is shown in his reports from the Cape: he found the sight of the gibbets in front of the Castle 'a sad example of vindictive justice . . . a melancholy reflection . . . of the inattention of one of the mildest governments of the world [his predecessors, the Batavians] to the humane and enlightened suggestions of Beccaria [the penal reformer whose opposition to capital punishment was shared by Caledon]'; and thought it 'gratifying to every benevolent mind, and highly honourable to our country' that the previous British administration had frowned on 'the idea of commandoes' – a fine example of contemporary liberal phraseology. All this was in advance of most public opinion of the time, which then, as now, was composed of disparate strands. On the extreme right, to adopt an anachronism, a fiercely reactionary group represented by Lord Eldon strove for rigid repression, especially in Ireland, and the continuance of existing restrictions of the civil rights of Catholics. At the other extreme a small band of radicals, represented by Samuel Romilly and Francis Burdett, went as far as suggesting universal suffrage (for men only, of course). But political debate was overshadowed by the prosecution of the war – two wars from 1812, when the United States joined in – the immense impact of which froze all other schemes of expenditure and reform.

Of these the most important was the abolition of slavery, a cause supported by the great mass of the British people, which united even those who differed on other subjects. The slave trade was banned in 1807, but putting an end to slavery itself was more difficult, since both commercial equity and the survival of key colonial industries – the valuable West Indian sugar trade was dependent on slave labour – demanded that slave-owners should be compensated for the loss of capital value. Such large sums were not available during an expensive war, but for many years the total abolition of slavery remained a passionately advocated cause.

Closely allied to the question of slavery was the British attitude to the non-white races. British law did not admit of different treatment on grounds of race; but sharp distinctions were made on economic or social grounds. Voting was a privilege restricted to the prosperous, and laws, often fiercely protective of property, bore more heavily on the poor. Furthermore, in colonies taken from another power, existing laws were usually allowed to continue for some time. But decent Britons held as an article of faith that all men had an equal right to the protection of the law, and most accepted that all deserved equal treatment before it. Sharing such ideas, it was not surprising that Lord Caledon upset some colonial prejudices, in which he was reinforced by an equally reform-minded Colonial Secretary. Colonel Richard Bird was a Catholic, sympathetic to oppressed minorities, as well as being a conscientious civil servant, who remained in office for seventeen years and did much to underpin the new order at the Cape.[29] In doing so both Caledon and Bird were often opposed by the military commander, General George Grey, who was unwilling to admit the Governor's authority in army affairs. Since the general was influential, commanding one of the largest overseas garrisons, and was an uncle of

Earl Grey, the prominent Whig leader, clashes with the Tory Caledon were endemic.

Revolutionaries in black coats

Lord Caledon found himself responsible for eighty thousand people: colonists, Khoikhoi, slaves, and the increasingly numerous 'Bastaards', of mixed descent, spread over some ninety thousand square miles, an area rather greater than that of Great Britain. Not under British rule, but intermittently making themselves felt, were the remaining Bushmen, reduced to a fraction of their former numbers by disease and persecution, and a shifting population of Xhosa, concentrated in the Suurveld. At the Cape, in settled circumstances, were some twenty-five thousand burghers, among them all the most prosperous members of the community. Dutch, or at least that variant of Dutch known as the '*taal*', which developed into Afrikaans, was the common spoken language of the colonists, even though by origin many were French or German, and of the thirty thousand remaining slaves. To the north burgher settlement had reached the edge of the winter rainfall belt, beyond which adventurous Khoikhoi-Dutch Bastaards were forming communities in the arid Namib; on the eastern frontier the now far-distant outposts of the stockfarmers were at first little affected by the change of government at the Cape.

'The strongest attachment and respect toward the British nation is the prevailing sentiment,' Caledon reported on 30 May 1807.[30] This was pitching it a trifle strong, but at the time the new Governor had experience only of Cape Town, where the citizens quickly adapted themselves to the resumption of British rule. Poor Andrew Barnard got his old job back for only a few months before dying in harness, but the senior officials of the Cape administration remained in their posts. Van Ryneveld was joined by such pillars of society as Johannes Andreas Truter, who succeeded him as Fiscal and later became Chief Justice Sir John Truter. With their help, and with the influence he was able to exert in London, Caledon was able to effect some useful reforms, including the stabilization of the failing Loan Bank by a Treasury injection of a million dollars.

Caledon's optimistic view of the population's acceptance of British rule was justified insofar that only one civil disturbance ensued, and that a sad little incident in October 1808 when a band of slaves, led by one Louis, having heard of the abolition of the slave trade, took this as a signal of immediate emancipation, or at least of a sympathetic hearing. Louis had 'provided himself with a blue jacket with red collar and cuffs, two swords, two pairs of epaulettes and some black feathers', intending to 'establish a Government upon principles of their own'.[31] Idealism mixed with pure wild adventurism when they were joined by two deserters from the British East India Company, James Hooper and Michael Kelly. The rising was promptly suppressed by a squadron of cavalry, and the ringleaders, in spite of Caledon's principles, hanged (they were also sentenced to be quartered, but this part of the punishment was remitted, which may have been some relief). The eastern districts, hitherto a constant source of anxiety, remained tolerably quiet, assisted by the abilities of such energetic officials as Landdrosts Anders Stockenström of Uitenhage and Jacob Cuyler of Graaff-Reinet, under the command of Colonel Richard Collins, appointed as Commissioner for the Eastern Districts.

Colonel Collins' enquiring mind and ironic appreciation of human weaknesses, employed on his extensive travels, made him the best-informed authority on frontier affairs, and his reports to Caledon influenced official attitudes for many years thereafter.[32] Although relative stability was being maintained with no greater force than that of a troop of dragoons, Collins saw no hope of permanent peace in the east unless Xhosa and whites could be kept firmly apart. This, he submitted, could best be done on the line of the Fish River, where small arable farms might support a population large enough to repel any attacks, while the absence of cattle, those perennially attractive objects, would make incursions less likely. The settlers would need careful selection in order to avoid the danger of having such bad characters as the Zwartebergers, 'people of the worst description' who 'enticed the Hottentots' to work for bad wine and worse wages. If such settlers were backed by a small regular force, tranquillity could be assured. One difficulty was that the region between the *de facto* colonial boundary and the Fish River, the Suurveld, had been occupied by Khoikhoi and Xhosa, who, as General Dundas had discovered, showed little inclination to be moved. Collins brushed this aside. 'The Caffres,' he claimed, 'have not a single hut' in the area, and what rights they claimed could be satisfied by an appropriate payment in cattle. It was a reasonable enough suggestion at the time, and later administrations attempted to effect similar programmes; but soldiers less scrupulous than Collins, urged by land-hungry settlers, coincided with disruption and resentment among the 'Caffres' themselves to invalidate the idea of a formal differentiation between black and white territories on a basis of equal rights.

A more immediate problem was that of those Khoikhoi remaining within the colonial boundaries, now completely severed from their original mode of life (de-tribalized, in the later expression), without legal status, and dependent upon employment or charity from the white population. The few remaining independent Khoikhoi villages had been suppressed by the Batavians, anxious both to increase the numbers of their Corps of Pandours and to allow the establishment of approved missions. Reporting to the Governor in February 1812, C.J. Reyneveldt found that, apart from a handful still remaining near Swellendam and the new settlement of George, not the smallest vestiges of *kraals* were to be seen: the Khoikhoi were 'free in name [but] are more to be pitied than the slaves'. Caledon considered it imperative to afford the survivors some protection, and protection necessarily implied a degree of integration and regimentation, which was welcomed by the colonists, anxious to coerce as many potential labourers as possible. His 'Hottentot Proclamation' of 1 November 1809, a development of labour regulations originally drafted by the Batavians, became famous – quite inaccurately – as the 'Hottentot Magna Carta'. In fact Caledon's proclamation confirmed the inferior legal status of the colonial Khoikhoi, who were obliged to carry passes and permitted to change their residence only with the permission of the authorities, declaring 'not only the Individuals of the Hottentot Nation, in the same manner as the other inhabitants, should be subject to proper regularity in regard to their places of abode and occupations ... but that they should be encouraged to work rather than to leading an indolent life'. But the proclamation did establish equality of access to the law between whites and Khoikhoi, both appearing as equal in a civil case, and clear rights and obligations on both sides – a difficult pill for many colonists to swallow. Some writers, hoping to fix blame for later infamous pass laws on British administrations, have described Caledon's law as the prototype of these. This is a spurious argument, since the possession of a pass was a guarantee of legal status essential in a wandering and illiterate community. Hottentots continued to be exploited, but the sort of unscrupulous exploitation demanded by the Swellendam Patriots was made a little more difficult. The possibility of escaping this by moving north across the colonial boundaries, into territories still not settled, had tempted Khoikhoi and Bastaards for at least the preceding half-century, but was becoming more difficult as this region, in turn, filled up.[33]

Lord Caledon, in considering what was to be done about the Khoikhoi, had the doubtful benefit of missionary advice. Since missions were to become perhaps the most important external influence brought to bear upon South Africa, it is worth examining – especially since the subject has been both neglected and misunderstood – the nature of this influence.[34] In the first place almost all pioneer missionaries were Protestants, and nineteenth-century Protestants at that, convinced that the Bible was the ultimate source of wisdom, and that bringing the scriptures to the people their first responsibility. Education was therefore essential; the missionaries were the first to analyse native languages and construct their orthography, and for more than a century all but a tiny minority of black schools were missionary foundations. Again, most missionaries were English-speakers, Scottish and American, but for the most part English, who brought with them all the ideology of their nation, religion and class. Even the French and German missionaries were, of necessity, competent in English, and shared at least some of the same principles. Although the *taal* remained the spoken *lingua franca* of Dutch farmers, slaves and de-tribalized Khoikhoi, English became the language of literate blacks, and therefore of political discourse. It is therefore hardly surprising that almost all black cultural and political leaders, from Tiyo Soga to Nelson Mandela, have been English-speaking alumni of missionary schools. Which is not to say that missionary attitudes were uncritically adopted by blacks. When they were rejected, in order to defend traditional values, or because of repulsion for the often condescending and insensitive missionary attitudes, the reactions were equally formative. One, the emergence of independent black 'Ethiopian' churches, has provided an opportunity for blacks to construct and control institutions that gave them what they wanted, rather than that which others felt appropriate.

Often attacked as agents of colonialism and imperialism, many missionaries did indeed cooperate willingly with white authorities in controlling black groups, predictably enough, since churches and governments shared many values: the link between salvation, virtue, monogamy and trousers was universally acknowledged. Yet other missionaries were often at odds with authority – usually placing themselves on the sides of the blacks – and found themselves resented as traitors to the cause of European solidarity; the succession from van der Kemp to Huddleston is unbroken. Especially was this so when the authorities were Afrikaner rather than English, since a deep suspicion of missionaries quickly developed among Dutch-speakers.

One of the first actions of the breakaway Boer communities in the 1830s was to place a total ban on missionary activities, and a century later, when Afrikaners controlled the South African government, a priority was made of replacing all missionary education with a state system which could be guaranteed not to disseminate unsettling ideas of human equality.

The original group, the London Missionary Society, was to become a particular object of hostility to the Boers. It began when some ecumenical-minded clergymen met at Baker's Coffee House in the City of London on 4 November 1794, with the object of sending 'the Glorious Gospel of the Blessed God to the heathen'. It is with the LMS that the most famous missionary names of Africa are associated – Robert Moffat and David Livingstone – and from the narrower point of view of South African history, that of John Philip, who was to be the chief Boer bugbear. Theological differences strengthened the perception that British missionaries were anti-pathetic. The Dutch Church in South Africa was moving towards a rigid Calvinistic view, more extreme even than the Presbyterians of Scotland or the Netherlands churches. Jean Calvin had reasoned that if God were omnipotent and eternal, time had no meaning for Him, who must be conscious at one and the same time of all that had passed and was to come, and therefore, who was to be eventually 'saved' or 'damned'. That precise theologian, however, insisted that humans themselves could never tell who was to be numbered among the saved. Ignoring this, and reflecting popular prejudices, many within the Dutch churches in South Africa regarded it improbable that God intended non-whites to be among the elect. Had He not condemned the children of Ham, well-known to be blacks, to be the servants of servants? Which did not remove the obligation to treat such unfortunates with decency, but offered a tempting excuse for disregarding their interests when this suited. The very integration of the Dutch predikants into white society rendered them susceptible to social pressures: the large and comfortable manses still to be seen in Graaff-Reinet and Fort Beaufort were residences for prosperous clergymen, a world removed from the wild and primitive conditions in which the first missionaries operated.

In no part of the world had the Dutch Reformed Church ever been an enthusiastic missionary organization. Employed by the VOC, which kept a tight control on their activities, ministers had provided spiritual leadership to their existing European members, but had made little effort to convert the natives, and by the end of the eighteenth century there were not more than a score of ministers in all the Company's territories. The East Indies was an unpromising mission ground, being either Islamic or Buddhist and content to remain so. Rather more success was found in Ceylon, but in South Africa no missionary effort was made until the very end of the eighteenth century when Dominus M.C. Vos, Predikant of Tulbagh – and of part-slave descent – founded the Society for the Expansion of Christ's Kingdom (van de Uitbreiding van Christus Koninkryk).

Even this modest move was stimulated by the arrival in 1799 of the first representatives from the London Missionary Society and the formation of the South African Missionary Society. The Church of England had been almost as lethargic as the Dutch Reformed Church in spreading the evangel, until sparked into life, chiefly by the agency of John Wesley, founder of the Methodist Church. Wesley's theology, a powerful influence on English missionaries, Methodist, Anglican and Independent alike, was strikingly different from that of Calvin, and anathema to the staunch Calvinists of the Cape. Wesleyan teaching concentrated on the New Testament rather than the Old, emphasizing the freely-available 'Grace of God', which abolished distinctions between 'Jew and Greek, bond and free', and by which none was a 'stranger or foreigner'; uncomfortable ideas to the Dutch farmers, wedded to their self-image as God-chosen members of an elite.

Many members of the Church of England agreed with Wesley's theology, and they, being of a higher rank in society than the usually working-class Methodists, exercised correspondingly greater influence. After the turn of the century such politicians as Prime Minister Spencer Perceval, although on some issues starkly reactionary, and Lord Glenelg, a reforming Whig, were united in evangelical principles and prepared to support the efforts of missionary societies. A typical British reaction to what appears distressing was to bustle about and clear things up, affording whatever unwanted instruction seemed necessary in the process; an activity not always welcomed by those whose conduct is being reformed. Natives may be dirty, ignorant and given to unpleasant practices; they should therefore be cleaned, educated, and made to mend their ways. But they were, the British admitted, human, and, suitably dressed and instructed, no more unwelcome in society than, say, Irishmen or Portuguese. The Boers, on the other hand, as Janssens pointed out, habitually referred to Khoikhoi and blacks not as men ('*mensen*') but as creatures ('*schepsels*'), hardly accorded human status.

Although non-denominational, the LMS was in the tradition of English independency, of Cromwell and Bunyan, tolerant of other (Protestant) views, but resisting interference, each congregation inviting its own chosen pastor. Presbyterian church government, practised by the Church of Scotland and the Dutch Reformed Church at the Cape, although sharing the concept of ministers appointed by their church members, was more centralized, decisions being taken at a synod which enforced discipline; this was also to become an irritant to nineteenth-century Afrikaners attempting to escape external controls.

These different forms of church administration were reflected in the character of their representatives. Scottish Presbyterians (there were comparatively few English) tended to be more intellectual and better-educated than most English Independents or Wesleyans, at that time banned from English universities, while those in Scotland were acknowledged centres of academic excellence and open to all. The Glasgow Missionary Society, founded in 1796, insisted that all missionaries first learn the language of their flock. The Society's instructions exemplify missionary attitudes – superior, certainly, but hardly arrogant. Missionaries must 'not ridicule the pagan idols, nor their manner of worship; but calmly reason with them always showing the utmost benevolence; that they ought not to expose the innocent customs of the country, but as far as possible become all things to all men'.[35] Such advice was, of course, prepared by decent, enlightened eighteenth-century Britons who had never met an African, and had little conception of conditions far from the comforts of Cape Town. When these were encountered, after a painful learning process, missionary attitudes were modified, but it is a tribute to the qualities both of the teachers and their pupils that South Africa numbers few missionaries among its martyrs.

The third British missionary society, the Anglican Church Missionary Society, founded in 1799, cut its teeth in India before devoting much attention to Africa. As the established Church was almost a branch of government Anglican missions were more intimately linked with the colonial authorities, and tended to be represented by socially superior ministers; although it was some time before they were noticeably superior in any other way. Both Anglicans and their offspring, the Methodists, were more apt to take the side of the white settlers in any conflict with the blacks. They were followed by the Basle Society – decent Swiss Calvinists – and in 1822 by the interesting Paris Society, inspired by the work of the Scotsman Robert Haldane, midshipman and evangelist, whose representatives were more heterodox. The American Mission Society, founded in 1831 to coordinate Calvinist missions, sent its first parties to the 'Inland Zoolahs' and the 'Maritime Zoolahs' in 1835, soon limiting themselves to the latter.

Even the Dutch Reformed Church was affected by missionary enthusiasm, establishing in 1824 missions among the mixed population at the Cape rather than attempting to pioneer new fields.

The London Missionary Society's first arrivals were led by Dr Theodorus van der Kemp, a complex character, in no way typical of later missionaries.[36] Van der Kemp, a former Dutch cavalry officer, had led an irregular existence which included a notorious affair with the wife of The Hague's public executioner. He later trained in Edinburgh as a physician, and published a work on Parmenides before turning to religion (it was typical of van der Kemp's impractical brilliance that he had been attracted by Parmenides, of all philosophers most free from any taint of common sense). Failing in an attempt to work with the Xhosa across the Fish River, or the colonists at Graaff-Reinet, he established a mission to the Khoikhoi at Bethelsdorp, near Uitenhage, which soon became the focus of bitter criticisms from the neighbouring burghers. He was joined by the twenty-four-year-old James Read – 'a good-hearted man', according to the condescending Dr Lichtenstein, 'but like most of the missionaries extremely ignorant'[37] – a carpenter by trade (hardly a disqualification for a follower of Christ). The two men were fiercely protective of their flock; their Hottentots could do no wrong, while the colonists were guilty of the most abominable cruelties. As well as being blamed for teaching the Khoikhoi to read and write, and allowing them into a church also used by whites, the missionaries' popularity was not increased when van der Kemp married a young slave and Read a Khoikhoi girl. Attitudes to intermarriage had hardened since Commander van Riebeeck attended the marriage of Eva and Pieter van Meerhoff, but James Read the younger, an altogether stronger character than his father, carried on missionary work till the end of the century, and exerted a considerable influence on events.[38]

Bethelsdorp was not the first mission in South Africa. Genadendal, an idyllic spot in the foothills behind Swellendam, had been founded by George Schmit's Moravian Brethren, that idealistic and pious German community, seventy years previously, but had proved too liberal for the Dutch predikants, who had contrived their expulsion after only a short time. By 1792 the Moravians, feeling the times better suited, sent out a party to revive their mission. They found only one old Khoikhoi woman and an ancient pear tree, still remarkably flourishing today, but within a couple of years the Khoikhoi were returning in their hundreds. The Dutch, although differing in matters of theology with the Moravians – 'excellent men', according to Dr Lichtenstein – approved of their methods, which concentrated more on providing practical training than on giving the natives elevated ideas of their own significance in God's scheme of things, which the LMS men were accused of doing. Genadendal soon became famous for its excellent knives, and Lord Caledon followed the Batavian example of establishing missions on the site of Khoikhoi villages; mission-trained and biddable Khoikhoi were valuable assets to the colony.

The Bethelsdorp mission, by contrast, did not meet with much approval from the authorities, British or Batavian, and even their sponsors, the LMS, began to believe that van der Kemp and Read had 'gone native'. Careless of his own appearance or dignity, van der Kemp shocked visiting officials, living alongside the Khoikhoi in a hut eight feet square, and single-mindedly devoting his talents and fortunes to their welfare. Landdrost Jacob Cuyler of Uitenhage – an American loyalist who had come to the Cape with Baird's troops, and one of the first foreigners to be appointed to such a post – was unsympathetic and short-tempered, anxious to get the Khoikhoi to settle to work, while van der Kemp was equally determined that his charges should not be forced away from the security of the mission. Governor Janssens, at first sympathetic – he had known van der Kemp for over thirty years – became irritated by his old friend's vehemence. In its turn the British Colonial Office soon became inundated with charge and counter-charge.

Uitenhage being some four hundred miles from the Cape, with nothing much better than a track in between, it was difficult for the authorities there to investigate the missionaries' complaints of persecution. Colonel Collins found the mission station 'entirely calculated for the happiness of the Hottentots and other heathen', unlikely 'to promise great benefits from a continuance' – benefits to the colonials, of course – and recommended its closure, but Lord Caledon, not in principle unsympathetic to missions, could not avoid giving some credence to van der Kemp's statements, which found their way to the highest quarters in London. Investigating allegations, the Governor considered, should be the task of the judiciary, and he made it a priority to endow the colony with a proper judicial system which would, among other advantages, bring impartial justice to the frontier districts, where Heemraden were only too likely to side with their own folk against the Khoikhoi. Permission from London was needed in order to establish circuit courts on the English model, with High Court judges making regular tours, and an application for this to be done was one of Caledon's first acts. In the interim he was however able on his own authority to issue the Proclamation establishing the Khoikhoi's status before the law.

Quite unfairly, Caledon was much criticized in England for this well-intentioned intervention, both at the time and later, when the missionaries' reports of persecution were reinforced as a particularly luscious scandal swept London in November 1819.[39] An enterprising Afrikaner businessman had imported two curiosities from the Cape – a giraffe and a Khoikhoi girl, Saartje Baartman, the first of her race to reach England since Coree two centuries before. The 'Hottentot Venus' was put on exhibition in Piccadilly, clothed, but in such a way as to emphasize her impressive proportions. In order to guarantee fair play, spectators were entitled to feel her bottom, and a fee of two shillings was charged. Full of indignation, both at this insult to womankind and by the suspicion that the girl was held against her will, and 'exposed under such circumstances of indecency as must necessarily give great pain and unease to a Female', the reformer Zachary Macaulay took the case to the High Court. In an episode which illuminates early-nineteenth-century English sensibilities, and the willingness of society to react when these were affronted, it was dealt with remarkably expeditiously and at the highest level, with the Lord Chancellor's intervention. In the course of the proceedings Lord Caledon was accused of conniving at the girl's exportation; theoretically he had done so, since under the 1809 Act no Khoikhoi could leave the colony without the Governor's permission. The affair blew over, since on investigation the girl affirmed that she was perfectly willing to be exhibited – she got half the proceeds, two black servants, and a coach to ride in on Sundays – but the public were sensitized to the subject of Hottentot persecution, and Lord Caledon was upset. Saartje had a worse experience in Paris, where she was exhibited naked, caught cold and died; her genitalia were preserved by the eminent scientist Georges Cuvier.

Permission to institute the new circuit courts was received only in 1811, as Caledon was about to leave the colony. His proclamation of 16 May, establishing these courts, marked a major advance in extending government from the centre to the outlying areas. A quorum of two High Court judges was authorized to tour the colony, checking on the Landdrosts and trying the more important cases. The judges were former VOC and Batavian legal officers, van Ryneveld being the first chairman, John Truter his successor, and traditional Dutch law was applied. In spite of this conservative approach local powers were much diminished and the scope of the Heemraden reduced under the new system; it was not therefore unanimously welcome.

Not that the more distant colonists resisted the rule of law; as soon as a new village was formed petitions would be sent to the Cape for *drosdties* and churches to be established, and nurturing law cases was a favourite pastime. It was rather that the burghers had been comfortable with the old ways, under which the master's word was always accepted in the absence of any strong contrary evidence, and where the essential inferiority of all non-whites was an article of faith.

Nor were British conceptions of justice necessarily superior to Dutch, although English common law was more adapted to liberal interpretation than the Romano-Dutch system. Caledon, the idealistic young Irishman, had much in common with the conservative de Mist, and even with Jans-sens, who had written: 'Instruction! Instruction! is what they [the Boers] lack above all else; they call themselves Christians, and Kaffirs and Hotten-tots heathen, and for this reason they believe that they are permitted anything.'[40]

The first of the new circuit courts, in 1811, passed without incident, but the second, in the following year, became notorious as the 'Black Circuit'. In their anxiety to see justice done to their flock van der Kemp and Read had encouraged every possible complaint to be brought before the court. Over a hundred murders, they claimed, had been committed: 'Some of the falsely called Christian Boors are accused of 8 or 9 murders.'[41] This was stretching evidence well beyond reasonable bounds, and even less-biased courts – for the judges were one with the colonists in attaching little importance to purely Khoikhoi evidence – would have dismissed most of the cases. Nevertheless, some guilty verdicts were pronounced, enough to infuriate the colonists. Indignant at being asked to justify their behaviour, which they regarded as sanctioned by a hundred years of usage, and genu-inely hurt that so many false accusations had been levelled, the back-woodsmen were left sullenly discontented with British justice. What they saw as the fissure of understanding between European and Afrikaner was thus developed and deepened; it already existed between Hollanders and colonists, but a further note of acerbity had been established when the British replaced the Dutch. Furthermore, the interests of the *trekboers*, the outliers of colonial expansion, and the growing merchant community at the Cape were increasingly divergent.

SIX

Alarms and Excursions

Baneful radical influences

It took twenty years from the initial British landing on the Cape for that occupation to become permanent. In August 1814, following the first abdication of Napoleon, the Netherlands regained their independence with the Prince of Orange installed as Sovereign. Acknowledging these new conditions Britain undertook to restore those Dutch colonies taken during the war, but with the notable exception of the Cape. Not that the Cape of Good Hope seemed in itself such a desirable possession. The West Indian colonies with their profitable sugar trade were considered much more valuable, but it was regarded as vital to prevent the Cape being occupied by any other power, and especially by the French. Communications with British India had to be safeguarded, for India had become 'the Jewel in the Crown', with British supremacy now firmly established by the ejection of the French and the subjugation of many of the most powerful princes – and extended further by the acquisition in 1802 of Ceylon.

In 1803 Nelson may have argued that the Cape was not essential, but by 1815 no strategist would have agreed. Even if of little commercial interest the Cape must be retained as a strategic base; an immediate purpose being the need to protect St Helena, where the former Emperor Napoleon was now incarcerated, from any attempted raid.[1] For thirty years after 1814 Governors were therefore military men, and the Cape accounts published not with those of other colonies, but as part of the general government expenditure. In keeping with this policy the Cape was initially treated as in practice a Governor's fief, with locally almost unlimited powers and few constitutional restraints, responsible only to the Secretary for War and the Colonies in London, three months' sail away, and little interested in so minor a responsibility as the Cape.

For military and naval purposes only the Cape Peninsula and False Bay were needed, but with these assets came 'a too extensive colony' sparsely populated by a few unruly Dutch herdsmen, with a formidable black nation pressing on its borders and demoralized Khoikhoi and Bushmen scattered about. Only around the Cape were any of the amenities of civilization or settled forms of administration to be found. Uncomfortable facts soon began to assert themselves in London.

With the end of the war with France came a sharp reduction in defence expenditure. In common with other stations, the garrison of the Cape was reduced, from four thousand to 2,400 men, although a naval squadron was permanently stationed there to keep an eye on Napoleon. Public expectation was that such reductions in spending should be accompanied by the removal of wartime taxes, although Chancellor Nicholas Vansittart found this embarrassingly difficult when Parliament insisted. Colonies were meant to balance their own budgets, and the Cape in particular had been given important assistance by the free admission of Cape wines in 1813, which led to a rapid increase in sales – by 1821 more than 10 per cent of wine drunk in Britain came from the Cape. The chief source of colonial income however was that derived from Crown lands. Why, therefore, with so much territory, were the receipts from the Cape so low? It did not help that the fault lay with the British government itself. Years previously Lord Caledon had attempted to reform the system he had inherited from the Company, whereby freely-granted loan farms covered huge tracts of land and produced little if any income. Caledon had wanted to replace these with proper leases at moderate rents, but the Board of Trade delayed its reply for two years, when it was received by Caledon's successor, Sir John Cradock, later Lord Harden. Cradock had been dismissed from commands in both India and Portugal before being sent to the Cape, but he had been a member of the Irish Parliament and a staunch supporter of the government, and had to be found a place. Arriving in September 1811 he was horrified to discover that the Board had refused to accept Lord Caledon's proposals, arguing that since it had not yet been decided that the Cape should be permanently retained by Britain, under international law nothing could be done which might restrict any future government's freedom of action. Cradock was determined not only that the Cape should remain British but that its British character, still weak, must be reinforced. With considerable shrewdness he appreciated that this could be powerfully assisted by bringing the land, and therefore inevitably the farmers, under government control.

Laws relating to land tenure are not the most exciting of subjects, but they are central to any understanding of South African history – or of current events there for that matter.[2] Acting within the restraints imposed by the Board of Trade, Cradock proposed a system of 'perpetual quit rents', to apply to all future grants: no more loan farms, and no loan farmers to occupy new lands without converting their existing holdings to the new system. Rents were to be modest, not exceeding 250 rixdollars, adjusted to the extent and quality of the land, and giving security of tenure and freedom to dispose of the holding. Such a system would also enable Colonel Collins' suggestion of an intensively settled frontier to proceed, and, Cradock flattered himself, would bring about 'a new order of things' in which 'all Arts and Comforts of Civilization would be encouraged', and the Dutch brought to realize the benefits of British rule.

Admirable as were Cradock's intentions, they foundered on administrative rocks. Nowhere near the number of qualified surveyors could be found to define holdings over such an area, and the new Inspector of Lands, Charles D'Escury, in office from 1814 to 1827, was a conceited incompetent. Quiet disregard of official sanctions by farmers experienced in the arts of non-cooperation resulted in land continuing to be occupied without any authorization; and loan farms, renamed 'request claims', were introduced once more.

Although Cradock had little of Lord Caledon's youthful enthusiasm he shared his predecessor's commitment to equal rights before the law. 'In the dispensation of justice,' he wrote in his instructions to the Landdrosts, 'no distinction is to be admitted, whether between the man of wealth or the poor man, the master or the slave, the European or the Hottentot.' Such sentiments did not prevent Cradock from tightening the screws of colonial control in the interests of ensuring a supply of labour. An ordinance of 1812 provided that Khoikhoi children who had been brought up on farms could be 'apprenticed' to the householder until the age of eighteen, which apprenticeship could become difficult to distinguish from formal slavery.

Sir John needed to give no instructions on the treatment of Xhosa, having dealt, he believed, with *that* problem by driving them beyond the colonial boundaries. Colonel Collins, in his 1809 report, had recommended that there must be a defined boundary respected by both colonists and Xhosa, and that should be the Great Fish River. This military ideal, although pursued for many years, was impossible from the beginning. Colonial frontiers were a great deal more permeable than European ones, with colonists, Khoikhoi and their mixed descendants wandering further afield, always ready to trade tobacco, brandy and beads, and later manufactured goods and arms, for ivory, cattle and skins. Only a prominent military presence could have restricted meetings to the annual fairs that Collins envisaged, and such a force was never forthcoming.

The war, for which both sides were prepared, each convinced of the rightness of its cause, was begun with the murder of the virtuous Landdrost Stockenström in December 1811, revenged with efficient ruthlessness by the new Eastern Commissioner, Colonel John Graham, at the head of a mixed force of Boers, regulars and the newly-formed Khoikhoi Cape Regiment. 'Detestable work', he found it, 'forced to hunt them like wild beasts', but he ordered that 'every man Kaffir ... if possible the Chief [should be] destroyed'.[3] In his 1809 expedition Colonel Collins had reported finding not a single hut in the Suurveld, but five years later Graham's men found dozens of *kraals* and cultivated fields, all of which were burnt. The Suurveld was then formally attached to the Cape as the district of Albany, with the new settlement of Graham's Town as its centre. Albany was secured by a line of blockhouses although, as Collins had pointed out, these constituted no real protection in the absence of a military garrison without the support of a healthy number of colonists.

Graham's war was a decisive moment. Hitherto all the frontier inhabitants, Xhosa, Khoikhoi and white, had 'in some respect resembled a couple in a disastrous marriage; they would fear and fight each other, but neither would destroy the other – in fact their constant battle ... was what made their lives meaningful and morbidly filled their daily thoughts'. By exercising decisive force, now available for the first time, Graham had raised the stakes, and ensured continued strife, not to be settled for another half-century, and to which there could be only one eventual outcome. Not that negotiations and co-existence abruptly ceased – the very next year Xhosa were allowed back into the Suurveld to raise a crop – but the exercise of imperial power had demonstrated that a solution could be enforced in the teeth of any resistance.

London was not pleased: Cradock's job was to defend the Cape against the French, not to go chasing blacks. He should have taken proper precautions beforehand rather than being forced 'to resort to general and offensive hostilities'. Cradock's successor would have instructions to settle disputes more diplomatically, but the appointment in April 1814 of Lord Charles Somerset was made with little consideration of his suitability.[4] In the immediate aftermath of peace colonial governorships continued to be regarded as convenient places to put deserving friends of government, or even to reward them without their suffering the inconvenience of actually going there – on leaving Oxford without a degree Charles Greville, the diarist, was made Secretary to the Government of Jamaica at a salary of £3,000 a year, and never expected to leave London.

Lord Charles was the second son of the Duke of Beaufort, whose forebears, descendants of the Plantagenet kings, had lived comfortably at Badminton without attracting much attention during the eighteenth century, but had produced a crop of able sons in the nineteenth, both Lords Edward and Fitzroy being distinguished soldiers. A contemporary of Wellington, Lord Charles had proved that soldiering in drawing rooms was both safer and more profitable than exposing one's person on the field of battle. When Wellington was promoted to Major General in 1804 after ten years' hard campaigning in Holland and India, Lord Charles, never having heard a shot fired in anger, had already held that rank for six years and was also a paymaster general with the additional salary of £2,000 a year. This comfortable post depended on political favour, and Somerset's friends exerted themselves to find him something that might suit 'a man of rank and family looking to the means of support'.[5]

But if Lord Charles 'wasn't a general to other generals', he had other talents to recommend him. He looked splendid, especially on a horse, was an admirable companion to the King, the Prince Regent, the Duke of York and William Pitt, and had made a romantic runaway marriage with the beautiful Clara Courtney. Other sinecures, such as the constableship of the Tower of London, were suggested, but Prime Minister Greville did not know whether the Colonial Secretary William Windham 'would think him [Lord Charles] of sufficient calibre for the Cape'. Apparently Windham did not, and it was only six years later, under a different government, that Lord Charles got the job, at the handsome salary of £10,000.[6]

Throughout his term of office, from 1814 to 1826, Lord Charles reported to the same master. Earl Bathurst, a moderate and conscientious politician, had been in office since 1793, and remained as Colonial Secretary between 1812 and 1827, an unparalleled term, during which he had to cope with the considerable number of new colonies acquired at the end of the war. Both were Tories, but of a very different character. Somerset was little interested in politics, trade or government; he was intelligent enough, capable of charm and affability, but also of near-hysterical conduct when crossed or his vanity was damaged, conscious of his high rank in society and disinclined to administrative duties. Bathurst, descended not from kings but East India merchants, was serious-minded, devout and personally self-effacing, much occupied with the evils of slavery and concerned to avoid the oppression of subject peoples, while always conscious of the taxpayer's reluctance to provide a colonial budget. He was a member of the amiable Lord Liverpool's government, which during the early part of its twelve-year existence maintained a sometimes violently reactionary line.[7]

Most of the Dutch population of the Cape accepted the prospect of permanent British rule passively if not enthusiastically. The two nations had become allies once more, and fought side by side at Waterloo, where the Prince of Orange had commanded a division. Prominent Cape gentry, who had already shifted allegiance several times and knew on which side their bread was buttered, continued to support the British administration loyally. Lord Charles took some pains to conciliate the Cape Dutch. He had little personal sympathy for the influx of evangelical missionaries, disreputable, low enthusiasts for the most part, or for the irresistible pressure for slave emancipation. The respectable, prosperous burghers who followed decent Presbyterian doctrine – and Presbyterianism was, after all, the established Church in Scotland – were encouraged by subsidizing the recruitment of Scottish ministers, many of whom were to become influential in Cape society, mainly Dutch- and English-speakers.

Take, for example, the Faurés and the Murrays. Abraham Fauré, a Stellenbosch native – his great-grandfather came to South Africa as Governor de Chavonnes' Secretary – was educated in Holland and England. He married an English girl and became a reliable supporter of colonial government, as well as an enterprising journalist and educator. Fauré's successor as minister at Graaff-Reinet was Andrew Murray, a Scot, educated in Aberdeen and Utrecht, brought by Lord Charles to serve in the Dutch Church (he remained at Graaff-Reinet for forty-five years). He married the sixteen-year-old Maria Stegmann, who was to be the mother of five more dominees. One of these, Andrew junior, became the most significant influence in the Dutch Church through a long life, during which he lived to see one of his sons, John Neethling, fight for the Boers against the British in 1899.[8] Such a family history illustrates how quickly English- and Dutch-speakers could merge to become South Africans.

The frontiersmen however remained divided in their allegiances, and shortly after his arrival Lord Charles was faced by a resurgence of the troubles there. Field-Cornet van Wijk reported on 10 November 1815: 'some vagabonds in my district [were] busily employed in collecting as large a number of people as they can procure, in order to attack the various magistrates &c.'[9] Twenty-five years after the foundation of Graaff-Reinet, now a thriving little town, there was already an alarming number of 'vagabonds' in the area. The sagacious Landdrost Stockenström had reported that there were some eight to nine hundred colonists without farms who roamed about – *bywoners*, landless men who lived on the edges of poverty.[10] Prominent among the 'vagabonds' in the wild country over the hills from Graaff-Reinet was one Freek Bezuidenhout, a farmer with a reputation for treating his servants badly. Bezuidenhout was summonsed to answer complaints, refused, and a party was despatched to collect him. Johannes Auret, the Field-Cornet in charge, attempted conciliation, calling out: 'Father Bezuidenhout, I come not to arrest but only to summon you.' But Bezuidenhout, 'with his fist swaying to and fro made use of all curses and invectives', opened fire. In the subsequent action he was killed. Freek's brother Hans Jan, a poor white with a similar reputation, persuaded some farmers into armed defiance. In an unsuccessful effort to gain support – the solider burghers refusing to be implicated – Hans Jan attempted, unsuccessfully, to persuade Ngqika to join him.

Landdrost Cuyler was able to persuade most of the rebels to surrender, but a hard core refused, and were brought to bay by Khoikhoi troops, Hans Jan Bezuidenhout and one soldier being killed. After trial, by, it should be noted, Dutch judges, five of the most seriously implicated were hanged near Slagtersnek; during the execution the rope broke and four of the condemned men were forced to wait, amid scenes of much agitation, for some hours before their sentences were carried out. Under these circumstances Cuyler, a hard unyielding man, would have been better advised to commute the sentences, but at the time Afrikaner opinion was divided between those who applauded the trial as deserved retribution and those who regarded it as yet more British persecution – the employment of Khoikhoi soldiers being seen as an added affront.

More representative than the uncouth frontiersmen, if not entirely typical of the settled Dutch communities, were those found in the same year by Christian Latrobe. At Uitenhage he played Haydn and Mozart duets with Mr Van Buchenrodes, and conversed with the civilized Mr Slabbert of Langfonteyn, 'in many respects superior to most so-called Afrikaners in intellect and liberality of sentiment'.[11] Only later was the Slagtersnek inci-

dent incorporated, like that of the Black Circuit, into an anti-British mythology of heroic struggles against British oppression, enhanced by the fact
that Slagtersnek, or Slachter's Nek, is 'Butcher's Pass' in English, and that
'*nek*' is both 'pass' and 'neck'. As in most mythologies there was an element
of truth; but in this case not a great deal.[12]

Five years after Sir John Cradock's theoretical 'extermination' of the
Xhosa the new district of Albany had relapsed into its former state of unrest
and recrimination, exacerbated by a developing drought. Lord Charles
Somerset attempted to reach a solution by diplomacy, and arranged a
meeting with both Ngqika and his uncle Ndlambe. The conference that
took place on 2 April 1817, and is recorded at some length in the Parliamentary Blue Books, laboured under great difficulties.[13] No Xhosa spoke English,
while Cuyler and young Andries Stockenström, the murdered Landdrost's
son, had Dutch and some Xhosa; Dyani (Jan) Tshatsu, a minor chief and
Bethelsdorp convert, was the only one present with a close knowledge of
both communities. It was nevertheless a revealing meeting. Three Xhosa
participants represented differing reactions to the problems posed by the
European advance: Ngqika that of cautious cooperation, accepting presents
and making promises, seeking to use the colonists as allies to crush his
rival Ndlambe, who was therefore being pushed towards the second solution, violent opposition and extermination of the white men. Tshatsu had
embraced what seemed to be a third answer, that of joining the colonists
first as a lay preacher, later as a magistrate and delegate to the House of
Commons.

Similarly divided attitudes existed among the Europeans. Somerset and
his officials required tranquillity on the cheap, without a permanent garrison, trusting that their colonists and the Xhosa would go about their own
business without disturbing each other. The colonists believed in the '*lex
talionis*', and being allowed to exploit Xhosa and Khoikhoi without government interference – but with government protection when needed. The
British soldiers, hoping for a quiet life, trusted that they would not be
asked to intervene, although the Khoikhoi Cape Corps, in their smart green
uniforms, each man with his horse and gun, were probably looking for an
excuse to use them. Joseph Williams, the only missionary, well-meaning
but weak and poorly qualified, hoped vainly for better things.[14]

Somerset, following previous policy, insisted on dealing with Ngqika as
head of all Xhosa. This was little more than a polite fiction. Hintsa, three
hundred miles off over the Kei River, was acknowledged as the paramount

chief of all Xhosa; Ngqika was, in theory, head of the Rharhabe party, although in fact his uncle Ndlambe, abler and more aggressive, enjoyed much support. Ngqika attempted an explanation for his inability to control all the Xhosa – just as the Dutch and British had been unable to keep their own people in order – but the Governor refused to accept what he saw as prevarication. The Xhosa were to stay on their side of the Fish and the 'English were to drink on the other side of the river'. What was more, the old Scottish border institution of the 'hot trod' was to be introduced, under the local name of the 'Spoor law'. Cattle which disappeared were to be followed to the most likely *kraal*, which was to accept responsibility for restitution and punishment of the offenders; needless to say this was to apply to one side only.

Such unequal treatment of a people who regarded their cattle as their dearest possessions and the centre of their existence was guaranteed to lead to violent resistance, but the next disturbance was a savage confrontation between the rivals Ngqika and Ndlambe. This war, more drastic than any so far seen in the region, resulted in the destruction of Ngqika's forces at the battle of Amalinde towards the end of 1818, when a very great number of Xhosa warriors perished. By now inextricably involved in the Xhosa civil war, the British were obliged to support their ally Ngqika by sending an expedition under Colonel Thomas Brereton, an inexperienced and, as his subsequent career proved, incapable officer.[15] Since little resistance was offered the expedition was successful in capturing a huge number of cattle. Too successful, in fact, since Ndlambe's people were thereby reduced to desperation. Existence would be impossible without their cattle, and retaliation was inevitable.

The slow Xhosa drift south and west along the coast, which had continued for many years as the population expanded, had met with little opposition from the displaced Khoikhoi, who for the most part were able to fit comfortably into Xhosa society.[16] Those clans that, like the Gqunukhwebe, formed the van of the Xhosa advance acquired a considerable admixture of Khoikhoi – sometimes even a majority. The whites were not so accommodating, and new conflicts, hundreds of miles off, were beginning to add impetus to the westward movement of the Xhosa. Other forces too were at work: the ferocity of Ndlambe's attack on Ngqika, and his subsequent offensive against the British, owed much to the influence of a strangely numinous figure, Nxele, also known as Makana, and to the British as Lynx. Societies faced with bewildering changes, and feeling old certainties threatened, are open to new cults. In the next generation the Xhosa were brought to the brink of extinction by following charismatic prophets, in much the same way as the Taiping in China would attract millions of supporters in their violent efforts to replace the crumbling Ch'ing dynasty. Like the Taiping leader Hong Xiuqan, Nxele had picked up elements of Christianity,[17] identifying himself as Christ's brother, before inventing a mythology of his own, 'set on revenging the aggressions of the Christians and emancipating his country from their arrogant control'. With Nxele's encouragement Ndlambe launched an assault on the British themselves.

On 22 April 1819 ten thousand Xhosa warriors, their assegais shortened for close-quarter thrusting, rushed down on the village of Graham's Town, defended by a few hundred Boers, British and Khoikhoi troops. After a desperate fight, in which the Khoikhoi distinguished themselves, the Xhosa were repelled with heavy losses. The subsequent pursuit, which was carried right to paramount chief Hintsa's own *kraal*, resulted in the disintegration of Ndlambe's alliance and the surrender of Nxele. But Stockenström, the most perceptive participant, regretted the whole business, 'unfortunately brought on by our interference with a quarrel which did not concern us'.

Somerset, believing that Ngqika was now re-established as the real power in the land following his rival's defeat, arranged a verbal treaty with him in October 1819. Being verbal, it was capable of differing interpretations. To Ngqika, Somerset had declared the land between the Fish and Keiskamma Rivers, for a distance inland of some hundred miles to the Amatola mountains, to be sterilized, neither black nor white settlers being allowed; on the very same day Somerset reported to London that the territory was 'ceded', and 'together with the still unappropriated lands in the Zuurveld' might be suitable for 'systematic colonization'. Systematic colonization appealed to Lord Charles; two years earlier he had told the Colonial Office that he was 'much swayed in recommending this plan by a strong wish to be eventually able to withdraw the detachments' from the eastern frontier.[18] The Governor also agreed with Lord Bathurst that the Cape Dutch must realize that they were to live in a British colony, with British institutions, and accept the official use of English. A substantial influx of British colonists would powerfully assist these ambitions, and the new land of Albany and the 'Ceded Territories' would provide the farms for them to cultivate. Ngqika's Xhosa, forced out of what they had come to regard as their traditional lands, saw this as rank treachery by their colonial allies, but bided their time.

Post-war depression and increasing industrialization were causing great distress in Britain, and accompanying fears of serious unrest prompted the government to listen to proposals for spending taxpayers' money in South Africa, a rare occurrence. A reversal of the previous reactionary policies (sometimes almost unbelievably absurd policies commanded vociferous support; even the abolition of that time-honoured institution trial by battle was strongly opposed) was under way. Ultra-Tories led by Lords Eldon and Sidmouth lost influence to such younger men as George Canning and William Huskisson, advocates of a programme which might be summarized as encouragement of free trade, civil rights for Catholics, Jews and Dissenters, liberty of expression and repeal of the more restrictive laws; together with the near-unanimous anti-slavery sentiment, all these factors began to be reflected in colonial policy.

In July 1819, in an initiative which indicated that even the Tory government was taking the problem of the working classes seriously, Chancellor Nicholas Vansittart announced that in order to 'assist unemployed workmen, in removing to one of our colonies ... the not inconsiderable sum of £50,000 would be set aside to subsidize emigration to the Cape, where from the mildness of the climate and the fertility of the soil in these parts, a rapid and abundant return may reasonably be expected'.[19] An area had been selected on the south-east coast, at some distance from Cape Town, where a small town was already built. Since this was the region inland from Algoa Bay, including the Suurveld, from which the colonial authorities had been attempting to eject the Xhosa for forty years, the 'some distance' was five hundred miles, and the 'small town' the emergent village of Graham's Town, which had just survived a Xhosa attack by the skin of its teeth, it was apparent that the government in London had a feeble grasp of the real situation. Some Members of Parliament felt that so large a sum of money could be better spent on encouraging domestic agriculture, but the motion was agreed on 12 July. The departed Lord Caledon must be given some credit for the suggestion, since the outstandingly mediocre Vansittart started his career as the obedient Member for Caledon's own pocket borough of Old Sarum.

The influx of British and Irish immigrants that followed altered the whole character of the colony. In 1814 the Cape had been brought into what was becoming the second British Empire, the most powerful international influence of the time, the leader of opinion, the 'workshop of the world' and the controller of the sea routes. Now, for the first time the formerly Dutch Cape also had at least a substantial minority of English-speakers, and ones who had been brought up in the modern world. The division that developed was not so much between Dutch- and English-speakers as between those who had been insulated for generations from social and intellectual developments, and those who came with the concepts and techniques of post-war Europe; Britons who read Byron and Walter Scott and had strong views on the rights and privileges of British subjects, together with such Hollanders by birth or by education as Cristoffel Brand, godson of Sir Joseph Banks, twice doctor of the University of Leiden, founder of the first Dutch African newspaper, first Speaker of the Cape Parliament, knight, and father of the President of the Orange Free State. Although not unsympathetic to the back-country farmers, Brand and other sophisticated Dutch-speakers lived in a different world.[20]

In the five years since the peace there had been a trickle of British immigrants, the largest contingent being organized by the Shetland laird Benjamin Moodie, who came out with two hundred fellow-Scots to the Cape in 1817 (and whose brother Donald became one of the founders of Natal and a notable historian). The 1820 emigration was on an altogether larger scale, as tens of thousands of applicants came forward, anxious to escape the gloom of post-war Britain. In what was a painstakingly thought-out enterprise, the first modern attempt at a government-sponsored settle-ment colony, some four thousand individuals were selected from the ninety thousand applicants.[21] The criteria were strict: emigrants had to be organ-ized into parties, under directors, who were even required to make a finan-cial deposit to ensure the viability of their communities. Colonial conditions were designed to reproduce those of the home country, with a stiffening of gentry as leaders, who naturally would command the respect of the lower orders. In fact the selection criteria were rather too strict, in that whilst they produced a high proportion of educated and responsible citi-zens, there were too few of the labourers and artisans needed for the pioneering work.[22]

Workmen formed only a minority of settlers eventually selected. More than half – 542 heads of families – were described as 'agriculturalists', which term included unskilled labourers. Another seventy-two were shopkeepers; but 337 were artisans, mostly carpenters and masons, although numbering among them machinists (two) and mathematical instrument-makers (two);

perhaps most importantly, there were four printers.[23] Given that many of the so-called agriculturalists' expertise did not 'extend to raising a potatoe' (sic), and that the area chosen was completely lacking in amenities, Grahamstown, as it was now becoming known, and Uitenhage being nothing more than small villages, it was not surprising that there was a high proportion of misfits. The Scottish highlanders proved 'a most valuable addition to the Colony at large', but others (specifically the Irish, who in order to avoid trouble were located six hundred miles away from the rest, under the leadership of the irresponsible William Porter) drifted away towards Cape Town.[24]

Lord Charles was not in Africa to welcome the newcomers, having departed for two years' leave in London. The task devolved upon the acting Governor, Sir Rufane Donkin. A complete contrast to the Governor, Donkin was cultivated (a classicist, Fellow of the Royal Society and a founder-member of the Royal Geographical Society), an experienced fighting soldier (West Indies, Flanders, the Peninsula and India) and, unlike Lord Charles, a gentleman, as well as being a liberal Whig rather than an ultra-Tory.[25] He was supported by two naval officers, Captains Sir Jahleel Brenton, devoutly religious and in charge of the Cape Station, and Fairfax Moresby, commanding the frigate *Menai*.[26] When the immigrant ships touched at the Cape it became apparent to Moresby that there would be 'much delay confusion and expense' unless a support operation was organized. The *Menai* immediately sailed for Algoa Bay to assist Landdrost Cuyler in the disembarkation.

It was not without problems, but under Moresby's watchful eye two thousand immigrants and their belongings were landed through the surf, there being no dock installations or natural harbour at what is now Port Elizabeth – named after Donkin's recently deceased wife. The newcomers were accommodated in a camp of several hundred tents, pitched in regular rows or streets, where 'Bands of men and women were walking up and down, conversing and laughing' amid 'ramparts of packing cases and grindstones and bastions of frying-pans and camp kettles'. Moresby found that it did not require much perception to prognosticate the future of different parties; some were clearly unsuitable, but many, such as that led by Mr Thomas Philipps, banker, barrister and Freemason, late of Milford Haven, were 'sure of success'.

While this was true, many difficulties remained. The plots allocated were too small – a hundred acres was the standard, generous enough for the

English shires, but ridiculously inadequate in a land where seven thousand acres was the norm – while the Suurveld, misleadingly fertile in the summer, was sterile, even dangerous, for the rest of the year, and unsuitable for cultivating the wheat it was intended to grow. Donkin's charitable fund and government rations were needed for many months to keep the less successful from starvation, and by 1823, when the three years needed to validate the land grants had expired, only 438 of the original 1,004 families remained settled on their own farms.

The Eastern Cape had indeed received a substantial number of English farmers to work alongside their Boer neighbours, but the influx to Cape Town was considerably more significant. Future effects of this immigration, small by comparison with that going to the United States, were disproportionately large. Those immigrants who made a success of farming were more able and innovative than the conservative Dutch (the merino-pioneering Reitzes a notable exception), and gave a powerful impetus to improvements. On the other hand both English and Dutch farmers made common cause in resisting (and raiding) the Xhosa and in asserting Eastern Cape independence against the distant government in Cape Town. In this they were to have the powerful backing of an independent press. In 1834 Robert Godlonton, a young, energetically Methodist London printer who came with the immigrants, took over the *Graham's Town Journal*, which he rapidly made a mouthpiece of the most virulent and aggressive white settlers. Inevitably the newcomers' effectiveness and independence ensured future trouble with the Xhosa as their settlements pressed on the frontier. And finally, that majority who made for Cape Town, many of whom were well-educated, enterprising and influenced by the newer radical thinking, transformed that still submissive and sleepy society.

The success or failure of the immigrants greatly depended on the group leaders' personalities: the venturesome Northumbrian Bowker family speedily (and ruthlessly) made good; William Cock, who led ninety Cornishmen and women, founded Port Alfred, from which he ran a shipping line; Lt Walter Currie RN became a prosperous farmer and his son, Sir Walter, who 'could ride without a saddle, march without boots, but who could not move along with adjectives', founded the Frontier Mounted Police. At another end of the cultural spectrum was Thomas Pringle, head of the Berwickshire party settled on the farms previously owned by the Slagtersnek rebels (and who found no animosity among the rebels' relations). Pringle was a journalist of great ability and something of a poet.

So perceptive a critic as Coleridge acclaimed Pringle's 'Afar in the Desert' as 'a few lines being omitted or amended among the two or three most perfect lyric poems in our language,' and took the trouble to emend, very much for the better, some of Pringle's drafts. In Pringle's 'The Bechuana Boy',

> The Smile forsook him while I spoke:
> And when again he silence broke
> It was with many a stifled sigh

became in Coleridge's hands:

> His face grew sadder while I spoke
> The smile forsook it: and he broke
> Short silence with a sob-like sigh.[27]

Being self-selected as people of initiative, and many of them having what would be regarded as a respectable position in society – the level of Jane Austen's family, perhaps – the new settlers were not inclined to put up with much official intervention. In the days when income tax was regarded as an intolerable invasion of privacy (and promptly abolished in Britain as soon as the war with France was over), and in the absence of police and the apparatus of local government, the middling sort of Englishman was unused to dealing with officialdom, and impatient of it. When Lord Charles Somerset returned to the Cape in November 1821 he was faced with a less submissive new element in the population.

The Governor arrived in a high temper: Donkin had done nothing right, had meddled with Somerset's frontier arrangements, had allowed the Albany settlers too much freedom, permitted missionaries to travel outside the colony, and, worst of all, insulted Lord Charles's son Henry, the apple of his eye, but a man who invited insults. A furious row followed, ending with Donkin storming back to London to initiate a damaging anti-Somerset campaign. Everyone at the Cape seemed to have sided with Donkin, from Colonial Secretary Christopher Bird down, and Lord Charles fulminated that the new arrivals were no better than Radicals, 'whose chief object is to sow the seeds of discontent wherever their baneful influence can extend'. Many of them were dangerous Dissenters, who, it was well-known, would 'soon move on to democracy'; a fearful thing.[28]

Such seeds of discontent began to be disseminated as public opinion at the Cape found a means of expression through the press. Among the immigrants who had found frontier life disagreeable and moved to Cape Town was Thomas Pringle, appointed by Donkin to head the new public library.[29] Like other ambitious authors poet Pringle attempted to establish his own journal, for which official permission was needed. Reluctantly, after a year's delay, Lord Charles – 'a determined foe to free discussion', according to Pringle[30] – agreed to allow the *South African Journal* to be published, with alternate monthly numbers in Dutch and English. By 1824, when the first number appeared, the home government had become more relaxed about the press; prosecutions, numerous hitherto, almost ceased. Somerset's high-handedness was beginning to run counter to the spirit of the time. The irascible Governor quickly suppressed Pringle's English edition, allowing the Dutch version, the *Nederduitsch Zuid-Afrikaansche Tijdschrift*, edited by the conservative Rev. Abraham Fauré, to continue; Lord Charles could not read Dutch, and Fauré was careful to avoid controversy.

Not so John Fairbairn, another Berwickshire man, and a friend of Pringle's. The *South African Commercial Advertiser*, which had been established by the newly-arrived George Greig – Scots again – ran into similar censorship trouble, whereupon Pringle and Fairbairn assumed joint editorship. Within six months the authorities again forced the newspaper to close.

Deprived of these outlets, public agitation grew. Lord Charles complained to Bathurst that the settlers had 'the temerity to attempt a public meeting'. At this even the conservative Thomas Philipps became disillusioned with Somerset, four hundred miles away at Cape Town: 'with no House of Assembly as in other of our colonies to control [him], Lord Charles we now have for life,' and protested at his 'arbitrary power to order people into local exile, or to be expelled from the colony'.[31]

Having lost both his journals, Pringle took ship to England to join forces with Donkin in agitation against Lord Charles' autocratic rule. For an impoverished journalist, Pringle had friends in some unlikely places – Sir Walter Scott found him 'a worthy creature, but conceited withal'.[32] On 8 September 1819 John Wilson Croker, then Secretary to the Admiralty, wrote in a lively letter to Henry Goulburn, Under Secretary at the Colonial Office, of one 'Pringle a Scotch Tory, born lame, dedicates himself to literature'.[33] Pringle was no Tory, as both Croker and Goulburn were, but both were in their twenties, and the bright young rising Tories were a very different breed from those of the *ancien régime*, personified by Lord Charles. The

Cape democrats were reinforced in Whitehall by the former Colonial Secretary Colonel Bird, who had, after more than twenty years' service at the Cape, been dismissed by the Governor on the pretext of his being a Catholic. A severe and upright man, Bird could count on the support of Lord Caledon, John Barrow and William Windham, all powerful allies.[34]

They found support in the Treasury, which was shocked to discover that Lord Charles had continued to issue paper money, and only two years after the unprecedented grant of £50,000, pleading, among other things, for compensation for damage to his stables caused by a storm, was asking for a loan of £125,000. The currency of the colony, as was a usual practice, remained the rixdollar of the Company period, a cause of frequent confusion since official salaries were paid in sterling. The published accounts showed that a loan of a quarter of a million rixdollars (now worth only eighteen pence each) from the East India Company had been needed to balance the books, and such constant expenditure as nine hundred dollars to 'G. Muller, for meat &c. for lions' was exposed to public scrutiny. Such a drain on the public purse could not be allowed to continue, and in 1823 two Commissioners were despatched to the Cape to make a report direct to the British government; very much in the style of the VOC sending a director to sort out the muddles made by its Governors.

The leading Commissioner, John Bigge, deserves a place among the architects of empire; he had already prepared a far-reaching study of Australian conditions, and now spent four years on a thorough investigation before producing a massive report on the Cape. The salient recommendations of this were that an Advisory Council must curb the Governor's previously autocratic powers, and a root-and-branch reform of the legal system be effected. The Heemraaden he found 'much perverted by the prejudices and habits that have become hereditary among them'. Chief Justice John Truter had 'stunned the whole colony' by sentencing one Wilhelm Gebhart, son of a predikant, to death for the particularly heinous killing of a slave. Somerset refused to commute the sentence: the 'impression made by the execution presented an opportunity not to be lost'. The 'strong prejudices . . . and imperfect sense of religious and civil obligation . . . that distinguished the white population' could only be amended by the introduction of English law.[35]

This was duly done: an Advisory Council, which was to include two civilian 'non-official' members, was appointed, and two Charters of Justice, promulgated in 1827 and 1832, established a Supreme Court and a network

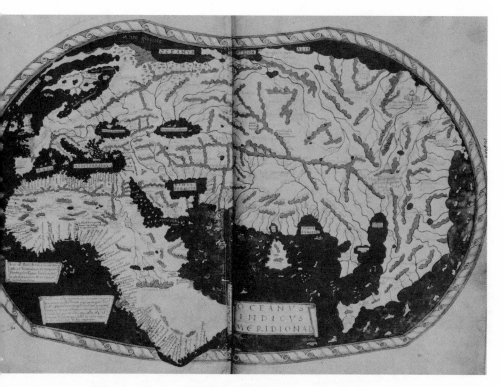

The cartographer Martellus prepared his world map in about 1490. The news of Bartolomeu Dias' voyage reached Europe only after the map had been drawn, necessitating a cut through the lower border to accommodate the Cape of Good Hope.

Seventeenth-century sketch of Khoikhoi women dancing.

This engraving of 1742 shows Kaapstad as a modest settlement, but one well-equipped with gallows. The execution wheels are just to the right of the Castle; on the extreme right the scaffold is occupied by a hanging body.

Left Lady Anne Barnard's sketch shows a Coloured wetnurse suckling a white baby. Her own child and a Newfoundland dog are in attendance.
Above Rosina, a Khoi-San girl photographed in 1860.

STATE OF CRADOCK'S PASS IN 1848

A distinguished soldier as well as a competent architect and surveyor, Colonel Charles Michell designed a new road (Montagu's Pass) to replace this horrific crossing of the Outeniekwaberge, near the town of George.

Right This magnificent Zulu warrior is in parade, rather than fighting-dress. The man-size oxhide shield was of little use in hand-to-hand combat.

Below Contrasting with the Zulu, the small shield, or target, of Moshoeshoe's Sotho encouraged close combat, and together with the Sotho battle-axe was well adapted to cavalry use.

OPPOSITE
Above This meeting of the Anti-Slavery Convention was held in Exeter Hall, London, in 1840. By that time slavery had been abolished in the British Empire, and some of the initial enthusiasm had been dispersed; but the fight against slavery remained a powerful influence on Imperial politics.

Below One of a series of cartoons by Frederick l'Ons published in 1838 as anti-Stockenström propaganda. On the left, Dr Philip is talking to T.F. Buxton, with Stockenström peeping around the curtain. Both versions of contemporary Hottentot life reflected some reality.

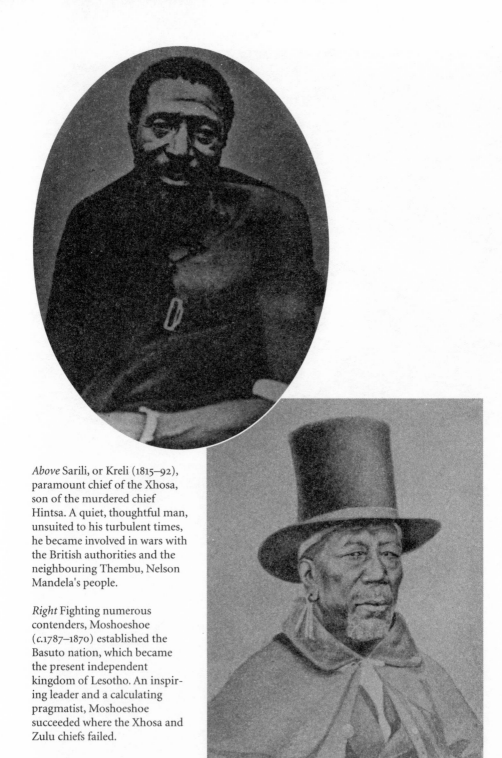

Above Sarili, or Kreli (1815–92), paramount chief of the Xhosa, son of the murdered chief Hintsa. A quiet, thoughtful man, unsuited to his turbulent times, he became involved in wars with the British authorities and the neighbouring Thembu, Nelson Mandela's people.

Right Fighting numerous contenders, Moshoeshoe (*c.*1787–1870) established the Basuto nation, which became the present independent kingdom of Lesotho. An inspiring leader and a calculating pragmatist, Moshoeshoe succeeded where the Xhosa and Zulu chiefs failed.

Adam Kok III (1811–75), *above*, Griqua chief, and Langalibalele (1818–89), *right*, leader of the Natalian Hlubi people, were both betrayed by the white authorities, and ended their lives disappointed men.

Boer republicans indignantly denied British accusations of slavery, but this Thomas Baines sketch of 1870 – and documentary evidence – substantiates the charges.

Above Sir Harry Smith, arrogant and swashbuckling, might serve as a model for George Macdonald Fraser's Flashman.

Left Painted towards the end of his long life, this portrait of Sir George Grey (1812–98) shows that most talented of colonial governors having failed in almost all his endeavours; and through his own defects.

of resident magistrates to replace the old system of Landdrosts and Heem-raden. All the characteristics of English law, including trial by jury and cross-examination in open court, were reproduced; and all cases were to be heard in English. Such innovations upset the rural Dutch, who could not rely upon the new magistrates to be as sympathetic as their own neighbours, while the insistence on English was a cause for well-grounded annoyance. Nor were the substantial burghers of the Cape best pleased: their control of the old Company institutions, the banks, the Orphan Chamber and the Burgher Senate, and their operation as allies of the British authorities, had given them power and prestige which were now threatened. Lord Charles was blamed for all this, but in fact it was the Colonial Office that insisted the Cape should become an English-speaking colony, as Simon van der Stel had done, more successfully, in forcing the Huguenots to adopt Dutch.[36]

Even more irritating was the English insistence on equality before the law, specifically expressed in the famous Ordinance 50 of 1828, which firmly stated that 'Hottentots and other free persons of colour' enjoyed 'all the rights of law ... to which any other of His Majesty's subjects are entitled', including the freedom to buy land in any region. Many Dutch farmers had treated Khoi-San kindly, but never for a moment had they acknowledged even a theoretical equality. Watching the public flogging of an English thief by two Khoikhoi, 'dancing in acting their part', Thomas Hodgson, a Wesleyan missionary, reported hearing 'a most strange sentiment' from a bystander 'who I supposed considered himself a rational being, that he had rather be *hung* by a white man than flogged by a black'.[37]

In practice the new liberty was tempered by the advantages (still not unknown in British courts) enjoyed by the astute, respectable and rich, and the white monopoly of the mechanics of the law. Apart from principals and witnesses, the only non-white faces to be seen in a court were those of jurymen, always a minority and soon a diminishing one. Clearly-guilty whites could still be cleared of atrocious crimes by prejudiced juries, but at least the presiding judge could make his displeasure at such miscarriages of justice public. This they did, often in the teeth of government opposition, when civil liberties were under attack. However imperfect, the rule of law and the independence of the judiciary have frequently been the only defences of the oppressed.

Combined with the retention of Romano-Dutch law in civil cases, in which the Dutch language could also be used, these innovations might have won general, if grudging, acceptance, but the new spirit of reform in Britain was about to produce more disturbing changes. The Great Reform Act of 1832, levered through, over dogged opposition, by the Whig government of Earl Grey, stands as a landmark in British constitutional history, the first extension of many hesitant moves towards a democratic society. Reforms, however, began five years earlier when liberal Tories gained office. Between 1827 and 1830 two reforming Colonial Secretaries, William Huskisson, famous as the first man to be killed by a railway train, and Sir George Murray, an intellectual soldier, were matched by a Whig reformer in Cape Town, General Sir Richard Bourke. Holding the fort from March 1826 to September 1828, Bourke was quickly receptive to Colonial Office encouragement in restricting the white colonists' powers to exploit the Khoikhoi and slave populations. At the Cape, Lord Charles Somerset's recall also defined the start of a movement towards colonial self-government, reflecting the changes in Britain's colonial empire. The end of the protracted wars against the French had brought Britain new colonies in the West Indies and the opportunity to develop the emerging 'settlement' colonies of New South Wales, New Zealand and the Cape.

A settlement colony was one where the original inhabitants had been supplanted by immigrants who thenceforward formed a majority. Anticipating the emancipation of the slaves, which was clearly imminent, and since – officially at least – no Xhosa lived within the colonial boundaries, the whites and freed slaves would constitute a massive majority over the only native peoples, the remaining Khoikhoi. The Cape at that time would have therefore possessed the characteristics of a settlement colony, one of which was that, sooner or later, it would have some degree of self-government. A potentially embarrassing result was that all inhabitants would have to enjoy, according to British colonial practice, equal legal rights; and former slaves and Khoikhoi might be in a majority, reducing the white colonists to a minority of potential citizens and, eventually, voters.

Since the abolition of the trade in 1807, no slaves had been imported.[38] In large part the slave population was therefore creole, born and brought up in Africa, speaking only the emergent pidgin Dutch, the *taal*, and increasingly integrated into the colonial society, albeit on a subordinate level. Many had been well-treated by their owners, and some fortunate individuals had attained a modest prosperity; others, when given the opportunity to leave, preferred to stay with their masters. New officials, Protectors of Slaves, had been appointed to watch over their interests, and the inevitability of emancipation was accepted. It was the underlying principle that proved hard to swallow, the idea that a freed slave would have the same rights as a European, would be able to buy land, sell his own labour or employ that of others, move freely about as he chose, bring charges and give evidence in open court against his master, and generally behave as a normal human being.

It was easy for the discontented Dutch farmers to find a scapegoat: missionaries generally, those of the London Society in particular, with Dr John Philip, its superintendent in South Africa, as prime villain. Dr Philip (the doctorate was from an American university, and not substantiated by academic merit, a further irritation to the farmers, admirers of intellectual ability[39]) was a stubborn self-educated Scot, possessing immense energy and powers of persuasion. A Congregationalist minister, he had been commissioned to reorganize the missionary effort brought into question by van der Kemp and Read (Read had an extra-marital affair with another Khoikhoi girl, which stretched London's tolerance too far[40]). This he did, and the later missionaries sent from Britain were more carefully selected and afforded greater support; of these Robert Moffat and his son-in-law David Livingstone were the best-known of Philip's protégés. Remaining in South Africa for the rest of his life, a source of inspiration and irritation in similar measure, Philip was a gifted publicist, but never one to be diverted by inconvenient facts. He could rely for support in London from Fowell Buxton, the rich leader of the anti-slavery campaign, and in South Africa from his son-in-law, John Fairbairn.

Philip's indignation was directed against slavery and oppression in all its forms, and he detected these particularly among the Dutch-speaking farmers. He was frequently right, but his intemperate and generalized accusations aroused equally hostile reactions from those who were conscious of no evil motives in their own treatment of slaves and servants. The patriarchal Boer society was perfectly capable of respecting the rights of all individuals, even if its interpretation of those rights differed from that of the missionaries. Respectable Dutch farmers could be as fierce in their condemnation of cruelty as any missionary; but they were less likely to arraign one of their own in courts of law.

Washing the spears

In the closing years of the twentieth century seven million Zulu formed a nation within a nation, the most homogeneous and cohesive division of South Africa's population. Two hundred years previously only a small tribe, perhaps two thousand souls in the foothills of the Drakensberg, acknowledged the name. This dramatic transformation, perhaps without parallel in modern times, was only the most outstanding of the many radical changes which shook southern Africa in the early 1800s.[41]

Arguments, sometimes fierce, rage about the causes of the *mfecane*, or *difaqane* – variously translated as 'clubbing', 'crushing', 'scattering', 'time of emptiness' – a want of unanimity typical of writings on the subject, but all with connotations of violence, hunger and forced removal – which transformed southern African society, but there is no doubt as to its stark reality.[42] From an epicentre in the lands of the northern Nguni, shockwaves shot out more than a thousand miles, displacing hundreds of thousands, with accompanying violence, death and painful readjustment. Old tribes were scattered and dissolved, emerging as peoples who, like the Bhaca or the Mfengu, had lost their previous traditions, and retained an imperfect collective memory of their past, or reforming into new peoples, sometimes with an identity amounting to nationhood. The Basuto, the Swazi and the Zulu themselves have been established as well-defined peoples – and in the first instances as independent states – only since the *mfecane*.

In the late eighteenth century competition for control over the trade routes from Delagoa Bay to the hinterland intensified as trade to that port increased. First ivory, in great quantities, followed by beef bought by American whalers, together with some slaves, found their way to the coast. Two northern Nguni tribes, the Mthethwa and the Ndwande, emerged as the most powerful in the region south of the Phongolo River, in what is now KwaZulu. Speaking a similar language and sharing many customs with the Xhosa, but separated from the Dutch and English by eight hundred miles, the expanding tribes began to change their character. Whereas previously, subjected communities had been absorbed into the dominant society, they were now increasingly characterized as an inferior caste within a stratified polity. Centralized control of the larger political units was reinforced by a major cultural development, the replacement of circumcision ceremonies and schools by larger units of young men obliged to perform years of service before attaining the status of manhood, symbolized not by circumcision but by the headring of the proved warrior. These new age-groups, the *amabutho* – the word is often translated as 'regiments', but 'corps' might be better, since they spent most of their time on collective tasks in the royal service, including hunting or merely working on the chiefs' estates, as well as raiding and disciplining recalcitrant vassals – lived in separate barracks, and were released to marriage and a civilian life only when the chief permitted.

By 1816 the two chiefs, Zwide of the Ndwandwe and Dingiswayo of the Mthethwa, were prepared for a final confrontation. Both chiefs had developed centralized systems – Zwide probably more so – and adopted different methods of combat. Nguni clashes had traditionally been settled by using the assegai, the universal short spear of all southern Africa, as a javelin, which could usually be deflected by an oxhide shield, and was only therefore effective against a retreating enemy. In the *mfecane* wars the assegai was shortened, given a broader blade, and used as a thrusting weapon at close quarters in a much deadlier fashion – as the Xhosa were doing at the same time.

For some years Dingiswayo had been able to consolidate his position without the necessity for more fighting, the demonstration of superior force usually being sufficient to persuade other chiefs to accept him as overlord. In this expansion his most effective follower was a young man known as Shaka, commander of the IziCwe regiment, who had established himself as chief of his own ancestral group, the Zulu. At that time there were probably not many more than two or three thousand Zulu, traditional feudatories of the Mthethwa, but their numbers were quickly enlarged as Shaka subdued neighbouring tribes, including the Buthelezi, who became particularly close to the Zulu rulers. When in 1817 the final clash with Zwide ended in Dingiswayo's defeat and death, Shaka had avoided involvement, and was able, three years later, to inflict a shattering defeat on Zwide and emerge as the unquestioned dominant power in the region, ruler of a more numerous population and a more extensive territory than any previous Southern African leader. In his short reign of less than ten years Shaka consolidated his position and founded a nation by reversing older traditions and establishing what amounted to a new society.

Traditionally the authority of Bantu chiefs had been circumscribed by law and custom, by the existence of sorcerers, diviners, thaumaturges and rainmakers whose magical authority rivalled that of the chief, by the status of hereditary councillors, and by the ready availability of qualified contenders for the chieftainship. Among the Nguni it was further diluted by the dispersed nature of society, in which independent groups of homesteads quietly got on with their own lives, receiving the chief with due respect when he paid his regular, expensive, visits, and following him to war – limited war – when necessary. Shaka gathered his people together in their thousands, under his own control, exercising supreme autocratic power. Cherished traditions, central to black African life, were jettisoned. Circumcision rites, the central point in a man's life, were replaced by enlistment in the *amabutho*. Marriage was no longer settled by families but by the king's will. Not only young men, but girls were forbidden to marry until the king permitted; in this way the whole productive capacity of the community could be harnessed into the royal service. Discipline was rigid and enforced by institutionalized terror; not only shirkers, but any unfortunate who happened to be in the wrong place might be instantly killed by the omnipresent executioners. Warfare ceased to be limited, and whole communities could be massacred; raids were made in all directions to create a *cordon sanitaire* around the Zulu heartland and to provide the young warriors a chance to prove themselves, 'washing their spears' in the enemy's blood. This became less necessary as Shaka's opponents chose surrender rather than annihilation; they could then expect to be absorbed into the Zulu community and treated as Shaka's people, although never allowed the same standing as the original members of the royal clan, resplendent in their parade garb of feathers and skins, inflamed with pride springing from an unbroken succession of victories, the young men of Shaka's *impis* looked down on the people of the vassal states on the borders of the Zulu empire as 'menials', 'destitutes', 'those with strange hairstyles'.

There are always those ready to admire unbridled violence, and Shaka has been compared, hysterically enough, to Genghis Khan, Alfred the Great and Napoleon. One writer has described him as being as 'sublime a moral teacher as martial genius. Submission to authority, obedience to the law, respect for superiors, order and self-restraint, fearlessness and self-sacrifice, constant work and civic duty – in a word all the noblest disciplines of life were the very foundation stones upon which he built his nation.' Today this sounds as though it might be from a handbook for the Hitler Youth, who were exhorted to exactly such virtues, but Arthur Bryant was writing in 1929, before such heroes as Hitler, Stalin, Mao and Pol Pot had made us more sensitive to these issues. Later apologists for Shaka, understandably protective of black Africans, have questioned the accuracy of the few contemporary European descriptions which formed the conventional highly-coloured portrait of a bloodthirsty tyrant. But other evidence supports this assessment. The accounts recorded in the Stuart archive, collected at the turn of the century from those who had survived Shaka, all describe the Zulu king as a 'tyrant, a marauder, a destroyer and a madman ... a wild beast'.[43]

There can be no question however that Shaka began the formation of what can only be called a nation. Some seven million Africans today define themselves as Zulu, and many enthusiastically accept the Shakan traditions. Shaka's Day is celebrated every year by parades in traditional dress, some-what unconvincingly led by tubby bespectacled leaders, more comfortable in collars and ties; gangs of thugs perpetuate his traditions by massacring opponents with clubs and spears, as well as more effective modern weapons. Like the similar mythology encrusted around the Boer pioneers, the Zulu inheritance is a potent, and usually dangerous, influence in modern South Africa.[44]

By the time Shaka was, predictably enough, assassinated by his half-brother in 1828 the Zulu, from being a minor sub-tribe, had imposed their own customs and will upon all the territory from the Drakensberg to the sea, between the Phongolo and Mzimkulu Rivers. The defeated fled in every direction, and in turn dispossessed others. Soshangane, one of Zwide's commanders, escaped to Delagoa Bay to begin a career of conquest that matched Shaka's own. Attacking in turn Tsonga, Portuguese, Shona and Boers, he finally established his rule over an area from the Zambezi to the sea. His people became the Shangaans – amaShangane, the people of Soshangane. Another of Zwide's chiefs, Zwangendaba, picking up some Swazi followers, raided into Shona territory and settled his followers, the Ngoni, in what is now Malawi and Tanzania. When such bands reached their final resting place they had, by conquest or by assimilation, included Swazi, Tonga, Sotho and Kalmaga as well as the original Ngoni.[45]

Zwide's grandson Mzilikazi became the best-known of the new men. Deserting Zwide, he temporarily joined Shaka, before falling out with the Zulu king and being driven north over the Vaal River. Attacking and dispossessing the local inhabitants, Mzilikazi's followers, the Ndebele or Matabele, were in turn pursued by Zulu and raided first by Griquas, before being harassed by Boers who were then setting out on the Great Trek of the 1830s.[46] Eventually, after a thousand-mile odyssey which deserves to rank with that of the Mormons or the Boers themselves, accompanied by much misery and bloodshed, the wanderers settled in what is now Zimbabwe, where they formed a heterogeneous collection with the original Ndwanda, Sotho, and, at the bottom of the pecking order, the Shona. Mzilikazi's dynasty lasted for only one more generation, coming to a violent end when his son Lobengula was dispossessed by Cecil Rhodes' South Africa Company.

Yet another chief, Sobhuza, an early victim of Zwide's, moved off north into present-day Swaziland, where he established another dynasty, which still survives. Sobhuza was a diplomatist, who made peace whenever possible with both Shaka and Soshangane, and continued to adapt his own traditions to the different customs of his new people. His army, organized according to Shakan custom, remained a powerful force. Another successful state was formed from a collection of refugees organized under the leadership of the Sotho leader Moshoeshoe, the founder of the independent protectorate of Basutoland, today's Lesotho, centred on the impregnable mountain holds of the Drakensberg. Such islands of relative stability were rare, and a generation of homeless refugees was doomed to wander about South Africa seeking temporary refuge and food, but being driven to cannibalism and starvation.

The passage of such armies led to widespread devastation. European writers spoke of travelling for days through a deserted countryside past the scattered bones of the dead. Into the geographical void left by the killing and dispossession moved the *trekboers*, the pioneers of what became the Afrikaner republics. Although few in numbers they were able to fend off the aggressive black conquerors, and were therefore, at any rate initially, welcomed by the remnants of the scattered population who appreciated both the possibility of protection and the likely consequences of resistance. Another void was however developing, as a result of the disruption to traditional societies and cultures. Shaka, Mzilikazi and the other warlords gave a simple choice – join us and accept our new and revolutionary communities, or perish; an alternative was beginning to be offered by the missionaries. A good deal more complex, this included access to European society, and the subsequent possession of horses and firearms – those solid guarantees of security (and of loot) – as well as the Christian ideals, always attractive to the dispossessed. Most important was the personality of the missionaries themselves, and among that mixed and often quarrelsome group were some of commanding stature and open generosity.

The most remarkable of these was the large and imposing, not to say dictatorial, figure of Robert Moffat, who established a London Missionary

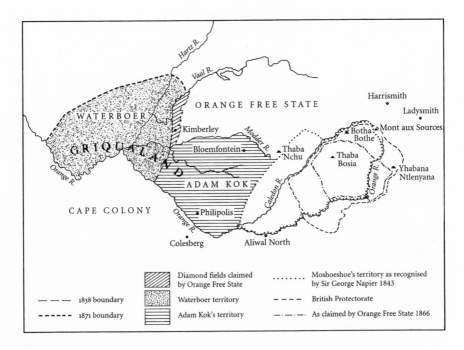

Map legend:

— — — 1838 boundary	Diamond fields claimed by Orange Free State
- - - - - - 1871 boundary	Waterboer territory
	Adam Kok's territory

....	Moshoeshoe's territory as recognised by Sir George Napier 1843
- - - -	British Protectorate
—·—·—·	As claimed by Orange Free State 1866

MAP 4 *Basutoland*

Society station well north of any settlement, on the fringes of the desert at Kuruman. Moffat and his family, which included David Livingstone, his son-in-law, made Kuruman not only a missionary centre, but a base for exploration and learning, where Moffat prepared a Tswana translation of the Bible and his successful account of *Missionary Labours.* Kuruman also served as a strong point from which to reach out to the conquerors and survivors of the *mfecane.* Mzilikazi never succumbed to Moffat's evangelism, but he held the missionary in high regard, recognizing in him a very similar towering personality to his own.

South of the Drakensberg the effects of the *mfecane* were less dramatic, the adjacent Nguni tribes either accepting Zulu chieftainship or moving themselves south of the Tukela River out of harm's way. At the time of Shaka's death in 1828, the Zulu kingdom was firmly established within clear territorial limits with a population of perhaps a hundred thousand. It was not geographically extensive, comprising about eighteen thousand square miles of good cattle country, but within it the power of the king was absolute in a way previously unknown to the Nguni. Zululand proper was

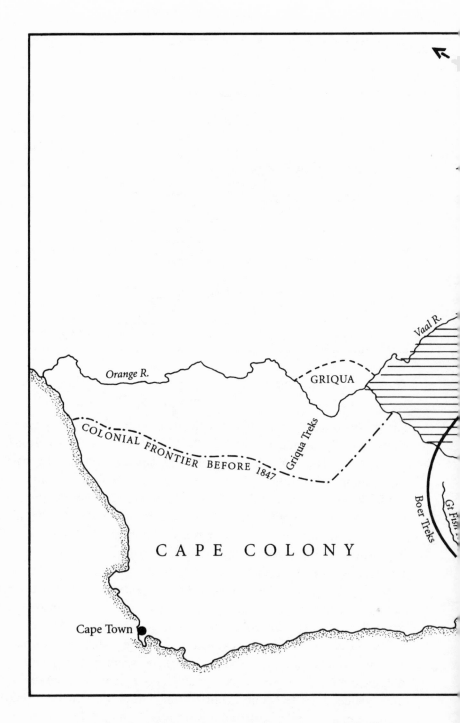

MAP 5 Mfecane *incursions (northern section overleaf)*

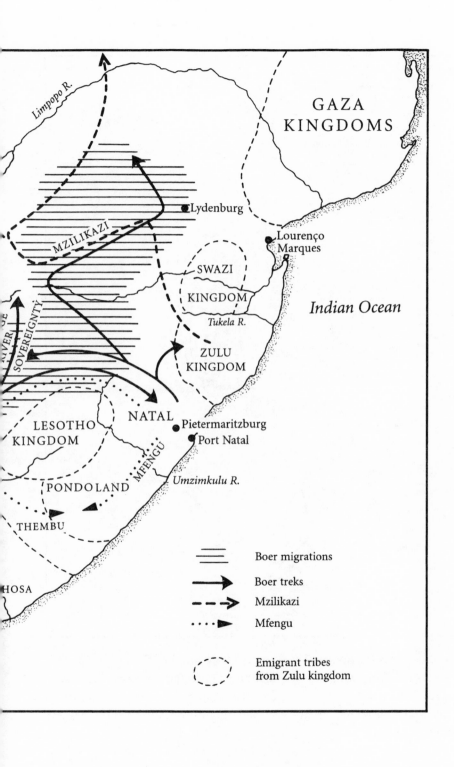

GAZA
KINGDOMS

Limpopo R.

Lydenburg

Lourenço
Marques

MZILIKAZI

SWAZI

KINGDOM

Tukela R.

Indian Ocean

ZULU
KINGDOM

SOVEREIGNTY

NATAL

LESOTHO
KINGDOM

MFENGU

Pietermaritzburg
Port Natal

Umzimkulu R.

PONDOLAND

THEMBU

HOSA

	Boer migrations
	Boer treks
	Mzilikazi
	Mfengu
	Emigrant tribes from Zulu kingdom

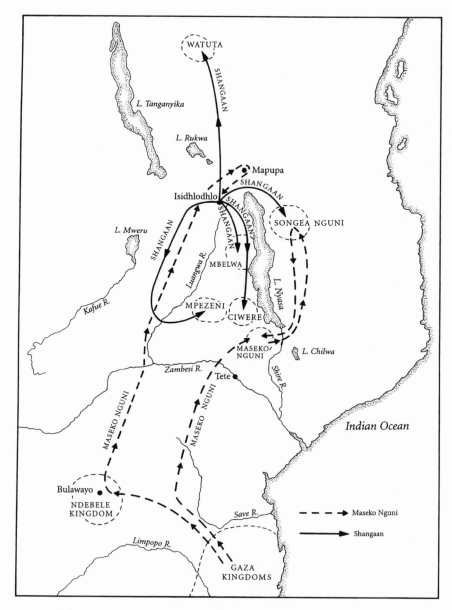

surrounded by a depopulated area, particularly south of the Tukela in what
became Natal, from which the population had fled further south, increasing
the pressure on the already overcrowded Xhosa, who found themselves
further squeezed up against the consolidating Europeans on their western
borders.

Matiwane, chief of the independent Ngwane clan, after having been attacked by both Zwide and Shaka, moved through Natal, Basutoland and the Cape in a protracted campaign of terror and devastation, which gained him the name 'who reddens his mouth by drinking the blood of men'. This lasted for ten years before Matiwane was finally stopped by the Thembu, assisted by colonial forces under Colonel Somerset, Lord Charles's son, who remained in the colony after his father left. Thereafter both the Thembu and their neighbours, the Mpondo, formed stable communities, dividing the Xhosa from the Zulu and usually cooperating with the colonial authorities.

The Mpondo, under their chief Faku, who remained in power for half a century before his death in 1867, acted as hosts for the wave of refugees that flowed through from Natal. Many of these were to return when stability was established in 1840s, but at least twenty thousand remained in Kaffraria and the colony. Cut off from their traditional society, these Mfengu – also known as the Fingoes, the dispossessed – quickly adapted to European ways, and both as soldiers and farmers showed qualities of intelligence and tenacity; but those blacks who remained faithful to their own culture looked on Fingoes as renegades.

Another refugee people emerged from the *mfecane*: the Bhaca – homeless ones – who established an identity under their aggressive chief Madzikane and his son Ncaphayi. Living alongside the Mpondo and Thembu, the Bhaca shared a common influence, in that Wesleyan missionaries were accepted by all three peoples. The Methodist influence made for a stability that survived many quarrels (Ncaphayi was killed fighting his father-in-law Faku's Mpondo), which gave a shape to the future Transkei and provided in due course an education for the Thembu nobleman Nelson Mandela.

At the time of Shaka's death the situation along the southern Nguni was that the coastal boundary of the colony was still that claimed by the VOC, the Fish River, extended to include the 'Ceded Territory'. This boundary was secured by the 1820 settlements centred around Grahamstown, with further movement – in theory at any rate – checked by Fort Wiltshire. For three hundred miles up the coast the land was occupied by the South Nguni people, of whom the most important groups were the Rharhabe and Gcaleka Xhosa, Thembu, Mpondo and Pondomise, with the newly-arrived Bhaca and Mfengu. Then, from the Uzimkulu to the Tukela, was the area of devastation, sparsely inhabited, that was to become Natal.

SEVEN

The Myth of the Great Trek

Nerves and bowels in agitation

In the twenty years after 1835 no fewer than fifteen thousand people left the Cape Colony to settle in areas outside British control. The Great Trek, as it became known, is a central point in African history. Siphoning off so many Dutch-speakers, it removed from the Cape not only the more aggressively anti-British and reactionary elements, but also those who had contributed most to the defence of the frontiers. The tenacious and independent character of the '*voortrekkers*' ensured that the communities they established would be awkward neighbours both for a generally liberal imperial power and for those whom they elbowed out of the way. But the emergence of a powerful 'white tribe' brought a measure of stability to some scattered survivors of the *mfecane*, albeit a stability offered only on condition of submission to the new chiefs.

If the Trek itself is a significant historical fact, the myth that has accrued around it has assumed even greater importance. To Afrikaners in the twentieth century, who perceived themselves to be humiliated and oppressed by the British, and often felt condescended to as culturally inferior by usually richer English-speakers, it was a comfort to remember – with considerable advantages – their earlier exploits. In just such a recreation of history that led the Zulu to fashion a Shaka myth to compensate for their own later exploitation and degradation, Afrikaners presented the Trek as a bold defiance of the British Empire, a courageous endeavour to find freedom from persecution in the great spaces of Africa. Symbolized by the huge *voortrekker* monument at Pretoria, commemorated in national holidays, re-enacted with much enthusiasm in the centenary year of 1938 (and markedly less fifty years later), and providing a name – the 'Ossewa Brandwag' – for the Afrikaner fascist organization, the Trek has taken a place at the centre of Afrikaner national consciousness.

Fanie Uys and Nick Fourie bore names made famous in the Trek. These pathetic, fat young men who in 1994 took part in an attempted coup against the new democratic regime, only to be shot down by black policemen in Bophuthatswana, saw themselves as acting in a heroic tradition, descendants of the *voortrekkers*, struggling for their liberties and privileges against liberal oppression and its consequence, black domination.[1] Never appreciated in quite the same light by the majority of the population, by the end of the twentieth century the myth looks tattered and disreputable, but retains something of its power. Without denying the dogged heroism of the pioneers, the very considerable accretions and romantic re-interpretations that have disguised the facts need scraping away. Leaving aside such points as the active participation of the Khoikhoi and Bastaards, and a number of British fighting alongside the Boers, and the protection afforded to the trekkers by such black leaders as Moroka of the Rolong, which rather blur the generally accepted picture, the nagging truth remains that within a single generation the Great Trek looked uncomfortably like a Great Illusion.

Although the individual leaders of the Trek were brave and often principled, they were usually quite incapable of cooperating with each other. Temporary alliances were followed by often permanent discord: Gert Maritz, townsman, trader and wagon builder, who led a party in his own blue-painted wagons with their distinctive square tilts, was irascibly ready to quarrel with anyone, especially the rugged frontiersman Hendrik Potgieter, who in turn found the slippery Andries Pretorius impossible to deal with. Their followers divided on almost every issue, whether of religion, principle, destination or personality. Within four years three of the first trekker parties – those of Retief, Tregardt and van Rensburg – had been wiped out; within forty the republics of Natalia, Lydenburg, Winburg, Utrecht, the Transvaal, Stellaland, the Land of Goschen, the Orange Free State and the New Republic had all commemorated Boer divisions and disappointments. None, except the Orange Free State, was viable; the largest, the Transvaal, was bankrupt; internecine quarrels at least once turned into civil war. The only factors preserving the identity of the Afrikaner people from obliteration were the resistance of the blacks they displaced, which forced a unity on the individualistic parties, the vacillating incompetence of British governments, and the discovery of gold in the Transvaal.

It is instructive to compare the initial failure of the Great Trek to the migration of the Mormons, which took place at the same time, for similar reasons, in the same way and over much the same distance. While the Afrikaners squabbled, starved and divided, Brigham Young succeeded in keeping the unity of his people and founded in Utah a prosperous and orderly state, which has stood the test of time.

The reasons for the migration have been much canvassed and variously explained. At the time, and still more later, when the myth developed, British actions were blamed. Most colonists, English as well as Dutch, were unhappy about the 1828 Ordinance 50. It was all very well, they maintained, to allow Hottentots theoretically equal legal rights, but given their propensity for wandering about and creating nuisances, and their reluctance to work hard for twelve months of the year for next to nothing, something must be done to protect the settler and guarantee him cheap labour. Sir Benjamin D'Urban, another Peninsular War general sent out as Governor in 1834, was convinced, and prepared just such a vagrancy order, only to have it cancelled by the Colonial Office, fulfilling their role of protecting non-whites from too-evident exploitation. D'Urban had been preceeded by Sir Lowry Cole (1827–33), a well-connected part-time soldier (son of an earl and married to an earl's daughter, an MP for over twenty years) who had also served in the Peninsula and who figures in many social memoirs of the time. Cole, chosen as a safe pair of hands, did what was required of him by avoiding trouble in the delicate period leading up to slave emancipation.[2]

It had been apparent for many years that the final step, the emancipation of all slaves used in the British Empire, was inevitable, but the constitutional upheaval surrounding the Great Reform Bill of 1830–2 postponed the final act. As an interim measure, Protectors of Slaves were appointed in all slave-holding colonies. In South Africa there were few matters of more than administrative importance to occupy the Protectors, although at least one alternative to immediate emancipation was advanced for discussion. As no slaves had been imported since the ban on the slave trade had taken effect in 1808, by 1834, when emancipation was finally proclaimed, most of the Cape slaves had been born in the colony, of mixed descent, speaking the *patois* that became Afrikaans, and increasingly integrated into the community, although in a clearly subordinate role. In Cape Town almost all women slaves were employed in domestic service, while many men carried on skilled trades, often on their own account, or as a joint venture with their owners. In a real sense, a distinct 'Coloured' community was waiting to be called into being by slave emancipation.[3]

The arrangements for compensating slave-owners added an irritation (leaving aside the question raised by some as to the necessity of any compensation at all for those who had benefited from that inhuman institution: owners of rotten boroughs had not been compensated when they were abolished in 1831, and one of those unrepresentative parliamentary seats changed hands at the price of half-a-hundred adult slaves). It was West Indian slavery that had excited most British indignation, since those slaves comprised the large majority of all in British ownership, and it was from Jamaica that the most horrifying reports of brutality came. South Africa was a secondary consideration to the legislators. Arrangements were therefore made, reasonably enough, for compensation payments to be made in London, where West Indian planters had long-established connections. Most Cape colonists had not yet had occasion to appoint such agents, and some were badly served, receiving only a fraction of what they claimed: the total requested of just over £3 million was slightly reduced on examination, but of this agreed sum less than half was actually received in the Cape. Yet most trekkers were not affected, for while some had possessed slaves, Maritz, for example owning twelve, the great majority of slave-owners lived near the Cape – twenty-one thousand of the total thirty-nine thousand slaves were in Cape Town and Stellenbosch alone; only 2,400 were found living in the extensive districts of Graaff-Reinet and Uitenhage, whence many of the *voortrekkers* came. Almost certainly a good deal of 'creative accountancy' took place, the valuation of slaves allowing much freedom of interpretation. In 1825 Mr de Mock was paid 1,600 rixdollars – say £140 – as compensation when his slave Adam was emancipated by the government; it was not likely to have been an excessive sum. Conservative farmers like Michiel van Breda, who in 1830 owned slaves valued from between £200 to £1,500 – an enormous sum – had written this entire human stock down to £64 by 1836.[4] And whatever individual farmers might have reason to resent in the sums they eventually received, the injection of so great an amount of cash compensation acted as a first-class stimulus to the economy, contributing to the general prosperity of the colony.

It was rather the liberal philosophy behind emancipation that produced hysterical reactions: the burghers of Stellenbosch found their 'Nerves and Bowels in agitation' at the 'revolting . . . shuddering idea' that a slave could bring his master to court.[5] In July 1826, 350 Cape Towners petitioned the

Burgher Senate, not even against emancipation, but against an ordinance allowing slaves to testify against their masters, fearing to see 'our streets . . . full of streams of blood . . . slaughtered by the steel of incited heathen slaves'. Even such a pillar of the establishment as Christoffel Brand complained that 'the very idea . . . of giving slaves a Protector or Guardian . . . with such extraordinary powers is ridiculous and dangerous . . . Some people accuse us Afrikaners of being vicious oafs.'[6] Correspondence between discontented farmers and Andries Stockenström makes it quite clear that British insistence 'on equal justice for all classes of the community' was 'profoundly rejected . . . as amounting to *gelykstelling*, a levelling or equalization of existing status distinctions'. Anna Steenkamp, a trekker, confirmed this: it was not slave emancipation, but the fact that blacks were 'being placed on an equal footing with Christians, contrary to the laws of God and the natural distinction of race and religion'.[7] That was both a root cause of the Trek and an attitude that underlay much Afrikaner action for long after. While the British were, quite naturally as the colonial authority, blamed, it is highly likely that any reasonably liberal administration, including the Batavians, would have enforced similar rules, and received similar reproaches from the intensely conservative frontiersmen.

Their insistence on the essential inequality of black and white was however accompanied by a strong sense of justice; the Boers were much concerned with fairness. Paulus Zietsman, a Natalian burgher, exemplified both these attitudes when he wrote to Andries Pretorius accusing him of flogging Zietsman's blacks: 'Do you think it would be possible for me to have my subordinate creatures . . . punished and chastised without the least semblance of a trial, and not to defend their rights?' But they were still 'subordinate creatures' and not men, and as Landdrost Stockenström – himself, as he pointed out, a frontier farmer – made clear, this attitude could never be acceptable. He wrote to one N.T. van der Walt, who had complained of the difficulty of making Bushmen work for him: 'Let me tell you this – and you may rely upon it, my dear friend – we will never again see the day when under British rule different degrees of rights and privileges will exist for different classes of His Majesty's subjects.'[8]

More mundane than such great issues of human rights is the sheer incompetence of the British administration in that most important of all areas, land tenure. Charles D'Escury's fourteen-year term as Inspector of Lands had been disastrous. Many of those conscientious applicants who had applied for registration of their holdings and paid deposits had to wait for years before receiving their deeds. Papers could be lost in the muddle of the government offices; one application made in 1817 was still being vainly searched for in 1850. Naturally enough, farmers did not bother to apply: 'Every proprietor claims his ancient boundaries, keeps his money in his pocket, and possesses the government ground in the same manner as if he had a title deed.'

When Charles Michell was appointed as Surveyor General in 1828 his conscientious efforts to reduce the backlog were thwarted by the lack of competent surveyors. In D'Escury's fourteen years just over five million acres were granted; Michell increased this to over a million a year by 1835, but these were concentrated in accessible areas near the Cape. Between 1828 and 1834 inhabitants of all the frontier districts (Colesberg, Cradock, Somerset, Graaff-Reinet and Albany), an area approaching the size of England, received titles to only 1,432,000 acres; in Graaff-Reinet, in the whole of that period, one single title had been formalized. By contrast, in the already well-settled restricted regions near the Cape over two million acres were allocated in the same period. After 1835 performance improved, nearly a million acres a year being allocated in Graaff-Reinet, but that was too late for the disillusioned *voortrekkers*.[9]

Insult was added to injury by crass British politicians who attempted to insist on discrimination against Dutch settlers. As early as 1820 the Colonial Secretary Lord Bathurst had decided that farms 'on the frontiers of Caffreland' should be worked only by free labourers; since slaves were owned only by Dutch farmers, this was equivalent to banning them from the new district of Albany. Such an offensive instruction was quietly ignored at the Cape until in 1826 Bathurst put his foot down and insisted on his edict being enforced within thirty miles of the colonial border. Since no survey of the border area had been made, this resulted in an undefined area being effectively prohibited to official settlement; of which opportunity unofficial squatters made speedy use.

Bathurst's successor Lord Goderich (later Lord Ripon), an amiable ditherer known as 'Goody' Goderich, went further, and in May 1831 announced that he would decidedly object to allowing the 'Boors' of the colony any of the lands in territory 'ceded' in 1819, which 'should be granted to Englishmen and to Hottentots only'. Lord Goderich's orthography illustrated an inbuilt British prejudice. A '*boer*' in Dutch is merely a farmer, a countryman (although it, like the French '*paysan*' has acquired pejorative overtones in Holland, but not in South Africa). In English, 'boor' had long been used as a synonym for 'churl', or even 'lout', a rough, uncultivated and coarse fellow. It was invitingly convenient to anyone disapproving of the South African Dutch to dismiss them as *boers*, or boors, an example of giving a dog a bad name and hanging it. Isie Smuts, who can be taken as an authority on the subject, explained that 'Boers' were properly-speaking inhabitants of the Dutch republics; colonial Dutch were 'boers'; but for convenience 'Boer' will do very well as a synonym for the emigrant farmers.[10] Goderich's policy, like his spelling, indicated an alarming ignorance of South Africa, since only during the liberal British regime there had any Hottentots been granted land outside mission stations – and then only half a dozen families in all – while the Xhosa living in the area would have taken violent exception to Khoikhoi intruders. That despatch was succeeded by a flurry of typically confused directives, the purport of which seemed to be that all land must in future be auctioned, and hinting that no more titles should be given to Dutch farmers. Such a combination of anti-Boer prejudice and sheer incompetence must have been a powerful spur to emigration, and future events indicated that the main interest, amounting to an obsession, of the trekkers was the acquisition of unlimited land. A necessary corollary of this was that the emigrants must be able to deal with any other claimants to the land in their own decisive fashion.

In contast to the amiable, slightly eccentric Lowry Cole, Benjamin D'Urban, whose background was a good deal less brilliant (no aristocratic connections, and having served with the Portuguese, not the British, in the Peninsula, emerging only with the rank of colonel) had been appointed as Governor by Lord Stanley (later the fourteenth Earl of Derby), Goderich's successor at the Colonial Office. Stanley, a restless, brilliant, but essentially superficial politician, who soon abandoned the Whigs to join the Tory opposition, had given D'Urban instructions to agree a series of treaties with the chiefs beyond the colonial frontiers. It was a policy that had been initiated by Cole, and had worked in India, where indeed it continued to function until independence, but African chiefly powers were more limited than those of Indian princes or Pathan leaders, and India had no acquisitive, land-hungry settlers ever pressing for expansion. Before he had a chance to develop agreements D'Urban was overtaken by events.

However potent were the underlying discontents of Dutch colonists, affecting some one-third of the colony's farming population, a powerful immediate impetus was needed in order to spark off so great an emigration. This was given by the behaviour of the British authorities in 1835. A decade of comparative peace on the eastern frontier, with the Xhosa permitted to live in the territory taken over in 1819 and 1824, being shattered at Christmas 1834, when over ten thousand warriors dashed over the Keiskamma River, devastating everything before them. It was a disciplined dash: no woman, child or missionary was harmed by the terrifying warriors, seven feet tall in their white plumes, but men were cut to pieces, farms destroyed and cattle taken in their tens of thousands. For the first time the whole Xhosa nation, reunited in the face of white expansion, was, if not in arms, at least supporting the offensive.[11]

A damaging drought had, as usual in South Africa, been the culminating factor. While the Xhosa themselves had not been subjected to a Zulu invasion, they had to suffer the consequences as those who had survived the onslaught poured into their lands. The Mfengu refugees were accommodated with traditional hospitality: somewhat condescending and not unlimited, but nonetheless straining Xhosa resources. Added to the pressure, less demanding but insistent, of the white farmers, the Xhosa were also faced with what appeared to be a revival of the Khoikhoi.

Lowry Cole's term of office had seen a shift away from Somerset's suspicion of missionaries towards a realization that they had become the best sources of intelligence on the black communities, and might serve as useful agents of government policy. This position missionaries were often reluctant to accept, seeing their first responsibility as being towards the welfare of their flocks. It was however true that missionaries and British government officials shared many of the same values, which might be summed up as a belief that the imposition of English Protestant ideals and standards was in the best interests of all the inhabitants of southern Africa. Such convictions were shared only in part by the colonists, much more concerned with the problems of survival in a challenging country on the fringe of enormous black populations. Under such conditions the missionaries continued often to be opposed by both English and Dutch settlers, despised as negrophilists, or *kaffirboeties*.

One important Lowry Cole initiative was the foundation of the Kat River Settlement; more accurately, although given the Governor's blessing, the scheme was originated by Andries Stockenström. Recognizing that the Khoikhoi were no longer free and distinctive people, but had become dependent on white employment, or had formed part of the developing 'Griqua' communities, Stockenström believed that 'some small portion of their native country' should be preserved for them, and selected for this

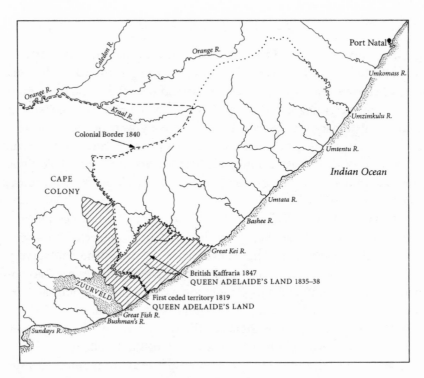

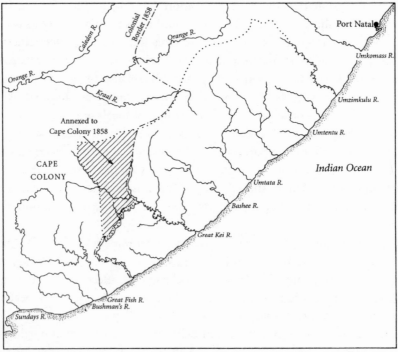

MAP 6   *Xhosa land losses*

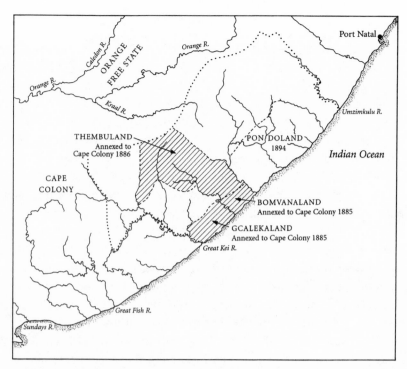

Orange R.
Caledon R.
ORANGE FREE STATE
Orange R.
Orange R.
Kraal R.
Umzimkulu R.
Port Natal

THEMBULAND
Annexed to
Cape Colony 1886

PON DOLAND
1894

Indian Ocean

CAPE COLONY

BOMVANALAND
Annexed to Cape Colony 1885

GCALEKALAND
Annexed to Cape Colony 1885

Great Kei R.

Great Fish R.

Sundays R.

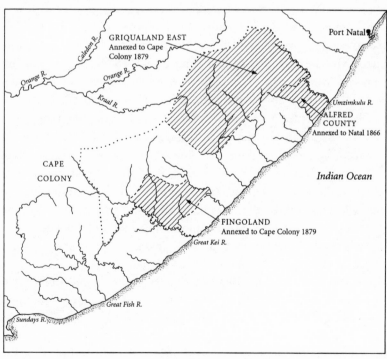

Caledon R.
GRIQUALAND EAST
Annexed to Cape Colony 1879
Port Natal

Orange R.
Orange R.
Kraal R.
Umzimkulu R.

ALFRED COUNTY
Annexed to Natal 1866

CAPE COLONY

Indian Ocean

FINGOLAND
Annexed to Cape Colony 1879

Great Kei R.

Great Fish R.

Sundays R.

purpose the pleasant region of the upper Kat River, a tributary of the Fish. Working under strict conditions, the new settlers rapidly developed a thriving community, with remarkable social and educational standards (girls as well as boys could learn Greek), and within five years seven hundred children were at the school. Without a colonial magistrate, the descendants of the Khoikhoi managed their affairs themselves, to general satisfaction.[12] To the British authorities it seemed that the Kat River Settlement might become a model for the future, but neither the Xhosa, in whose territory it had been placed, nor the white settlers, whose reliance on their own innate superiority was strengthened by nervous apprehensions, were equally enthusiastic.

Since 1819 there had been constant arguments, raids and brawls between Xhosa and whites in the ceded territories, where only sporadic control was ever exercised by the colonial authorities. Policies were constantly altered in response to events, as personalities at the Cape changed (there were five Governors, substantive or acting, between 1827 and 1834, all with different views on how to handle the Kaffirs). By 1830 the old rivals Ndlambe and Ngqika were dead, and a new leader had emerged, Ngqika's able son Macoma, perhaps the most talented soldier in nineteenth-century Africa.

Both Macoma and Sir Benjamin D'Urban were obliged by their own people to seek a permanent definition of frontier relations. The western Rharhabe Xhosa, freed from the old enmity between Ngqika and Ndlambe, were pressed into unity by the twin forces of colonial expansion and *mfecane* refugees. Although many of the 1820 settlers had moved off to the Cape, those who had settled were well established and lusting after more land. Grahamstown, with a population of three thousand, was the base of such exponents of aggression as Robert Godlonton, editor of the *Graham's Town Journal*, 'waiting for an opportunity to excite a quarrel that might furnish a pretext to the government to drive them [the Xhosa] from their lands . . . In such a colony there are numbers of toadeaters, civil servants who want estates.' Commandant Henry Somerset, a vain and amiable man, far from any firm authority in distant Cape Town, blew hot and cold in his treatment of the Xhosa, at one time allowing parties to resettle, and then, as Thomas Pringle had described, 'blundering about and attacking one peaceable party of Caffres after another'. Harry Smith was even less complimentary: 'Somerset's imbecility in war is equal to his vacillation and love of intrigue in peace.'[13]

D'Urban had been charged by Lord Stanley to do justice both to colonists and Xhosa; an impossible task. On his arrival at the Cape in 1834 the new Governor sought Dr Philip's advice, which when tendered was somewhat surprising. After another visit to the Xhosa, Philip, usually a staunch defender of native freedoms, recommended not treaties but annexation and the imposition of civilized rule; but before any action could be taken, Macoma struck. Some chiefs, who had an accurate idea of the likely outcome of such action, were not enthusiastic. Both Hintsa and Macoma's mother advised against war, and many leaders refused to take part, but popular feeling was too strong, and on 21 December 1834 Macoma's warriors invaded the colony on a broad front.[14]

As in 1824, terrified farming families fled to the safety of Grahamstown, while a scratch force was quickly assembled to confront the Xhosa, organized by Colonel Harry Smith, a picturesque, hard-swearing, opinionated and gifted fighting veteran of the Peninsular War.[15] It consisted of a few hundred regulars, reinforced by burgher commandos and Khoikhoi, riding as the Cape Mounted Rifles, the successors of the Corps of Pandours. The subsequent war was bloody and unpleasant, often fought with bayonet and assegai in the hilly bush of the Amatola hills, with the Khoikhoi 'Totties' in the thick of it. It took Smith's Spanish 'guerrilla rabidity', and all of four months, to push through beyond the Kei to the 'great place' of the paramount chief, Hintsa. For the first time the eastern, Gcaleka, Xhosa were brought face to face with the Imperial power.

The peace conference held in May 1835 was stage-managed by Colonel Smith, who had an impresario's eye for such events, and led to the unhappy Hintsa, who had taken no active part in the war, and whose people had lived in peace on their lands for a century, being forced to agree impossibly stringent conditions. The negotiations were complicated by the arrival of nearly twenty thousand Fingoes, who saw the opportunity to escape from their dependence on the Xhosa and claimed to risk being slaughtered by them in punishment for their disobedience. D'Urban agreed that they would be allowed to move, cattle and all, into the Cape Colony, a massive population transfer which was to have far-reaching results.

Lasting agreement, even had D'Urban and Smith been less headstrong, was hampered by the old white misunderstanding of a Xhosa chief's powers. Unlike Zulu kings, Hintsa could not impose his will on other chiefs: his was a pre-eminent, but not an authoritative rule. Faced with a demand for reparations so extravagant – fifty thousand cattle and ten thousand horses – as to be impossible, Hintsa agreed to everything, and attempted to escape.

In the course of this he was brutally killed by young George Southey, a local volunteer, and his body mutilated. For the Xhosa people this was an incredible insult, never forgotten, and much dwelt upon in later years. Sir Charles Bunbury, a perceptive, scholarly young liberal visitor, believed the Xhosa 'have been beaten just enough to increase their caution, to improve their knowledge of war, and to teach them safer and more efficacious ways of attacking us'.[16] He was proved absolutely right.

As D'Urban foretold, there was much indignation in England at this unnecessary war, but before any reaction could come from home, the Governor made matters worse by taking it upon himself to annex all the land up to the Kei as Queen Adelaide's Land (named after King William IV's wife). The chiefs, settled on defined reserves, would rule under supervision, reduced to 'the most wholesome position of subordinate magistrates (or field-cornets) acting under prescribed rulers and limits' – and under the sagacious direction of their new paramount chief, Colonel Harry Smith. Surprisingly enough, it nearly worked. Hintsa's son Sarili (Sarhili, Kreli) succeeded to his father's rule, and even Macoma accepted British authority.

A more formidable enemy

Sir Benjamin had to face a more formidable enemy than the Xhosa nation in arms; the British Colonial Office was roused against him.

Seldom has one small group exercised more power than did the score or so of civil servants, operating from a single house in Whitehall, who comprised the nineteenth-century Colonial Office. The Indian Empire was the responsibility of another department, the Board of Control, but the Secretary for War and the Colonies had the task of administering the mixed collection of colonies that spread from Van Diemen's Land to Canada. Some had been Imperial possessions for many years – Newfoundland and Jamaica from the sixteenth and seventeenth centuries – but many were recent acquisitions. Ceylon, Guiana, Mauritius and the Cape were conquests; New South Wales, Van Diemen's Land, Canada and Nova Scotia, later to be joined by New Zealand and Victoria, were evolving as settlement colonies; and other small but sensitive spots such as Labuan, Prince Edward Island and Hong Kong all required attention.

In Parliament the post of Secretary of State, commonly known as the Colonial Secretary, frequently changed hands. Eighteen months was the average tenure between 1830 and 1845, and the single year of 1855 saw no fewer than five Colonial Secretaries hold office. They were often younger men on their way up (both Gladstone and Churchill served an apprenticeship in the Colonial Office), or politicians passed over for better things. When these sat in the House of Lords their junior Parliamentary Under-Secretaries in the Commons had much influence, but significantly greater power was held by the permanent career civil servants. They were a diversely talented group, which included poets, playwrights, scholars and an Oxford Professor of Political Economy, and in which the commanding figure since 1813 had been the devout and industrious James Stephen – who was also Virginia Woolf's grandfather. Stephen's earnest evangelical character determined much colonial policy during his twenty-five years of office as legal counsel and Permanent Under-Secretary.[17]

British officials and politicians had learned the lessons of two wars with the United States. The old restrictive commercial policies were dismantled and the civil rights of colonists acknowledged; or acknowledged insofar as they did not conflict with values cherished by British public opinion. Slavery had been abolished by the pressure of such opinion, and clashes between colonists' insistence on independence and Colonial Office principles, usually over the exploitation of the native population, were to be a constant factor in South African politics.

Many commentators assume that 'imperialism' 'colonialism' and capitalism were actual malign forces combined to exploit other peoples all over the world. As far as Britain, prior to about 1880, is concerned, this is a wildly distorted picture. Those in power, politicians and civil servants, had a lively distrust for all forms of business – 'a set of popinjays ... worthy cheesemongers and paltry shabroons' were some of the epithets applied to those most distinguished of tradespeople, the directors of the Honorable East India Company. What must be ensured, it was generally agreed, was the free passage of goods, capital and services throughout the world, by which, it was considered, everyone must benefit. Of such sums only a small proportion, some 15 per cent, was directed to British colonies, while by contrast nearly two thirds went to Europe and the Americas.[18]

Public expenditure on protecting these investments was both low and static; severely restricted budgets absorbed only between 5 and 6 per cent of the national income between 1860 and 1900, of which modest sum army and navy costs remained between a third and a half until the re-armament moves after 1885. A low level of interest in colonial matters was reflected in the sparse attendance, often criticized, at House of Commons colonial debates. Much more important were foreign relations, and the avoidance of any large-scale conflict for which Britain, with a small standing army, was always unprepared, together with such fascinating questions as the admission of Jews and atheists to the House of Commons, the insidious advance of the Roman Church, and the perennially argumentative Irish, who, with one fifth of the total of House of Commons seats, were able to make and break governments.

Colonies were, and remained until the closing years of the nineteenth century, something to be avoided as productive only of expenditure and embarrassment. And the most difficult problems were often encountered in South Africa. It is worth noting, too, that the Colonial Office was usually highly critical of the other two departments of state responsible for external affairs, the Foreign Office and the India Office. But the main antagonists of the worried men in Whitehall were always the colonists themselves.

D'Urban excited Colonial Office wrath by his extravagant use of language as well as his actions. Having previously described the Xhosa as 'irreclaimable savages', he announced, in May 1835, his policy of 'exterminating' them. The term was meant to be taken in its classic, and then current, meaning of 'to thrust beyond the boundaries', rather than 'to extirpate', but Bunbury quoted an anonymous British officer who pronounced 'the imperious necessity, dictated alike by reason, justice and humanity, of exterminating, from off the face of the earth, a race of monsters'. Both D'Urban's language and his policies came under attack in London, where Lord Stanley had been succeeded as Colonial Secretary by Charles Grant, Lord Glenelg, irritatingly serious and devout, and a close friend of James Stephen. Glenelg was influenced by Thomas Fowell Buxton, the Parliamentary leader of the anti-slavery campaign, something of a fanatic in the good cause of human rights, and in close touch with Dr Philip. Politicians and civil servants were therefore at one in denouncing D'Urban, whose treatment of the Xhosa was pronounced 'equal in horror, to the French revolutionary "Reign of Terror"'.

Bolstered by the deliberations of a House of Commons Committee of Enquiry into the relations of Europeans with 'Aborigines' throughout the Empire, Lord Glenelg drafted a majestic despatch on this 'most foolish and wicked business'. 'The Caffres,' the Colonial Secretary considered, 'had ample justification for the war,' since they had only 'endeavoured justly, though impatiently, to avenge a series of encroachments'.[19] D'Urban had, the Colonial Secretary continued, totally failed to understand British policy, as shown in his claim that annexation was in some way a compensation for the expenses involved: 'to the assumption ... that an enlargement of the British dominion in Southern Africa is a national advantage, I find myself unable to assent.' Expansionism was morally wrong; and expensive to boot.

Inexplicably, D'Urban neglected to offer any defence of his actions, which had been enthusiastically supported by most colonists, until it was too late. James Read, with his talented son, also named James, and Jan Tshatsu, who had met Somerset in April 1817, visited London, where they made a great impression on the public at large as well as the House of Commons, reinforcing the official view that the rights of blacks to their historic lands was 'the only policy which it becomes this country to observe'. Accordingly Andries Stockenström, staunch advocate of black rights, who had advocated not only the abandonment of Queen Adelaide's Land but the ceded territories as well, relying instead on enforceable treaties with the Xhosa chiefs, was despatched as Lieutenant Governor of the eastern part of the colony, with his headquarters at Grahamstown.

The news of Stockenström's appointment, recognized as a complete check to the colonists' ambitions and the equivalent of a call for D'Urban's resignation, was received with consternation. The easterners had indeed agitated for some form of separate recognition, but not under Stockenström, whom they regarded as irrevocably biased in favour of the blacks. Even the Cape Towners were discontented, and raised money to publish a collection of documents which would put the settlers' case; this eventually became the influential 'Record' of Donald Moodie. But London was implacable, and in October 1836 Queen Adelaide's Land's short existence was terminated, and the territory restored to the Xhosa. Treaties were negotiated, and government agents appointed to ensure that any difficulties that might arise could be settled on the spot. It was a policy that might perhaps have worked had the British government been prepared to select and pay enough competent agents, and to respond to their reports, but the frontier was a long way from London and its well-intentioned but parsimonious administrators.

One prominent frontiersman made his objections clear to Stockenström in person. Pieter (Piet) Retief, an able and well-educated man who wrote in English as well as Dutch, had been appointed field-commandant, the senior burgher post, after a chequered career in which he had experienced a number of disappointments.[20] Failing to obtain any reassurances from Stockenström, he came to the reasonable conclusion that the British authorities could not be relied upon to commit themselves to a clear and sustainable frontier policy which might offer the prospect of stability. The only solution was to move on, and to carve out a dominion where the interests of the white farmers would be paramount.

Piet Retief openly published his reasons for trekking in a 'Manifesto' of February 1837: the 'turbulent and dishonest conduct' of wandering Khoikhoi and Xhosa; the financial losses suffered by the abolition of slavery; Xhosa incursions and 'the unjustifiable odium which has been cast upon us by interested and dishonest persons, under the cloak of religion, whose testimony is believed in England'. He solemnly declared: 'we quit this colony with a desire to lead a more quiet life . . . We will not molest any people, or deprive them of the smallest property; but if attacked, we shall consider ourselves fully justified in defending our persons and effects, to the utmost of our ability, against every enemy.'

Given 'the natural distinction of race and religion', this was an honest statement, and the *voortrekkers* – in Retief's party at any rate – adhered to his principles. But it begged a very important question. The lands outside the colonial boundaries were all under at least the loose control of black rulers. To some extent accommodation with these might be possible, and the trekkers prided themselves on reaching agreements with chiefs. But in spite of the ravages of the *mfecane*, there was simply not enough land to accommodate for long two cultures, both without any tradition of observing fixed boundaries and accustomed to expansive methods of farming. By this time every Boer saw the standard seven-thousand-acre farm as a birthright, and larger acreages were not uncommon. With vigorous Afrikaner fecundity – families of ten or more were the norm, with more than twenty not unknown, young men coming of age at sixteen and girls marrying as young as thirteen – wide tracts of land could be populated within two generations.[21] Nguni methods of exploiting arable land without manuring, moving on when their maize patches were exhausted, was similarly demanding; and both cultures enthusiastically stripped their environment clean of game. Fifty years of war had proved the impracticability of expansion into Xhosa territory across the Fish River, but attractive alternatives existed.

There was no question in the emigrants' minds that the land was waiting to be claimed, both to the north of the colonial boundary and further east beyond the Xhosa lands. A number of expeditions, '*kommissie-treks*', 'patrollies' and plain hunting trips had penetrated deeply into the interior. In 1828 the colonial boundary was officially extended to the Orange River, but enterprising farmers had already settled even beyond the new limits. The arid country near the western coast was attractive only to bands of Khoikhoi who sought freedom from colonial restrictions and could subsist on land where thirty acres were needed to support a single beast. Dutch trekkers preferred the country three hundred miles or so inland, where higher rainfall resulted in better pasture and allowed arable farming, upstream of the confluence of the Orange and the Vaal. A number of families were settled there, theoretically illegally, but in practice paying their taxes to the colonial government and acknowledging the authority of Field-Cornet Michiel Oberholster. They were reasonable and tractable people, often taking pains to regularize their occupation by 'purchasing' their land from the putative owners, the Bushmen.

Tranquillity was less common further downstream, where extensive tracts had been claimed by the Bastaard captains, the Kok and Barends dynasties. Some of the earliest British missionaries had made for the north rather than the turbulent eastern frontier, and had persuaded the Bastaards to take the name of Griquas, assisting them to form reasonably stable communities. Speaking the *taal*, the slave language that became Afrikaans, organized with their own elected officers and observing colonial law, but too willing to part with their land to whites for a fraction of its value so that they might live in leisure with a supply of brandy and tobacco, these mixed-race people sometimes appeared a caricature of Boer society; but they were the equals of Boers in battle and the hunt, and their captains were capable of making as honest efforts to rule justly as were any Boer commandants.[22]

John Campbell of the London Missionary Society, who had provided a Griqua constitution, succeeded in having a convert, the lay preacher Andries Waterboer, appointed as Griqua chief in 1820 and recognized by the colonial authorities, leaving the Barends and Koks to set up their own communities. Yet others, less peaceable Bastaards, formed roving bands, the 'Bergenaars', who recognized no authority and raided indiscriminately, finding their easiest victims in the Sotho and Tswana communities, scattered by the *mfecane*. All the Griquas, legally and illegally, were eager traders, moving manufactured goods, especially arms and ammunition, to the black communities on the high veld. In this racial and sociological melting-pot the names given to the sections were flexible and approximate. Bergenaars and

Kora (Koranna), the other less settled bands, had Khoikhoi, Bastaard and even white members. Griqua statelets spread for three hundred miles along the Orange River, with their centre at the missionary stations of Philipolis and Griquatown, protected by treaty arrangements with the Cape government. Between them and the sea the Namaqua Khoikhoi chief Jager Afrikaner, the latest in succession, led a predatory group who raided indiscriminately on both sides of the river.

Emigrants intending to push on past the Griqua lands would move along a well-defined route from the colonial outpost of Colesberg, over the Orange and along the valley of the Caledon River, whence they might press on to the great open spaces of the high veld or turn south, back over the mountains, to the land of Natal, having safely avoided the Xhosa territory.

Natal seemed an attractive destination. In 1832 Dr Andrew Smith, a distinguished zoologist, first director of the Cape Museum, was commissioned to visit Shaka's successor Dingane (Dingaan).[23] The record of his journey from Grahamstown to Zululand was widely reported, and Smith's account of a wide area of almost deserted country, the profusion of rivers and the fine grass, aroused much interest at the Cape.

The camp at Thaba Nchu

The last outpost north of the Orange River on the emigrant route was at Thaba Nchu, beyond the Griqua communities, the site of a Methodist mission station and capital of Moroka, chief of the Rolong tribe of the Sotho. A few years previously Moroka had negotiated a treaty with the Sotho leader Moshoeshoe, whose mountain fastness of Thaba Bosigo gave him effective power in the region, by which Moroka's people were allotted an extensive tract of land. The treaty had been facilitated by the chiefs' missionary advisers, James Archbell for Moroka and Jean-Eugene Casalis and Thomas Arbousset for Moshoeshoe. Archbell, a worldly and persuasive Wesleyan, and Casalis, a pious, scholarly French Calvinist, were later both to be influential figures. Moshoeshoe, perhaps the most interesting and able black ruler of the nineteenth century, struggled to maintain his ascendancy and independence against all comers, being either a good friend or a redoubtable enemy.

On the northern edge of Moshoeshoe's impregnable massif the Tlokwe chief Sekonyela, son of the formidable warrior queen Mmanthatisi, led a brigand-like existence, but was usually wary enough to avoid attacking anyone in a position to retaliate, and left the trekkers undisturbed. The first parties to take to the road in 1835 were those of 'Lang Hans' van Rensburg and Louis Tregardt (or Trichardt). They were an ill-matched expedition, Tregardt a prosperous farmer, with well over a thousand cattle and ten slaves, his family accustomed to life's comforts, and van Rensburg an illiterate frontiersman, bent on hunting rather than settling. In what was to become a customary sequence, the leaders quarrelled, and the parties split. Van Rensburg's turned south for the sea to dispose of its loads of ivory, and was wiped out by a Zulu force, apart from two children who sheltered under a warrior's shield. Tregardt, who had previously attempted to settle in Hintsa's land – with, it should be said, the chief's consent – felt himself persecuted by the colonial authorities, and was anxious to get as far away from them as possible. His party did succeed in establishing a settlement near the modern town of Louis Trichardt in the far north of the present Transvaal, a thousand miles beyond the colonial boundary, but was soon discouraged by privation and ill-health, and moved off in turn for the coast. Still bickering among themselves, none of the men being trusted by Tregardt, the trek reached Lourenço Marques. Only twenty-eight from the original party of over a hundred survived, Tregardt and his family being among the dead, before being rescued by the British brig *Mazeppa* in July 1839.

A few months after Tregardt left, two other major parties trekked, led by Hendrik Potgieter and Gert Maritz. They were by no means a representative selection of Dutch African society. A substantial minority were slaves or Khoikhoi who had become, to varying degrees, integrated into the white community, usually in a subordinate position – although the first *voortrekker* official Secretary, Jan Bantjes, was of mixed blood. Their numbers contained none of the prosperous western Cape families who were making good under the British regime – no Truters, Cloetes, Brands, van Rynevelds or de Villiers; for that matter no professional men at all – no doctors, lawyers, surveyors, ministers or journalists. The Dutch Church was generally opposed to the Trek: Tobias Herold, minister of Stellenbosch, wrote a harsh denunciation. Apart from some agriculturalists and tradesmen, the trekkers were predominantly herdsmen, tough, self-reliant and quarrelsome, adept hunters and marksmen, fond of discussion and disputation. Their families could, if necessary – and it proved necessary – live in their wagons for years on end, cultivating a little ground when a long halt looked likely. Many had experience of commando service, and those who did not – among whom Gert Maritz, a wagon-builder who owned books, stood out – found themselves often in opposition to the military leaders.

Coming as they did from frontier districts, the emigrant farmers – the most favoured description – were accustomed to the simple life, far from centres of population, and dependent upon peddlers for any goods they could not provide themselves. Of these the most vital were coffee, sugar and ammunition – although Erasmus Smit bought three pairs of socks from a '*smous*', something of a reflection on his wife's ability to knit. Whatever her defects as a housewife, Susanna Smit proved one of the most influential of the trekkers, a formidable woman, although only one of many always ready to stiffen the fibres of male resistance.[24] Deprived of a roof over their heads and the comforts of a settled existence, and with none of the compensations their menfolk found in unlimited hunting, the women suffered most, but often held out longest. Fighting alongside their men, Boer wives, and even children such as Hendrina Botha, were to be acknowledged as powerful forces in Afrikaner society.

Most trekkers were active churchmen, and the absence of a Calvinist minister, to say nothing of official Church disapproval, was a severe trial. The quarterly celebration of communion, the *nagmaal*, had become a valued ritual, both religious and social, and depended on the presence of an ordained minister. A substantial minority of the trekkers, including such leaders as Hendrik Potgieter and Caspar Kruger (who was accompanied by his ten-year-old son Paul), were Doppers, fundamentalists who abominated hymn-singing, long coats and belts and regarded the orthodox Calvinists as dangerously permissive liberals. Families divided on the merits of the trek. Joshua Joubert left a missionary post to join Retief's party; his uncle, Commandant Gideon, was against the whole idea as morally dangerous (and with some reason).

Although resentful of condescending British attitudes and distrustful of government actions, the trekkers were not specifically anti-British, nor the British colonists unsympathetic to the trekkers. The highly-esteemed Thomas Philipps, who had protested to the Select Committee of the House of Commons against some of the accusations levelled against the colonists, formally presented a Bible and an address of sympathy to the Uys party as they passed through Grahamstown (an event recorded for posterity in the Voortrekker memorial frieze). In spite of theological differences many emigrants sat at the feet of the Wesleyan minister James Archbell, and when later the first *voortrekker* government attempted negotiations with the colonial authorities, they stated that all they wished for was 'the liberties of British subjects'.

Differences also existed on the best destination. Potgieter intended to make for the high veld, that vast area of grassland which stretches for six hundred miles north to the Zoutpansberg mountains, and had been, it seemed, depopulated and ruined by the *mfecane*. That had been Louis Tregardt's destination, and the fate of his party was not yet known when Potgieter crossed the Orange River in February 1836. Others decided to skirt the highest peaks of the Drakensberg before descending the escarpment into Natal.

The dictatorial and aggressive Hendrik Potgieter, with Sarel Cilliers, a younger, more conciliatory character who acted as deacon and as a spiritual leader of the trekkers, were the first to move north-east in search of Tregardt's trek into lands which had, only a few years previously, been conquered by Mzilikazi. Although Mzilikazi had previously shown himself ready to welcome individual whites, and had formed a friendship with the missionary Robert Moffat, who had helped the Ndebele chief send a mission to Cape Town, where it was well received, he was not about to tolerate such an unannounced invasion. Leaving most of his followers scattered around the Vaal River, Potgieter left for an exploration as far north as the Limpopo, searching for likely places of settlement, and meeting, in a journey of 1,500 miles, little opposition. During his absence the Ndebele attacked the camps on the Vaal, and wiped out several of them. The survivors were met by Potgieter at Vegkop, south of Heilbron, where he organized a defence. This was done by forming and reinforcing a circle with the wagons; not a new device – the '*wagenburg*' of the fifteenth-century Hussites is an earlier example – the laager remains extremely effective: British tanks still take the precaution of 'laagering up' at their halts. A fight followed in which the Ndebele, charging in the customary Zulu fashion, were shot down by the laagered trekkers; although outnumbered by over a hundred to one Potgieter lost only two men, but all the Boer cattle were carried off.

Making their way back south to Thaba Nchu, the surviving *voortrekkers* were relieved by Moroka, who provided cattle to replace those lost – a dignified chiefly gesture, which reflects Moroka's perception of the Boers as allies against their mutual enemy Mzilikazi. The trekkers' numbers had been increased by the arrival of the biggest party, some seven hundred strong, that of Gert Maritz, who speedily found himself at odds with Potgieter. Maritz was an educated man who had led a relatively sheltered life, never moving far from Graaff-Reinet, where he had carried out his duties as field-cornet conscientiously, 'cautioning Landdrost Andries Stockenström very seriously when stray horses belonging to the landdrost became a danger to young children in the streets of the town'.

At Thaba Nchu the emigrants endeavoured to agree a form of government. It was to be a *'Maatschappij'* (Afrikaans *'maatskappy'*, a society or company), and indeed the first constitution was not unlike that of a commercial company. No trekker had more than a superficial knowledge of constitutional theory or law, nor indeed was there any settled intention of founding an alternative state. The result was an *ad hoc* patchwork, with no clarification of individual responsibilities and a confusion of legislative, executive and judicial functions. The deficiencies of this, and of subsequent more formal trekker constitutions, were to be a source of many difficulties and an important cause of that great disaster, the Anglo–Boer war of 1899.[25] Every adult white Protestant male who cared to join the company was a member; laws were made and unmade by the assembled *volk* – not too difficult on trek, but impracticable when the voters were widely dispersed. An elected *volksraad* acted as interim executive and judiciary, combined with Maritz as both President and Landdrost. Potgieter, acknowledged to be the best fighting leader, was elected commandant general and chairman of the *krygsraad* (military council).

The agreement was short-lived. In January 1837 a joint Boer–Griqua–Rolong commando under Potgieter was successful in attacking Ndebele *kraals* and carrying off a great number of cattle, and as a result displacing those American missionaries who had just arrived hoping to convert the 'Inland Zoolahs'; but Potgieter and Maritz continued on poor terms. They disagreed about the distribution of the captured animals, and about the position of poor worried Smit, whom Maritz wanted to install as predikant, while Potgieter, much to Mrs Smit's disgust, supported Archbell, who, although no Calvinist, was at least properly ordained. To complicate matters, in April 1837 Piet Retief's party arrived at Thaba Nchu. Retief, older and a more emollient personality than Maritz, and certainly than Potgieter, was invited by Maritz to become 'Governor and Head Commandant' while Maritz remained civil head. Potgieter was not re-elected, and remained discontented on the sidelines while the trek moved slowly forwards. A general meeting in June confirmed Smit, ordained or not, as predikant, and agreed to nine articles of association. Within days these were questioned when another group led by Piet Uys, an affable Albany horse-breeder and racing man who had already made an exploratory visit to Natal, arrived. The newcomers would have nothing to do with any of Retief's or Maritz's regulations, which they believed would only reduce them 'to a state of slavery'. 'Men shouted and stormed and flourished their guns, Retiefs and Maritzes on one side, Potgieters and Uyses on the other,' while Sarel Cilliers contrived to divide Retief's followers by a furious quarrel with the unfortunate Smit.

Largely due to Retief's diplomacy, the parties patched up their differences well enough to permit a joint expedition in September to settle with Mzilikazi. After a battle that lasted nine days, inflicting thousands of Ndebele casualties, the commando returned with enormous booty (on the division of which the customary fierce dissension raged). By December the whole expedition, now two thousand strong, with Retief in the van, was ready to move off not for the dangerous north, but to the promised land of Natal.

The Republic of Natalia

The territory south of the Drakensberg that was to form the Boer Republic of Natalia consisted of the land between the mountains and the sea, well-watered and fertile, divided by a series of parallel rivers. The northernmost, the Black Mfolozi, was well inside what was recognized as Shaka's kingdom of Zululand, the boundary of which was customarily accepted as the Tukela (Tugela), seventy miles to the south. Shaka's bloodthirsty and arbitrary rule had finally driven his subjects to rebellion, and in 1828 the founder of the Zulu kingdom was murdered by his half-brother Dingane.

The new king shared many of Shaka's psychological abnormalities – he was sterile and quite probably impotent – but being grossly fat and slothful was less inclined to warlike activity, delegating much responsibility to his ministers. Even before Shaka's death the tradition of Zulu invincibility seemed to be wavering. The last *impis* despatched to punish Soshangane returned badly battered, Mzilikazi was pursued indecisively across the mountains, and a campaign against the unfortunate Hlubi displaced that people from their ancestral home, a persecution later completed by the British in what became known as the *'izwekufa'*, the destruction of the nation. While Shaka had maintained friendly relations with the few Europeans he encountered, a bold and successful raid on the Portuguese port of Lourenço Marques, in which the Governor was killed, may have served to give Dingane a false idea of European weakness.

Europeans had shown only sporadic interest in the region since it was first named Natal by Vasco da Gama on Christmas Day 1497. The VOC had noted the splendid natural harbour that later became Port Natal and then Durban, and attempted to purchase it from the local ruler, but its impossible access – the entrance channel could be as shallow as one foot – discouraged exploration. It was only in 1824 that British traders, led by a naval officer, Francis Farewell, established a post at the port, with Shaka's consent. The inevitable missionary followed, despatched by the Anglican Church Missionary Society. Francis Owen, a pleasant but unworldly Cambridge graduate ('truly well-informed, estimable ... who knows nothing of this world and is determined to have as little to do with it as possible' was the American missionary Daniel Lindley's very accurate description[26]), was a thoroughly unsuitable choice if any hopes of converting the formidable Dingane were cherished.

Hoping for British recognition, with a degree of protection and possible annexation to follow, the Port Natal community changed its name to Durban, after the Governor. Enthused by Dr Smith's report, an impressive number of Cape merchants supported them, petitioning King William 'to occupy Port Natal and the depopulated country in its vicinity'. The Colonial Office would have none of it, being 'persuaded of the inexpedience of engaging in any scheme of colonization or of acquiring any further territory in South Africa'. The 'too-extensive' colony of the Cape of Good Hope was trouble enough. The little settlement at Durban clung on precariously, dependent on Dingane's goodwill, which was growing more doubtful. Although he appreciated the opportunities for trade offered by the port, the Zulu king was beginning to resent the number of his people – more than two thousand of them – who had deserted his country to live with the traders.

Piet Uys, checking on Dr Smith's report two years later, agreed on the region's desirability. 'Allemagtig! I have never in my life seen such a fine place,' one of his companions had exclaimed. It seemed – quite erroneously – that the Zulu king might be ready to allow the trekkers, approaching from the north, to settle on his lands, as Shaka had encouraged the British traders from the Cape. In October 1837, therefore, Retief, with an advance party of six men, made his way through Natal to Port Natal, where he met with a friendly reception, before making for Dingane's capital. There the king seemed to be disposed to listen; he had heard of Potgieter's brisk treatment of Mzilikazi and appeared ready to accept the formidable Boers as allies, and to permit them to inhabit the land south of the Tukela River – Natal as distinct from Zululand, and the region which had been depopulated by Shaka's and Dingane's wars. A preliminary test of the newcomers' reliability being required, Retief was ordered to 'recover' a thousand head of Zulu cattle which, Dingane claimed, had been stolen by the disreputable Sikonyela.

On his way back over the Drakensberg Retief reported on his discussions with Dingane to the assembled trekkers – now over two thousand in the camp – but warned them not to venture too far from the mountains until he had secured a formal agreement from the Zulu king. Disregarding this, hundreds of emigrants poured over the border, looking for land and blatantly hunting over the Tukela River into the heart of Dingane's territory. When Retief returned in February 1838 to formalize, as he thought, the agreement with Dingane, accompanied not this time by six men but by a strong force of seventy horsemen – too many for an embassy and too few to overawe – no difficulties were made about signing the piece of paper he had brought with him. Dingane waited until the Boers were relaxed and unsuspicious before having them seized and killed, one by one, before the eyes of the horrified Francis Owen, who was himself unharmed.

Retief's faith in the written word, which he had shown in publishing his 'Manifesto', had been his undoing. He believed that having obtained Dingane's mark on a paper granting the Boers all the district between the Tukela and Mzimvubu Rivers, a considerable part of Zulu territory, all would be well. Such trust may have been optimistically *naïf*, but it was not quite without foundation, for Xhosa chiefs had previously shown themselves ready to cede territory over which they exercised some control in exchange for white support in their own quarrels, and both Dingane and Shaka himself had permitted the Europeans to settle at Port Natal, insisting in return that they help in the Zulu's wars. But once Dingane realized the scale of the Boer advance, supported as it was by a blatantly threatening show of strength from Retief, the European influx, previously a peripheral concern of the Zulu monarchy, assumed a new importance. Dingane changed the strategy of cooperation to one of annihilation.

Eleven days after Retief's massacre, on 17 February 1838, the Zulu fell on the unsuspecting trekkers camped in the foothills. More than five hundred, including 186 children, were massacred in the district thereafter known as

Weenen – 'weeping'. Attempting a clean sweep of the whites, a Zulu *impi* sacked Durban, slaughtering all those who had not been able to get away by sea. In Zulu terms this was probably the correct strategy. Only by making conquest too costly could the nation's independence be secured, but the trekkers had invested too much effort and lost too many lives to be repelled. Women and children had usually been spared in all African warfare (at least, that is, by black fighters), and this massacre shocked the whole white community.

Eventual retribution was drastic, but delayed. Once more the Boer leaders disagreed. Potgieter had enlisted the help of Piet Uys in his quarrel with Maritz, but the two, who together in April 1838 led the first punitive expedition against the Zulu, soon fell into disagreement. It was hardly surprising therefore that their force was defeated in a fight during which both Uys and his son were killed. Pursued by accusations of treachery, Potgieter took off for the high veld, where, having cleared the region of the Ndebele, he proposed to found his own state, in which he would tolerate no querulous opposition and reach agreements with the neighbouring black communities which would enable the Boers to live peaceably among them. Violence was never a preferred option, and Potgieter was ready to acknowledge existing rights; as he once told Adam Kok, 'we desire to be regarded as neither more nor less than your fellow emigrants.'[27]

Back at the Cape, D'Urban had been replaced in January 1838 by General Sir George Napier, a member of that extraordinary Scottish family which invented modern mathematics and produced batches of generals and statesmen. Napiers tended to eccentricity, and Sir George was no exception.[28] A humane and decent man, he was prepared to be conciliatory but still insisted that the emigrants must return to the colony they had left. In October Gideon Joubert was sent to recover those slaves who had left with the trekkers and who would now be due for emancipation. He found only forty of 140 choosing to leave their masters – something of a testimony to the much-criticized Boers. Joubert was followed in December by Major Charters, with a small force and instructions to offer protection to those British who remained in the region, to persuade the trekkers to return to the colony, and to render any relief that might be needed. He found very few who were willing to go back even after the dangers and hardships they had experienced; a 'spirit of dislike to the English way was remarkably dominant among the women', who 'rejected with scorn the idea of returning to the Colony. If any of the men began to droop or lose courage, they urged them on to fresh exertions, and kept alive the spirit of resistance within them.' Charters was a few days too late to be of much use, for the emigrants had been reinforced by the arrival of a new leader, Andries Pretorius, with sixty men and a field-gun.

A substantial Graaff-Reinet farmer, Pretorius was as opinionated as any *voortrekker* leader, self-confident, unwilling to accept orders, and capable of wilful pettiness. But he was immediately effective, and was given undivided authority, which he used vigorously. Within three weeks the new Commandant had assembled a new force – the Wen Kommando of 470 men and two cannon – invaded Zululand and met Dingane's army in the battle of Blood River. The Boers laagered, and in the subsequent fight on 16 December 1838, some three thousand Zulu, charging regardless of danger – or of sense – were killed, at the cost of only three Boers wounded.

It was a decisive enough victory, and one which secured relative peace for the next forty years, but it did not gain Natal for the Afrikaners: six years later many of them found themselves trekking back over the Drakensberg. But the battle, and more particularly the ceremony that took place before it, assumed a central position in Afrikaner mythology. One week before the fight, on 9 December, the commando vowed, if victory were granted, to build a church and to commemorate the event in perpetuity. The church was indeed later built in Pietermaritzburg, but was soon abandoned for such mundane purposes as bottling mineral water, and the commemoration forgotten, until the myth-construction aimed at defining an Afrikaner national identity rescued the idea, and elevated it to the most important date of the state calendar, Dingane's Day.[29]

Grudgingly enough, being convinced that the British had no business in the land he had conquered, Pretorius accepted the assistance of Captain Jervis, Charters' successor, in arranging a treaty with Dingane. One of the more interesting documents of the period is a sketch by an officer of the British force, J.A. Harding, showing Pretorius haranguing the Zulu envoys: the Boer leader, in plumed hat and sash, waves a sabre, utterly unlike the dour figure of official portraits; a Khoikhoi warrior in the forefront of the attentive trekkers; the gnome-like Jan Bantjes acting as Secretary and a gloomy Mevrouw Pretorius sitting at the Commandant's right hand, make this a unique picture.

It was a perilous business being an ambassador to Pretorius, since he shot two of Dingane's representatives out of hand. Neither he nor Dingane intended the treaty to be permanent, and the Boers soon enlisted the help of Mpande, Dingane's half-brother. When the Swedish naturalist Johan Wahlberg met Mpande in November 1839 the Zulu leader told him that 'it was high time he had Dingane killed'.[30] Within a few weeks, with the assistance of the Boers, this was done. Pretorius' price for cooperation was the extortion of enormous reparations of forty thousand cattle, with nearly a thousand children to be 'apprenticed' to Boer families; the by now usual quarrels over the division of loot followed. In return Pretorius solemnly inducted Mpande as king, and was himself acknowledged as paramount chief of the Zulu people.

Being thus convinced of their legal rights, and in undisputed *de facto* possession of all the territory claimed by Retief, together with a substantial slice of Zululand north of the Tukela, the Republic of Natalia was now in a position to negotiate with the British authorities. Pretorius wrote accordingly – less elegantly than had Retief – sending a copy of the treaty found on Retief's body, in order to prove 'that we did not go out with aggressive purpose, but had sworn by the living God to do no harm to the cruel Dingane', and that 'as we left our motherland behind with concern and sorrow, so we hope now not to be troubled nor opposed by anyone'.[31] It was by no means impossible that this hope might be realized.

Even after their traumatic experiences the Natalians found unity difficult. Pretorius was the obvious choice as leader, but many detested the idea of any formal command. This faction was led by Gert Maritz until his death in September 1838, thereafter by his brother Stephanus and Jacobus (Kootjie) Burger. The republic began its life with a constitution drafted by Jacobus Boshof, a young clerk on leave from Graaff-Reinet. Since the trekkers were unlikely ever to agree on a President, no successor to Retief was ever named, the new state remaining without a head, other than Commandant General Pretorius, who was in charge only of military affairs. Legislative and judicial powers were entrusted to a twenty-four-member Volksraad, meeting regularly in the new village of Pietermaritzburg. Since strictly speaking there was no one able to take any decisions when the Volksraad was not sitting – and these busy farmers met only once a quarter – things arranged themselves locally. The familiar Company system of Landdrost and Heemraden was recreated, along with an Orphan Chamber and Marriage Commissioner. When a difficult task emerged Pretorius was summoned, but he was not entrusted with any permanent office or even allowed membership of the Volksraad, which ensured permanent antagonism between the Commandant General and that body.

Maritz and Retief had been the best-informed of the migrants, and there were few if any others with a talent for administration. Dogged and courageous folk, they were unhappily conscious of their need for help. Erasmus Smit had done his faithful best to minister to their needs, and with his redoubtable wife had taught their children, but he was '*oud en zwak*' (old and weak). By a fortunate chance, the right man was on the spot.

As a body they are ignorant and wicked

Borne on the same wave of missionary enthusiasm that initiated the London and Glasgow Societies, the American Board of Commissioners for Foreign Missions comprised both Presbyterians and Congregationalists.[32] Driven from their original station with Mzilikazi's people after the Boer attacks in 1837, the Americans had switched their attention to the 'Maritime Zoolahs', where their representative was Daniel Lindley. Lindley had qualified as a Presbyterian minister, with all the intellectual stringency that ordination required, but also with an upbringing in the American West, which had conferred the much more important advantages of being a dead shot and a fearless horseman, qualities which won him instant acceptance among the Boers of Natal.

He arrived there in July 1837, in time to meet Piet Retief, 'a worthy man', and to translate his letter to Dingane. It soon became clear to him that the Boers needed missionaries quite as much as the Zulu: 'As a body they are ignorant and wicked. Without schools, without teachers, without ministers – what will become of them?' George Champion, another American missionary, agreed: when they had finished being 'scourges of the natives ... perhaps they will be mutual scourges of each other'.[33]

British missionaries would almost certainly have been rejected by the trekkers, but they showed every sign of friendship towards Lindley. In January 1841, when things had settled down after the defeat of Dingane, the new Natalian Volksraad formally invited Lindley to become their minister. For the brief period of the republic's existence, Lindley was the calm centre of its turbulent affairs, discussing its constitution with Boshof, attempting to restrain aggressive commandos and to dissuade the 'credulous and the wild untameable young Boers'. No sign of the Afrikaners' reputed hostility towards missionaries appeared in their relations with Lindley, or with any of the other American missionaries travelling all over Natal. Susanna Smit objected that Lindley 'openly in the name of the Reformed Church preached the doctrines of Wesley', but the American baptized and confirmed thousands of Boers, including Paul Kruger, who was to become the most famous Afrikaner of his time, President of the South African Republic, the Transvaal, and staunch opponent of imperialism.

Another difficulty arose about the boundaries of the new republic. The settlers in Natal considered that they represented all the emigrant farmers outside the Cape Colony, which included those who had followed Potgieter to the north; but most of those northerners did not share that opinion. Potgieter claimed Winburg, an area larger than Holland 'bought' for forty-nine cows, as his personal fief; and by right of conquest from Mzilikazi a much more extensive but undefined region north of the Vaal.

Dingane's original concession, which he had no intention of keeping, had been for the lands south of the Tukela. His successor Mpande, a more emollient character, showed willingness to let the farmers settle well beyond that line as part of the price of his quiet thirty-year reign, during which time his people regained some of the prosperity lost to the Boers in the 'reparations'; an era of comparative tranquillity constituting something of a triumph in those disturbed times.

Compared to Mpande's long reign, the Republic of Natalia had only an ephemeral existence. Although the handful of British at Port Natal had fled before Dingane's *impis* they returned within three years. In the meantime the Volksraad attempted, within the self-imposed limits of their unworkable arrangements, to govern, and in doing so developed themes which underlay subsequent Afrikaner constitutions. Their main problems, and these were to prove permanent, were those of land and labour. It should have been possible in so extensive and fertile a territory to settle the small number of *voortrekkers* several times over, but the wasteful method of land grants and the primitive agricultural methods of Company days militated against this. In Natalia waste was allied with plain greed. Each man was entitled to two standard farms, amounting to some fourteen thousand acres; seven such farms would cover the English county of Rutlandshire. As every boy of fifteen was to be given his own farm, it would not take many families to absorb the area of Rhode Island. Men pressed claims for extra land according to their own estimation of their merits. In the absence of any executive authority, free grants were indiscriminately showered on those with most influence. Commandant Gert Rudolph, who succeeded Pretorius, contrived to be allocated a quarter of a million acres. Such huge tracts could not be, and were not, ever occupied, let alone cultivated.

Still bruised by the horrible experience of Weenen, the Boers remained nervous of so many black neighbours – a population soon increased tenfold from its original ten thousand – but still needed their labour, it being understood that white men must not demean themselves by working for wages. Accordingly the Volksraad legislated for compulsory black labour – a maximum of five allotted to each farm, all to carry passes, those without to be sent off to black reserves. This policy proved both ineffective and unnecessary; ineffective because no police existed to enforce it, and unnecessary because the communities driven south by Dingane had settled down quietly enough. The question remaining was whether any action might be expected from the emigrant farmers' previous rulers, the Cape Town government.

It soon became evident that the British were not content to leave the new republic to its own devices. The Trek had caused wrath and embarrassment. Believing none of the emigrants' protestations, the pious Lord Glenelg wrote angrily to Governor Napier: 'The same motives have, in all ages, compelled the strong to encroach on the weak, and the powerful and unprincipled to wrest by force or fraud, from the comparatively feeble and defenceless, wealth or property or dominion, richer pastures, more numerous herds, and a wider range of territory – opportunities for uncontrolled self-indulgence and freedom from the restraints of law and settled society.'[34]

More practically, General Napier was concerned that thousands of British subjects, who had paid taxes and formed the mainstay of the colony's defence, had taken themselves off. Those English settlers who lived near the eastern border were sympathetic: 'the circumstances of the frontier farmers require the most attentive and humane consideration on the part of the government; hitherto they have been treated without the slightest regard to their personal feelings or their prejudices', wrote the *Graham's Town Journal* in July 1836. Further off, opinion was more cynical: 'to obtain land for nothing, and to escape taxation' were the trekkers' motives, the Cape Town *Commercial Advertiser* claimed in September. Support for the *voortrekkers* was offered by the *Zuid-Afrikaan*, edited by the learned Christoffel Brand, who appealed to the example of Cyrus and the Marsigetae, which must have been a comfort to the farmers.

Official opinion was convinced that footloose Boers, whatever Pretorius and Retief might claim, would come into violent conflict with the blacks, a cause for concern on several grounds. Although they might claim to be independent the Boers were still, in British eyes, British subjects. Their tendency to bully and enslave natives was, as missionaries insisted, abundantly proved. Not only the missionaries, but neutral observers like Johan Wahlberg described such incidents as Louwrens du Plessis flogging a Khoikhoi to death, Potgieter sjamboking a Khoikhoi girl, and the return of a plundering expedition where 'not so many Kaffers (about 130) were killed, but on the other hand [others] were beaten with the sjambok in the most frightful manner. On one occasion a whole party of them; who from terror and pain could not keep back their excrements, so that the ground all round the place where this devilish deed was committed was covered with them.'[35]

Apart from being morally objectionable, such conduct would lead to wars, which, if they demanded intervention, would entail expense. Colonial Office sympathy for the Boers was therefore limited, and Lord Glenelg was not surprised at the news of Retief's death: 'Much as I lament the fate of these misguided men, it was not to be expected that the Natives of the countries adjacent to the Colony would suffer themselves to be overrun by those invaders.' Stockenström advocated firm action 'against those of His Majesty's subjects who had exterminated whole tribes of blacks'.[36]

The ticklish question then arose as to how far British jurisdiction should extend into the still unexplored interior of the continent. Governor Napier realized the absurdity of claiming that the emigrants remained British subjects, while making no attempt to exercise any control. Either they should be recognized as independent, or annexed. He believed annexation to be the only answer, affirming as early as October 1838 that 'the British nation will never consent either to allow the emigrants to perish from want or the sword, or to permit them to attack and slaughter the natives of the countries they invaded.'[37] Which was, in a nutshell, the British view: the trekkers were invading countries that rightly belonged to the blacks, and the slaughter on both sides was taking place even as Napier wrote. While the battle at Blood River might be admitted as no more than a legitimate punishment for the massacres at Weenen, it was the sanguinary expulsion of Mzilikazi, four hundred miles north across the Vaal, that had angered the Colonial Office. The legal position was temporarily defined by extending British jurisdiction to twenty-five degrees south latitude, some fifty miles north of Pretoria. Since this left an area of half a million square miles –

the size of northern Europe from the Atlantic to the Polish border – to be policed by two thousand troops, any jurisdiction was theoretical, to say the least.

It was also a cause for concern that the Boers had reached the coast. Susceptibilities were not at that time much aroused by penetration inland. The interior was largely unexplored, and British interests were not threatened by what went on there, but the littoral was a more sensitive area. Insofar as any consideration had been given to the subject it was assumed that any part of the southern African coast not already occupied by Portugal should not be allowed to fall under the control of any other Europeans. Admiral Campbell had reported in 1835 that it was not improbable that 'the USA might be interested in forming settlements on the Eastern Coast . . . which . . . may be anything but beneficial to England.'[38] The annexation of Natal, although separated by hundreds of miles from British settlements, was therefore a possibility which forced itself upon the attention of a reluctant Colonial Office.

The situation in Natal was considerably more complex than anyone realized at the time. Incursion had not been a simple case of white colonialists forcibly dispossessing established black communities, since these had been previously shattered by Shaka's aggression. A later inquiry identified ninety-four tribes which had occupied the territory before Shaka, of which some fifty were destroyed or dispersed while twenty moved more or less entire to other regions. Large areas, which corresponded approximately to the land first taken by the Boers, were left nearly empty. Most of the remaining Natalian blacks welcomed the peaceable conditions established by the *voortrekkers*, so much so that thousands more flocked south from Zululand to join them, causing considerable congestion. Nor, if the Afrikaner concept of innate black inferiority was accepted, could the Boers reasonably be accused of intolerable oppression, as distinct from casual brutality: their taking children into near-slavery was not accompanied by gross abuse and, once apprenticed or enslaved, there was little buying and selling of the victims, perhaps the most repugnant feature of American slavery. But the British persisted, backed by public opinion at home, in distrusting Afrikaner willingness to treat blacks decently; although it should be said that as soon as British newcomers themselves became farmers their views quickly approximated to those of the Afrikaners.

London's suspicions were confirmed when in December 1840 the Revd William Shaw accused a Natal commando, under Pretorius' command, of attacking Ncaphayi, who had led a group now known as the Bhaca – the homeless ones – formed from fugitives from Shaka's aggression. Shaw, a Wesleyan, was on good terms with the Cape government, and his report that not only had the Bhaca been savagely attacked by the Boers but women and children carried off to what could only be described as slavery – all quite true, although Ncaphayi was himself no innocent – had to be taken seriously, and indeed was taken seriously even by the Natal Volksraad, where a vote of censure was moved, but not carried, against the Commandant himself.[39]

Lacking permission from London, Napier could not move quickly to intervene in Natalia. Glenelg had been succeeded in February 1839 by Constantine Phipps, Lord Normanby, a deservedly neglected novelist and a useless minister, whose instinct was to let sleeping dogs lie. After a few months Normanby was replaced by the much more forceful Lord John Russell, who deprecated both the despoliation of Mpande and the attack on the Bhaca, and was concerned about possible European interest in Natal, where the French were said to be contemplating interference. His instruction to Napier that Port Natal should be reoccupied was not immediately acted on, but in January 1841 Captain Thomas Smith of the Inniskillings, a Waterloo veteran, was sent to take up a position on the borders of the lands claimed by the republic. His instructions were 'to afford the native tribes of Africa the protection of British arms against the aggression of Her Majesty's subjects'. Specifically this was to guard the interests of the Mpondo chief Faku, whose people had occupied their present land for at least two centuries, and who had sheltered many refugees from the *mfecane*.

Meanwhile Napier attempted to negotiate with the Natalian Volksraad, with little success. In September 1840 the Volksraad had asked that it might 'graciously please Her Majesty to declare us a free and independent people'. By January 1841 they were requesting an alliance, guaranteeing to abstain from the slave trade and from attacking their neighbours without warning the British, and to give British citizens equal rights. There might have been a possibility of this proposal being accepted. The Permanent Secretary at the Colonial Office, still James Stephen, was anxious to avoid any moves which were likely to involve Britain in 'warfare alike inglorious, unprofitable and afflicting'; but once again the emigrants ruined their chances of independence.[40] In April 1841 they extended their territorial claims south, first to the Mmzimkulu and then to the Mzimvubu Rivers, well beyond any lands ever claimed by Dingane or Mpande, and seriously encroaching on the territory of peoples whose independence was recognized by the British. By so doing the Republic of Natalia ensured a strong British reaction.

When in December 1841 the Volksraad were confronted by Napier's warning of impending British occupation, negotiations were entrusted to Jacobus Boshof, who had decided to make his home in Natal. Quickly recognized as one of the few men in the republic with any administrative capacity, Boshof was appointed both Landdrost of Pietermaritzburg and President of the Volksraad. Boshof wrote an able reply to Napier: 'May we not ask where there is a Colony or conquered possession of Great Britain, or any other Power, to which a stronger claim or right [for independence] can be asserted?'[41] Two months later he tried again, assuring Napier 'that we will cherish friendship and peace with the tribes and would wish to do so with the country we have left', although he admitted that 'as long as . . . the chimerical philanthropy, so generally raging in Europe' continued, this was unlikely.

In March 1842 Captain Smith eventually arrived at Port Natal with a force of some three hundred regulars and the ubiquitous Cape Mounted Rifles. Making the mistake of attempting a night attack on Pretorius' camp, Smith's troops were ambushed and spent an uncomfortable three weeks before reinforcements – summoned by Dick King, one of the Port Natal pioneers, after a famous hundred-mile-a-day ride together with his groom Ndongeni – arrived escorted by the frigate *Southampton*. However reluctant the Colonial Office were – and they were very uneasy about the prospect of extending their responsibilities eight hundred miles from Cape Town, and separated from it by three hundred miles of black settlements – it was only a question of what arrangements would finally be made for British control; but making these took another three years.

Public opinion in Britain was not unsympathetic to the Boers, considering, as *The Times* put it in July, that 'imperfect protection offered by the Colonial government against the incursions of the Kaffirs' and its 'temporizing and irresolute policy' had been to blame. Nor was the government feeling as protective towards wronged blacks as it had been in Glenelg's day. Once the abolition of slavery had been achieved, something of the humanitarian impetus was lost. With the establishment in 1839 of the Aboriginals Protection Association, philanthropic attention turned to native peoples; but the great days of Exeter Hall, that 'Sanhedrin of the evangelicals', were numbered.

Lord John Russell found himself out of office in 1841 as a consequence of the replacement of the exhausted Whig government by a strong reforming Tory administration led by Sir Robert Peel, with Lord Stanley as Colonial Secretary once more. Stanley began in April 1842 by insisting on a U-turn: the emigrants should be ordered to return, and the Cape government must 'immediately ... take the most prompt and effective measures' to withdraw the troops sent the previous month to Port Natal. Napier sensibly ignored the instruction, and replied arguing that Natal should rather be annexed and colonized. The Colonial Secretary considered this at leisure for three months before agreeing in December. The inhabitants should be consulted as to the future form of government, but this must include three essential principles: no colour bar of any sort; no attacks on neighbours; and, of course, no slavery, 'in any shape or under any modification'.[42]

James Stephen's objections were thereby overruled, but the Permanent Secretary was spending less time at the Colonial Office and after 1846 had entirely withdrawn. The new brooms there were more aware of the 'hatred expressed' towards them by so many colonists, who saw their system as 'a vague and occult influence'.[43] A new influence on national opinion was that of John Delane, who succeeded the amiable Thomas Barnes as editor of *The Times* in 1841. Delane, who was to hold the post for thirty-five years, made the newspaper the 'Fourth Estate', a massive influence on the public and on governments, often adopting an aggressive and 'forward' policy.

Such success as the negotiations between the British authorities and the Volksraad attained was largely due to two brothers, Josias and Henry Cloete. Both were fifth-generation Afrikaners, descendants of one of van Riebeeck's companions, and diplomats of considerable ability. General Sir Josias, the soldier, was trained in England and on his return to the Cape became ADC to Lord Charles Somerset. Despatched to England to negotiate a loan for the colony, he succeeded in persuading Lord Bathurst, not an easy touch, to part with the considerable sum of £125,000. Less diplomatically, he became the only dragoon ever known to fight a duel with a woman. Not that he was aware of her sex, for Surgeon Major James Barry, Inspector General of the Army Medical Department, passed seventy years of her life disguised as a man. In July 1842, immediately Smith was relieved, Josias negotiated the surrender of the Volksraad, leaving the details to be settled later, when the Colonial Office had decided the shape of Natal's future.

Until this decision came the loyal but dispirited Boshof attempted to tidy things up. Half the Volksraad members took themselves off; Pretorius resigned, having mislaid a number of the title claims, thus stultifying Boshof's efforts to get these registered in advance of the British takeover. Recalcitrant burgers at Weenen refused to accept the Volksraad's capitulation; others took comfort in the hope that the King of Holland might intervene to protect Dutch-speakers. This engaging possibility had been put about by one Johann Arnold Smellekamp, supercargo of a Dutch brig, who had visited Port Natal in the spring of 1842. There was never any possibility of this happening, but the rumour was enough to confirm the Foreign Office's hereditary suspicions that the French must be at the back of it.[44]

It was another year before an authorized Commissioner came to inform the Volksraad of the British government's intentions. This was the second Cloete brother, Henry, the lawyer, who had studied at Leiden and at Lincoln's Inn, and back in Cape Town married the sister of Colonel John Graham of Fintry – and of Grahamstown – founder of the Cape Mounted Rifles, whose Khoikhoi troopers made it one of the most effective South African fighting units. Henry's task was made difficult by Natalian public opinion, which was strongly against the settlement already agreed by the Volksraad. Stephanus Maritz, Gert's brother, had been elected President, and tried vainly to gain some concessions, 'to beg that some shadow of a colour bar, some little inequality between white and black before the law be retained'.[45]

The leading voice of anti-British opinion was the strong one of Maritz's sister-in-law Susanna Smit. In an impassioned two-hour harangue she threatened to walk barefoot back over the Drakensberg rather than submit to British jurisdiction. The phrase became widely quoted as an example of Boer defiance, and took its part in the Afrikaner mythology. In one of history's little ironies, however, Susanna did no such thing, but continued to live for many years with Erasmus in Pietermaritzburg, on a pension from the British authorities. Her defiance appears in most history books; the outcome in none.

183

EIGHT

Ruthless Worthless Savages

The surrender of the Republic of Natalia in August 1843 formalized the division that had already developed between it and the Highveld Boers. After the unsuccessful commando against Dingane, Potgieter had left Natal in a huff, furious at Maritz. He led his followers the better part of three hundred miles back over the Drakensberg to the Mooi River. There he established what was to become the Republic of Winburg/Potchefstroom, on reasonably good terms with the local inhabitants. Although he reacted vigorously when attacked, Potgieter, more so than his rival Pretorius, tended to reach agreement with neighbouring black rulers, who appreciated the Boers as more tolerable than Mzilikazi's Ndebele or the sporadic fillibustering Koranna expeditions. In October 1840 the Natalians approached Potgieter in an attempt to unite the republic with the Winburg and Potchefstroom communities. Unenthusiastic, but encouraged by Caspar Kruger, whose son Paul was already making a name for himself, Potgieter agreed, and Potchefstroom became a region of Natalia. Potgieter was given the title of Commandant en Bestieder ('*bestuuder*': governor, director), but with only limited powers.

In April 1844, after the British occupation of Natal, the Potchefstroomers and Winburgers formally established a new state, free and independent, with a constitution of thirty-three articles, designed for a primitive farming community, and which excluded all non-whites. 'Constitution' is too grand a description of what was no more than an elementary guide to litigation and punishments, little different from those then being adopted by the Griqua states; *trekboers* had no taste for governing or being governed. Potgieter, always unwilling to tolerate even the most basic constitutional restraints, only remained there for a year before moving his headquarters to Andries-Ohrigstadt, another three hundred miles to the north.

Almost immediately a split developed between his followers and those of the new Volksraad leader, that same Jacobus (Kootjie) Burger who had been Secretary of the Natal Volksraad, and was elected to the equivalent post in Ohrigstadt. Antagonism between Potgieter's devoted followers and those, many ex-Natalians, who wanted a more democratic regime, led to Potgieter's attempting a *coup d'état* by arresting Burger and requisitioning official files. For some months the rival governments, a military command under Potgieter and the Volksraad following Burger, each claiming its own constitution, argued it out. The frustrated Potgieter, getting the worst of it, moved off yet again in 1848 to establish a patriarchal society in the far-northern Zoutpansberg. Pretorius meanwhile had settled in Potchefst-room, where he belligerently organized resistance against British claims in the Orange River area, a policy opposed by both the Ohrigstadt Volksraad and Potgieter, for once united, as well as the mainly Boer farmers further south, led by Michiel Oberholster. In this fashion three little Boer communities found themselves spread over an area the size of France, with each district fending for itself.

For six months after the departures of Napier and Stockenström the frontiers were in the sole charge of Colonel John Hare, until another decayed Waterloo veteran, Sir Peregrine Maitland, 'a very pious man', according to Daniel Lindley, arrived in August 1844. He immediately ran into trouble on all sides.

The first crisis arose in the north, where the Griqua Captain Adam Kok of Philipolis attempted to arrest a Boer resident. By virtue of his recognition by the colonial government Kok had legal powers in his own territory. While the land remained in Griqua hands enforcement presented few difficulties, but once granted to whites all the traditional Boer resentment at being subject to any black authority was aroused, and for three years past the more recalcitrant trekkers led by Jan Mocke had been threatening Kok's people. At a meeting on 31 December 1842 between Lieutenant Governor Hare, Oberholster and Kok, Hare had reinstated British protection, and Hendrik Hendriks, Kok's Secretary, thankfully acknowledged, 'It was the English who made the Hottentot free ... And never, never, will there be security for the Griquas and the black natives of Africa until England continues to hold her hand over the whole country' – sentiments with which many British officials would have agreed.[1]

Subsequently Mocke and Potgieter, after the British takeover of Natal, attempted to negotiate a treaty with Kok, which he refused to accept without

British agreement. The eventual, inevitable Boer attack on Kok's Griquas in April 1845 was met by colonial reinforcements, and a cavalry charge at Swartkoppies ended the incident with the Boers being scattered; the British dragoons had to be reminded that this time their enemies were white, and their allies, the Cape Mounted Rifles and Kok's Griqua cavalry, were brown. Painfully riding the four hundred miles to the scene, the seventy-year-old Sir Peregrine met the Griquas together with Moshoeshoe at Touwfontein, where treaties were signed protecting 'the prosperity and even existence of the rising Native communities'. Kok's territory was divided into a core area south of the Riet River, where the land had to continue in Griqua owner-ship, and a part on which the trekkers might be accommodated. The newly-appointed British Resident – a post analogous to those in British India – Captain Warden, established a suitable base at 'a place called Bloem Fontein', which he bought from a Cape farmer, one J.N. Brits, for five hundred rixdollars.

Sir Peregrine was less successful in the east. He started off badly by succumbing to the colonists' demands and denouncing the treaties entered into by Andries Stockenström, which inevitably exacerbated ill-feeling among the Xhosa. Even the great warrior Macoma had sworn to abide by the treaties, and shown every sign of keeping his word, in spite of the running sore caused by seeing Thembu and Khoikhoi occupying lands which had been his own. Discontent among the white settlers had been heightened by the growth of profitable merino sheep-farming, which was then turning wool into the main export of the Cape Colony, increasing the demand for access to new land. They saw no reason why they should not be allowed to clear the region of a 'few thousand of ruthless worthless savages', free of the restraints imposed by the British government represen-tatives at the Cape. Port Elizabeth was now second only to Cape Town, handling a third of all the colony's exports. If only they had a separate Eastern Provincial administration of their own, formed by men who really understood the Kaffirs, peace and prosperity would surely supervene, and the present miserable state of things improve. Back at the Cape, William Porter, Attorney General and the most sensible man in white South Africa, one who was to lend support to every wise move of the next thirty years, wryly observed that the colonists must be extraordinarily enterprising, since in spite of the fearsome conditions of which they complained the value of frontier property had never been as high as it was then.[2]

The dilemma of the colonists was that without vigorous backing from

Britain and the deployment of strong bodies of troops, there was no hope of decisively defeating the Xhosa and ejecting them from their lands – in the way Shaka had done – which was what Godlonton and his supporters all cried out for. But no British government was prepared to attempt so blatant a piece of aggression, especially since it would necessitate spending huge sums of taxpayers' money for the benefit of ungrateful and unprofitable colonists. Had, as those colonists cynically observed, the Xhosa been sitting on mounds of silver, the aggression might have been countenanced.

Among the Xhosa, desperation was setting in. When Macoma had attended the conference with Lord Charles Somerset in April 1817, the Southern Nguni, although bitterly divided among themselves, were able to move their herds freely through the whole coastal area of South Africa from the Tukela to the Fish River. A generation later the disappointed, now drink-addicted, leader saw his people penned in a much smaller area between the Transkeian Xhosa and the advancing Cape settlers, reinforced by the Khoikhoi on the Kat River. Encroaching on even this restricted domain were the peoples displaced in the *mfecane* and now settled in the north of Xhosaland – the Bhaca and Thembu recognizing their own chiefs, and the Mfengu allied to the colonists, and particularly in the Ciskei, bitterly resented by the ejected Xhosa.[3] To some extent the physical clashes with the colonists, the frontier wars, were less damaging – a deal less bloody than those between the Xhosa themselves – than the constant pressure of new rules, boundaries and disciplines; and ideas. The missionaries may have had limited success in converting people to their own forms of Christianity, but the messages they preached were powerful and disturbing, and were absorbed, causing the ancient and comforting certainties of the Nguni to begin crumbling.

In such an atmosphere another war was inevitable, and that which took place between 1846 and 1847, known both as the Seventh Frontier War and the War of the Axe, needed only the flimsiest of excuses to break out,[4] but became the longest and most ferocious of any to date. The Xhosa protagonist was the twenty-five-year-old Sandile, Ngqika's successor, and half-brother of the much abler Macoma, who did his best to stay neutral, as did Hintsa's successor as paramount chief Sarili (Kreli), who ruled the Transkeian, Gcaleka, Xhosa from 1835 until his deposition in 1877 (he lived on until 1892), a decent, worried man who had the misfortune to live through troubled times. Sandile, by contrast, was a more impressionable character, susceptible to pressure – invariably disastrous – from his more militant counsellors. Since the influence of paramountcy was by now much reduced, Sarili was unable to prevent some of his own followers breaking away to join in the war.

Stockenström – Sir Andries since his baronetcy of 1840 – who had been recalled as the only man able to negotiate with the Xhosa leaders, and the most experienced in fighting them, made an unopposed expedition in August 1846 to argue things out with Sarili, who defended himself emphatically, convincing Stockenström of his good intentions. Not convincingly enough, however, to satisfy Maitland, who demanded indemnities from the Xhosa chief. Both Sarili and Stockenström were infuriated; Sarili withdrew out of reach of the British and Stockenström resigned in disgust.

With the Xhosa paramount neutral, Sandile's only supporters were Phato, chief of the Gqunukhwebe, whose brother Kama, on the other hand, fought on the colonial side, and Maphasa, a Thembu leader. Neither Phato nor Maphasa could count on being followed by all his people, since the Thembu paramount chief Mthikrakra (Mtirara, Umtirara) joined with Kama in cooperating with the colonists. Other Xhosa who had settled themselves in the colony at Blinkwater, near Fort Cox, had served on commando with the whites in 1835, and were to do so again.

It therefore turned out to be a vicious little civil war, fought in well-covered country. The Xhosa had learned to avoid headlong charges, included a number of experienced shots, and were skilled in ambush and harassment; a British army supply column was quickly ambushed and raided, with more than twenty British regulars killed. Once again over twelve thousand warriors invaded the colony, to be halted only with difficulty, as the British units had to learn the principles of guerrilla warfare, one of the first of which was to leave the most disagreeable and dangerous activities to those who best understood them – the allied Khoikhoi and Mfengu. For the first time, fighting was accompanied by the brutal torture of prisoners; one unlucky British sergeant was spitted on a stake and roasted, surviving for three days after he was rescued. Captured Xhosa were disposed of less brutally, but just as finally.

When news of the war reached England – the sanitized official despatches countered by the dramatization of those from missionaries – there was anxiety and annoyance. Campaigns like this were both expensive and inglorious, unlike that being waged at the same time in north India against the Sikhs. Those were proper wars, with foot, horse and guns arranged against each other in respectable fashion, won against the odds by the

Anglo-Indian armies – and not paid for by the British taxpayer. The war in the African bush had no such appeal, and its cost hurt; a military expenditure of about £250,000 per annum suddenly quadrupled to a total of £1 million in 1847.

A firm hand was needed, and was provided by the third Earl Grey, who took office in July 1846 as Colonial Secretary in the Whig government of Lord John Russell. Grey was the most efficient of all nineteenth-century Colonial Secretaries, and the only one to leave a detailed account of his stewardship.[5] Cool and self-possessed to the point of arrogance, he had a mastery of detail, and was entirely uninfluenced by party political considerations. Needless to say these qualities did not contribute to his popularity.

Grey's choice as a successor to the incompetent Sir Peregrine Maitland fell on Sir Henry Pottinger, fresh from his triumph over the Chinese Empire, which had led to the opening of that country's ports to international trade and the cession of Hong Kong to Britain. Pottinger, a choleric and arrogant man, was reluctant to come to Africa to tidy up another Imperial muddle, and did so only on the firm promise of reward, and of being invested with the widest powers. In China he had been a Plenipotentiary, and he now insisted on an appointment as High Commissioner – the first of a series that ran until the Union of South Africa was established in 1911 and, with different responsibilities and a gap between 1960 and 1994, continues today. High Commissioners were responsible directly to London for 'settling and adjusting the affairs of the territories in Southern Africa adjacent or contiguous to the Eastern and Northern frontier', and 'promoting the good order, civilization and moral and religious instructions of the tribes'. Something of a tall order, covering as it did the scattered populations, Boer, black and brown, outside colonial boundaries. Within the colonies, acting as governor, Pottinger and his successors were constrained by the colonial governments, constraints which increased as these governments were given greater powers, and which led to regular clashes between them and their governors, with the Colonial Office often caught in the crossfire.[6] Outside these boundaries High Commissioners had unfettered powers, and frequently used them: Pottinger had been given instructions that reliance on treaties was believed to have been misplaced, and that the Xhosa must be made to accept their subordinate status.

Maitland believed as early as October 1846 that he had successfully negotiated a peace, but when Pottinger arrived in the following January he quickly not only found this illusory, but the colonists uncooperative. In Hong Kong his distaste for the British merchants had been reciprocated with cordial dislike; the Cape, he decided, was worse. Never had he seen, 'even in an Indian native state . . . such extensive corruption and idleness'. The burgher militia was nothing more than riff-raff such as 'merchants, tailors, shop-keepers, editors of newspapers, hotel-keepers &c &c . . . all dignified with military titles of captains, lieutenants and ensigns'. Responding in kind, newspaper editors described Pottinger as a 'Crocodile', a 'black compound of malice and misrepresentation'. Thrashing around for objects of wrath, he also turned on the Kat River Khoikhoi, entirely misunderstanding the nature and value of their contribution to the war, in a display of petulance which soon had tragic consequences and was a major cause of the later rebellions.

The inhabitants of 'this ill-conditioned and hitherto worse-than-useless settlement' were bullied and oppressed by the High Commissioner to an extent that left Stockenström, the founder of the community, permanently furious. But the war petered out, its end marked by the virtual kidnap of Sandile in a longer-remembered act of near-treachery. As Sir Charles Adder-ley later remarked, 'No Kaffir war had ever been really concluded, but each was patched up *"flagrante bello"*.'[7]

If the savages retaliate no one can blame them

Pottinger left after only a few months, to be replaced by a very different character, the popular hero Sir Harry Smith, who had ten years previously served in the last frontier war. An experienced and dashing Rifleman, next to the Foot Guards the most highly esteemed of infantry, Sir Harry had faced the finest armies of his day – Massena and Soult in the Peninsula, Napoleon at Waterloo, the Sikhs throughout the recent war, and – less successfully – Andrew Jackson at New Orleans; but he *had* helped to burn the new capital of Washington. His rescue of and marriage to a beautiful Spaniard inspired romances, and his dramatic gifts captivated sober states-men – Lord Grey was said to be 'entranced'. In 1847 Smith was fresh from a successful victory against the Sikhs at Aliwal, where he led the final charge in a battle which killed nearly six thousand of the enemy, a triumph acknowledged by enthusiastic public recognition, including the freedom of the City of London, the thanks of the Houses of Parliament, a Cambridge doctorate and a baronetcy. He therefore arrived at the Cape in December 1847 even fuller of himself than ever.[8]

By then, somewhat to his disappointment, the war had ended, not by any military victory, but by the exhaustion and near-starvation of the Xhosa. Pottinger had brought with him General Sir George Berkeley, a capable soldier who instituted a system of long-range patrols in strength, which devastated the Xhosa hinterland, destroying crops and villages and capturing cattle: 'A disgrace to the age we live in,' as one observer described the British campaign, 'and, if the savages retaliate hereafter no one can blame them.' The disgusted Stockenström wrote to the Colonial Secretary: 'A miserable starving chief has surrendered and we are as elated as if the battle of Waterloo had been fought and won ... will the nation consider Africa as far as Suez worth the dead?'[9]

Disappointed with one war, Smith set about making a second inevitable. With monumental insensitivity, no sooner had he landed than he sent for Macoma, forced the chief to his knees, and put his boot on the kneeling man's neck, to teach him that 'I am chief and master here.' In future Smith was 'Inkosi Inkhulu', the Great Chief, who hoped to impress the Xhosa by dramatic gestures and 'bullying interviews' (as his own ADC described them), typified by his erection of a well-sharpened halberd, the staff of war, and a knobbed pole, the staff of peace, and demanding that the chiefs make their choice.[10]

After many years of British government resistance, Lord Grey had reluctantly come to the conclusion that a limited extension of British territory was inevitable. It was decided that the land west of the Keiskamma, the old Ceded Territory, was to be settled by both whites and Mfengu and annexed by the Cape as the district of Victoria, while that between the Keiskamma and Kei was to become the new crown colony of British Kaffraria. The power of the chiefs was to be circumscribed by a Chief Commissioner with two assistants, one for each section of the Rharhabe Xhosa people, but customary law was to continue except where this conflicted with what the British saw as the dictates of humanity. Both the Assistant Commissioners, Charles Brownlee and John Maclean, were decent and sympathetic men who did their best to serve the interests of the Xhosa. Brownlee in particular, a native of the country, brought up among the Xhosa, son of a Scottish missionary, was to be an important influence for good.

Before proclaiming his new colony, and within days of his arrival at

Port Elizabeth, Sir Harry made a four-hundred-mile dash to the northern frontier. His first action was to extend the colonial boundary beyond the old Plettenberg line in the west to the Orange River, followed the next month by the acquisition of the Stormberg; not a particularly significant expansion, as it did nothing more than confirm existing realities, but enough to alarm the Colonial Office. Once at Bloemfontein Smith had to deal with many separate groups: the still independent but rapidly diminishing bands of Bushmen, Adam Kok's Griquas, the white settlers between the Orange and Bloemfontein (in the main faithful colonial subjects, unlike those further north at Winburg, recalcitrant *voortrekkers* all), and finally Moshoeshoe, ensconced in his mountain fortress, surrounded by minor chiefs, including the gentle Moroka; to say nothing of the Koranna, Waterboer's Griquas, and a number of outlaws lurking in the Orange River islands, the chief of whom was the current head of the Afrikaner family, one Jonker. Francis Galton saw the results in 1851 of an attack by Jonker Afrikaner's band: 'two women, with legs cut off at the ankles', dragging themselves along, as 'one of Jonker's sons, a hopeful youth ... leisurely gouged out [a child's eyes] with a small stick'.

Arriving at Philipolis, Sir Harry bullied the respectable Captain Adam Kok, threatening 'to hang the black fellow on this beam', and made him renounce all authority outside his reserve. He intervened more deferentially with Moshoeshoe, and told the Bushmen that they had not been created by God to run after game, but to work. Since he went no further north, Smith met only the amenable southerners, who assured him of their devotion to the British flag, and heard little of the Winburg northerners' very different sentiments.[11]

He had the opportunity to do this only a few days later, when after another four-hundred-mile ride across the Drakensberg – still only seven weeks after his arrival in Africa – he came across Andries Pretorius on the Tukela River in Natal. Unaware of, or merely disregarding, the difference between the friendly emigrant Boers of Transorangia and the ambitious Pretorius – rendered more suspicious since Pottinger had stupidly refused to meet the Boer leader when he came to Cape Town for that purpose – Sir Harry chose that moment to proclaim the 'Orange River Sovereignty'. This extension of British territory comprised a region larger than England, including 'the territories of Moshoeshoe, Moroko, Molitsani, Sinkonyala, Adam Kok, Gert Taaybosch and other minor chiefs so far north as to the Vaal River ... with the sole view of establishing an amicable relationship with these chiefs ... and protecting them from any further aggression'. Since the feared aggression was specifically that of the Boers, Pretorius was understandably annoyed, and attempted to reason with Smith, but had to record that 'His Excellency proceeded without taking notice of anything in this world, neither begging nor praying could stop His Excellency.'[12]

Returning to Winburg, Pretorius established that the community there was almost unanimously opposed to the new Sovereignty, and found that Smith had no intention of sticking to the pledge that he had made to withdraw unless supported by four fifths of the burghers. Pretorius then assembled some one thousand like-minded farmers, who turfed the British Resident, Major Warden, out of Bloemfontein and back into the Cape, accompanied by alarmed missionaries and apprehensive Griqua.

Sir Harry Smith asked no better excuse for a fight. With a company of his old Rifle Brigade comrades, Argyle and Sutherland Highlanders and Sherwood Foresters, supported by the Cape Mounted Rifles and an assortment of colonists and Griquas, he rushed for Pretorius' force at Boomplats, in Griqua territory. A typical dashing charge, more successful than it deserved to be, dispersed the Boers. Sir Harry had a couple of deserters he found in the Boer ranks executed, a move of doubtful legality which formed in due course another cause of contention (typical of that contrary character, Smith worried himself about the welfare of one, Michael Quigley's, widow, 'poor creature'[13]).

The Orange River Sovereignty accordingly became part of the British Empire, but its welcome there was cool. South African military expenditure now exceeded £2 million, an enormous sum, and the Colonial Office permanent staff gloomily saw nothing in prospect but increased responsibilities and further expenditure. Lord Grey was more optimistic, since it was left up to the newcomers themselves to arrange their own form of government and to pay its costs. Many of the Europeans remaining in the Sovereignty were prepared to accept British rule, while those who were not had the alternative of trekking over the Vaal and taking their pick between Potgieter and Pretorius. Warden, reinstated as Resident with greatly increased powers, proved himself a man of uncertain judgement. While the Orange and Vaal Rivers formed natural boundaries, those of the colony and Moshoeshoe's people were not defined.

That remarkable man, who had contrived to survive the dangers of Matabele, Boers and Griqua, and the uncertain support of the British authorities, emerges as perhaps the greatest African of his time – certainly superior to Shaka, or any of his white contemporaries. His upbringing had been unconventional, largely by his relative the Sotho chief Mohlomi, who together with his pupil began a change among the Sotho quite as revolutionary as that started by Shaka among the Nguni. A 'profound contempt' for witchcraft, a prudent generosity in providing cattle to poor men, and a preference for negotiation, if necessary accompanied by a graceful submission to superior forces, rather than damaging war, characterized Moshoeshoe's plans to found a new state: 'Let us first render ourselves popular by mighty deeds, and afterwards we will speak of peace and clemency. In the disputes of others let us always put ourselves on the side of the stronger. If we would become rich in men and cattle, we cannot help making enemies; but they will not roar for ever.'

When the *mfecane* (the *difaqane* in Sotho) came, Moshoeshoe was still no more than a promising young man among the Sotho chiefs of the Caledon Valley. Within ten years his military skill, his impregnable base on the mountain of Thabu Bosiu and, above all, his good sense in realizing when fighting could best give place to diplomacy, had established his influence in South African affairs.

Like many other African rulers, Moshoeshoe regarded the land as inalienable: he could grant temporary possession of it, and had done so to many farmers, black and white, but this did not constitute an abandonment of his people's heritage. In his usual airy fashion, Smith had given his word that 'neither white nor black should be removed from their present habitations ... but that they should both drink out of the same fountain and live in peace'. But Warden's settlement, which was imposed in 1849, was grossly unfair to Moshoeshoe, who lost a considerable area of his people's best land. Warden had fallen in line with the Wesleyan missionaries, supporters of Moroka and the white settlers, who, led by his brother-in-law the Revd Mr Cameron, 'with distinguished acrimony and no feeling of Christian charity' resented their French rivals, stout supporters of Moshoeshoe. Trouble was inevitable, and not long delayed, but for the next eighteen months Sir Harry was free to devote himself to his responsibilities as Governor of the Cape; until fighting broke out, yet again, on the eastern frontier.[14]

We want no more church-going niggers

There the colonists' persecution of the blacks had become more vicious. 'Moral Bob' Godlonton's prose in the *Graham's Town Journal* was hysterical, demanding: 'every institution where a number of the coloured races are, or can be drawn together, shall be broken up . . . If we destroy, or prevent the building of the nest, we shall not be liable to the incursions of the brood.' Even the totally unthreatening Kat River community was attacked by two successive magistrates, Thomas Biddulph, a vile man, and Holden Bowker, corrupt and unsympathetic, who made it their business to persecute that inoffensive community to the extent that John Freeman, the London Missionary Society Secretary then in South Africa, warned that such 'flagrant injustice, cruelty and oppression . . . if left unchecked will so multiply that the whole of the native border tribes will be provoked into a battle of dangerous exasperation'. The colonists responded by blaming the missionaries for 'inflating the native mind', and took potshots at the Philipton belfry, shouting, 'Shoot the damned bell, we want no more church-going niggers.'[15]

Not all missionaries were sympathetic to the blacks; at least one went further than the most racist of colonists. The appalling Patrick Griffith, the first Roman Catholic South African bishop, an Irishman, found 'Boschmen, Fingoes, Caffers, Hottentots, all base and barbarous . . . deluding the English Fanatics [i.e. Protestant missionaries] by professions of Christianity'. The Bishop had often thought '*seriously* if indeed they [the Bushmen] might not be the unnatural products of Baboon and man'. Not surprisingly, the Catholic missions did not do well.[16]

Equally unsurprising was the resurgence of Xhosa resistance. A new prophet, Mlanjeni, the Riverman, had ignited the desperate Xhosa, promising that the English could be driven back to the sea if witches were purified and dun cattle slaughtered, and guaranteeing invulnerability to those warriors who rose up against the invaders. In December 1850 two British forces were attacked and the inhabitants of the recently-established Victoria villages slaughtered. This time Phato stayed out of the fray, but others joined in. Ndlambe's son Mhala, together with his nephew Sixolo, and Maphasa's Thembu followers, always ready for a fight, joined with Sandile. More seriously, and much to the disappointment of their supporters, many of the Khoikhoi who had been settled by Stockenström on the Kat River threw in their lot with the Xhosa. They had been infuriated by Pottinger's insensitive treatment and by the foolish brutality of his magistrate, Biddulph, to the extent that even some troopers of the Cape Mounted Rifles rebelled, those same 'Totties' whose fighting qualities had been so admired by the British regulars.

Conflict with the proud and independent Xhosa would have been inevitable, however skilful Cape rule had been, but the British administration had made a genuine, and sometimes successful, effort to treat the remnants of Khoikhoi communities fairly. Kok's people were flourishing modestly, and the Kat River community had settled well. Khoikhoi, refugee blacks and mixed-race leaders had formed a tranquil, civilized, self-governing community, before the severe damage inflicted on them during the War of the Axe and the persecutions of Bowker and Biddulph. In spite of the efforts of the two James Reads, several hundred fighting men took sides with the Xhosa, among them old Andries Botha, who had fought alongside the British for thirty years, and was now to be tried for high treason; his friend James Read the elder died lamenting the destruction of the work on which he had spent half a century.[17]

Sir Harry Smith himself, the veteran of so many wars, was besieged in Fort Cox as Hermanus Matroos, an independent Kat River raider, attacked Forts Beaufort and Hare. Macoma, with a small force of Xhosa and Khoikhoi, fought a brilliant guerrilla campaign, while Sixolo, one of the most able and determined fighters the Xhosa ever produced, ambushed a detachment of the Queen's Regiment, leaving sixty British soldiers dead. Charles Bell described one struggle when a soldier, grabbed by his haversack, was rescued by a 'grenadier who rammed the muzzle of his flintlock through the Kaffir's skull'.[18] It was altogether a thoroughly vicious war, which continued for over two years. Xhosa and Khoikhoi attacks on any fortified place could never succeed, nor could colonial forces drive their opponents from their wooded and mountainous fastnesses. Ingenious tortures inflicted by Xhosa women on the wounded were followed by massacres of Xhosa women and children. With many Xhosa neutral, and the Mfengu actively helping the British (the decisive battle at Fort Hare was almost a straightforward Mfengu v. Xhosa affair), it had, once more, many of the characteristics of a civil war, while the participation of the Cape Mounted Rifles on both sides foreshadowed the Indian Mutiny, then only five years off.[19]

This was all too much for London. Reluctant though Lord Grey was to abandon Sir Harry, public opinion had turned against him. Unpleasant – largely true – stories of atrocities by colonials and even by British regulars made themselves heard. William Molesworth, an influential Radical, pilloried Smith's 'fantastic mountebank tricks . . . aping the manners of the savage . . . the effects of which were that . . . the Kaffirs laughed at him, turned him to ridicule'. The cost to the home country amounted to half a million pounds a year, and even at that rate it was deemed 'uncommonly difficult to kill Kaffirs'. Gladstone found the cost 'frightful and almost incredible'. The country's treasury had been 'squandered and the lives of its subjects lost for no conceivable purpose of policy'. *The Times* attributed the disastrous state of affairs to Lord Grey's conduct, which amounted to 'mischievous meddling'.[20]

Covering his rear, Lord Grey despatched two Commissioners, Major Hogge of the Dragoons, who had fought in the previous war, and Mostyn Owen, superintendent of the Kaffir police, ostensibly to investigate the causes of the Khoikhoi rebellion and to organize the new Orange River Sovereignty, but also to report privately to Grey. Their reports were devastating: 'The defection of Hermanus, the Kat River, the Caffre insurrection' – all were probably caused 'by acts of omission or commission by the present authority'. Lord Grey had 'been systematically kept in the dark as to the real state of affairs'. Complaints from the loyalists were relayed: 'We are all in the dam'dest mess possible in the Sovereignty.' Hogge's criticisms of Sir Harry's 'Harlequinades' were not however the only reason for Grey's decision to recall the High Commissioner. Sir Harry had also contrived to irritate the population in the Cape.[21]

The idealistic Governor of Bermuda, Captain Charles Elliot – who had earlier, and much to Lord Palmerston's distaste, landed Britain with the 'Barren Island of Hong Kong' – had conceived the idea of sending former prisoners, sentenced for their part in the Irish disturbances of 1848, mostly young men innocent of any grave offence, to settle at the Cape. The Colonial Office and Sir Harry both agreed, but the Cape inhabitants reacted with fierce indignation. Riots more like 'the chase of wolves than of human beings', 'neither more nor less than an application of Lynch law', were widespread. The Governor's annual ball had to be protected from the wrath of the population by soldiers with fixed bayonets, and Adderley Street in Cape Town was given its name in honour of Sir Charles Adderley, a pious and energetic Tory colonial reformer whose passionate objection to transportation was credited with making Lord Grey change his mind, although some credit should go to those ladies of Stellenbosch who, 'laying aside that modest reserve', petitioned the Colonial Secretary to 'preserve them from that dire pollution' that had distressed their Sydney sisters.[22]

Sir Harry was dismissed, although he returned to a hero's welcome in Britain and the approbation of the Duke of Wellington. He was succeeded by yet another Waterloo veteran, Sir George Cathcart, who successfully brought the Frontier War to an end. Cathcart, in contrast to his predecessor, was a decent and intelligent soldier, who knew when not to press things too far, and attempted a reasonable settlement with the Xhosa. Macoma and Sandile were firmly pushed over the Kei, and those Thembu who had taken part in the war placed under the vigorous rule of Queen Nonensi (who was, by a dynastic quirk, the daughter of Faku of the Mpondo).

London was happy enough to allow the Xhosa settled over the Kei to manage their own affairs, and indeed wanted to restrict British responsibilities even further, for the war had been excessively expensive. Sir John Pakington, one of the mayfly Colonial Secretaries (he lasted only nine months, under Lord Derby), wanted to abandon Smith's new colony of British Kaffraria, pulling back within the now-traditional boundaries of the Cape, but plain-speaking Cathcart dissuaded him from so 'impolitic and disastrous' a measure. Successive governments, however, remained wary of adding any more territory or subjects to their already unrewarding and embarrassing responsibilities, agreeing with Gladstone that 'it was frightful and almost incredible . . . that any government should go a-hunting to the uttermost ends of the earth to find means and opportunities of squandering its treasure . . . for no conceivable purpose of policy.'[23]

And the future of the Orange River Sovereignty was by no means settled.

Representative government

'No man's station, in this free country, [is] determined by the accident of his colour.'

William Porter, Cape Attorney General, 29 August 1848[24]

One method of at least shifting responsibility for the seemingly insuperable African problems would be to make the colonists themselves look after their own interests, instead of getting themselves in trouble and relying on London to come to their rescue. It was, James Stephen sadly reflected,

'impossible that such a society . . . should be well governed', but if government was left to the inhabitants they could at least take some initiative in
solving their own problems – and in paying for the remedies.

While beyond the eastern borders of the Cape the 1830s and forties had
been a time of upheaval and tumult, the colony had enjoyed a modest
prosperity. Even though the slave compensation payments had been diluted,
they still represented an unprecedented influx of cash, providing a vigorous
stimulus to the economy. The rixdollar had been abandoned for the pound
sterling and the Cape Colony brought into the heart of Imperial commerce.
The first successful bank, the Cape of Good Hope Bank, was set up in 1838,
followed by the Eastern Province Bank, the South Africa Bank, the South
African Mutual Insurance Company and a number of joint-stock trading
companies. Established Cape Town merchants such as John Ebden, shipwrecked in Table Bay at the age of eighteen, first chairman of the Cape of
Good Hope Bank, and Hamilton Ross, his colleague there, who had hoisted
the Union flag over the Castle in 1795, were joined by such enterprising
Afrikaners as Francis William Reitz. Intermarriage between English- and
Dutch-speakers brought the emergent middle class closer together; Ross
eloped, with Lady Anne Barnard's help, with a van der Berg girl; Ebden
married into a German family; both Cloetes married British girls. Increasingly property became dependent on sheep, fine-wooled merino imported
principally by the 1820 British settlers. The eastern Cape, from Grahamstown to the Karoo, became a centre of wool production, which by 1851
represented over half of all Cape exports. By then regular steamship services
had made communication both with Britain and along the coast more
dependable, and an energetic programme of roadbuilding – Sir Lowry's
Pass, constructed with much effort over the Hottentots Holland mountains
in 1830, being the most prominent example – made internal road communications speedier. The *Illustrated London News* could comment in March
1849 that at the Cape 'trade and commerce continue to flow in a stately
current . . . the local institutions, too numerous to be noted in detail, have
enjoyed uninterrupted prosperity'.

Education was, after a period of neglect, developing. There had been
English schools at the Cape at least since 1797, when one J. Wearing, of
Pembroke College, Oxford, had begun a successful establishment, but the
first serious attempt to establish state education, inspired by the distinguished astronomer Sir John Herschel, had been made on the basis of the
remarkable Prussian system. 'Pupils,' Herschel insisted, 'must not be mere

passive listeners but active respondents,' and teachers must be properly paid, members of 'an independent profession; one within the pale of which an ample reward may be found'.[25]

But the Cape still lagged well behind other British colonies, in spite of nearly two centuries of development. Emigrants went by preference to the United States or Canada – even Australia, much further off, was preferred. The city of Melbourne, empty scrubland in 1835, had a larger population than Cape Town within seventeen years. To British governments and public, the Cape Colony remained a place from which nothing but trouble might be expected.

Progress towards local self-government was cautious. A classic crown colony constitution had been established in 1834 with an Executive Council (the Governor and his senior officials) and a Legislative Council (which included five civilians – 'unofficials' – all nominated by the Governor). Municipal governments with elected Boards of Commissioners were founded: Beaufort West was the first, in 1838, with Cape Town electing its first local authority two years later. Other evidences of respectability – the South African College, gas lighting, and the establishment of an Anglican see, with Robert Gray as its first Bishop, installed in an elegant classical cathedral – helped to persuade Lord Grey that his predecessor, the Tory Lord Stanley (later the 14th Earl Derby), was wrong to dismiss the idea of a 'legislature composed exclusively of persons elected by the people at large [which] is utterly unknown to the constitution of this kingdom'; and that a modest extension of democracy was possible.[26]

Moreover the permanent Cape officials, John Montagu, the Colonial Secretary and William Porter, the Attorney General, were both reliable and experienced men in whom the home government had confidence to guide the colonials on their first steps to self-rule. Lord Grey would have preferred that such men should themselves constitute the membership of any Cape council, but Cape opinion, headed by the veteran John Fairbairn and Andries Stockenström, challenged this concept.

Accordingly a revised draft constitution was agreed in 1853 which provided for two elected Houses of Parliament – 'representative' government, the first step towards full colonial self-government, 'responsible' government, in which the executive was dependent upon a parliamentary majority. It was felt, both at the Cape and in London, that a period of learning the skills necessary for a parliamentary administration was needed; indeed, it was only after twenty years, and then with much reluctance, that the Cape

Parliament agreed to accept the grant of responsible government. The example might have been borne in mind when preparing colonies in the twentieth century for self-government, but was not, with many tragic consequences.

Porter, together with other colonists, was concerned about the unwieldy extent of the Cape Colony, and argued for its division into East and West. Lord Grey advocated moving the capital to a more central location – Uitenhage was his favourite. It was left, democratically enough, to the new representative government to decide on these matters, in a constitution which provided a bicameral assembly elected by all those possessing a minimum income or capital, a principle already established by the 1828 qualifications for jury service being solely based on the ownership or tenancy of a house with a minimum annual valuation of £10. All 'civilized' men, black or white, living in the colony were therefore to be eligible to vote, and Dr John Philip's definition of civilization as 'the way of life enjoyed by labourers and artisans in ... the manufacturing districts of northern Britain' was generally accepted; which might be characterized as literacy, trousers and the proper employment of a fork.[27] The British government insisted on equality, expressing their 'earnest desire' that all Her Majesty's 'subjects at the Cape, without distinction of class or colour, should be united by one bond of loyalty and common interest, and we believe that the exercise of political rights enjoyed by all alike will prove one of the best methods of attaining this object'.

Wise words, which the next century contrived to ignore; but while being impressed by the sagacity of Victorian statesmen, one must also be struck by their ignorance of the facts of life in Africa. Although the income qualification was kept low enough to allow the vote to 'those of the coloured classes who in point of intelligence are qualified for the exercise of political power',[28] most non-whites of the Crown Colony of British Kaffraria remained too poor to meet it. It would be some years before they could exercise a significant degree of power – and indeed no non-white was ever elected to the legislature – but the money qualification accurately reflected British opinion at the time: that the vote was a privilege that ought to be restricted to those with a stake in the community. Lord Stanley had been correct in stating that a government 'elected by the people at large' was 'utterly unknown' to Britain; it was not until after the Second World War that the principle of one adult, one vote was accepted there (by the suppression of the university Parliamentary seats and the reorganization of local government), and all governments still (in 1998) include unelected peers. These electoral qualifications were the foundation of the distinctive 'Cape Franchise', the only colour-blind electoral system ever to be allowed in South Africa before 1994, and for that congeries of former slaves, Khoikhoi and mixed-bloods becoming identified as 'Cape Coloureds' it was the opening of a new door after the suppression of the Kat River Settlement closed an old one.

The Legislative Assembly elected in 1854 was a good mix of Afrikaners and English, easterners and westerners, liberals and conservatives, young and old. Cristoffel Brand, former editor of the *Zuid-Afrikaan* and Somerset's old adversary, was Speaker, with the old allies Fairbairn and Stockenström acting as Council members. The young Francis Reitz, a progressive scientific farmer, and Saul Solomon, a crippled newspaperman, held liberal views in sympathy with the officials, while the veteran anti-black Godlonton, strenuously arguing for eastern rights and a firm hand on the frontier, was supported by the brothers Holden and Robert Bowker in defending farming interests in the House of Assembly.[29] The opposite point of view, that of unity and the supremacy of trade and financial interests, and the consequent retention of Cape Town as the sole seat of government, was advocated by the self-confident John Molteno, a rich farmer and banker who had formed, during the frontier wars, a low opinion of Imperial officials and was 'very apt to be led away by excessive zeal for anti-government attacks'. It is worth noticing the ease with which Dutch- and English-speakers moved between colonies and republics; sons of both Reitz and Brand became Presidents of the Orange Free State, and a son-in-law of Reitz's, William Schreiner, Prime Minister of Cape Colony. At any rate for the first sessions of the Legislature, Dutch was but rarely spoken, most members being fluent English-speakers, and many Dutch farmers remaining distrustful of parliamentary institutions.

Representation was geographical. Insofar as any parties could be defined, they were westerners and easterners: those nearer the Cape English and Dutch merchants and farmers – the latter overwhelmingly Dutch – the more aggressive easterners mostly English, the 1820 and other settlers. Apart from a few 'free blacks' there were no black voters in the west, but a number of 'Cape Coloureds', of whom the best-organized were those of the well-established Muslim community, qualified for the vote in the east. Black voters, mainly Mfengu, increased in numbers following the annexation of the district of Victoria, much to the alarm of the hostile section of whites led by Godlonton, violently expressed in a series of hysterical newspaper articles. The divide between easterners, apprehensive of being 'swamped' by those black voters that the Cape Franchise might eventually bring, and the westerners, becoming skilled in using Coloured votes to their own advantage, and pleased with the approbation their racially equal policies brought them from the home country, became more strongly marked.

Some visitors commented on the division between increasingly urbane, anglified Cape Town and the hinterland. Ivan Alexandrovich Goncharov, creator of the immortal Oblomov, visited the Cape with Lieutenant Rimsky-Korsakoff of the *Vostok* in 1853. The reforms initiated by John Herschel were already showing results, with a flourishing high school at Stellenbosch, and in Cape Town the Russians found 'omnibuses drive about . . . brandy is distilled and there are hotels, shops, young ladies in curls and pianos – can final triumph be far off?' But no further off than Paarl they discovered 'dour, Anglophobe Dutch, still resentful of British tenderness towards the "Kaffirs"'.

Seven years later further naval visitors were equally taken with the Cape. Captain Charles Jacquelot de Moncets arrived in February 1860 with the French expedition to join the Allied force in China, and admired everything he saw – the 'château' of the Chief Justice, 'Monsieur Clouted's' Constantia vineyard, even the 'excellent champagne *du pays*'. Lady Duff Gordon, at the same time, found more relaxed relations between the races than she had expected: on one building site, 'the foreman is a Caffre, black as ink, 6'3" high . . . and *Englishmen working under him!!!*'[30]

Transorangia: the Empire draws back

Lord Grey had originally been reluctant to let the Orange River Sovereignty fly the coop, but the Prime Minister Lord Russell grew increasingly adamant that this must ultimately be done. The Colonial Secretary was obliged therefore to write to Sir Harry on 15 September 1851: 'I have to instruct you to adopt the earliest and most decisive measures in your power for putting an end to any expenses to be incurred in the Orange River Sovereignty.' In the meantime at least Pretorius might be conciliated, a considerable potential economy, which Hogge and Owen proceeded to do in January 1852 at a meeting on the Sand River. Their agreement indicated that, even

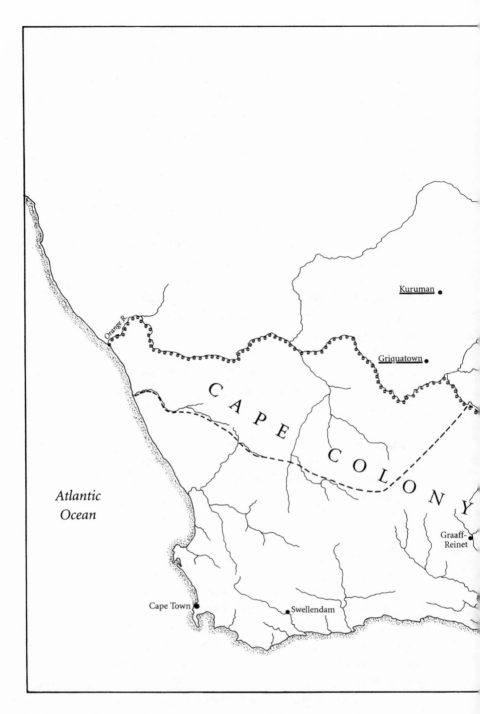

MAP 7 *Cape Colony: pre-1848 and post-1854 borders*

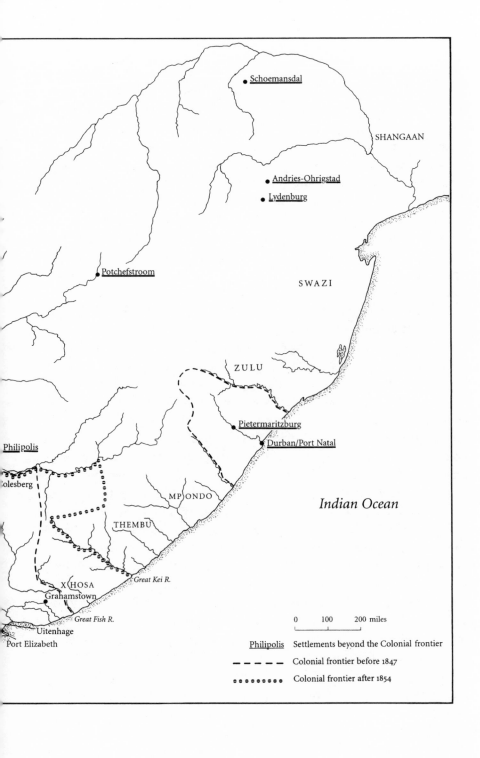

Schoemansdal

SHANGAAN

Andries-Ohrigstad

Lydenburg

Potchefstroom

SWAZI

ZULU

Pietermaritzburg

Durban/Port Natal

Philipolis

Colesberg

MPONDO

Indian Ocean

THEMBU

XHOSA
Grahamstown

Great Kei R.

Great Fish R.

Uitenhage

Port Elizabeth

0   100   200 miles

Philipolis   Settlements beyond the Colonial frontier

– – – – –   Colonial frontier before 1847

∘∘∘∘∘∘∘∘∘   Colonial frontier after 1854

before the future of the Orange River Sovereignty was settled, the British were prepared to recognize the potential existence of another Boer state, north of the Vaal River. The 'emigrant farmers' in that region were accorded 'the right to manage their own affairs and to govern themselves according to their own laws, without any interference on the part of the British Government'. The Sand River Convention was an easy agreement since all parties were convinced white supremacists, free of any liberal London prejudices: Hogge had recorded his conviction that the 'unalterable law . . . of Providence' dictated that the 'black race' must inevitably disappear before the advance of the whites. An obligatory nod was given in the direction of a ban on slavery, but the most significant item in the Convention was the British disclaimer of 'all alliances whatever and with whomsoever of the coloured nations to the north of the Vaal River', a concession that gave the Boers a free hand in settling their relations with any black communities they met in an enormous – and undefined – area.

Hogge and Owen were acting on their own initiative, without any specific authorization from London or from the High Commissioner, but they correctly interpreted Colonial Office thinking at a time of rapid change – there were three separate British governments in that year. Sixteen years after the first trekkers left the colony, it seemed as though their ambition for independence was to be fulfilled. Protecting black races outside colonial boundaries was henceforward to be a lower priority for Imperial governments: their work would be cut out in protecting their own non-white subjects from their white compatriots. The Commissioners then turned their attention to the Orange River Sovereignty, but their effectiveness was much diminished by Hogge's sudden death in May 1852. An elected convention, chaired by Dr A.J. Fraser, agreed in supporting a continuance of British administration in the Sovereignty, but the matter was put on hold pending the arrival of Sir Harry Smith's successor.[31]

Lord John Russell's ministry fell in February 1852, and Lord Grey was succeeded, after a brief interval of Conservative government, by the Duke of Newcastle, a decent enough man and, as a Duke, less susceptible to party pressures, but one not given to bold imaginative strokes. Sir George Cathcart, fully occupied with the eastern frontier, agreed that the task of disengaging from trans-Orange responsibilities should be delegated to Sir George Clerk, a cynically realistic Indian civil servant. Made responsible for what he described as 'a vast territory, possessing nothing that can sanction its being added to a frontier already inconveniently extended', inhabited by 'self-interested and prejudiced' colonists with 'cormorants' appetite for public money', Clerk was determined to withdraw, 'if possible in a friendly manner, if not, to withdraw anyhow'.[32] He proposed that the Sovereignty should be replaced by a Free State, a change which aroused the spirited objections of some of the population. The only responsibility Clerk recognized was to hand over power to some properly constituted authority capable of ensuring order. If loyalists were reluctant to do this, then the anti-imperialist burghers must be convinced, which proved not too easy. Many wanted either a continuation of the informal trekker arrangements and a continued accommodation with Moshoeshoe, or a unification with the Transvaal Boers.

The missionaries were particularly nervous. Jacques Pelissier of the Paris Mission wrote: 'The future alarms and troubles me. A terrible storm is brewing . . . I cannot see that our mission will survive . . . The antipathy which the colonists feel towards the natives and the missionaries is so great.'[33] Dr Fraser, accompanied by the influential Scots minister of the Dutch Reformed Church Dr Andrew Murray Jr, presented their views in London, but the by then once-more Liberal government would not be moved. It was a critical moment in African history. If the British government had, however reluctantly, taken action – and its anxiety to relinquish responsibility is yet another example of how far Britain was from being an expansive imperialist power – future events must have been greatly altered. The Sovereignty's population was so minute and scattered that union with the Cape would have been almost certain; and the Cape Franchise would therefore have been applied. Recalcitrant Boers had the assurance of possessing their own community north of the Vaal, whither they might remove, and any resistance was therefore unlikely. Without an ally, the Transvaal would never have entered into the war which eventually brought about the Union of South Africa under Afrikaner domination; but the existence of two independent Boer states presaged a very different future.

The Bloemfontein Convention was signed in February 1854 by Clerk and Johannes Hoffman, the first President of the new Orange Free State. Hoffman, a shrewd and able merchant, crippled by an accident, was nothing of a fundamentalist *voortrekker*. A friend of Moshoeshoe, conciliatory towards the Griquas and distrustful of Pretorius' militant Boers, Hoffman would have preferred the British to remain, but shouldered instead the considerable burden of founding a new country.

As the Sand River Agreement had done for the Transvaalers, the Transorangians were given a free hand, the British renouncing any 'alliance whatever with any native Chief or Tribes northward of the Orange River, with the exception of the Griqua Chief, Captain Adam Kok'. Just as previously recalcitrant Boers had trekked on over the Vaal, now disappointed English settlers moved back to the Cape. The new state was left with three cannon, together with 'tables, chairs, desks, shelves, inkstands, green baize, safes . . . freely sacrificed in the cause of peace', as *The Times* cynically reported.[34]

The Free State's inheritance also comprised the unresolved problems of Moshoeshoe's Basuto. Previous definitions of his borders had left everyone concerned dissatisfied. Major Warden had attempted to reach a solution by force of arms in July 1851, but was repulsed at the battle of Viervot with considerable losses – some 150 killed, most from Moroka's Rolong, who formed the bulk of Warden's force. In December of the following year Sir George Cathcart himself, who had fought against Napoleon's armies in 1812–13, now with a considerably superior force, was again completely defeated by Moshoeshoe, losing, among other casualties, twenty-seven of his British lancers. The Basuto light cavalry, which Sir George compared to the Cossacks he had served with, were a formidable enemy. Showing more sense than Sir George, the undefeated Moshoeshoe, as skilled in diplomacy as in war, immediately offered to make peace: 'You have chastised, let it be enough: and let me be no longer considered as an enemy of the Queen'; an offer which was gratefully accepted.[35] Without further interference Moshoeshoe was then able to dispose of his old antagonists Sekonyela and Taaibosch, making himself undisputed master of what is now Lesotho, independent of both Boers and British.

Absolute independence for a people now wedged between Dutch communities was, as Moshoeshoe well understood, dangerous. He therefore earnestly requested a British agent to be appointed, formalizing the relationship. Clerk supported the proposal: Moshoeshoe 'ought not to be left alone. He does not desire or deserve to be regarded with that degree of indifference or neglect.' But London, always nervous of extending British commitments, refused. In a speech which clearly defined mid-century opinion, Frederick Peel, speaking for the Colonial Office, claimed that no 'object of interest, honour or dignity' justified 'going to the enormous expense of maintaining peace between the aborigines and the Europeans'. The change in sentiments from those of only ten years before, when Natal had been annexed, was striking, but the fact that Natal had a tempting and vulnerable coastline would, even in Peel's view, have made British control imperative. The Orange Free State was landlocked and dispensable.[36]

Within two months of its independence the tiny new republic, with a white population of not much over ten thousand, perhaps thirty thousand blacks and Griqua, the blacks mostly Moroka's Rolong, but occupying together some fifty thousand square miles, had evolved a constitution much more sophisticated and advanced than that subsequently adopted by the Transvaal. A Dutch teacher, Jacob Groenendaal, and Joseph Orpen, a twenty-six-year-old Irish surveyor who had fought hard for the continuation of British rule but remained to become a member of the Volksraad, were its chief architects. Unlike previous trekker programmes, the Orange Free State imposed no religious tests, had a clear separation of powers, a declaration of basic rights, and a strict limitation on the powers of future assemblies to change the fundamental law. Moroka was left in control of his small area around Thaba Nchu, but isolated from the white community. At a time when a colour- if not money-blind franchise was being established south of the Orange River, the black man to the north was to have none of the rights of citizenship for another 140 years.

Natal: the peace and security which a good government affords

When the British formally took over in May 1845 the missionary Daniel Lindley, who had been a good friend to the emigrants, wanted to 'shout as many a weather-beaten sailor has done with a joyful heart – Land ho! ... the Natal country is now under British authority and we shall very soon enjoy all the peace and security which a good government affords.' He was perhaps over-optimistic.[37]

The Republic of Natalia expired slowly and without dramatic incidents. The Volksraad continued in being until December 1845 when Natal was formally annexed, not by Britain, but by an unenthusiastic Cape Colony. Henry Cloete continued as sole judge and recorder for nine years, superintending the complex questions of land registration and ownership. Tranquillity seemed assured: he was able to report that there had been no serious crimes for twenty months, and that all previous sentences of capital punishment for murder had been commuted.[38]

As well as Erasmus and Susanna Smit, many other trekkers decided to stay on, and prospered: Paulus Zietsman, Pretorius' Secretary and a Volksraad member, became Natal's foremost trader; the prospective board of the Bank of Natal (banks, like amateur dramatic societies and racecourses, were at that time the priorities of any British colony) in 1854 included such men as former Volksraad member P.A.R. Otto, who farmed forty thousand acres, and Zulu-fighter Johannes van der Plank. Faku's Mpondo had the territory taken from them by the Boers restored, and Mpande was left in undisturbed possession of Zululand east of the Tukela/Buffalo, with the exception of the little territory around Blood River, where he allowed some remaining emigrants to form yet another republic, that of Utrecht.

With the transformation of Natalia into the colony of Natal the British government assumed responsibility for a territory with an overwhelming majority of blacks, presenting new opportunities and challenges. Unlike the Cape's turbulent borders, those of Natal were defined and peaceable. The Mpondo on the south and Mpande's Zulu on the north had few aggressive intentions. Black Natalians were fragmented, many having lost their own chiefs and ready to welcome a government offering security and tranquillity. But there were a great and increasing number of them, far in excess of the white colonists, whereas at the Cape the citizens, including the freed slaves, Khoikhoi and Mfengu were much more evenly balanced.

Imperial policy was much argued in London. If it proved necessary to incorporate some part of the world into the Empire – something mid-nineteenth-century British governments were usually reluctant to do – two alternatives were possible. Either it was right to work for as rapid an assimilation of races and cultures as possible, or the existing population must be protected by assigning a proportion of the land to them in which existing rulers could run matters in the traditional style. Whichever system was chosen it was assumed that the white colonists could not be left to exploit the natives, and that the Imperial government must reserve the right to protect these interests.

A century later, South African Nationalist governments were to develop a very different system of reservations. Black 'homelands' were created, usually absurd collections of plots where blacks were impounded, and outside which no political or social rights were allowed. The Victorian reservations were protected zones, where whites were not allowed to own land. Blacks could, and did, settle in the remainder of the country and were, in due course, allowed to choose whether they wanted to remain in

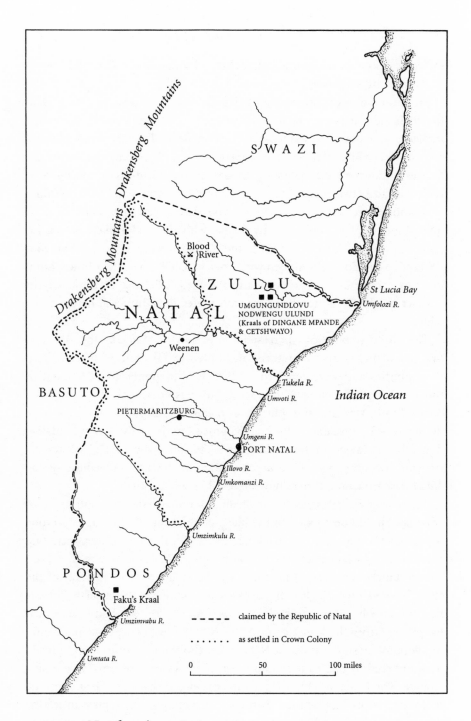

MAP 8 *Natal region, 1846*

the reservations or to assume citizenship, with the same rights and obligations as white settlers.[39]

From the point of view of the black Natalians there was much to be said
for their new masters. Traditional societies had been shattered by the
mfecane, and the new state did in fact provide the peace and physical
security for which Lindley had hoped. The black population, from the
fourteen thousand estimated by Cloete in 1843, had risen, voting with
their feet, to between sixty and seventy thousand five years later; within a
generation there were more than 300,000. These were the '*amalala*', conquered and kept in subjection by Shaka, who retained a lively hatred for
their oppressors. When war with the Zulu came in 1879 the Natalians
('Kafirs' to the Zulu) responded with alacrity. Chief Phakadet of the Chunu
lost three sons and two grandsons in the British defence of Rorke's Drift
– a fact quickly forgotten by those who prefer their Imperial heroes to be
white.[40]

The white population increased more slowly. Many of the Boers at
first persuaded to stay or return later opted to join one of the northern
communities and were replaced by British immigrants, five thousand of
them arriving between 1848 and 1851. Natal thus became the most 'English'
of the South African states, but by no means the most liberal. There were
no Reads or Philips among the Natalian missionaries, a more representative
figure being James Archbell, Moroka's old ally, who had given up his
original vocation to become a prosperous landowner and editor of the
Natal Independent, a generally white-establishment organ.

As soon as British rule was formally announced the question arose of
what law should be applied to the black population. At the Cape everyone
was subject to the same Anglo-Dutch law, and influential voices, including
that of Henry Cloete, wanted the same system in Natal, where, however,
circumstances were very different.[41] The heterogeneous population of the
Cape, where Dutch, English, freed slaves, Khoikhoi and those defying classification, now beginning to be known as 'Cape Coloured', had been joined
by refugees from the Xhosa country, the Mfengu or Fingoes, the first Nguni
to adopt Western customs. In Natal a few thousand colonists were greatly
outnumbered by blacks, to whom European laws and customs were totally
strange. The Colonial Office therefore considered that they must continue
to govern themselves by their own laws, excepting those 'repugnant to the
general principles of humanity': witch-killing and torture, for example,
were to be suppressed, but polygamy and *lobola* – commonly but mislead-

ingly known as 'bride-price' – allowed. Blacks on the reservations were expected to look after themselves, under their own chiefs, subject only to the loose supervision of a government agent.

Most pressing, however, was the question of how the country should be divided. Under the trekker Republic of Natalia every habitable square inch of the land had been allocated to whites. Martin West, the first lieutenant-governor, appointed a Land Commission to plan the whole settlement and ensure a reasonable division, which the three Commissioners were well placed to do, since they included Lindley and the enigmatic Theophilus Shepstone, first government agent to the Natalian blacks, who was responsible for the successful insistence that his charges should be allowed to retain their traditional law. Reflecting William Blake's Proverb of Hell, 'One Law for the Lion and Ox is oppression,' Shepstone claimed that 'equality meant deprivation'.[42] The Commissioners succeeded in identifying five of the ten locations they believed necessary to reserve for black occupation, which would have comprised in all some two million acres, over thirty acres for every black man, woman and child then resident: not the best of land, by any means, but enough to permit a decent living for the population as it was then.

Such recommendations were bitterly opposed by the white colonists, who demanded that blacks be allowed only enough land to provide basic subsistence, which would force them into working for whites at minimum wages. Nor was the British government enthusiastic. Earl Grey, while being 'fully sensible' of the arguments, refused to countenance any 'large expense'. A final stopper on the Land Commissioners' reasonable solution was placed by Harry Smith's arrival. A new Land Commission was appointed, much less likely to be sympathetic to the blacks. 250,000 acres, the Commissioners declared, would be quite enough to reserve for them, and even a hundred thousand would suffice, since more generous allotments would only encourage the blacks' 'habitual indolence' and make them free not to work for the white farmers. Sir Harry's high-handed methods infuriated Martin West, who had been forced to dismiss his own more liberal Commissioners, and London's support for West might have modified the settlement, had it not been for his premature death in 1849.

Daniel Lindley accurately described West's successor, Benjamin Chilley Pine, as 'very clever, very nervous, very fickle, and wanting in courage and *firm* principle'. Pine was aggressively pro-colonist, convinced that even the existing reserves were too large and should be split up, scattering the population among the white farms. So reactionary a proposal aroused a storm of protests from the normally acquiescent missionaries, and in particular from Theophilus Shepstone. Governments, local and Imperial, they insisted, had pledged their word that blacks in Natal would be fairly treated. They won the day, and the two million acres were allocated for reserves, but accompanied by little in the way of government support. Apart from the missionaries, American, British and German, the displaced blacks were left to fend for themselves; and did surprisingly well, with some support from David Dale Buchanan, liberal editor of the *Natal Witness*.[43]

By 1854 Natal had a population of some 120,000 blacks and six thousand whites, who were determined to have things their own way in spite of Shepstone and his allies. Pine adopted the 'very clever dodge' of packing another commission with settlers to report on 'the past and present state of the Kafirs' and to recommend arrangements for their future. When the report was finalized its proposals were so absurdly reactionary, and so clearly aimed at reducing the great majority of the population to absolute dependence, that it was quickly set aside, and the problem left for a representative government to consider. This status was conferred in 1857, with the majority of legislative councillors subject to election, but with a government-appointed executive. Even though the franchise was, as that of the Cape had been four years earlier, 'colour-blind', the British government, justly suspicious of the legislature's intentions towards the black population, specifically exempted Shepstone from its power. Shepstone was accordingly allowed almost unfettered control over the black population as Secretary for Native Affairs, with the support of Pine's successor John Scott, 'a frank affable gentleman' who was the first governor of the new colony.

There was an element of self-indulgence in Shepstone's enthusiastic adoption of the title of Great Chief; he enjoyed the reverence and affection in which he was held by at least a vocal part of the population and the respect shown to him by the Colonial Office as an undoubted expert on South African affairs, but he stoutly defended the interests of the blacks against the rapacity of the whites, always convinced, however, that the master knew best. For better and for worse, the Shepstone system developed in Natal was a model for many subsequent arrangements: blacks were to be governed by their own chiefs – who had to be acceptable to the colonial authorities – according to customary law, on lands which were communally held. Qualified individuals could apply for exemption to live under British law, which included access to the franchise. Shepstone saw this as leading in time to majority control, but to the white settlers the idea was anathema, and exemptions were rarely granted, as the Natal legislature fought bitterly to restrict black rights and force blacks on to the labour market. 'It is impossible,' John Scott observed to the Colonial Secretary, 'for white men to live with the coloured races without adopting a conviction that . . . they have the right to command the services of the less civilized.' The Colonial Secretary agreed: 'If practicable I should be disposed to look to the withdrawal of the European population as the best solution.'[44]

Scott became Governor of Natal in 1856, when the colony passed under direct Imperial rule; in the previous year two prominent figures made their first appearance in African and British history. The Revd John William Colenso took up his post as the first Anglican Bishop of Natal, and Cetshwayo kaMpande, the Zulu king's first son and probable heir, distinguished himself in combat against the Swazis.

NINE

First Steps
to Self-Government

The infant Cape Parliament was not allowed a peaceful first session. In December 1854 a new High Commissioner arrived. Sir George Grey – confusingly no relation to either Earl Grey or Sir Charles Grey, later Colonial Secretary – was a man of impressive intelligence and personality, a very different character from any of his predecessors, and one whose period in Africa left such substantial memorials as the Grey Library in Cape Town and the Grey Hospital at King William's Town. He had already built up a considerable reputation, having been appointed, as a junior army officer, to the governorship of South Australia at the age of twenty-six, followed by a nine-year stint as Governor General of New Zealand. His reputation in Whitehall was of the highest – assisted by the fact that he was every bit as cultivated as the permanent civil servants who often looked upon military governors with cool condescension – but it was to be marred as his wilfulness, arrogance and capacity for deception made themselves apparent.[1]

On Grey's arrival the new parliamentarians, led by Molteno and Bowker, expressed fears that trouble was brewing on the borders. Grey could appreciate that the unhappy Xhosa must have cause for 'constant uneasiness and annoyance', and suggested that only an organized campaign to improve the conditions under which they existed would ensure peace. 'In a few years,' he optimistically reported, 'our frontier defence will consist of a strong European population of young men, accustomed from childhood to the country, mixed up with a civilized coloured race won from heathenism and barbarism by our exertions.'[2] The young white men were to be the offspring of a chain of new villages along the Buffalo River, settled by retired soldiers. The 'mixing up' was to be done by assimilating the Xhosa into the rest of the community, bringing them under British law, and providing education and social services which would convert them from 'apparently irreclaimable foes into friends who have common interests with ourselves'.

In theory it was an admirable ideal, and even in practice something was done. The Grey Hospital, opened in 1855 under the guidance of Dr J.P. Fitzgerald, was an immediate success. Fitzgerald was an ophthalmologist, a branch of surgery which permits many quick and dramatic cures, but 'scarcely less wonderful was the fact that the natives were treated in the same way as the Europeans; they queued up together, had to share the same beds, the same doctors . . . and the same careful attention'. The admirable Lovedale, which was to produce a great number of black leaders, was founded in 1841 by William Govan, a Scots Presbyterian who believed in a good classical education – 'that commonly given to a Scottish gentleman' – for black and white alike; and Anglican mission schools were added to the existing Dissenting stations. A realistic attempt was made to eradicate the murder of witches: since a substantial part of any chief's income, and much of his power, lay in sequestering the property of those unfortunates sniffed out as witches, the Xhosa chiefs were given modest salaries in return for ceasing this traditional practice, thereby increasing their dependence on government, and much decreasing their status.[3]

Lord John Russell, at that time passing through the office of Colonial Secretary – a four-month stint before being succeeded by Sir William Molesworth for a similar period – agreed with Sir George's proposals, making it plain that as far as he was concerned, British Kaffraria could be abandoned, and welcome, were it not that 'an honourable duty to British colonists . . . and . . . views of comprehensive and vigilant humanity' forbade such a course. He would agree to a temporary annual subsidy, but Grey must realize that 'Great Britain will not defray the expense of another war in British Caffraria.' In supporting the subsidy, Molesworth pointed out that it represented only 1 per cent of the cost of a single year's war in South Africa. As for the rest of Kaffraria's costs, since the Cape now had representative government, the colonists could also have the privilege of paying some of their own bills; a suggestion which the Cape Parliament was reluctant to accept.[4]

Difficulties, which Grey seldom allowed to deflect him, soon arose. Veterans proved unwilling to volunteer for settlement – only 107 names were put forward, many quite unsuitable – and unrest developed on the frontier as Xhosa cattle began to suffer an epidemic of lung sickness. This virulent disease combined a variable incubation period, which could be as long as two years, with a high mortality. In spite of drastic measures by the chiefs, which included the executions both of quarantine-breakers and of the witches, clearly responsible for the catastrophe, and the more scientific, but equally ineffective remedies suggested by the Cape government, absolute destitution was widespread as tens of thousands of cattle died – Phato's herd was nearly wiped out.

Archdeacon Nathaniel Merriman, who was close to the Xhosa, wrote of their 'depression and great sense of loss'. Forced into a restricted area, banned from much of their ancestral land, with their cherished cattle dying miserably, their time-honoured customs traduced, the Xhosa were ready to listen to any promise that might relieve their desperate lives. Such a promise came in April 1856 when an adolescent girl, Nongqawuse, one of Sarili's people, was approached by two strangers, 'new people, from over the sea'. They instructed her that all the dead would rise again on an appointed day, and bring with them great gifts, including herds of magnificent cattle, and that the English would disappear from the face of Africa. Witchcraft, the strangers explained, was to blame for the current distress; in order to purge the people's crimes, and to prove themselves worthy of such wonders, all the surviving cattle must be slaughtered, after which all would be well. Westerners scornful of such wild notions might observe the Christian overtones, and recall that something very similar happened to a French girl of the same age two years later, in a cave near Lourdes, and recall the 'great disappointment' of the fifty thousand Americans who, only a little earlier, had confidently expected the end of the world.

Nongqawuse's followers were as firm believers as those of Bernadette Soubirous. Excitement heightened as rumours of the Crimean War led to hopes that the Russians, believed to be another black tribe, having defeated the British, would come to liberate their oppressed brothers. Cattle-killing began immediately, and spread rapidly through the Transkei and British Kaffraria. Not all chiefs were true believers – some, notably those who had already accepted Christianity, being scornfully sceptical – but each household made its own decision, not invariably that of their chief. Euphoria spread among the believers; the people had seen the light, there was no need to take thought for the morrow, to sow or cultivate the crops. On Resurrection Day felicity would be complete; but month after month passed, and no miracle came. In spite of the failure of the ancestors to return, hope fed on disillusion. The non-fulfilment of the prophecy could only be because some unbelievers were holding out; all cattle must be destroyed. Great pressure was put on those who kept their beasts alive; all animals, even goats and chickens, were slaughtered.

Some chiefs held out for some time. Sandile, in Kaffraria, bolstered by his Commissioner, Charles Brownlee, prevaricated until the end of 1856, but then gave in, while Brownlee 'covered my face with my hands and wept'. Much earlier Sarili, the paramount chief, son of the murdered Hintsa, who had never forgiven the English for their crime, had thrown the weight of his authority behind the movement. The quiet, deliberate Sarili was much attached to tradition and dedicated to the welfare of his subjects, capable of spending two days listening to the complaint of a Mfengu against one of Sarili's own people, and found it difficult to resist the influence of more aggressive councillors. By 18 February 1857, the last date promised by Nongqawuse, even the most devoted believers had to give up and prepare to pay for their delusions; the price was to be the destruction of the Xhosa nation.[5]

The number of those who died from disease and starvation is unclear, but this last, self-inflicted wound must have caused more damage than all the previous wars and incursions put together (not that responsibility for the event has not to be shared; had it not been for the colonial pressures, the Xhosa would never have been reduced to such straits). During 1857 the Xhosa population of British Kaffraria dropped from 105,000 to 37,500, and in the following year to 26,916. Many of the departed had become refugees, but in all it is likely that some forty thousand perished, and ten times that number of cattle were slaughtered.

The indirect consequences were perhaps even more damaging. For nearly a century the Xhosa had been divided among themselves, and now further splits developed between believers and non-believers. Any hope the chiefs might have had of establishing a quasi-independent state, as Shaka had done, and Moshoeshoe was even then doing, were permanently shattered. While missionaries and charitably-inclined folk led by Fitzgerald and Bishop Cotterell worked devotedly to help the starving refugees, Grey spurned their assistance. It was not the way he had hoped for, but the plight of the Xhosa made their assimilation into colonial organization inevitable. It suited the Governor that the desperate state of the Xhosa forced them onto the labour market. 'A restless nation,' he told the Cape Assembly on 7 April 1857, 'who for years have harassed the frontier, may now to a great extent be changed into useful labourers.'[6]

Both revisionist writers and Marxists have tended to dismiss Grey's actions as cynically calculated to destroy black independence and bring the people into the colonial labour market, which is a fundamental misunderstanding of his intentions. Like most of his contemporaries Grey held as an article of faith that it was his duty to advance primitive peoples to the standards of mid-Victorian Britain. Human dignity and happiness were synonymous with literacy, steam transport and hospitals. Hindus and Mahomedans could be – were best, in fact – left to follow their own doctrines, but less formal religions should be discouraged, especially when they included witch-murder. Unlike later, twentieth-century views of black education, Grey wanted black leaders to be in all respects as well educated as whites, but it was assumed that the *polloi* would be, as in Britain, encouraged rather to be literate labourers and artisans, useful hands in the great commercial and industrial Empire. Hence, the provision of hospitals and libraries of the highest standards was not incompatible with pouncing upon the opportunity offered by the cattle-killing to force Xhosa into the colonial economy. Only by such assimilation could they be extracted from their unhygienic and ill-disciplined existence and formed into 'the civilized coloured people' Grey had always wanted.

Sir George went on to point out that while Kaffraria had hitherto been overpopulated, the convenient absence of Xhosa now made it possible to fill the gaps with European settlers. These were to form those military villages which he had first envisaged three years previously. The end of the Crimean War had produced unemployed veterans of the German and Swiss legions, who could be resettled in Kaffraria; a suggestion which had the blessing of the Queen herself.

At first the experiment looked like being a success, as some 2,400 German soldiers arrived, led by their former commander Baron von Stutterheim. But Grey, without informing the War Office, decided to keep all the men under arms, and on full pay, in order to allow some units of the existing Cape Command to be sent off to assist in the suppression of the Indian Mutiny. Many of the legionaries also volunteered for Indian service, leaving fewer than a thousand in the villages, most without wives and families. Grey's efforts to persuade the British government to fund the provision of suitable females, and further settlers, were largely unsuccessful, but eventually a number of prosperous little German communities emerged along the banks of the Tyumi River.[7]

Other projects were more far-reaching. During the cattle-killing the colonists had been apprehensive of a unified assault, and perceived the Xhosa's present disorganization as an opportunity to destroy their power. In what seemed to one twenty-three-year-old officer, Lieutenant George Colley of the Queen's Regiment, 'a filibustering expedition . . . invading a country at peace with us', Grey had Sarili's people expelled from their traditional lands, where they had been settled for over a century, and confined them to a twenty-mile-wide strip of the coast east of the Kei. The northern part of their territories was then allocated to the Mfengu – the despised refugees sheltered by the Gcalekas a generation ago. Among the Thembu, Joyi, the paramount regent, had scornfully rejected the cattle-killers: 'What fools have you become, thus to pour out your beauty on the ground!' but many of his people had believed, provoking another 'filibustering' expedition against Chief Fadana, and fighting between the Thembu and Sarili's people. When this had been subdued many of the Thembu were moved on across the Indura River, into what had also been Gcaleka territory, and was now to be known as Emigrant Thembuland.[8]

The emergent republics

In spite of Grey's belief that an extensive conspiracy aimed at destroying colonial control connected Moshoeshoe with the Xhosa, Transorangia was little affected by the cattle-killing, although the area had its fair share of troubles. Both the struggling little states behind the Orange and the Vaal shared one potential, and nearly unassailable, enemy in the shape of Moshoeshoe, as well as a number of only somewhat less threatening other black and brown tribes. Having received assurances of British neutrality, an alliance, or preferably a union, between the small Boer states would seem a prudent move, and this was first suggested by the Orange Free State Volksraad in 1854. This initiative was premature, since there was at the time no united, organized society over the Vaal to deal with, but nothing more than a collection of widely separated quarrelsome communities without a constitution. Moshoeshoe was, however, also a potential threat to the British colonies, and the renewal of British rule was an attractive alternative to many worried Free State burghers.

To the north of the colonial boundaries the agreements at Sand River and Bloemfontein had liberated the scattered communities from British control and left one, the Orange Free State, as recognizably a viable state.

North of the Vaal the situation remained confused. The boundaries of that roughly four-hundred-mile-square block of land were for the most part definable: to the north and west the Limpopo River and its tributaries, and to the south the Vaal. The western perimeter was formed by the Lembotho mountains, behind which lay the Portuguese colony of Mozambique. The boundaries were reinforced by another, invisible, line, that of the westward limit of the tsetse fly, the carrier of sleeping sickness. In this area, the valley of the Limpopo and its tributary the Olifants, cattle-farming was impossible, and hunting the only practicable activity (which has resulted in the Kruger National Park, the biggest wildlife sanctuary in the world, now being sited there).

Since the upheaval of the *difaqane* a generation earlier, new black groupings had emerged. Sekwati, talented son of the great Thulare, founder of the Pedi empire which at the turn of the nineteenth century comprised most of the Transvaal, succeeded (after a number of his siblings had murdered each other) in reuniting many of his fellow-Sotho in the east, beyond the Steelport River. By the same mixture of diplomacy and resistance so successfully employed by his contemporary Moshoeshoe he remained independent of Boers and Zulu. Unfortunately for the Pedi, their missionaries from the Berlin Society were less supportive than Moshoeshoe's Frenchmen, nor did their territories adjoin a British colony. When Sekhukhune succeeded his father in 1862 the previous stability began to disintegrate.

Two smaller chiefdoms, Mako's Sotho and Mapoch's (Mabhogo's) Ndebele, descendants of those who had crossed the Drakensberg more peacefully and two generations earlier than Mzilikazi, were recognized by their Boer neighbours. Further north in the Zoutpansberg, where hunting and slave raiding continued to be popular, the Venda retained effectual independence, while the Lovedu succumbed to Boer raiders, acting with the Tsonga Knobnoses. Needless to say the areas where the whites settled tended to be those most suited for farming, the less desirable areas being left for the blacks.[9]

It was a time of change, as the first generation of *voortrekkers* died out to be replaced by the first generation of settled Afrikaners, and as the *taal* developed into what became in the 1860s the Afrikaans language. Hendrik Potgieter died in 1852, and his son Pieter Johannes was killed in the following year. Young Martinus Wessel Pretorius, a politician who gained little wisdom as he grew older, succeeded his father as Commandant General of the Transvaal in 1853, but lacked weight and credibility: 'A fine-looking man, but very weak-minded and uneducated,' was one assessment. Two years later, when a constitution had been agreed, he became the first President of what was known as the Transvaal or South African Republic, but which in reality existed largely on paper. The constitution reflected both the prejudices of the trekkers and their unsettled condition. Article 9 stated: 'The people desire to permit no equality between coloured people and white inhabitants, either in church or state.' Article 12 provided a period of three months to elapse between laws being passed in the Volksraad and their enactment, in order to enable the voice of the people to be heard. In spite of these prohibitions Coloured men, like Rudolf du Plooy, could be appointed as *heemraden*, and even as an acting *landdrost*. The Volksraad was peripatetic, and frequently unable to muster enough members to conduct its business. Potgieter's followers supported Stephanus Schoeman, who had succeeded him as Commandant and General, and remained distrustful of Pretorius, as another division opened among the Afrikaner community.[10]

All Western Christian Churches underwent agonizing reviews of their beliefs in the nineteenth century as they strove to adapt to the new liberal ideas that took root after the French Revolution – reviews which involved the most intricate of intellectual about-turns as the horrid truth that the world was not founded in 4006 BC began to thrust itself forward. Presbyterian Churches, the most democratically organized, had shown fissiparous tendencies: by 1820 the Church of Scotland had split into a dozen disputatious factions – burghers and antiburghers, Moderates and Evangelicals, Relief and Secession churches, Auld Licht and New Licht, Sandemans and Glasites. In 1843 the great schism came with the secession of the Free Church of Scotland, which considerably reduced the once monolithic established Church of Scotland.

The closely-allied Dutch Churches followed a similar pattern as the new ideas drove conservatives into more reactionary positions; and since many of the most influential dominees were themselves Scots, the divisions followed similar lines. Ds Andrew Murray Jr, although theologically adventurous himself, defended the orthodox Nederduitse Gereformeede Kerk (NGK), as established at the Cape. More liberal were such ministers as J.J. Kotze and D.P. Faure, who both ended up as Unitarians; while the extreme conservatives contended amongst themselves for the most vigorous purity. Most of the contention took place in the new republics. The trekkers, as Daniel Lindsay appreciated, were not greatly interested in theology, and tended quickly to slide away from religion altogether; twentieth-century

Afrikaner Calvinism, that highly individual system, began to develop in the Transvaal, but reached its perfection only after the Second World War. Pretorius and the Potchefstroomers had cast off allegiance to the NGK and founded their own sect, the Nederduitse Hervormde Kerk (NHK), initially led by the sharp-tempered Hollander Dirk van der Hoff. In 1859 Dominus Dirk Postma, another Hollander and a member of the secessionist 'Affscheiding' Dutch Church, set up a Church of his own, the Gereformeerde Kerk, better known as the Doppers, who frowned on such degenerate frivolities as hymn-singing and long coats. Zoutpansbergers and Utrechters would have none of these, and remained on the whole faithful to the Cape NGK, whose Transvaal congregations were socially liberal, friendly with the Methodists, often in sympathy with the British, and enthusiastic about missions, which the NHK deplored.[11]

Divided both religiously and politically, the two major communities, the Schoemanites of Lydenburg/Zoutpansberg and the Pretorians of Potchefstroom, moved painfully from an actual state of war in 1857 to an agreed constitution in 1859. It was, from the start, unworkable, little more than a restatement of the trekkers' thirty-three articles. The Volksraad – at first restricted to members of the Hervormde Kerk – was supreme, and took to passing simple resolutions which had the force of law, ignoring what constitutional restrictions existed when it suited them, so storing up trouble for the future. The first united Volksraad, which also included representatives from the little republic of Utrecht, met for the first time on 4 April 1860. Its unity and concord were short-lived. By October Acting State President Schoeman resorted to a *coup d'état* to unseat Acting State President J.H. Grobler, and a civil war began at once to simmer. The combatants themselves would probably not have recognized the fighting as 'war': a tradition was developing that discontented burghers could saddle up and brandish their rifles in a '*wapende protes*'. More legally-minded British administrators, though, could well take this to be war, and act accordingly.

It was the ambitious and intractable Pretorius whose actions caused the strife. In 1856 he had entered Bloemfontein to demand that the Free State unite with the Transvaal. This singularly unappetizing prospect appalled the sensible President Boshof, who was then strenuously erecting a workable modern administration, and was convinced that if union with anyone was needed, it could only be with the economically sound and politically stable Cape Colony.

This Grey was enthusiastically prepared to accept, believing that withdrawal from Transorangia had been a serious error, and that the permanent solution for South Africa must be unity between the widely differing communities. The only power able to control these communities was Britain, acting through the Cape; but neither Britain nor the Cape was willing to accept more responsibility. Reacting to a series of despatches urging closer ties with the Boer republics, the Liberal Foreign Secretary Henry Labouchere was unenthusiastic, insisting that on the contrary their independence must be 'vigorously observed'. Nor were the Tories, when they came to office in February 1858, more helpful. Both the Colonial Secretary Edward Bulwer-Lytton (later Lord Lytton) and his influential lieutenant Lord Carnarvon agreed that some amendment to the Convention was overdue, but that any political union was out of the question; it was 'the old story of the giant and the dwarf', where 'the dwarf could be thrusting his Dutch nose into all sorts of black squabbles', from which the British taxpayer would have to extricate him.[12]

Grey saw an opportunity of bypassing the home government in December 1858 when, having successfully negotiated an end to a war between Moshoeshoe and the Orange Free State, the Free State Volksraad and President formally asked him for discussions on 'a Union or alliance with the Cape Colony', either on the plan of federation or otherwise, which they were convinced was 'desirable'.[13] Quite contrary to his instructions, Grey gave his blessing and passed the project on to the Cape Parliament for their consideration. This was too much for the Colonial Secretary, who wrote in the severest terms that Grey had placed the government in a position of extreme embarrassment and difficulty, and that he was to be sacked. But Sir George was saved by the bell as the Conservative government was replaced by a Liberal ministry, with the Duke of Newcastle back in his former post. Grey was sternly spoken to – in person, since he came to London on leave – but allowed to stay in post, and was back at the Cape in June 1860.

With no possibility of union with the Cape, and with many of the more anti-British burghers pressing the unattractive alternative of joining the Transvaal, the disillusioned Boshof resigned, opting for the more settled life of colonial Natal, where he became a member of the legislature. Martinus Pretorius saw the opportunity to unite the two republics, and in December 1859 was elected to succeed Boshof as President of the Free State, whereupon the Transvaal Volksraad took umbrage, and in the first session of April 1860 suspended Pretorius as Transvaal President. The subsequent four years saw the Transvaal reduced to a travesty of a state, in which the Potchefst-room/Zoutpansberg government fought the Rustenberg/Lydenburgers and Staatsleger fought Volksleger. The civil war that followed was not a bloody affair, but only subsided when Pretorius resigned as Orange Free State President and was readmitted to the Transvaal, which was by then bankrupt and disillusioned. In the decisive action of January 1864, the Volksleger ('*Volksleer*' in Afrikaans) under Jan Viljoen got the worst of it, losing five dead. Viljoen was a fiery individual, who later sjamboked Ds. F. Lion Cachet of the NGK on account of their theological differences. Paul Kruger was the successful commander, and became henceforward the most influential figure in Transvaal affairs.

Returning to reality, in February 1864 the Orange Free State chose as President the excellent John Henry Brand, son of Christoffel, who was to hold the office for the rest of his life, and who established the Free State as a stable and successful – within its own peculiar terms – independent country. Certainly life there was more agreeable than in the Transvaal, where church-going remained the only cultural activity on offer. There were no schools, education being in the hands of itinerant teachers, no newspapers or libraries, nor indeed any recognizable towns. Widely scat-tered farmers came together in one of the centres for a rare meeting of the Volksraad, attendance at the locally preferred church, or to join one of the leaders on commando against the blacks or, as in 1857, against their fellow-Boers on the other side of the Vaal.

It did appear that the Freestaters had the best of things.[14] Their highveld lands were fertile, the people were more united, although quarrels in the Volksraad were not uncommon, and Bloemfontein was developing into a pleasant little town, with its churches, schools and a newspaper, the *Friend of the Free State*. More importantly, the black and white populations were moving towards a more satisfactory equilibrium, with the major black groupings retaining a good deal of independence. John Mackenzie recorded in 1859 that it was 'not unusual for a Dutchman to give his hand in greeting to a Griqua, and call him "oom" or "neef"'; but he also noted that by 1871 attitudes had hardened. Moroka, 'that stately Black gentleman' remembered by little Sophie Leviseur, continued to rule in Thaba Nchu, and the Queen's birthday remained an official holiday in the Boer republic. But none of the Boer states – four until 1864, thereafter for some time only two, the Free State and the South African Republic – were anything but appendages to the much larger and infinitely more developed Cape Colony.

There it was incumbent upon the – hopefully chastened – Sir George Grey to settle the unaddressed agenda awaiting his return in June 1860 from an unpleasant leave in London (rendered more distressing since on the return passage Lady Grey began a shipboard liaison which led to the couple being separated for the next thirty years). A complex situation, burgeoning with difficulties, marked by a series of false starts and backward steps, greeted him. It was still uncertain whether the Cape Colony would be divided into East and West; Queen Adelaide's Land had been annexed, disannexed, and reappeared as British Kaffraria with the Ciskeian Xhosa under Sandile now colonial subjects and its own lieutenant governor, John Maclean. Grey was enthusiastic for extending its boundaries to the Natal frontier, bringing all the Xhosa and the other South Nguni under British rule, and had convinced the Duke of Newcastle, who agreed that 'A glance at the map and a knowledge of the habit of our fellow-countrymen must at once convince anybody that the whole of Kaffiraria must in a few years become British.' But the Duke exemplified mid-Victorian attitudes when he went on: 'Annexation is an ugly word, and ugly deeds have been done under it – but the word need not frighten us and the deeds by no means be repeated.' It was, however, to be more than twenty years before the inevitable happened.[15]

The northern border of the colony had been defined only as far as the central Orange River – and many within the Orange Free State were hoping to be readmitted into the fold; while to the west of Kok's Griquas the followers of Waterboer had uncertain status, and to the east Moshoeshoe remained unsubduable; Natal was occupied with its own affairs, on the first stage of representative government from 1856; and strung between the colonies were a number of native states which accepted varying degrees of British authority – Fingoland, Thembuland and Emigrant Thembuland, Pondoland, Nomansland, Bovambaland and Gcalekaland, where Sarili's Xhosas led a confined and unhappy existence. Only on the perimeter, where the powerful Zulu kingdom under Mpande was still quiet, and over the Vaal, where the widely scattered Boers were too busy fighting among themselves, were there no immediate Imperial concerns.

Thirty-five years after the historic meeting between Somerset, Ngqika and Ndlambe, it was evident that the blacks who had adapted to the colonial presence had chosen a more profitable strategy than those who had resisted. After the frontier wars and the cattle-killing, Macoma, the great opponent of the British, was imprisoned on Robben Island. His people and those of

Sarili, reduced to a fragment of their former strength, were squeezed out of their old lands, partly by white settlers, but more so by the successful Mfengu and Thembu, who had opted for collaboration.

A personal comparison might be made between Macoma, his brother-in-law Phato, and Phato's brother Kama, both sons of Chungwa, the Gqunukhwebe chief. Phato had been present at the 1819 conference, and in spite of many colonial aggressions and privations had either remained neutral or allied himself with the colonists until the 1846 war, which his people anticipated by killing a missionary in November 1845 – an unprecedented event – and in which he joined Macoma's attack. This was followed by Phato's adhesion to the cattle-killing cause, which left his people starving and scattered, and he himself exiled on Robben Island with Macoma. Kama, on the other hand, was an early convert of the Wesleyan missionary William Shaw, and continued to collaborate with the colonial authorities. By 1864, having survived all the frontier wars and kept his people from the cattle-killing, he had flourished to become one of the most respected Xhosa chiefs, with some sixteen thousand followers. Such an attitude was less glorious than that of Macoma's dogged resistance, but Kama's people were doubtless grateful that they had followed a Methodist lay preacher rather than a great warrior.

Sir George Grey gave impetus to the Europeanization of the chiefs by a well-planned piece of social engineering. Zonnenbloem was founded by the autocratic and ceaselessly energetic Bishop Gray as a school for the children of chiefs near Cape Town, a sort of black Haileybury where boys and girls could be turned into decent, preferably cricket-playing, British administrators.[16] It had mixed success, but both the Bishop's and the Governor's efforts were in accordance with the spirit of British governments. Any policy that promised the minimum of trouble and expense would recommend itself to London. The new Liberal government in office from 1859 to 1866 had brought with it as Chancellor of the Exchequer William Ewart Gladstone, who was dedicated to reducing public expenditure, especially defence spending, even in the teeth of his Prime Minister, the pugnacious Lord Palmerston. Based on his own previous brief experience as Colonial Secretary, Gladstone had earlier written: 'the test of a good colonial policy is that it shall prepare colonies for independent self-government.'[17] Such a combination of principle and economy and expediency was powerful, and when in 1864 the Duke of Newcastle was succeeded at the Colonial Office by Edward Cardwell, a disagreeable but very capable reformer, firm action was inevitable. Cardwell had accepted the clear advice of J.R. Godley, an accepted authority on colonial defence and a senior official at the War Office, that any British troops stationed in a colony should be paid for by the colony itself, and that the accounting would be on a uniform basis for all colonies. Colonists must, Godley insisted, realize that the British government was determined 'to make a sufficient *colonial* contribution a condition *sine qua non* of ours'.[18] It was obvious that money was going to be tight as never before; war must be avoided if possible, but if inevitable, then a fixed proportion of the cost would be charged to the colonies. At the same time public opinion at home must not be outraged by either English or Boer colonists behaving too aggressively. The 'negrophile' lobby was not as powerful as it had been, but any too-obvious oppression of the blacks remained certain to raise a storm of protest.

Both the Cape and Natal now had representative governments supported by public opinion of their own. These administrations could be overruled by the High Commissioner and Governors, but any such assertion of Imperial authority brought with it responsibility for footing the bill; a powerful restraint. Since the 1860s began with a period of economic crisis it was an unpropitious time for initiatives. A serious drought in 1861–62 more than decimated the flocks. Bank deposits slumped, and small local banks looked precarious.

Sir Philip Wodehouse, a cousin of Lord Kimberley, who replaced Grey in January 1862, was the first governor without a military background. Brisk, decisive and authoritarian, but humane and competent, he remained for more than eight years, and guided South Africa through difficult times. He needed persistence and tact to deal with the Cape, where the split between Westerners, primarily Molteno and Saul Solomon, who pressed for an advance to 'responsible' government, and Easterners, led by the indefatigable Godlonton, who resisted it as handing power to the West, showed no signs of healing. Between the two a prudent financial policy was nearly impossible. Wodehouse also soon found himself trapped between his masters in London and his local legislators. The Treasury, insistent that the subsidies to British Kaffraria could not be allowed to continue, combined with the Colonial Office, which was unable to explain why the Cape, with less than 4 per cent of the British colonial population, absorbed more than a quarter of all colonial military expenditure; the obvious solution was that Kaffraria be annexed to the Cape, but the Cape Parliament was reluctant to accept the responsibility and expense.

By 1864, partly by agreeing to hold a parliamentary session in Grahamstown, so conciliating the Easterners, Wodehouse had managed to persuade
the Cape legislature to authorize enough taxation, and to cut expenditure
sufficiently, to balance the budget. It was hard to argue for the separate
existence of British Kaffraria, and the white settlers there weakened their
case for independence by agitating for expansion to the east, establishing
a protective cordon of military settlements in Sarili's country. This had
been anticipated by Sir George Grey who had despatched the aggressive,
hard-swearing Walter Currie to instruct a nervous Sarili that he should
prepare to move not only well behind the Kei, but to the Mbashi, or even
into Pondoland, and the Duke of Newcastle had agreed quite specifically
that British Kaffraria should annex the Kei-Mbashi lands. Sarili therefore
reluctantly withdrew behind the Mbashi, but the prospective settlers (who
would have to accept a militia obligation) were not forthcoming. Currie
attempted to push things along by a disgraceful little plot, claiming (what
he later admitted was 'not the T—th but a L-e') that Sarili was planning
an invasion. Wodehouse saw through the deception, and indignantly
ordered that the planned annexation would be cancelled and that the
Transkei would remain a black reserve; but not for the Xhosa alone.[19]

An effort was made to persuade the Ciskeian (Gaika) Xhosa, under
Sandile's leadership, to cross the Kei. Sandile refused, fearing to lose the
support of Brownlee: 'What had he sinned that Charles should be taken
from him?' He went on: 'I do not know the land beyond the Kei. I have not
grown up there . . . We like to die here . . . I am satisfied with chieftainship I
have here, and if it is small I do not care so long as I am taken care of by
the English.' But he admitted that even if he moved, many of his people
would not go with him, 'and I will be there a common Kafir'.[20]

By this time the abrasive Cardwell had arrived at the Colonial Office,
and put his food down firmly. The projected expense was intolerable: 'A
proposal to extend our frontier to the Bashee', much less to the Umtata,
would entail a cost proposal 'as unacceptable as it would have been possible
for any Minister to make'. The frontier was to be the Kei, and the lands
between that and the Natal frontier would remain black. Within that twenty
thousand square miles were the still independent Mpondo kingdom,
together with Thembu, Xhosa, Mfengu and Mpondomise, under chiefly
rule. The region, the Transkei, continued predominantly black, becoming
in 1959 the first independent black homeland. The main beneficiaries of
this reserved territory were not however the traditional occupants of the

land, Sarili's Gcaleka Xhosa, but forty thousand Mfengu, who agreed to move on condition that they did not lose their British citizenship, and that they should be given a resident magistrate.

Having reduced as much as possible the population of Kaffraria, who would have to be accorded all the privileges of British citizenship (it is instructive to see how these privileges, modest though they may have been, were insisted on by those blacks, like the Mfengu, who had previously qualified for them), the British government annexed British Kaffraria to the Cape. It was not a popular action there: 'arbitrary interference', Solomon complained. Persuaded by the invaluable Attorney General William Porter, who pointed out that the Cape, dependent on the British taxpayer, could not 'look big and talk big', the Cape Assembly grudgingly agreed to accept Kaffraria, and the borders of the Cape Colony were extended to the Kei. Throughout the episode it should be noted that no outright coercion was used. If black communities objected to a move, they stayed where they were; this was Imperial policy, however, and by no means popular with the white colonists, most of whom would have much preferred that blacks were made to live where it best suited the settlers. After the end of Imperial rule the settlers, represented by Nationalist governments, got their way.

It was not only the eastern boundary of the Cape Colony that was defined in the mid-1860s, for this was a time when much of South Africa assumed the shape it has since held. Natal's western frontier was fixed – to the annoyance of the Natalians, who coveted Pondoland – very much where it was before, with the exception of a strip of coastline to include the new Port Edward. More significantly, the boundaries of what was to become first the British protectorate of Basutoland, and then the independent kingdom of Lesotho, were finally established. These abutted on the Free State, Natal, the Cape Colony and the black Transkeian communities. Those areas originally claimed by Moshoeshoe were open to some dispute – he had, after all, only established his people there in the 1820s when Griqua, white, other Sotho-Tswana and Khoikhoi communities were also staking claims in Transorangia – but had been severely restricted first by the Warden line, which had taken the best lands of the Caledon Valley from the Basuto.

These lost lands were not immediately occupied by Free State farmers, and many continued to be farmed by the Sotho, but as President Brand gradually succeeded in improving his administration, Free State power, and willingness to exert it, increased, while Moshoeshoe was growing older, often ill and unable to control his active sons. The old chief had already asked that 'his people should be taken care of by the Government of the Queen as all people are taken care of by it', and Wodehouse was very willing that this should be done. Given successive British governments' antipathy to any extension of colonial responsibilities, evidenced by the refusal to extend the Kaffrarian boundaries, this was likely to be difficult. Only after a protracted and damaging war between the Free State and the Sotho, which dragged on from 1865 to 1868, was any progress made. Moshoeshoe renewed his pleas for British protection, suggesting annexation by Natal, to which the Colonial Secretary, by then the sensible Duke of Buckingham, was prepared to accede. It was Wodehouse who, not trusting the Natal colonists to treat any black properly, put a stop to this.

In what was a bold step for even a High Commissioner, Wodehouse struck out on his own, on 12 March 1868 announcing Basutoland to be a British territory and the Sotho British subjects. The resulting row took time to subside. Brand, understandably indignant, sent a delegation to London, but Buckingham decided to back Wodehouse. Indeed, the Duke considered, questioning the previously received wisdom that had produced the Sand River and Bloemfontein Conventions, it might well be that any future overtures from the Boer states to be brought 'in some form or another under British authority' should be accepted.[21]

The agreement between the Orange Free State and Britain took much negotiation before the Convention of Aliwal North was signed on 12 February 1869, and ratified on 19 March 1870. Moshoeshoe had died one week previously, believing that although even most of the territory he claimed rightfully to have belonged to his people had been given to the Free State farmers, the future of the nation he had founded was assured. Which, after some vicissitudes, proved to be so; but the Basuto were penned in a mountainous region with limited resources, secure perhaps, but doomed to comparative poverty.

One more movement of peoples was effected in that decade of displacement and boundary definitions. Adam Kok's position had become impossible when the British withdrew from Transorangia. The British negotiator Sir George Clerk had, quite deliberately, deceived Kok in a secret arrangement made with the Boer delegates in February 1854 in which Clerk made it clear that ensuring the Griquas left the Free State was a prime objective of the agreement. The published proposals – which Kok fought doggedly to improve – merely mentioned that 'should circumstances at any future time render it more conducive to the welfare and comfort of Adam Kok to remove to the south of the Orange River', the British would help him establish elsewhere. The secret proposal's wording, suggested by the Free State representatives, was that '*When* [my italics] Adam Kok departs from his territory the treaty between Her Majesty's Government and him lapses' – his lands would then become part of the Free State. Clerk agreed, but cynically asked, 'Will this be productive of any advantage to the Orange River, or will the knowledge of the consequence being inevitable upon his migration not rather tend to keep Kok longer where he is?'[22]

The plan worked; faced with the gradual disappearance of his lands, Kok, a man of courage and determination, decided to initiate his own Great Trek. In the century that had elapsed since the first Adam Kok led his people over the Orange River, the Griqua had established a society equal in many respects to the Dutch settlements, and superior in some. John Mackenzie had remarked on the quality of their houses and possessions, and their administration was in many respects a viable political entity. Their betrayal by the British authorities was a disgraceful act.[23] Leaving their lands, more than two thousand Griqua moved over the Drakensberg to Nomansland, the foothills of the Drakensberg, hitherto claimed by Faku, but which had indeed been largely abandoned. There they were to be British subjects, and not, Governor Grey assured them, to be left to the tender mercies of Natal. Nomansland became, and continues to be, Griqualand East, and although the Griqua have been absorbed into the population their influence is still visible.[24] Once again the Griqua began to construct a decent life for themselves, to replant their orchards, sow new crops and repair the depredations to their flocks made during their two-year peregrination.

TEN

Uncertain Imperialists

The rock on which South Africa will be built

Sir Philip Wodehouse had reason to congratulate himself when he left the Cape in May 1870. During his term of office, he claimed, not a shot had been fired by a British soldier – a great change from the turbulent 1840s and fifties. He had, however, had less luck with the Cape Parliament, which he unsympathetically described as 'an infernal machine'; and there were serious economic problems in the colony.

Sir George Grey had spent freely on public works, and 1860 had been something of an *annus mirabilis*, marked by the visit of Queen Victoria's favourite son, Affie, Midshipman Prince Alfred. A pretty boy – his portrait hangs in the splendid Grey Library – Affie was a great success. Even Sandile was impressed that a son of so great a chief should do menial work – washing the decks – under strict discipline. Affie's opening of the new docks, which were to make Cape Town at last a safe haven, gave rise to a national celebration. Grey jokingly suggested that if the Prince 'would only marry Emma Sandile he would have the means of ending Kafir wars for ever'.[1]

But it all cost money, and the public debt rose as the euphoria of 1860 evaporated. Droughts cut back the wool crop, and borrowers and lenders both began to suffer the consequences of too-rapid expansion. Railway-building, which had made a tentative start, ground to a halt, and failures proliferated; even the Standard Bank had to pass its dividend. The conclusion of the American Civil War ended the demand for uniform cloth and plunged sheep farmers into crisis. 1865 saw many banks, having made loans on the security of temporarily-inflated land values – up to 300 per cent in a few years – on the brink of failure. Immigration dried up – for some years more left than arrived – exacerbating the chronic labour shortage.

The first indication that South Africa might develop more than an agricultural economy came in 1867 when a fine diamond was found at Hopetown, near the Orange Free State border, and placed on the table of the Cape Assembly by Sir Richard Southey, the Colonial Secretary, with the words, 'Gentlemen, this is the rock on which the future success of South Africa will be built.' This was more accurate than most such prophecies, although gold soon supplanted diamonds as South Africa's most valuable mineral resource. Within twenty years four farms, ninety miles north of the Orange River, had become the centre of the world's diamond industry, and that under the effective control of one man.

Events on the diamond fields during that period foreshadowed much of the country's future. Many features which were to become characteristic of South Africa developed around the mines: the deployment, for the first time, of large-scale international capital; the introduction of modern industrial techniques; the employment of immigrant blacks on short-term contracts and their segregation into confined locations, with their movement controlled by complex pass laws; all contributed to radically changed attitudes. The theory that the basic necessities of black existence could continue to be provided by their family farms, leaving the menfolk free to earn cash wages, which might therefore be regarded almost in the light of pocket money, developed from a reasonable assumption into what became an irrational dogma; liberal Imperial rules of equality before the law were supplanted by exploitative colonial capitalism to leave non-whites subordinate and degraded; the first strikes were savagely suppressed; and the prime mover in colonial expansionism, Cecil Rhodes, initiated his African empire.

Southey's diamond was an alluvial stone, found by 'panning' silt from watercourses, an operation well-fitted for individuals with limited capital. More stones were soon discovered as prospectors were drawn to the banks of the Vaal River. Blacks and whites from the Orange Free State and the Cape foraged assiduously from the confluence of the Vaal and the Harts at Debtor's Hope, through Bad Hope and Gong Gong to Fool's Rush, near what is now the city of Kimberley. There the diamonds were found in a deposit of blue shale, and had to be dug from the ground, a very different operation from the extraction of alluvial stones. Immediately the problem arose of which state owned this interesting but highly debatable territory in a hitherto neglected area of indifferent farmland. Hopetown, where the original stone was found, was just within the Cape Colony, but the diamond fields lay north of the Orange River.

The removal of Adam Kok's Griquas to Griqualand East had left Nicholas Waterboer and his people uneasily exposed in a salient of territory projecting into the Free State and the Tswana tribes of the Kalahari. Waterboer's lands being less attractive than those of Adam Kok, his people had suffered less from white pressure, their main rivals being the Tswana. In the Free State the solid work put in by Presidents Boshof and Brand to create an effective administration had been damagingly undermined by the Basuto troubles. Moshoeshoe had been a dangerous enemy, and one of the best Boer leaders, Louis Wepener, had been killed in the fighting. Brand had to balance as best he might the interests of Dutch farmers and English merchants, who had been offended by Britain's brusque rejection of their offer of union. Although generally less backward than the Transvaal burghers, Free State whites could be equally primitive in their attitudes towards blacks. In 1863 one Volksraad member, J.A.D. Serfontein, reproved another for referring to the 'zwart goed' (black things) as 'menschen' (human beings): they were simply Kaffirs. With such men in positions of power the pool of talent on which Brand could draw was limited, and importations from the Cape continued to be essential.[2]

In 1865 the surly mindcast of some burghers brought about both the expulsion of the Standard Bank, which had set up business only four years previously, and of the missionaries. This did nothing to promote prosperity, and contributed to leaving the Free State in a poor position to cope with the sudden eruption of an invasion of diggers from 1870 onwards. These came from all corners of the world: English-speakers from the Cape, Natal and Britain, from Australia and California, with experience of gold mines; local Afrikaners, Thlaping, Rolong and Basuto; Pedi and Tsonga from the Transvaal and Mozambique. And from all walks of life: 'a young officer who lost his commission, a young surgeon with an insufficient practice . . . fellows retrenched by the depression in trade', to say nothing of at least four Cape MPs, including John Xavier Merriman, who arrived in February 1872.

One of the fortune-seekers was the eighteen-year-old Cecil Rhodes, who sat in his tent reading for his Oxford matriculation and having philosophical conversations with Merriman, his senior by fourteen years. Rhodes and Merriman were to become first friends and then opponents: Rhodes, the arch-imperialist, dedicated to advancing the English-speaking nations' world leadership; and Merriman, the archbishop's son, ironic and idealistic, who placed unity in South Africa first.[3] At the diggings, however, they were nothing more than two ambitious young men developing their ideas and seeking their fortunes – an operation in which Rhodes was much the more successful.

In a sprawling camp of tents and huts, with a few timber buildings including dozens of bars, a music hall and a newspaper office, this very mixed society ran itself under 'diggers' law', developed on the goldfields of Australia and California and more or less officially recognized. Every man – black or white – was entitled to register up to three claims, thirty-one feet square, which could be subdivided into plots as little as five square yards; claims not worked for three days could be 'jumped'. From its inception the camp at the 'dry diggings' was superintended – from a distance – by a capable Free State official, Oloff Truter, who happened to have had previous experience of the Victoria goldfields; but there were others contending for control.

No powerful chiefdom like that of Moshoeshoe exercised sovereignty over the region. Between them the Tswana and the Griqua had killed, enslaved or absorbed the original Khoi-San inhabitants. The Thlaping chief Mahura claimed a large area, but was in a poor position to assert his ownership, leaving the Orange Free State as indeed the most likely owner. Alexander Fullarton's map of 1860 showed all the land south of the Vaal as being part of the Free State, an area which included the Berlin Mission settlement at Pniel, and the farms of Bultfontein, Dutoitspan and De Beers; these, and the Pniel missions, had formerly been part of the Orange River Sovereignty and had recognized the successor authority of the Free State magistrates. Others, however, had their eyes on the diamond fields.

The ever-ambitious and unrealistic President Pretorius unilaterally claimed not only all the diamond diggings, but the newly-discovered Tati goldfields, although both lay well outside recognized Transvaal borders (but the Transvaalers' attitude to boundaries was famously flexible). When Pretorius then granted a monopoly over the diamond fields to three of his friends, Messrs Webb, Posno and Munnich, the diggers' indignation was ferocious. The self-appointed local government, the Free Diamond Republic, with Stafford Parker, owner of the local music hall and ex-able seaman, as President took over the Klipdrift diggings and for the best part of a year ensured order. A London reporter wrote that Parker 'behaved modestly and does honour to his position . . . the order of the day – is stolid civility – listen to, but say nothing, and dig away'.[4]

Another unlikely claimant to the diggings was the Griqua Captain

Nicholas Waterboer. By this time his subjects, scattered over a wide but ill-defined area, 'numbered less than a thousand poor and listless people', well outnumbered by Afrikaner farmers, Tswana and Khoikhoi. Waterboer may have had neither the power, nor much inclination, to meddle, but his agent David Arnot, an intelligent and vigorous lawyer, not too hampered by scruples, had for some years previously amassed voluminous, if doubtful, evidence to prove that all the land was rightfully Waterboer's, nine thousand square miles of it. Arnot now stepped in to claim the diamond fields on behalf of the Griqua. He was himself 'Coloured', which adds some savour to the conflict, although it probably had little influence on Arnot himself.

Two years previously Sir Charles Dilke had prophesied that if gold was found anywhere on the globe, that region would shortly be governed by English-speakers; it seemed that this was equally true of diamonds. Waterboer was persuaded by Arnot and Richard Southey, a committed imperialist, to ask for British 'protection' against acquisitive Boers.

The incoming High Commissioner, Sir Henry Barkly, was a brisk authoritarian, a commanding figure with enormous black whiskers, a former Member of Parliament and an experienced governor, who enjoyed a high reputation at the Colonial Office, which was to prove essential in persuading London to accept Waterboer's offer.[5] Two years of Conservative government there, which included Benjamin Disraeli's first, brief, stint as Prime Minister, had ended in December 1868 with Gladstone heading *his* first government. From July 1870 the Colonial Secretary was Earl Kimberley, the most professional of Colonial Secretaries, who brought twenty years of government experience to the post and was never less than thoughtful and industrious. Gladstone's government was deeply unwilling to accept the trouble and expense of more colonies. Army reform, new Education Acts and the perennial difficulties in Ireland were all proving expensive. Only Kimberley's conviction that Afrikaner control of the diamond fields would result in the extension of slavery (a reasonable enough fear, given the prevalence of 'apprenticeship' in the republics, fed by continued raids from the Transvaal) led to the reluctant British agreement that Waterboer's lands could be annexed, not by London, but by the Cape.[6]

This the Cape Parliament was reluctant to do. Little enthusiasm existed there for seizing the opportunity to grab the diamonds, while there was much sympathy for Brand's case: characters as dissimilar as Merriman, Thomas Bowker and Robert Moffat condemned the idea of annexation, and the principle was rejected by the Legislature in June 1872. This did not deter Barkly, who as High Commissioner could act independently, and who could foresee only trouble if the ebullient diggers were not brought under British control; he had after all spent seven years in Victoria, Australia, where memories of the Ballarat rebellion were fresh.

A pretext lay conveniently to hand. Pursuing his doubtful claim, President Pretorius had formally requested a British adjudication of the western border of the Transvaal, which offered the opportunity to send a Cape magistrate to the diggings. President Brand, who had demanded an international arbitration, was infuriated at this action, and appointed Truter to the Pniel magistracy with a commando to back him up. For a few months Landdrost Truter on the dry diggings faced Magistrate Campbell on the river, until the result of the arbitration requested by Pretorius was received. This had been confided to Robert Keate, Lieutenant Governor of Natal, who, much to Pretorius' chagrin – he was forced to resign the presidency as a result – pushed back the Transvaal frontiers to benefit the Thlaping, and awarded the diamond fields to Waterboer.

Barkly thereupon immediately (on 17 November 1871) annexed Waterboer's lands as the new Crown Colony of Griqualand West (Griqualand East being Adam Kok's Natalian district). With every justification, Brand and the Free Staters were enraged. Legally their case was strong – apart from their *de facto* occupation, had not the Bloemfontein Convention expressly disclaimed any treaties with native rulers north of the Orange? Only President Parker seemed satisfied, and willingly handed over the reins of power.

Both the annexation of Basutoland and that of Griqualand West were forced upon a reluctant British government by High Commissioners. British Kaffraria had been disposed of, and in 1871 Basutoland had also been temporarily palmed off on the Cape (until 1884), but for the moment at least Great Britain was landed with an expensive and unworkably small third colony. 'It will require great patience to bring South Africa under a satisfactory general system of government,' Lord Kimberley, with some percipience, regretted.

President Brand persisted, badgering the British government for a more equitable settlement. This was eventually conceded when a Conservative government succeeded in 1876 under Disraeli, with Henry Herbert, Lord Carnarvon, as Colonial Secretary.[7] Since incoming governments always find it easy to acknowledge the errors of their predecessors, Carnarvon settled the Orange Free State claim by a payment of £90,000, which was used as the initial capital of the new National Bank.

When Judge Andries Stockenström, son of Sir Andries, and equally controversial, began the task of sorting out land titles in Griqualand West, he concluded that chiefs had personal jurisdiction over their people but not, given their wandering pattern of life, territorial jurisdiction over specific areas, and that the Free State claim to the diamond fields was probably valid. His decision angered the Griqua to the point of rebellion, but the British annexation of the region remained. The strategic consequences were that by its northward extension the Cape Colony effectively sealed off the Free State from any possibility of expansion westwards, and served a similar notice to the Transvaal. The 'missionary road' to the north, to the territories of the Tswana and beyond them to Mzilikazi's Ndebele and their subject Shona, was to be a British route; and the railway from the Cape would be extended to Kimberley, the ramshackle capital of the new colony.

It might be said that the Orange Free State got something of a bargain since the unfortunate Southey, sent to administer the new Crown Colony in January 1873, a reward he had been anxious to acquire, found nothing but trouble. Rebellious diggers, unacceptable exploitation of black labour, rampant crime, combined with little support from Britain, made his task harrowing and frustrating. He attempted to apply the more liberal Cape Regulations, by which blacks were allowed to undertake digging, much to the indignation of whites. An attempt to emulate the Ballarat rising had to be suppressed by British troops, followed by the recall of Sir Richard.

Griqualand West[8]

The first deposits of blue diamond-bearing clay were excavated by simple open-cast methods, cutting out saucer-shaped holes progressively wider and deeper into the breccia pipe. As the excavation of the largest mine, the Kimberley, proceeded – a depth of a hundred feet was reached by 1874, with a circumference of seven hundred feet, and nearly three hundred feet in depth by 1878 – horse-driven 'whims' and 'whips' replaced manual windlasses, and stationary steam engines made an early appearance, although at the poorer mines of Dutoitspan and Bultfontein ox-carts continued to draw the earth for many years.

Such primitive methods made enormous demands on labour. By 1872 the camp population was between thirty and fifty thousand, of whom thirteen thousand were Europeans. The manual effort of the diggers was quickly assumed by Africans, mainly Pedi from the northern Transvaal and Tsonga (Shangaan) from Mozambique, with an organized contingent from Basutoland – 'Moshoeshoe's people'. Three to six months' work at twenty-five shillings a week in cash, or ten shillings plus food, was enough to buy a good gun – sturdy and easily repairable British Army muskets cost £4, while a breech-loading Snider could be had for £12 – and to contribute towards *lobola*. Wages were supplemented by the sale of diamonds stolen from the diggings, and quickly purchased by touts who abounded in the camp.[9]

While all the labourers were volunteers, they were at first organized by the chiefs, eager to seize the opportunity of increasing their own power and wealth. Sekhukhune (Secocoeni), who succeeded Sekwati as chief of the Pedi in 1861, had his brother Marmaree stationed at Kimberley to represent Pedi interests. In emergencies, such as the Pedi War with the Transvaal in 1876 and the 1880 Gun War in Basutoland, thousands of labourers left the mines at their chief's summons, but as the pattern developed of working for some months at the diggings, then returning to their villages with wealth enough to buy cattle, ploughs and implements, young men began to feel a new independence from traditional ties. The first large-scale enlistment of the black populations into the white cash economy had begun.

Evidence too was available that a black man could prosper, at least in the British colonies. Once Griqualand West became a crown colony the authorities distinguished between those 'honest, intelligent and respectable men' who 'must of course be treated in every way similar to the whites', and 'raw Kaffirs . . . who must be treated as children incapable of governing themselves'. Joseph Moss, a Mfengu High Court interpreter, was a highly respected man of unimpeachable character and considerable wealth, who took the lead in organizing those black voters who had the franchise as Cape citizens. Africa Kinde invested the money he made as a digger in 'farms of considerable value and herds of cattle the envy of many of his neighbours'.[10]

Divisions of this sort between full citizens and illiterate foreign transients posed serious problems to authority. A vocal group of white diggers resented any blacks being treated as equals, and agitated for an independent republic, affiliated to the Orange Free State, where such liberal follies would not be tolerated and 'swell niggers' would be kept in their place. The malcontents, united in Alfred Aylward and Albury Paddon's 'Diggers' Protection Association', attempted an armed uprising; the 1875 'Black Flag' revolt was a singularly timid affair which collapsed without a shot being fired. Aylward and his followers proclaimed that diggers' rights were only for whites, although there were many black diggers: Bulfontein Diggers' Committee had black members in 1874 – 'persons of indifferent character and similar colour', according to Aylward.[11] Bearing in mind that Aylward, together with the great majority of the diggers, was an immigrant, it is clear that racism was by no means entirely a native South African growth.

The clash of attitudes between Imperial officials and colonists was as apparent in Griqualand West as it had been on the eastern frontier. The colonial authorities attempted some form of control over the constantly shifting population (up to ninety thousand blacks visited the diggings in a single year) by issuing passes. Some form of control was essential. Diamonds being easily stolen, secreted and sold, robbery was endemic; diggers were separated from their money by bar-keepers and prostitutes; murder became commonplace. In theory the pass system, defined by Proclamation 14 of 1872 and aimed at controlling diamond theft, was related to contracts of employment. Every employee was liable to carry a certificate of employment, but since almost without exception white employees refused to register, such certificates were only ever carried by blacks, and only blacks were ever examined by police. Blacks of independent means were obliged to carry certificates of Cape citizenship or 'protection certificates' proving their exemption from pass laws – a pass to avoid a pass. 'Most European diggers found the law wanting and remembered with nostalgia the period of Orange Free State rule, when servants knew their places and Europeans were able to enforce a purely racial colonial order,' and 'Truter's Law', when it was sufficient that a suspect be black to be 'proof enough of his guilt, and punishment was sure'.

Aylward's supporters had reason to fear for 'diggers' democracy', which had only a brief existence as improving technology led to increased capital investment. Human and animal power were replaced by steam for haulage and for the vital task of pumping, necessary both to keep the diggings dry and to provide water for processing the excavated clay. After 1878, when open-cast working began to be superseded by deep mining, steam power for lifting, drilling and, after a few years, lighting, became universal, and provided employment for reliable and sober men – not easy to come by in the still wild atmosphere of Kimberley. It was the Kimberley Central mine that led the way, sinking its shaft in 1885 and immediately multiplying its output more than tenfold. Deep mining required skills and experience not locally available, and thousands of British miners were imported, supplanting the colonial diggers.

Responsible government

After many years of cajoling by successive British governments the Cape Parliament finally voted to accept 'responsible government' in 1872. If they had not taken this step, the alternative would have been to move in the opposite direction, by reducing the limited power the Cape legislature already had – the patience of Gladstone's government was wearing thin. Cardwell at the War Office had put his foot down: certainly the harbour facilities at the Cape were essential, as a commission on the Defence of the Cape of Good Hope had reported in 1868,[12] but unless the Cape government began to pay their fair share all British troops, Cardwell insisted, except for the Simonstown garrison, would be withdrawn in 1870. Wodehouse, who never wavered in his belief that the colonists at the Cape, and more especially those of Natal, could not be trusted to govern blacks honourably, had been firmly against responsible government, but his successor Sir Henry Barkly was more flexible.

Barkly had been sent to the Cape with specific instructions to install responsible government. As Governor of Victoria from 1856 to 1863 he had coped both with an initially chaotic Assembly, in which the government could rely on only eleven votes out of fifty-seven, and with troublesome goldminers; after which the Cape, with nearly twenty years' experience of representative government, posed little challenge against a stubborn resistance. It was however only by a single vote that the Cape Legislative Council accepted self-government in June 1872, with John Molteno as Prime Minister and, in a link with the past, old Christoffel Brand, born in the eighteenth century, founder of the *Zuid-Afrikaan*, opponent of Charles Somerset and father of the Orange Free State President, as Speaker.[13]

Molteno healed the east/west division by appointing members from all regions to the cabinet, and reorganizing the constituencies. William Porter, that most creatively liberal Attorney General, was succeeded by J.H. de Villiers, who was to become a major influence on the formation of South African law. Apart from de Villiers, who considered himself more French than Dutch, there were no Afrikaners in the cabinet, nor was there over-much interest in the new situation from the Afrikaner population. This was to change during the next few years, as was the importance of non-white voters. Already in 1865 thirty Mfengu farmers in the native district of Peddie in the Ciskei worked between five hundred and a thousand acres each, and by 1870 it was judged that Peddie surpassed the European district of Albany in its productive capacity – which argued a rapidly-increasing number of black voters.[14] Although there were to be no non-white members of the Cape or any other South African parliament until 1994 (if the ludicrous quadripartite parliament fabricated in 1984 is excepted), the non-white voters did, later in the century, constitute a significant interest. In this respect the Cape did no more than reflect contemporary realities: few non-whites in 1872 were politically conscious. Sir Henry Barkly was a convinced democrat who believed that 'in every case the remedy was a wider franchise and the greater freedom of public expression' – a considerable change of attitude for a Cape governor.

Although responsible government came comparatively late for so developed a society as the Cape Colony – the better part of twenty years after New Zealand and Victoria, both brash newcomers, achieved the same status – the transition was in some ways still too early. Apart from the irreconcilable Easterners there were no stable groupings, and widely differing personalities made cooperation difficult. From the old days the staunchly liberal William Porter and the proto-racist Godlonton still had seats. Among the rising stars was F.W. Reitz Jr, briefly member for Beaufort West at the age of twenty-eight, and Merriman, a member since 1869, who joined Molteno's cabinet in 1875, still only thirty-three. Tall – six feet four – and striking, with an acerbic wit, Merriman was often erratic, but his instincts for decency and human sympathy made him one of the most attractive figures of his time. More than any other man he bridged the gap between Boer and Briton; but, although intellectually convinced of the brotherhood of man, he found it impossible to deal with blacks on a sympathetic basis.[15] The less attractive Gordon Sprigg, small, conceited and ambitious, capable of considerable folly and deception, had yet to make his presence felt. Saul Solomon continued Porter's tradition, and usually supported the undisputed leader of the house, the impressive Lion of

Beaufort, John Molteno, who farmed there on a ducal scale – a hundred thousand acres of well-tended land, backed by a thriving commercial business. Charles Brownlee, experienced and sympathetic but feeling the strain of an active life, and J.H. de Villiers, the locally-born Chief Justice, were the two most distinguished members of the first responsible government.

Parliamentary life in Natal was less advanced. From the beginning white settlers had shown a bitterly racist attitude, even more xenophobic than that of the Cape Easterners, and one that was to continue for many years. Every step the British government took to protect black interests was fiercely resisted. Blacks, as in the Cape, had to be given the vote, but every stratagem was employed to weaken this right. The initial property qualification was high enough, but other restrictions were added in 1865, when blacks were not allowed even to petition for admission to the electoral roll until they had overcome a series of hurdles – seven years of exemption from customary law, the approval of three whites (a condition entirely negating the 'colour-blind' principle), and a public inquiry – before the eventual decision of the Lieutenant Governor. Political repression was reinforced by economic exploitation. The tiny sum of £5,000 per annum hypothecated for black communities by the home government was never fully spent. Taxes which bore most heavily on the blacks – hut taxes, dog taxes, marriage registration fees, customs duties on basic implements like hoes being higher than those on ploughs – all made it imperative for blacks to earn a cash income.[16]

In spite of these encouragements for the blacks to engage in healthy agricultural labour for the whites, this did not transpire. Some of this reluctance was attributed to the unreasonable preference of blacks for cultivating their own gardens in tranquillity and enjoying unaccustomed relaxation.[17] Added to this was the existence of more profitable opportunities: jobs as transport riders – muleteers or wagon drivers – and labourers on public works paid considerably better wages than did farmers: 'They are policemen, government messengers and post carriers ... cooks, nurses, grooms and general house servants ... farm labourers and waggoners, and in short perform nearly the whole of the unskilled labour of the colony.' Then, the cultivation of their gardens was proving unexpectedly profitable to the black farmers. Protected from land speculators by the existence of the reserves, and freed from the worst exactions of chiefs (a man could no longer be ruined and murdered by an accusation of witchcraft, and might therefore feel safe in prosperity), a substantial black peasantry emerged, taking the more regular exactions of the colonial government in its stride. Magistrates and Natal officials, solidly behind the white settlers and opposed to all those who attempted to shelter the blacks, attempted to coerce labour for the farmers. They were legally entitled to demand that chiefs furnish labour for public works (six man-months for every eleven huts), but their efforts to extend this to private service were usually stopped by Imperial officials. Natalian settlers were furious – 'Creatures having fewer legs than insects, and commonly called Kaffirs, are practically the greatest hindrances to successful agriculture' – since the blacks refused to work for a pittance on white farms.[18]

In the first years of colonial rule there was little shortage of land for black occupation, even as the population expanded, since unallocated 'Crown' lands (all land was deemed to belong to the state until allocated to individuals or institutions) were quietly, and without official objection, taken over by enterprising blacks. The 'Kaffirs' were much more ready to work on a profit-sharing basis, occupying white-owned lands and contributing part of the proceeds of their work to the landowner, a custom confusingly known in South Africa as 'squatting', although 'share-cropping' would be a more accurate term. Substantial acreages were still owned by absentee landlords and land companies, often ready to welcome black farmers. By the 1870s there were some 375,000 black Natalians, forty-three thousand 'squatting' on crown lands, the remainder divided almost equally between reserves, missions and private white-owned land. Missionary stations, which encouraged individual black farmers and modern techniques, increased steadily. Edendale became a conspicuous example, and some Edendale blacks set up a farming company for themselves which became one of the larger and most successful of such enterprises, owning more than thirty thousand acres. Such an enterprising man as William Africa could own 1,600 acres, as well as having shares in several other farms.[19]

Although blacks could become decently prosperous in Natal there was no question of them enjoying those political or social rights, limited though they were, available at the Cape. The career, for example, of Tiyo Soga would have been impossible in Natal. One of thirty-nine children of Ngqika's senior counsellor, usually known as Old Soga, his mother one of Jan Tshatsu's people, Tiyo was educated first at Lovedale and then in Glasgow and Edinburgh, being ordained in 1856. Coming back to South Africa with a Scots wife, he was able to work for only a few years before his early death in 1871. Any black with a white wife was an unusual and alarming phenomenon, but Soga's dignity, and his publicly-expressed pride in his ancestry, made him the first of those who were able to accept colonial standards while not rejecting their black heritage. Soga's remarkable children, who included Alan Soga, a prominent publicist, and John Henderson, a historian also married to a Scotswoman (who survived to be killed in a German air raid on Southampton, an unlikely end for the grandson of a Xhosa chief), were predecessors of such eventually successful black politicians as Oliver Tambo and Albert Lutuli.[20]

Kaffir law: guilty until proved innocent[21]

The problems caused by the reluctance of black Africans to work for next to nothing on white farms were solved to some extent by the importation of Indian labour, primarily to service the new sugar industry. Sugar was indigenous to Natal, and one of the first crops to be cultivated by the British settlers, who found the whole littoral suitable for growing it. At first the government of India was happy to cooperate by facilitating emigration, but when the treatment accorded to the unfortunate Indians by the white Natalians became known the Indian authorities objected and forbade further emigration until the government of Natal ensured better conditions. The fact that the Indian government was responsible to a different department of the British government in London, and had both a good deal of independence in administering its own affairs and a readiness to stand up for the rights of its subjects, was to lead to constant friction between Indian and African authorities.

Since Indian workers were allowed by the terms of their contracts to stay in Natal once their time was up, when they would be allotted land to the value of their return passage, and since the Indian government insisted that a proportion of the immigrants should be women, a permanent Indian community soon developed. Traders, artisans and even professionals began to make their own way from India to Natal as 'Passenger Indians', where they integrated into the white community much more readily than did the blacks; but always as servants or subordinates to white masters. Indians did not attract missionary attention and protection in the same measure as Africans. As was the custom in India the many Hindu – but with a fair proportion of Muslim and some Christian – immigrants were left to their own devices, and began to contribute to the modest prosperity of Natal.[22]

Sections of the farming community other than the sugar producers remained starved of labour, particularly after the diamond fields began to exercise their seductive influence.

Settler attitudes in Natal were reinforced when, in July 1873, Sir Benjamin Pine was reappointed as Lieutenant Governor. He had learned little in his absence, and immediately on his return stumbled into a first-class crisis, the Langalibalele affair.

Since Pine had left Natal in 1855 a new figure of outstanding importance had emerged. John William Colenso had struggled up the Anglican hierarchy, financing his own education, schoolmastering and publishing textbooks before being appointed as the first Bishop of Natal in 1858. A man of impressive intellectual honesty, he felt forced to answer truthfully the questions posed by his black flock. Were the Bible stories true? Were they meant to be taken literally? Or were they – and this was easily comprehensible to people with their own rich traditions – poetic expressions of an underlying truth? Colenso investigated, and came up with the unsurprising answer that the Old Testament was not to be swallowed whole as in the King James Version. This was a conclusion that serious scholars had already reached, but there were few such scholars in the Church of England, and conventional wisdom was hysterically upset. Colenso was charged with heresy, and his Archbishop, the High Church Robert Gray of Cape Town, an arrogant man and a superficial thinker, deposed him. Colenso appealed to the Privy Council, and had the judgement overturned. More concerned with ecclesiastical modishness than serious theology, Gray had appointed a sympathizer, James Green, as Dean of Pietermaritzburg. As a result Dean and Bishop inhabited the same little town for twenty years without speaking to each other, both distrusting the inoffensive William Macrorie, despatched as alternative bishop.[23]

A man of immense energy, Colenso remained primarily a missionary, devoting himself to the welfare of the blacks and becoming 'undoubtedly the most outstanding figure in Zulu literary work in the nineteenth century', acclaimed as 'Father of the people', and being at all times ready to champion black causes against the whites. In Natal the necessity for this was permanent, for although thirty years of peace succeeded the British annexation, Natalian whites were nervously conscious of being a tiny minority surrounded by blacks, and in particular by the well-organized and united Zulu and Basuto nations.

The calm that Natal enjoyed after its annexation was something of a tribute to Theophilus Shepstone. Although as Secretary for Native Affairs he had no force other than a handful of police, and a miserly contribution from the colonial government, Shepstone was able to use his intimate knowledge of black languages and customs – by 1870 he had spent half a century among Xhosa- and Zulu-speakers – to act the part of a Zulu paramount, rewarding cooperative chiefs and dispossessing those who showed signs of recalcitrance, all with a high degree of firm diplomacy. The occasional dissidents came from those communities which had retained their identities and chiefly lines; those which had been regrouped by Shepstone from fragmented peoples were naturally more cooperative. Shepstone's system had achieved a fair measure of tranquillity, but little in the way of advancement. Natal's economic resources were nothing like adequate to provide training and education for its third of a million blacks, and there was no likelihood of a subsidy from any British government. Colenso and Shepstone were both powerful advocates of Natalian black rights, although their approaches were strikingly different, Colenso's being fraternal while Shepstone remained unambiguously paternal. Neither, naturally, enjoyed good relations with many of the white colonists, although each had a number of influential supporters.

Among those chiefs whose people had remained united was one Langalibalele, whose Hlubi had originally settled near the border of Zululand before being despatched by Shepstone to the Drakensberg foothills in order to act as a barrier against the Bushmen incursions. There the Hlubi prospered under Langalibalele, a chief of considerable dignity with a high reputation as a rainmaker, and materially assisted by their strategic position on a convenient route to the diamond mines. Like their Basuto neighbours, returning Hlubi brought guns and horses with them, increasing Langalibalele's power to the extent that he began to show signs of independence. Traditional ceremonial rights had not been interfered with by Shepstone: the great first-fruits ceremony, the annual public assertion of chiefly supremacy, and the raising of age-regiments for non-military purposes were allowed to continue, only the more revolting aspects such as ritual murder being banned. One ceremony frowned on by the colonial authorities was 'doctoring', the ceremonial induction of the age-regiments which involved cutting off the hind leg of a live ox and observing the animal's agony; the subsequent tasting of the gall-bladder indicated the future strength of the young men. The performance of such cruel rituals could have been dismissed with a caution, but there was a strong reaction when Langalibalele, called upon to register the guns owned by some of his followers, took flight in October 1873. A colonial expedition led by the decent but unlucky sapper officer Anthony Durnford misfired, with Durnford losing an arm and five of his men being killed. The white colonial reaction, not only in Natal but throughout South Africa, was hysterical. Although Langalibalele himself had been handed over by the Sotho, a virtual massacre of some two hundred Hlubi, mainly old men, took place.

Langalibalele was put on trial by a colonial court, quite irregularly presided over by Governor Pine, and sentenced to death – a punishment commuted to exile. The whole proceedings were so unconstitutional and manifestly unfair as to provoke a serious row in Britain. Lord Derby, then Foreign Secretary, wrote in his diary that the Cabinet had discussed 'at considerable length' what to do about 'Langalibe, or something like it', who had been 'very unjustly sentenced by a court which had no authority to try him, for the offence of murder which he had not committed'.[24] Bishop Colenso was an impressive advocate for Langalibalele, and he and Durnford, himself the most intimately concerned, both made their protests, with considerable effect in London. There had been trouble before, in 1866, when the Natal Legislative Council had been rebuked by London, and the restricted rights given under the 1872 charter were intended as a 'punishment' to the colonists. Clearly it had not been punishment enough.

The affair brought about the parting of the ways between fraternity and paternalism. Shepstone indignantly broke with Colenso, insisting on the propriety of punishing a revolt, however irregularly. Queen Victoria supported Colenso's 'noble, disinterested conduct', and expressed her appreciation of the Bishop of Natal's action, adding that she wished '*all* her Colonial *governors* should know her feelings on *this subject*'.[25] Robert Herbert, the Permanent Under-Secretary at the Colonial Office, minuted that the whole of Natal law and administration called for attention.

Twitters at the helm

In London the buck landed on the desk of Disraeli's new Colonial Secretary, Lord Carnarvon, who made South Africa the most important item on his agenda; with very mixed results for the region.[26] Carnarvon was a fine example of a now extinct type, the aristocrat in serious politics. Rich, cultivated, not only translating Homer – a commonplace among Victorian statesmen – but an expert on early Gnosticism, Carnarvon was sensitive, enthusiastic and industrious. Gladstone wrote that he 'had a cacoethes of action, or stir, in him'; Grant Duff, acting for Kimberley in the Commons, commented in 1881 that 'half the calamities of life had their origin in people not being able to sit still in a room. If Lord Carnarvon had had this power . . . we should have been saved most of the troubles which have afflicted this part of the world [i.e. South Africa].' Carnarvon was inspired by an ideal of public service rather than party political pragmatism. His aptitude for seeing all sides of a question, and his readiness to resign, explained his nickname, 'Twitters'. He was no stranger to the Colonial Office, having been both Under-Secretary during Lytton's tenure of office and Secretary in Lord Derby's 1868 government, where he had gained much prestige by finalizing the union of seven previously independent provinces, each with its own legislature, into the self-governing Dominion of Canada. The new dominion had extensive powers and a fully responsible government, with the London parliament retaining only residual powers, mainly in defence and foreign policy. Although Carnarvon was at the Colonial Office for only nine months before resigning, and a good deal of the work had been done by his Whig predecessor, Edward Cardwell, much of the credit accrued to him.

Lord Carnarvon took immediate action in Natal, and dismissed Pine – a rare occurrence in colonial affairs – with the enthusiastic backing of his civil servants (it was on this occasion that the Colonial Office's Edward Fairfield wrote sarcastically of South African magistrates' 'very popular principle that a Kafir is guilty until proved innocent'). It appeared clear in London that the ever-distrusted Natalians had finally proved unfit to rule themselves, and that therefore their recent representative constitution must be downgraded. An example had already been made of Jamaica, where, after a similar scandal, the long-established 'responsible' constitution had been reduced in status to that of a crown colony. The colonists must however be persuaded to accept this, and General Sir Garnet Wolseley was despatched with special powers to do so.[27]

A 'modern' soldier, Wolseley irritated the royal family and the Horse Guards, but his dashing, open-collared appearance and adept public relations had made him a favourite with public and politicians.[28] Accompanied by a brilliant staff, which included that young Captain Colley who had criticized Harry Smith, the General found Natalians unsympathetic: 'such people and such dresses! . . . scarcely anything approaching an English gentleman here.' Gritting his teeth to perform his 'disagreeable duty', Wolseley manoeuvred between 'howling humanitarian fanatics' and local politicians, 'self-seeking, or failures in every walk of life'. By means of his imperturbable affability – 'Drowning objections in a sea of sherry' – and some judicious bribery which included suborning a local newspaper, Wolseley succeeded in winning over the colonists. Natal reverted to something close to its former status, and civil service control of the legislature, stifling the wilder spirits, was ensured. African opinion was however not conciliated, in spite of Langalibalele's release from Robben Island; Cetshwayo, King of the Zulu himself, complained that he had hitherto regarded the British as being strictly fair, but that this faith had been gravely damaged.

Faced with a situation in South Africa superficially similar to that in Canada – a widespread territory inhabited by two sets of European colonists with different traditions and mutual distrust (the French Canadians being yet more recalcitrant than the Boers, some breaking out in armed rebellion even as the new dominion was being formed), it seemed sensible to attempt to imitate the Canadian solution. This thought had previously occurred both to Sir George Grey and to Lord Kimberley, and had even gained Gladstone's agreement – always, of course, on condition that there should be no extra expense. It was left, however, for Lord Carnarvon to discover that there were considerable differences, for whereas Canada was primarily a federation between two states of similar importance, Upper and Lower Canada – Ontario and Quebec – together with others considerably smaller, the Cape far outweighed all other South African states in every respect. It contained most of the white population, some 240,000 of 365,000, and possessed the lion's share of the income, £2,100,000 against £580,000 for the other five communities. Again, while all the Canadian provinces were British possessions, two of the South African states were republics, with inconveniently independent ideas, and the Cape's now responsible government was not always, or even usually, inclined to cooperate willingly with London. Moreover, while the indigenous Canadians were few in number and widely dispersed, the black population of South Africa considerably outnumbered the white, and had interests which London fully understood were likely to be trampled underfoot by any strong white colonial government. Finally, some of the still-independent black states were in a position to make their objections felt, most notably the Zulu and the Basuto.

Marxist historians and conspiracy theorists have seen Carnarvon's confederation policy as an attempt to make South Africa safe for capitalism. In reality he had no concept of economics. He was regarded as an unreliable eccentric by his Conservative colleagues, liable to fly off the handle for some abstruse reason. He owed his political reputation to the Canadian confederation, and, as a dog with one trick, was enthusiastic to repeat it.[29] It was accepted that the Cape itself was vital as a coaling station for both naval and merchant shipping – no steamers of the period had bunkerage enough to allow long ocean passages without refuelling – but no enthusiasm was manifested by Disraeli's government for extending the expensive and large territory attached to it. When it was discussed at a Cabinet meeting on 28 April 1875 Lord Derby reported: 'the scheme was sharply criticised, and I think no member of the Cabinet quite likes it . . . my apprehensions are shared by many of my colleagues.'[30]

When the famous historian James Anthony Froude volunteered to research the subject on the ground Carnarvon enthusiastically agreed, although without much backing from his civil servants. Robert Herbert deplored Froude's 'rather outré views of the Imperial connection', but felt he could do no harm if he went 'quite on his own account'.[31] This Froude failed to do. Travelling widely, from Cape Town to Pretoria, between June and September 1874, he returned critical of past policies and enthusiastic about the proposals for a new federation along Canadian lines.

Lord Carnarvon drafted a despatch to High Commissioner Barkly suggesting a conference to discuss a similar arrangement for South Africa. Although well-meant, it was a lamentable document. Carnarvon had little concept of colonial rivalries, or the fretful susceptibilities of such local celebrities as Prime Minister Molteno. The guests refused to come to the party: Molteno was annoyed at being put on the same level as Jock Paterson, the self-elected leader of the Easterners, and was suspicious of what he regarded as Lord Carnarvon's naïvety. Barkly, perhaps correctly judged by Carnarvon to be 'cold-blooded and at heart opposed to all my policy', agreed to put the Colonial Secretary's despatch to the Cape Parliament before publication. In that assembly the proposals for federation were contemptuously rejected with 'coarse and brutal invective' that pained the sensitive Lord Carnarvon. Merriman was furious at what he later called Carnarvon's 'insane desire to add to his reputation by founding what he pleased to call a Dominion out here' – which he believed to be the root cause of all the troubles Africa was then (February 1879) experiencing after Isandhlwana.[32] It was little consolation that the Natalians and Griqualand

Westerners accepted the suggestion of confederation enthusiastically.

Afrikaner leaders were also wary. President Brand refused to come to any meeting at which a representative of Griqualand West was present. The Transvaal Volksraad was a little more accommodating, and accepted the invitation 'with all caution for the interests of this state'. Any alteration in the affairs of that republic was likely to be for the better; there had been some progress, but the Transvaal remained in a parlous condition. Within its commonly accepted borders some independently-inclined black tribes remained, of whom Sekhukhune's Pedi were the strongest. On its northern frontiers Venda communities cooperated in slave-raiding operations (strenuously denied and industriously covered up by the Transvaal authorities), varied by skirmishes with the Boers. Smaller units, such as the surviving Koranna of David Stuurman, were suppressed as occasion offered, and their children 'apprenticed'.[33]

In the settled areas of the high veld the farmers were making a good beginning, rejoicing in the space available. There were no important urban centres: a few hundred houses, churches representing the rival denominations, and a court house were all that could be found in Potchefstroom or Lydenburg. Pretoria, the new capital, had not as much. There was no currency apart from paper notes of doubtful value, expressed in British pounds, shillings and pence. Gold sovereigns were much prized, but hard to come by. The traditional reluctance to pay taxes resulted in there being almost no government income. In 1872 the revenue of the South African Republic of Natal was less than £41,000. Land sales were the only backing for state credit. Since there was no professional civil service and no army, the lack of income was of less importance than might be expected. Education remained rudimentary – there were four state schools in the whole country, and the total annual expenditure remained less than £5,000 as late as 1877 – although from 1867 there was one newspaper; it was, of course, in English.[34]

Recognizing the imperative need for some guiding hand, other than that of the erratic Pretorius, who admitted that his 'capabilities were now quite inadequate', President Brand was approached to unite the two Afrikaner states. Wisely, he declined, whereupon the Volksraad invited Thomas François Burgers, a liberal Cape predikant, to become the new head of state of the South African Republic. It was an odd choice. Like Colenso, Burgers had been accused of heresy, but similarly supported by the Privy Council. Educated in Utrecht, married to a Scots girl, the sophisticated and intellectual Burgers was an unlikely character to appeal to the dour Transvaalers: 'A good man indeed but thirty years ahead of his time,' judged one of his people, with some accuracy.[35]

On his arrival there in 1872 the new President found much to occupy him. The Transvaal had been recognized by the European powers and by the USA as a sovereign state, but it remained unrecognizable as a functioning country. One possibility for improvement opened when the status of Delagoa Bay, claimed by both Britain and Portugal and eyed covetously by the Transvaal, was settled in favour of Portugal, so leaving Burgers free to negotiate for a railway from Pretoria to the bay which would make the Transvaal independent of the Cape – should the near-bankrupt republic ever be able to raise the money.

Meanwhile the Orange Free State was almost flourishing. Similar difficulties of currency had been experienced, but these were to be solved with the British payment for the diamond fields. Education had been made a priority, a system of public schools being begun in 1872, supplemented by Church education. The unfortunate first Bishop of Bloemfontein, one of Colenso's opponents, who took a great interest in children, was forced to flee in advance of a warrant for arrest for pederasty, seeking refuge suitably enough in Clifton, but by the early 1870s there were Church of England schools, segregated by race, for blacks, whites and Coloureds, with a crocodile of black girls in school uniforms going to Sunday matins in the Anglican cathedral. A notable addition to the almost cosmopolitan society was effected when young Francis Reitz arrived from the Cape in 1872 to head an appeal court and became head of an organized judiciary.[36]

Pursuing a settlement to his diamond fields claim, Brand was at least prepared to cooperate with London in discussing possible confederation. Froude, sent out again to rally support for London's proposals, did not succeed in forwarding the cause, appearing 'most insolent and confident', demanding the recall of the Cape Parliament, and denouncing the 'forms of constitutional etiquette as a dangerous doctrine'. The 'eminent historian', as Merriman, who was appointed to the Cape Ministry in order to give Froude a worthy opponent, ironically termed him, openly admired the Transvaal's brisk methods of dealing with their black population, and suggested that Basutoland ought to be given to the Orange Free State in return for the diamond fields. Barkly was infuriated by Froude's interference, and Merriman and the Cape liberals found his ideas 'detestable'; they were working steadily to advance the natives, and resented a 'mountebank who scampers through the country and can make a glib after-dinner speech'. Froude reciprocated by describing the 'Cape people' as 'slow thinkers and easily upset'.[37]

But the Colonial Secretary was full of enthusiasm; he 'devoured, rather than read' Froude's report,[38] and enough concessions were made to the unbelievers to enable a conference to be held in London in 1876. President Brand argued his case well – he was, after all, a barrister, and one with many highly-placed friends, including the Duke of Manchester – and got his compensation in the form of £90,000 cash, but declined to take part in further discussions, and Molteno refused to take over Griqualand West. Carnarvon denied the Cape's request to annex Thembuland, although the acquisition of Walvis Bay, a tiny enclave far away on the west coast, the only possible harbour between the Cape and Angola, was approved. Some progress was made, in that Brand agreed to prepare a memorandum on possible federation, and Merriman suggested a gradual tidying-up of the Cape dependencies. For his part the Colonial Secretary introduced a Bill permitting unification of the South African states, should they so wish, to the House of Commons. It was passed only with the greatest difficulty, since Charles Stuart Parnell took advantage of the opportunity to show the strength of the Irish party by mounting a sustained filibuster. The Act that so painfully resulted was hardly worth the effort, since none of the South African states showed any inclination to take advantage of the permission.[39]

But direct action was also undertaken, with immediate and enduring consequences. During his thirty years' labours Theophilus Shepstone had shown himself adept at controlling the black population of Natal, and impressed Lord Carnarvon as 'heaven born for the object in view', the object being the Colonial Secretary's new policy of simply taking over the Transvaal. If the British colonies could not be cajoled, perhaps the republics could be coerced, for it seemed that the Orange Free State would inevitably follow the Transvaal. Without consulting the cabinet, and with only a hastily scrawled agreement from Prime Minister Disraeli, Lord Carnarvon now entrusted Sir Theophilus (knighted for the occasion) with the task of annexing the white burghers of the Transvaal to the British Empire. Since these were the self-same *voortrekkers* who had emigrated a thousand miles to liberate themselves from British rule, scorning the compromises of the Orange Free State, it seemed an unlikely project, but Shepstone had no difficulty in persuading the Colonial Secretary that it could be done, and that he, 'Sometseu', the Inkosi, the great white chief of the Zulu, with his reserved manner and distant gaze, was the man to do it. Henry Rider Haggard, who served as a young clerk on Shepstone's staff and later wrote the perennial bestseller *King Solomon's Mines*, recorded something of Shepstone's charisma, and also experienced his incompetence as an administrator. Shepstone fascinated his contemporaries: 'an Africander Talleyrand, shrewd, observant, silent, self-contained, immobile ... a curious, silent man, who had acquired many of the characteristics of the natives among whom he lived.'[40]

It was true that the Transvaal was in a bad way. President Burgers had made himself unpopular by his modern theology, liberal ways and optimistic financing. Education had scarcely moved at all: the novelist Anthony Trollope, who had travelled in South Africa, noted that in 1877, after Burgers' reforms, there were a mere five pupils in the New High School, only three hundred more in all the republic's junior schools, and annual expenditure on education was less than £5,000. Hoping to raise money for a railway, the new President had made a prolonged and expensive foreign tour, which did not help matters back in the Transvaal. He did not succeed, and had to be content with £60,000 borrowed from a Cape bank. This was rapidly exhausted and the state treasury emptied, insult being added to injury by Burgers' hubris in causing gold sovereigns to be struck with his own effigy.

The Transvaal having few inhabitants capable of even simple office work, administration inevitably had to be carried out by Cape Afrikaners or imported Hollanders such as State Attorney E.J.P. Jorissen, also Secretary of Education, a disciple of John Stuart Mill, State Secretary N.J.R. Swart, who actually deserted the Dutch Reformed Church to join the Church of England, and Coenraad Juta, Secretary for War, brother-in-law to Karl Marx himself. Liberal intellectuals of this sort, who imported such distressing habits as tennis parties and dances, were anathema to the '*platteland*' Boers of the backveld, whose indignation had burgeoned on being called out against the Pedi chief Sekhukhune, who had developed a mountain state similar to that of Moshoeshoe in the northern Transvaal.[41]

Nourished by wages from the diamond diggings, Sekhukhune's young men were well-equipped, and pushed beyond the previously agreed boundaries to threaten Lydenburg. President Burgers insisted on leading the commando himself. After an initial success the Transvaalers were repulsed, and fled in panic to Pretoria, causing Burgers' reputation to plummet further.[42] On the southern border the Zulu, considerably more powerful than the triumphant Pedi, were regarded apprehensively, so it was not surprising that the worried Lydenburgers actually asked for British protection. Lord Carnarvon was elated by this 'singular fulfilment'. Natalians too were concerned, Governor Bulwer writing that with this defeat 'the Boers were no longer to be hated and feared; they were to be hated and defied' by the black nations who would no longer need English protection from 'the aggression or injustice of the Government of the Republic'.

When therefore Shepstone turned up in Pretoria in January 1877, ostensibly to confer with the Transvaal government, accompanied only by twenty-five policemen, he was cordially welcomed, recording that the horses of the state carriage, which had been sent to welcome him, were taken from the shafts and replaced by cheering onlookers singing 'God Save the Queen'.[43] That, like all Shepstone's subsequent reports, was a blinkered exaggeration. It was probably true that a majority of the Transvaal's voters – in all some 6,500 Afrikaners and 1,500 English – were sufficiently discontented not to object forcibly to at least a temporary annexation; but any suggestion of wholehearted majority support was false. In spite of this, after much negotiation with the President and his advisers, but no consultation with the people, Shepstone formally announced the annexation of the Transvaal to the British Crown on 12 April 1877.[44]

His proclamation to this effect, read publicly by Rider Haggard, rehearsed the adverse circumstances – all confidence destroyed, the country bankrupt, the government 'in helpless paralysis', expected 'anarchy and bloodshed' – that led the territory 'heretofore known as the South African Republic' now to become British territory. The Transvaal would however 'enjoy the fullest legislative privileges compatible with the circumstance of the country and the intelligence of its people'. President Burgers objected formally, Vice-President Paul Kruger more decisively, but the Transvaalers' action was limited to sending a two-man delegation – Jorissen and Kruger – to protest in London.

Two weeks before Shepstone had pronounced the annexation, a new chief landed at Cape Town in succession to Henry Barkly. Few visitors to the Temple Gardens in London now recognize one of the statues there, that of Sir H.E.B. Frere, Bt, High Commissioner to South Africa, and Governor of the Cape Colony. In his day, however, Bartle Frere was a great figure.[45] As an Indian civil servant he had kept the vital province of Sind quiet during the Indian Mutiny, and as Governor of Bombay had put in hand much of that city's infrastructure. A man of integrity and quiet, even diffident charm, Frere was a personal friend of the royal family, a Privy

Councillor with honours showered upon him. To Carnarvon he seemed the ideal man to settle the quarrelsome and individualistic South African communities; but he was an 'Indian', not an 'African', and attempted to apply the techniques of control he had found effective in dealing with sophisticated and worldly Indian rulers and merchants to the straightforward, uncomplicated but pugnacious colonists, Afrikaners and Africans.[46] In the few years he spent in South Africa one can sense the disintegration of the man as he fell into self-deception, irrationality and arbitrariness. (It is a measure of Disraeli's perception, and his lack of sympathy with Carnarvon, that he formed 'a dismally low opinion of Sir Bartle'.[47])

For some time after his arrival Frere was occupied with the latest of the century-long series of Xhosa wars. It began in August with a quarrel between the Xhosa and the Mfengu and Thembu over a wedding party, starting with attacks led by Sarili against those Mfengu and Thembu who had been resettled in once-Xhosa country. The division between colonial blacks, who had adopted up-to-date farming techniques, accepted colonial rule and sent their children to school, and the still-independent, disillusioned and unhappy Xhosa over the Kei had developed into a cultural chasm.[48] It was matched by a split between the colonial ministers, determined to maintain their independence from London, and Frere as High Commissioner with plenipotentiary powers outside colonial territories and as at least titular commander-in-chief. Exacerbated by one of the worst droughts on record, a full-scale war developed as Sandile's Ngqika Xhosa joined in.

From the start there was dissension between the colonial forces, raised as traditional commando troops together with their Mfengu, Thembu, Mpondo and even some Batlokwa allies, experienced in bush warfare and ruthless in their pursuit of looted cattle, and the more cautious British soldiers (more disciplined but not necessarily less murderous: the Xhosa lost five hundred killed in the battle of Kentari in February 1878). Sandile was killed resisting the British as his father Hintsa had been before him, and his skull was taken to adorn Colonel Frederick Carrington's mantelpiece.[49]

At sixty-three, Frere was too old for the rigours of campaigning, and unable to keep his self-possession when faced with the stubborn Molteno and the brilliant young Merriman, who acted as colonial Minister of War and who insisted on retaining control of the local forces. Seeing Molteno and Merriman's independence as a challenge to any plans for confederation, and hoping to establish a more biddable government in Cape Town, Frere precipitated a constitutional crisis in January 1878. Insisting on his own plenipotentiary powers, he curtly dismissed the Molteno ministry. Gordon Sprigg, always thirsty for office, accepted Frere's policy and was only too delighted to take it over. Both he and Frere went on to make a series of grossly damaging errors that affected the whole course of South African history.

The collapse of the rebellion in June 1878 signalled the end of Xhosa resistance, although not of all black African armed opposition in the Cape Colony. The final campaign of the hundred years' war began in 1880, when the furious reaction against the Cape government's disarmament (see pp. 277–8) provoked what was truly unified action, in which Sotho, Pondomisi and even some Thembu launched a well-planned attack. To be denied their rifles was to forfeit their last protection, as the obedient Mfengu who had complied with the government directive discovered. 'Government is a wolf,' they complained, and even the loyalists who had done everything government had asked were angry but impotent.[50] One more short but devastating war began with the killing of the Qumbu resident magistrate in October 1880. It was another horrible little campaign, made worse since new military technologies were now available. Captain Sidney Turner of the Durban Mounted Volunteers wrote: 'To describe what I have seen and done ... would be impossible ... What a sight! Killed and wounded Kafirs in heaps; some blasted by the rockets almost white, others' legs and heads blown off by the shells.' However new the weapons, the war ended in the same way as had all its predecessors in March the following year, to be succeeded by the customary relocation of the communities, to reward the virtuous and punish the rebellious.

The Xhosa, exhausted, had remained neutral.[51] For a century they had shown their determination to resist colonial encroachment and had fought their enemies to a standstill. The Xhosa wars were a much more prolonged struggle than that of Moshoeshoe, and were fought with more ingenuity and skill than the Zulu ever mustered, but they ended in unmitigated failure and bitter division. Many black leaders had taken the decision to cooperate with the whites rather than to challenge them, and their people had reason to be thankful, but at every critical point there had been further divisions, which left the black communities splintered; Moshoeshoe's secret weapon, and that of other tenacious societies such as the Venda, had been unity.

Nathaniel Umhala, Ndlambe's grandson, may serve as an example of divided loyalties. It was to be expected that Mfengu, such as the Revd Peter

Resistance and collaboration.

The Xhosa warrior Macomo (1798–1873), *left*, chose resistance; Kgama (*c.*1830–1923), *below*, cooperated with the British and founded the independent country of Botswana.

Contrasts: Tause Soga, an elegant Victorian young lady, *left*, and the Xhosa girls Nongqawuse and Nonkosi, whose visions led to the tragic cattle-killings.

Kimberley, 1875. The hundreds of individual workings were soon to be superseded by monopoly capitalism in the shape of Cecil Rhodes.

Unlikely allies: Zulu king Cetshwayo (1826–84) and Bishop Colenso(1814–83).

Cetshwayo's brother Dabulamanzi, a competent horseman (although this animal is unimpressive), led the disastrous Zulu attack on Rorke's Drift in January 1879.

Many of John Dunn's Scouts, part of Lord Chelmsford's force in 1879, were themselves Zulu warriors, wearing the headring. The front rank carry the British Martini-Henry rifle.

Above The Raad (council) of the Rehoboth (Namibia) Bastaard community before the German acquisition.

Right The emergence of a Coloured middle class: Minnie Adonis and her young man.

Boer leaders in the First War of Independence, 1880–81. General J.P. Joubert, Kruger's rival for the presidency, is third from left, second row; General N.J. Smit, 'victor of Majuba' and Vice-President of the Transvaal, is second from right, front row.

There is much in common between Jan Smuts' Boer War commando (Smuts is seated, holding a sjambok) and the Bondelswarts chief Morenga's officers (1905), armed with Lee-Enfield rifles.

The Cape Colony Cabinet in 1884: J.X. Merriman, J.W. Sauer, J.W. Leonard, the thirty-one-year-old Cecil Rhodes and Prime Minister Scanlen.

Masiza, the first black South African to become an Anglican priest, might believe that 'the pride of the Kaffirs had destroyed themselves. They looked down upon the Fingoes as dogs';[52] but Umhala was a Xhosa aristocrat. His father Mhala had fought against the whites in the frontier wars, and joined in the cattle-killing, but his son Nathaniel – named after Bishop Merriman – had been through the course of British indoctrination at Zonnenbloem and at St Augustine's, Canterbury. Umhala was an impressive figure, sincerely religious and an active member of both the Church and the colonial administration. When the 1877–8 war broke out many of his friends and relations took up arms against the whites – nine Lovedale alumni joined in – but he remained on the sidelines. In his diary his painful predicament is obvious: such entries as 'Oh Lord! God Almighty! Let my people be as one man!' and 'God grant that the Kaffirs be united to make common cause of their trouble' indicate his grief at the divisions. 'I am sure Kaffir life is no life; it is actually being dead whilst one lives . . . nothing to animate the mind or quicken the intellect. God! Save me from this dull forgetfulness of thy gifts.'[53] Umhala later contrived to combine his fight for black rights with his support of British institutions and values by his editorship of the influential newspaper *Izwi Labantu* (The Voice of the People), whose voice was particularly that of the movement which later became the African National Congress.

For others, who had not Umhala's opportunities for action, the only answer was to retreat into myth-making. Just as the Afrikaners began to construct their ideal of a divinely inspired Great Trek to a Promised Land, and the Zulu theirs of a heroic Shaka, the Xhosa accepted a version of history even more remote from the facts. According to Fatima Meer in her biography of Nelson Mandela, this is history as passed on to the young Mandela. It relates to the cattle-killing:

> For a hundred years the Xhosa fought the white people to save their land and their customs. Growing impatient, the white people decided to destroy the Xhosa by perpetrating an unimaginable evil. They simulated the *izinyanya* [the ancestral spirits] and tricked them into destroying themselves.
>
> Sarhili's most renowned councillor was Mhlakaza, the wisest of all the seers of the Xhosa. Sarhili respected and believed him. So the white people set a trap for Mhlakaza. One day when his niece was fetching water from the stream she heard voices and saw strange men, and when she was about to run in fear they restrained her and asked her to send her uncle, Mhlakaza, to them. She did. He

came and the trick was so clever that he believed they were the *izinyanya*. He saw among them his dead brother who had been an even greater seer than he, and his brother told him of the Russians, the powerful enemy of the English, who would come to liberate the Xhosa. He asked them to prepare for the coming by killing the cattle and leaving the fields fallow.

Tatu Joyi said that to this day they were unable to explain how so wise a man as Mhlakaza could have fallen for so terrible a trick. He must have been bewitched and in turn he bewitched Sarhili, the king, who ordered his people to do as the *izinyanya* had directed.[54]

Zululand delenda est

The last Xhosa war ended, as had the others, not by outright military victory, but by starvation and exhaustion. Sandile was killed, and Sarhili became a refugee in Pondoland. Frere, having overcome both black and white opposition in the Cape, turned his attention to Natal.

Before Mpande died, in 1872, he had already proclaimed his son Cetshwayo as his successor. Tall, handsome and dignified, as to be expected from a Zulu aristocrat, Cetshwayo was also prudent and capable, with a wry sense of humour. Before making good his claim, however, Cetshwayo had to assert it with widespread slaughter, destroying thousands of his half-brother Mboyazi's followers and murdering Nomantshali, mother of another potential claimant, Mthonga. Having taken these precautions, in September 1873 Cetshwayo was ceremoniously installed by Theophilus Shepstone as ruler over some 300,000 subjects, whom he proceeded to govern in an absolute but reasonable fashion, as however an acknowledged satellite of Natal, with no aggressive intentions towards the republican burghers (although he was highly suspicious, and with some reason, of Boer ambitions). Arbitrary executions became rarer, and a range of measures including fines, confiscation and punishment served to maintain discipline (although Cetshwayo aroused much criticism when he had some girls killed who refused to marry older men[55]).

Certainly Cetshwayo gave no indication of hostility to the English. The Zulu, he said, were 'like relations of the English ... and wanted their help [against the Boers]'. This was, admittedly, after his defeat, but the deposed King was a good witness at the Cape Inquiry on Native Laws and Customs, and Bulwer had earlier reported that Cetshwayo had asked for 'the Shelter of the Great House should bad times come upon him'. Anthony Trollope found the Zulu he met 'singularly amiable . . . docile and well-mannered, and as Savages are not uncomfortable neighbours'.[56]

Natal's new governor, Sir Henry Bulwer, and Bishop Colenso agreed on the unthreatening attitude of Cetshwayo,[57] but Shepstone, always a major influence, had changed sides. Now appointed to head the new Transvaal administration, he backed the interests of his new subjects against the Zulu in the border areas disputed with the Boers. A boundary commission met at Rorke's Drift (soon to become famous) in March 1878, and settled the question by defining the Transvaal boundary in favour of the Zulu.

Frere had other ideas.[58] With a duplicity not unknown among colonial administrators he suppressed the commission's inconvenient report for some months, and fired off a series of alarmist despatches to the Colonial Office. Cetshwayo, he claimed, supported by perhaps sixty thousand fierce warriors, held Shaka as his avowed model and presented a permanent threat to the whole of southern Africa: *Zululand delenda est*. Writing to the Queen's Private Secretary Colonel Ponsonby, Sir Bartle claimed – hysterically inaccurately – that 'no language indeed would be too strong for the horrible state of things prevailing across the river not seventy miles from this.' It was the High Commissioner's Indian experience that dictated his conclusions: the British Raj was maintained by watchfully upholding prestige, by force sometimes but by bluff always, and this was one of those regrettable instances when force was needed – 'I cannot see anything but disaster in delaying to let the natives know that if the English government is non-aggressive it is so from a sense of justice, and from no want of power,' Frere warned in November 1878.

The evidence for the imminence of war was scanty. Whether or not it was immediately necessary might be debatable, but Frere was convinced that it was only a matter of time before it became inevitable. He determined to make an example of Cetshwayo, and in this was enthusiastically backed by popular opinion in Natal. Only Colenso, Bulwer and such 'half-informed and prejudiced people who [show] a curious sort of sympathy for Cetshwayo', as Frere patronizingly put it, stood out against warmongering. Since Cetshwayo had followed his father's example in discouraging missionaries, this potentially valuable source of support, which had been so useful to Moshoeshoe, was not available. Having two regiments left over from the Xhosa war, giving him over five thousand regulars, Frere's general, Frederick Thesiger, felt confident of overcoming any undisciplined blacks, even if they were as numerous as the Zulu were said to be. Thesiger was a society, rather than a fighting, soldier. His father Lord Chelmsford (Thesiger succeeded to the title in the course of the campaign) had been a prominent Conservative politician, and Frederick had served on a succession of staff appointments. What he had seen of actual fighting had convinced him that the traditional stand-and-fire techniques that the British Army had practised for the last two centuries were still the best. Informed local opinion – which included that of Paul Kruger, transmitted by Sir Bartle – attempted to persuade him of the proven advisability of always forming a defensible position at every halt, but such sensible advice was disregarded.

Frere adopted the device of an impossibly unacceptable ultimatum to start his war.[59] A banal criminal case provided an excuse for him to demand the disbanding of the Zulu army, abolition of the military system and acceptance of the ultimate authority of the British government over all Zululand. Bearing in mind the constant civil unrest and the number of claimants to the throne, no Zulu chief could accept such conditions and survive, but it was Thesiger who, as soon as the thirty days allowed in the ultimatum expired, made the first aggressive move.

On 11 January 1879 an army increased by 1,200 colonial volunteers, black and white, and nine thousand Natalian blacks, crossed the Tukela River to invade Zululand.[60] Within a fortnight the British had suffered their most dramatic tactical defeat for half a century. An entire regiment, the First Battalion of the Twenty-Fourth, the South Wales Borderers and a similar number of supporting troops had been wiped out in a massive Zulu attack at Isandhlwana. Colonel Durnford, who with Colenso – he was engaged to the Bishop's daughter Frances – had protested against the war, was amongst the dead.[61] Although relieved to some extent by the successful defence the next day of a border post at Rorke's Drift, which evened the body-count and resulted in eleven Victoria Crosses being awarded, a hysterical case of overcompensation, British public indignation seethed at the news of the worst defeat for forty years. It was the very scale of the disaster that in fact marked the end of the Zulu power. The logic of prestige demanded that so signal a reverse had to be avenged by the set-piece slaughter of an appropriate number of Zulu: and the following six months saw the process completed.

Encouraged by two subsequent defeats of small British parties (minor but very disconcerting – fifteen officers and seventy-nine men dead in a fight at Hlobane), the *impis* continued their headlong assaults. Attacks on Colonel Eveyln Wood's force, prudently encamped at Kambula, and Thesiger's at Gingindlovu left more than three thousand Zulu dead for a British loss of forty-one. Cetshwayo, realizing the fact of defeat, sent a series of envoys to Frere: 'What have I done? I want peace, I ask for peace.'[62] But Frere and Thesiger both insisted on a demonstration of British supremacy in a battle of extinction, Thesiger being spurred on by the knowledge that Sir Garnet Wolseley was on the way to replace him. This they got in July at Ulundi (Ondini), when the last of the Zulu *impis* obligingly charged Thesiger's reinforced army, formed in a defensive array protected by quick-firing field-guns and Gatling machine-guns. More than a thousand warriors died for a British loss of twelve.

For Thesiger it was only just in time. He had already been superseded by the dashing Wolseley, who had been given the command in spite of Queen Victoria's reservations. The news of Isandhlwana had devastated Britain. Disraeli was greatly stricken by the 'horrible disaster', and took to his bed. The cabinet were now unanimous for sending out a 'dictator' to replace Frere as High Commissioner, leaving him in charge only at the Cape. But Queen Victoria did not agree with anything that might discourage 'poor Sir Bartle Frere', and Disraeli commented: 'the Horse Guards are furious, and the Princes all raging, and every mediocrity . . . jealous as if we had prevented him from conquering the world.'[63]

Too late to effect any military success, Wolseley had to content himself with tidying up and reconstruction. The 'howling societies' at home would, he regretted, prevent his preferred solution, which was encouraging the Swazis to attack the surviving Zulu, since beyond 'shooting and wounding some ten thousand men we have not really punished the people as a nation'. This omission Sir Garnet proceeded to rectify. Cetshwayo was captured and packed off to the Cape, with his rule replaced by that of thirteen independent chiefs under the guardianship of a British resident, Melmoth Osborn. This was an attempt to set the clock back to pre-Shaka days and to ensure that the most powerful of the new chiefs acquiesced in British hegemony, without the Imperial government having to accept any real responsibility for subsequent events.

Among the most powerful of the newly-appointed chiefs was the British elephant-hunter John Dunn. He had already established himself as a notable figure under Cetshwayo, but served with the British during the war, and was awarded the Reserve, nearly a third of Zululand, as his new fief.[64] Zibhebhu, who had fought bravely in the war, was given the guardianship of the King's family, and Hamu, another of Mpande's sons, rewarded for his support of the British with another independent chiefdom, but many of the other chieftains were personages of little consequence. Designed to fragment the Zulu state, Wolseley's plan was criticized at the time by many well-informed figures, including Bulwer, Colenso and Dunn himself. Nor was it well received by the Natalian whites, who had hoped to be able to settle Zululand themselves, as Wolseley well appreciated; their plans were 'all based on the assumption that the land belongs to the white man and that the native was designed to be the settler's servant'.[65]

The division of Zululand into thirteen chieftainships might have worked had it been accompanied by a strong central direction, for the removal of the royal house had left a vacuum in the power structure which demanded filling. This the British government, shying away from any more involvement after the horrifying war, and faced with many other colonial troubles, refused to contemplate.[66]

But Colenso, that indefatigable crusader for justice, insisted that Cetshwayo must be returned to his country. With Gladstone in power again from April 1880, a more sympathetic hearing from London might be expected. Lord Kimberley, convinced that the war had been unjust and unnecessary, was willing to listen, but on no account would he countenance the only action that would have assured security, the establishment of a British protectorate in Zululand (Kimberley needed no persuasion to realize that incorporating Zululand into Natal would be purely prejudicial to the Zulu).

Cetshwayo had been allowed a reasonably comfortable imprisonment in Cape Town castle with four of his wives, allowed to receive visitors and communicate freely. Many supporters rallied to the former king – Colenso, of course, but also William H. Russell, the influential *Times* correspondent, and the young Robert Samuelson, who acted as the deposed monarch's adviser. Cetshwayo's powerful personality and innate dignity, assisted by some skilful publicity, ensured that he made a good impression when he was permitted to visit London, the British public always being ready to lionize a brave enemy – at least after he had been successfully defeated. Gladstone personally welcomed Cetshwayo, even offering him the use of his own house in Harley Street, and the Queen received him at Windsor; there was an element of relief in that the visit gave the opportunity gracefully to permit Cetshwayo's return to Zululand.[67]

He returned in February 1883, but with sovereignty over only a fraction of the country. Dunn's and Hamu's lands were consolidated into a Native Reserve with some degree of British control (but the idea of protection was resolutely avoided) and a strategic territory allocated to Zibhebhu, perhaps the most formidable Zulu fighter since Shaka, having made himself a bold horseman and a fine shot, and trained his people in these methods. Both before and after Cetshwayo's return Zibhebhu harassed the '*usuthu*', the Zulu loyal to their former king, culminating in a massacre at Ondini in which probably more Zulu were killed than in the previous fight with the British Army, and in which fifty-nine of the leaders perished. Cetshwayo was wounded, narrowly escaping with his life, and died shortly afterwards, a refugee seeking sanctuary with the British from his own people. The Zulu had been able to recover quickly enough from the first battle of Ondini, allowed to keep their stock and provisions, but were now debilitated by five years of war, divided and devastated.[68]

Majuba

At the outset, the acquisition of the new crown colony of the Transvaal announced on 12 April 1877 elicited little interest in Britain; it was not the first time the country had been asked to take over some failing African polity, as both Griqualand West and Basutoland had recently demonstrated. Was the report of annexation true?, asked Lord Kimberley on 7 May, nearly a month later. Nothing official had been heard, Carnarvon replied, but he understood that the Transvaal had 'passed under British protection' after Shepstone had 'carried forbearance to the limit'. Were there any protests?, Mr Courtney enquired in the Commons. James Lowther, the Under-Secretary, admitted that the President and the Executive Council of the republic were not in accordance, but that 'the generality of the populace cordially accepted.'

Assisted by a tiny staff, which included Jorissen and John Gilbert Kotzé, Chief and only Justice at the age of twenty-seven, Shepstone contrived at least to keep things moving; but no progress was made towards the promised rapid advance to self-government, undertakings which were reiterated during Kruger's visit to England in July 1877. Had Sir Theophilus and his successor Owen Lanyon made a success of the administration, and the British government been more generous with financial assistance, the annexation might have been more successful. Young Rider Haggard wrote a sarcastic note on the Volksraad proceedings: ' "Let's consider finance" says somebody, and they all proceed to consider finance, but finding out that all the vouchers are missing for at least three or four months, they give it up as a bad job ... Anything more childish, more futile, or more disconnected it is impossible to imagine.'[69]

Kruger set off for England to argue the case for restoring the Transvaal's independence, together with Jorissen and accompanied by Edward Bok – yet another young Hollander who had come to the Transvaal civil service – acting as interpreter. The delegates were cordially received by Carnarvon,[70] who entertained them at his country house, listened to them civilly, and took them on a river trip to Gravesend with Gladstone as a fellow-guest, but refused to budge (and it might be noted that there was no question of Kruger being offered a Prime Minister's hospitality; a hotel was good enough for him). Completely deluded by Shepstone's inaccurate despatches, Carnarvon insisted that most of Paul Kruger's compatriots welcomed the British occupation, but refused any referendum to test this assertion. It would be 'in the highest degree inexpedient', he wrote in July 1877, 'to place on record that an extremely small minority of the community, as I believe you agree with me, is opposed to an acceptance of the Queen's rule'.

Kruger, who was still being paid as a member of the Executive Council, showed little of the uncompromising anti-Britishness he later demonstrated. Probably overwhelmed by the splendours of Whitehall and Highclere House, and with his colleague Jorissen pressing for a compromise, he acceded in an almost deferential letter from the delegation to Carnarvon, expressing themselves convinced that 'your Lordship's views are very promising for the welfare of the country.'[71] For his part the Colonial Secretary was so satisfied with the delegates' demeanour that he wrote to Shepstone recommending their future employment in government.[72] On their return to Pretoria in November Jorissen resumed his duties as Attorney General, but Kruger confirmed his own resignation from the Executive Council, though not before extracting an extra £100 from the colonial authorities in compensation for the additional time he had spent. He then very quickly set about disproving the myth that only an 'insignificant minority' refused to welcome annexation. Walking delicately between the furious intransigents who wanted to shoot eight Englishmen as a preliminary warning and the wrath of the British, Kruger organized an unofficial plebiscite which produced 6,591 signatures against the annexation, with only 587 in favour.

Fortified by this evidence, and assuming that the British government had meant what it said when it undertook only to annex if a majority of the inhabitants approved, Kruger set off again for London in June 1878, accompanied this time by Piet Joubert, who was to be his arch-rival for the next twenty years, the useful Edward Bok and Sir Donald Currie, a Liberal ship-owner, founder of the Union Castle Line, and a supporter of Transvaal independence. By the time they arrived Lord Carnarvon had been replaced by Sir Michael Hicks Beach, a tougher customer and one preoccupied with more pressing concerns and much influenced by his Permanent Under-Secretary, Robert Herbert, who despised the 'weak and cowardly' Boers. Although Bartle Frere wrote to Sir Michael, pointing out that the Boers had valid complaints of Shepstone's maladministration – promises on retaining the Dutch language had not been kept, there was still no elected Volksraad, or indeed any visible government – Hicks Beach was constrained by party politics. Discredited though Carnarvon was – 'every day brings forward a new blunder of Twitters,' complained Disraeli – his proceedings could not be denounced by a Conservative government, especially one that by then was looking decidedly shaky. Support for the Transvaalers was developing among the opposition, led by Currie and Leonard Courtney, an influential *Times* leader-writer and Professor of Political Economy at University College, London. Any concessions to the delegation would be seen as a surrender, and its members were therefore allowed a single grudging interview before being dismissed by Sir Michael.

Boer indignation at this rejection, exacerbated by Shepstone's dilatory regime, moved a substantial number to muster under arms, prepared to assert their independence by force. Frere was immersed in his disastrous Zulu war, but made time to meet the burghers in April 1879. After some difficult preliminaries Sir Bartle, who was nothing if not a master of the grand gesture, showed the qualities that had won his reputation. After a ride of more than three hundred miles he was met by a recalcitrant Boer assembly at Erasmus's Spruit, near Pretoria. Leaving his staff behind, the old civilian cantered alone into their camp, and insisted on beginning the deliberations with a prayer. Although nothing was decided, the burghers departed peacefully in a better frame of mind. Whatever benefit might have come from Frere's intervention was undone by his recall and Wolseley's arrival in the Transvaal. Moving quickly to subdue the Boers' old enemy Sekhukhune, warning him that the English now had a new weapon – the lyddite shell – which would destroy all neighbouring life, Wolseley considered his work done. In his usual style the new High Commissioner insisted, 'so long as the sun shines, the Transvaal will remain British terri- tory.' That was in December 1879: within six months British forces had been decisively defeated, their general killed, and the Transvaal was once more independent.

This astonishing reversal might have come sooner had it not been for political events in Britain. Weakened by the expensive Zulu war (the sinking fund had to be suspended in order to avoid a tax on tea, a sure recipe for revolution) and another disaster in Afghanistan, and the resignation of Lords Derby and Carnarvon (Twitters finally left over what he regarded as British provocation in the Russo–Turkish War), Disraeli's government lost the election of April 1880. While in opposition Gladstone, during his famous Midlothian campaigns, had made his support of Kruger clear: 'were the Transvaal as valuable as it is valueless', he would still 'utterly repudiate' its acquisition as being obtained 'by means dishonourable to the character of the Country'.[73]

Reasonably enough, the Transvaalers expected the new Prime Minister to keep his word: 'They were confident that one day or another, by the mercy of the Lord, the views of the Imperial government would be entrusted to men who look out for the honour and glory of England, not by acts of injustice and crushing force, but by the way of justice and good faith.' They were to be disappointed. The new Liberal government was formed on 23 April 1880; on 10 May Kruger reminded Gladstone of his promise; the Prime Minister passed the letter to Lord Kimberley, saying that he was 'at a loss how to answer it'; on 12 May the Cabinet decided to renege. In spite of pressure from the radicals, including such influential persons as Joseph Chamberlain – who foresaw the danger of a war with the Boers: 'the most costly, unsatisfactory, and difficult of all the little wars which we can possibly undertake' – John Bright and Charles Dilke, and of a petition signed by such great men as Ernest Renan, the historian of Christianity, and Victor Hugo, all that the new Liberal government was prepared to do was to implement the promises made four years earlier of 'the fullest liberty to manage their own affairs'.[74] While it is always easier for a government to do nothing rather than something, both Gladstone and Kimberley, back at his desk as Colonial Secretary, were greatly influenced by Wolseley, who had pointed out that gold had already been discovered in the Transvaal, and 'there can be little doubt that larger and still more valuable goldfields will sooner or later be discovered', which should bring British immigrants in such numbers as to swamp the Boers. Surely it would be a very short-sighted policy to give the Transvaal up merely to save the cost of keeping a garrison of some two or three thousand troops?[75]

By the end of the year the Transvaalers' resentment was unstoppable. Kruger called together the tail of the Volksraad on 10 December 1880, and the Proclamation of Pardekraal was published three days later. Although the demand that independence be restored was made clear, it was by no means an intransigent document: boundaries were to be subject to arbitration, and native policy to be decided upon 'after deliberation with the Colonies and States of South Africa'. But martial law was proclaimed, and a triumvirate of Kruger, Joubert and old Pretorius appointed as an executive.

The subsequent war was nothing more than one ambush and a couple of skirmishes, but it rocked Britain, and caught the attention of the world. Sir George Colley, who as a subaltern twenty years before had complained of Harry Smith's brutality, now High Commissioner and Governor of the Transvaal and Natal, in succession to Frere and Wolesley took personal command of his forces. Colley's active service was limited to a couple of minor campaigns in the China expedition of 1860, very much a walkover, and Wolseley's Ashanti campaign, where he had been in charge of transport; but he was the most distinguished academic soldier in Britain, greatly learned, a professor at Sandhurst and author of the long 'Army' entry in the *Encyclopaedia Britannica*. In this exhaustive study of the military, past and present, he disposes of 'militia' in a few sentences: 'History abounds with lessons that such forces can never carry on sustained operations against trained armies. They may show brilliant courage; but they want the mutual knowledge and reliance, the constancy in defeat, and the instinctive discipline which can be acquired by habit alone . . . opposed to trained armies, they invite defeat.'

Sir George proved himself mistaken in the most personal way. In the third of the skirmishes, at Majuba Hill on the Natal border, on 27 February 1881, he led a mixed force of Gordon Highlanders, the Northamptonshires — the Fifty-Eighth, who had stormed Quebec with Wolfe – and Bluejackets, supported by artillery, rockets and Gatling guns, into a disastrous fight against a considerably smaller force of Boer 'militia'. Ninety-three Britons died for one Boer, and among the British dead was Sir George, killed by a single bullet through the head. The picture of panic-stricken Highlanders and sailors, the most renowned of fighting men, rushing down the slopes of Majuba Hill became an icon of British humiliation. A further irony lay in the fact that eleven days previously Lord Kimberley and Kruger had agreed on a ceasefire and the appointment of a Royal Commission to adjudicate on the future of the Transvaal – the latter being a tacit acknowledgement of *de facto* British hegemony there. It was Colley's own impatience and folly that had led him to disaster at Majuba.

Imperial policy would normally have dictated that the triumphant Boers should be shattered, as had been the Zulu, in a demonstration of British superiority. More than enough troops were on their way to South Africa – six regiments of infantry and three of cavalry led by Lord Roberts, the hero of Afghanistan and a genuine fighter. Evelyn Wood, now knighted and a general, in command on the ground, was 'humanly speaking confident of certain victory'. But the Boers were white, and the importance of keeping 'face' was less than if they had been brown or black. Given the possibility of a fairly honourable deal, and the certainty that further fighting would inflame the Free State and Cape Afrikaners, together with the pacific influence of President Brand, Gladstone's cabinet agreed to back down.[76]

It was a gift to the Conservative opposition, and hay was duly made in Parliament. 'Why,' the formidable ex-Lord Chancellor Cairns demanded, 'had the government spent the blood and treasure of our country like water, only to surrender at the end what they had refused at the outset?' Feebly justifying their concession of defeat to an indignant Queen Victoria, the cabinet pleaded: 'in requiring the dispersion of the Boers to their homes, they will have made the necessary provision for the vindication of Your Majesty's authority.' The Queen was not impressed: at the end of a '*cruel civil war* – for so it is, the Boers being my *subjects*', it appeared that the Boers had 'obtained all they fought for'.[77]

Negotiations between Kruger and the Commission dragged on for some months before reaching a conclusion in the Convention of Pretoria, signed on 3 August 1881. By this agreement, 'complete self-government, subject to the suzerainty of Her Majesty' was to be accorded to the Transvaalers. An odd word, devoid of any precise meaning, 'suzerainty' only entered the language in the nineteenth century, and was popular chiefly among romantic novelists until shifted into politics by the romantic novelist who happened also to be a Prime Minister, Benjamin Disraeli. Meaning some sort of rather vague authority, it seems to have been inserted in the Convention largely to please the Queen. A more accurate definition was given in Article II, as including 'the control of external relations ... and the conduct of diplomatic intercourse with foreign powers, such intercourse being carried out through Her Majesty's diplomatic and consular officers abroad'.[78]

Kruger had a hard time of it convincing the Volksraad to accept the agreement. Joubert was especially bitter, claiming that the terms 'opened up every wound of the past, instead of, as we hoped, closing them up for ever'. Only at the last minute did the Volksraad, 'provisionally submitting the articles of the convention to a practical test' agree to ratify the agreement on 13 October 1881.

Picking up the Pieces

Colonel Stanley has asked for some notes of instances in which there has been vacillation in the policy of this country towards South Africa. To tell the story in full would be to re-write the history of the country.

So began a long, sarcastic memorandum dated 4 August 1885 from Edward Fairfield of the Colonial Office. Fairfield was unquestionably right, and his indignation was heightened since the preceding ten years had seen a catalogue of misfortune and incompetence. British politicians and officials had contrived to:

1 Begin an expensive and, to the Zulu, disastrous war

2 Fail to prevent an equally damaging Xhosa war

3 Shuffle off responsibility for the Basuto onto the Cape government, and subsequently be obliged to take it back again, after yet another war

4 Unilaterally annex the Transvaal and muddle the subsequent administration

5 Stumble into an armed clash with the Transvaal, and get much the worst of it

6 Arbitrarily dismiss an elected Cape government

7 Irritate the Orange Free State by a doubtful annexation of the diamond fields

8 Be obliged, by dubious means, to suspend the constitution of Natal

Westminster

After the failure of his attempt at a South African federation, Lord Carnarvon left the colonial scene; his only subsequent government post was Ireland, that graveyard of reputations. All the violence that marked South Africa in the late 1870s and early 1880s can be attributed either to the Conservative government's mistaken policies or their Liberal successors' failure to rectify them, aggravated by the clumsiness of their self-willed representatives. Frere's recall and the withdrawal from the Transvaal reflected the mood of Gladstone's cabinet, in which Lord Kimberley was succeeded in December 1882 by Lord Derby (who as Lord Stanley had been Foreign Secretary in his father's – also Lord Derby, for the nobility were ubiquitous in nineteenth-century British government). Lord Derby, who would always have preferred to be on his estates in Lancashire, or on a racecourse, was one of those nineteenth-century aristocrats who sacrificed their inclinations for public duty; up to a point. 'He was a very big fish to land,' wrote Gladstone's Private Secretary, 'but has been worth all the trouble.' Others disagreed: Derby was 'for letting everything drift . . . always trying to evade responsibility . . . hopeless . . . dreadful . . . never will decide anything . . . never states his case to his colleagues', according to one senior civil servant, Sir Robert Meade. Much of the muddle and many of the poor decisions made by the British government between 1882 and 1885 must be attributed to Derby's faults, allied to overwhelming pressure of events in other areas.[1]

With the follies of Frere and Shepstone acknowledged, the massacre at Isandhlwana satisfactorily avenged by the slaughter of several thousand more Zulu, and the defeat of Majuba written off to experience (subsequently neglected), British attention switched from South to North Africa, and in particular to Egypt, where a nationalist revolt against the corrupt and inefficient Khedive flared up in 1881. When France, the other party of the Egyptian condominium, declined to take action, the Royal Navy bombarded Alexandria, and the British Army, under Sir Garnet Wolseley, destroyed the Egyptian forces in a textbook battle outside Cairo. If the British government had faced the responsibilities that these actions had thrust upon it many subsequent problems might have been avoided, but Gladstone's government shied away from such involvements, and contented itself with appointing Evelyn Baring (later Lord Cromer) as Consul General, with great influence but limited power. When in 1884 General Gordon got himself cut off in Khartoum, and the reluctantly-despatched relief expedition arrived too late to save this popular hero, it was the last straw. Colonial adventures were henceforward firmly off the agenda of the Gladstonian Liberals.

Other more pressing issues faced the government. In May 1882 the Irish Viceroy, Lord Frederick Cavendish, an irreproachable young man, was assassinated, sliced to death with surgical knives. Like many subsequent Irish terrorist acts this was a mistake – the assassins did not know who he was – and counter-productive, since both British and Irish opinion was horrified. The horror was intensified three months later when a whole family, including three children, were stabbed and beaten to death by terrorists. The previous understanding between Liberals and Parnell's Irish MPs evaporated in the subsequent repression, and in 1885 the Irish members voted with the Conservatives to defeat Gladstone. During the seven months in which Lord Salisbury governed with a minority Gladstone studied the Irish question, with the result that when the November 1885 election produced an Irish vote of eighty-six members solidly (for the moment) behind Parnell, Gladstone prepared his plan to offer Ireland self-government (Home Rule), a radical reform which, if effected, would have changed all subsequent history. But the Liberal cabinet were not willing to accept so drastic a measure; led by the radical Joseph Chamberlain, now fiercely opposed to what he saw as the disintegration of the Union, many Liberals voted against the Home Rule Bill.

By August 1886 Lord Salisbury was firmly back in power, with Gladstone, after more than half a century in Parliament, apparently a spent force. Salisbury, a stout and cultivated patrician, acted as his own Foreign Secretary, a post in which his unequalled proficiency was acknowledged. Colonial affairs, which he regarded as tedious, were relegated to the reliable but unenterprising hands of, successively, Edward Stanhope and Henry Holland, an experienced former colonial civil servant. Holland had come to politics late in life, and this was his first cabinet post (at the age of sixty-three). An agreeable man, but lacking in firmness, he found the hurly-burly of the Commons too much, and quickly accepted a transfer to the upper house as Lord Knutsford.

A mistake as well as a crime

Even had any of these Colonial Secretaries possessed the forcefulness of Lord Kimberley, their rapid succession would have made it difficult for them to exercise much influence. Initiative rapidly passed to the other players, of whom the most important were increasingly the South Africans themselves.

There agreements, once made, quickly became unravelled. Moshoeshoe and the British Colonial Office knew that the only hope for independence for the Sotho people lay in direct British rule, but Basutoland had been handed over to the Cape. The old chief had been succeeded by his son Letsie, who found himself unable to impose the same authority over his relations and allies, of whom the most prominent was the famous old warrior Moroosi of the Phuti. Moroosi was over eighty when in 1879 Frere's appointee, Cape Prime Minister Gordon Sprigg, made a fatuous demand that all guns owned by blacks should be handed over to the authorities. Since guns, together with horses, were not only prized possessions, bought with hard-earned wages in the diamond fields, but also guarantees of freedom, the demand was scornfully rejected. Only after six months' fighting was the rebellion quelled, and Moroosi killed and decapitated. Pompous little Sprigg, describing himself as 'Premier and Master of the Colony', then attempted to browbeat all the Basuto into surrendering their weapons. Wolseley, well aware what a difficult proposition the Basuto would be, wrote agitatedly to the War Office blaming Bartle Frere for starting a war which would be 'a mistake as well as a crime', but his warning came too late since most of the chiefs were already united in revolt under Letsie's son Lerotholi.[2] Sprigg's forces soon experienced the difficulties of fighting a colonial war on their own account without British assistance, and at an eventual cost to the colony of the enormous sum of £3 million. Since looting and confiscation were forbidden there was no reward for the militia, who speedily deserted. Lerotholi proved a superb guerrilla leader – 'the bravest of the brave,' Merriman called him – and fought an intelligent campaign with minimum losses. Greatly distressed by this unconscionable attack on *his* people, the French missionary Pelissier hurried to London, and was successful in convincing Lord Kimberley that something must be done. With the troubles spilling over the Drakensberg into British-administered territory and threatening, it was thought, to spread to Zululand, Westminster was forced to find a solution.[3]

The Liberal government did not need much persuading. Gladstone's secretary Edward Hamilton feared 'a repetition of the Zulu War', and called the disarmament 'a monstrous act of injustice mainly attributable to the handiwork of that "fire-eating" Sir Bartle Frere . . . it would be difficult to conceive a proceeding more calculated to wound the pride of a high-spirited race.'[4]

The 'gun war' was settled after the arrival in August 1880 of the new High Commissioner, Sir Hercules Robinson. A more considerable figure than the usual run of colonial Governors, Sir Hercules, later ennobled as Lord Rosmead, had proved himself under difficult circumstances in both Hong Kong and Australia as an emollient and intelligent administrator, but one consistently faithful to the interests of Sir Hercules Robinson. Basutoland, in spite of the settlement, remained an intractable problem facing the incoming government, since once the pressure of war was removed the chiefs returned to internecine bickering, combined with persecution of those who had remained loyal to the Cape during the war. Even Joseph Orpen, Moshoeshoe's old friend and historian of the Basuto, who resigned his parliamentary seat in order to become resident agent, could neither persuade nor coerce Chief Masupha, Letsie's brother, and prime source of trouble, to a settlement. Nor were the Cape parliamentarians more united, options ranging from an unconditional scuttle, leaving the Basuto to their own devices, through a plan for the territory's 'home rule', to persuading the British government to take back the responsibility they had originally accepted in 1871. A desperate attempt was made to have General Gordon, the hero of the hour after his exploits in China, apply his talents to Basutoland. With considerable perception Gordon realized that the Basuto saw themselves as a nation, one of the few identifiable as such in South Africa, but his suggested solution, of indirect rule through Masupha, was diametrically opposed to that preferred by the Cape government. A '*pitso*', the Basuto general council, held in April 1883 rejected Cape rule, Gordon went off to his glorious death in Khartoum, and nothing remained for it but to persuade the Colonial Office to assume responsibility for Basutoland. Merriman was therefore sent to London in May 1883 to make the attempt. He found Lord Derby, Kimberley's successor, receptive enough, insisting only that the Cape should make some contribution to administrative expenses and that the chiefs should agree.

In 1884 therefore Basutoland became a state with many characteristics of independence, ruled by its own chiefs, the descendants of Moshoeshoe, supervised by a resident British Commissioner and neglected by British governments. Economically the Basuto were dependent upon employment in the surrounding territories, and regarded suspiciously by successive South African governments who believed that Basutoland should be part of their territory, and not ruled by 'negrophiles' in London; but London continued to resist, and Basutoland survived to become the independent country of Lesotho.

Gladstone's agreement to accepting another colonial responsibility was obtained only with difficulty; had it not been for Sprigg's gun war there would have been little possibility of his consent. Far from scrambling for Africa, both Cape Town and London were deeply reluctant to take on more responsibilities. Merriman even harboured a hope, which the Colonial Office did not discourage, that the Transkei could also be given a similar status to Basutoland, but this the Liberal government firmly declined.

Clarifying the Transvaal agreement was almost as difficult as settling the Basuto's future. Relations with the Transvaal – now once more the South African Republic – had temporarily been patched up in the Pretoria Convention of 1881, but the republic's Volksraad accepted it only for the time being and provisionally, and President Paul Kruger had to exert himself to obtain even this grudging assent. Although the boundaries of the South African Republic were supposed to have been defined, they were speedily, and in several directions, broken. Transvaalers were ebullient at what seemed to be the defeat of British imperialism, and within months had set up three new republics: Stellaland and Goshen (from Genesis – 'the best of the land of Egypt given to Joseph') in the Tswana lands on the west frontier, and the New Republic between Natal and Zululand.

The loss of this huge slice of Zululand was the result of the angry young Usuthu warriors supporting Cetshwayo's successor, the sixteen-year-old Dinizulu, and seeking revenge on Zibhebhu for his treachery to the former king. In April 1884 the young prince, taken into protection for his own good by the Boer 'Committee of Dinizulu's volunteers', was, as his grandfather Mpande had been, solemnly installed as King of Zululand by the Boer expedition. Their price had been Dinizulu's agreement to cede as much of Zululand as they 'may consider necessary for establishing an independent self-government'. In the following month an Usuthu *impi*, powerfully reinforced by Boer firepower, inflicted a crushing defeat on Dinizulu's rival Zibhebhu at the battle of Chaneni (Etshaneni), where Zulu casualties were higher even than at Isandhlwana; Louis Botha, the future

Prime Minister of the Union of South Africa, who was there, said he had never seen so many dead men.

Claiming their reward, the Transvaalers proclaimed the 'New Republic' with Piet Joubert, who had encouraged the enterprise, elected as President. Natal's Governor Sir Henry Bulwer was angry and humiliated, for Zibhebhu had been a 'faithful ally' and his people 'the finest and bravest', but the Colonial Office was not disposed to make an issue of it, so long as the protected reserve was not interfered with. The whole episode was admittedly an 'insolent disregard' of the British, but since 'we have decided to acquiesce in it, it may be best to do so without words'.[5] Lord Derby, the Colonial Secretary, was a peace-at-any-price man, who had left the Conservatives in protest at Disraeli's aggressive foreign policy, and was anxious to avoid trouble at all costs; especially if it meant adding to his responsibilities. 'We want no more black men' was one of his favourite remarks, and he was happy to allow the Boers to assume responsibility for however many Zulu they wanted. Prime Minister Gladstone agreed: 'Is it unreasonable to think that the Dutch . . . are perhaps better qualified to solve the Zulu problem outside the reserves, than we can do in dealing with it from Downing Street? If Natal was a real self-governing colony it would be another matter.'[6]

This Bechuana business

With very great reluctance Lord Derby found that he could not be so permissive about Boer expansion to the west. Transvaalers, always looking out for new horizons, had made sorties since the 1850s, annexing the Tati area in 1866, causing the Tswana chiefs to make appeals for British protection, which had been spasmodically accorded. Little attention had been paid in London, but a first-class row had erupted in the House of Commons in March 1883 when the news of 'cruel and treacherous attacks . . . by . . . lawless bands of Boer banditti, the scum of the Transvaal' had been received. Lord Randolph Churchill suggested the formation of a corps on the lines of the Texas Rangers to deal with such 'ruffianly Boer aggressions'.

The 'ruffianly' Boers had pushed across the 1871 Keate Line at two places to establish the Stellaland Republic, with its capital at Vryburg, and the Republic of Goshen, with no capital at all other than the farm Rooi Grond, later glorified with the appellation of Heliopolis, further north near Mafikeng (Mafeking). A form of government had been established, and land allocated to whites. Sensible Lord Kimberley pointed out that 'unless we are prepared to use frequent force we must put up with things being done ... that the majority of people in this country do not approve,' and Lord Derby, rather lamely, suggested that the chiefs should be compensated for any land taken by the Boers.[7] These incursions threatened the established missionary – and trade (the two had always been near-synonymous) – route to the interior of the continent, but London might well have dithered had not Van Plettius, leader of the Gosheners ('freebooters' to London, 'volunteers' to Pretoria), issued a decree in September 1884 annexing Goshen to the South African Republic.

Although hedged about, this looked suspiciously like a deliberate insult, coming only days after the Transvaal Volksraad had ratified the latest agreement with Britain, the London Convention. Anxious to establish the completed independence of the South African Republic, Kruger had come again to London with two other envoys, General Nicolas Smit, the victor of Majuba, and Ds Stephanus du Toit, to renegotiate the existing Pretoria Convention. Much more pressing concerns were engaging the cabinet – Egypt and Ireland foremost amongst them – and only superficial attention was paid to the importunate Boers. The eventual agreement had many ambiguities, with the concept of 'suzerainty' carefully glossed over – although the Transvaal was forbidden to conclude agreements with foreign states without British agreement – and the veto on native legislation removed. Although Kruger fought hard for Stellaland and Goshen to be included in the South African Republic this was not granted, and the boundary as finally drawn up allocated only a small part of the two splinter states to the Transvaal.

Agreement was only reached after four months' hard negotiation, in February 1884. Kruger then made a tour through Europe, where he was warmly received by the Dutch King, the German Emperor and the President of France, and returned to Pretoria only a month before the Convention had to be ratified. This was only achieved after the President disguised to the point of deception the details of his agreement with Lord Derby: 'We have got back our independence,' he claimed. 'The suzerainty is abolished.' In London the Colonial Office tended to agree: Robert Herbert minuted: 'It is intended that we should understand that the South African Republic will not carry out the portions objected to,' but the more optimistic Derby 'read this as a general ratification'. There the matter was allowed to rest.[8]

When, just days after the Volksraad ratified the London Convention, the

Revd. Stephanus du Toit, who had himself been one of the delegation responsible for the boundaries' agreement, went off to Goshen and raised the South African Republic's flag, it was too much even for the peaceful Lord Derby. He had acquiesced in the dismemberment of Zululand, a clear breach of the London Convention, but he was not ready to climb down again. 'To eat humble pie once is one thing, to have a second helping of it another,' Edward Hamilton wrote. 'The more I look at this Bechuana business,' Derby told the premier, 'the more unsatisfactory it appears . . . it seems to leave no choice between accepting what is undoubtedly a humiliating defeat, or persisting in our refusal . . . and the risk of a Boer War. And this when we have Egypt on our hands!' The War Office, however, insisted the risk had to be taken, and assumed 'that Her Majesty's Government is prepared to enforce – if necessary by arms – the terms of the convention'.[9]

Gladstone took some convincing. In the same month of August 1884 he had, with the utmost reluctance, and after four months' procrastination, authorized a force to rescue Gordon from Khartoum; and this additional expense would mean another penny on the income tax. But the map of Southern Africa was to be greatly changed, and the pressing necessity for action made obvious, when on 7 August 1884 Chancellor Bismarck announced that the whole of the coastline of South-West Africa, with the exception of the British enclave of Walvis Bay, was henceforward to constitute Imperial German territory. How far this annexation extended inland was not made clear, but it was obvious that German influence was being brought uncomfortably close to the Transvaal. Such an event worried Gladstone not at all: 'I should be extremely glad,' he wrote, 'to see the Germans become our neighbours in South Africa, or even the neighbours of the Transvaal.'[10]

Until a few months previously Bismarck had also appeared indifferent to the notion of colonies: 'My map of Africa is here in Europe,' he claimed, adding that 'colonies for Germany would be like the silks and sables of the Polish nobles who had no shirts to wear under them.' The Chancellor's conversion had begun in 1879, when a series of customs duties were imposed on imports in order to protect German agriculture and industry. A corollary of this was the need to find new markets which could similarly be closed to competition. Respectable institutions such as the Kolonialverein, the Colonial Union, founded in 1882, urged that 'colonization was a matter of life and death'; disreputable bodies such as the Gesellschaft für Deutsche

Kolonisation (Society for German Colonization) founded by the 'mounte-bank, patriot and Jew-baiter' Carl Peters were even more vehement.[11]

The British cabinet was shocked. Only the previous year Bismarck's son Count Herbert had insisted that Germany 'had not the least design to establish any footing in Africa'. In spite of this assurance a German expedition occupied the bay of Angra Pequena (Luderitz Bay), between Walvis Bay and the Cape boundary. It was followed by a warship, and a quite unnecessary diplomatic crisis. At Merriman's instigation Lord Derby agreed to the Cape's annexing the disputed coastline, but the Foreign Secretary, Lord Granville, reached a settlement with Bismarck in return for German support in Egypt. Both Bismarck, who could not understand that a colony with responsible government was in most respects independent of the parent country, and the Cape politicians were furious; but German South-West Africa had become an established fact, and its threatening presence drew attention to the imperative need for a buffer between it and the Transvaal.

'This Bechuana business' that Lord Derby had worried about concerned that territory, today divided between the independent country of Botswana and the northern Cape, controlled by the BaTswana – Bechuana to the nineteenth century. The region, arid and largely profitless, had received little attention hitherto, other than that of the missionaries, who, beginning with Robert Moffat, had pressed north from Griquatown first to Kuruman and thence to Molepole, where David Livingstone made his first, and best-known convert, Sechele (Setshele), a Tswana chief. Missionary influence was strongest in the eastern part of the region, nearest the Transvaal and Orange borders. By 1840, when the tumult of the *mfecane* had subsided, and the Ndebele settled well away to the north-east, the Tswana peoples had recovered a measure of stability as those who had fled to the desert returned to the more hospitable east. Linguistically close to the Sotho, the Tswana were differentiated by some customs, including that of supporting a system of permanent subordination equivalent to slavery. Among other African communities foreign elements, including Khoi-San and white, were absorbed into the parent society, perhaps after a period of clientship. Even the huge influx of Mfengu into Hintsa's Xhosa, which must have placed a considerable strain on the community, had been accepted on terms of at least potential equality. But the subordinate status of the Khoi-San Sarwa among the Tswana was distinct and permanent. Slavery in Southern Africa had elsewhere been practised only by whites, but the Sarwa had been held in servitude since the seventeenth century and were, at the time of the first accounts, 'virtually enslaved' and treated with startling brutality – cutting off ears and plunging hands in boiling fat were not unusual punishments.[12]

By the beginning of the nineteenth century the Tswana had experienced dozens of divisions into different lineages and chiefdoms, usually fighting among themselves, the literally vital watering-places being a great object of contention, and were spread for a thousand miles in a great arc around the eastern boundaries of the Kalahari. Unlike their Sotho cousins, the Tswana had thrown up no outstanding leader until the emergence in 1875 of Kgama, chief of the Ngwato branch of the Tswana people. Kgama, one of the most remarkable Africans of his time, had been converted by Lutheran missionaries, and appreciated that the best hope for the survival of his people was to enlist British support against Boer encroachments. Sandwiched in among the Tswana on the edge of the Transvaal settlements was another Christian community, the last surviving independent Khoikhoi people, the Taaibosch Koranna, led by their captain David Massouw. More than a century earlier, under the leadership of Gaaner Gaauex, the Koranna, pushed from their own homeland by Dutch expansion, had in turn displaced the Tswana from the Harts River area around Taung.

Public opinion in Britain was formed from missionary accounts. When Moffat wrote his *Encyclopaedia Britannica* (ninth edition, 1885) article on Bechuanaland, he described the Tswana as 'a people of industrious habits, attentive to whatever may increase their property and comfort', and was, together with most other missionaries, generally – and with some justice – critical of the Boers. By 1880 the missionary road ran two thousand miles north from the Cape to Matabeleland, Mzilikazi's kingdom, where even that fierce old warrior had responded to the uncompromising Moffat with warm friendship. Linked by the only available water, and not much of that, the missionary road was the only practicable route from the Cape to the north.

Kgama quickly sought British protection, appreciating that his people stood a much better chance with London than with Cape Town. In this he had initially to overcome the opposition of Cecil Rhodes, who considered Kgama 'the most remarkable Kaffir this or any other century has seen',[13] but who wanted to keep the initiative with the Cape government. Fortified by the millions he had made in the diamond mines, Rhodes had in 1880 become member for the new Griqualand West seat of Barkly West in the Cape parliament. Lacking any of the normal parliamentary skills of well-organized argument and fluent debate, Rhodes nevertheless had an incomparable gift for gaining influence, his remarkable personality being aided by more direct commercial methods. He had recognized that the most dangerous opponent to his own imperial dreams of British hegemony in Africa was the Imperial power itself, with its perennial reluctance to assume new responsibilities and its nervous distrust of colonial attitudes towards human rights. If the Bechuana became an Imperial responsibility, as had the Basuto, it would be more difficult to arrive at the first step in Rhodes' programme, unity with the republics. 'The only method,' Rhodes had written, 'of checking the expansion of the Boer Republics is to enclose them by the Cape Colony.' In an attempt to reach some agreement with the Boers, an increasingly angry series of negotiations and confrontations took place between Rhodes, acting on behalf of the Cape government, and John McKenzie, the missionary appointed by the Colonial Office as Deputy High Commissioner with responsibility for Bechuanaland. McKenzie was altogether too dedicated to supporting black interests to resist either the Cape or the Colonial Office, who accused him of acting as 'an honest schoolboy'.[14]

Eventually, and most reluctantly, the British cabinet, gritting its collective teeth, hoping that the Cape government would assume responsibility for this new acquisition, and 'as much afraid at least, of Sir Charles Warren as of the Germans',[15] despatched that unorthodox soldier, Fellow of the Royal Society, distinguished archaeologist and veteran of the last frontier war to settle the Bechuanaland business. General Warren was given a force of some four thousand volunteers to expel the freebooters, bag and baggage, while Gladstone and his government looked on with apprehension.

As it turned out, no force was needed. President Kruger and Rhodes met Warren in January 1885 at Fourteen Streams in the Transvaal and agreed to withdraw the Transvaal annexation; indeed, the 'freebooters' happily charged exorbitant rates for transporting the British supplies north. The annexation, Kruger explained, was always intended to have been subject to British agreement, and Ds du Toit's initiative had been sponsored by Joubert, Kruger's rival, against the President's better judgement. Acting on his own initiative, and justifying Gladstone's forebodings, General Warren then proclaimed the whole of the region south of 22 degrees south and east of 20 degrees east, as far as the Transvaal border, to be under British protection. An alarmed Hercules Robinson succeeded in having this modified so that the smaller part south of the Molopo, and now part of the Republic of South Africa, was formed into a crown colony, with the northern part, now the independent country of Botswana, left with only an indeterminate degree of British protection.

With their western borders sealed off by British Bechuanaland, the sole remaining possible route which could connect the Transvaal – since the London Convention officially known as the South African Republic – to the sea would be through the still-unclaimed strip of coast between Zululand and Mozambique to St Lucia Bay. Anticipating a Transvaal move in this direction the British took over the bay in 1885, following this two years later by the annexation of the remainder of Zululand. Access to the exterior being denied, the Boer republics were now effectively sealed in, although individual efforts to trek off into the dusty wastes of the Kalahari continued. The best-known of these was the 'Thirstland Trek' of Louwrens du Plessis, which struggled through into South-West Africa, where his people were rescued by the extraordinary W.W. Jordan, a self-taught young 'Coloured' therapist who helped them to found yet another Boer polity, the Republic of Upingtonia, while others were allowed to settle in Angola.

This question of access was to remain outstanding among South African concerns for the next ten years. The Free State was entirely dependent on routes to the sea ports of Natal, closer to hand, or the Cape, which was the more important centre. So for that matter was the Transvaal, but while the Free State habitually remained on good terms with the Cape, President Kruger became doggedly determined to create his own railway system, as an essential requirement to preserve Transvaal independence. Until that came – and there was little sign of it in 1884 – all the lands north of the Drakensberg must remain dependent on the ox-cart for transport, a sure means of ensuring commercial stagnation.

The Cape Parliament

Queen Victoria still sits in majesty outside the Republic of South Africa's Parliament in Cape Town. Fittingly so, since it was in her name and in those buildings that South African parliamentary government was born. Perverted over the years and grossly undemocratic for much of the period, parliamentary rule has nevertheless survived, and Speaker has succeeded Speaker, until the present day. After its rude interruption by Sir Bartle Frere political life at the Cape returned to normality, but it was about to undergo a transformation, which had begun in 1875.

Language and nationality are intimately linked, and one development of the last two centuries has been the revival of moribund languages in order to bolster nationalisms. The artificial respiration accorded to Irish and Welsh may not have established those tongues as useful media for communication (one can travel far in either country before seeing an advertisement in anything other than English; money talks), but it has kept those two ancient and beautiful languages from disappearing completely. Afrikaans, on the other hand, is a modern development that has become the accepted method of communication among millions of people, and has acquired a body of modern literature greater than that of any recently revived language.[16]

Basic Dutch was quickly adopted by slaves, Khoikhoi and colonists alike. As early as the 1680s Commissioner van Rheede had cause to complain that the colonists were polluting the mother tongue by the introduction of Malay, Khoikhoi, Bantu, French and German words and grammar (including a double negative which does not exist in Dutch and probably came from the Huguenot refugees). When printed versions of the *taal* appeared in the early nineteenth century they were essentially comic, put into the mouths of Christianized Khoikhoi by such non-Dutch writers as playwright and journalist Charles Etienne Boniface, and the more talented Andrew Geddes Baines, whose 'Kaatje Keekelbek' became famous. The first semi-serious use of the *taal* was in 1860 by Louis Meurant, a magistrate at Cradock and another native non-Dutch-speaker, and the first book to be printed in the *taal* was, oddly enough, an 1856 Muslim children's catechism: the little Malay boys learned their '*Lat Muhammed Allah sain Poeroefiets*' not in Arabic but the *taal*.

Educated South African Dutch-speakers continued to dismiss the *taal* as 'kitchen Dutch'. It needed immigrant Hollanders to recognize the possibility of ordering and disciplining the language. Arnold Pannevis, a philologist and preacher, the genial schoolmaster C.P. Hoogenvoet and especially the weighty Dr Johannes Brill, rector of Grey College in Bloemfontein, the first to appreciate the potential of the new language, were all born and educated in Holland and provided the impetus for the transformation of the *taal* into Afrikaans. They were joined in 1875 by some local Dutch-speakers in Paarl to form the Genoodskap van Regte Afrikaans, a nationalist society with its own newspaper, *Die Patriot*, and a policy of defending Dutch rights and of developing the use of Afrikaans. '*Kom uit*', encouraged the first issue of *Die Patriot*, '*skrywe julle taal*' ('write in your own language'), observing that most 'Afrikaanders' could write neither correct Dutch nor English.

Encouraging acceptance of the language was an uphill task for many years. Leaders of Dutch-speaking opinion tended to be bilingual, and English remained the language of fashionably cultivated circles. Many Dutch-speakers had married into English families, and leaders were increasingly often educated in England; even many of the sermons in the Dutch Reformed Church were preached in English. The new movement did however lend an impetus to another Afrikaner institution. Founded in 1878, the Boeren Beschermings Verneeniging (BBV) was specifically a farmers' lobby, intended to combat an excise duty on wine and spirits, and having a membership initially of western Cape wine-makers. Jan Hofmeyr – 'Onze Jan', our Jan – its somewhat unlikely instigator, had been a successful and precocious journalist, beginning at the age of seventeen.[17] He was a subtle, even slippery character with little sympathy for the new Afrikaans language movement, and a distinct distaste for the demagogic and increasingly anti-English stance of Dominus Stephanus du Toit, of Goshen notoriety, and his brother Daniel Francis, 'Oom Lokomotiv'. The du Toits had been founding members of the Genoodskap van Regte Afrikaans, and had gone on to establish, in 1880, the Afrikaner Bond. Hofmeyr correctly saw this new organization as a rival to his own successful BBV, which already had a solid block of supporters in the Assembly.

It was not too difficult for Hofmeyr to outmanoeuvre the unstable du Toit, and when a union of the Bond and the BBV was arranged in 1883 the new institution, which retained the name of the Afrikaner Bond, reflected Hofmeyr's moderate views: it was to be a party of English- as well as Dutch-speakers, and dedicated to the ideal of South African unity. With its strongest support coming from the farmers, the Bond was given impetus by a collapse in cereal prices – wheat dropped from twelve shillings a bushel in 1881 to five shillings seven years later. The Bond's attitude to the non-whites reflected Afrikaner rather than English liberal views, but Hofmeyr was always a supporter of a non-racial franchise, and became skilled in the manipulation of black and Coloured votes. Under his leadership – he was a member of the Cape Assembly from 1879 to 1895 – the Afrikaner Bond became the only organized party and the most powerful single force in parliament. Partly due to Hofmeyr's own temperament – Merriman christened him 'the Mole' for his liking for working quietly behind the scenes – and since the Bond never had an absolute majority, Hofmeyr relied on negotiating specific issues with amenable English-speaking leaders. Spriggs' undistinguished successors Thomas Scanlen and Thomas Upington always had to rely on Bond support, although Bond policies did not always prevail in coalition governments.

A striking demonstration of the separation of the Bond from the more reactionary Afrikaners of the Genoodskap was given in 1889 when Hofmeyr agreed to support that incarnation of British imperialism, Cecil John Rhodes.[18]

Nearly a century after his death, Rhodes remains an enigma. His influence on the history of Southern Africa was decisive. Some seven hundred thousand square miles, an area about the size of Western Europe, had their boundaries defined and much of their future decided by him. His success was made possible by an ability to bully or cajole most people he came across. He could inspire both admiration and irritation, but many of those who came within the magic of his presence rendered an uncritical love. Although not obviously brilliant – he was a poor speaker and could hardly write a clear paragraph – Rhodes had two invaluable gifts: an ability to concentrate all his energies on a single objective, and a tangential relationship with the real world. Nothing seemed impossible to Rhodes, convinced of his own infallibility. Awkward questions of morality, truth or practicability could be banished from his calculations and replaced by a cynical reliance on his ability to 'fix' opponents. In all this he was perhaps not very different from many prominent businessman – the names of Murdoch, Maxwell and Beaverbrook come to mind. The added factor was that Rhodes worked on an imperial scale, devoted to the ideal of bringing all Africa under British influence and as much as possible under British rule.

Among nineteenth-century Europeans it was a commonplace that the benefits of their civilization should be brought to those who languished in barbaric darkness. France had its '*mission civilatrice*'; Germany warned the Chinese that the 'German Michael' was 'firmly planted on the Chinese dragon', and that the doctrine of the Kaiser's 'hallowed person' was to be preached to them, whether they liked it or not. Exemplifying their genius for exploding pretentiousness, American infantrymen sang 'We'll civilize the bastards with a Krag [the standard army-issue rifle]' as they marched to suppress nationalist opposition in the Philippines. America and England went further than others in believing that it was the specific responsibility of 'the Anglo-Saxon race' to influence, if not to rule, the rest of the world. Teddy Roosevelt and Alfred Milner, who was to exert so decisive an influence on South Africa, in spite of their non-Anglo-Saxon forebears, were at one with Rhodes on this subject. Such a conviction differed greatly from that earlier one, the missionary desire expressed by the Glasgow ministers: 'not to ridicule the pagan idols, nor their manner of worship; but calmly reason with them always showing the utmost benevolence; that they ought not to expose the innocent customs of the country, but as far as possible become all things to all men'. It was though identical with that of the slightly later communist idealists who fervently believed that anything was permissible in the interests of furthering their revolution, which alone could establish universal felicity. A century later, with McDonald's dispensing nourishment in every land, and English the world's most widely spoken language, it might seem that Rhodes and Roosevelt have been at least partly successful.

Rhodes was however unique in that he was not only a business genius, but a leading democratic politician, Prime Minister of the Cape, and a shaper of empires, a man of action, albeit slightly at second hand. There seemed to be little in common between Rhodes and Jan Hofmeyr, but they did in fact share similar aims.

Rhodes became member for the new constituency of Barkly West in 1880, when Griqualand West found itslf absorbed into the Cape Colony; persuaded to accept the reponsibility with a sweetener of £200,000 from London. As part of the larger state, Kimberley settled down, and by the end of 1881 more than £10 million had been raised to finance the diamond mines, mainly from the Cape, and a stock exchange established. It did not, however, gain immediate respectability. Cecil Rhodes' standards of commercial probity were no higher than those of his Kimberley contemporaries. The Standard Bank was horrified by the Beaconsfield company's flotation, in which a lot of notoriously dud claims were palmed off by Robert Graham, Rhodes and others for four times their value, whilst the new London and South African Company was also stuffed with useless De Beers claims.

Rhodes' Griqualand colleagues in the Cape parliament pressed for new laws which would allow the segregation of African workers in compounds under conditions of strict security. Although some of the mine-owners' demands were met – the Diamond Trade Act (1882) established a special court, without a jury, to control illicit diamond buying – their most important demand, for the installation of secure compounds, was turned down for the moment. But by 1885 De Beers were able to enclose their workers, beginning with convicts contracted to them by the government, in 'model' compounds. Other workers were, more or less, volunteers, although many were sent willy-nilly by their chiefs, but all were kept immured for the duration of their contracts in conditions which varied from good to atrocious, but over which they had themselves no control. This pattern was faithfully followed in the Transvaal goldfields.

Another diamond fields first was the emergence of combative trades unions. Beginning with the 1882 Working Men's Association, miners, black and white, successfully resisted the owners' attempts to lower their wages. But when in 1884 the owners attempted to enforce strip-searches, after previously having promised not to do so, the strikers were fired upon by volunteers commanded by the mine directors. Six white workers were killed in this, the first major clash between representatives of labour and capital. Blacks who had joined with their white colleagues were left with a clear signal of their own likely fate if they should attempt similar action.

With the sinking of the first deep mines in 1885 the composition of the labour force changed, as the amateur diggers were replaced by skilled workers, usually imported from Britain, who could not be dealt with at gunpoint. Within months the locals found themselves unemployed, and a 'poor white' community emerged. With it came the inevitable demand that white employment be protected by the designation of certain occupations as 'whites only' – the colour bar that was to become entrenched in South African industry. By 1889 legal regulations provided that no 'native', except under the responsible charge of some particular white man as his master, or '*baas*', might be employed in the mines.

Rhodes continued to defend the owners' interests as member for Barkly West until 1895. His first ministerial appointment was in Thomas Scanlen's 1881–84 government, in which Hofmeyr also briefly held a post. The alliance between Rhodes and Hofmeyr, while it lasted, united English-speaking imperialists and Afrikaner farmers with pragmatic merchants. The opposition was of individuals rather than organized parties. Liberals found themselves uncomfortable with the Bond's attitude to non-whites: Merriman, the third powerful figure in Cape politics, also a member of Scanlen's cabinet, was allying himself with such sympathizers as William Schreiner, brother of the novelist Olive, James Rose Innes and Jacobus Sauer. This grouping was beginning to cohere as a liberal third bloc, aligning itself with Bondsmen or Rhodes supporters on specific issues.

All members of parliament were white, but black and Coloured voters were, increasingly, flexing their muscles. After the collapse of the Zulu kingdom and the last, miserable, frontier war, the only available strategy open to black leaders was that of cooperation, and only in the Cape was this possible on anything like a basis of equality. Blacks in the republics had no political rights at all, and the best they could hope for was to be left alone under the few remaining chiefs, or to accept a permanent subordination in the white community. Theoretically they should have been better off in Natal, but whites continued to exclude them from any exercise of political power, and the increasingly prosperous Indian community was gaining the lion's share of any economic and social benefits that might be going.

The consequences of a century of war, fragmentation and change, though, were working themselves out. Embittered and disillusioned by defeat and dispossession, many of the Xhosa (the Ngqika–Gcaleka Xhosa of Hintsa's paramountcy, as distinct from the other Xhosa-speaking peoples: Thembu, Mfengu, Mpondo etc.) retreated into what remained of their traditional areas and habits, holding aloof from missions and colonial authorities. Others – 'schoolmen', to distinguish them from 'red men' – who had been dispossessed by the *mfecane* found refuge in colonial society, attended mission schools and took their place in the European scheme of things. Naturally enough the Mfengu, who from their origin in the 1840s had thrown their lot in with the colonists, were prominent among the schoolmen, a fact which led to continuing tension between collaborating Mfengu and recalcitrant Xhosa.[19]

The first black to contribute to political life in the Cape, and a great contribution it proved to be, was John Tengo Jabavu. Jabavu was a Mfengu, a second-generation convert and, like many other black leaders, a pupil of William Govan's Lovedale. He was a man of great honesty and consistency, a Methodist local preacher and a gifted journalist; just such a man as his English contemporary Thomas Burt, the Methodist trades unionist and Liberal and Labour MP, who would go far to avoid controversy but would fight hard when necessary.

Reflecting his conventional background, Jabavu was not always popular with those who wanted faster progress, but when in 1881, at the age of twenty-two, he was appointed to edit the Lovedale journal *Sigidimi Sama*

Xosa (the Xhosa Messenger), his views proved sufficiently militant to irritate the principal, the staid Dr James Stewart, whose appointment in 1870 had led to a larger component of practical work in the school's curriculum. Lovedale, in the tradition of contemporary British public schools – Thomas Hughes' Rugby is a fair example – did not encourage dissent, but it remained multi-racial at a time when other schools were increasingly segregated. Mother Cecile's Anglican order, for example, founded separate schools in the Ciskei for white, Coloured and black children during the 1880s and nineties, but as late as the 1920s the greatly-esteemed anthropologist Monica Wilson attended Lovedale. In 1888 the Cape government decided to limit grants for mission schools to those which ceased to teach the senior grades, except for teacher training, and insisted on students performing manual labour.[20] Langham Dale, the government Superintendent of Education, who did much to improve white educational facilities, had little sympathy for black education. His first duty was 'to see that the sons and daughters of the [European] colonists . . . have at least such an education . . . as will fit them to maintain their unquestioned superiority in this land'.

Jabavu did not have long to wait before being offered, in 1884, the editorship of another newspaper. *Imvo Zabantsunu* (Views of the Bantu People), the first black vernacular newspaper, was financed with the help of another young man making his way in politics, James Rose Innes, a third-generation African who was to become the best-known lawyer in South Africa, and Chief Justice of the Union. Innes was then attempting to enter parliament, and although it would have been possible for Jabavu himself to stand, the accepted strategy was one of working through 'friends of the natives'. The condescending implications of the phrase were accurate: the relationship between politically active blacks and white liberals was not one of absolute equals. At the time when they were closest, Rose Innes wrote to 'My dear Jabavu', while Jabavu never ventured further than 'My dear Mr Innes' – a distance was always maintained. Merriman was even more superior in his attitudes to the black races, referring, in the same year of 1884, to 'the dim stirrings of their imperfectly developed intellects'. James Bryce, the astute and multi-talented politician and historian, who visited Africa in 1897, was 'astonished at the strong feeling of dislike and contempt – I might almost say hatred – which the bulk of the whites have for their black neighbours', and recorded that when the Duke of Westminster entertained the Bechuana chief Kgama to lunch, it 'excited annoyance and disgust among the whites in South Africa' – very few of whom might have expected to be given hospitality at Grosvenor House.[21]

The 'natives' certainly needed friends, for their political rights were coming under attack from the Sprigg and Scanlen ministries, with the powerful backing of Rhodes, who wanted to treat blacks as children: 'We should be lords over them . . . these are the politics of South Africa.' It was a constant preoccupation of the Colonial Office to cure this attitude; in 1874 Lord Carnarvon had been forced to protest against a proposed Cape law, on grass-burning, 'which makes offences when committed by one class of Her Majesty's subjects liable in a manner different from that [of] another class'.[22] In 1884, after the conclusion of the rebellion, the Transkei was formally annexed, much against Merriman's advice and inclination, and half a million blacks became Cape citizens, entitled to the vote on the same grounds as whites, although in fact only some 2,500 would qualify. This was enough to upset the white supremacists; already in two constituencies – one being Victoria East, which Rose Innes held with Jabavu's support – there was a majority of black voters, and it was only a matter of time before enough blacks and Coloureds became sufficiently prosperous to qualify for the franchise to outnumber the whites. Against powerful opposition led by Merriman, a shabby Bill which became the 1887 Registration Act – described by Jabavu as the 'natives' disrepresentative bill' – was passed. This disenfranchised anyone who held any land on common tribal tenure, and who inevitably therefore was black, removing about a quarter of the black electorate. It was the first act of a long-drawn-out destruction of non-white political rights, continued in 1898 with the Liquor Act, which banned the sale of alcohol to 'Aboriginal Natives', while allowing it to Coloureds.[23]

Some effective protection was given by the law. J.H. De Villiers, Chief Justice from 1874, and the great William Porter's disciple, insisted that 'no man's fundamental rights should depend on the colour of his skin.' As far as judges were able to do so, this principle was observed; but juries were another matter, often showing great reluctance to convict whites even on the clearest evidence. Some cases became scandals, particularly the 'Koegas atrocities' of 1879, when Bushmen prisoners were shot by white farmers, and the failure to convict Willem Pelser of the murder of a black man, Zachariah Gqishela, in 1885, a case taken up with vigour by Jabavu and a Presbyterian minister, John Davidson Don.[24] The very fact that such blatant injustices did arouse judicial and public indignation is evidence that they were comparatively infrequent. Viewed in the light of recent European or

American experience, the late-Victorian Cape was admirably impartial and commendably restrained. The prison population remained about three thousand; wardens and policemen were firmly disciplined – three hundred sentenced for various offences in the single year of 1894; capital punishment was rare – a single execution in that same year. Above all, while blacks are today charged and sentenced out of all proportion to their numbers, this was hardly so in the Cape Colony of the 1890s. Non-whites, who formed three-quarters of the population, were charged with 84 per cent of offences – no great disproportion.

Jabavu's *Imvo* took the lead outside parliament in the struggle over the franchise, establishing itself thereby as an authentic voice of educated black opinion, and not only that of the Mfengu people. Jabavu himself was concerned to establish links with other communities, sending two of his children to learn Sotho at the Paris Mission's Morija College and naming his eldest son Davidson Don, in commemoration of the Pelser case. From its earliest days *Imvo* pushed for black political rights, organizing in April 1885 a petition to the Colonial Office protesting against the 'disrepresentative bill' and asking that Britain take as a crown colony 'all the native territories beyond the Cape Colony'. Sir Henry Holland was not impressed, insisting that if there was any injustice, then the Cape Parliament was the proper forum for its rectification; but at least Jabavu had established that his 'Native Committee' had to be taken seriously by the Colonial Office.

Even in the imperialist heartland, Rhodes' domain of Griqualand West, 'friends of the native' could be effective. Henry Burton, a young Kimberley lawyer, was able to obtain a judgement that blacks could not be arrested for having no pass (it might have helped that he was acting for the – black – chairman of the Eccentrics Cricket Club). The most liberal of white South Africans were convinced that full participation of blacks in political life was a question for the distant future; and no great enthusiasm for hastening that future was evident. Anthony Trollope expressed the English view: 'Certainly let the black man have the franchise on the same terms as the white man,' but while 'a Kaffir may make as good a Prime Minister as Lord Beaconsfield, for at least the next hundred years we shall not choose to be ruled by him.'[25] That was in 1877. Trollope was not far wrong, since it was 117 years later that all South Africans voted on equal terms, and chose a 'Kaffir' – the Thembu Nelson Rohila Mandela – to represent them.

For the moment, however unfairly the non-whites were treated, there was always hope; in the Cape Colony things could improve, visible signs of success were to be seen, political effort could defend rights and perhaps extend them. But elsewhere in South Africa hope was a commodity in short supply.

The wretched little colony

That 'wretched little colony', as the exasperated Lord Carnarvon described Natal, remained sulkily regretting the prosperity that war profiteering had brought to its inhabitants and resentful of its lost status. Bulwer, whose decency had made him unpopular with Natalians, was reinstated as Governor and Special Commissioner in 1882, with instructions to introduce 'responsible government', in order to remove this embarrassing colony as far as possible from Colonial Office jurisdiction.

Most of the administrative work had been done by C.B.H. Mitchell, first as Colonial Secretary and then as Governor, over a long period from 1878 to 1893, with two years' interval. During this time the insistent demands of the whites, especially the farmers, for more restrictions on blacks were decently damped down. Pressure on the reserves grew as the black population increased, and when Crown lands were released for sale blacks were encouraged to buy, both as individuals and as chiefs on behalf of their people. Between 1878 and 1890 black Africans, more usually the missionary-educated 'Kholwa', the emerging middle classes typified by the Luthuli family, increased their holdings from eighty-three thousand to 211,000 acres, and in the next decade to 328,000; but this was still much less than the area acquired by white farmers. More blacks still depended on share-cropping or 'squatting' on Crown or privately-held lands.[26]

Although the blacks – not many fewer than 300,000 – were entitled to the sole use of only some 20 per cent of Natal's twelve million acres, the forty thousand white settlers were casting envious eyes on this productive area. The original sin of the *voortrekkers* in alienating large tracts of land had led to no less than half of Natal being held, largely uncultivated, by a few hundred white families and land companies. By 1860 fifteen speculators held between them 700,000 acres; fourteen years later a single London-based company owned very nearly as much. New arrivals therefore found farms hard to come by, but the absentee landlords were ready to welcome easily-removable black tenants. Not only did such tenants prosper, but a further cause for irritation was black willingness to content themselves with a traditional subsistence economy, doing only as much as necessary for a comfortable life, and evincing no interest in working for wages. Such inaction, contrary to every instinct of the Protestant work ethic, had to be remedied by forcing the blacks into a cash economy and thereby towards the benefits of nineteenth-century civilization. Surely they 'must at least see that a continuance of this easy, happy, idle sort of life, without those stimulating elements of labour and hardship and danger . . . must only end in degeneration and demoralization?'

After the hectic prosperity of the war years, blacks did less well. Partly due to innate conservatism, and much assisted by the reluctance of the authorities to spend any of the allocated funds on education or improvements, the quality of black lands deteriorated. Grain cultivation – maize and sorghum were still the staple crops – rapidly exhausted the land. Indian competitors – the number of Indians was rising rapidly – were experienced agriculturalists, practising crop rotation and fertilization, and were able to supplant the conservative blacks. They also came from a society which had enjoyed the benefit of paying taxes for hundreds of years, a necessity which accustomed them to monetary transactions, which were only beginning to be understood by black Africans. Indian traders soon established themselves in Natal, and much further afield. It is something of a challenge to explain why those in the west have often excelled in trade, while Africans of the south and east rarely managed to succeed, seemingly content to leave this to their Indian neighbours.[27]

Areas suitable only for grazing became overgrazed, and the stock deteriorated as traditional culture forbade culling excess herds. Custom influenced other habits that infuriated white farmers. Blacks much preferred to work for short periods – day hire was especially popular – for only as long as they needed to earn a certain sum: enough for a plough, a rifle, a wagon, or cash to pay their taxes. Gold and coal soon joined the diamond mines in offering lucrative short-term contracts, and blacks were reluctant to commit themselves, usually for lower wages, to the extended terms of service necessary on a farm.

The situation of the chiefs grew progressively more uncomfortable. Nearly half were government appointees rather than hereditary successors, and all were finding their authority undermined by the magistracy, who had jurisdiction over all criminal cases, and whose courts attracted many black civil cases. The end of the power to try 'witchcraft' cases, which had been the main prop of chiefly power, 'equivalent to the possession of a standing army', much reduced the chiefs' status, and the shortage of land devalued the other important currency of chiefly influence, the ability to allocate property. Only a handful of chiefs managed to maintain the system of age-regiments, and these in a much diminished form. It became more difficult for them to allow even related families admission to their regions, and some were driven to badgering the colonial authorities to relocate their people, or to allow them to move to the still-independent Basutoland or Pondoland.

Sir Theophilus Shepstone had been succeeded by his brother John and then by his son Henrique as Secretary for Native Affairs in 1884, but Henrique was no 'Sometsu', and became notorious for rarely visiting the locations, although he managed to prevent the now inadequate reservations from being reduced even further. Michael Gallwey, an attractive and liberal Cork man, was as Attorney General a more effective defender of black rights, and was influential in blocking the more reactionary moves before the grant of 'responsible government' in 1893 removed most of the officials' powers.

Paternalism without a credible father-figure is useless, and morale in the black communities crumbled after Theophilus Shepstone retired. Missions as well as chiefdoms saw their previously accepted authority dwindle as the young took to drink, faction fighting and prostitution. With no political power reinforcing black leadership, black political activity lagged well behind that of the Cape, but in that same year of 1893 a new figure arrived at Durban: one Mohandas Karamchand Gandhi, LL.B., who was to transform future developments.

The Orange Free State

Under the sagacious and moderate President Brand – Sir John Brand, GCMG, from 1872 – the Orange Free State had experienced twenty years of tranquillity and modest prosperity. After Britain had accepted responsibility for Basutoland and Griqualand West few internal problems remained in this rural community, with a Dutch-speaking majority among the burghers, but little friction between them and their English compatriots. Nor, after the troubled earlier times, was there serious difficulty with the other races. Blacks had few rights, the Free State being decidedly unfree in this respect, and were not permitted to own land, but with the independent

Basutoland as a neighbour, and the reserve around Thaba Nchu quiescent and moderately prosperous under the guidance of Moroka II, these restrictions provoked little obvious discontent – which would have been pointless, since the numbers of whites and non-whites were evenly balanced. It would have been possible, were it not for its strategic position, to dismiss as negligible a state with a population of less than 140,000, smaller than most English counties. But the Free State was considerably bigger than England, and lying as it did to the south of the Transvaal, controlled all access between there and the Cape.

In 1884 this was of particular importance. Railways had got off to a very slow start in South Africa. At the beginning of that year there were only 1,318 miles of track in operation, of which 1,213 were in the Cape Colony and the remainder in Natal. By contrast, 5,133 miles had been built in Australia (although with typical independence the states had selected their own gauge of track). Even New Zealand had a greater extent of track (1,486 miles) than the whole of South Africa. All Cape lines ran north from termini at Cape Town, Port Elizabeth and East London, financed by a £7 million loan initiated by Merriman in 1872.[28] By 1884 the lines were nearing Kimberley, but there progress was blocked. Neither the Orange Free State nor the Transvaal was in a position to raise finance of the sort that the Cape had contrived, and the Free State government found itself dithering between the obvious advantages of allowing an extension from the Kimberley line, or yielding to Kruger's pressure to delay a decision until the (at that time purely hypothetical) link between Pretoria and the sea was opened.

TWELVE

War

The City of Gold

The triumvirate of Kruger, Joubert and Pretorius that had seen through the successful confrontation with Britain had soon dissolved. Pretorius had never been of much account, and Joubert, highly critical of Kruger, lost the first presidential election in 1883 to his rival, thereafter sulking in his tent, supplanted as Vice-President and a reluctant member of the government as Commandant General, but always ready to oppose the President. For eighteen years, sometimes precariously, with one very narrow scrape in 1893, Kruger remained entrenched in power, baffling his antagonists and often irritating his allies, but overshadowing with his massive personality all with whom he came into contact. The ill-at-ease backwoodsman, deferential to Lord Carnarvon amid the splendours of Whitehall, developed into the embodiment of solid Afrikaner qualities, willing to defend them against any opposition, but at the same time a master of negotiation and persuasion.

English officials often found him amusing – 'a rugged version of our own Edward Cardwell', according to Bartle Frere – or uncouth and repulsive, but they soon learned to respect his tenacity, although they were rarely able to appreciate his real capacity for tolerance and kindness. It was these virtues, combined with political astuteness and his simple habits, which included keeping open house for all burghers – coffee for forty always on call – that kept 'Oom Paul', Uncle Paul, in power.

The first years of Kruger's presidency were spent in settling external affairs – revising the Pretoria Convention and hammering out agreements on the boundaries of the South African Republic. It was only in 1886 that the first indications came that the ugly duckling, the most impoverished and backward of the white South African states, was to be transformed, if not into a swan, at least into a very plump and prosperous goose. For some years the existence of gold-bearing areas had been known, and in 1884 alluvial deposits were discovered in the Lydenburg hills, two hundred miles east of Pretoria, where the goldrush town of Barberton sprang up. Barberton quickly became the biggest town in the Transvaal, with a population of fifteen thousand and a stock exchange, the first in the country. But the Barberton boom was short-lived, and prospectors were soon diverted to the Witwatersrand, a ridge thirty miles south of the capital, where what were to become the most extensive gold deposits in the world were first recognized in 1886. The existence of these deposits, and their nature, soon changed the face of South Africa.

The Rand deposits are a series of gold-bearing conglomerate bands, or 'bankets' stretching for nearly two hundred miles. Bankets are found at varying distances from the surface, down to depths of over a thousand fathoms; the Village Deep mine reached 7,630 feet, but was still capable of producing gold at a profit. Unlike alluvial gold, which can be extracted by quite primitive equipment – the Californian prospector 'panning' a stream being the best-known example – deep mining is both capital- and labour-intensive, demanding complex industrial organization and substantial capital.

Figures for the earliest years are doubtful, a fair percentage of the gold being unofficially abstracted, but by 1890 half a million ounces were produced. This was still a modest proportion of the world total of some 5.7 million ounces, of which 1.5 million came from Australia and New Zealand, with a similar amount from the United States. It was, however, hope – ultimately to be fulfilled – rather than immediate dividends, that powered the Transvaal goldrush: a mining company with accepted reserves can command heavy share premiums before a single ounce of metal has been refined. Even land which might possibly have had gold below it shot up in value: before the boom was over nearly a third of the whole country had been sold to the growing '*uitlander*' – off-comer – population who had formed the mushrooming new settlement of Johannesburg, with a stock exchange, clubs including that majestic institution the Rand Club and a Canton Club for the Chinese, a racecourse and cricket field. The *uitlanders*' contribution to the state treasury was striking: revenue in 1882 had been £177,000; by 1889 it was well over £1,500,000 (the Transvaal had always adopted the British monetary system of coinage).[1]

Although the gold-bearing strata are so extensive, laterally as well as vertically, the percentage of gold contained is very small, less than in any other comparable fields, averaging then about £2-worth of gold per ton.

Profitable operation of such deposits demanded extensive plant, which was just then becoming available as steam-powered crushing, grinding, drilling and mechanical handling equipment were developed. Even so, the labour needed was also considerable, and the viability of operations was highly sensitive to this, the only potentially variable cost. While the first mines were the most accessible, and therefore the least costly, it was apparent that both capital and labour in hitherto unknown quantities would be needed to exploit the Transvaal's new asset.

Inevitably, given the great power of the City of London in international finance, and the fact that British firms had an overwhelming holding in the diamond industry, most external capital was likely to come via London, and just as over half the £12 million invested in the Kimberley mines had come from the Cape, the same held true on the Rand.[2] The capitalists, well-named the 'Randlords', who formed the Chamber of Mines, were equally inevitably mainly British subjects, although the best-known were frequently of German Jewish or Lutheran origin. British too were most of the skilled men, engineers and mechanics (although a fair proportion came from the other goldfields of America and Australia), and a high proportion of the ancillary occupations and professions – accountants, hotel-keepers, clerks, teachers, lawyers and doctors – were from Britain, the rest from Europe and the Cape. Due to the almost complete absence of education there were very few Transvaalers with any such skills. Manual labourers, who were to be required in great numbers, would have to be sought, as had been the case in the diamond mines, among the South African blacks. The 1896 census showed the white population of Johannesburg as 50,907, of whom 6,205 were Transvaalers, well outnumbered by the 16,265 from England and the 15,162 from the Cape Colony (the next-largest population was that of 'Russian' – more properly Baltic – Jews).[3]

The Transvaal burghers, sitting only thirty miles off this new cosmopolitan city in the still small town of Pretoria, were therefore presented with both a challenge and an opportunity. Prosperity, and acceptance by the international community, could bring a new stability and reinforce their country's independence; at the price, however, of a radical change from the old trekker customs. If the Transvaal was to benefit from its newfound potential it must develop the apparatus of a modern state. Had the Transvaal been blessed with so intelligent and adaptive leader as the Free State's President Brand, and a Volksraad less blinkered, the changes might have been made, but Kruger had few of the necessary qualities, and when he did appreciate the necessity for unpopular moves, often had difficulty in forcing them through. The failure of the successive Kruger administrations to grasp the nettle of change, exacerbated by the inspired stupidity of some of its opponents, was the fundamental cause of the 1899 war that brought down the South African Republic.[4]

Paul Kruger, uncouth, given to table- and Bible-thumping, shouting and spitting on the floor, weeping to order, was nevertheless a skilled politician, capable of retaining power for eighteen years, getting the better of British statesmen in negotiations, and, within the traditions of his people, and the standards applicable to politicians, reliable and honourable. His was a very personal rule: Volksraad committees were held in the President's house, lit by two frugal candles, with Oom Paul wandering around between the two tables.[5] Almost alone in the 1880s among Transvaal politicians in having a knowledge of the great world outside the high veld, it was only after 1895 that such capable young men as Jan Smuts were able to match President Kruger. The Volksraad, packed with back-country *takhaars*, often found their President too liberal and advanced for their liking, and took some persuading to abolish such time-honoured diversions as public executions. It was only by a one-vote majority that the Volksraad decided that locust control was not an offence against the Lord; trams (unless drawn by horses), museums, parks and similar amenities were also objects of grave suspicion – the park proposal was lost by twenty-two votes to eleven. Likewise firmly rejected was the impious idea that births, marriages and deaths should be registered. The proposal that Jews and Roman Catholics should be given equal civil rights was thrown out even more decisively – only three dissidents, and they voting for a firmer rejection, to still the terror in each Christian's heart at the growing power of the Whore of Babylon.

Kruger had also to cope with what might be called a left-wing party, loosely grouped around his old rival, the unattractive but less hidebound Piet Joubert, and his eventual successor, Schalk Burger, a moderate third-generation Transvaaler.[6] These 'Progressives' were often, but not invariably, supported by the imported Dutch officials, 'Hollanders', who had since President Burgers' time been recruited to supplement the inadequate Transvaalers. Their frivolous ways, tennis parties and dances, their obvious disdain for the Boers and their occupation of positions of importance made Hollanders as unpopular as the English: 'Flippant drunkards, and modernists who infected the country like a dangerous disease . . . the whole country is infested with Hollanders.' Since the restoration of the South African

Republic in 1880 the position of State Secretary, the highest executive post, had been filled by Hollanders – Willem Bok and the elegant young Dr Willem Leyds. Kruger would have preferred Transvaalers (certainly not Cape Afrikaners, whom he distrusted); even such senior posts as those of departmental heads were therefore usually given to 'those with some pretensions to education, and often those without it . . . utterly incompetent to write a letter or frame a report'.[7]

Opportunities for personal gain were rarely resisted. Kruger's salary as President was raised over the years from £5,000 to £7,000,* and jobs were found for many friends and relations. In order to keep important persons sweet, gifts of shares in new projects were handed out as a matter of course, and presents freely distributed; practices not unknown in neighbouring states, but carried on to an excessive extent in the Transvaal, thereby stultifying efforts to construct an efficient administration. An investigation in 1898 disclosed that the enormous sum of £2.4 million had been 'advanced' to officials and not accounted for. The atmosphere of corruption discouraged the Deutsche Bank from proceeding with a proposed loan, because they could not reconcile rank bribery with their position. In spite of their agent's best efforts – which included bribing the editor of the *Volkstem* – by the late 1890s even the friendly German government 'had apparently realized that the Kruger regime was incapable of establishing a well-ordered policy'.[8] Monopolies were granted on excessively favourable terms to friends of the President: a wily Hungarian, Alois Nellmapius, realized £120,000 on the liquor monopoly,[9] and when eventually sentenced for fraud was released, against the objections of the judge, by executive order; the dynamite monopoly proved a lucrative source of income to its holder, but substantially increased mining expenses.[10]

Two examples of the way in which graft, conservatism and Kruger's own prejudices militated against the Transvaal's rapid development into a modern state were the construction of a railway system and the establishment of a national bank. While both the Cape and Natal had made some progress in track-laying, the Transvaal had lagged behind. By the time the Cape line reached Kimberley, 650 miles from its terminus, in 1885, no construction at all had been started within the Transvaal. Kruger appreciated that a railway link to the sea that did not cross colonial soil was a

---

* Between 1914 and 1995 a factor of fifty should be applied to equate values, and can be taken as a guide to earlier periods, giving the equivalent of £350,000 as the presidential emoluments.

powerful prop to independence, but made two attempts to enlist the help of the Cape. In 1885 and 1886, recognizing the perilous state of the Transvaal, he had asked for a customs union, in return for which he would allow the Cape railways to run direct to Johannesburg. This offer was, with great folly, rejected by the Upington ministry, but even after this rebuff General Joubert and Ds S. Du Toit, who had much modified his views, attempted to reopen negotiations. Kruger never forgave this insult, telling Merriman that he had 'made you a most liberal offer, was prepared to throw myself into your hands, but you not only refused to meet me but slapped me in the face'. It was a great opportunity lost: had the customs union gone ahead, the subsequent war would very probably not have taken place, and the whole course of African history would have changed. But as it was, particularly after the development of the goldmines, Kruger's policy had to be the development, as quickly as possible, of the Transvaal's own rail link.

Responsibility for this, the Delagoa Bay line, had been divided between concessions from Portugal, covering their portion of the track, from the Lourenço Marques terminal to the Transvaal border, with the republic responsible from the border crossing to Pretoria. Initially neither section did well. The southern concession, begun in 1883, dragged along until the Portuguese government was forced to take it over six years later. Even then it moved more rapidly than the Transvaal's section, contracted to a Dutch company, and originally financed by President Burgers in the previous decade. By 1891 the colonial lines were far ahead, poised on the Transvaal border, while the Dutch line was enmired in financial crises which obliged Kruger – unwilling to ask for British money – to seek an international loan through a shady French financier. This proved impossible, even at the high rate of 5 per cent, and the Transvaal was forced to turn to the Cape government, which obliged with a loan at 4 per cent, but at the price of obtaining the right to run their line on to Johannesburg, a mortification for Kruger, whose critics accused him of having sold the republic in 'bondage to England'. Moving smartly, the Cape line pressed forward to open the following year; it was another two years before the Delagoa Bay line reached Pretoria, twenty years after its inception.

In addition to the railway connection to the outside world, another essential institution for an emergent state was an efficient national bank. Until 1890 all Transvaal banking business had been carried out by 'foreign' banks, either colonial or Dutch, of which the Standard Bank was the most important. Again, when looking for investors in a Transvaal bank, Kruger sought a major French participation. In the event, the foundation capital was arranged through the London firm of Schroders, backed by Wernher Beit, the most prominent of the recently-arrived Rand capitalists, also London-based; in all twenty-four thousand of the forty thousand non-government shares were placed in London. The gifts made to the President and other officials in order to secure the business of floating the bank were estimated by Wernher Beit as costing £30,000 (£1,500,000 in modern terms). In spite of early bad management – government faces being set sternly against British managers, and the first German manager, Hermann Militz, making 'an ass of himself' – the value of a national bank was demonstrated when in 1892 it succeeded in raising a £2.5 million loan; but again in London, and with the backing of Cecil Rhodes and Rothschilds.[11]

It was hardly surprising that an active opposition developed. Within the government itself, Joubert, who had himself become extremely wealthy, with an 'enviable estate' valued at £280,000 in 1902, not including the livestock,[12] looked for any opportunity to discredit Kruger, in which he was often joined by his rival and successor as Vice-President, N.J. Smit, who had gained much kudos by his defeat of Colley at Majuba. Regarding the new national bank as Kruger's creation, within a month of its inception Smit had inspired a prospectus for a rival institution, the Transvaalsche Bank, with a directorate mainly drawn from other state officials. In opposition Joubert's Progressive Party was loosely composed of those dissatisfied with the Krugerites. Its policy and membership varied, but in general it was concerned to modernize, without liberalizing, the ramshackle Transvaal state, and it attracted younger and more sophisticated members such as Koos de la Rey and Louis Botha, elected to the Volksraad in 1896. One measure of the potential support for the Progressives was the narrow margin by which Joubert lost the 1893 presidential election – by 7,009 against Kruger's winning 7,854 (the figures indicate how limited was the electorate). Considerably less popular personally than Kruger, regarded by many voters as devious and untrustworthy, Joubert himself was something of a disadvantage to his party.

Bartle Frere had prophesied in 1881 that if a 'really good goldfield' was discovered in Southern Africa it would 'induce an influx of gold diggers who would not be content until they had removed all difficulties, political as well as physical, which at present limit this branch of industry'.[13] Proving the accuracy of his forecast, a third centre of political activity formed itself around the new immigrants, the *uitlanders*. Their grievances were genuine enough – the rapacity of concessionaires and officials, the insistence on the use of Dutch in schools, and, most importantly, the lack of political rights in a society where they were producing the lion's share of the income. In earlier years the franchise had been available after one year's residence, raised in 1882 to five years. The great influx of immigrants that followed the opening of the Rand mines, coming as they did in such large numbers, threatened to overwhelm the original Boer element if they were to be allowed to take up citizenship on the same terms. By 1896 there were already probably more non-Dutch than Dutch potential voters in the Transvaal, although the Boers, who tended to have large families, were still in an actual majority – and the number of off-comers was daily increasing. In order to prevent their becoming an electoral majority a drastic new regulation was issued in 1890 allowing the franchise only after a residence period of fourteen years, during which time most applicants, who were required to renounce existing allegiances, were virtually stateless. As a sop to public opinion a Second Volksraad was created, voting for which could be allowed after two years' residence; but it had only quasi-municipal powers, and acted as little more than a sounding-board. Perhaps more important was the continuance of the old trekker constitution by means of which the Volksraad, never the most reliable of institutions and susceptible to whims, could – and did – alter fundamental laws at a stroke, without any provision for legal review, a situation dramatized when in 1897 Chief Justice Kotzé attempted to assert some judicial control, only to be suppressed by the Volksraad's swift gagging order.[14]

We have got the Maxim gun, and they have not

Unfair as these arrangements were, internal pressures would probably have led to their amendment, as the less inflexible Progressives assumed greater influence. William Hall, the Californian State Engineer, commissioned to report by the Chamber of Mines, concluded that 'the administration of laws on the Rand must be greatly changed; or there can be no very great advances.'[15] Lord Salisbury had no doubts: 'Leave our people [the *uitlanders*] alone ... in a few years it will be our people that will be the masters, it will be our commerce that will prevail, it will be our capital that will rule'[16] – which was, of course, exactly what Kruger feared. *Uitlander* discontent was primarily economic. They had come to the Transvaal to make money, and government seediness and incapacity were restricting their opportunities to do so. The remedy must lie in democratic institutions, where the constantly-increasing numbers of *uitlanders* could exercise due weight; but the same reasons that led Kruger to restrict the franchise worked in reverse on those who wanted to see the Transvaal evolve by natural growth into a state with an English-speaking majority. The domestic question of *uitlanders'* votes became therefore a subject of international importance.

Not, however, for some time. The British government had other things to worry about at home, including social and industrial unrest accompanying the rise of organized labour (the most violent demonstration was suppressed by General Sir Charles Warren, now translated to Commissioner of Metropolitan Police), financial difficulties exemplified by the Baring crisis of 1890, and the overshadowing problem of Ireland. By insisting, quite rightly, that Ireland be allowed self-government rather than continued incorporation into the British system, Gladstone had split the Liberal Party. Many of the most influential members – including Joseph Chamberlain, changed from a radical liberal to an enthusiastic imperialist – left to become Liberal Unionists, voting with the Conservatives. The division ensured nearly twenty years of Conservative government, broken only by a Liberal interlude between 1892 and 1895.

After the split the Colonial Office underwent one of its unstable periods, with five chiefs in eighteen months between June 1885 and January 1887 – Lord Derby, Sir F.A. Stanley, Lord Granville, Edward Stanhope and Lord Knutsford, who then held the post until 1892. During this time the most pressing Southern African concern was not the *uitlanders'* grievances but the question of what should be done about expansion into Bechuanaland and beyond, an area which Cecil Rhodes had firmly in his sights.

By his ingenious financial manoeuvrings Rhodes had made his diamond monopoly De Beers one of the richest companies in the world, and his colleagues Alfred Beit, Charles Rudd and Barney Barnato multi-millionaires. Although he missed the initial Rand opportunity, being called away by the illness of his friend Neville Pickering, Rhodes quickly recovered to form the Consolidated Goldfields Company in 1887.[17] The governing articles of both this company and De Beers contained the same freedom to apply the company's funds to all types of expansion – a licence to use shareholders' cash to finance Rhodes' imperialist ambitions.

In 1890 Rhodes had become Prime Minister of the Cape, in an unparalleled combination of financial and political power. This was contrived by nurturing the support of Jan Hofmeyr and the Afrikaner Bond, with judicious offers of farms in Matabeleland, some straightforward bribery, and a promise to support farming interests. At the same time the Rhodes ministry included such liberals as Merriman, the most able, and completely upright, although irritating, man of his time; young James Rose Innes; and J.W. Sauer; together with the tougher and unscrupulous James Sivewright. This improbable coalition held until May 1893, when an election entrenched Rhodes' power and enabled him to govern without worrying about liberal sensibilities.

The liberals had contrived to resist an Afrikaner attempt to have blacks flogged for such offences as riding on their master's horse (the Strop Bill), and weakened another effort to restrict the black franchise (the 1892 Franchise Bill), but found themselves in two minds about the 1894 Glen Grey Act. That attractive area of the Eastern Cape was populated by Thembu, and had been coveted by white farmers for some time. The intention of the Bill was to secure black rights to the land, but in such a way as to limit the size of holdings, thereby encouraging the owners to work for cash wages – an intention underlined by a proposal, dropped under pressure, to tax those owners who did not work outside the district. Rhodes was entirely open about his motives: 'It is our duty as a Government to remove these poor children [the Thembu] from [a] life of sloth and laziness, and to give them some gentle stimulus to come forth and find out the dignity of labour.' His Bill proposed that this should be done by imposing the labour tax, and, in order 'to occupy their minds, allow them a measure of local self-government'. A new form of individual land ownership was therefore proposed in the Glen Grey district which limited the size of holdings to less than four acres, and imposed restrictions on sale and mortgaging designed to prevent alienation of the original grant. A similar idea had been rejected ten years previously, but was now taken up with much enthusiasm when it was appreciated that it could be an ingenious method of restricting the black franchise, since 'Glen Grey' title was specifically excluded from qualifying for the vote. It was not however without attraction to potential owners, since some security of tenure was offered, and participation in local government encouraged, through a system which later developed into the Transkei General Council, commonly known as the Bunga. Liberal opposition to the Bill was divided; even Rose Innes felt that 'the giving of a vote to a native is a small thing for which he could very well wait, while the breaking up of these huge locations which at present serve as reservoirs of labour would be disastrous both to the natives and to ourselves.' Merriman however fought hard against the restriction of the franchise.[18]

Rhodes' political balancing act, combining huge wealth – his personal income was a million pounds a year – and political power, enabled him to begin translating his dreams of empire into reality by pushing through Bechuanaland to the open spaces of the north (open to European powers, at any rate). By accepting the British protectorate the Tswana chief Kgama (Khama) had ensured that the route to the north – the Suez Canal of South Africa, as Rhodes had described it – lay under British control. Kgama had secured all the region's people from the raids of his neighbours, both the Transvaal Boers and the Matabele. The founder of the Matabele-Ndebele polity, Mzilikazi, had been succeeded in 1863 by his son Lobengula, who had contrived to retain his people's independence in the face of considerable Transvaal expansionist pressure and British commercial initiatives. The Transvaal got there first, with a grant of concessions, in 1887, but were quickly trumped by the British High Commissioner, Sir Hercules Robinson, who used the good offices of Robert Moffat's son John to persuade Lobengula not to alienate any of his land without British agreement.

Ndebele land extended from the Bechuanaland Protectorate border – the current frontier between Botswana and Zimbabwe – towards the Zambesi River and Portuguese territory. The Ndebele themselves were centred around Lobengula's *kraal* at Bulawayo, 'the place of slaughter', with the subjugated and rebellious Shona over in the north-east, the two regions being known to the British as Matabeleland and Mashonaland.

Rhodes' agents were by a narrow margin the first to take advantage of Sir Hercules' diplomacy.[19] Led by Charles Rudd, who had saved Rhodes' Kimberley venture from collapse, an odd party which included Rochfort Maguire, a suave Irish lawyer and a Fellow of All Souls College, Oxford, secured 'a complete and exclusive' right to all mineral exploitation in Lobengula's lands in return for a thousand rifles, a subsidy and a gunboat. Lobengula, illiterate and unused to Western ways, was thoroughly misled by the verbal explanations, but being an intelligent and receptive man, soon appreciated that he had been duped. To Rhodes' consternation, the Matabele chief was allowed to send a delegation to London. The British government was suspicious – those rifles sounded sinister to Lord Knutsford, but the officials were not pleased: 'those guileless old men have got round him [the Colonial Secretary].' On Lobengula's request for a British agent to be stationed in his territory, as had been done in Bechuanaland and elsewhere, the cynical Colonial Office minute read that the only point in so doing would be 'with a view to his [the agent] being killed', which would give an excuse to send a punitive expedition 'to conquer the . . . country for the benefit of the gold companies'. It was only after the Colonial Secretary and the Queen had received a Matabele deputation – those 'guileless old men' – and an urgent amalgamation had been contrived between Rhodes' interests and those of his British competitors, that a Royal Charter was given authorizing the new British South Africa Company to take advantage of Lobengula's concession. Outward respectability had been given to the BSAC by the presence on the board of two dukes, Fife and Abercorn, but they were correctly seen as 'dummies and figureheads', and another director, Sir Horace Farquhar, as a man 'whose business morals were highly questionable'.[20]

The device of a chartered company, along the lines of the old East India Company, was revived in the last decades of the nineteenth century as an economic method of establishing favourable trading conditions in Africa. Sir George Goldie's Royal Niger Company, which had been granted a charter three years previously, served as a model, with similar reservations intended to protect the existing communities' rights. On the other side of the continent, the Imperial British East Africa company was chartered in August 1888 by Sir William MacKinnon. None of the new charters lasted long before being replaced by an Imperial authority, but all three succeeded in drawing huge tracts of Africa into British control. From the date of the BSAC's charter – October 1889 – a new quasi-sovereign state began to emerge in Southern Africa.

As far as colonial matters went, it seemed that these had been settled in 1890 when Lord Salisbury, at the height of his very considerable powers, had negotiated with the Germans and Belgians to secure a British-controlled through-route from the Cape to the headwaters of the Nile, and thence eventually to the Mediterranean. The Portuguese, who hoped to establish an east–west link between their colonies of Mozambique and Angola, were brushed aside, much to their resentment. At the same time the French were satisfied with several million square miles of the Sahara, and the partition of Africa among the European powers was thereby substantially completed. In Britain the Colonial Conference of 1884 and the foundation of the Colonial League to advocate colonial interests foreshadowed a confederation of self-governing British colonies united in preserving common interests; that the Orange Free State and the Transvaal were not numbered among them seemed a matter of small importance. To put this in perspective, it should be remembered that as late as 1893 there were fewer than twenty thousand electors in the Transvaal, less than in the City of Newcastle-upon-Tyne; that its total revenue of £1,700,000 was not much greater than the product of a rate at par of that town; and that the republic's export trade, even swollen by gold receipts, was of no greater value than that of Tyneside.

High Commissioner Sir Henry Loch succeeded Hercules Robinson in December 1889. An energetic and opinionated Scot, Loch, whose adventurous youth included the command of cavalry in India and Bulgaria and capture and torture by the Chinese in 1860, had not been much tamed by a respectable career in colonial government.[21] In 1893 he visited the Transvaal in order to settle the remaining boundary questions. Perennially discontented burghers had continued to make attempts to trek into new areas. Some of these were not unacceptable to the British authorities – the successive 'thirstland treks' were not objected to – but an attempt to settle over the northern border was resisted, and President Kruger agreed to stop the 1890 'Banjailand trek' (the more willingly since it was organized by his political rival Joubert). On the other hand, Boer ambitions in Swaziland were considered reasonable, and by 1894 a settlement was reached which gave the Transvaal a protectorate in that much-exploited territory, a settlement earnestly backed by Natal. The white population in that colony, dissatisfied with their own boundaries, jealous of the Cape and concerned about the increasingly large black and Indian majority, had been making overtures to the Transvaal for some time, hoping to advance the prospects of their railway, which did provide the shortest route from the Rand to what was now the major port of Durban. By 1891 the Natal railway was nearing the Transvaal border, and Kruger was feted and flattered during a visit he made in April of that year. When three years later Natal's 'sucking up to Kruger' was successful, and permission was given for the extension of the Durban line to Johannesburg, it seemed to many that the British colonies were now hopelessly divided. Natal's conduct was viewed suspiciously by both the Colonial Office and the Johannesburgers.[22]

During his visits Sir Henry had been made vividly aware of the *uitlanders'* feelings, and was convinced by such enthusiasts as Percy Fitzpatrick that discontent was reaching the pitch of open rebellion. Another visit the following year resulted in a noisy demonstration of enthusiasm, with Sir

Henry's carriage dragged by cheering *uitlanders*. 'The political atmosphere,' he reported, 'was charged with such an amount of electricity that every moment an explosion was imminent.' Appealing for guidance to Lord Ripon, the veteran radical Colonial Secretary in the fading Liberal government of Lord Rosebery, Gladstone's successor after the Grand Old Man's retirement in March 1894, Sir Henry suggested some ways in which a rebellion might be assisted. In so doing he was acting within what he believed to be his rights. As High Commissioner he was charged with securing the welfare of all British subjects – and of all natives – wherever they might be. The London Convention explicitly claimed 'suzerainty' over the Transvaal, which could well be interpreted as the right to intervene. In Pretoria, needless to say, they saw things rather differently.[23]

Lord Ripon would have none of it. Negotiations with Kruger had produced results; the old President had backed down on one of the most contentious issues, that of forcing commando service on the *uitlanders*, and a new Convention had been agreed. All was well, to the extent that Ripon suggested that Kruger should be given the highest rank in the Order of St Michael and St George, a Grand Cross, which would have made him Sir Paul.

The young Lord Rosebery, on the other hand, was a convinced imperialist, and not unsympathetic to intervention in the Transvaal. During a visit to London in 1893 the case for this was advanced by Cecil Rhodes, then at the height of his powers. Prime Minister of the Cape, Chairman of De Beers, one of the world's largest firms, and of Consolidated Goldfields, unquestioned chief of the British South Africa Company's operations in Africa, empowered by Royal Charter to acquire land in Africa wherever it might be had, Rhodes was by far the most influential man in that continent. In spite of reservations about his vulgarity, even Gladstone was impressed: 'Rhodes wants nothing,' he had written, in what must be one of the most astounding misjudgements of his career. In spite of Henry Loch's warnings, and the lively muck-raking journal *Truth*'s attacks on 'a wretched, rotten, bankrupt set of marauders and murderers', Rhodes' extraordinary persuasiveness, reinforced where necessary by a carefully-calculated distribution of shares at considerably less than their real value, combined with the great sweep of his vision of a British Africa from Cairo to the Cape and a capacity for striking memorable phrases, won widespread support. He was made a Privy Councillor, at that time a signal mark of respectability (but he *had* given £5,000 to the Liberal Party); yet he had been blackballed by the Travellers' Club.[24]

In June 1895 the Liberal ministry tottered to an end, to be replaced by a Conservative and Liberal-Unionist government under Lord Salisbury. When Joseph Chamberlain opted to take the Colonial Office rather than a more dignified department of state, which could have been his for the asking, there was some surprise, but 'Radical Joe' was convinced that the future lay with the British Empire overseas, rather than the stately progress of negotiations with other powers, of which Lord Salisbury was an acknowledged master. As a businessman himself, Chamberlain was perhaps less sniffily critical of Rhodes' methods than were his more aristocratic colleagues.

On the surface it appeared that the British South Africa Company was continuing to do well. With the assent of Loch, the advantage of their British government charter and a very dubious agreement with Lobengula and Kgama, the company had occupied Mashonaland, in the east of what came to be known as Rhodesia, and established settlements at Victoria and Salisbury.[25] But hopes of quick profits from this expensive enterprise – founding a new country does not come cheap – soon faded, as did hopes of discovering a new Witwatersrand, and the company found itself highly illiquid, on the brink of a financial crisis. This was avoided only by some shabby manoeuvring by the BSAC, with the tacit agreement of the Colonial Office.

Heir to the aggressive traditions of his father Mzilikazi, Lobengula's *impis* were constantly anxious to wet their spears, an experience now denied to them as far as the Tswana were concerned by the British protectorate of Bechuanaland. Having no illusions as to the outcome of a fight with the British, being well aware of his kinsman Cetshwayo's fate, Lobengula did his best to restrain the hotheads from massacring the wrong people. Mashonaland had been entrusted to Dr Leander Starr Jameson, 'Dr Jim', whose career – from his medical studies, through the diamond diggings with Rhodes, his lackadaisical administration of the British South Africa Company's acquisition, his pure adventurism and sojourn in prison, to eventually becoming Prime Minister of the Cape Colony – is difficult to parallel. With few special gifts besides an extraordinary power to charm, Jameson had that most essential requisite, luck, combined with a nearly complete lack of scruples. It did not take him long, with the assistance of a particularly brutal officer, one Captain Lendy, to manufacture an excuse for a war with Lobengula.

Sir Henry Loch, who by now had come thoroughly to distrust Rhodes, would have preferred any intervention to be his own, rather than the company's, and despatched a force of Tswana, led by their impressive

Chief Kgama, more than willing to revenge themselves on the persecuting Matabele, and strengthened by a contingent of Bechuanaland police. Unfortunately for the Matabele, Jameson's force of mercenaries got there first, massacring thousands of young warriors, who rushed in old Zulu fashion on the rifles and machine guns. A not entirely satisfactory outcome, according to one officer, who would have liked 'to lay out about 2000 more Matabele as we have not killed enough of them'. When Lobengula's *kraal* of Bulawayo became the company's town a brutal sense of humour caused the hotel to be named 'The Maxim'. The *Natal Witness* celebrated the glorious victory:

> On Afric's shores, where England furled her sullied flag in shame,
> And memories are bitter fraught at dread Majuba's name,
> The pride of race, of birth, which *was* the British boast,
> Is born anew through the valour of the Charter's host.[26]

A fiasco would be most disastrous

While the occupation of Matabeleland saved the company's fortunes, their new state of Rhodesia remained cut off from the Cape by the Crown Colony of Bechuanaland and the British Protectorate. 1895 saw the colony absorbed by the Cape, but the Tswana chiefs resisted any alteration in their protected status. Kgama, one of the great Africans, a man of prudence and integrity, led a delegation to London and convinced Chamberlain that the company should be given no more than a narrow strip along the eastern border with the Transvaal (conveniently in the hands of minor chiefs). The ostensible reason for the company's insistence on this was the need to protect the new railway which would link Salisbury and Bulawayo to the Cape.

Only ostensible, for even while the chiefs were negotiating in London it was being made clear to the Colonial Secretary exactly why the whites wanted to control the border. Rhodes had persuaded Albert, fourth Earl Grey, 'the paladin of his generation' and a man of unquestioned rectitude, to become a director of the British South Africa Company, lending some much-needed credibility to that doubtful institution, and Lord Grey felt it incumbent on him to warn Chamberlain of Rhodes' intentions. In April 1895 Grey had forecast that 'rough times' lay ahead, and in August he had a private meeting with the Colonial Secretary in which the reason for the Bechuanaland base was made plain: it was to be the starting point for a company raid into the Transvaal with the aim of bringing down Kruger's government.[27] Grey maintained, as Loch had maintained two years before, that this would only occur if there were a rebellion of discontented *uitlanders* in the Transvaal which threatened to disturb the peace of Southern Africa and perhaps provoke foreign intercession – the Germans again. It was hardly clear why the intervention should be made from a railway station by a commercial company rather than by an Imperial force, but the explanation was that access to the Rand from the Bechuanaland border was very much quicker than the direct alternative from Natal; which might be thought an inadequate reason for contemplating an attack on a friendly power.

Chamberlain, who might reasonably have been expected to express horror at Lord Grey's news, merely remarked that he took it for granted 'no movement will take place unless success is certain, a fiasco would be most disastrous'. He then went on a prolonged holiday, leaving South Africa in the tremulous hands of a newly-arrived High Commissioner. This was, once again, Sir Hercules Robinson, chosen as a pliant instrument to replace the difficult Loch at the behest of Cecil Rhodes. Sir Hercules, who always had an eye for personal gain, was a director of the BSAC, although his appointment had been bitterly criticized by many, including Chamberlain himself while still in opposition as 'little short of scandalous', and something to which 'only Americans would stoop'. Once in office, however, Chamberlain was willing enough to work with Robinson.[28]

An excuse for intervention was quickly provided by President Kruger himself. His cherished railway from the sea having reached Pretoria in 1894, and the Rand in the following year, a rates war broke out between that line and the established Cape railway. As part of their tactics in the commercial struggle the Cape railway avoided paying extortionate Transvaal railway rates by offloading goods at their Vaal River station and shipping them onwards by ox-cart. In an attempt to stop this President Kruger ordered in November 1895 that the Vaal drifts – fords – be blocked to non-African imports, a violation of the London Convention which aroused Whitehall's indignation. Chamberlain, refreshed from his holiday, made it clear that this 'drift crisis' could lead to war, whereon Kruger prudently backed down. This was most disappointing for Rhodes, depriving him as it did of the open support of the British government in furthering his ambitions.

But at least tacit encouragement seemed to be forthcoming. Flora Shaw, that remarkable woman, then *The Times'* colonial correspondent, and later Lady Lugard, telegraphed to Rhodes on 12 October the result of a conversation with Chamberlain: 'Joe sound . . . but have special reason to believe wishes you do it imm[ediately].'[29] 'It' should have been an armed rising in Johannesburg such as had been discussed two years previously; but the conspirators were divided and uncertain 'reluctant revolutionaries'.[30] There was, it was true, less to lose since the 'Kaffir' market had slumped alarmingly in October, but it is not easy to take to the streets, shooting at police, of a modern city where one has been living for some years on civil terms, without some sort of dramatic pretext, and none of the *uitlander* 'Reformers' had the qualities that might have fired the others, being mostly commercial gentlemen of urban habits. Merriman, who was not unsympathetic, had warned Charles Leonard, a prominent conspirator, that 'Revolutions are not made by those who live soft,' and he was right. Leonard himself denied being influenced by Rhodes: 'there is no room for Imperialism, and their Rhodesian principles have been flung back at them . . . we want nothing more than a Republic in deed and in fact,' he proclaimed in July 1894.[31]

Christmas came and went without a rising – the plans were put off one week for the races – while Dr Jameson, who had been charged with organizing the intervention, and provided with a plausible letter of appeal from the reputedly desperate *uitlanders*, was fuming with impatience, chain-smoking at the Pitsani railway station. Four hundred horsemen, accompanied by the same Maxim guns that had so satisfactorily accounted for the thousands of Matabele, had been mustered at Pitsani awaiting the signal from Johannesburg, which never came. On 30 December, entirely on his own initiative, Dr Jameson led his men across the border. They never reached Johannesburg, being stopped a few miles outside it four days later, with many casualties, by a hastily-raised commando at Doornkop. The survivors were taken to Pretoria Jail, Jameson, since 'poor Uncle Lee was suffering terribly from haemorrhoids', being conveyed in a cart. The alarmed Johannesburg 'Reformers' put on a show, distributed guns, and hoisted the Transvaal flag upside down to symbolize their new republic, but were persuaded by Robinson, summoned to Pretoria for the purpose by President Kruger and assisted by the Pretorian magistrate, to disarm. The revolt quickly subsided; a most disastrous fiasco.

The effects of the Jameson Raid were devastating. Rhodes' personal involvement was clear – he resigned as Cape Prime Minister the following day – and that of the British government strongly suspected. All Dutch-speaking South Africa, which had in varying degrees evinced considerable respect for British integrity, however much it might have disliked characteristics of British rule, was immeasurably shocked. Young Jan Christiaan Smuts, a graduate of Stellenbosch and Cambridge, son of a liberal Cape MP and a passionate admirer of Cecil Rhodes, was forced to reappraise all his previous ideas. Merriman suspected the worst, and was shocked by Rhodes' blatant lack of regret; his political career, Rhodes boasted only two weeks after his enforced resignation, was 'only just beginning'.[32]

An angry reaction to the raid was only to be expected from the two republics; that it caused similar fury in Cape Colony should have worried the British government more than it did. Even so liberal an Afrikaner as the Unitarian clergyman Pieter Fauré, one of Rhodes' cabinet colleagues, wrote that faith in British justice was 'shattered'. Only a minority of the Cape English, headed by Merriman and Percy Molteno, spoke out with the Afrikaners, the others adopting even more fervent jingoism, at a time when only a decent repentance would have conciliated Boer feelings.[33] Sprigg, once more leading the government after Rhodes' resignation, vacillated, sipping warm water from his mittened hands, and being badgered from all sides.

Although it took months, even years, for the truth to emerge, their suspicions were more than enough to make Afrikaners and colonial liberals deeply distrustful of Imperial integrity, and drove their opponents, the 'jingos', into increasingly bellicose postures. Channelled into a new organization, the South Africa League, English-speaking imperialists reviled any who dared criticize Jameson or Rhodes. 'Dr Jim' became a music-hall hero, and Alfred Austin, Poet Laureate, wrote an ode of ineffable badness in his honour:

> There are girls in the gold-reef city,
> There are mothers and children too,
> And they cry: 'Hurry up! For pity!'
> So what can a brave man do?[34]

Chamberlain survived by claiming: 'I never had any knowledge, or, until, I think it was the day before the actual raid took place, the slightest suspicion, of anything in the nature of a hostile or armed invasion of the Transvaal' – which, taking Lord Grey's testimony into account, can only be called a lie. From that time onwards Chamberlain had a vested personal interest in forcing the Transvaal into a British South Africa.[35]

The international consequences of the raid quickly faded. Kaiser Wilhelm's tactless telegram of congratulation to Kruger and his offer to send marines to Pretoria was sternly reproved by his grandmother, Queen Victoria, and gave the opportunity for Britain to send a warning fleet to Delagoa Bay. Fortunately she did not know of Dr Leyds' audience on 6 February with the Kaiser, in which the German monarch assured the State Secretary that the English suzerainty 'did not exist', and that if the Transvaal had not been able to repel the raid, 'He would have made it a *casus belli*.'[36] France, Russia and the United States similarly fell into line, thereby effectively recognizing British hegemony in Southern Africa. On the ground, matters were less satisfactory. The incompetent veteran Sprigg and a weak cabinet were bullied by Merriman and Hofmeyr into establishing a committee of inquiry which eventually found Rhodes guilty. So, with reservations, did the British parliamentary inquiry, written off as the 'Lying-in-State at Westminster'. Sir Hercules was exonerated – 'Everyone,' *The Times* said on 6 May 1897, 'will accept Mr Chamberlain's account of the incident, and believe his scruple and straightforward tale' – and was given the usual reward for successful slipperiness, a peerage.

The blame was taken by his faithful Secretary Graham Bower, who was consoled with a knighthood and exiled to the governorship of Mauritius. Ten years later, in March 1906, Bower wrote to Merriman revealing his bitterness: 'I fear that both parties have an interest in putting the blame on the innocent subordinates, and to the end of my life I will have to bear the blame of a crime I never committed and against which I had warned my superior in the strongest terms.'[37] The truth was also told by Bower's daughter Maude, who wrote at his dictation that Fairfield and Meade of the Colonial Office both knew of the probability of a rising, and that in October 1895 he had warned Sir Hercules Robinson that 'the less you and I have to do with these damned conspiracies of Rhodes and Chamberlain the better.' After the raid, Chamberlain 'swore to be even with Kruger and was prepared to go very far' if the truth leaked out.

It did not take long for Rhodes to bounce back. Arriving in London on 4 February 1896, he had a friendly interview with his fellow-conspirator Chamberlain, in which, astonishingly enough, the raid was not mentioned. While Rhodes was returning unscathed to Africa, the news broke out that the Ndebele had claimed their revenge: an *impi* had descended into the company's land and massacred every white person they could find. Some two hundred men, women and children were killed in an attack far more deadly than any since Dingane's descent on Weenen. It was suppressed with grim brutality, as was a slightly later rising by the Shona.

The colony of Rhodesia had an unpromisingly bloody start.[38]

Prospects for reconciliation between the colonies and the republics were improved in October 1898 when a Cape election resulted in a precarious but markedly liberal administration headed by William Schreiner, brother of the writer Olive, whose *The Story of an African Farm* remains one of the best-known novels to have come from South Africa, and which included Merriman, Sauer, Richard Solomon – Saul's son – and Dr Thomas te Water. All were on good terms with the new President of the Orange Free State, Martinus Steyn, elected in February 1898 at the age of thirty-eight. Steyn, a man of immense moral staunchness, was married to a Scots girl and was, like Schreiner, a barrister of the Inner Temple, but remained a staunch republican; his influence was immediately brought to bear on old Kruger to encourage the Transvaal along the route to reform.

From Pretoria's point of view all might have been forgiven. The Jameson Raid and its aftermath had, after all, been a moral and psychological triumph. The four most prominent of the Transvaal conspirators were sentenced to death (by Judge Gregorowski, a barrister of Gray's Inn, son of a German pastor, married to a Scots woman, all serving to indicate the oversimplicity of the Dutch v. English equation), rapidly commuted to short terms of imprisonment. The winning side could afford to be gracious. A year after the Raid Kruger was, quite sincerely, felicitating Queen Victoria on her Diamond Jubilee.

For the British, however, this was the second time in a generation that the Empire had been humiliated by a handful of peasants. To some extent injured pride was salved by triumphs elsewhere. Just as Arabi Pasha had served in 1882 by being defeated at Tel-el-Kebir, the slaughter of thousands of Dervishes by Kitchener at Omdurman in 1898 (an action in which Lieutenant Winston Churchill distinguished himself) soothed British public opinion and avenged the death of Gordon. But Joseph Chamberlain was not comforted; although officially cleared, the Colonial Secretary himself and some others knew, and many more suspected, his involvement in the Rhodes-Jameson fiasco. That the extent of Chamberlain's culpability was unclear led only to its being exaggerated. Bringing the Boers to heel was brought well up Chamberlain's agenda, and a new instrument to effect their punishment was selected.

This was Sir Alfred Milner, the star of British officialdom. A man of intellectual brilliance and immense industry, with a cosmopolitan background – a German mother and education – he had advanced without any advantages of birth or wealth.[39] Essentially a numbers man, he had been given effective charge of Egyptian finances at the age of thirty-three; sorting out *that* muddle within three years, Milner was placed in charge of the British Inland Revenue, with the responsibility of assisting Sir William Harcourt, Chancellor of the Exchequer, in preparing the budget. Still in his thirties, he was acclaimed as the most distinguished public servant of his day, a Fellow of New College, Oxford and a Knight Commander of the Order of the Bath. Beneath a cool and disciplined exterior Milner's emotional life was turbulent and complex: living with an alcoholic sister and through a harrowing and unsuccessful love affair with Margot Tennant – who eventually married another achiever, Herbert Asquith – reinforced the glittering protective shell Milner had formed around himself.

Chamberlain of course had never been to Africa – very few politicians of his time had ventured outside Europe: Gladstone, preoccupied as he was for twenty years with the problems of Ireland, visited that island once – and did not realize how eccentric a choice he had made for the post of High Commissioner in South Africa. Sir Alfred's experience of finance had not prepared this urbane, office-centred administrator, conscious of his own intellectual superiority but with no experience of commerce or industry, no particular liking for an outdoor life, and no wife – an essential part of a colonial Governor's equipment – to face a number of assorted countries where farming and mining were the stuff of life. Milner had been spared the rigours of an English education, and operated within the highly-structured Imperial civil service, where everybody knew their place.

All for a people whom we despise

But the war that ensued in 1899, and altered African history, was not simply Milner's war, nor Chamberlain's, nor Kruger's, and certainly not an imperialist war fought at the behest of the Randlords, as Marxists have claimed. Nor even was it quite an Anglo–Boer war, at least not if 'Boer' is taken to include all Dutch-speakers. (Mrs Smuts pointed out that Boers were inhabitants of the republics, while Dutch-speakers – she held no notion of Afrikaans – in the colonies were boers: 'I always consider myself a typical Boer woman (though not half as good and religious as the Boer women usually are) and I certainly differ very much from Tant Sannie, *who got into bed with all her clothes on and snored loudly at night after eating sheep's trotters.'*[40]) Many Cape Afrikaners remained loyal or neutral, while many English-speakers were bitterly critical of the British government, to the point that Milner agitated vehemently for the suppression of the Cape Parliament as a hotbed of treason. Some of the most energetic of the Boer fighters, moreover, were Irish, French or German. Nor, again, was it a war between two colonies and two republics. A worrying number of Cape Dutch joined or assisted the commandos, while a majority of urban Transvaalers fled to Natal or the Cape. To a considerable extent the Boer War resembled the American Civil War thirty-five years previously. One side was upholding the traditional values of its communities, including the denial of political rights to non-whites, which were subsumed into a struggle for independence against a superior power, more modern both in technology and ideology.

A notable difference was that whereas the War Between the States was fought between whites, with the black minority participating only on the Union side, in Africa the non-whites were in a majority – five million to two – and were forced to stand aside from most of the fighting. There was however no doubt which side held out the best hope for their future: black and Coloured voters were found only in the British colonies, and it was to British justice that they looked for future protection; but looked, as it turned out, largely in vain. Milner had little concern for them, except as pawns in his game: 'You have only to sacrifice the "nigger" absolutely and the game is easy.'[41]

In the last decade of the nineteenth century the great powers agreed that war was the continuation of diplomacy by other means: France and England came near to a war in 1893 over Siam, and in 1898 over the Fashoda incident, when a little expedition under Captain Marchand struggled across the continent to the Nile, only to be met by Kitchener's gunboats. In the same year Chamberlain threatened Europe with an Anglo–American alliance, saying that war would be 'cheaply purchased if this were the result'.

Lord Salisbury's cabinet was particularly distant from the experience of war. Salisbury himself, although one of the few British politicians of his time who had seen anything of the world apart from Europe, was the most peaceable of men, devout and intellectual, avoiding adventures of any kind; his nephew and successor Arthur Balfour was something of a dilettante, enthusiastic chiefly about tennis and golf; Lord Lansdowne, Secretary of War, had been both Governor General of Canada and Viceroy of India, during generally tranquil periods. Lord Salisbury had indeed been a

Member of Parliament during the Crimean War, but at a time when Chamberlain was prominent only in the Birmingham and Edgbaston Debating Society. They were therefore able to talk easily about a small war on the lines perhaps of the Chitral Campaign of 1893–94.

Not that a war was considered at all likely. Certainly the Transvaal had spent very large sums on modern equipment (a great deal of it pointlessly, building forts to defend Pretoria which never were used) and State Secretary Leyds had attempted to drum up European support for the Transvaal, discovering much public sympathy – stimulated by bribes to such newspapers as *Le Temps* and *La Liberté* – but had to report: 'while France would gladly cause England difficulties, but is not to be relied upon . . . Germany will do nothing.' The odds were surely too great for the Boers not to back down at the last moment when the whole might of the British Empire threatened to descend on a scattered population of 200,000 farmers whose only professional army was the eight hundred men of the Staatsartillerie. As late as June 1899 Chamberlain was convinced that 'there will be no fighting. We know that these fellows won't fight . . . we are playing a game.' From a more junior level, George Wyndham, Under-Secretary of State for War, was told by his nephew, Bend'Or Grosvenor, Milner's ADC, that 'the Boers will blooming well fall down – directly there is any military demonstration . . . to back up an ultimatum.'[42]

Explaining the causes of wars has always been a popular subject for examiners to set. The combination of gold on the grandest scale, the might of the British Empire at its apogee opposing little Afrikaner communities, the first of the modern anti-colonial struggles (if one ignores the fact that most of the population, the non-whites, were backing the colonialists), is all too seductive. Marxists and anti-Semites have combined to paint a picture of a grand conspiracy between gold millionaires, Jewish financiers and corrupt politicians ganging up to subdue simple farmers. Afrikaner apologists, assisted by foreign sympathizers, mostly French and Irish, preferred a version of an anti-colonialist struggle against predatory imperialism. Those concerned with a black perspective have concentrated on the fight between two bands of settlers to decide who would gain the ascendancy over the blacks. There is something, but not much, to be said for these, and other, perspectives.

The Marxist theory prompts the reflection that while such an incompetent gang of conspirators as those who contrived ('organized' is altogether an inappropriate word) the Jameson Raid could not be trusted to manage the proverbial event in a brewery, there is little evidence for the prosecution, at least of the millionaires. The 'Randlords' were a competitive and disparate bunch. Alfred Beit was a Rhodes man through and through; he had put up £20,000 of his own money to fund the Raid, but after 1895 had withdrawn from active management, leaving the direction to his level-headed German partner Julius Wernher. Their Johannesburg partners certainly did much to stimulate *uitlander* solidarity, but showed little appetite for adventure. As late as March 1899 Wernher wrote to François Rouliot, the partner in charge in Johannesburg, that he was 'more convinced than ever that our salvation was with the Government [of the Transvaal]'. Two months later he was writing that war would be 'a great misfortune', and that what was needed was a redrafting of the London Convention together with '*a renewed guarantee of independence*' (my italics). Which hardly suggests aggressive imperialism on the part of these, the most influential of the Randlords. Only Percy Fitzpatrick, no Randlord but a talented publicist, head of Wernher Beit's intelligence, worked closely with the High Commissioner, Alfred Milner, to precipitate a crisis. Of the other houses, Consolidated Goldfields, Rhodes' own company, was solidly against political intervention; Rhodes himself frequently said that he had no intention of deposing Kruger in order to have Barney Barnato or Joseph Robinson as President. Robinson, disagreeable and disliked by all the other mine-owners, was consistently sympathetic to the Afrikaners, while Abe Bailey, an enthusiastic reformer, had at that time little influence with the British authorities. War is a desperately risky business for such heavy capital investments as those in the deep-mining and processing industries; if they could be said to have a common aim, the capitalists looked for a competent republican regime on good terms with its neighbours.

Nor could it be said that there was pressure from British financial interests to secure supplies of gold. Certainly Chancellor of the Exchequer Goshen had been worried about supplies of gold in 1891, but that was at the height of the first Barings banking crisis. In 1899 there was no possible threat to the gold supplies – the Bank of England was the customer who fixed the world price – *except* in the event of war.[43] As war appeared inevitable the City became jittery. Consols fell to their lowest since the Raid; the bank rate went up suddenly on 3 October from 3½ per cent to 4½. Once war was declared, however, the Stock Exchange was swept by patriotic fervour, exhibited by the beating of a pro-Boer member on the floor of the Exchange.[44]

The last thing the mine-owners needed was a war. Millions of pounds of investment in plant and equipment, together with all the mine-workings, would be at risk; there was no question of war leading to increased prices or more sales after the fighting was over; the best that could be hoped for would be that production would not stop for too long, and that at least running costs would be reduced, although the considerable expenses of servicing capital and maintenance would remain. As it happened, and contrary to any prudent expectation, the mines were undamaged. When the war came the excitable young Judge Kock was all for destruction, and even Smuts wanted to lead a scorched-earth commando, but Kock was locked up by Dr Crause, the sensible commandant of the Witwatersrand, and Smuts was discouraged by Botha. A fair proportion of the black workers stayed on and production continued, to the benefit of the Boer treasury.

In the face of this the claim made by some Marxists, even such eminent historians as Dr Eric Hobsbawm, that 'the motive for war was gold' hardly deserves serious consideration. Milner, who exerted himself to bring about a conflict, had a quasi-religious belief in the British mission to bring civilization and peace, which was not shared by the capitalists or many of the politicians. The Bank of England, which might have been expected to be interested as the gold price arbiter, and was indeed concerned about the world supply, showed no sign of unease, and the price of gold remained steady throughout the war.

It should not be forgotten, either, that the Boer War – or the Second War of Independence – was, like the American Civil War and the Franco–Prussian conflict of 1870–71, begun by the eventual loser. Up till the last minute there was a strong possibility that the British government would not assume responsibility for giving the order to fire the first shot; their attitude was either that the threat of war would suffice, or that if the worst came to the worst, and the republics began hostilities, there would be enough British troops on the scene to ensure a quick victory. Each side had aims of different magnitude: that of the British was to establish hegemony in Southern Africa to the exclusion of the European powers; the constitutional position of the Republics was hardly in question. But the Transvaal burghers saw themselves as fighting for national independence and the preservation of a distinctive native Afrikaner culture. Their whole way of life and ideology was menaced directly by the increasing influx of English-speaking immigrants, and threatened in the longer term by the British insistence on constitutional equality between races (although this insistence was rapidly losing impetus by the 1890s).

Nor should the influence of muddle be neglected. All previous colonial history had shown how the sporadic and cursory attention given to colonial affairs by British legislatures and governments had led to a succession of expedients produced to mollify a particular crisis. The muddle over sovereignty/suzerainty, evolved to placate Queen Victoria and to gloss over a British defeat, was reviving eighteen years later as Cabinet Ministers debated among themselves what precisely was involved, and whether the claim was still in existence.

When the war did, at nearly the last moment, appear inevitable, those most concerned in London were surprised and alarmed; it had never been their plan that actual fighting should break out, and the British were lamentably unprepared. It was a period when wars *almost* began with impressive frequency. Wars between Britain and France, Portugal, Germany and even the United States (over, of all things, the Venezuelan border) were threatened in the decade of the 1890s alone. Governments became habituated to thinking of wars as inevitable, but also skilled at avoiding them when they would clearly be disadvantageous. Certainly there were many potential causes of conflict in South Africa, some of them deep-rooted enough, but it needed specific actions by identifiable individuals to make the fighting start.

Of these individuals the most interesting was Jan Christiaan Smuts, who made his name in the war and became thereafter a figure of international importance. A man of quite extraordinary talents – double first at Cambridge, a brilliant and ruthless guerrilla leader and a British Field Marshal, one of the founders of the Union of South Africa, the League of Nations and the United Nations, the originator of a philosophy, holism, which continues to exercise fascination for many – Smuts attracted bitter enmity and fervent admiration in similar proportions. As early as June 1897 Smuts, who had just set up a legal practice in Johannesburg, was convinced that the Cape Boers 'are absolutely committed to the support of the Republic ... and should an ambitious Colonial Minister choose to bring his "vigorous" policy into operation in South Africa the entire South African continent would be speedily involved in a final conflagration'. It was a conflagration Smuts did a great deal to avoid. Appointed Attorney-General in 1898, he at first did everything possible to accommodate British demands, even though he had little hope of success.[45]

Martinus Steyn, in contrast to Smuts, was admired by supporters and opponents alike. Like Smuts and his own predecessors as President of the

Orange Free State, Brand and Reitz, Steyn was an English-educated lawyer, but unlike the lively and humorous Reitz he was a dour and lugubrious character. Utterly unswerving and brave, he exerted every effort to avoid war,[46] but once engaged refused to surrender. Nor was there an innate bellicosity in Britain. Kipling had written his 'Recessional' in 1897. *Punch*, that other accurate barometer of public opinion, published a sympathetic cartoon on 21 June 1899 showing a respectable Kruger demanding of a ruffianly Chamberlain what his 'Dogs of War' were intended for.

For most of 1898 and 1899, all those involved engaged in war-avoidance manoeuvres, while endeavouring to force a favourable decision on the only real issue, which was that of South African hegemony. That much-discussed London Convention had omitted any reference to 'suzerainty'. Lord Kimberley, Foreign Secretary in the previous Liberal government, who had been Colonial Secretary when the Convention had been agreed, was willing to admit: 'We gave up the clause as to suzerainty,' to which the Law Officers of the Crown were 'inclined to assent'. Lord Ripon also agreed: 'practically this is probably true, but we never said so to the Transvaal and should not now [February 1895] publicly admit'. Conservatives took an opposite view, for the idea was still cherished by Chamberlain and anyone concerned to push Imperial ambition; but in communications between the British politicians the word 'paramountcy' was frequently used, as Salisbury did when he insisted on 6 October 1899 that he was prepared to face war 'sooner than not get out of Kruger terms that will secure good government at Johannesburg and make the Boers feel that we are and must be the paramount power in South Africa' – which is much less than a suggestion that the Transvaal ought to become British, the ideal to which Milner was personally committed. Chamberlain did not need to force his colleagues into considering war – although they did not do much to prepare for it – but few believed that war would actually break out, and none that it would be as damaging and decisive as it turned out to be.

None, that is, except that engaging Irishman General Sir William Butler, who was left in charge during Milner's absence in London between November 1898 and February 1899. An experienced soldier, Butler appreciated that a war would need to be taken seriously, and would require a much bigger effort than anything anticipated by the War Office, and as many as a hundred thousand troops. Believing that if it came it would be 'the greatest calamity that ever occurred in South Africa',[47] the acting High Commissioner and commander-in-chief absolutely refused to discuss what preparations should be undertaken. Much to Milner's annoyance a potential *casus belli*, which aroused a great deal of somewhat synthetic indignation, was dismissed by Butler as a 'drunken brawl', and good relations with the Transvaal restored. This was the shooting of one Tom Edgar by a Transvaal policeman, a case which did warrant investigation but which had been hysterically exaggerated by the jingo press. 'Either Butler or I must go,' Milner grimly decided, and Butler went, leaving a clear stage for the bellicose Milner.

An extravagant and widely publicized despatch in which Milner described the prosperous *uitlanders* as being kept in the position of 'helots' aroused Chamberlain's ire; he asked Milner to 'doctor' it, and began to send increasingly cross despatches to his High Commissioner. He had written to Milner on 16 March 1898: 'the principal object . . . at present is peace. Nothing but a most flagrant offence could justify the use of force.' Flagrant offences were not forthcoming, but Milner's only likely fox, the fate of the drunken Edgar, which had been shot by General Butler, was given new life when the Transvaal government chose to have the case tried by twenty-eight-year-old Judge Kock, a political appointee who later proved to be clinically insane. Merriman, now in office again under the gloomy, slow-moving Schreiner, shuttled between the Cape, Bloemfontein and Pretoria, talking with the two Presidents, and with Smuts and Abraham Fischer, Steyn's link with the Transvaal, pressing the need for some sensible reforms. In a separate series of negotiations Smuts and Lippert, the dynamite concessionaire, outlined to Percy Fitzpatrick what became known as 'The Great Deal'.

It was not all that much of a deal: a five-year waiting period for franchise, but only after an initial application, which meant freezing the lack of rights for that period, and an undertaking to behave according to Afrikaner standards in future, including such things as suppressing pushy Coloured and Indian traders. The mine-owners were equivocal: Rhodes' men were for accepting, but Fitzpatrick persuaded Wernher that it should not be taken seriously, since the Volksraad would never accept it – which might well have been so. All the Randlords were however anxious to arrive at some solution, especially since a surge of investment was being experienced. Lionel Philips detected in 'the present eagerness for shares' a 'tendency . . . distinctly in the direction of running wild'.[48]

The nearest approach to avoiding war was the meeting arranged with great difficulty at Bloemfontein, in the first week of June 1899 between President Kruger, the High Commissioner and President Steyn. Assisted by the Cape liberals, Schreiner, Hofmeyr and Merriman, together with

Smuts and Reitz, had succeeded in bringing Milner and Kruger together, considerably against Milner's inclinations. The meeting had been arranged by Milner to exclude all those who might help smooth the discussions; Steyn himself was allowed to take no part. Not that it would have made much difference, since Milner was determined not to reach agreement. From his first appearance, when the elegantly correct High Commissioner made his entrance and, obeying social conventions, made straight for Mrs Steyn, ignoring the old President, it was obvious to Steyn that Milner was prepared to be intransigent.[49] Such an attitude came naturally enough, for Milner was no hand at negotiations, which Kruger enjoyed. Good stock-farmer as he was, chaffering was a pleasure to Kruger, and he had much experience of it. For two days he rambled on, 'very old, blind in one eye, wearing green spectacles ... weeping crocodile tears' about the infamous Raid, before producing a cut-and-dried reform plan, doubtless drafted by Smuts, which would give, under conditions, a franchise after seven years.[50]

When he heard of this Chamberlain was delighted, and wrote to Milner congratulating him 'on a great victory ... No one could dream of fighting over a two year qualification period. We ought to accept this as a settlement.' Too late, for congratulations were not in order: Milner had rejected Kruger's terms almost out of hand, and declared the conference closed. The Prime Minister was not pleased at this news, writing to Lord Lansdowne: 'Milner and his jingo supporters would force the Government to make a considerable military effort – all for a people whom we despise, and for something which will bring no profit and no power to England,' but gloomily determined nevertheless to face war in order to be acknowledged as 'the paramount power in South Africa'.[51]

Efforts, increasingly desperate, were still made to avoid war. *Punch*, again, carried a scathing article on 28 June, criticizing Milner's 'helots' despatch as 'ridiculous ... preposterously frothy ... tawdry ... which had caused Jingoes ... to wave flags and shout for blood', while 'calm and sober Englishmen who had trusted you ... were struck with shame'. Chamberlain endeavoured to persuade Kruger to hold a joint inquiry on the franchise proposals, and Kruger, to everyone's surprise, came up with an acceptance of the five-year franchise. Steyn and Smuts had been persuasive, but it was no use. Milner's 'jingo supporters' – who included Lord Salisbury's own son-in-law, Lord Selborne, second-in-command at the War Office, worked on Chamberlain. Selborne wrote to Milner: 'Far the best thing ... is that the Boers should ... commence the war by invading our territory.' And that happy result is exactly what Chamberlain's insulting rebuff, delivered on 28 August, ensured.

Stimulated by the knowledge that British reinforcements were at sea, with more to follow, the Boer leaders decided to attack while they still had what should have been a decisive superiority on the ground. A swift surgical strike down to Durban and the sea would deny the British their port and constitute an irreparable humiliation. Like their opposite numbers in London, the men in Pretoria envisaged a short war. President Steyn had little alternative but to agree, although with misgivings. Not only formal agreements but Afrikaner solidarity dictated that the Orange Free State would act with the Transvaal. Abraham Fischer, who had shuttled between Bloemfontein and Pretoria in his untiring efforts to find a compromise, had to admit on 13 September 1899 that he 'could not be party to further humiliation of the Transvaal'. On 9 October, when the republics had completed their preparations, an ultimatum designed to be incapable of acceptance was presented to the British representative in Pretoria. Drafted almost certainly by Smuts, it insisted that all British troops be withdrawn from the republic's borders, that no reinforcements be landed and that all disputes should be subject to arbitration; and only forty-eight hours were given for acceptance. Failure to do so would be regarded as a declaration of war. 'They have done it,' Chamberlain rejoiced, spared the odium of issuing his own already-prepared ultimatum. 'Tipping the black spot' was Reitz's jocular description, but it was the last joke to be made for some time.[52]

The progress of the war was simple enough; its effects were to be both complex and enduring. Hostilities began on 12 October 1899 with a Boer invasion of the British colonies closely following the plans originally suggested by Smuts.[53] The main thrust was over the Drakensberg into Natal, twenty-one thousand men in three columns from both republics. At the same time a smaller force pushed into the Northern Cape and invested Mafeking and Kimberley. Within a month the impetus had slowed to a stalemate. Twelve thousand British soldiers were besieged in Ladysmith, with the main Boer armies well-entrenched further forward on the banks of the Tukela, faced by General Buller, one of Wolseley's former young men who had distinguished himself in the Zulu War, grounded on the other side. In this way a large proportion of what should have been the splendidly mobile Boer forces were firmly stuck, giving time for the British to assemble their greatly superior forces.

Before these could have their full effect there were some fierce little actions which shook British morale. Public opinion had become used to a series of picturesque victories – Roberts' march from Kabul to Kandahar, the storming of the Ethiopian emperor's mountain fastness of Magdala, and only a year before, Kitchener's almost bloodless (for the Anglo-Egyptians) victory over the Dervishes at Omdurman. Such triumphs were extravagantly rewarded – Napier of Magdala and Kitchener of Khartoum both receiving peerages after their actions – while such reverses as Majuba, nothing more than skirmishes, aroused hysterical popular reactions. Much worse was to come.

In 'Black Week', 10–15 December 1899, nearly three thousand casualties were suffered in the three battles of Magersfontein, Stormberg and Colenso; of these fewer than a thousand were killed. To put this in perspective, Ulysses S. Grant lost 17,700 men in the two-day Chancellorsville fight of May 1864; on the first day of the Somme offensive in July 1916, the British suffered sixty thousand casualties, over nineteen thousand of them dead – three times the number killed in action during three whole years of fighting against the Boers. But this was the first war to be reported by telegraph in a widely-read popular press; the first in which almost all the soldiery were literate, and letters home reliably delivered; the first in which photographs – discreetly censored – of the carnage were widely reproduced in journals. Most disturbingly, this was a war in which British troops actually surrendered, and that with increasing frequency.

Helped by the Boers' mistaken strategy – wasting most of their energy investing three relatively unimportant towns instead of pressing on to capture Durban, which would have been a devastating moral and practical blow – the British soon recovered. By March 1900 Lord Roberts – little Bobs, hero of the Indian Mutiny and one of the few generals ever decisively to have beaten the Afghans – recalled for the occasion and assisted (not very effectively, since he had little gift for field command) by Lord Kitchener, had marched into Bloemfontein. By May the British 'steamroller' entered Johannesburg, and on 5 June Lord Roberts held a victory parade in Pretoria. Kruger fled – he was, after all, seventy-five years old – to Holland, and the last Boer field army was defeated by 9 June, not much more than six months after the first shots had been fired. The Free State and the Transvaal were annexed; and that, by all the rules and customs, should have been that.

Kruger may have gone, but the indomitable Steyn refused to give in. For the next two years a handful of brilliant guerrilla commanders – de Wet, Botha, Smuts, de la Rey – carried on the fight, raiding all over South

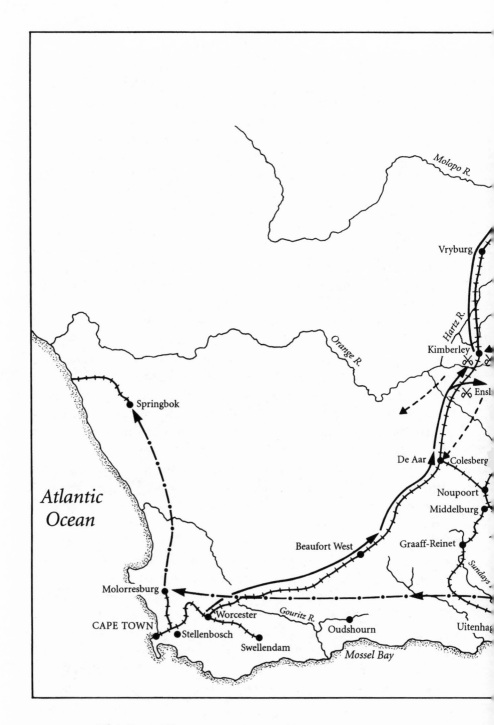

MAP 9 *The Boer War*

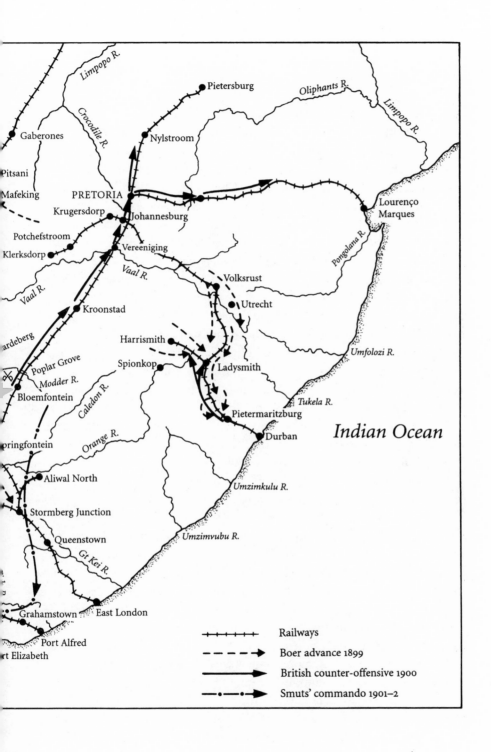

Limpopo R.

● Pietersburg

Oliphants R.

Limpopo R.

Crocodile R.

● Gaberones

● Nylstroom

Pitsani

PRETORIA

Mafeking

Lourenço
Marques

Krugersdorp ● ● Johannesburg

Pongolana R.

Potchefstroom

● Vereeniging

Klerksdorp ●

Vaal R.

Vaal R.

● Kroonstad

Volksrust

● Utrecht

Umfolozi R.

● Harrismith

● Spionkop

● Ladysmith

ardeberg

Poplar Grove

Modder R.

● Bloemfontein

Caledon R.

Tukela R.

Pietermaritzburg

● Durban

Indian Ocean

springfontein

Orange R.

● Aliwal North

Umzimkulu R.

● Stormberg Junction

● Queenstown

Umzimvubu R.

Gt Kei R.

● Grahamstown ● East London

Port Alfred

t Elizabeth

+++++++	Railways
- - - ➤	Boer advance 1899
——➤	British counter-offensive 1900
—•—•➤	Smuts' commando 1901–2

Africa, passing through British armies almost unnoticed. Smuts led his commando right across Cape Colony to the Atlantic, and Botha nearly reached the Indian Ocean. They were impossible, it seemed, to catch and defeat; contradicting all the axioms of military science, the Boer commandos were magnificently successful.

Lord Salisbury had taken advantage of the capture of Pretoria to call a general election in September 1900, 'the Khaki Election', which was fought on a blatantly imperialist policy. Such slogans as 'If you want Colonies for your Sons, vote Conservative!', 'To Vote for a Liberal is to Vote for a Boer!', 'Bobs for Pretoria, Soames for South Norfolk' were successful enough to return a slightly increased Conservative majority with a mandate to win the war.

It took dogged, expensive and widespread British action under the direction of Lord Kitchener, cutting off all possible sources of supply, laying 3,700 miles of barbed wire, defended by a chain of eight thousand fortified blockhouses, eventually to bring the Boer commandos to the point of even discussing surrender. The cost of reaching that point had been enormous. From start to finish not many fewer than half a million Imperial troops, regulars and volunteers, British, Canadian, Australian, South African and Indian, had been engaged. Deaths from disease, three times as common as those in battle, brought the total British fatalities to twenty-two thousand. Financially, the war cost more than £200 million to the Exchequer, a far cry from the originally estimated few millions.

Proportionately to the population, the losses on the other side were enormously greater. As a result of Kitchener's policy of denying supplies to the Boers, all country dwellers who might, willingly or not, support the commandos were rounded up and housed in refugee or 'concentration' camps, following a plan pursued by the Spaniards in their Cuban war six years earlier. When all the explanations and excuses are offered – some camps were well-run, with knitting lessons and organized games; prisoners presented an illuminated testimonial to one commander; others were ineffective; all were plagued by disease; strenuous efforts were made by concerned Englishmen and women, especially by *that Miss Hobhouse* – the cold statistic remains that more than twenty thousand Boer women and children died in the concentration camps. From a population of perhaps half a million, this was a terrifying proportion. Fighters do not find it too difficult to forgive those they have met in battle, but the deaths of so many innocents left a bitterness that has not yet disappeared a century later. Cold comment from officials such as Edward Ward, who referred to 'undesirables' being placed in the camps, rubbed salt into very painful wounds.[54]

Other causes for resentment existed. The British Army executed 'war criminals' – those who infringed accepted practices, such as firing on white flags or shooting prisoners – both their own (the case of the Australian 'Breaker' Morant is famous) and the enemy's (Commandant Gideon Scheepers is perhaps the best-known of the Boer victims). Both Morant and Scheepers were unprincipled murderers, which did not, of course, prevent their posthumous conversion to heroes, but there were others less obviously guilty.[55]

By no means all the Boers went on fighting. Generals de Wet and Cronje had the humiliation of seeing their brothers, Piet de Wet and Andries Cronje, become not only '*handsoppers*', but 'joiners'. Piet de Wet in particular had fought well, once capturing a whole regiment of Irish yeomanry after a fierce little fight – over five hundred prisoners, including four peers – but went over with Cronje to form the 'National Scouts'. 'Bitterenders' railed furiously against the Scouts, many of whom were shot when captured, as were several well-intentioned peace emissaries, which did nothing to help Boer morale or solidarity.

It was meant to be a 'white man's' war, but the Coloured and black races were often anxious to join in, almost always on the British side. There were exceptions; as in the American Civil War, when slaves sometimes accompanied their owners into battle, some of the Boer leaders had their *agterryters* – 'grooms' might be a fair translation – riding with them. Often these grooms had been compelled to join, and many thousands of labourers were forced to work for the Boers, although some blacks in the republics were willing to offer their services as scouts, especially in the Orange Free State; but the enthusiastic participation was on behalf of the British. However restrictive the social constraints on black advancement might be – and even in the Cape these were coming under increasing pressure – it was clear that British victory promised some hope, while that of the Boers held none. Coloured town guards took part in front-line actions, and were sometimes atrociously treated when their posts were overrun by the Boer commandos, the most famous case being that of Abraham Esau of Calvinia, a bold resistance fighter who was flogged and dragged behind a horse before being finally shot.[56] There was one prominent exception to the black support for the British, Jabavu's principled opposition to what he saw, with much justice, as an unnecessary war, an opposition which led to his personal unpopularity and the temporary suppression of *Imvo*.[57]

Black communities and nations reacted in different fashions to the spectacle of the whites fighting among themselves. Those in the Orange Free State, who had been decently treated by the government, according to their lights, and were for the most part secluded in their own areas, offered no resistance to the commandos, and usually assisted them with supplies. Their kinsmen over the border in Basutoland obeyed British orders to close their frontiers against the republics, and so contributed to one important Boer defeat in July 1900. In the Transvaal the only strategy available to blacks was to try to stay out of trouble.

Only the more noteworthy massacres, such as that of the population of Modderfontein by Smuts' commando, were recorded, but numerous instances exist of the Boers 'shooting niggers like dogs'.[58] At least one opportunity for retaliation occurred when Chief Linchwe led his Kgata Tswana in a successful charge against a Boer *laager* at Derdepoort, on the Bechuanaland borders, while in September 1901 an outnumbered force of British and Zulu repelled Botha's second attempt to invade Natal, and two months later Captain Elliot's Thembu drove off Commandant Bezuidenhout's commando.[59]

With both commandos and the British burning crops and removing cattle, the high-veld blacks had only the alternative of refugee camps, formed around the railway lines, where at least they were able to cultivate some small plots. As a matter of routine, black scouts accompanied British columns and rendered invaluable intelligence, but often participated in significant numbers. Colonel Henry Rawlinson, one of the most enterprising British commanders, who specialized in dawn charges on unsuspecting Boer *laagers*, had 453 blacks among his 1,900 mounted infantry. Thomas Pakenham estimates that all together as many as twenty thousand blacks were on active service.

Other Coloured and black men took an active part in transport as muleteers and wagon drivers, treated with disdain by some but with open camaraderie by others. Polo games with the cavalry and guards, cricket and football matches all contributed, together with good wages, to the self-esteem of the non-whites. The original intention to employ non-whites on non-combatant duties only – and many did serve in such capacities – was soon abandoned as blacks fought not only as scouts but alongside British colonial troops. Without the Rolong fighters at Mafeking, the 'Black Watch', Baden-Powell could never have held out during the famous seven-month siege of that little town.

In the Cape the situation was more complex. The commando expeditions, although brilliantly executed and giving rise to much apprehension, had little influence on the result of the war; that had to be decided in the republics. Some Cape Afrikaners joined the commandos, at the considerable risk of execution as rebels-in-arms, and many more prudently limited their support to giving shelter and provisions. To a man and to a woman the non-whites had resisted, and had been brutally treated by the commandos as a result. In the wake of what appeared to be victory, after the occupation of the republics the revenge began in the colonies. Under martial law hundreds of Cape rebels were sentenced to death. Most were reprieved, but enough public executions took place to delight the non-whites: 'Trial sessions and the carrying out of sentences generally took place in an unruly, almost carnivalesque atmosphere, with excited and demonstrative crowds jostling to taunt Boer prisoners, occasionally pelting them with dung and rotten fruit,' while such enterprising Coloureds as Mohamed Allie offered haircuts to onlookers, and flowers were pressed on the firing squads. Inevitably, this strengthened the Afrikaners' resolve never to allow such things to happen again.[60]

English-speaking colonials were almost as horrified. It was all very well for the army to encourage the natives in 'cheeky' (a favourite adjective) attitudes, but the soldiers would go home, while the colonists had to live among the blacks. The contrasting attitudes had been obvious throughout the war: colonial officers kept blacks in what was considered to be their place, whilst Imperial troops had no such inhibitions and generally remained on friendly terms with their 'niggers'. The better the regiment, the better, usually, were the relations: Dombey and Pickwick, two muleteers, became regimental boxing champions of the Coldstream Guards.

In the tide of new self-confidence that came with the knowledge of being on the winning side, the satisfaction of a visible triumph over former persecutors, and the expectation – sadly to be disappointed – of a brighter future, some new organizations appeared. Mambe, to the north of Cape Town, saw a Coloured Political Association formed two years before Cape Town itself launched the African Political Association with F.Z.S. Peregrino, Ghanaian editor of the cautiously conservative *South Africa Spectator*, and the Coloured labour pioneer John Tobin as its first leaders, soon to be succeeded by the more effective Dr Abdullah Abdurahman. The Boers, for so long upholders of white supremacy, were being defeated; should not the Coloured and blacks now begin to have their say?

THIRTEEN

Peace

A shameful peace

Hounded unremittingly over the plains and mountains by British forces grown more skilled in mobile warfare, the Boer commanders were forced into peace discussions in May 1902. These were by no means the first; Lord Kitchener had wanted to start negotiations after the occupation of the republics in November 1900. Kitchener clearly realized the difficulty he faced in running the guerrillas finally to earth in the face of a general expectation that the serious fighting was over, and that the British taxpayers' money would cease to flow in such excessive amounts – then £2 million a week. Any further delay would only imperil his reputation, but it was not easy to establish contact with the Boers since, after previous well-meaning emissaries had been flogged and shot, others were, not unnaturally, reluctant to come forward. Eventually Botha was brought to a discussion through Mrs Botha's agreeing to take the risk of visiting her husband. She succeeded, and a meeting was arranged on 28 February 1901.[1]

Sir Alfred Milner was much less anxious for peace than Kitchener. As far as reputations went, his was also in jeopardy. Bearing as he did the responsibility for getting Britain involved in a damaging and inglorious war, it was essential that Milner made it all worthwhile by a successful post-war reconstruction. He therefore wanted the slate wiped clean, with no restrictions imposed on his ambitious plans for the future of South Africa; that of the republics in particular, but he also had in mind doing something about those irritating liberals in the Cape. When Winston Churchill, who had escaped from his Boer captivity with a high regard for the enemy, wrote to Milner suggesting an early peace and a general amnesty for the Cape rebels, the High Commissioner replied on 6 February 1901 with twenty-two handwritten pages pleading to be left alone: 'it is a serious matter to have suggestions of pacification coming from you, with your ability, popularity and special South African experience.'[2]

In spite of Milner's objections the terms Kitchener offered to the Boers at Middleburg the following month were generous enough – the annexed republics to become self-governing, no indemnity exacted but, on the contrary, grants to be made to assist the burghers in re-establishing themselves. On one point the British government differed: Kitchener had suggested that there could be no extension of the franchise to 'Kaffirs' in the old republics before representative government. Chamberlain objected, insisting: 'we cannot consent to purchase a shameful peace by leaving the coloured population in a position in which they stood before the war with not even the ordinary civil rights which the government of the Cape Colony has long conceded.'

These terms had been rejected by the Boers, and Kitchener began his policy of clearing the veld and forcing the Boer civilians into concentration camps. Over a year later, after all the misery of the camps and the brutalities of a bitter war, Botha was willing to talk. On 11 April 1902 a delegation of both republics, including Botha, Steyn and Smuts, came to Pretoria to negotiate terms of peace. They were not united, the Free Staters being all for continuing the war, while the Transvaalers were anxious to finish it. On the British side Kitchener was impatient. After tremendous effort and at some cost to his professional reputation, he had at last brought the truculent Boers to the point of surrender. His next appointment beckoned, the magnificent prospect of being commander-in-chief of the Indian Army, second in rank but first in power (he succeeded in forcing Viceroy Curzon's retirement within three years of his arrival in the subcontinent). Within the limits accorded to him, Kitchener would make any concessions to ensure an agreement with the Boers. Milner, on the other hand, was still unwilling to concede anything. He had enjoyed eighteen months of limited reconstruction in the republics unhampered by the war, and wanted no limitation to his future authority to finish the work.[3]

After a month of negotiations at Pretoria the two sides moved to Vereeniging, on the frontier of the Free State and the Transvaal, where a delegation of sixty republicans elected five negotiators, three of whom were to be future Prime Ministers of South Africa: Louis Botha, Jan Smuts and Judge J.M. Hertzog. The final terms were in fact drafted by a committee of three lawyers – Smuts and Hertzog, with Richard Solomon – and offered little more to the Boers than had been available fourteen months before.

Financial arrangements were improved, increasing grants and offering loans to the republicans, while the Cape rank-and-file rebels were to be amnestied. On one point the new terms were less favourable. Middleburg had allowed English and Dutch to be treated as joint official languages, a concession much diluted by the 1902 terms, on Milner's insistence. A typescript of the agreed terms was prepared, including a variation paragraph on the original item dealing with the franchise, which now read: 'the franchise will not be given to natives until after the introduction of self-government.' When Smuts, that extraordinary combination of Cambridge, the Temple and guerrilla warfare, received his copy, he displayed the skills that earned him the name of 'Slim Jannie' by pencilling in an innocuous-seeming alteration: 'the question of granting the franchise to natives will not be decided until after the introduction of self-government,' thus transforming the assumption that the franchise would be granted to a very open question indeed.[4]

None of those present was interested in the preservation, still less the extension, of non-white rights. The great matter was to sign a document and finish the fighting. Only the irreconcilable Steyn would not sign. That tenacious man, who had been so earnest in his endeavours to prevent a war but who had supported the Transvaalers loyally once it was inevitable, had ridden with his burghers throughout the conflict, a rare act for a country's head of state in modern times; now that defeat was accepted by almost all, Steyn refused to submit. 'We must be ready to forgive and forget,' said Schalk Burger, head of the Transvaal delegation; Steyn could forgive, but never forget. As acting President, Burger, an amiable man, was nominally in charge, but it was Botha aided by Smuts who were the real leaders of the Transvaal Afrikaners. Both had showed outstanding qualities during the war, and had in abundance the qualities of persuasive charm and decisiveness. Smuts, decisive to a fault, allied to this an intellectual arrogance which lost him much support. Great men, and Smuts was certainly one in his influence on history and personal genius, cannot be expected to be faultless, and Smuts' career to 1902 gives cause for some serious criticism.

Only thirty-two at the time of Vereeniging, Smuts had done much to modernize the stale South African Republic, and made earnest attempts to avoid a war. He had proved, on a small scale, an effective guerrilla leader, and sufficient of a realist to support an eventual settlement. On the debit side, he exerted himself to refuse the earlier peace proposals made at Middleburg, by invading Cape Colony helped to prolong the war, and placed the Cape colonials who joined him in serious jeopardy. By holding on for an extra year great misery was caused. Had the earlier proposals been accepted the concentration camps and methodical scorched-earth policies would never have taken place. Botha and Smuts, together with their supporters, must therefore bear a major responsibility for the sufferings of that period.

It might be claimed that an amnesty for the leaders of the Cape rebels had been obtained at Vereeniging, but had it not been for the invasions of the Cape the amnesty would not have been needed. To that extent the executions of such commando leaders as Scheepers, Lotter and some forty others may also be ascribed to their Generals' actions. Whether the black and Coloured jubilation at the executions, and the humiliation of the Boers, goes to the credit or debit side, that also has much to do with Smuts' conduct. More tangentially, Smuts personally did more to raise Afrikaner feeling against the British than any of his contemporaries by writing *A Hundred Years of Wrong*, published in 1899. A compendium of all the Afrikaner myths from Slagtersnek and the Black Circuit, the book was an immediate propaganda success, and accepted, historical perversion though it was, as a work of authority.

While in Britain the physical effects of the war were negligible, there were other, highly important results. Jingoism, which had been rampant during the first phase, culminating in the triumphant march on Pretoria, was subdued by the two years' hard, expensive and unglamorous slog that followed. Photography and the telegraph had enabled quick and graphic reports to touch sensibilities; the hysterical rejoicing over the relief of Mafeking was only one result. Sir Arthur Conan Doyle's brilliantly-written history was obligatory reading for all admirers of Sherlock Holmes. The Boers, formerly reviled as bearded thugs shooting on white flags, earned themselves heroic status in the estimation of the British people, always ready to admire courageous – and safely beaten – enemies. Public and politicians alike were in a mood to be generous, and to avoid any repetition of such an expensive and uncomfortable episode.

In official circles the inquest was long and detailed. Two successive Conservative War Ministers, Broderick and Arnold-Forster, made flurried attempts at reorganizing the army, before the much more able Liberal, R.B. Haldane, set in hand root-and-branch reforms. Deficiencies in the troops' performance were carefully analysed and, for once, not fudged. Infantry tactics were adapted to those of the Boer, with more emphasis on musketry and the deployment of smaller units, permitting fire-and-movement advances rather than the heroic rush with fixed bayonets. Twelve years of training at all levels produced the British Expeditionary Force of August 1914, the most efficient army in Europe. One unfortunate development was the survival of cavalry as a major assault force rather than as mounted infantry. General French's cavalry division had won one of the most spectacular actions of the war by a quick circuit of Cronje's army at Paardeberg, which forced a largely bloodless surrender, a success which diverted much expenditure towards a largely useless cavalry arm, and the perfection in 1904, twenty years after Gladstone fired the first Maxim gun, and after much technical work by an industrious committee, of the ideal sword.

A Royal Commission report, in four volumes, described much that was unpalatable. Wolseley's unpreparedness was criticized; the intelligence and physical fitness of the rank-and-file were commented on adversely. Only one applicant in ten met the army standards; 565 in every thousand recruits were below five feet six inches tall, whilst two generations previously, in 1845, the figure was only 105.[5] 'Young Colonels' were blamed by Lord Roberts for undue enthusiasm in burning towns; but in his summing-up for King Edward VII, Lord Esher had to admit too that the final report was 'not favourable' to Roberts, 'and not wholly favourable to Your Majesty's Ministers', and that if the pre-war recommendations of the Liberal government had been acted upon, 'hundreds of lives, and expenditure of 200 millions would have been saved'.[6]

Reconstruction took obviously different forms in the two colonies, representatives of the victorious Imperial power, and the two former republics, now defeated and occupied territories; on paper at least. On the ground this was hardly evident. War indemnities, considerable enough, grants of £7 million and a loan of £35 million were paid, but paid by the winning side. The defeated Generals Botha, de la Rey and de Wet visited London to be welcomed by the affable King Edward VII. In Africa Milner was now supreme, Governor of the Transvaal and the Orange River Colony, each with a new Crown Colony constitution of the classic type, which enabled him to show the qualities of a superlative administrator that had been masked by his defects as a diplomatist.

Assisted by those talented young men ironically described (by Merriman, in reference to Sir Alfred's Teutonic habits and German blood) as 'Milner's Kindergarten', reconstruction, which had begun as soon as the British occupied the republics in 1901, moved rapidly ahead. In the Transvaal the priority had to be restoring gold production, the motor of the state's prosperity, which by 1904 had regained its pre-war level. The new colonial government and the Chamber of Mines worked closely, almost indistinguishably, together, but the mine-owners were not amused by an increase in their profits' tax to twice that which Kruger had wanted to levy. Edmund Bright, a morose American mining engineer, wrote: 'the mining people, who caused the conflict, would give anything to have the old times back. They are now so fenced in and bound by red tape and laws that only the richest mines can be worked at a profit.'[7] If the war had indeed been waged to benefit capitalists, it could not be called successful: new investment remained reluctant for some years.

Farms took longer to restore, for the devastation had been complete, especially in the Orange Free State. Kitchener's scorched-earth campaign meant that 'the whole fabric of the former rural society had been swept away'. Outside the largest towns there was hardly a building intact, except where, in a refinement of offensiveness, the animals had been driven into the houses before being slaughtered. Perhaps a tenth of the pre-war stock remained, and away from the strip of cultivated land that followed the railway, on which the black refugee camps had been placed, no crops had been sown for two years. Delays were inevitable, but within months of the peace treaty most farmers were reinstated, and provided with tents, stock and veterinary services, seeds and equipment; by 1904 maize production on Sammy Marks' Vereeniging Estates was approaching twice its pre-war level, and the Orange River Colony, the worst hit, was practically self-supporting; but malnourishment and poverty were still evident when Emily Hobhouse, who had, to the vast indignation of Lord Kitchener, done so much to alleviate conditions in the concentration camps, returned in May 1903.[8]

By that time no refugee camps remained. The vigorous action needed to clear up the appalling conditions in them had been entrusted to the youngest of the Kindergarten, John Buchan, the future novelist and Governor General of Canada. The horrifying death rate fell from the peak of 34 per cent in October 1901 to 4 per cent in the following March. One less prominent worker was Edmund Sargant, the brilliantly erratic Transvaal Director of Education who contrived, with the aid of enthusiastic volunteers, to give the camp children more instruction than they had received before the war. With the limited rail network and the enormous reduction in the number of draught animals, poor transport facilities constituted a

major obstacle to physical reconstruction, a problem addressed by a conference in 1903 which led to an expansion and rationalization of South Africa's
rail network; the same year saw the establishment of an experimental free
trade zone.

Milner was rewarded for his efforts by the offer of the Colonial Secretaryship in September 1903, but, knowing that much still remained to be
done in South Africa, he refused. Little progress had been made towards
his one essential goal: the Transvaal and Orange Free State remained Dutch,
whereas Milner's intention had been to flood the areas with immigrants
to form an English-speaking majority. A million and a half acres were set
aside for English settler families, ten thousand of whom were expected, but
only some fifteen hundred turned up, after a great deal of effort and
expense, and at the cost of arousing the distrust of the Afrikaners. Probably
the worst of Milner's errors was to insist that English should be the language
of instruction in all state schools; Dutch was to be used only to teach
English. This struck a sensitive nerve, as it seemed that military defeat was
to be followed by cultural domination.[9]

Although in the long run the failure to ensure an English-speaking
majority was to be the ruin of Milner's plans, a more immediate crisis was
caused by the mining industry's insatiable hunger for labour. As the deeper
levels were exploited the quality of the ore worsened and costs increased.
Thousands of tons of rock had to be brought to the surface and treated,
requiring a high proportion of less-skilled labour. Whites demanded high
wages – £25 per month – while blacks would work for a tenth of that sum.
And they were so easily disposable. Edmund Bright again, after describing
a mine riot, wrote: 'The only other exciting thing that happened this week
was a dog fight . . . oh yes, a Kaffir was killed in the shaft.'[10] But Kaffirs
refused permanent employment; colonial blacks still had the prospect of
working the land, progressing towards actual ownership of farms, and
tended to accept mining jobs only as long as they needed to earn whatever
funds were required. In all probability they would not long remain content
with their conditions; the Transvaal Indigency Committee reported in 1908
that it was 'clearly proved to us that the restriction of the native to the
sphere of unskilled work cannot be permanent. His intense desire for
education is everywhere the subject of comment.'[11] Attempts were made
to organize recruitment from Mozambique, but by the end of 1903 more
than 120,000 mining jobs remained to be filled.

The mine-owners were agitated, and pressed for labour to be imported;

and when the mine-owners insisted, the Transvaal colonial government obeyed. Rightly suspicious of the treatment Indians were likely to receive, the Indian government was reluctant to cooperate. The alternative seemed to be China, as a deputation sent to California and China reported. It was not a popular decision in many quarters. White workers complained, 'Is this what we spilled our blood for?' and were supported by a Trades Union Congress rally in Hyde Park in March 1904, at which eighty thousand protested. Nevertheless, the Chinese and British governments concluded an agreement in May.

Earnings remitted from Chinese working overseas had been an important source of income to that country ever since the English East India Company had taken over the Singapore station in 1822, and had increased greatly with new demands from the Californian goldfields. Efficient organizations had developed enabling large numbers of labourers to be transferred. Unlike the Natal Indians, the Chinese were not to be given the option of remaining in South Africa; at the end of their three-year term they either re-enlisted or were repatriated. The experiment was quickly successful; the first of an eventual 63,695 Chinese labourers arrived in June 1904, and by 1906 the gold output had doubled.[12]

Naturally enough the mine-owners were relieved. The Chinese were 'very steady fellows, quite as powerful physically as the Kaffirs and, endowed with a higher intelligence . . . a very happy lot taken all round'. The owners remained, however, seriously apprehensive that they might be accused of displacing white workers. As things turned out, it was not the objections of the white workers in South Africa that put a stop to Chinese labour, but political changes in London.

Expansion in mining and railway construction, together with the ancillary industries, brought benefits to farmers, but more especially to those in a position to finance expansion. Prosperous landed gentry like the Bothas were being joined by such enterprising individuals as the Lithuanian Lazarus family, who ended up employing over two thousand workers on their modern farms; those Randlords who stayed in South Africa, Sammy Marks and Abe Bailey prominent among them, ran extensive estates. Blacks enjoyed, not their fair share – *that* never happened – but *a* share of the prosperity, either as tenant farmers or, more rarely, owners. Seth Ramanbe bought a Middleburg farm in 1905, and the Ramagaga family acquired over eleven thousand acres of good land nearly half a century later; but black owners remained rare in the Transvaal and almost non-existent in the

Orange Free State. Even so, share-cropping could bring reasonable returns: after a lifetime of hard work, and a number of errors and misfortunes, the old patriarch Kas Maine, whose life is described in Charles van Onselen's fine book *The Seed is Mine*, was able to provide satisfactorily for his numerous dependants.[13]

Efforts were made, both by private owners and public institutions, to help small farmers. The Vereeniging Estates provided loans to assist their black tenants, together with stock and implements. A proportion of British loans and grants went to republican farmers. Inevitably, however, small independent farmers – almost all white – were squeezed out, forced into share-cropping alongside blacks, working for 'low wages, or declining into abject poverty'. Poor whites were no new phenomenon – lack of pigmentation did not inevitably bring prosperity. Anthony Trollope in 1877 had found English beggars and white navvies working for less than half black wages, and impoverished, wandering, unqualified '*meesters*' had characterized rural society for longer; but white poverty became increasingly evident after 1902, and a fertile ground for discontent, exacerbated by a series of droughts and poor harvests between 1903 and 1908.[14]

While the crown colony form of government established in the former republics allowed no popular representation, the Legislative and Executive Councils being entirely government-nominated, the rights of free speech and free press were assured and, in the Transvaal, improved. New political parties were able to appear headed by Botha, Smuts and Hertzog, all former commando leaders. Louis Botha, forty years old in 1902, was unquestionably the senior. A burly fighter of great personal charm and natural gifts, but subject to fits of depression, he made an ideal partner for the more capable Smuts. Botha's bluff honesty gave credibility to Smuts' equivocal pronouncements; like many intellectuals, Smuts expressed himself in such a way that he could justify one set of opinions to himself while seeming to satisfy entirely opposite views; he was frequently, for example, called upon to explain away policies offensive to non-whites to such friends of the natives as the English Quaker Clarke family. Both Smuts and Botha put themselves firmly behind the new order, and became imperialists, to a sometimes embarrassing degree. But Hertzog remained an Afrikaner nationalist, defending the language and traditions of his people, an honourable man, but with few immediately attractive qualities. Between them these three were to be continuously in power for the first thirty years of the new South Africa, until Smuts' electoral defeat in 1948.

Botha and Smuts in the Transvaal led the formation of a new party, 'Het Volk', while in the Orange Free State Hertzog inspired a parallel organization, 'Orangia Unie'. Reflecting both the character of the leaders and the more recalcitrant Orange attitudes towards the peace settlement, Het Volk was less anti-British than Orangia Unie, but both parties attached much importance to reinforcing the status of Dutch, or, as it was rapidly becoming, Afrikaans, and vigorously opposing Milner's efforts to establish English as the major language.

Giving a foretaste of what was to happen forty years later in Europe, the victors in South Africa paid heavily for their success. Between 1902 and 1910 the Cape accumulated a deficit of nearly £3 million and Natal a smaller one of £700,000, while the Transvaal was in credit every year, ending £5,750,000 to the good, and even the Orange River Colony, on a much smaller scale, was in surplus each of the first six years, ending up with a modest surplus of £170,000.

To Milner, once peace had been signed, the real enemy were the liberals in Cape Colony. Schreiner's government fell in June 1900 after the liberals, headed by Merriman, insisted on leniency for rebellious Cape nationals. It was succeeded by the pliant Sprigg, fortified by the unopposed election to the Kimberley seat of Dr Jameson. Sprigg, old and indecisive though he was, was capable of resisting Milner when, in the middle of the Vereeniging negotiations, the High Commissioner took himself off to Cape Town in an attempt to get the constitution suspended. Success would have given him the same extensive powers that he enjoyed in the ex-republics, and avoided the danger that Merriman would press for inquiries into the dubious practices that had taken place under martial law. Backed first by Rhodes and then by Jameson and Rhodes' successor in his old seat of Barkly West, the irrepressible Abe Bailey, Milner organized a petition to London from the Cape Parliament, requesting its own dissolution. This was too much even for the usually accommodating Sprigg, who happened to be in London for the 1902 Colonial Conference, where he made a brave defence of constitutional rights. As it happened, Milner had already scuppered his own case by publishing a letter advocating suspension only twelve days after Chamberlain had told the House of Commons that Milner was not so doing. The Colonial Secretary was furious, 'dismayed and seriously embarrassed'; Milner's credibility in London was seriously damaged, and Chamberlain decided to visit South Africa for himself. He arrived in December 1902, to be horrified by the 'ravages of war, worse than he anticipated', and to find himself often at odds with Milner, sympathetic to the Afrikaners, 'almost more to his liking than the British on the Rand', and infuriating Jameson, who called him 'that callous devil from Birmingham'.[15]

Milner's campaign had been supported by the Progressives, now – after Rhodes' death in 1902, worn out at the age of forty-seven – headed by his old lieutenant, Jameson. Thirsting to push imperialism and punish the Cape rebels, the Progressives were opposed by an alliance of Hofmeyr's Bond and Merriman's liberals, the South African Party. Leaving aside peculiarly South African questions, the division between Progressives and the South African Party followed much the same lines as that between British Conservatives and the pro-Boer Liberals. At an election held between October 1903 and February 1904 – Cape elections were long-drawn-out affairs – the Progressives stormed home, Jameson's natural vivacity and warmth going a long way to make up for his political naïveté and incompetence. Merriman, Sauer, Sprigg and all the cabinet lost their seats, and Jameson, eight years out of Holloway Prison, became Prime Minister of the Cape. Lord Milner was content. He may have been unsuccessful in getting the constitution suspended, but the Cape had returned a government he could work with.

You have only to sacrifice the 'nigger'

It was a defeat for the non-whites as well as the South African Party. The black vote was not high – less than 5 per cent of the total – but it was critical in all the marginal seats, and Jabavu, who continued to support the 'friends of the natives', was beginning to face opposition from more radical elements. Vereeniging had placed the whole question of black political rights on hold. The South African Native Affairs Commission (SANAC) was set up to recommend future policy; being appointed by Milner – 'You have only to sacrifice the "nigger"' – it was unlikely to be unduly sympathetic to African aspirations.[16] As previous hopes of a gradual extension of the franchise faded rapidly, new organizations multiplied. Many were sectional: the Natal Native Congress, founded by Martin Lutuli, uncle of the Nobel Peace Prize winner Albert Lutuli, and Harriet Colenso, daughter of the Bishop, naturally promoting Zulu interests. At the Cape the APO (African People's Organization), under the energetic leadership of Dr Abdurahman, was primarily interested in protecting Coloured rights, while no fewer than four separate organizations divided support in the Transvaal.

During the war black political groups had received significant encouragement from British liberals. The first Pan-African Conference was opened by Mandell Creighton, Bishop of London, in June 1901, and supported (ironically in view of the propaganda use later made of his name by the Smith regime in Rhodesia) by sympathizers such as the hunter F.C. Selous and influential journalists like W.J. Stead. But political weight was lacking, the Liberal Party being divided between Liberal Imperialists, supporting the government, and the more pro-Boers led by Henry Campbell-Bannerman. The conference sent a petition to the Queen, which was dismissed by Chamberlain with nothing but the assurance that 'native interests would not be overlooked'.[17]

The self-help associations were backed by an increasingly professional press. *Imvo* had been joined in 1897 by *Izwi Labantu*, originally fervently imperialist, very much opposed to Jabavu's pro-Boer stand, but becoming more radical under the editorship of Alan Soga. Sol Plaatje, a talented journalist by any standards, produced a Tswana paper, while the eccentric F.Z.S Peregrino, editor of the Cape *South Africa Spectator*, founded the Coloured Men's Protectorate and Political Association. Natal had *Ipepa lo Hlanga* and, more significant, *Ilanga lase Natal*, this last founded by one of the most distinguished of Africans, the Reverend John Dube. Son of a Nguni chief, educated at Oberlin College, Ohio, Dube returned to Natal to found the Ohlange Institute, on the model of Booker T. Washington's Tuskegee Institute.

Natalians had no need to worry about conciliating black voters, since by 1903, after more than thirty years of theoretical access to the franchise, there appeared to be only two or perhaps – opinions differ – three of them. It had been perhaps the most successful piece of gerrymandering in the history of elections. There had, however, been disappointments. Natal had harboured designs on adjacent Pondoland, the last independent polity before the Cape frontier, for some years. Successive British governments, always reluctant to let more blacks slip into Natalian hands, considered a protectorate, but could never reach a decision, agreeing with Gladstone's objection to 'creeping up the coast' to nibble off more territory. When Thembuland was eventually peacefully incorporated into the Cape Colony in 1884, rendered apprehensive by incursions of Boer farmers after 1880 – the Thembuland Trek – Pondoland remained the only quasi-independent coastal black state. As had happened with the Xhosa, the Mpondo had suffered the endemic dislocation between the 'great house' and the 'right-hand house' and had, on the death of the redoubtable Faku, split between Mqikela and his successor Sigcawu on the one side, and Ndamese and his son Nqiliso. More dissension ensued when a civil war broke out between Sigcawu and his senior counsellor Mhlangaso, accompanied by the Bhaca and the Xesibe, hitherto reluctant subjects of the Mpondo going over to the Cape.

The Mpondo were well aware of their predicament. Apprehensive about possible German intervention in 1886, the Cape government had forced the sale of Port St Johns. In reply Mhlangaso took the extraordinary initiative of writing to the Tsar: 'We are independent Nation subject to no other power up to the present self independent.' Complaining about the Xesibe's delinquencies and the annexation of Port St Johns, the Chief Minister suggested a Russian protectorate, in return for mineral concessions. The letter arrived safely in St Petersburg but, not surprisingly, went unanswered. Mhlangoso did a little better with the German Consul in Cape Town, and signed an agreement making concessions to the German Land and Colonization Company. Combined with Mhlangoso's constant quarrels with his neighbours and his enmity towards Sigcawu, this pushed the Cape government towards annexation. Sigcawu would have preferred an Imperial protectorate, but bowed to the inevitable, and the last independent Xhosa-speaking people were obliged to accept the tender mercies of Cecil Rhodes' government. One interesting sequel took place in 1894. The Cape government passed an Act allowing arrests without subsequent trial, the object being the exile of Sigcawu. Appealing to the courts, Sigcawu was able to secure his release and a stinging condemnation of Rhodes' action: the rule of law was holding at the Cape.[18]

Natalians had also harboured hopes of an eastward expansion into Swaziland. For much of the nineteenth century the Swazi had survived by maintaining a balance between Zulu and Boer pressures, under two outstanding leaders. The first of these, Sobhuza I, kept his flank secure by a treaty with Zwide while extending his power north among the Pedi of the Transvaal. After the Boers established themselves in Natal, the Swazi entered into a series of treaties with the newcomers. Sobhuza's son Mswati was able to reorganize his army along Zulu lines, creating a powerful and mobile force without resorting to Shaka's absolutism, and launched an even more extensive series of raids as far north as Zimbabwe and eastward along the coast, reaping a harvest of loot and slaves, but allowing the Transvaalers some concessions.

After Mswati's death in 1869 the Pedi and Tsonga carried the war into the enemy Swazi camp, a struggle which ended ten years later when the Swazis were 'let loose' by Wolseley in his final defeat of the Pedi. Under the terms of the London Convention the nominally independent Swaziland was tacitly recognized as a Transvaal sphere of influence, a corridor potentially linking the republic to the coast, and a source of land. With the young Mbandzeni's accession in 1874 the infiltration accelerated as, tempted by a series of presents 'ranging from champagne to greyhounds', and persuaded by glib concession-seekers, the gross and sluggish Mbandzeni signed away 'almost all the reserves of the kingdom, actual and potential': 'Practically the whole area of the country was covered two, three or even four deep by concessions.' Swazi monarchs suffered by lacking the type of disinterested missionary support that Moshoeshoe had been given by the French, relying instead on the doubtful advice of 'Offy' Shepstone, Sir Theophilus' lawyer son. An appeal for British protection was rejected in 1885, and on his death in 1889 Mbandzeni lamented, 'The Swazi kingship ends with me.'

He was nearly right, since in 1894 Swaziland was unilaterally proclaimed a 'protected dependency of the Transvaal', and the young King Bhunu forced to seek refuge in Natal. The Transvaal and British governments agreed a joint administration of Swaziland, with Offy Shepstone retaining his post as representative of the Swazi regent. Such an arrangement offered the Swazis no protection at all, merely substituting the Transvaal government for most of the individual concessionaires; after another appeal for incorporation as a British protectorate had been rejected, and with the assent of the British, the Transvaal simply took over Swaziland as a 'protected dependency'.

It proved a doubtful and short-lived asset, reverting to British protection within seven years, and not affording the Transvaal access to the sea. Lord Kimberley, at the Foreign Office for a few months in 1894, had secured the last possible harbour south of Lourenço Marques, at Koosibai. For once aggressive, the Earl anticipated German interest on behalf of the Transvaal by suggesting that a gunboat might 'accidentally appear' there: the eight-hundred-ton HMS *Thrush*, almost as inoffensive as her name implied, did so. It was enough, and that uninviting swamp became part of Natal.[19] Since the British had already taken over the coastal strip between the Portuguese colonial and Natalian borders, the Boer annexation of Swaziland did not give Kruger what he wanted, an independent access to the sea.

By 1902, when it became a British responsibility following the defeat of the Transvaal, interest in Swaziland had waned, and in the era of stability that followed the Swazi showed that they shared the considerable powers of recuperation that characterized so many of South Africa's black societies. During their century of evolution, in the course of which Sotho and Pedi influences had been at work, Swazi society had taken an individual form. Circumcision had been abandoned and the puberty ceremonies curtailed, but the most significant innovations were the development of royal ritual and the elevation of the Queen Mother, the Great She-Elephant, to a position of authority equal in many respects to that of the king, the two often being referred to as twins. It was the Queen Regent Lomawa (Gwamile Mduli) who held the country together until the young King Sobhuza II, born in 1899, came of age, eventually in 1968 to become king of an independent Swaziland.

Natal's disappointment over Pondoland and Swaziland was assuaged by the acquisition of Zululand. Dinizulu, Cetshwayo's successor, had been exiled to St Helena on the very dubious charge of treason (provoked once again by colonial action in allowing Zibhebhu, bent on revenge, back into his old territory, out of British control). He returned in 1897 only as a headman, a great falling off from royal status. In 1889 the rump of Zululand not already ceded to the New Republic had been reluctantly annexed by Britain and put under the personal rule of the Governor of Natal, who had himself steamrollered through the annexation. The new colony of British Zululand was yet another embarrassment. The country had been devastated by ten years of war, drought and several complete upheavals of the administration. A serious sustained and expensive programme of rehabilitation was essential, and it was not enforced. The British failure to assume responsibility for the future of Zululand after a war provoked by its own representative must be one of the most heinous of colonial misdemeanours; it was neglect, and lack of commitment, that caused much greater damage than any colonial aggressions. Ten years later British Zululand was incorporated into Natal and two-thirds of the land sold off, almost all to white settlers, who were by then the driving force behind the colonial government.[20]

In Natal itself Shepstone's system had been savaged partly by manipulation of the laws to damage both the traditional black communities and the 'kholwa', Christian converts striving towards a Western manner of life, the 'amarespectables', who were emerging as a literate middle class, but also by its own success. In addition the stability and security undeniably brought by colonial government had encouraged dramatic population growth, to over 500,000 blacks in 1891. An area that had been adequate enough in 1850 for a hundred thousand was dangerously overcrowded forty years on, even with increases in black land ownership outside the reserves – and this was limited when in 1903 the government, succumbing to white pressure, prohibited the sale of Crown lands to blacks. Overcrowding was exacerbated by successive natural disasters – drought, plagues of locusts, and the first invasion of rinderpest, a devastation known to Asia since the Middle Ages, but which penetrated Africa only in the nineteenth century. Less ready to take preventative measures, and with much less access to credit than the white farmers, blacks were proportionately worse hit. One perceptive magistrate wrote that 'old men and fathers would cry like children . . . at the sight of their cattle and calves, their sole asset upon earth . . . drop down and die in scores before them, cleaning out the coveted collection of a lifetime . . . the food for their children, and the wives for their young men taken from them.' Governments took decisive action: a barbed wire fence a thousand miles long was erected to barricade the rinderpest-free area; compulsory sheepdipping was enforced to eradicate tick-borne diseases. These measures, imperfectly explained, aroused indignant and sometimes violent protests from the affected blacks.

In a reflection of the Xhosa cattle-killing, this natural catastrophe undermined the whole traditional pattern of life. The old men and fathers had to rely upon the young to leave home and seek wages in the goldmines, where they quickly adapted to the values of the compound and lost respect for the impotent chiefs and elders on the reserves. The war brought an opportunity for black resilience to assert itself, with prices for produce and services shooting up and the restoration of self-esteem given by working and fighting alongside the English against the Boers, who were seen as very much the greater evil. As in the Cape the influence of the soldiers, whose camaraderie – and gratitude – were gravely damaging to the superior attitudes adopted by white Natalians, was an important factor. When it became clear after the war that blacks were meant to resume their inferior status without complaining, and indeed to accept increased taxes, a disappointed reaction was experienced. Not only taxes, but an array of new fines were calculated to intimidate blacks: in a foretaste of what was to happen under apartheid, in one year 40 per cent of the black population of Durban were arrested at one time or another. In a particularly hurtful manifestation of settler superiority, the silver medal which the British War Office had decreed should be offered to all those who had served was transformed by Natalian ordinance into bronze for non-whites. Even those *kholwa* who had risen to comparable prosperity, such as Martin Lutuli, and the survivors of those who had fought with the British against the Zulu were forced to realize that there was no hope for any movement towards freedom and equality. 'How is it,' one complained, 'you come to treat us thus, seeing that we are your people . . . When you went to fight Cetshwayo, you called us to help; we did so, and marched off to fight with you as allies. Had you called on us to fight in this last war we would readily have done so, but no demand was made for our services . . . What is it that we do that bars and negatives our belonging to you?'[21]

In such an atmosphere the old enmities between the Zulu and their former subjects who had moved to Natal dissolved. The Zulu royal house, although much diminished in authority, became a symbol of potential unity, in which the same sort of pride that the Basuto had achieved under Moshoeshoe could be invested; a pride for which the Xhosa, with their history of fragmentation, could not find a centre.

Among those who helped the British in the Boer War was Mohandas Gandhi, who, true to his non-violent principles, formed an ambulance corps composed mainly of Natalian Indians, a fine gesture, since Indians had much to complain of in their treatment by the Natal government. New language tests were introduced for immigrants, restrictions on Indian trading and a denial of the franchise were introduced and opposed by the indignant young lawyer's foundation of the Natal Indian Congress in the following year. Even more than the black opposition movements, Gandhi's was concerned only with his own people. Every bit as racist – if not more so – as the whites, Gandhi at that period despised 'Kaffirs', as he generally termed all blacks. Sir Mancherjee Bhownaggree, Liberal MP for Bethnal Green in London's East End, and Gandhi's principal ally in fighting for Indian rights in South Africa, put the Indian point of view to Colonial Secretary Lord Lyttelton on 21 December 1903. His complaint was that Indians, who enjoyed the franchise in India, deserved to be treated equally with whites, and not bracketed with 'uncivilized or semi-civilized African tribes and with American negroes', well-known for their 'lawless gratification of sensual passion'. It was 'degrading for Indians sprung from an ancient civilization to be associated with semi-savage, backward and demoralized peoples'.[22] Whilst there were understandable reasons for Indians not making common cause with blacks – their grounds for resistance were not the same, and their power bases different – the growing assertion of undiluted white supremacy everywhere except in the Cape Colony began to force Indians, Coloureds and blacks into a degree of unity.

After 1902 all South Africa south of the Zambesi was under British rule, with the worrying exception of the Germans in the west and the less bothersome Portuguese in the east. Three protectorates – Basutoland, Swaziland and Bechuanaland – four colonies – the Cape, Natal, the Transvaal and the Orange River Colony – and the British South Africa Company territory of Rhodesia were susceptible to influence from London. Lord Carnarvon's dream of a South African federation might now become a reality.

Whitehall's influence was, however, nowhere decisive; the Cape and Natal retained their own governments, quiescent and cooperative at the moment, but capable of asserting their independence in anything that affected their own interests. The two former republics called for sensitive treatment, which would lead to their quickly attaining a similar degree of autonomy. Theoretically at least, the protectorates and the British South Africa Company's territory were subject to actual control by the Colonial Office, but the paramount importance of consulting the inhabitants' wishes had been thoroughly underlined by successive parliaments; and those wishes emphatically did not include being subjected to the mercies of colonist government.

The same did not apply to the millions of other non-whites. Their interests might not be entirely ignored, but could certainly be subordinated to more pressing concerns. Only in the Cape did non-whites deploy any direct political power, with some 15 per cent of the total parliamentary vote (about 10 per cent Coloured and 5 per cent black voters). These votes were used well and thoughtfully, and were eagerly canvassed by white politicians. Coloured political activity, which in the Cape included the Indian population, centred around the African People's Organization (APO), which elected the talented and personable Dr Abdullah Abdurahman as its President in 1905. The Coloured and black share of the vote was patchy, nonexistent in many constituencies, but capable of swinging an election in others. A major opportunity was however missed when Abdurahman declined the offer of a safe seat in parliament. Although he was elected both to Cape Town City Council and later the Cape Provincial Council, this failure of the Coloured voters to return so distinguished a representative to the Cape legislature furnished a convincing argument when the right of non-whites to sit in parliament was eventually quashed.

Coloured political influence was bolstered by industrial power. In at least one sector of industry, the building trade, Coloured labour was predominant, and beginning to be well-organized. Wages, which had traditionally been somewhat less than those of whites, were being brought into balance under somewhat reluctant pressure, and when the Cape Federation of Labour Unions was eventually set up in 1918 its committee was elected without regard to race.[23]

Socially the Coloureds were also being threatened, partly because they covered so wide a social stratum, from Abdurahman, himself descendant of Malay slaves, Glasgow-trained, married to a Scots girl, with an extensive and prosperous medical practice, to drunken dropouts; all of those who were recognizable by their colour were judged by the lowest common denominator. Theatres, hotels and even churches began to close their doors against all Coloured people. At the same time privileges denied to blacks, such as those contained in the 1898 Liquor Act and the 1902 Morality Act, set aside the Coloured population as a separate community, regarded as superior to the 'aboriginal Natives', and often so regarding themselves.[24]

There had never been any question of such amenities being open to blacks, even though such emerging leaders as the Reverend Walter Rubusana, who joined Abdurahman as the only non-white members of the Cape Provincial Council, were beginning to make themselves felt. When Rubusana and others founded the South African National Native Congress in 1909 a new current of black activity began to be perceptible, but at the end of the Boer War many Cape blacks continued to follow Jabavu in cooperating with liberal whites such as Hofmeyr and Merriman in working towards a gradual improvement in their position.

A different view was beginning to be expressed in the Eastern Cape. Jabavu's supporters were Mfengu, committed supporters of the British since the 1830s. Xhosa, whose resistance had continued longer, and the Thembu were not so patient. They found an able propagandist in Tiyo Soga's son Alan, adopting a less cooperative attitude in his paper *Izwi Labantu* and looking to the Progressives for backing. *Izwi* was financially supported by Cecil Rhodes as something of a counter to Jabavu, who refused to support the Progressives. This division was exemplified in the 1904 election, when the old liberal Merriman lost his seat in spite

"DOGS OF WAR."

THE BOER AT BAY.

THE SULLIED WHITE FLAG.

Punch, an accurate barometer of British public opinion, marked the progress of South African events. The first cartoon, published in June 1899, shows a ruffianly Chamberlain and a sympathetically drawn Kruger; the second, two weeks later (5 July), has nervous *uitlander* curs facing a belligerent Boer boar; but when hostilities had begun (20 December), and the British were getting the worst of it, the Boer was immediately villainous and treacherous.

Foreign attitudes to the Boer War varied.

Left New York's *Punch* has France and Russia taking advantage of the British lion's singed paws to clip his tail.

Below Le Rire of Paris countered British criticism of its caricatures of the Queen by publishing an earlier English cartoon of Victoria, Disraeli and Gladstone.

Left 'Another two victories like this and we will have to quit the Cape,' ran the caption to this cartoon from *Simplicissimus* of Munich.

Below Given Kruger's detestation of tennis, the caption from Vienna's *Humoristiche Blätter* is apt: 'The English smart set like lawn-tennis . . . So do I.' But Kruger is shown playing badminton.

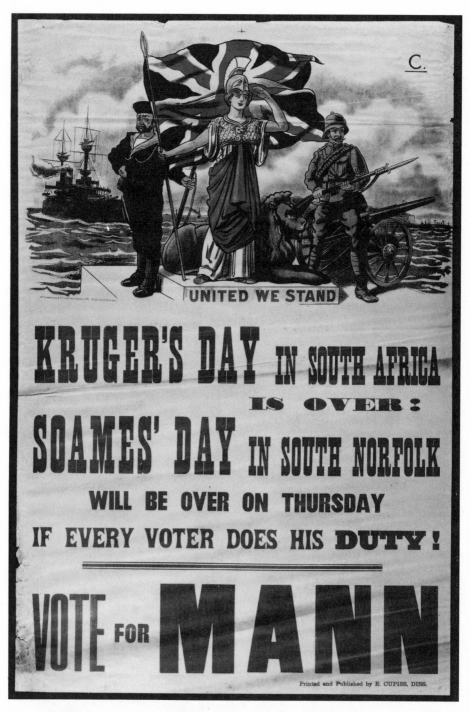

Britain's 'khaki' election of October 1900 was won by the Conservatives; but the Liberals held this seat in spite of their opponents' jingoist propaganda.

Such discouraging images as this Boer photograph of British dead on Spion Kop did not appear in British journals.

The only professional soldiers in the Boer armies were the gunners of the Staatsartillerie, here ranging their Crensot 155mm 'Long Tom' on the British besieged in Mafeking.

Emily Hobhouse's spirited attacks on the administration of Kitchener's 'concentation' camps did something to assuage Boer anger at the appalling number of civilian deaths.

Below Sir Alfred, later Lord, Milner. A study in cold arrogance.

Right Jan Christiaan Smuts:
Prime Minister, philosopher,
Boer General, British Field
Marshal.

Below The first Nationalist
Cabinet, in 1948: all Afrikaner,
all Broeders. Prime Minister
Malan is third from left, front
row. The three men seated
on the right are Havenga,
Strydom and P.O. Sauer.

The Sharpeville massacre of March 1960 was not the only, nor the worst, outrage perpetrated against civilians by police in the post-war world: but the callous attitude of the South African authorities did much to ensure international condemnation.

Right Private Eye's comment on Verwoerd's assassination.

of Mfengu support, because the Thembu vote was solidly against him.[25]

Black leadership was still being drawn from the students of Lovedale and similar missionary schools, all of whom shared to differing degrees the English Nonconformist tradition of discussion, accommodation and compromise, but some more vigorous philosophies were beginning to be on offer. Methodism transplanted to South Africa had lost much of its loyalty to principles of equality, never as strong in Wesley's authoritarian foundation as among the Nonconformists. The Methodist system of entrusting most pastoral work to local lay preachers – almost all black – under the strict control of superintendent white ordained ministers had given blacks invaluable experience, but led both to the subordination of blacks and their separation from white congregations. Such a betrayal of Christian principles led to defections, and the adoption of more relevant and valuable standards. Nehemiah Tile had left the Methodists to establish a national Church among the Thembu, working with the young paramount chief Dalindeyebo to foster an institutional expression of a specifically African Christianity. Mangena Mokone left the Methodist ministry in disgust, seeing there no 'Justice, Brotherly Love, or Christian Sympathy', to work with other Methodist ministers in founding the first 'Ethiopian' Church, an orthodox Methodist institution, 'John Wesley's legitimate child'. For the first time American influences, such as the success of institutions like Tuskegee and its inspiration Booker T. Washington, whose book *Up from Slavery* was published in 1901, began to affect South African blacks. Bishop Henry Turner visited South Africa in 1898 and ordained James Dwane, another disillusioned Methodist minister, as Bishop. Dwane, however, found that as a black he was regarded as less acceptable than American 'blacks' of mixed race and lighter complexion, and soon took his congregations into the Anglican South African communion, but the links between the influential and politically moderate American Church and the similarly inclined South African congregations contributed to a solidly-based non-colonial black Christian community.[26]

The return of the Liberals

The writing on the wall heralding the end of Milner's regime appeared in July 1904, with Chamberlain's resignation, only eighteen months after his visit to South Africa. Chamberlain was moving towards a shift in policy away from free trade to the creation of an empire protected by tariffs, a chimera destined, with the encouragement of Lord Beaverbrook, for a long life. With his most influential supporter gone Milner was discouraged, and made known his intention to resign, although he did not actually leave until March 1905, to be replaced by Chamberlain's right-hand man, Lord Selborne, a more emollient character than the edgy Milner.

Lord Milner left South Africa amid a rising chorus of criticism. While the importation of Chinese had enabled the goldmines to expand production (although the economy was still depressed), stories of conditions within the compounds were engaging much attention. Always ready to enjoy scandals, the British public were enthralled by horrifying accounts of buggery, prostitution, opium addiction and sadism. Six to 7 per cent of the Chinese were 'buggerboys' – most of them barbers or actors ('Acting and immorality go hand in hand,' one Mr Bucknill reported[27]).

After the resignation of the Conservative government in December 1905, the party having been drastically split over Chamberlain's conversion to tariff reform (Winston Churchill having crossed the floor of the House on this issue), a general election was held in January 1906. Going to the country with a cry against 'Chinese slavery' – which Churchill admitted to be 'a terminological inexactitude' – the Liberals romped home with a clear majority over all other parties, their first for twenty years, and with the Tories reduced to an unhappy minority of 167. The new Prime Minister was Henry Campbell-Bannerman, who had made his Boer sympathies clear during the war, especially by his condemnation of Kitchener's methods: 'War is not war when it is carried out by methods of barbarism.'

Although 'Chinese slavery' had been a useful electoral slogan, the Chinese workers, now repatriated as per contract, had been efficient, and their replacement by blacks, which was completed by 1907, caused no interruption to production. In the interim effective recruitment procedures had been established, bringing over 180,000 black Africans to the Rand by 1910. Goldmining's future was assured, but subject to maintaining a permanent supply of cheap labour.

On constitutional questions the new administration was able to deploy some relevant practical experience. The Colonial Office was now headed by Lord Elgin, a plodding, decent man, but as a peer banished to the House of Lords; his Under-Secretary of State, Winston Churchill, was therefore in a position of great influence in the Commons. Churchill had seen enough of South Africa as a war correspondent and prisoner of the Boers – a very rare exposure to the facts of colonial life for a minister – to be assured that a rapid development of self-government in the former republics was essential.[28] The Prime Minister was equally convinced – a conviction reinforced by an interview with Smuts in January 1906, but anathematized by Milner. Such an attitude was in contrast to that of the previous Colonial Secretary, Alfred Lyttelton, a first-class cricketer but lightweight politician. Acting on Milner's recommendation, Lyttelton had decided that the Transvaal could be offered only a modest advance towards self-government (the Orange River Colony would automatically follow), with an elected legislature and an executive of nominated officials – representative, rather than responsible, government. Ominously for black hopes, the franchise in the former republics was to be awarded to white men only.

From the Liberals, traditional supporters of black rights, something much better might have been expected; but such expectations were to be disappointed, for the parliamentary Liberals were preoccupied with other issues. In preparing their plans for responsible government the priority was so to arrange the electoral system as to give the English-speaking Transvaalers, concentrated in the Rand, a majority. The Boer leaders were not so firmly against this as might have been thought; their priority was to ensure that the Randlords were not able to ally political predominance to their financial power. Botha could speak with the knowledge that almost all Transvaal Afrikaners were solidly behind him, while the Transvaal English were divided between the Progressives, very much the mine-owners' party, the 'Responsibles', who allied themselves with Het Volk, and a number of labour groups, who also showed themselves ready to side with the Afrikaners. However the franchise was fixed, therefore, it was likely that the Afrikaners would find themselves in the driving seat of any 'responsible' government, although this uncomfortable possibility was not realized at the time by the British cabinet.

Black concerns engaged the attention of none of these groupings. No such liberals as Merriman and Sauer, old Cape partisans of black rights, were to be found in the Transvaal, and even Merriman was less than lukewarm towards non-Europeans: 'I wish we had no black men in South Africa,' he lamented, but since such was the unhappy reality, to ignore it would be 'to build on a volcano, the suppressed force of which must some day burst forth in a destroying flood, as history warns us it has always done'. The political fact was that, if a qualified franchise as in the Cape was to be given in the Transvaal, a good number of poor whites, mainly

Afrikaners, would be excluded on grounds of poverty or illiteracy. Only universal white male voting would give Afrikaners a chance of a majority.

Percy Molteno, old Sir John's nephew, exerted what influence he could as a Liberal MP supporting Campbell-Bannerman's government. Writing to the Lord Chancellor, Lord Loreburn, on 20 March 1906, he listed the injuries already inflicted on the blacks by Milner's Transvaal government: severe and costly pass laws, increased taxation, flogging permitted, walking on footpaths prohibited, restrictive labour legislation, and the offensive 'Morality Act' which provided for death for black rapists, but comparatively brief terms of imprisonment for whites[29] – most of the worst features of the apartheid laws of the 1950s and sixties already enacted by a British (not a colonial) government in the Transvaal. The taxation issue was less emotive, but staggeringly unjust. Of £446,000 raised from native taxation, £5,000 was spent specifically on the blacks, whereas in the Cape the respective figures were a rather more respectable £267,000 and £67,000.

Replying to appeals from Molteno, Merriman and their supporters, Smuts took refuge in what has been well described as 'an undefined and abstract altruism, a confused philosophic escapism': 'When I consider the political future of the Natives in South Africa I must say that I look into shadows and darkness, and then I feel inclined to shift the intolerable burden of solving that sphinx problem to the ampler shoulders and stronger brains of the future.' The essential, Smuts went on, was to keep 'Hoggenheimer' (the anti-Semitic caricature figure of the capitalist) 'in his right place politically', which could only be done by giving 'the general population and not the mining population the balance of power' – equivalent to insisting on arranging the franchise to ensure that the Rand voters were discriminated against.

Steyn wrote at the same time, rather more straightforwardly, that 'native rights' formed a vital question 'for the whole of S. Africa unless we hold with the Magnates that the natives have no other rights than to work for such wages as will increase the already bloated dividends. I am not one of those who hold that no native, however civilized, should ever get the franchise, but I will all the same object most strongly to any provision of that kind being put in the Bill for Responsible Government because if the natives have to get the franchise they must get it from our parliament, so that the natives be not brought under the delusion that only the Englishman is their friend.'[30] In fact there was no prospect at all of either of the former republics willingly acceding to demands for a non-white franchise; the

'Englishman' might be a weak, unreliable and condescending friend, but he was the only one available.

This unreliability was evidenced by the British government hiding behind the Vereeniging agreement and agreeing with the former President that the 'native question' could only be solved by a responsible government. In the meantime any black legislation would be subject to an Imperial veto, a poor protection since it was difficult to exercise against the legislation of a responsible government, and impossible to use against its executive acts. There was not only no discussion about the black vote; in none of Churchill's lively and clear memoranda concerning the Transvaal constitution was there even a *mention* of the subject. Unconsciously, but precisely, Churchill put not only his, but the whole cabinet's view of the situation when he wrote to King Edward VII on 15 August 1906: 'As I see South Africa in the years that are immediately to come, it will be racially a piebald country. Dutch and British will have to live together side by side.' In this view blacks, Coloureds and Indians did not exist.[31]

A commission sent to investigate the subject (the West-Ridgeway Committee) attempted to provide a fair distribution of seats and at the same time to ensure an English-speaking majority. The key was the weighting of votes between urban and rural constituencies. If all constituencies contained similar numbers of votes the urban, chiefly English-speaking constituencies would do well. If rural constituencies were allowed to be smaller, then the Afrikaners would produce more members; and so, astonishingly, it was arranged. Rural voters had an effective advantage of 30 per cent, a bad arithmetical mistake of the committee's. In the first election of March 1907 Het Volk won thirty-seven seats, with the divided opposition split between twenty-one Progressives, six Responsibles (now the National Association), three labour representatives and two independents. In the Orange River Colony Hertzog's Afrikaner Orangia Unie did even better, winning thirty seats to the opposition's eight. With the two republics once again under Afrikaner control, less than five years after the Boers had surrendered, hopes of British hegemony in South Africa were shattered.

As Prime Minister of the new colony of the Transvaal, Botha attended the London Colonial Conference in April 1907, taking his place among the premiers of Canada, Australia and New Zealand, entertained by Winston Churchill. A few years previously he had been at war with all those countries, but now he headed an independent government with a Boer majority in parliament. 'British interests,' he assured the world, 'would be absolutely safe in the hands of the new [Transvaal] cabinet ... Was it possible for the Boers ever to forget such generosity?'

It would have made little difference to the eventual results, but supporters of a black franchise were undermined by a sad little rebellion in Natal.[32] It began with a protest against a poll tax in which two white policemen were killed. A furious reaction followed as suspects were summarily shot, or executed – in public – after a drumhead court martial. This served only to provoke a full-scale revolt headed by a discontented and aggressive minor chief, Bambatha, supported by two great names from the past, Sigananda, who had fought alongside Shaka, and Mehlokazulu, who had precipitated the 1879 war. Assured of protection against bullets by a doctoring which included the genitals of one slain policeman, some thousands of followers joined with Bambatha. The Kaiser, anxious to show that he knew how to handle the natives, offered the services of German troops; Churchill declined, observing that 'in Natal our chief difficulty had not been to kill the rebellious natives, but to prevent our Colonists (*who so thoroughly understood native wars*) from killing too many of them.' Most of the insurgents were massacred by 10 June when they were caught in a mountain gorge and shredded by shrapnel and rifle fire against which the portions of the late Sergeant Brown offered little protection.

A secondary uprising lasted for another month before being crushed. In all over three thousand blacks had been killed, fewer than thirty whites; and it was noteworthy that these included no women and children. But white Natal had been badly frightened, and took a savage revenge. The British government objected to the first executions – 'This wretched Natal government on its hind legs again', Churchill growled – causing the Natal administration to resign in a huff.[33] Accepting London's explanations they took up office once again, but were more discreet in the eventual trials, the violent death of some thousands of blacks having mollified white indignation. In the final massacres in the Insuzi Valley the pursuers found that 'The natives were cowed and made no reply either with spears or guns. They tried to secrete themselves in caves, under stones and even up some of the taller trees;' which was of no avail, for they were shot down in their hundreds. There were no more executions. Only a few thousand of the remaining culprits were imprisoned and flogged. Natal's Governor Sir Henry MacCullum suggested a medal should be struck to commemorate the rebellion's suppression, prompting a sarcastic minute from Churchill: 'there were, I think, nearly one dozen casualties among those devoted men in the course of their prolonged operations and more than four or even five are dead on the field of honour . . . A copper medal bearing Bambatha's head' – the chief had been decapitated – 'might be suitable.' The decoration was not, needless to say, produced, but the Governor did tell Sergeant Major Gandhi of his 'appreciation of the patriotic movement made by the Indian community in providing a stretcher-bearer squad'.[34]

It should have been argued that it was the constant government persecution of Natal blacks and the denial of civil rights that had caused the violence. Nothing similar had been threatened in the more liberal climate of the Cape, and there was little in common between a warlike leader like Bambatha, renewing memories of Zulu martial achievements, and a pacific country gentleman like Martin Lutuli or so intellectual and pious a clergyman as the Revd John Dube; but continued repression and persecution would provide a uniting force.

FOURTEEN

The Union of South Africa

Flabby friends

When in February 1908 an election in Cape Colony brought in Merriman as Prime Minister the way was opened, after thirty years of controversy, for real progress towards union of the four colonies – and possibly of Rhodesia and the protectorates as well. Merriman was respected by Afrikaners in the Boer republics following his principled stand during the war, was a constant correspondent of Steyn, and represented a Cape Colony that they could accept as a partner – although Natal still remained a stumbling block. A detailed draft constitution for a united South Africa had been prepared by young Lionel Curtis, assisted by other members of the 'Kindergarten', and financed by the only slightly older Abe Bailey, now with a seat in the Transvaal parliament, who was later to work with Curtis to establish the Royal Institute of International Affairs. Curtis' eventual memorandum was edited by Lord Selborne and published under his name in July 1907. Merriman, Steyn and Smuts had also been active, both in correspondence and personal discussions, clarifying their ideas on South Africa's future. As practical politicians they did not wish to show their hands until they were in a position to control events, and held themselves aloof from the Curtis–Bailey–Selborne initiative. Putting aside the question of black rights, on which no agreement was possible, Smuts and Merriman together shaped a future constitution, not on federal lines, as in Canada and Australia, which would have been comparatively easy, but as a single strong political entity.

To a great extent it was a question of hanging together rather than hanging separately; economic jealousies between the states were leading to something approaching a trade war. Wartime prosperity had been followed by post-war depression in the old colonies, affected both by the decline in customs revenue – Cape imports fell from £32 million in 1902 to £14 million in 1908 – and railway receipts, because of the increased use of the Rand–Delagoa Bay line. Since these two sources represented something like 80 per cent of each colony's income an attempt was made to secure improvements, and an inter-colonial customs agreement was reluctantly signed in June 1906.[1] Almost as soon as the Transvaal secured responsible government Botha announced that he proposed to withdraw from the agreement, raising the spectre of a protracted economic dispute, to which the only alternative was unification. In such a debate the Orange Free State would agree with anything the Transvaal accepted, while Natal would, however reluctantly, have no alternative but to fall in with the other three. Whereas previously Cape Afrikaners, members of the Bond, had always been in favour of unification, republican Afrikaners had distrusted the idea as meaning Cape domination; but now it was the Transvaal, at last secure in Boer hands, that was acknowledged to be the most important region of South Africa, the centre of industry and commerce, with a rapidly expanding white population. Moreover, as long as the colonies had separate governments the frequent disputes between them could only be settled by Britain, in the shape of the High Commissioner, Lord Selborne. Only by unification could a real independence be gained.

With three of the colonies controlled by anti-imperialists accepting the principle of unity, a National Convention was held between October 1908 and February 1909, with delegates nominated by the colonial parliaments to consider what form a Union of South Africa might take. They were a heterogeneous assortment: fourteen Afrikaners and sixteen English-speakers, ranging from out-and-out white supremacists like General de la Rey and the Natal delegates to such dedicated liberals as Walter Stanford, a former Lovedale boy who had spent his life in the Transkei; there being no non-white members of any parliament, there were no non-white members of the National Convention.[2]

The Natalians were reluctant participants, suspicious of the whole idea, but had once again weakened their case by an outbreak of nervous aggression in which the Zulu king – now demoted to chief – Dinizulu was tried on trumped-up charges. Their preference for a federal state was firmly overruled; the existing colonies, all now with responsible governments, would, under the constitution eventually agreed, become mere provinces, with elected councils headed by an administrator. The central government would be along Westminster lines, with a Governor General taking the place of the monarch, a senate with a majority of elected members, but others nominated by the government, and a parliament in which the government would have to command a majority. In a compromise to suit regional sensibilities, Parliament was to continue to sit in Cape Town, with the executive an inconvenient thousand miles off in Pretoria, and the supreme court in Bloemfontein. The allocation of seats was skewed in favour of Natal and the Orange Free State in order to mollify the dissidents in those colonies. Most controversy centred around the number of voters to be included in each constituency. Rural voters succeeded, after much wrangling, in establishing that, as in the Transvaal, they would have a 30 per cent advantage over urban constituencies – i.e. that they might have up to 15 per cent fewer than the average number of voters in each constituency, while towns might be loaded with the same percentage in excess. This could, and eventually in 1948 did, in a historic fashion, result in a government being elected with a minority of votes cast. Reluctant backwoodsmen in the old republics were comforted by this concession, and also by the unexpected lack of opposition to giving equal status to the English and Dutch languages.

In the light of subsequent events, the key discussions were those concerning the franchise, although at the time these were treated as almost of secondary importance. Anything but a compromise on this was, in truth, impossible. The four colonies had developed in different directions to an extent that made an agreed common policy out of the question. In the smallest colony, the Orange Free State, 175,000 whites and 326,000 blacks formed together 95 per cent of the population. Although blacks there were completely excluded from political life there was some willingness among both Dutch- and English-speakers to allow modest progress. Cornelius Wessels – later Sir Cornelius – a jovial Volksraad leader, felt that 'intelligent coloured men and intelligent African land owners' should have a vote;[3] but no Free State politician was prepared to sit in a legislature alongside non-white members. Wessels' liberalism found little echo among his fellow-burghers, not least since the disproportionate increase of the black population created the menacing spectre of an eventual overwhelming black preponderance if any franchise was allowed. In 1904 the respective white and black percentages of the population were 37 and 58 per cent, but within seven years this had changed to 33 and 62 per cent.

Another picture was presented by the largest province, Cape Colony. In 1911 there were 582,000 whites, 462,000 Coloured/Asians and 1,520,000 blacks, a distribution which might be analysed as 77 per cent non-white or as 40 per cent non-black, but all having the potential to become enfranchised on equal terms. Any male adult, being a British subject, who could write his name, address and occupation and who either earned £50 a year in wages or occupied property worth £75 or more was entitled to the vote. This was no less democratic than contemporary British qualifications, which, although much more complex, were also arranged to ensure that electors were men of some substance, but did exclude most of the blacks, who still occupied tribal land. In 1909, 85 per cent of the Cape electorate was white, 10 per cent Coloured and 5 per cent black. The formula had preserved tranquillity in the Western Cape for half a century, and there remained the possibility that the eastern districts, where most of the blacks lived, would in time pass peacefully into the same system. While political power remained firmly in the hands of a white minority, hope, that invaluable factor, was pervasive.

Conditions in the other colony, Natal, were very different. The white population was but 8 per cent of the whole, somewhat outnumbered by the Indians at 11 per cent, and dwarfed by the 80 per cent of blacks. By 1907 the non-white population, more than 90 per cent of the whole, could claim between them only two hundred qualified voters, six of whom were black, and it was painfully clear that the whites were determined to so twist and contrive the laws as to allow no hope of improvement.

Hopes had never been high in the Transvaal. The Coloured/Indian population was a mere 3 per cent, with 25 per cent white and 72 per cent black. Non-whites, in addition to being denied any political rights, were discriminated against in diverse and ingenious ways. Almost the only voice raised there on behalf of non-whites was that of the imperialist Percy Fitzpatrick, the other whites, Afrikaner and English, being united in wanting to keep the native in his place; although few went as far as the abominable E.A.O. Schwikkard, representing the Natal Farmers' Congress, who claimed that 'the thing that should be used very freely is the lash, for it is bodily pain the native fears. He fears nothing else.' Natalians could usually be relied upon to be more extreme than anyone else. Smuts attempted to be all things to all men; writing to the liberal Merriman on 13 March 1906, he cordially agreed with many of Merriman's views, sympathizing profoundly with the native races, 'whose land it was long before we came here', but going on to say that he did not believe in politics for them – 'perhaps I do not believe in politics at all for the attainment of the highest end' – and was sure that the blacks would only be 'unsettled' by being allowed the franchise.[4]

There was therefore no question whatsoever of the Natal, Orange Free State or Transvaal delegates to the Convention allowing the possibility of a black franchise, while at the same time the Cape delegates were equally determined that their own black and Coloured voters should not lose their existing rights. Since eventually whatever the Convention decided would have to be approved by the British Parliament, Sir Henry de Villiers, the chairman, kept in touch with Lord Selborne, the High Commissioner, to ascertain what the Liberal government's views might be. In transmitting these, Lord Selborne, who was a Conservative, inevitably flavoured his advice with his own prejudices.

Another circumstance affecting the final recommendations was the absence of black participation. Coloureds, with Dr Abdurahman in the lead, did present their case forcibly, but the politically active blacks in the Cape, regarding themselves perhaps with a certain smugness as privileged citizens, did not. It was felt that any agitation, such as holding a parallel Native National Convention, would be counterproductive; the Cape parliamentary delegates could be relied upon to ensure black rights were protected. So indeed they could, but as it proved, with one important exception. Transvaal blacks were less sanguine, and did form a Transvaal Natives' Union, a significant development since its programme foreshadowed that which was later adopted by the African National Congress.

Attacks by Botha, de la Rey, de Wet and Frederick Moor of Natal, an unpleasant and dictatorial character, who claimed that the history of the world proved that the black man was incapable of civilization, were resisted by the Cape parliamentarians. The admirable Walter Stanford, who had become a member of the Cape Parliament in the 1908 election, asserted: 'there must be a just native policy or the white man would go under in South Africa.' Some absurdly complex compromises were explored, including one suggested by the historian Dr Godée-Molsbergen and supported by Lord Selborne, whereby a non-European would be able to qualify for the vote at the age of thirty-one if he passed the 'civilization' test, but his vote would be given only one-tenth the weight of a European's. His son would be able to qualify at thirty, with a two-tenths vote, until in ten generations, about the year 2200, a black university professor would be the full equivalent of a white labourer. Coloureds would be dealt with by having, on a sliding scale of multiple votes, half those of white men.[5]

The Convention's final decision, to leave the franchise as it was in the four provinces, was inevitable, and at least held out the possibility of future change. The Cape was a special case; its franchise had been imposed by London as a condition of the grant of representative government, and nurtured by a series of Imperial officials ready to intervene on behalf of the non-whites. Such intervention had been, sometimes reluctantly, accepted by the colonists, the most influential of whom were in sympathy with Britain, shared British ideals, and were emotionally loyal to the monarchy – although by the 1890s preventing encroachments on established rights had become more difficult. The existence of a separate class of Coloureds, who tended to follow white customs and to share similar values, made it possible to face the black majority with equanimity; at the then rate of progress it would be many years before that predominance became reflected in political power.

In Natal circumstances differed, as the fears provoked by the huge black majority led whites into defensive counter-measures that had contrived to circumvent criticism and intervention from Britain. That experience had proved how impossible it was for a British government to force the hand of what had become effectively an independent country, even when such factors as attachment to the mother country and shared values were taken into consideration. Neither of these conditions were present in the ex-republics, which had been accorded this independence without any provision for non-white rights being included in their constitutions, and where consideration of such subjects was conspicuously absent.

Few bones were made about Afrikaner intentions not only never to accord political rights to blacks in their provinces, but to remove the franchise from Cape non-whites as soon as possible. Smuts hinted strongly, and Botha stated more straightforwardly, that this would be high on their agenda. Any other attitude would have cost them their parliamentary support; democracies are not kind to unpopular high-mindedness, and throughout the twentieth century South Africa remained a parliamentary democracy in that governments succeeded each other by winning a majority of elected seats in a legislative assembly, without *coups d'état* or revolutions. The fact that apartheid governments had to play by the rules (cheating, naturally, as much as they could) while excluding most of the population from any participation has to be appreciated in any account of South African history; but then, all British electorates were composed of a minority of the adult population until 1918.

More destructive than the lack of progress on black rights was the Convention's decision that only British subjects of European descent would be allowed to sit in parliament. The question of what constituted European descent was wisely left vague. Many Afrikaners had non-European forebears, including the chairman Sir Henry de Villiers himself. Was Turkey part of Europe? Its capital was, and Ahmed Ataoullah Effendi, with a Kurdish father and a Yorkshire mother, claimed reasonably enough to be European when he stood, unsuccessfully, for a parliamentary seat in 1893. If not Turkey, why Russia? The Cape liberals could not well oppose such a ban: they had contrived to work a theoretically colour-blind franchise for half a century, without electing a single black or (officially) Coloured representative. Botha declared that 'on one point there must be no manner of doubt – they could only have Europeans in Parliament.' In the face of an absolute refusal of the two northern republics and Natal to consider the possibility of non-whites sitting in parliament, the Cape delegates backed down.

When the draft constitution was made public in February 1909, black and Coloured reaction was predictably hostile and disappointed. Although, given the implacable attitude of the former republics, there never was any hope of progress there, the prohibition of non-white membership of either house of parliament was an actual step backwards, deeply hurtful to those who had previously prided themselves on their status as electors. It brought however the start of a unified black opposition, although Jabavu still held himself aloof; he had for twenty-five years enjoyed a position of power and influence, been part of the political machinery of the Cape, working closely with the liberals. The new constitution, while freezing prospects of advance in the other provinces, protected Cape privileges. Other black leaders were not content to sit on their hands and organized regional congresses, which culminated in a formal South African Native Convention, chaired by the Revd Walter Rubusana, and held in Bloemfontein in March, at the same time that the final agreements to the Constitutional Convention were being settled there. Their objections were echoed by a conference of the APO in Cape Town, who decided to send a protest delegation to England. They agreed for the first time that 'The time has arrived for the cooperation of coloured races,' and resolved that their executive would work with the black organizations 'to act unitedly to protect the rights of all coloured races and secure an extension of civil and political liberty to all qualified men irrespective of race, colour or creed throughout the contemplated

Union'. It was not yet a claim for any liberalization of the franchise, which would have been beyond anyone's ambition at the time, but a sober and realistic plea for the extension of the limited Cape franchise to the other provinces.

It was therefore two separate delegations that left South Africa for London in June 1908: an official one led by Sir Henry de Villiers, and a second of black and Coloured protesters headed by William Schreiner, former Cape Prime Minister, Dinizulu's advocate, brother of the novelist, a man of high liberal principles but never a flexible politician.[6] Jabavu had agreed to accompany the delegation, as had the handsome and abrasive Abdurahman. They were politely received at the Colonial Office, but Botha and Smuts had been there before them. After Smuts' visit in January 1906 Botha had attended the Colonial Conference the following year, and had impressed the assembled ministers and colonial premiers with his massive presence. It was a tribute to the bonds of empire and, British politicians liked to think, their own generosity, that the General who only six years before had been fighting a dogged campaign against them was now one of their own number, pledged to loyalty to the Crown; and Miss Botha was very attractive, said to have won the heart of Winston Churchill. Confidence, it was generally felt, could be placed in Botha to do the right thing, and Botha himself was 'a sugar bun'.[7]

Schreiner's delegation was also undermined by the Cape liberals, who had in the past supported black rights, but who now considered the Union more important. Even Stanford pressed on the Colonial Secretary, Lord Crewe, that 'although he shared Schreiner's objection . . . and regarded it as a blot on the Constitution he is strongly of the opinion that the considered decision of the Convention . . . ought to be accepted.' Stanford went on to say that he was assured of 'a growing feeling and intention' among white Africans 'in favour of promoting the interests of the Natives . . . and he is confident that in the end all will work out for their true interests'.[8] Merriman, torn between a consistent, if cool and academic, attachment to equal rights and a desperate anxiety to heal the breach between Boer and Briton which Union would effect, threw his weight against Schreiner. In a memorandum to the Colonial Secretary he suggested that 'the best prospect for the elevation of the Native to the ranks of citizenship' would be in local self-government as in the Transkei, rather than through a common franchise.

If even Merriman was prepared to take that line there was no great hope for Schreiner's delegation. With the exception of the *Manchester Guardian* there was little press support; sympathy was expressed by the Quakers and the much-diminished inheritors of the evangelical 'negrophilist' tradition, the Anti-Slavery Society. Public opinion and intellectual fashions had undergone many changes since the serious, soul-searching days of the High Victorian age, of James Stephen and Gladstone. 'Social Darwinism' was pervasive, the notion that mankind was evolving from the 'lower' races, being Australian Aborigines and Bushmen, towards the higher, being whatever community the thinker happened to belong to. The Chinese, it was true, presented a problem, and the French would not agree with President Teddy Roosevelt's description of them as 'deserving extinction'.

Decent people accepted that powerful societies had responsibilities towards weaker, developing ones, and the idea of 'trusteeship', with the connotation of the trustee surrendering control, albeit at some unspecified but distant time, was scarcely dishonourable. But in 1909 other factors were at work in Britain. The Boer War had not been a glorious episode, and there was some sense of shame remaining which could be comfortably assuaged by a magnanimous gesture towards the Afrikaners, an emotion on which Botha and Smuts played powerfully. Given the atrocities committed by the Belgians in the Congo, and the behaviour of the Germans in their parts of Africa, there was not much to feel ashamed of in British treatment of 'their' blacks; nowhere else on that continent were there black doctors and lawyers able to cast a vote, in the same way as had their grandparents. They were, it could be argued, 'evolving' nicely.

When Schreiner's deputation had their meeting with Lord Crewe, Elgin's courtly successor at the Colonial Office, the minister was civil, but non-committal. The delegates were not invited to take part in the Colonial Secretary's two-day conference, which was opened by Lord Crewe's stating that the government was 'prepared to see the Bill through as it stands both as to franchise and to representation', the issues most likely to be contentious. It had already been agreed that protection should be given to existing black and Coloured rights by requiring a two-thirds majority of both houses of the new Union parliament to assent to any alteration in these. The only other point on which the British were prepared to be adamant was that of the future of the protectorates, the populations of which had 'begged not to be handed over'; their future was therefore to be subject to later discussions, it being pledged that nothing should be done until after consultation with their inhabitants. This was not done without some fuss. Lord

Selborne had 'so often assured [the government] that the conditions of transfer must be embodied in the constitution Act' that the complete exclusion of the subject was an object of considerable debate.[9]

Not much more than a propaganda success could therefore be hoped for from the debate in the House of Commons on 16 August. Both Liberal government and Conservative opposition treated South Africa as a bipartisan issue, although there were differences of emphasis. Moving the motion for the government, Colonel Seely regretted the 'colour-bar', while Alfred Lyttelton congratulated the South Africans on avoiding the error which 'had had such disastrous effects upon the American people', by 'facing the real facts' and acknowledging 'that the black races are not the equal of the whites'. Arthur Balfour agreed: 'to suppose that the races of Africa are in any sense the equals of men of European descent, so far as government, as society, as the higher interests of civilization are concerned, is really, I think, an absurdity.'

Although the radical Charles Dilke and some Liberal backbenchers opposed the restrictions on black representation, it was left to the members of the new Labour Party to retrieve some scraps of the disappearing Victorian morality. At least Campbell-Bannerman, that innocently decent old-fashioned Liberal, comforted the dissidents and showed a touching optimism in his introduction to the last reading of the Union Bill, expressing 'not only the hope but the expectation' that the new South African parliament would 'sooner or later, and sooner rather than later', agree to modify what 'almost all of us, regard as unnecessary restrictions ... from the electoral rights of our fellow-citizens'. The Bill was passed without a division, and the new state, the Union of South Africa, came into being on 31 May 1910, with the newly-created peer Lord Gladstone – Herbert, the Grand Old Man's son – as Governor General and Louis Botha appointed as head of a temporary government pending a general election.

The September 1910 election, the first for the Union of South Africa, was fought mainly between the supporters of Botha, the old provincial parties of Het Volk in the Transvaal, Orangia Unie, and the Cape Afrikaner Bond, which was in the process of uniting with the liberals into a new South African National Party, and those of Jameson, the new Unionist Party of South Africa. Botha himself lost his seat, to Percy Fitzpatrick, but his party achieved a sufficient success – sixty-six seats out of 121, with the emergent Labour Party, led by Colonel F.H.P. Creswell, DSO, gaining four seats. Although the Unionists were almost all English, Botha's supporters were an amalgam of English and Dutch, the substantial English-speaking contingent headed by the veteran John Xavier Merriman, a strong candidate for the premiership. But in spite of Merriman's long record of support for equality among the Europeans, he suffered the defect of being too English – he was known to refer to England as 'home', anathema to rigid Afrikaners – as well as too old, too acerbic, and perhaps just too clever. Botha, quickly having himself elected to a safe parliamentary seat, therefore became Prime Minister of the first elected Union government, the first in a series of Afrikaner Prime Ministers and Presidents which was to continue unbroken until 1994.

As a convinced supporter of white unity, Botha chose a cabinet which, on paper, gave equal representation to English- and Dutch-speakers and a balance between the provinces. In practice the Dutch – Botha, Smuts, Sauer, F.S. Malan, Abraham Fischer, Judge Hertzog – were of higher calibre than the English contingent. Merriman, who could not be expected to serve under anyone else, and who was suspicious of Botha's intentions towards the blacks, was omitted, and at least one minister, Dr Sir Charles Decimus O'Grady Gubbins, was a frank makeweight. More significant than the separation between English- and Dutch-speakers was the division between those who were committed to making a success of union, who included many Dutch-speakers, and those – all being Afrikaners – who still resented the Vereeniging treaty and were dedicated, in the fullness of time, to establishing a republic under Afrikaner hegemony. Judge Hertzog, who had as Education Minister in the Orange River Colony gone near to ruining the education system by his high-handed adhesion to compulsory Dutch, was the natural leader of these dissidents, and made an impossibly awkward colleague for the rest of Botha's ministry.

Chiefs of royal blood and gentlemen of our race

The divide corresponded to a differing view on the position of blacks. Botha's supporters realized that the question had to be faced at some time, and that Britain expected positive action, as had been made clear in the reservations about the future of the protectorates. But, like St Augustine, they prayed that the reforms should not come yet. Unrepentant Boers saw no 'native problem'; all that was needed was firm handling to keep them under control, which could only be done by proven Afrikaner methods.

Nowhere was there an indication of any easy contact between whites and non-whites. Even such an admirable liberal as young Jan Hofmeyr, protégé and kinsman of Onze Jan, was startled when first arriving at Oxford to find himself sitting next to an Indian.[10] On his return to South Africa Hofmeyr, who was to become the great hope of South African liberalism, lived for many years in an entirely white world, never meeting a member of another race on equal terms. He went to a white church, and spent his leisure helping boys' clubs – all white. Only the few blacks who went abroad to be educated, to Britain or the United States, were able to exchange views with influential people on normal human terms. Returning to South Africa was for them to come to a different world.

Indications that the Union government was to evince little tenderness for the majority of its people were given by a number of minor acts, of which the most significant was the creation of an all-white Citizen's Defence Force. Real discrimination began only two years later, when in December 1912 Hertzog was ejected from the ministry after a series of speeches which contained some near-hysterical attacks on a cabinet colleague. Accompanied by old General de Wet, who had never become reconciled to the new order, Hertzog founded a new party, the Nationalists. Drawing their strength from the country districts of the Orange Free State and the Transvaal, the new party contained a number of horny-handed primitives, emotionally distrustful of anything English, and especially of that turncoat Smuts, 'Slim Jannie' – Sly Jannie – too clever by half. Hertzog himself was an honourable, fair and reasonable man, but one who suppressed within himself a dangerous flow of Afrikaner nationalist emotion, rendering his political activity and even morality suspect when driven too hard. In the speech which really marked his break with Botha, Hertzog said: 'I am not one of those who always talk of conciliation and loyalty: these are idle words which deceive no one. I have always said that I do not know what concilation means.'[11] Intellectual backing to the Nationalists was given by the misleadingly unimpressive figure of Dr Daniel François Malan, a contemporary of Smuts at Stellenbosch who had sat out the war in Holland, and became the editor of the Cape newspaper *De Burger*.

Understandably worried about Hertzog's defection, the reorganized Botha government attempted to conciliate its country supporters by passing the first really significant piece of legislation designed to deal with the 'native problem', the Natives' Land Act of 1913, somewhat surprisingly introduced by J.W. Sauer, one of the Cape liberals and generally pro-black.

The Act's intention was to effect a geographic separation between blacks and whites by restricting black land purchases outside the reserves – which were to be increased – and other designated areas. Share-cropping was to be forbidden, forcing blacks into paid employment by ending their cooperation with white owners.

The immediate influence of the Act was restricted by its not being applied in the Transvaal or Natal until a commission – the Beaumont Commission – had recommended what extensions to the reserves should be made. In the Orange Free State, however, where reserves were minimal – some 160,000 acres accommodating only seventeen thousand of the 224,000 blacks – the effect was much more quickly felt. Farmers had been successfully and prosperously 'farming on the halves' – sharing the proceeds between landlord and tenant – especially on such investor-owned lands as the Vereeniging Estates. Spans of oxen, horses and modern machinery were common, in both the Transvaal and the Free State. All these were jeopardized at a stroke by the Act. Driven off the lands they had made to flourish, the black population was converted into a great labour pool. Sol Plaatje encountered the evicted families in the northern Free State, moved off their homesteads to wander with 'their attenuated flocks emaciated by lack of fodder . . . the little children shivering . . . I could scarcely suppress a tear'.[12]

There had been much disillusion among South African blacks after the British had proved themselves, in Abdurahman's bitter phrase, 'flabby friends', but new blood was stimulating resistance. Two barristers, Alfred Magena, who had attacked the Natal government's actions after the Bambatha rebellion, and George Montsioa, with a solicitor, Richard Msimang, one of John Dube's first pupils, became the first blacks to work professionally in the South African legal system. They were joined by the most influential black man of his time, Pixley Seme, a lawyer with degrees from Colombia and Oxford, connected to the Swazi and Zulu royal families – he married a daughter of Dinizulu. Very sure of himself – he once pulled a gun on some whites who tried to throw him out of a first-class railway carriage – and with no inhibiting obligations to any existing political groups, Seme had already suggested to Schreiner's London deputation the formation of an African Native Congress, and on his return to Johannesburg he lost no time in making the idea reality. 'The demon of racialism,' he wrote in *Imvo* on 24 October 1911, using the word in an unfamiliar sense, 'the aberrations of the Xhosa–Fingo feud, the animosity that exists between the Zulus and the Tongas, between the Basuto and every other Native must be buried, and forgotten. We are one people.'

Jabavu, in the process of founding his own South African Races Congress, was still being difficult, but other leaders flocked to Bloemfontein for the first meeting of the South African Native National Congress in January 1912. It was a sedate affair, a middle-class, Christian, missionary-educated assembly, combining 'chiefs of royal blood and gentlemen of our race', in Seme's opening words. All paramount chiefs, including those of the Thembu, Rolong, Basuto, Bechuana, and Mpondo, along with the demoted Dinizulu, were to form a sort of upper house, representing the blacks still living under traditional law, 'in a state of transition from barbarism to civilization'. In spite of their disappointment over the Union Constitution, the delegates at Bloemfontein were still prone to rely on what Dube, the first President, called 'the sense of common justice and love of freedom so innate in the British character'. Of the first officers – Seme being Treasurer and Rubusana a Vice-President – only the Secretary, Sol Plaatje, was approaching a properly cynical realism. It did not take long for disillusionment to set in.

The Natives' Land Act provided the first major cause. It was not the principle of segregation that was in itself objectionable; that had proved a valuable protection in Natal. The annual meeting of the new Native Congress voted to send another delegation to London, protesting against the other aspects of the Act, but asking that the territorial segregation policy should formally be agreed, to 'form the basis of an undertaking as a native policy by the Imperial and South African Governments'.

With only a limited constituency in England – the expiring Aboriginal Protection Association and the emergent Labour Party – black objections had little force. J.H. Harris, Secretary of the APS, was particularly unhelpful, and supported Botha in spite of the spirited objections of Saul Solomon's splendid widow Georgiana and Jane Unwin, daughter of Richard Cobden.[13] The complaints of the South African Indians, however, had powerful backing from the Viceroy himself, Lord Hardinge, in Delhi, and the remarkable talents of Mohandas Gandhi on the spot. There was reason for complaint, since Indians had suffered an ingenious series of discriminatory laws. Natal had imposed an annual tax on those Indian labourers who exercised their right to remain, and denied their tenuous right to vote on the excuse that India did not have representative government (but the male population did have a franchise, albeit limited). Further immigration was reduced by insisting on a test in a European language (which could be chosen by the authorities: few Indians were fluent in Norwegian). The Transvaal had passed discriminatory pass, trading and property laws, and the Orange Free State had since the 1880s enforced strict limitations on Indian immigration and enterprise. After Union little improvement had taken place, and indeed an iniquitous judgement in 1913 had banned the entry of all non-Christian wives – and Christians formed only a modest proportion of Indian wives.

Gandhi had been developing his method of passive resistance – *satyagraha* – for some years. Drawing upon great reserves of patience and determination, this involved simply refusing to obey unjust laws, and quietly taking the consequences. In a society in which the rule of law was respected, and where official violence was strictly limited, passive resistance worked well; that it would not do so in the face of more violent regimes has since been abundantly proved. Thousands of men and women were gaoled for tearing up passes and other minor infringements. In a speech made in November 1913 Lord Hardinge declared 'the sympathy of India, deep and burning, for those passive resisters who were being dealt with by measures which could not for a moment be tolerated in any country that claims to be civilized'. The South African government, backed to the hilt by the Governor General, was furious. Lord Gladstone was not cut from the same stuff as his father: 'Is there nobody better?' King Edward had asked when his name had been advanced; 'a poor specimen', 'human but stupid', according to Merriman. While Gladstone worried, Lord Crewe, now at the India Office, supporting Hardinge, and 'Lulu' Harcourt at the Colonial Office, backing Botha, snarled politely at each other across Whitehall. Lord Ampthill, a former acting viceroy, intervened, backing Gandhi and attacking Gladstone's 'prejudiced and one-sided views'.[14]

Reluctantly, Botha agreed to a joint commission to examine South African Indian rights, as long as there were no brown Indians on it, which caused a wave of natural indignation among Indians; but Gandhi worked for a compromise which ended some aggravating restrictions while leaving others, especially those on residence and trading, unreformed. Lord Crewe mollified a deputation led by the able and 'very gentlemanlike' G.K. Gokhale, a member of the Viceroy's council. Crewe, the innocent idealist, explained that the South African ministers were anxious to deal out fair treatment, but were 'hampered by public opinion . . . and a degree of racial prejudice of which they themselves, as individuals, are largely free'. Racial prejudice, rather than a disinterested struggle for equality, was very much at the bottom of the Indian case. Quite as much as any white, Gandhi and his followers resented the 'mixing of the Kaffirs with the Indians'. Smuts, at least, was able to sympathize with these sentiments. He and Gandhi, who was 'if anything more deeply in love than Smuts was with the British constitution and the habit of British compromise',[15] maintained a friendly relationship throughout their disputes. Gandhi left South Africa in July 1914, as other events began to occupy the attention of all concerned.

'You cannot govern South Africa by trampling on the Dutch' – Cecil Rhodes

The outbreak of war in Europe in August 1914 provoked an immediate crisis in South Africa. Just over twelve years previously Afrikaners and Britons had been at war, a war which the British had all but forgotten about, but which was still a bitter and recent memory for numerous Afrikaners. German support for the Boers, both moral and material, had been enthusiastic, many Afrikaners were themselves of German descent, and the Germans in South-West Africa were on the border, although not presenting much of a threat. Good reasons could be advanced for staying out of a thoroughly unnecessary war, and most Afrikaners – 95 per cent, according to one of Merriman's correspondents – wanted to remain neutral; but Botha and Smuts were enthusiastically, even perhaps romantically, dedicated to Imperial solidarity. They had sat together on the steps of the throne when the Act of Union was proclaimed, and Smuts continued to the end of his long life to be a symbol of Empire and Commonwealth unity. As soldiers they had pledged loyalty to the King Emperor, and they kept their words.

Other old soldiers had more flexible notions of honour. Colonel Manie Maritz, although an officer in the new Defence Force, had been plotting a rebellion at least since 1913. Maritz, who survived to become an enthusiastic admirer of Adolf Hitler, protesting against the 'rule of Englishmen, niggers and Jews', lost no time in taking his supporters to the safety of German South-West Africa, leaving the fighting to be done by other rebels, including old General Koos de la Rey, veteran of many wars since the 1865 fight against the Basuto. It seemed to these dedicated republicans that an opportunity had arrived to dissolve the Union and regain their former independence. De la Rey, by then quivering on the brink of senility, was accidentally shot in a police block before he could take the field. General Beyers, the commanding officer of the Defence Force, protested on 20 September that he had no thought of rebellion, but was under arms a month later. Maritz was joined by another renegade, Major J.C.G. Kemp, who also fled to the Germans. Another old General, Christiaan de Wet, joined the rebellion, but was soon captured.* Although the rebellion was quickly suppressed by the government, using only Afrikaners as far as possible in order to minimize bad feeling, the moral effect was ruined by the subsequent execution of one young officer, Captain Jopie Fourie, on something of a technicality. Abundant reasons could be found for shooting the ringleaders, but they were too popular to be harried, and were allowed to drift back into political life. Fourie's death, at the hands of an Afrikaner firing squad, on the orders of General Jan Smuts, after his capture by President Pretorius' grandson, nevertheless joined the mythology of British persecution, to be treasured as yet another example of British wickedness. While fewer Afrikaners joined the rebellion than elected to fight the Germans, there was much resentment of what seemed to be government policy dragging behind British coat-tails. The rebellion had been almost a party affair – Deneys Reitz described it as 'a domestic dispute ... while not every Nationalist was a rebel, it is literally true that every rebel was a Nationalist'. Hertzog, who had been ambivalent about the rebellion, took advantage of this, and reaped the benefit in the October 1915 election when his party polled seventy-seven thousand votes against Botha's ninety-five thousand, although the Nationalists only gained twenty-seven of the 130 seats – sixteen of these in the Orange Free State, Hertzog's home ground, where only one seat was not won by a Nationalist.

Reason enough could be found for Afrikaner bitterness. Twelve years had not been long enough to repair the damage to farms or to efface memories of concentration camps. New, more expensive methods of farming, greater use of machinery, increased fencing as agriculturalists displaced pastoralists, exerted new pressures on small farmers. When farms were divided equally among all heirs according to Dutch law, valid in the republics until 1902, fragmented holdings were often too small for viable working. One heir found himself entitled to a 148,141th share in a farm; thirteen

---

* The decidedly shaky grasp of legal and moral issues that survived half a century later is demonstrated by Dr van Schoor's article on de Wet in the *South African Dictionary of National Biography*, where his capture by the forces of the government he was in rebellion against, having jettisoned his oath of loyalty, is ascribed as due to 'treason'.

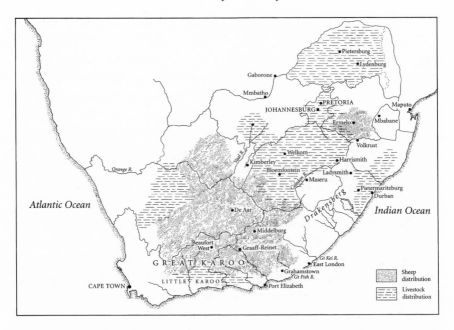

MAP 10   *Livestock distribution*

others shared the same seventeen acres of land. Independent farms grew
rarer, and landless labourers, '*bywoners*', more common. Their poverty was
often absolute – malnutrition and lack of clothes were frequently reported
– and even when only relative was contrasted with the comparative affluence
of the English-speakers. A consciousness of economic inferiority was added
to the resentment of cultural superiority assumed by the English-speaking
gentry, even those who were Afrikaner by birth; Smuts, for example, always
wrote to his wife in English, and was considerably more fluent in English
than in Dutch.

Unlike their leaders, the rank and file rebels had taken no oaths of loyalty
to the Union. Suspecting, correctly enough, that the apparent magnanimity
of the British in restoring self-government was also the disposal of an
embarrassing inheritance and represented a considerable convenience,
especially to the Johannesburg businessmen, the *bywoners* had little sympathy with either Botha or Smuts; Hertzog, with the increasingly influential
Cape support of Dr Malan and *De Burger*, was their only political hope
for the restoration of republican rule. Comfort was sought by recalling past
exploits and finding new martyrs to commemorate. Beyers, drowned in the

rebellion, and Jopie Fourie, executed by his own people, became prominent among these. New organizations, 'Helpmekaar', and Ds J.F. Naudé's labour colony were established to relieve poverty and to pay the fines levied on the rebels. When labour opportunities were available, however, they were often rejected as 'Kaffir work', not fit for white men, however poor and illiterate they might be.

If it was bad enough feeling inferior to white English-speakers, it was much worse being confronted by blacks and Indians who were richer, better-educated, and immersed in English culture. Such men as Silas Molema, owner of prosperous farms and businesses, who cooperated with Jameson in his raid, or his son Dr Joshua, or Dr Alfred Xuma, with qualifications from the United States, Hungary and Britain, driving round Johannesburg in a new motor car, were objects of intense jealousy, and concrete proof that blacks were capable of rising to the highest level. It became essential for unsuccessful whites to keep the blacks 'in their place' and ruthlessly assert white '*baaskap*' – absolute supremacy.

Running parallel to the assertion of white supremacy was the development of organized white labour, fighting their corner against the employers on the one hand and black competition on the other. A modest degree of solidarity between Afrikaner and English workers was achieved, it being accepted that British-trained – mostly in fact Scots – organizers were most effective, but the divide between the mainly English-speaking industrial workers and the Afrikaner farmers remained wide. The first strike action, in July 1913, was an unqualified success, Botha and Smuts being forced into a meeting with the strikers. Thomas Baines' Transvaal Federation of Trades was recognized, the strikers reinstated, and a government grant of £50,000 made to those strike-breakers – 'blacklegs' – whose dismissal had been forced.

A repeat performance attempted in 1914 proved an equally clear failure. When the railwaymen sparked off a general strike in January, Smuts, as Minister of Defence, declared martial law and called out the new Defence Force. As de la Rey's burghers rode in 'as if they had come straight from the veld with their dirty old patched trousers and shaggy beards', one irate Scotchman commented: 'They're a dirty lot of buggers . . . Just fancy their commin' in to pit doon us Britishers.'[16] Smuts followed up the military intervention by the deportation of the strike's leaders, a dubiously legal act, and the passage of legislation greatly increasing strike-breaking powers. Black strikes were dealt with a good deal more harshly than white. Disturbances in Johannesburg during July 1913 were brutally suppressed, more than twenty strikers being shot dead. One witness reported: 'I was through the war with the 1st Cavalry Brigade but I have never seen such a sight.' Less formally, in January 1914 sixteen blacks were killed by white workers in the Jagersfontein diamond mines.

One result of the disturbance was a boost to the fortunes of the South African Labour Party. Like the British party, the South African equivalent, founded by Colonel Creswell, was never very socialist – the left-wingers soon left – remaining committed to the Crown and constitution. *Unlike* the British party, which worked closely with the trades unions in the sectional pursuit both of labour interests and a wider, more generous political liberalism (with occasional lapses), the South African Parliamentary Labour Party combined with the *white* trades unions to press for *white* workers' advantages, often to the detriment of the great majority of wage-earners, and in most decidedly illiberal ways.

Black conditions in the Rand mines were frequently deplorable; wages were a fraction of those accorded to whites, the death rate reached 6 per cent a year, accidents were frequent and lung diseases and malnutrition endemic. Some improvement resulted from government regulation in 1905 and the introduction of controlled compounds, following the Kimberley example, but six years later a worried Lionel Philips, old 'Reformer' and partner in Wernher Beit, was still pressing for bacteriological research and lamenting the carelessness of managers which had resulted in the damning indictment constituted by the mortality figures. The low-yielding Reef deposits demanded quantities of cheap labour, be it Chinese or black, for their profitable exploitation. Creswell had made an effort to run a mine without black labour, but found it economically impossible. The problem of reconciling this economic imperative with a degree of social and political equity remained to plague South Africa, and to some extent remains still.[17]

Once the rebellion had been crushed, Botha began a successful little war in South-West Africa. It was not too difficult, since the Germans were outnumbered ten to one, and the total casualties – 530 killed and wounded – were fewer than those incurred in the rebellion; but the spectacle of British and Boer cooperating within weeks of the suppression of the rebellion was hopeful. Former followers of Rhodes, unrepentant capitalists like Abe Bailey, who had been a conspiratorial 'Reformer' and served with General Pole-Carew in the Anglo–Boer War, were now fighting alongside their old enemies (Bailey was on Botha's staff, receiving the Croix de Guerre for his part in the final action). Some differences continued between the British troops, who complained that the burghers only fought when it suited them, and the burghers, who resented what they saw as stupid regulations and unnecessary discipline. Smuts, holding the fort in Pretoria, had to cope with supply problems, which included a shortage of toilet paper. Horseshoes were used as a substitute; understandably, one officer reported that his men complained, 'Ik kak onder protest.' Smuts promised to do his best.[18]

Sound strategic reasons could be advanced for the war in South-West Africa – it would have been impossible for South Africa, not only as an ally, but as a constituent of the British Empire, to have left the German forces there undisturbed, and the eventual inevitable addition, in whatever form, of South-West Africa to the Union was seen as correcting the British government's earlier failure so to do. South African troops also took part in the German East Africa (Tanganyika) campaign with Indian and British contingents, this time under Smuts, now acting as a British General,[19] and on the Western Front, where the South Africa Brigade suffered terrible losses in the 1917 Somme offensive. Brigadier Henry Lukin, who had fought at Ulundi thirty eight years before, took the South Africans into Delville Wood on 14 July with 121 officers and 3,032 men; a week later five officers and 750 men reported for duty. Such imperialist exploits by the 'damned khakis' were looked upon with scorn by many Nationalists, more than ever convinced that Smuts and Botha were traitors to the *volk*.

On the outbreak of war thirty-four thousand blacks volunteered for the South-West Africa campaign, but were employed only on non-combatant duties. More than twenty thousand went overseas as members of the South African Native Labour Contingent. 865 of them died, including 615 calmly singing hymns in the best Imperial tradition when the steamer *Mendi* was lost off the Isle of Wight. Those who returned had learned much from their experience, which had been one of welcome from many of the rank and file, especially from their colleagues of the British labour battalions, and much condescending and illiberal treatment from officialdom. Blacks were segregated, locked in compounds and banned from fraternization with Europeans as 'subversive to discipline'; and at least one fatal riot had to be suppressed. On the other hand Jason Jingoes, one of the volunteers, remembered how impressed they all were by the King himself visiting their unit, telling them that 'You also are part of my great armies fighting for the liberty and freedom of all my subjects of all races and creeds throughout the Empire'; fine words, but never translated into actions for South African blacks. One of the most positive aspects of the Native Labour Contingent was that blacks from many African communities worked together in a different atmosphere, doing much to break down traditional enmities.[20]

Black enthusiasm was severely damaged when the Beaumont Commission, set up to investigate potential reserves, finally reported. The commission admitted that the existing reserves could accommodate no more than half the black population; even the good arable land – not that there was much of that – was rapidly exhausted by poor farming methods. Over one and a quarter million blacks lived on European land, and it was estimated that another 17.6 million acres must be allocated to blacks if the policy of segregation was to be implemented. Given the power of the farming lobby, and the general lack of concern, this was an impossible target, and was never remotely approached; but segregation nevertheless continued to be enforced. A Native Administration Bill attempted to separate 'native' from European administration. It was the kernel of what later became the fully-fledged system of apartheid, with separate legislative bodies and administrations for blacks, leaving the parliamentary system for whites – and perhaps Coloureds.

Opposition to the Bill was widespread. The old Cape liberals were still led by Merriman, who, quite accurately, wrote: 'this most ill-judged measure will reduce the Natives to the condition of serfs.'[21] Chief Kgama obtained a judgement against it – the courts continued to afford some protection; and the SANNC revoked its support of segregation. Congress's June 1917 meeting was stormy; Sol Plaatje was offered, but rejected, the presidency, and both John Dube and Selope Thema resigned, to be replaced by Sefako Makgatho, a moderate Methodist lay preacher, and Saul Msane, an outspoken Zulu opponent of Dube, also a Methodist lay preacher. Makgatho was a man of outstanding ability who for many years provided much-needed stability to the Congress.

There were other, less visible, signs that the whites had little intention of sharing power. Isaiah Bud-M'belle, the first black to be accepted into the Cape Civil Service, was sacked in December 1915; Plaatje, taking his sick daughter to the Aliwal North hot springs, was refused admittance.

In spite of previous disappointments, the SANNC decided at the end of the war to send another deputation to London. There were the added incentives of countering a deputation which Hertzog as leader of the parliamentary opposition planned to take, and of the possibility of raising their case at the Versailles Peace Conference. The Hertzog Freedom Deputation of Nationalists pleading for revocation of the Act of Union and the restoration of the republics had no chance of success, and was dismissed with little sympathy; the SANNC delegation had not much better prospects, but did achieve a moral victory. It was given a fair wind by the liberal South African minister F.S. Malan, and courteously received by the Colonial Office. Leo Amery, at that time second in command there, knew Africa well; he had been the *Times* correspondent during the Boer War, had written the seven-volume history of the war and had worked closely with Milner. Now Colonial Secretary and in the House of Lords, Milner had been rehabilitated and invited to become one of the war cabinet, where, by an ironic turn of fate, he was placed next to Smuts. Although Amery was privately convinced that the South African government was following a dangerous path by their attack on non-white rights, he could, being bound by the constitutional doctrine of 'responsible' government, do nothing other than repeat the impossibility of British interference in South African domestic affairs.

The deputation was soothed by their polite reception in London and an enthusiastic welcome on Tyneside, chaired by Sir Hamar Greenwood, the local MP and a supporter of black rights, who, by another quirk of fate, was shortly to launch the Black and Tans on the Irish. A sharp reminder of South African realities was administered when, leaving Plaatje in London, the rest of the delegation attempted to board the Union Castle liner *Edinburgh Castle* for their return. They were met by resentful South African ex-servicemen, angry that mere blacks should be allowed to travel in relative comfort while they were crowded in hammocks; in order to avoid a riot the deputation was not allowed to board. Hertzog's delegation had suffered a similar affront, when the Union Castle sailors at Cape Town refused to carry them, forcing the republicans to proceed via New York, but that provoked little sympathy in England. The insult to the blacks, in contrast, caused a considerable stir, with questions asked in the House of Commons, which at least served to alert the Prime Minister David Lloyd George to the problems faced by South African blacks.

When Plaatje's deputation – Selope Thema was the most important member – came to Downing Street they were well received. Plaatje was a persuasive publicist, and Lloyd George was impressed. Ignoring Colonial Office advice that 'the less said the better', Lloyd George listened 'with some distress' to 'their very clear and able and temperate speeches', and wrote to Smuts presenting the deputation's case:

> I was greatly impressed by the ability shown by the speakers. They presented their case with moderation, with evident sincerity, and with power. It is evident that you have in Africa men who can speak for native opinion and make themselves felt, not only within their country, but outside. I am sure you will be impressed by them, and I am equally sure that you will be able to remove the impression which seems to rest there at present, that they cannot get people in authority to listen to them with sympathy.

Although the Prime Minister's confidence was misplaced, it was a remarkable tribute that he compared Plaatje's delegation favourably to that of Hertzog. 'The contrast between the case made by these black men and by the deputation headed by General Hertzog, was very striking,' he wrote in a private letter to Smuts, and concluded: 'if they do suffer under disabilities and if they have no effective mode of expression it is obvious that sooner or later serious results must ensue'.[22]

If the failure of the London delegation was not enough alone to convince the SANNC that constitutional advance was unlikely, changes in South African politics reinforced the message. In August 1919 Louis Botha died, and was succeeded as Prime Minister by Smuts. During the war Botha had remained at the helm while Smuts was first leading his less than entirely successful campaign in German East Africa (Merriman scathingly described it as two sets of blacks killing each other for the privilege of deciding who was going to rule them) against General von Lettow-Vorbeck, one of the ablest commanders of Word War I, and subsequently establishing himself as an international statesman.

Botha and Smuts together represented South Africa at the Versailles Peace Conference, where they were much concerned at the contrast between the revengeful Allied treatment of the defeated Germans and that of the Boers by the British. Smuts made his objections to the harshest terms manifestly clear, warning the British delegation in May 1919 that he would hesitate to sign a treaty which would only ensure that 'the fires will be kept burning and the pot be kept boiling until it again boils over, either in a new war, or in the breakdown of the European system under the onslaught of social and industrial anarchy'. He also made personal appeals to President Wilson and Lloyd George, ending one with an emotional appeal to the Prime Minister: 'This treaty breathes a poisonous spirit of revenge, which may yet scorch the fair face – not of a corner of Europe, but of Europe.'

If Smuts had little success in modifying the Versailles terms, he was influential in the formation of the League of Nations. The idea of such a post-war settlement had been floated for some time, but Smuts' pamphlet 'The League of Nations – A Practical Suggestion', if not a blueprint, was a detailed sketch of what the League was to become, indicating the machinery that would be necessary, and foreshadowing such institutions as an International Labour Office. One point in particular is interesting – the insistence that the League should not be a mere debating society: 'We want an instrument of government which, however much talk is put into it, will grind out decisions at the other end.' To effect this, boycotts, although powerful, would not be sufficient: 'A powerful military state may think that a sudden military blow will achieve its objects . . . the obligation on the members of the League to use force . . . should therefore be absolute.'[23]

The post-war settlement in Africa was a disappointment to Smuts. He and Botha had hoped for a major expansion of South Africa, to include the protectorates, Southern Rhodesia and German South-West Africa; having eventually taken German East Africa, Smuts also hoped that this might be exchanged with the Portuguese for Mozambique. Had this been possible South Africa would have ended up with a huge block of Southern Africa – and a great many more problems. Rhodesians, however, resisted the invitation, voting instead for responsible government, and the Portuguese were not tempted. Nor was the British government sufficiently convinced of the South African administration's good intentions towards the blacks to cede responsibility for their future. Control of South-West Africa did however pass to South Africa, but in a limited fashion under a mandate of the League of Nations. (The mandate system, later to be a source of great difficulties, was devised by Smuts himself.) As eventually formulated the South-West Africa mandate allowed the territory to be administered according to South African law, which placed its inhabitants at a considerable disadvantage compared to those of the protectorates.

However considerable a figure he cut on the international stage – and his contribution was great – Smuts had a much less sure grasp of domestic politics. A general election in March 1920 gave Hertzog's Nationalists a major share of the seats – forty-four – with Creswell's Labour Party winning twenty-one and Smartt's Unionists twenty-five. Reitz's analysis still held good, in that while all the Nationalists were Afrikaners, not all the other parties were English-speaking. Many of Smuts' South African Party were

Afrikaners, although Natal support for the Unionists made that party as exclusively English as the Nationalists were Afrikaner. Stability in such a situation could only be assured by some inter-party arrangement, which was effected by the Unionists coming over *en bloc* to join Smuts. A snap election the following year gave the enlarged South African Party a secure majority of twenty-four, the Labour Party having fared badly.

Within weeks of the election Smuts had left South Africa to reassume his role as international statesman. Chaim Weizmann asked for his services in settling the Palestine question; Lloyd George despatched him to Dublin to reach agreement with De Valera; he was everyone's honest broker, except in South Africa.

FIFTEEN

Pact and Fusion

Post-war traumas

South Africa was undergoing the same post-war stresses as other Western states, with one or two extra of its own. The war had increased industrialization, with the consequent demand for labour, and rises in both prices and wages. Organized labour, inspired by the example of the Russian Revolution, was preparing to fight, in the same way that unions in Britain and the United States were becoming more militant. Black wages had failed more blatantly to keep pace with the cost of living than had white, but when black municipal workers in Johannesburg with the unpleasant job of removing domestic sewage attempted a strike they were prosecuted under the Masters and Servants Act and given prison sentences for breach of contract. Whites, theoretically governed by the same legislation, were never so treated, and SANNC members led the protests.

Strikes and protests against the pass laws were widespread, with discontent affecting even Lovedale, that shrine of non-racial education, where a riot, partly provoked by the really horrible food, broke out. In October 1919 a large crowd demonstrating against low wages in Port Elizabeth was fired on by panicking civilians 'assisting the police'; twenty-three blacks died. A major strike by black miners was broken, with loss of life, in February 1920. Particular indignation was aroused by women being required to carry passes; hundreds of women were gaoled, until a delegation led by the redoubtable Mrs Charlotte Maxeke, President of the SANNC Women's League, a graduate of Wilberforce University in Ohio and the first black woman to make a reputation in politics, persuaded the Prime Minister to modify the system.[1]

This did not satisfy the SANNC, who wanted a complete abolition of passes. Peaceful protests, following Gandhi's example, with the demonstrators singing 'God Save the King' and the hymn that was to become the national anthem, 'Nkosi Sikelel'i Africa', were frequent. Feelings ran high, and violence broke out in skirmishes between protesters and the police. Compared to later troubles it was all comparatively low-key, with the SANNC exercising a moderating influence, and ended with formal discussions with a new government committee investigating the pass laws, which were resented not so much in principle – with more than a hundred thousand temporary workers on the Rand alone, some form of identification was needed – but on their unjust and unequal application. Congress President Sefako Makgatho, who had earlier convinced the Transvaal authorities that blacks should be allowed to use the pavements, a very considerable advance, won a number of cases in the courts for African and Indian rights, including amendments to segregation in railway coaches.

Industrial unrest took a more violent turn. In November 1921 the employers, hoping to reduce wage costs, announced their intention of ending the colour bar in semi-skilled work, which had hitherto protected white jobs. Mine-owners were never in favour of a colour bar, from no idealistic motives, but because they much preferred to use cheap labour whenever they could. After a ballot miners, engineers and power workers – all white – came out on strike, backed, logically enough, by the Labour Party, but also by Nationalists scenting an opportunity to embarrass the government. Following abortive negotiations between employers, government and unions the Revolutionary Miners' Council of Action took over; while most of the traditional unionists were still English, a good number of the revolutionary leaders were Afrikaners, who readily organized themselves into armed commandos.

Martial law was declared in February 1922. Smuts took personal charge, and a couple of days' fierce fighting ensued, with the government forces using machine-guns, tanks and artillery. There were many casualties, the fighting being widespread; among the dead were fifty from government forces, 138 strikers and bystanders, and thirty-eight 'natives'. Some of these were 'blacklegs' shot by strikers, since black miners and management contrived to keep the coalmines operating. It was hardly a triumph for working-class solidarity – one strikers' banner proclaimed: 'Workers of the World Unite, and fight for a White South Africa' – but the violence gave an opportunity for Smuts' enemies to attack him once more as a bloodthirsty tyrant.

The Nationalists made much of what could credibly be portrayed as an unholy alliance between Smuts, the murderer of Afrikaner workers, and the capitalists, still represented by the cartoon character Hoggenheimer, invariably depicted as bloated and Jewish. An alliance with Colonel Creswell's small Labour Party, equally angry with Smuts' government, presented an attractive opportunity for the Nationalists to win power, a proposal finally effected in April 1923 with the formation of a United Front between Nationalists, Labour, and communists – the latter a fact which the Nationalists subsequently did their best to forget.

Their embarrassment was soon eased by the communist alliance being spurned by the Labour Party. The Communist Party of South Africa (CPSA), founded in 1921, was beginning to influence events, but had a difficult time for some years, swayed by changes in the party line and uncertainty as to whether members' duty was primarily to white labour, which would inevitably be adverse to the interests of the great majority of workers, or whether blacks deserved specific consideration. The party began as an odd institution, a broad church sheltering many different ideas, and including some members who would anywhere else be plain liberals. Sidney Bunting was such a one, an unlikely figure as communist leader, from Magdalen College, son of Sir Percy Bunting and grandson of Jabez, the Methodist leader, he fought for the inclusion of blacks into first the International Socialist League, the left-wing malcontents from the Labour Party, and then the CPSA. He had an uphill struggle, and a purge in 1923 ensured that the executive was packed and that Bunting would not be allowed to protest against what he called the 'worship' of white workers 'to the exclusion of all others'.[2]

Smuts was always tempted by international opportunities and philosophical excursions to ignore or gloss over domestic problems. With respect to what Merriman, almost alone among senior politicians, had kept insisting was the gravest of these, the future of the blacks, Smuts prevaricated. Torn between the liberal qualities he liked to show such friends in England as the Quaker Clarke family, and the necessity to avoid alienating white votes, the Prime Minister shelved the problem as being too difficult, and best left to future generations to solve. The maintenance of public order, he considered, was a priority and an undeniable necessity, and this was done with a considerable degree of ruthlessness.

As had previously happened in times of stress, visionary charismatics flourished among the rural black communities. Some were relatively harmless. 'Dr' – the title was self-conferred – Wellington Buthelezi persuaded

Transkeians to part with their half-crowns in return for the promise that American blacks would come in aeroplanes to free them from white rule and end the compulsory dipping of livestock.[3] With more serious results a millenary sect of 'Israelites' announced that Halley's comet portended the expulsion of the whites. Armed only with sticks and assegais they gathered at Bulhoek in the Eastern Cape; refusing to be ejected from their encampment, 170 were shot dead within minutes. Similar official viciousness was shown in the suppression of a revolt in the newly-mandated territory of South-West Africa. A quiet group of Khoikhoi/Bastaards, the Bondelswarts, who had mounted a courageous resistance against the Germans in South-West Africa, protested against the imposition of a new and insupportably heavy tax on dogs.[4] The administrator, G.R. Hofmeyr, previously a parliamentary clerk, and with little relevant experience, called on aircraft to bomb the Bondelswart flocks, killing women and children, and driving the men into open rebellion. This was bloodily suppressed, again using aircraft (a tactic pioneered by the RAF in Afghanistan and Mesopotamia), leaving sixty-four Bondelswarts dead. A storm of protest was aroused, in South Africa itself, in the British House of Commons, and in the League of Nations. Smuts felt obliged to support the incompetent Hofmeyr, sidestepping the embarrassing question of how in a single incident fifty-two men had been shot dead and only one wounded, earning the criticism of the League of Nations, and adding to his own reputation for ruthlessness.

None of these events directly influenced the SANNC, which had done its best to persuade the Israelites to disperse, and deplored such charlatans as Wellington Buthelezi, but they did serve to indicate the need to develop other methods of protecting black interests. Of these the most encouraging was the Industrial and Commercial Workers' Union (ICU), founded in the Cape to represent Coloured and black workers, with Clements Kadalie as its moving spirit. Although missionary-educated and of chiefly stock, Kadalie was a very different character from the SANNC leaders. Being a 'foreign native', born in what is now Malawi, Kadalie spoke no black South African language, but proved a persuasive orator, finding it possible to establish good relations with English-speaking liberals and exercising a charismatic fascination over many; even General Hertzog made a donation to Kadalie's organization. Grassroots support was provided by the Zulu George Champion. In addition to his trades union activities the enterprising Champion also functioned as clerk, policeman, butcher, general shopkeeper, cobbler, land speculator, mail-order herbalist, farmer and general broker.[5]

Smuts' sporadic attempts to grapple with the 'native problem' consisted of a series of measures, all of which, however benevolently intended, were posited on the assumption that blacks had to be dealt with separately from whites. Although the two philosopher-statesmen were regarded with veneration, both Smuts and Gandhi were, from their different standpoints, unequivocally racist. Smuts could be insufferably condescending about 'this child-like human, the African', in whom 'there is much good which ought to be preserved and developed'. 'The natives' were always dangerously different, the principal axiom being 'that it is dishonourable to mix white and black blood'.

Believing such pernicious nonsense, Smuts' 1920 Native Affairs Act was segregationist. Providing for a Native Affairs Commission, the members of which were, of course, all to be white, it envisaged a system of black councils, with a headquarters in Umtata, in the Transkei, where the Bunga had been established in 1908. As a device for allowing a degree of self-government in such tribal territories as the Transkei, the Bunga was not without merit. Composed of chiefs, government nominees and some elected members, sitting under the chief magistrate as its chairman, debate in the Bunga was often lively. Despite the evident fact that it was little more than a talking-shop, the real power remaining with the magistrates, the very existence of such an institution preserved the traditions of debate, and did something to spread political awareness among the country people. Arising out of the Act, a commission headed by the Natalian Colonel Stallard recommended that the towns ought to be regarded as white enclaves, with blacks admitted as needed to 'minister to the needs' of the white population, confined to residence in specified areas and 'deported therefrom when he ceases to minister'.[6] The 1923 Natives Urban Areas Act confirmed these proposals while attempting to ensure that proper housing was provided. It had little effect at the time, but a dangerous principle was established.

When Merriman retired from political life in 1921 the Cape liberal tradition lost its most prominent advocate; but a new generation, prepared to work on more equal terms with blacks – Merriman never found non-whites sympathetic – was emerging. Many of these were from liberal dynasties – Justice Oliver Schreiner, Richard Solomon and the young prodigy Jan Hofmeyr, who was to become the great hope of liberal change. A visit in 1921 by the Revd James Aggrey, a spellbinding American-trained Methodist missionary and idealist from the Gold Coast who preached racial harmony, gave an impetus to liberals that led to the establishment of unofficial Joint

Councils of Africans and Europeans,[7] which in time led to the creation, in 1929, of the South African Institute of Race Relations. The members of these bodies were all dedicated, decent people, South African versions of the Colensos and Clarkes who continued to support the black cause in England, and used their influence to counsel moderation and cooperation. Given the implacable opposition of the Nationalists and the lukewarm theoretical acknowledgements of common humanity made by the South African Party, they would have done better to be more aggressive.

Aggression was still far from the minds of the SANNC leaders. In 1925 a reorganization was carried out which gave Congress new colours – black, green and gold – and a new name, the African National Congress, but no new energy. Divisions between the provinces developed. The new President of what was shortly to be the ANC, the Revd Zaccheus Mahabane, a Methodist minister, typified the patient decency that continued to inspire the institution. When it came to consider the proposals for the Native Affairs Council the Congress did not find unanimity easy. The Cape was anxious to defend its franchise, but willing to consider some arrangement for separate representation. Natal and the Transvaal, where non-whites had no political rights, were readier to cooperate with the proposed system of native councils, which the Natalian John Dube considered 'the best attempt yet made to meet the requirements of the bulk of the native people'.

With a general election due, the parliamentary parties began to manoeuvre for position. The SAP had to avoid the Scylla of losing black votes and the Charybdis of offending white racialists by paying some attention to black complaints. In the past much support had been due to Botha's personal popularity, whilst Smuts was viewed with suspicion and even hatred by irredentist nationalists as having sold out to the British. Treading delicately, Smuts gave a friendly interview to Sol Plaatje, who in turn shared the hustings with Sir Ernest Oppenheimer, the South Africa Party candidate for Kimberley. It was an interesting example both of the residual power of the Cape black vote – Sir Ernest was elected by a large majority – and the shape of political alliances. As Nationalists joined with white labour to present a firm front against black interests, only the alliance between the SAP/Unionists and the employers held out any hope for progress. Oppenheimer was not the only employer to offer encouragement to blacks: the Chamber of Mines had extended themselves to support Joint Councils and to finance such enterprises as the newspaper *Umteteli wa Bantu*, a reasonable and liberal journal. The employers hoped that calm debate would damp down discontent and agitation and avoid – above all – the need to pay higher wages, but the element of genuine concern for black advancement should not be wholly discounted.

When it came, in June 1924, however, the election was decisive. Hertzog's Nationalists won sixty-three seats, and their Labour allies eighteen, giving a majority of twenty-eight seats to what became a coalition 'Pact' government with Hertzog as Prime Minister. Many of the more liberal SAP members lost their seats, including F.S. Malan, Henry Burton, Plaatje's old ally from the 1890s, and Smuts himself, who then devoted himself for some years to philosophy, producing a book, *Holism and Evolution*, remarkable in itself, but even more so as being written by a soldier-politician. Later writers, including Arthur Koestler, have not given Smuts the credit he deserves for his originality, admittedly often disguised under some woolly prose, and it is ironic that many of the later anti-apartheid demonstrators were adherents of holism, yet ignorant of its creation by so consistent a supporter of white hegemony.

Smuts' opponent, James Barry Munik Hertzog, was to be at the head of successive South African governments from June 1924 to September 1939, a longer period than any British Prime Minister, although always with a coalition cabinet including members of other parties. Compared with the brilliant, masterful Smuts, Hertzog was a grey, subfusc character, a man of painful personal decency and modesty, his self-control sometimes breaking out into near-hysteria, but capable of inspiring trust and affection not only among those prepared to share his unyielding views but in his political opponents. Where Smuts had been a scintillating Cambridge success, an army commander, international statesman, Hertzog had an undistinguished degree from Amsterdam University (but Merriman found him 'one of the most cultivated men in South Africa') and, although accorded the title of general, had never commanded more than a few hundred men in the Boer War. His international experience was limited and hardly noteworthy: the unsuccessful Boer Freedom Delegation being only the second time he had been abroad. Hertzog was an uncompromising, unashamed South African, first and last.

In order to retain power Hertzog had to accommodate both Labour's pressure for workers' interests and the more extreme nationalists clamouring to reverse the outcome of the Boer War and to assert '*baaskap*' on the basis of the mythical traditions of the *volk*. Hertzog himself shared some of these attitudes. A dedicated supporter of Afrikaans, he habitually used the language (Smuts thought and wrote now exclusively in English), encouraged its teaching and institutionalized its use in government service. While passionately desiring a republic, Hertzog was prepared to accept the titular role of the monarchy implied in dominion status in order to placate the English-speaking community. Africa, he insisted, should be the home of all who considered themselves true Afrikaners, and this included English-speakers.

But not blacks. Although subject to normal democratic rules, liable to be turned out of power by electoral shifts, Hertzog and his successors could afford to disregard the great majority of the population, the voteless blacks. The Coloureds, it was admitted, were somewhat different, set aside by their precious admixture of 'white blood', and in his early years of power Hertzog attempted to conciliate the Coloured vote. Repressive anti-black legislation, however, was soon proposed. The Cape Franchise, he declared in December 1925 would have to go. The parliamentary system was 'the fount of centuries of civilized government, and [the European] is the result and the heir of a civilization in which the Native does not share'.

Hertzog's formal programme to extinguish black rights and perpetuate white supremacy comprised four Bills. The Coloured Persons Rights Bill confirmed the Coloured Cape Franchise and offered the possibility of having this extended to other provinces after seven years; but blacks were to be excluded, their interests to be represented by seven white MPs indirectly elected by a nominated black college, and able to vote only on 'Native Matters'. A Union Native Council was proposed as an advisory body, with nominated and indirectly elected members. Finally the Native Land (Amendment) Bill, proposed as some consolation for the loss of the black Cape Franchise, allowed – theoretically, that is – for another eleven million acres to be allocated to blacks.

Due to the provision in the 1910 Act of Union requiring a two-thirds majority in both Houses of Parliament for any Act removing the franchise, these four bills did not become law, in spite of many efforts and subterfuges, for ten years; but the challenge to black interests was clear, and reinforced by Bills which were quickly passed. The 1926 Mines and Works Amendment Act gave the Labour Party its reward by establishing a statutory 'colour bar', banning blacks from most well-paid jobs, and reversing previous court judgements that had declared this illegal; the Immorality Act of 1927, welcomed on all sides in parliament, made sexual relations between blacks and whites outside marriage a criminal offence; the Masters and Servants

Acts increased the powers of employers; and the Native Administration Act gave extensive powers restricting political activity in tribal areas. Ironically, under this Act anyone 'promoting any feeling of hostility between Natives and Europeans' was liable to a year in prison; if it had ever been applied, the National Party would have had few MPs left in freedom.

So concentrated an attack served to unite black opposition. Previous agreement to the principle of segregation, always somewhat half-hearted, was unanimously revoked. Plaatje, ever ready with a good convincing metaphor, told Tielman Roos, acting Minister of Native Affairs: 'When a Dutchman wants to trap a jackal he puts down poisoned meat. But the jackal usually walks round and round the meat and does not take it.' Blacks were not prepared to accept the bait of extra land in return for surrendering political rights. Plaatje, versatile and observant, was the equal of any white journalist, and a new generation of able speakers were coming on the scene, of whom the most impressive was Davidson Don Jabavu, John Tengo's son, named after the minister who had sought justice in the Pelser case in 1885. Another Lovedale Methodist, Jabavu junior had graduated from London and Birmingham Universities. A delightful character with great personal presence, and like Plaatje a talented musician, Jabavu, had he been inclined to say it, could have claimed that *his* father was a newspaper editor, working with such men as John Merriman, at a time when Hertzog's father was a modestly successful Kimberley baker – a comparison which would have put Hertzog's remarks about the 'heirs of civilization' in their place.[8]

The University of Fort Hare, of which Jabavu was the first member, remains a remarkable institution, having survived many vicissitudes and government hostility. Intended to provide university facilities for blacks and Coloureds, increasingly denied access to higher education, the university was a development of Lovedale, situated on the other side of the main road in the town of Alice, and was infused with the same missionary ethos. Methodists, Scottish Presbyterians and Anglican mission societies each provided a hall of residence and funds, enabling the new project to be run on a shoestring budget, but to maintain a high standard. Among its first pupils was Z.K. Matthews, who was to become the most authoritative black spokesman of his time. Such men as Jabavu and Matthews were so obviously the equal of any white South African, and superior to most, as to make comparisons uncomfortable. Matthews, with post-graduate studies at the London School of Economics and Yale, taking as his leisure reading classical texts, was able to face down even Jan Hofmeyr, the uncomfortable liberal prodigy of the Afrikaners. In the forty years or so of its independent activity an impressive number of black African leaders passed through Fort Hare, and were exposed to its specifically tolerant and liberal ethos.

Afrikaner resurgence

The 'native question' was not a priority for the Pact government; it would have been agreeable if the Bills could have been passed, but there was no urgency in the matter. The wilder republican fringe of the Nationalists was still pressing for complete independence, but the Labour Party insisted on remaining within the Commonwealth. The establishment beyond dispute of South African independence as a dominion was for Hertzog the lowest common factor that would satisfy most of his supporters. At the 1926 Imperial Conference in London the pace was set not so much by Hertzog as by William Mackenzie King of Canada, who pressed for a precise definition of dominion status, which must accommodate South African and Irish insistence on virtual independence as well as New Zealand's emotional loyalty to the Crown. That master of elegant imprecision Lord Balfour, as chairman of the Inter-Imperial Relations Committee, obliged by defining the mother country and dominions as 'autonomous communities within the British Empire, equal in status, in no way subordinate one to another in any aspect of their domestic or internal affairs, though united by a common allegiance to the Crown, and freely associated as members of the British Commonwealth of Nations'.

Hertzog was able to claim this as a triumph for the Afrikaner cause, although Smuts protested, with some reason, that Balfour's words in no way altered the previous position, arrived at in 1919. Many nationalists, who could be satisfied with nothing less than a republic, would have agreed that this was so. Hertzog attempted to mollify them by some symbolic changes, of which the most visible was the adoption, after much angry debate, of a new flag, insisted on by Dr Malan, which contained, as a concession to the English-speakers, an almost invisibly small Union flag. South Africa's independent status was underlined by the creation in 1927 of a Foreign Ministry – the Department of External Affairs – the appointment of Ambassadors and Trade Commissioners, and the separation of the office of Governor General, the King's deputy as head of state, from that of High Commissioner, the equivalent of a British Ambassador. When this was eventually done, in 1937, Hertzog, with considerable acumen, appointed as Governor General the English-speaking Unionist Patrick Duncan, one of Milner's old colleagues.

Less prominent, but of eventually greater importance in establishing the precedence of Afrikaner over English, was the careful encouragement of an Afrikaner business sector.[9] This had begun after the Boer War, inspired by a group of Stellenbosch wine merchants who founded the Nasionale Pers – the National Press – publishing newspapers and journals in Afrikaans. The arable farmers and wine growers centred around Stellenbosch represented one of the most important sources of capital in South Africa, and such men as Jannie Marais, who represented the constituency in the Cape parliament, had investments in many companies, and provided funds both for the foundation of Stellenbosch University and the Nasionale Pers. Marais died just before the first issue of *De Burger*, under Malan's editorship, appeared in July 1915, and was succeeded by Willie Hofmeyr, another of that famous clan, who became first chairman of the Nasionale Pers. Three years later the Nasionale Pers was able to provide £20,000 in order to found two new projects, Santam, a mutual insurance company, and its subsidiary Sanlam, an investment bank. Both grew to become enormously influential institutions under Afrikaner management, and provided services specifically targeted at encouraging small Afrikaner businesses.

All these initiatives came from the Cape rather than Johannesburg, the leading commercial centre but still dominated by English-speakers. Around the University of Stellenbosch (previously Victoria College), an entirely Afrikaner institution (in notable contrast to the University of Cape Town, English-speaking and mildly multiracial), and the person of Dr D.F. Malan, the seeds of Afrikaner hegemony were sown, of which the most influential was the foundation in 1919 of the Afrikaner Broederbond. In due course this secret society, under the leadership of L.J. du Plessis, an eccentric philosopher who combined National Socialist ideals with a belief in Coloured rights, became an invasively potent force in Afrikaner society. Membership, widespread throughout all levels of teaching, the professions and government, was restricted to 'ware' Afrikaners without a taint of English blood. Parallel organizations were formed to counter the Boy Scouts, Chambers of Commerce, the Red Cross, the Teachers' Association and Students' Union, in a 'corrugated iron curtain'. Everything possible was done to ensure that senior positions were filled by 'reliable' (i.e. narrow-minded and bigoted) Afrikaners.

The formation of the Federasie van Afrikaanse Kultuurverenigings (the Federation of Afrikaans Cultural Organizations – FAK) in 1929 was a Broederbond initiative, operating openly to encourage the development of Afrikaans and to foster the myths that served to unite the *volk*. Like the Broederbond, the FAK became a pervasive influence as Afrikaans replaced Dutch as an official language, which took place in 1925. This did not happen without dissension. Conservative Dutch-speakers still thought of Afrikaans as a 'kitchen' language, but to a child such as even the precociously intellectual Jan Hofmeyr, Dutch was 'a highly artificial language used only in church and reading the Bible'.[10] Once the spelling had been sorted out – and this took some time, since there were two ways of spelling even the invariable definite article, as *De Burger* transmuted into *Die Burger* – Afrikaans was a much easier language to learn than Dutch.

Hertzog's Pact government was at its best in matters of trade and industry; helped by Creswell, who forced through the creation of the Iron and Steel Corporation of South Africa (ISCOR) against bitter opposition, and Nicholas Havenga, the solidly able Finance Minister, South Africa began to diversify and to regulate its industry. Iscor became the base for a rapid expansion of manufacturing industry, which increased five-fold between 1925 and 1929, from twenty-six thousand workers to 149,000. The Industrial Conciliation Act and the Wage Act, well-thought-out and successful pieces of legislation, enabled South Africa to avoid repetitions of the previous damaging strikes and the labour unrest that plagued other industrial countries. Both Acts, however, were not taken to apply to black labour, and industries that employed higher percentages of 'civilized' labour (legislators were still too coy to call it 'white', and indeed Coloureds still enjoyed some protection) were allowed preferential treatment.[11]

Attempts were made to alleviate the 'poor whites'' condition but the problem was basically insoluble. As the report of the Economic and Wage Commissions accurately described it in 1925, the white community were being 'enabled to maintain a standard of life approximating rather to that of America than to that of Europe, in a country that is poorer than most of the countries of Central Europe, solely because they have at their disposal these masses of docile, low-paid native labourers'. By making manual jobs effectively unavailable to whites, those who were not fitted for more skilled or responsible jobs – increasingly Afrikaners – were thereby deprived of any sort of employment. An exhaustive report made by a Carnegie Commission in 1932 found that 300,000 of 1,800,000 whites, almost all

Afrikaners, could be classified as 'very poor', and attached much blame to poor education and a reluctance to take 'Kaffir' jobs, the only work for which they were in fact competent.

It did appear, however, that the docility of black labour could be guaranteed, in spite of their wretched conditions. Objections to repressive actions continued to be constitutional. Indian complaints, stimulated by efforts to tighten segregation and to control trading, were considered by a joint conference between officials and Indian representatives in January 1927. Some of the more repressive conditions were lifted, and a degree of future harmony was secured by the appointment of V.S.S. Sastri, a member of the Indian Legislative Council, a man of almost hypnotic personal charm, and one not given to excessive demands for justice, as agent general. But neither this agreement, nor soothing overtures by the shifty Dr D.F. Malan to Coloureds and Indians alike, convinced those communities; Abdurahman had been promised 'a raised status . . . equal rights, economic as well as political' by Malan in 1923: two years later Malan assured Malays that the government 'would always try to give Malays equal rights with the white man', and in 1931 he was to say that the Coloureds 'must have the same political rights as we give the Europeans . . . in principle': but Malan's principles were fluid. Some degree of unity between non-whites was sketched in a joint conference chaired by Jabavu and Abdurahman in June 1927, but a common front was not established.

The ANC reacted against the failure to make any impression on the government by moving to the left. The old missionary-influenced, mainly Methodist and Nonconformist leadership was challenged by such colourful individuals as Professor James Thaele, with his 'white sun helmet, white suit, white spats, and white gloves', and Elliot Tonjeni, inclined to communism, who spoke darkly of the need for bloodshed before the rightful owners of South Africa were restored. Both men, although at odds on policies, were like many others influenced by Marcus Garvey, a plausible but fundamentally flawed Jamaican (he was to be imprisoned for fraud in 1925) who had made a reputation in the USA as a black racist in opposition to such more conservative leaders as W.E.B. du Bois. In 1927 Josiah Gumede, who had been a member of the 1919 delegation to London, together with the communist James La Guma, visited Russia and returned full of enthusiasm – this was before the worst of Stalinism became apparent – for the 'New Jerusalem', a land of equality and freedom.

Clements Kadalie's ICU resisted leftward pressure. Kadalie's reaction to the Hertzog proposals was to call a day of prayer and to organize support in London and Geneva. Pressed to take more positive action by the communists on his national executive, Kadalie had them all – five of eleven members – expelled, an action reinforced by the 1927 annual conference, which by a majority of two hundred to five banned any member from identifying themselves in any way with the Communist Party. The ANC proved somewhat more sympathetic to communism. When, at a combined ANC/communist meeting, Gumede called on the people of Africa 'to unite with the only country in the world where freedom existed ... Workers' Russia', the conservative chiefs were horrified, but Gumede did succeed in being elected President General in succession to Mahabane, with a card-carrying communist, E.J. Khaile, as Secretary General.

A similar division between left and right in the government deepened at the same time. The – largely English – Labour movement had never been entirely comfortable with its members sitting in a Nationalist government that seemed to be growing progressively more anti-British. When the controversial Native Franchise Bills eventually, after a tediously long passage in committee, came before the House in February 1929, having been considerably altered in a more restrictive way, they were rejected pending further consideration. The government resigned and called a general election, in which, for the first time, 'Native Policy' was to be the main issue.

The jovial and lightly-principled Thielman Roos ('I regard politics as a game'[12]) and the sinister Dr Malan joined in raising the spectre of libidinous blacks intoxicated by power ravaging helpless white females. Electoral propaganda depicted shame and misery as the inevitable consequences of miscegenation. Smuts, they claimed – quite erroneously, for he was as dedicated to white supremacy as any Nationalist – wanted a 'Kaffir state ... a black hegemony in which we are all to be on an equal footing'. Oswald Pirow, brilliant as a lawyer, and an accomplished sportsman, horrified voters with talk of – equally non-existent – red terror. It was all thoroughly disgraceful, but it worked. The Nationalists were returned with an overall majority, the Labour Party having split between those prepared to collaborate with Hertzog and those, like Creswell, who were becoming disgusted with the alliance.

Pirow became Minister of Justice, and immediately set about imposing the strong-arm tactics which he later admired in Germany. The Riotous Assembly Act of 1929 gave extensive powers to the police and the minister to banish suspects from any district. It was to be used widely thereafter.

Pirow showed his style with an armed raid in Durban black areas to round up tax defaulters. Protests were widespread, and at a meeting in Potchefstroom, a place venerated by Nationalists as Munich was by the Nazis, several blacks were shot by a brother of the location superintendent; tried for murder with clear evidence against him, the man was acquitted. It was not the first time that such a blatant miscarriage of justice had taken place, and it was certainly not the last.

The black organizations were poorly placed to withstand government attacks. Kadalie at the ICU had concentrated on pressing for international support at the expense of nuts-and-bolts administration at home. George Champion in Natal, with Jason Jingoes and Thomas Mbeki, an energetic realist in the Transvaal and Northern Cape, drummed up members, but subscriptions melted away, until Champion, whose own finances were chaotic, charged Kadalie with maladministration and started his own Union, ICU yase Natal. Realism had become tainted with millenarianism, arousing in turn suspicion among the masses of religious countrymen and women. After 1929 the core ICU had ceased to function as an effective body, having, according to Jingoes, 'ground to a halt because of their internal wrangling . . . the real purpose had become obscured and clouded by side issues'. One result of Kadalie's last-minute appeal had however succeeded in bringing an English union organizer, William Ballinger and his exceptional wife Margaret, out to South Africa; too late to save the ICU, but able to help significantly in what was developing into a straightforward struggle between blacks and a white-supremacist government.

Similar squabbles had affected the ANC. Gumede's flirtations with communism had irritated the conservative chiefs and clergymen. In April 1930 he was replaced by Pixley Seme, the original founder of the SANNC, now grown autocratic and set in his ways. The communists, who had become a source of much-needed energy and realism, were beginning to slide into fractionalism as the party line was imposed by Moscow against the better judgement of South African members. In 1928 the Moscow Comintern resolved that the South African party must work for 'an independent native South African republic as a stage towards a workers' and peasants' republic'. Foreseeing that this would result in exacerbating the conflict between white and black workers, the more reasonable members objected, but agreed to toe the line. Sidney Bunting, who had committed the crime of speaking from the same platform as ANC members, was soon expelled as a 'right-wing deviationist', along with the best members of the party, including Bill

Andrews and Solly Sachs, the energetic garment-workers' organizer.

Economic crisis, however, diverted the new Nationalist government from pursuing internal repression too vigorously. The Wall Street collapse of 1929 and the subsequent Depression reduced demand for South African products. Australia, in a similar situation, devalued in February 1931, and in September that year Britain abandoned the gold standard, the convertibility of paper currency into gold. South Africa, the world's largest producer of gold, was placed in a dilemma as to whether or not its currency should remain tied to gold, thereby being grossly overvalued and placing a heavy burden on the economy, but reinforcing the country's prestige. Gold was very much an emotional as well as a practical problem. In 1925 the Vissering-Kemmerer Committee had recommended that South Africa should return to the gold standard, which had been generally abandoned during the First World War, and that this decision should be taken independently of Britain. Delighted at the prospect of the colonial tail wagging the Imperial dog, Hertzog's government agreed, much to the consternation of the Bank of England, which was forced to follow suit against the inclinations of its Governor, Montagu Norman. The temptation to cling to gold in 1931 was irresistible.[13]

For more than a year the South African pound stayed linked to the gold standard. Havenga, Minister of Finance, an honest man, efficient within his abilities, something of a counterpart to Philip Snowden in Britain, insisted that this was a demonstration of economic independence, an assertion of South Africa's individuality and freedom from Imperial ties. If so, it was an expensive one. As the consequences of an overvalued currency bit, mines closed down and unemployment increased. Eventually Thielman Roos, playing his own hand, precipitated a crisis by openly advocating devaluation, and within a fortnight at the end of December 1932 South Africa abandoned the gold standard. The result was immediate as the price of gold shot from £4 to £7 an ounce, enabling low-yield mines to reopen, and new ones to be developed.

The purified politicians

Borne on by the success of his initiative, Roos attempted to displace Hertzog as leader of the Nationalists by means of a coalition with Smuts, thus reconciling the Afrikaner *volk*. Hertzog countered by making a similar offer which was, after some serious debate, accepted by both Nationalists and South African Party members in March 1933. The common ground between the two parties was clarified: the few diehard imperialists were confined to Natal, and everyone else agreed on what had for so long been inflammatory issues, the replacement of the Union flag by new South African colours, and equal language rights; the native problem was to be settled following the established principle of higher-paid jobs reserved for whites and the maintenance of white hegemony, which mollified Labour. Details of how this might be done were lacking, left for the new government to be elected in May 1933 to settle.

The Parliamentary Select Committee which had spent so long considering and reconsidering the 1926 Bills had reported its conclusions in 1931. These were in large part inspired by a SAP representative, the Natalian Heaton Nicholls, immensely conceited and irredeemably anti-black, and were, in essence, to restrict black representation to the Senate and to add a Grand Committee on Native Affairs with a mixed membership.[14] Most of the SAP Select Committee members, including Smuts, disagreed, holding out for some element of the existing franchise to be retained. The report was set to one side until resuscitated by Hertzog in 1935.

The new coalition cabinet included such fundamentally diverse characters as Oswald Pirow, developing an increased admiration for Herr Hitler's German policies, and Jan Hofmeyr, worried and uncertain, emerging from the influence of a monstrous mother and fumbling towards solutions which would satisfy both his increasingly liberal conscience and the demands of the white electorate, now much increased by the enfranchisement of white women, and to a lesser degree by the abandonment of the property qualification for white voters. That reluctant convert to Commonwealth unity, Hertzog, remained Prime Minister and Foreign Minister, with Smuts as Deputy and Minister of Justice.

When the coalition agreement was tested in the election held in May 1933 the coalition was endorsed overwhelmingly, with seventy-five Nationalists and sixty-one SAP members returned out of a total of 158 seats, the opposition being reduced to half a dozen irreconcilables, who included the surviving Natal Home Rulers. But the Nationalists were a divided party. Dr Malan had a considerable following, amounting to nearly half the new MPs, who shared a deep aversion to Smuts and regarded Jan Hofmeyr, now seen as his heir-apparent, with near-hatred for his weak tendencies towards a belief in political rights for non-whites. When the parties began to consider actual combination – fusion – rather than mere coalition, the Malanites put their feet down. Although the concept of fusion was accepted, with convincing majorities, by party caucuses in the Free State, Transvaal and Natal, Nationalists at the Cape, Malan's base and stronghold, voted overwhelmingly against – 142 votes to five. Torn between Malan, pressing for ultimate republican independence, and Smuts, insisting on retaining connections with King and Commonwealth, Hertzog sided with Smuts, and the provisions of the Statute of Westminster, which now formalized the sovereign independence of the dominions, were enacted. To most intents and purposes South Africa was now an independent state, the only stages remaining before nationalist hopes could be fully realized being the ultimate severing of links with Britain by the establishment of a republic, and the removal of that irksome constitutional restraint, the 1910 restrictions on removing non-white franchises, the last barrier to complete white supremacy.

The combination of the Nationalists and the SAP into the new United Party took place in December 1934. It was too much for the Malanites, who began to work together on a new 'purified' nationalist party, free of any taint of liberalism or attachment to Britain. Colonel Stallard, moving in the opposite direction, was unable to swallow the rhetoric of republican nationalists and formed a Dominion Party to work for the preservation of the British connection.

When the 'fusion' government brought the proposals for Native Representation before the House in February 1936 – ten years after Hertzog's original measures were drafted – the original four Bills had been reduced to two and had changed, from the black point of view, substantially for the worse. The land-acquisition programmes were maintained, with a pledge by the state to acquire the land that had first been identified twenty years before as the minimum needed to accommodate blacks, but the new political proposal was to abolish the Cape Franchise altogether, although allowing current voters to remain on the electoral roll, and to have a Native Representative Council in place of Nicholls' Grand Committee.

Once again, black organizations were roused from disarray into new activity. By that time the ANC had declined to a total membership of under four hundred. The 1933 annual meeting had, under Seme's lack of leadership and blatant packing of the delegates, degenerated into a farce, and thereafter the congress seemed to slide into oblivion, 'in the death pangs', according to the communist ANC leader Moses Kotane. The revival began with the election in 1936 of an Anglican priest, the Revd James Calata, to become General Secretary of the ANC, and Zaccheus Mahabane, that reliable veteran, returned as President General; both positions were now held by realistic clergymen.

During the period of the ANC's decline opposition to the Bills centred around a new *ad hoc* organization, the All African Convention (AAC) led by Davidson Don Jabavu and Dr Xuma. Under Jabavu's inspiring chairmanship the AAC was able to unite an imposing body of Africans. Professor Matthews, Dr Joshua Molema, grandson of old Chief Molema of Mafeking, and Dr James Moroka, grandson of the Thaba Nchu chief who had succoured the *voortrekkers*, were emerging as leaders who would have lent distinction – much-needed distinction – to the South African parliament, and who resented being fobbed off with the most indirect and muted offers of political influence. The AAC resolution was searching and well-argued. The co-existence in the same country of two nations, one perilously subjected, was an impossible concept: 'The interests of the racial groups are inextricably interwoven.' The only solution was a political unity which would ensure 'a single South African nation, allowing liberty for racial groups to develop along their own lines socially and culturally . . . bound together by the pursuit of common political objectives'.

Predictably, black objections had no effect upon the passage of the Representation of Natives Bill through parliament. Only eleven members voted against it in the combined final vote of Assembly and Senate, as against 169 voting for the extinction of non-white participation in the national political life. The names of the eleven are worth recording – they were the survivors of Merriman liberalism: F.S. Malan, fellow undergraduate at Christ's College with Smuts, imprisoned by the British for revealing conditions in the concentration camps, a minister since 1910, an ardent supporter of Afrikaans and a consistent defender of black rights; Jan Hofmeyr, finally out of the closet; Morris Alexander, born in Germany, educated at St John's College, Cambridge, a Zionist and friend of Gandhi; R.J. Du Toit; J.M. Chalmers; and A.J. MacCullum – six from the United Party; together with all the members of the Dominion Party: Colonel Stallard, R.M. Christopher, J.G. Derbyshire, C.W. Coulter and J.S. Marwick, who had led his charges to safety at the start of the Boer War. Three Afrikaners, one German Jew, and seven Englishmen forming a tiny minority for decency.[15]

With the Bill passed, the question of whether the non-represented majority should cooperate with the new arrangements was raised. In spite of thirty years of disappointed hopes the whole tenor of AAC and ANC members' opinion was to make the best of what was on offer. Jabavu lamented: 'the structure of European morality [had] tottered and collapsed . . . down to its pristine level of the jungle that obtained two thousand years ago,' but advised cooperation nevertheless. Selby Msimang, the most moderate of men, who had volunteered for war service in 1914, wrote angrily that 'Parliament and the white people of South Africa, have disowned us, flirted and trifled with our loyalty,' and suggested that only a revolution could prevail against 'the most pagan militarism'. But Msimang accepted that the only feasible strategy was to make the best possible use of the new machinery. The sort of action Gumede and the communists advocated – industrial pressure and defiance of the pass regulations – depended on the backing of an organized mass movement, which the ANC had never been. The ICU, which had for a time possessed such support, was now moribund, its surviving members split between Dube in Natal and Kadalie, hanging on to a splinter group in East London. Indians and Coloureds, although they may have sympathized, had their own agendas to pursue. Individual bursts of anger against the ever more repressive action taken by police and their white civilian supporters led to violent incidents, which were savagely suppressed and followed by blatantly unjust trials.

However restrictive the government's policies might be, they would not have been effective without willing administrative support. This local officials, police and the greater part of the white community enthusiastically provided. Hertzog's period of rule had seen an influx of Afrikaners into the police, and the previous readiness to charge into white demonstrators became decidedly modified. Legal protection was patchy. The courts, at their highest levels, remained impartial. One of the most consistent defenders of non-white rights was old Sir James Rose Innes, former Chief Justice, a colleague of Rhodes and Merriman, grandson of the James Rose Innes sent out by Lord Bathurst a century before to organize Cape education, who founded the Non-Racial Franchise Association together with that other veteran, Henry Burton, in order to combat Hertzog's Bills. Many local authorities (largely English-speaking) were reluctant to apply segregation, and had opposed the principle in evidence to the preliminary fact-finding committee. The Native Laws Amendment Bill of 1937 reinforced controls on blacks' access to towns, where they were confined to fenced localities. More severe restrictions, enabling local authorities to expel men from towns, were enforced by rigorous pass laws, forcing blacks to become law-breakers in the same way that parking controls can produce thousands of hardly-criminal offenders; but the penalties on blacks breaking pass laws were considerably more rigorous – and whites were not affected at all.

If local government was ineffective, or reactionary, or simply corrupt, the results for the blacks could be grave. Maize farmers' demand for labour in the North-East Transvaal spawned what was almost a revival of the old blackbirding days as immigrants from the north, from Rhodesia and Nyasaland, lured by the prospect of mine work, were cajoled and bullied into working for the farmers. It was admitted that the conditions in which they were held were inhuman and amounted to forced labour, but the Department of Native Affairs officials turned a blind eye, and even cooperated in what were entirely illegal activities.

Despite repression, patience, exuberance and sheer criminality were able to provide an outlet for frustration. Alcohol was an obvious source of relief, exploited by local government to raise money through the taxing of beer-halls. Plaatje had been sufficiently worried – his sons had become heavy drinkers – to join the Order of True Templars, a total-abstinence organization. Another non-racialist group, the South African Templars, were headed by James Mushet, one of Smuts' faithful parliamentarians. An entertaining contrast to the Templars' good works is provided by Elias Kuzwayo, former General Secretary of the ICU's Pietermaritzburg branch. The remarkable career of Kuzwayo, who turned to managing dance-halls, teaching, establishing phoney medical schemes, running (as Qwabe Chief Shadrack M. Gumede kaMseni) a Cooperative Society and masquerading as a cleric was less that of an enterprising petty criminal than a paradigm of the underdog's creativity.

In the ferment of the period one cohesive group which might, on past form, have been expected to show a high degree of activity was remarkably absent. The Zulu had provided many leaders of constitutional action and debate, including John Dube, George Champion, Pixley Seme and Richard Msimang, but what might be called the Bambatha tradition of violent action had fizzled out. What could have been a centre of resistance, the Zulu royal house, was in a period of decline. Denied the official recognition given to other hereditary chiefs, Dinizulu's successor Solomon was an uncertain ruler, gifted but weak, another victim of alcohol. Nevertheless, the visit in 1925 of Queen Victoria's grandson, the Prince of Wales, did much to revive memories of past glories. Received by Solomon and a majestic array of sixty thousand warriors raising the royal salute, '*Bayete*,' the fading glory of Shaka's house and its links with Imperial Britain were to some degree strengthened.

A few months earlier a seminal gathering had taken place which led to the foundation of Inkatha ka Zulu – the name refers to the 'rope of grass', the sacred coil symbolizing Zulu unity. With John Dube and another ANC member, William Bhulose, as its first chairmen, Inkatha started its existence as a respectable conservative association, an alliance of the *kholwa* middle classes and the chiefs, working together with such whites as Nicholls and Marwick, who appreciated the merits of supporting blacks who would cooperate rather than resist. Only after its revival thirty years later by the redoubtable Mangosuthu Buthelezi did Inkatha become a real power in the land, concentrating and expressing revived Zulu aspirations.[16]

Apart from the anxieties raised by the repressive new Acts, which were not accompanied by any widespread unrest, the Fusion government enjoyed a period of economic prosperity. In the five years after 1933 South Africa's GNP grew by 70 per cent, with little increase in prices. Fired by the gold price rise, industry expanded. The Iscor steel plant came on stream in 1933, and expanding industries created something like half a million new jobs between 1932 and 1939. Of these 400,000 were non-white, creating, if not a degree of prosperity, some alleviation of poverty. Conditions on the reserves made such contributions essential. The millions of extra acres promised in the Hertzog Bills since 1926 were not forthcoming, and over-crowding and soil erosion were becoming critical. Reports spoke of 'poverty, congestion and chaos . . . starvation, endemic typhus and almost chronic scurvy . . . desert conditions . . . a process of ruination'. The statistics were appalling. In one Ciskei district the average family income had declined over fifty years to a quarter of what it had previously been. By 1936 the death rate in the reserves was 40 per cent higher than it had been fifteen years previously. Infant mortality was approaching 50 per cent, and 'practically all diseases prevalent in the Native Reserves are associated with malnutrition and personal poverty . . . they are all preventable'.

The condition of the poor whites, on the other hand, was slowly improving. Large grants were made available for training and relief, and non-whites were increasingly moved out of semi-skilled jobs to make room for Afrikaners. The earlier actions taken to stimulate Afrikaner participation in commerce and industry were also having an effect. 1934 saw the formation of the Volkskas, with L.J. du Plessis, formerly head of the Broederbond, as its first chairman. That organization had secured a hold on many institutions, and recruited a whole new generation of militant Afrikaners supporting Dr D.F. Malan and his Purified Nationalists. Every South African Prime Minister between 1948 and 1994, between Smuts and Mandela, was a member of that sinister institution.

Hertzog himself was violently against the whole principle of conspiratorial secret societies, as he made clear in a long speech in November 1935, in which the aims of the Broederbond were fully exposed. He read from a circular issued the previous year by the society's chairman, Professor J.C. van Rooy: in order to ensure that 'Afrikanerdom will reach its ultimate destiny of domination [*baaskap*] in South Africa it was necessary that the Afrikaner Broederbond shall govern South Africa'. Hertzog poured scorn on this negation of his ideal of two streams, English and Afrikaners, coming together to govern the country justly (which, according to his lights, he always attempted to do). His loathing for Dr Malan, who had 'watched the Anglo–Boer war from the comfort of the Netherlands', and now sat 'making pronouncements in the Koffiehuis in Cape Town', was 'unmitigated and complete'.[17]

But Malan and his disciples were the men of the future. His new Purified Nationalists, who soon officially changed the name to the National Party, usually known as the Nationalists, took up any convenient stick with which to beat the Hertzog–Smuts alliance. Malan, middle-aged and portly, mounted a black horse to attend a rally of the anti-Semitic Greyshirts, one of the multiplying quasi-fascist organizations. *Die Burger*, reflecting the views of its German namesake, denied that German Jews were being persecuted, and demanded restrictions on Jewish immigration; very quickly bending to the storm, the government acted to control the arrival of Jews, with a handful of liberals protesting to no avail.

Liberal views in parliament received some reinforcement after the 1938 election, which brought the first Native Representatives into the two houses. In the Senate these included Edgar Brookes and J.D. Rheinallt Jones, founder members of the Institute of Race Relations. A distinguished historian, Brookes performed a political pilgrimage lasting fifty years in which he became more consciously liberal as events hardened him, eventually taking Holy Orders at the age of seventy-six. In the lower house Margaret Ballinger, who had come out with her husband to reorganize the ICU, and Donald Molteno, grandson of Sir John, acted closely together with Jones and Brookes to form a pressure group effective out of all proportion to their numbers. Some of the more offensive proposals, such as the ban on marriages between whites and Indians or Coloureds, were defeated, but that particular pass had already been sold, in that marriages between black and white had previously been made illegal. Although the Mixed Marriages Bill was defeated, traditional attitudes prevailed among even the most advanced Afrikaners: Hofmeyr, the most prominent liberal by far, admitted that he found racial mixing repugnant. More Nationalist horror was expressed when it was discovered that four of the undergraduates at Witwatersrand University were not white; and it was with some difficulty that the government was able to maintain the principle of university freedom. Hardening attitudes among the Afrikaners, accompanied by growing self-confidence, were to find their apotheosis in 1938, with the celebrations of the Great Trek's centenary.

SIXTEEN

The Shadows of Apartheid

Homespun fascists

The policies adopted by successive South African governments after 1948 were so repellent to most of the country's population and to the rest of the world that a special effort must be made to understand how they came about. The doctrines and practices of apartheid – 'separate development', as the system was usually described – did not suddenly begin in 1948. Their origins, in some part, go back to much earlier days, to the first efforts of different cultures to live together, peacefully or otherwise, in Southern Africa, and in particular to the British attempts to systematize government and reconcile contrary interests. Segregation, which had been the policy adopted in Natal from the beginning of colonial rule, and which was accepted as late as the 1930s by leaders of the ANC, was the rationale behind the protectorates, and was intended to provide exactly that – protection from the worst exploitation. A somewhat weaker version of the same principle was generally adopted by Smuts and the South African Party as the best way of dealing with the 'native problem'.

Apartheid, on the other hand, is primarily an affirmation of Afrikaner identity, and 1938 was its year of glory, the centenary of the oath-taking before the battle of Blood River, when the *voortrekkers* committed themselves to constructing an independent society. Such inconvenient facts as the presence of non-white *voortrekkers*, the quick ejection from Natal and the subsequent quarrels between trekker governments were set aside, to be subsumed in a new version of history. In this revised account freedom-loving Dutch-speakers had battled against the climate, savage attacks, British assaults on their liberties, capitalist oppression and both cultural and commercial imperialism. Slagtersnek, the Black Circuit, Boomplats, the annexation of Natal and Griqualand West, the attempt to subdue the Transvaal and the sequel of Majuba, the Jameson Raid, the second War of Independence, the concentration camps, Veereniging, the 1914 Rebellion, the 1922 strike, were all remembered, with advantages (Smuts must have regretted his 'Hundred Years of Wrong'). Only Hertzog, many felt, who had surrendered to the persuasions of Sly Jannie Smuts, and his nigger-loving lieutenant Hofmeyr, stood between the Afrikaner *volk*, the *eie*, 'our own flesh and blood', and complete independence; and absolute power.

That essential of national identity, a language, had made a powerful impact with the publication of the first Afrikaans Bible in 1933. Much more than merely simplified Dutch, Afrikaans is a magnificent language for passionate sincerities, probably the finest and most important linguistic construct of modern times. Its powerful rhythms are those of seventeenth-century English: here, for example, is the 1933 Afrikaans Bible version of the 23rd Psalm.

Die HERE is my herder; niks sal my ontbreek nie.
Hy laat my neerle in groen weivelde; na waters waar rus is, lei Hy my
  heen.
Hy verkwik my siel; Hy lei my in die spore van geregtigheid, om sy
  Naam ontwil.
Al gaan ek ook in 'n dal van doodskaduwee, ek sal geen onheil vrees nie;
  want U is met my: u stok en u staf dié vertroos my.
U berei die tafel voor my aangesig teenoor my teenstanders; u maak my
  hoof vet met olie; my beker loop oor.
Net goedheid en guns sal my volg al die dae van my lewe; en ek sal in
  die huis van die HERE bly in lengte van dae.

On a less elevated plane, Afrikaans is also a fine vehicle for robust insults: '*tweegatsjakkals*' and '*soutspiel*', for a hypocrite and an English-speaker (frequently regarded as synonymous) are two examples.[1] John Bunyan would have been quite at home with Afrikaans, although hardly his contemporary John Milton. In politics, fluency in Afrikaans became a shibboleth. Hofmeyr was taunted with his reputed failure to use Afrikaans in his everyday affairs; Smuts was beyond redemption, with his voluminous writings in English and his measured debate.

With language went religion. All supporters of apartheid, including most of the dominees of the Dutch Churches, constantly invoked divine authority for the separation of races and the right – the duty – of the white races to govern, a duty which English-speakers had betrayed by thrusting political rights on unprepared blacks. It was 'the Christian duty of the whites to act as guardians over the non-white races until such time as they have reached that level where they can look after their own affairs'. Superficially this closely resembles the old British doctrine of trusteeship, with a dash of Roosevelt/Rhodes racism. In reality the differences were vital. The Imperial concept of trusteeship applied to both black and white: colonists had to show themselves capable of self-government (or prove extraordinarily and expensively difficult for Whitehall) before this was conferred, and when they were 'left to look after their own affairs' the franchise was allocated impartially. It was the individual who qualified for political participation, and not his race.

Of course this was a doctrine of perfection, well-muddied by prejudice, incompetence and, as Natalian colonists had abundantly proved, sheer chicanery. But it had not been entirely ineffective. Black, Coloured and Indian men and women, capable of competent and honest leadership, had over eighty years of working in a parliamentary system proved themselves as effective as any whites. If that fatal initial error of the Act of Union, the restriction of parliamentary membership to whites, had been avoided, men like Abdurahman and Z.K. Matthews would have had the opportunity of demonstrating their personal capacities in the national arena as British Indians had been doing – with many limitations – for some years.

The experience of India's progress towards self-government was instructive. In 1917 'the progressive realization of responsible government in India' was announced as the policy of the British government, a development which would give India the same status as the other dominions. As had been done in the Cape, the Indian franchise was limited to the educated and prosperous, but nevertheless in 1921 one million Indians were entitled to vote for the Legislative Council, and over five million for the provincial governments. In South Africa the opposite was happening, as Indian votes were being squeezed out, to disappear completely in 1951.

Christian Nationalism, the doctrine evolved from many earnest conferences between Afrikaner churchmen and academics, which gave moral strength to the doctrines of apartheid, was hardly either Christian or national in any sense that would be understood outside South Africa. The concept of racial inferiority had no foundation in Calvin, or even in the influential restatement of Calvinist doctrine made by Abraham Kuyper, the nineteenth-century Dutch philosopher/theologian whose idea of 'autonomy within a particular sphere' was extended by such Afrikaner intellectuals as Dominus A.P. Treurnicht and Nicolaas Diederichs. When the terrifyingly sincere Hendrik Verwoerd wrote that perhaps the Afrikaners had been divinely sent to South Africa so that 'all that has been built up since the days of Christ may be maintained for the good of all mankind', he expressed sentiments that would have come more naturally from a mid-sixteenth- than a mid-twentieth-century politician.[2]

The idea of a nation had also to be understood in a very special sense – and a sense which underwent rapid change between 1938 and 1960. When in the centenary year old Father Kestell, who had ridden with the Boer commandos, spoke of 'my nation in peril' he meant only the *volk*, the Afrikaners; and only 'true' Afrikaners at that, not Smuts and Hofmeyr, traitors enmeshed with imperialism. Blacks were another matter; they had their rights and their dignity, but were another 'nation' – all of them, Zulu, Sotho, Xhosa, with their different languages, traditions and frequent mutual antipathies, lumped together as 'Bantu', to be dealt with separately from their white masters. As for the English-speakers, once they had been cut down to size, properly repentant for their past misdeeds, willing to learn Afrikaans and conform to the standards of the *volk*, they would be allowed their rightful place as associates in the white state.

These views were given a vigorous stimulus by in the 1938 celebrations. The eight oxcarts which dragged their way hundreds of miles to the site of the new *voortrekker* monument frowning over Pretoria were welcomed with tearful joy by hundreds of small communities *en route*. The excitement reached its peak on 16 December 1938, the centenary of Blood River, when the monument's foundation stone was laid, surrounded by ten thousand enthusiasts camped on the newly-named Voortrekkerhoogte, previously Roberts Heights. Hertzog as Prime Minister could not attend, since at a formal state occasion 'God Save the King' would have had to be sung; both the veritable Boer War heroes, the Prime Minister and his Deputy Smuts, therefore absented themselves. Hertzog was being abandoned and rejected by the new radical Malanites and their even more threatening allies, less committed than was Malan himself to normal democratic methods.

The enthusiasm generated by the celebrations was put to practical use in October 1939 by an Afrikaner Economic 'Volkskongres', with the support of Kestell, as a means for the redemption of the poor white, its aims being 'to employ the mobilized capital of the Afrikaner, in the furtherance of his national interests in the sphere of commerce and industry, and to capture key positions'. On the foundations built by Sanlam and Santam a new company, the Federale Volksbeleggings (People's Investments – FVB), was established, to provide finance for small Afrikaner businesses. A permanent overview was to be provided by the new Economic Institute, which reflected the rhetoric of the movement by setting up a Reddingsdaadbond (Rescue – or Salvation, 'De Redder' being one title of Christ the Saviour – League), an institution dedicated to 'making Afrikaners economically conscious' and to circumscribing the influence of trades unions, especially black ones. The 'capturing of key positions' was left to that rapidly spreading secret society, the Afrikaner Broederbond.

In political terms 1938 gave a modest boost to Malan and his purified followers, when in a general election they won twenty-seven seats; among the new members was one Hans Strydom. Outside parliament the effects were more marked. Since most Afrikaners had some German forebears and many leaders had studied in Germany, events in that country were watched with attention and excitement. From February 1939 the Ossewa Brandwag (Oxwagon Sentinels – OB) rapidly grew into a uniformed and armed organization along Nazi stormtrooper lines. A few months later the National Institute for Christian Education and Instruction was formed. Both these organizations were offshoots of the Broederbond: Hans van Rensburg, leader of the OB, a thoroughgoing Nazi admirer, remained on the boards on Sanlam and Santam; Professor van Rooy, Chairman of the National Institute, was also Chairman of the FAK, the Broederbond cultural front; and Dr Piet Meyer, Secretary of the Broederbond, held the same post in the FAK, the OB and the Reddingsdaadsbond.[3]

Actions provoking reactions, an upsurge in anti-Nationalist liberal organizations occurred. Libertas Bon, the Libertas League of Action, the South African Group for Good Government and the Democratic League all joined the Institute for Race Relations in challenging Afrikaner nationalism and pressing for recognition of black rights. Few of these, mainly young, people were Afrikaners, but it was to an Afrikaner that they looked for leadership. In June 1937 Jan Hofmeyr, who had steadily been growing unhappier with the Hertzog/Smuts coalition's race policy, resigned over a Bill designed to stop Indians buying land outside designated areas, introduced not by a Nationalist but a member of his own South Africa Party, Robert Stuttaford. Hofmeyr was then pressed to start a new Liberal Party, which would dissociate itself from the racist attitudes that now seemed to be common to all United Party members, but prevaricated, emotionally loyal to Smuts and sharing the General's unsureness as to what action other than gradual improvement was feasible.[4]

Events overtook these discussions when in September 1939 the outbreak of the Second World War immediately provoked the same controversy over South Africa's participation that had taken place twenty-five years before. It could be argued, as Hertzog did, that the question had been answered the previous year when the cabinet, discussing the crisis in Czechoslovakia, had decided that South Africa should remain neutral. A year later Smuts took a different view. For six years he had acted, often against his inclinations and beliefs, as a loyal member of a coalition, but there were some issues on which he was not prepared to compromise. Fascism was to Smuts an absolute evil, which had to be fought at every point, and unlike any other member of the fusion government he had extensive and detailed knowledge of European issues. Hertzog had assumed personal responsibility for foreign affairs, but had little inclination to enmesh himself too closely in any issue that did not involve South Africa. A dedicated parliamentarian with no personal sympathy for totalitarians, Hertzog had agreed to join the League of Nations sanctions against Italy after the invasion of Ethiopia, but was adamant that South Africa had no business interfering in a purely European quarrel. Whether Russia or Germany would be the first to invade Poland seemed, not unreasonably, to be no concern of South Africa; sympathetic neutrality was all that should be offered to Britain. That option (although some doubts as to the 'sympathy' are legitimate – one recalls the Irish Prime Minister commiserating with the Germans on the death of their beloved leader Herr Hitler) was chosen by Eire, and could have been chosen with excellent reason by South Africa.

But on this vital issue, Smuts, deploying the great moral authority that he had shown in previous crises, won the day. By eighty votes to sixty-seven in the House of Assembly South Africa declared war on Germany, and Hertzog resigned; with him went thirty-seven Afrikaner members of the United Party. White South Africa was again divided, with all the English behind Smuts, as well as a substantial minority of Afrikaners, and all those non-whites who could afford to take an interest in anything so far removed from their daily struggles. But the enthusiasm among non-whites for the British cause that had marked 1914 was absent in 1939. The reliance South Africa placed on Imperial goodwill and power had long evaporated, and the hundred thousand blacks and Coloureds who volunteered for service were often inspired only by hopes of better pay. Since the regular army was little more than a token force, less than five thousand all told, volunteers were essential, and over a third of the eligible European population –

Afrikaans- and English-speakers – came forward. 'Sailor Malan', the fighter pilot, was the most famous of the South African war heroes (although his compatriot Pat Pattle was actually the highest-scoring ace of any of the Allies, with forty-one victories), and Abe Bailey's son Jim survived four years' front-line action in fighter squadrons. South African forces drove the Italians out of Ethiopia and Somaliland and the Vichy French from Madagascar before joining with the Allies in North Africa and Italy. After fighting their way through the desert a whole division was captured by Rommel at Tobruk in one of the war's worst defeats, but South African soldiers also took part in the victory at El Alamein, and went on to participate in the invasion of Europe.

Strategically, the Simonstown base in False Bay assumed vital importance when the virtual closure of the Mediterranean forced Allied shipping to take the long route around the Cape. Rapid industrial expansion enabled South Africa to equip its own forces and provide munitions – chiefly rifle ammunition – for export. Morally, the influence of Field Marshal Smuts – the only non-Briton ever to attain the rank[5] – who was one of Churchill's closest friends and most consistent supporters ('two old lovebirds who can still peck' was Churchill's own description), was great. Smuts' Guildhall speech of 19 October 1943 was memorable, but exposed the basic vagueness of his feelings – 'thoughts' is too precise a word – on race and morality: 'the basic problem before our race is that of aggression . . . the Christian gospel still fights in vain against this earlier, more deeply founded gospel of our race . . . the blond beast, the superman of nature, still hurls defiance at the Christian code'. Any South African black might well identify with every word of that, but in a very different sense, especially when Smuts had previously spoken of the 'most brutal ruthlessness . . . of the Nazis who reduce enslaved populations . . . to destitution and despair . . . moved about like dumb cattle, far away from home and friends'.

On the home front the Malanites and Hertzogites were reunited at least in the parliamentary sense, having joined uneasily together in the new Re-United National or People's Party, the Herenigde Nasionale Party (HNP), supported by almost all the sixty-seven minority votes, but in the country the anti-war, anti-Smuts activists were divided. The OB under its Nazi leader van Rensburg, supported by the German propaganda machine, encouraged an ineffectual campaign of sabotage, joined by the Handhawersbond (League of Defenders). In the Free State the Nationalists rallied to attack Jews and capitalists and to cry for a republic. British servicemen and South Africans who had volunteered for foreign service were set upon in the streets, and bemused by the combination of sympathetic hospitality in Afrikaner homes and overt hostility in public places.

Opposed by Hertzog, still faithful to his twin streams of Afrikaners and English, first the Free State and then the Transvaal Nationalists moved towards the 'Purified' followers of Dr Malan. At the National Party congress of November 1940 Hertzog's statement of principle that national unity should be based on 'the equal rights of the Afrikaner and English-speaking populations, coupled with the recognition and appreciation of one another's heritage' was successfully opposed by the Malanites. The old statesman, Prime Minister for sixteen years, walked out into the wilderness in 'a moment of infinite hurt, bitterness and disappointment' left with the faithful Nicholas Havenga as his only serious supporter to form the new Afrikaner Party. Saddened and disillusioned, Hertzog, unable to cope with the crassness of the new men, resigned from parliament in December 1940, but lingered on for two more years before, in that unassuming fashion he had always adopted, checking himself quietly and anonymously into hospital to die. Smuts paid a final tribute to his old colleague and opponent when he described Hertzog: 'Ah, there was a man . . . If he gave you his word you could count on it.' Havenga survived to be reconciled with Malan and to merge the Afrikaner Party with Malan after the Nationalists' 1948 victory, but the Hertzog tradition was dead.

As committed to fascist doctrines as van Rensburg, Oswald Pirow also formed a splinter organization, the New Order Group, but the principal opposition to the Ossewa Brandwag came from Malan, determined not to allow a powerful competitor to challenge his leadership of what was left of the Purified Nationalists and the anti-Smuts Afrikaners. By now the most experienced Nationalist by far, and with the Cape Nationalist press and the Afrikaner business groups behind him, Malan was successful, and the OB knuckled under, gradually losing enthusiasm as it became clear that the Allies were not going to lose the war.

Having little to fear from parliamentary opposition, and not much from the amateurish terrorists, the government was able to concentrate on the war. Hofmeyr, now reconciled to his own leader, and the competent Scottish engineer Claude Sturrock, an experienced parliamentarian and an old ally of Hofmeyr, and Dr H.J. van der Byl, the able ISCOR chairman, were the most prominent in a talented war cabinet.

The end of the war brought a new opportunity for the non-whites to exert pressure for change. Just as he had done for the League of Nations, Smuts had exerted a powerful influence on the formation of the United Nations; it was he who had drafted the preamble to its Charter, which included a statement committing the organization 'To re-establish faith in fundamental human rights, in the sanctity and ultimate value of human personality, in the equal rights of men and women of nations large and small.' While this is nothing more than fine-sounding verbiage, which could mean a dozen different things, it reflected ideals very difficult for a South African Prime Minister to implement.

Dr Xuma, President General of the ANC from 1940, who had a better grasp of international affairs than most South Africans, lobbied the United Nations to ensure that formerly German South-West Africa be placed directly under United Nations rule, rather than being incorporated into the Union, as the South African government had asked. Together with the Indian Congress and the Indian government – Lord Wavell as viceroy making clear his support for moves against South Africa – Xuma was able to convince the United Nations to reject the South African request, and furthermore to censure South Africa for its past administration. Nevertheless the future of that extensive territory (more than 300,000 square miles) was confided to South Africa under a United Nations mandate. In one revealing meeting Smuts took Xuma aside and said, 'Look, Xuma, these people do not understand us. Let us go back home and sit down together and solve our problems.' It was typical of Smuts both to make the advance and then never to follow it up.

South African Indians emerged from the war in a more militant frame of mind. During the war Smuts had been able to rely on patriotic enthusiasm to support the government; in the 1943 election his United Party had won 110 seats, with Malan's Purified Nationalists reduced to forty-three. But with the coming of peace the Prime Minister had to placate Natalian voters permanently jealous of successful Indian enterprise. Immediately before the election a 'Pegging Act' had therefore been introduced in order to freeze all property transactions in Durban between Indians and whites. Much indignation was aroused: Hofmeyr nearly resigned, the furious Indian government, led by Wavell, threatened economic sanctions – this in the middle of a world war in which troops from the two countries were fighting side by side – and the Parsee owners of the magnificent Taj Mahal hotel in Bombay banned both white South Africans and dogs. The 1946 Asiatic Land Tenure and Indian Representation Bill suggested a compromise whereby Indian land ownership would be restricted but offering special Indian representation, by whites, in the Union parliament. This was scornfully rejected by the Natal Indians, now led by Dr G.M. Naicker, a devoted supporter of Gandhi, and led to the Indian recall of their High Commissioner, followed by a vote of censure in the United Nations. Naicker was joined by the Transvaal Indians under the communist Dr Yusuf Dadoo. In a revealing interlude which shows Smuts' stature as a world figure, Mrs Pandit, India's United Nations representative, 'asked his pardon lest anything she had done might have failed to match the high standard and conduct set by the Mahatma'. 'My child,' he replied, taking her hand in both of his, 'you have gained a hollow victory. This vote will put me out of power in our next election but you will have gained nothing.'[6] Serious riots ensued in Durban, in which white civilians attacked unresisting Indians and in which the Revd Michael Scott, who was to be a great figure in the fight against apartheid, made his first appearance (he was sentenced to prison for the grave offence of allowing himself to be knocked about). For the first time a realistic cooperation between black and Indian congresses seemed possible with the 'Doctors'' pact of March 1947 when Naicker, Dadoo and Xuma agreed to work together for a fair franchise and the end of all race-based restrictions. It was an illusory unity, since many newly-formed organizations, among them the largely-communist Non-European Unity Front, who regarded the Doctors' pact as 'despicable', the All African Convention and the African Democratic Party competed for support.

The Coloureds found themselves in a particular dilemma. Abdurahman, a fine and tested leader, had died in 1940, and with him had died the African People's Organization. Some of his followers supported his son-in-law and more radical rival Dr Goolam Gool, while others preferred to cooperate with the government in the Coloured Advisory Council, and could point to some beneficial results. Unlike Indians or blacks, Coloureds had been courted in the past by the Nationalists, who had always regarded their 'brown cousins' with a guilty indulgence and sometimes specifically sought their support.

Although the ANC retained its conservative constitutional aspect under Xuma's leadership, new influences were emerging. The Communist Party had acquired a new gloss during the war through its association with Russia, and was able greatly to increase its membership, even winning a Johannesburg Council seat. J.B. Marks and Moses Kotane, experienced communists since 1929, both educated in Moscow, joined the ANC National Executive in 1946, together with the young Anton Lembede, a former pupil of Adams College, at that time headed by Senator Edgar Brookes, where he had been taught by Z.K. Matthews and Albert Lutuli. More radical than his tutors, Lembede was an ardent Africanist, passionately concerned to assert the importance of African traditions and values. As expressed in the manifesto of the ANC Youth League, founded in 1944 some of these were almost purely Smuts' own, idealistic imprecision and all. Contrasted with the 'Whiteman's' world picture, 'The African . . . regards the Universe as one composite whole; an organic entity, progressively driving towards greater harmony and unity whose individual parts exist merely as interdependent aspects of one whole realizing their fullest value in the corporate life where communal contentment is the absolute measure of values.'

Lembede himself was more rigorous, but equally open to criticism. Future leaders, he insisted, must be black Africans, who had inhabited Africa 'from time immemorial' – a difficult proposition for the Arabs of the Maghreb or the remnants of the Khoi-San to accept. Nor was Lembede's enumeration of 'African heroes' who must be 'honoured and venerated as a source of inspiration' wholly convincing. Shaka, heading the list, was a poor example to the young, while the unfortunate Hintsa was hardly heroic (Macoma would have better represented Xhosa courage), although the worthier names of Moshoeshoe and Kgama were included. Not that the manifesto or Lembede's writings were to be taken as a basis for policy, but as an inspirational call to action; and in this they were immensely success-ful.[7] Few young blacks were tempted to emulate Shaka, and the Youth League acted within the conservative Christian culture – Lembede was an active Roman Catholic – but insisted on fighting not only for equal rights, but on asserting the supremacy that such rights would bring, while acknowl-edging that this would not be done without a long, vigorous and probably violent struggle. White assistance was not rejected, but it should not be relied upon, a fact that was becoming daily more obvious. Africans 'would be wasting their time . . . if they look up to the Europeans either for inspiration or help'. Europeans 'in the last analysis count for nothing': Africans must act for themselves. On the other hand Garveyism – Africa for the blacks alone – was explicitly rejected as 'extreme and ultra-revolutionary', since 'the different racial groups have come to stay'.

Accordingly, many of Lembede's followers were 'less inclined to worry about the dangers of engendering anti-white (or anti-Indian) attitudes, as long as an ideology could be developed that was dynamic enough to rouse the African masses to political awareness and action'. 'Africanists', who included Walter Sisulu and Nelson Mandela, gave priority to black interests (although Mandela had close Indian friends). Oliver Tambo, 'the Christian', a man of great charm and integrity, was conscious that the nation's one-third of non-blacks could not be dismissed. Lembede died in 1947, soon after the Youth League's foundation, but the three other men were to become the backbone of black resistance. Sisulu was a wise, self-educated trades unionist, married to Albertina, one of the great figures in the black resistance, while Tambo and Mandela were both lawyers, graduates of Fort Hare. Tambo came from a Mpondo peasant family whilst Mandela, by contrast, was an aristocrat, cousin of the Thembu paramount, suave and self-confident to the point of arrogance. Although differing on tactics, all three were united with Lembede in strongly opposing communism, to the point of persuading their provincial branch of the ANC in the Transvaal to accept their 1945 motion banning communists, many of whom were non-black, from membership.

Fortunately, this was not agreed by the central ANC, for in the following year Congress communists gave a striking demonstration of their energy and power. The war years had seen a threefold increase in the number of blacks employed in manufacturing and a commensurate increase in black trade unionism: at the end of the war 158,000 were organized in the Council of Non-European Trade Unions, including twenty-five thousand black mineworkers, represented by their own new union led by the genial communist J.B. Marks. Black mineworkers had good reason to complain of their treatment. A commission appointed to investigate their grievances during the war had seen its recommendations implemented only in part; black miners had a fixed daily minimum wage of only two shillings and three pence at the end of the war. Claiming ten shillings, widely recognized as reasonable, in 1947 Marks led seventy thousand black miners out on the biggest industrial action ever to have taken place in South Africa, and the most convincing demonstration yet of black industrial power. Wartime regulations making black strikes illegal had not been repealed, and Smuts reacted as he had twenty-four years previously. The strike was repressed with unnecessary violence by the police, leaving twelve miners killed, and the others forced back to work at bayonet-point.

As it happened, the Native Representative Council was in session during the strike. Having previously been ejected from the City Hall as sullying its Afrikaner purity, the Council was reduced to meeting in the Department of Labour, where they were not allowed to use the toilets; such acts of petty degradation were common, and served to give an example of the low esteem in which the Council was held in official circles. Since its inception in 1937 Council members had been left to stew in their own juice, rarely being consulted, with no power and very little influence – their current meeting was chaired by a young Under-Secretary. When refused a government statement on the strike the solidly conservative, gentlemanly councillors, who had patiently done their best during ten difficult years, revolted, passing a resolution condemning 'the policy of fascism which is the antithesis and negation of the letter and the spirit of the Atlantic Charter and the United Nations Charter' and calling for the government 'forthwith to abolish all discriminatory legislation affecting non-Europeans in this country'.

When the strike was over, and some hundreds of its leaders in gaol, Hofmeyr attempted to mend fences with the Native Representative Council, in a session that showed how fundamentally even that decent man failed to understand the black point of view. Why, he asked, did the natives not appreciate what had been done for them? Had not health, education and land-purchase measures proved the good intentions of a generous government? As for the removal of discriminatory legislation, it was 'simply not practicable'. Matthews replied, after due deliberation, that if that was all that could be said, Council proceedings should be suspended. Hofmeyr's statement was 'merely an apologia for the status quo, apparently oblivious of the progress in forces not only in the world in general but in South Africa itself'.[8] On 26 November 1946 the Council, the last hope of a reasonable dialogue, unanimously decided to end its meeting. 'We have been asked,' Paul Mosako, the youngest member, asserted, 'to cooperate with a toy telephone.'

The change in attitudes that this failure forced was exemplified by Dr Z.K. Matthews' son Joe, who in his presidential address to the Youth League said:

> The possibility of a liberal capitalist democracy in South Africa is exactly nil. The racialist propaganda amongst the whites and their desire to maintain what they imagine to be a profitable situation makes it utterly unthinkable that there can be a political alignment that favours a liberal white group. In any case the political immorality, cowardice and vacillation of the so-called progressives

amongst the whites render them utterly useless as a force against fascism.

Afrikaner apotheosis

If black political leaders assumed, quite correctly, that they could hope for little improvement from the Smuts/Hofmeyr United Party, the 1948 election starkly illustrated that any alternative was very much worse. Dr Malan had seen off the challenge of the extreme right by drawing the teeth of the Ossewa Brandwag and had reconciled Havenga's little Afrikaner Party, to the point where he could command forty-nine seats out of 153 in the Assembly. His party, which dropped the 'Purified' label to become simply the National Party, made 'native policy' the main issue of the election. Hofmeyr's very moderate liberalism was attacked at every point: he wanted, the Nationalists claimed, such horrifying and intolerable things as equal political rights, and social liberalism (which was then about as pejorative a phrase as it became during the 1980s and 1990s in the United States) to the point where black doctors could give instructions to white nurses! The spectacle of the chairman of the huge Anglo-American group Harry Oppenheimer sharing, as his father had done with Sol Plaatje, a platform with blacks and Coloureds was highlighted as the sort of outrage that could be expected.

The ideas of apartheid which had been made current in the 1930s were given political form in a report prepared by the talented Paul Sauer, who had drifted away from the principles of his father, Merriman's friend and colleague, and of his godmother Olive Schreiner. Sauer distinguished Coloureds, who had to be accommodated by virtue of their white blood, from Indians, thoroughly undesirable, to be suppressed and deported, and from blacks, who should be given a separate political system, on traditional lines, in the reserves. The Cape Franchise was to be suppressed, and education taken out of the hands of the dangerously seditious missionaries. Most importantly, the movement of blacks, and their places of residence, must be strictly controlled. All this was music to the ears of Afrikaners, especially the country-dwellers, and the Nationalists went to the polls on this manifesto. Malan had already sketched out his own ideas for the future, and extraordinary they were, harking back to Kruger's republic, and on to grand apartheid. All 'coloured races' – non whites – were to be strictly segregated, and membership of the state accorded only to white 'burghers'

– but only those 'of whom it can be expected that they will act as builders up of the state'.[9]

There was nothing precise about Sauer's plans, for at that point the construction of a new society took very much second place to the restoration of party unity. In 1940 Afrikaners had been in turmoil: 'hardly ever before had there been greater confusion, internal divisions, and political impotency.' The resounding success of the United Party in the 1943 election had underlined Nationalist weakness, and the visit in February and March 1947 by George VI and Queen Elizabeth, accompanied by Princesses Elizabeth and Margaret, had been met with general enthusiasm, although many recalcitrant Afrikaners held themselves aloof. The royal party's arrival in the new and powerful battleship *Vanguard* also served to reinforce the – by then fading – idea of British naval power. It seemed to many observers that Malan's men were doomed to permanent opposition. It would take 'a miracle' for them to win.

The result of the May 1948 election therefore came as a happy surprise to the Nationalists and a mortal blow to the United Party, as devastating as it was unexpected. Although the United Party attracted many more votes – nearly 60 per cent – while the Nationalists polled only a minority, the weighting given to the country seats in the 1910 constitution ensured the return of seventy-nine Nationalist supporters against an opposition of seventy-four – sixty-five United Party, six Labour Party and the three Native Representatives. In a personal humiliation, Smuts himself was defeated. Within six months the two most powerful United Party ministers, van der Bijl and the white hope of the liberals, Jan Hofmeyr, were dead. An era had passed, and half a century of oppression and confusion began.

The new government was pure Afrikaner, and committed to the principles of apartheid. But Malan, like his successors, was prepared to be flexible in his interpretation of the new principles; having at last gained control of the country the Nationalists were determined not to lose it, and were prepared to use any methods available in order to hang on to power.[10] In the interests of party unity pragmatic policies had to be adopted, and the Nationalists were by no means united; traditional rivalries between the Cape party and that in the Transvaal had existed for many years. Malan's Cape supporters, the 'Keeroomstraat clique', with the backing of the influential Nasionale Pers and *Die Burger* and the Afrikaner financial institutions, were regarded by the Transvaalers as capitalists and dangerous liberals. The Broederbond, now that power had passed into Afrikaner hands, changed its character. Where previously it had been, as Dr O'Meara put it, 'almost exclusively a petty-bourgeois organization', after 1948 the upper ranks of Afrikaner business and the members of the numerous influential para-statal institutions combined in a solid bloc, able to exercise massive financial and social pressure.

Given its precarious majority, the priority of Malan's government was to ensure its continued existence. One useful device ready to hand was the extension of parliamentary representation to South-West Africa, a doubtfully legal move but one which provided six, reliably nationalist, new members from an entirely white electorate. In the longer term a determined effort to Afrikanerize the army, police, judiciary and civil service was begun, which was to prove very effective. The danger that British immigrants might decrease the Afrikaner majority was diminished by a restrictive Citizenship Bill in 1949. A systematic purge of senior civil servants provided opportunities to promote Afrikaners, especially in the Department of Native Affairs, which was previously awash with liberals. Police numbers grew, but with the Afrikaner increase three times as great as that of English-speakers, leading to an overwhelmingly Afrikaner force. In the army, senior officers, who were understandably antagonistic to fascism, and who regarded the 'Malanazis' as little better than traitors, were dismissed and replaced by Broederbond-approved Afrikaners.[11] The saboteurs and terrorists who had been put in prison during the war – although some had committed capital crimes – were released and welcomed back into the bosom of the *volk*. Civil servants were allowed – even encouraged – to join the Broederbond and the OB; black trade unions were no longer to be recognized; African artisan training to build cheap housing was cancelled; even black school meals were stopped.

With the executive branches ever more firmly in control, legislation could be enacted with some confidence that it would not be sabotaged by unsympathetic officials. Malan was loyal to the form of parliamentary government, but no Nationalist minister accepted the unwritten but powerful traditions and customs that made the Westminster system workable. Those former members of the Cape parliament who had developed such habits had by now disappeared from the political scene, and the new Nationalists had no compunction in such matters as not consulting with the opposition on the choice of a Speaker or packing the Senate with uncritical appointees, to say nothing of such minor Nationalist vulgarities as hailing every ministerial speech with 'Dank die Minister' (seventeen thanks from one member alone in the course of a single speech, according to Helen Suzman, the Progressive MP).

Malan's own position differed from that of his predecessors. Generals Botha and Hertzog enjoyed unquestioned status as heroes of the Afrikaner people, although Smuts had sacrificed this distinction in many Boer eyes by his unflinching support of the Imperial ties. Malan, a portly unheroic figure, acquired such authority by elevating his position as leader of the Nationalist Party, the 'Volksleier' – the Leader of the People, thereby equating the Nationalists with the Afrikaner people, something very different from the modest status of a Westminster Prime Minister. Although the Afrikaans term has the same meaning as the German 'Führer', the equation with Nazism is inept. In all their actions the Nationalists had complete faith in the rectitude and benevolence of their own intentions. Cynicism was rare, leaders were expected to be, and often were, deeply religious, Godfearing men; which made them both more powerful and more frightening. Essentially too, they worked in a sort of democracy, and relied for their power on an electorate casting its votes in free elections.

The first Nationalist Acts were less concerned with the mechanics of apartheid than with the introduction of a completely segregated society. The Mixed Marriage Act of 1949 banned marriages between whites and any non-European; the following year's Immorality Act made any form of sexual relations between whites and others illegal (those between whites and blacks had already been prohibited in 1927). The same year saw the Population Registration Act, the basic weapon of apartheid, under which every person had to be classified as 'White', 'Asian and Indian' or 'Coloured'; and to carry an identity card showing their race. The Group Areas Act extended territorial segregation to allow any area to be nominated for the use only of one race. The Illegal Squatters Act of 1951 provided the machinery for ejecting surplus natives from urban areas, or indeed from anywhere they were not required. Further expansion of reserves, promised as long ago as 1916 and never fulfilled, was stopped at some seven million acres less than had then been judged necessary. The Abolition of Passes Act required all black men to carry passes at all times (Malan had nothing to learn from George Orwell on the art of double-speak).

This last Act was particularly resented by the black population, and their reaction was indignant. Almost by default – the All-Africa Convention, which had once looked like a real challenger, having drifted off to the Trotskyist left, the unions subjected to increased repression and the communists driven underground by the 1950 Suppression of Communists Act – the ANC was left as the sole representative of black opinion, with the Youth League its most active part. It was a remarkable feat for an organization which before the war had seemed moribund, and even now was less than flourishing, and was in large part due to Dr Xuma's nine-year presidency. Decisive and efficient, Xuma had imposed financial discipline and given a new clarity of purpose. Working closely with James Calata and Z.K. Matthews, he had prepared a clear non-racial constitution and drafted a definitive Bill of Rights, the 'Africans' Claims in South Africa', based on the Atlantic Charter. But despite their devoted efforts the ANC remained very small indeed: in 1949 there were only 2,755 members, and finances remained very shaky.

The Young Turks, however, felt that Xuma had been left behind by events, having 'presided over the era of delegations, deputations, letters and telegrams. Everything was done in the English manner, the idea being that despite our arguments we were all gentlemen.'[12] They appreciated they were no longer dealing with gentlemen, and the 1949 Congress meeting therefore saw Oliver Tambo and six other Youth Leaguers elected to the executive, and Dr Moroka elected as President in place of Dr Xuma, who was perceived as antipathetic to the Youth League and temperamentally autocratic. Walter Sisulu was elected full-time Secretary in place of the retiring Calata. Both Moroka and Sisulu were essentially Christian conservatives, very much as their predecessors had been, but both had been convinced by events that the Youth League was right in pressing for more positive action against the government's rapidly-increasing persecution. When Pixley Seme, Makgatho and Clements Kadalie died in 1951, and Champion was replaced in Natal by Chief Albert Lutuli, the older generation had almost passed away. With their successors came the acknowledgement that the policies of persuasion, conciliation and cooperation that had seemed reasonable in the days of Smuts and Hertzog would have to give place to open confrontation.

Mending fences with the Indians, after the severing of never-intimate relations by a bloody Durban riot in January 1949, when blacks savagely attacked the Indian community, leaving a total of 142 dead, was appreciated to be essential.[13] The African and Indian Congresses appealed for calm, and attempted to work together.

1952, the tercentenary of Jan van Riebeeck's landing, was a year of celebration for Afrikaners, but not for the majority of the South African population. Preparations for a counter-demonstration, stimulated by the Youth Leaguers, were put in hand as early as 1950 when the Indian and African Congresses decided to make 26 June – an arbitrarily chosen date – a day of protest. The same day was to mark the launch of the 1952 Defiance Campaign, a carefully-prepared programme of non-violent passive resistance. The campaign, which was superbly well organized and disciplined, led by Drs Moroka and Dadoo, did much to heal the inter-communal wounds inflicted by the Durban riots. With the young Nelson Mandela emerging in charge of the volunteer demonstrators, the campaign led to 8,500 demonstrators being imprisoned and inspired widespread international sympathy. It was notable that most of the demonstrations took place in the Eastern Cape, with its long tradition of black political participation and with the powerful support of Z.K. Matthews. White liberal opinion in South Africa was divided; most viewed mass action nervously, and tried to discourage Congress leaders. Their fears seemed justified when more riots erupted in the Eastern Cape and Kimberley. The violence was at its worst in East London, where police charged a prayer-meeting, and whites attempting to help the injured were beaten to death and mutilated. The more timid among the white liberals, understandably worried, were discouraged, but others supported the blacks.

Ex-servicemen, who had fought alongside and admired the Indian Division in North Africa and Italy, were indignant at Nationalist attempts to end non-European voting rights, and formed the 'Torch Commando', which included such famous figures as 'Sailor' Malan and General Brink – both, as it happened, Afrikaners. The Commando's disapproval of apartheid, however, stopped short of allowing Coloureds to join their ranks. Less dramatic, but in the long run more influential, was the new magazine *Drum*. Founded and owned by Abe Bailey's poet and historian son Jim, and first edited by Anthony Sampson, an Oxford friend of his, *Drum* was produced by blacks and Coloureds as a popular journal which reflected, in the liveliest fashion, and some years before Steve Biko made it more fashionable, pride and pleasure in Africanness.

In a fashion never before – and rarely afterwards – seen in South Africa, Bailey harnessed a distinguished advisory board, which included Dr Xuma, to produce a magazine that sold nearly half a million copies throughout sub-Saharan Africa. Over *Drum*'s thirty-three years Bailey was able to claim that a generation of black authors, journalists and photographers had proved a great popular educator for the broad mass of their fellow-citizens.

As well as exposing the crudities of apartheid, the magazine stimulated popular African cultures and provided a joyous celebration of such politically incorrect events as the Cape Town 'Coon Carnival', as well as expert writing on such subjects of official disapproval as jazz, shebeens and bathing beauties.

Although the Defiance Campaign led to no cessation in oppressive legislation, and although both old conservatives and young radicals were discontented, the ANC emerged much stronger, with quadrupled membership. Moroka, who had been a skilled and courageous leader, was thought to be too willing to work with the old system of deputations and petitions, and was replaced by Albert Lutuli in December 1952.[14] Not as intellectual as his predecessors – many of his finest speeches were written for him by the white novelist Alan Paton – Lutuli was nevertheless a man of absolute integrity and great moral force.

Other potential sources of support for black protesters were the growing number of former colonies now represented in the United Nations. Starting with the Gold Coast, which in 1951 began its transition to full independence as Ghana in 1957, Britain was committed to advancing all her African possessions to independence, raising the spectre of South Africa becoming eventually the only white-ruled state on the continent. Even those countries with responsible government were in peril: the Mau Mau rising in Kenya began in August 1952, foreshadowing the end of colonial rule there, and similar movements in Nyasaland and Northern Rhodesia were emerging.

For the time being India was the source of most pressure on South Africa, restating as an independent country the objections that had previously been forcefully made by British viceroys, with Nehru's sister Mrs Pandit, the Indian representative at the United Nations, making forceful attacks on South African policies. Such outside intervention was unlikely to be effective, since South Africa could claim that the United Nations had no right to interfere in domestic matters, and that India, whose people had killed millions of Muslims after partition, whose government ruled Kashmir against the wishes of most of its population, and where a rigid caste system obtained, was in no position to read lessons to anyone else. Britain and France, as permanent Security Council members, were also usually anxious to dampen black agitation and to protect South Africa.

The courts continued to offer some defence against the Nationalist government. Malan's attempts to remove the Coloured voters from the electoral roll were twice frustrated by Appeal Court judgements, much to the fury of the Prime Minister; the Supreme Court ruled that if separate facilities had to be provided for different races, they must be equal; Judge Rumpff, to the government's chagrin, gave only suspended prison sentences to the leaders of the 1952 Defiance Campaign. Counter-attacking, the government made prudent political appointments to the bench of judges which gave rise to much criticism and increasingly undermined the independence of the judiciary, but helped the government to gain the verdicts it wanted. Unfavourable judgements could be, and were, overruled by subsequent legislation, although the 1910 Act of Union continued to safeguard Coloured voting rights by its provision that they could only be altered by a two-thirds parliamentary majority, which Malan did not possess.

With the death of Smuts in 1950 and that of Hofmeyr in 1948 the United Party had found itself without any serious leader or successor. 'United' was increasingly a misnomer. The party contained at least three factions: the progressives, Harry Oppenheimer, Helen Suzman, and the eminent and experienced Harry Lawrence, were constant supporters of more equal rights; Natalians continued to press for increased provincial independence; and a majority (two-thirds of United Party MPs had Afrikaner names) sympathized with many National Party policies. Smuts had held these conflicting strands together, but J.G.N. Strauss, who took over, a decent parliamentarian, lacked his great predecessor's personal leadership qualities. The best that the United Party could offer non-Europeans was political rights 'after a long period of training in the ways of democracy', and with the approval of 'a decisive majority of the European electorate'. This slightly watered-down version of Nationalist policy served to do nothing more than assuage some liberal consciences, and to convince young blacks that the patient reasonableness of their elders, now extended for nearly a century, had produced less than nothing.

But the government, by so quickly fulfilling so many of its undertakings to establish white supremacy, had left little else to promise its more militant supporters; only the prospect of a republic, bound by no obligations or sentimental commitments to Britain, remained as a goal. Before moving on this, still an unlikely prospect with so precarious a majority, one last effort was made to take over the British protectorates.

The protectorates

A comparison between the history of the Republic of South Africa on the one hand and the three British High Commission territories on the other provides what is almost a controlled experiment in political and social development. Valid comparisons could be made between the three states under British administration and at least one of the Bantustans, the Transkei. All had clear tribal-national identities – Sotho in Basutoland, Tswana in Bechuanaland, Swazi in their country and Xhosa in the Transkei – all controlled solid blocks of territory, and the Transkei had a population considerably larger than any of the British protectorates.[15] Basutoland and Bechuanaland, the two black polities that had survived nineteenth-century imperialism more or less intact, had been left to their own devices in the twentieth century, very much at the bottom of any Colonial Office list of priorities. British policy had been to plod along with the minimum of expenditure, relying on the good sense of the chiefs to work with the handful of colonial administrators. Such an inglorious system had worked better than it deserved: the two countries had preserved their traditions and independence from their overpoweringly influential neighbour, South Africa, but the transition to self-government was hurried and sometimes painful. The great Moshoeshoe's twentieth-century successor and first king of the independent country of Lesotho, Moshoeshoe II, educated at Ampleforth and Oxford, described colonial rule accurately, and not without bitterness, as 'one empirical, "common-sense" decision after another', which rarely produced a definitive and lasting solution.[16]

Overhanging the future of Basutoland, as of the other protectorates, was the possibility that, as the Act of Union had envisaged, they should eventually be consolidated with South Africa. Hertzog had made an unsuccessful approach to Britain in 1926, on the basis that the new status envisaged by Lord Balfour had made the Act of Union provisions protecting the territories' status irrelevant. He tried again in 1935, and succeeded in convincing J.H. Thomas, the convivial Labour Dominions Secretary in the coalition government, that the South African case deserved consideration, a view supported by many influential figures, including Lionel Curtis, the former 'Kindergarten' member.[17] After the Second World War Smuts confidently expected that the protectorates would be transferred to the Union as a recognition of South Africa's wartime contribution. For some time it seemed that this might well come about, but after the Nationalist victory in the 1948 elections the possibility receded. Offering economic assistance, which would have been valuable, and threatening sanctions, Hertzog did manage to get a joint Advisory Conference established to study possible incorporation; but Britain adhered to the original pledge that the people of the territories must be consulted, and their opposition to transfer was adamant. Without much hope of success Malan reopened the issue in 1949, but by then Britain was already committed to making the protectorates independent, and no serious discussions were ever begun.

Swaziland was in a somewhat different position, having been abandoned to the Transvaal before coming under British rule in 1901. While the two protectorates had retained their land-holding structure essentially intact, apart from a few well-defined areas in Bechuanaland, occupied by the old Stellaland farmers, Swaziland had to cope with the effects of the previous shamefully extensive concessions. In contrast Basutoland had avoided any white settlement, and remained the state founded by Moshoeshoe, although within reduced boundaries. With the national territory acknowledged to be the property of the Basuto people, it was clear from the first that this almost entirely black country could only be administered by its own people, the exiguous British officials holding the lightest of reins. Sir Herbert Sloley, 'the chief who understands how to be silent', established a pattern of minimal interference, with the Basuto National Council having a massive majority (ninety-four of a hundred members) nominated by the Paramount Chief.[18]

Moshoeshoe's successors never sought to establish the priest-king identity that the Zulu, and even more the Swazi, 'royal' families had cultivated, their paramountcy being purely of a political character. The Sons of Moshoeshoe were a dominant group, but no more; the tradition of democratic discussion never died out entirely. The bitter rivalry between Moshoeshoe's sons Molapo, David Masupa and Letsie carried on to the next generation, but subsided in the long reign of Paramount Chief Griffith between 1913 and 1939. In the same period the constant strife between the minor chiefs – there were more than two thousand of them – was smoothed over and the authority of the Paramount under the rule of law was supported, although the traditional hegemony of Moshoeshoe's successors was modified to some extent by the existence of the Council, founded in 1910, which played a considerable part in budgeting.

Not that there was too much to budget. By the Act of Union Basutoland was entitled to a modest allocation – less than 1 per cent – of South African customs revenues, and the Colonial Office remained parsimonious, except in the matter of education. Basutoland had always, thanks to the French Protestant missionaries, reinforced by the Roman Catholics competing for influence, which increased sharply after the conversion of Chief Letsie II in 1913, had a more extensive educational system than any other part of South Africa. The colonial government assisted missionary work with an annual grant of £50,000, not an overly generous sum, but twenty times that spent in Swaziland. Facilities were concentrated in basic education, with five hundred elementary schools and a technical college. It was only in 1939 that the first high school was opened, but the population had wide access to basic instruction, and constituted one of the most literate communities in black Africa. Lord Selborne had found the Basuto 'the most intellectually able and the most sensible', and in the Union they held a high proportion of clerical and supervisory jobs – which did not make for popularity among the other black peoples.

And people were Basutoland's great resource, for their country was impoverished, lacking in natural resources, without any but the simplest industries and entirely surrounded by South Africa. In 1837 the Basuto had as much as eight years' grain in store, and even after the loss of their best agricultural lands to the Free State were able to export eight thousand tons of cereals in a single year; but the pressure of population and soil erosion had left the country entirely dependent on remittances from Basuto working in the Union – nearly half the menfolk by 1956.

Whatever the deficiencies of successive British governments in developing the economy of Basutoland, a fair measure of effort and goodwill went into the constitutional consolidation of Moshoeshoe's heritage as a nation. In the 1920s and thirties Colonial Office lethargy was stimulated by the realization that almost all their charges had to be prepared for eventual independence. An investigation in the Southern African territories was mounted by the industrious Sir Alan Pim of the Colonial Office, which resulted in financial assistance being provided for much-needed land rehabilitation, and the first steps towards self-government. One instructive episode was the protracted debate in the National Council and the Colonial Office on the exact nature and status of the customary law earlier codified as the Laws of Lerotli. Lord Harlech, Mr Justice Landsdown, the Resident Commissioner and the South African Attorney General debated the subject exhaustively with the National Council before decisions were reached – and all in the middle of the Second World War.

It was only after the end of the war that the pace quickened, set in train by Britain's Labour administrations of 1945–51 and the progressive grants of self-government to the African colonies, beginning with Ghana, and recognized in Harold Macmillan's 'wind of change' speech in February 1960.

Succession problems followed Griffith's death in 1939, and one contender, Bereng, a son of the chief, resorted to magic to obtain power as an outbreak of particularly horrible '*diretlo*' murders burst out.[19] Bereng's trial and execution cleared the air, but the traditionalists contrived to block moves towards local democracy until the new constitution was effected in 1960, with a modest element of elective qualification introduced into the National Council, which became a Legislative Council. Half its members were appointed by the chiefs, the others elected by members of the democratically-elected District Councils. The new Council had limited resources or power. In 1961 Britain's subsidy to its protectorate amounted to the miserable sum of £1 per head, and 'External Affairs and Defence, Internal Security, Currency, Public Loans, Customs and Excise, Posts and Telegraphs and the recruitment etc., of officers to the Public Service [and all such officers were expatriates]' were excluded from the Council's jurisdiction. It was not much of an advance, but the Basutoland Legislative Council was the first South African legislature to be elected by black voters.

As self-rule approached two major political parties evolved: the Basutoland National Congress (BNC), established in 1952, claiming the mantle of the banned ANC; and the more conservative Basuto National Party (BNP), headed by Chief Lebua Jonathan, Moshoeshoe's great-grandson; with the energetic and talented new monarch Moshoeshoe II fighting his own constitutional corner. The first election, in 1965, was won by the narrowest of margins by the BNP – 41.6 per cent against the Congress's 39.7 per cent – but five years later Chief Jonathan made sure of things by a *coup d'état*. The King was exiled and opposition bloodily suppressed, several hundred people being killed in disturbances on a scale unknown in the protectorate days. Although arbitrary arrest and torture were not uncommon, Chief Jonathan's rule was, compared to that of most contemporary African countries, remarkably mild: opposition parties were tolerated, the King returned and the law courts remained vigorously independent. The BNC lost much credibility when it formed the Lesotho Liberation Army with Libyan help, and then allowed it to be used by the South African government in schemes to destabilize the Lesotho government.

But however internal power shifted, the overwhelming problem facing any potential Lesotho administration after the new state's incorporation in 1965 was its relationship with South Africa. At first this was amicable enough – the Republic was easier dealing with a reasonable autocrat than with a black democracy in its midst – but it soon deteriorated when Jonathan, who was receiving large subsidies from international agencies, adopted a stronger attitude to Pretoria. Tension culminated in a savage South African attack on the capital Maseru in December 1982, which was followed by a further worsening of relations. Four years later South Africa engineered a military coup which left King Moshoeshoe as the lone guardian of constitutional rights. Most real power rested with General Lekhanya, who with the King's assent made some progress towards constitutional improvement. In 1990 the King was again expelled, to be replaced by his reluctant son Letsie III. In that year more military unrest led Letsie to suspend the constitution; Pretoria intervened, sending Archbishop Desmond Tutu to mediate, after which the Basuto Congress Party, which had been proved to enjoy the support of most of the electorate, was restored to power. Lesotho's was not a notably successful record, with a number of deaths at each political crisis, but at least the Basuto people had the satisfaction of making their own errors, rather than being subjected to the dictates of a South African government.

Bechuanaland/Botswana was in a less dependent position on geographical grounds than Basutoland/Lesotho, having borders with Rhodesia/Zimbabwe, Zambia and South-West Africa. Its huge, sparsely-populated territory, half a million inhabitants in a land the size of France, had some respectable pastoral country in the east and was known to have mineral potential, but its main advantage was the sensible and moderate character of its rulers.[20] Since old Kgama III had assumed the Ngwato chieftainship in 1875 there had been, apart from a brief interlude from 1923 to 1925, only one other ruler. This was Kgama's son Tshekedi Khama, who until his succession by his nephew Seretse in 1959 ruled wisely in the interests of his people. This extended guidance of two prudent and dependable leaders had given Bechuanaland stability and something approaching a national identity. Kgama had been a man of decided views: ferociously teetotal, with alcohol being banned in his territories, and staunchly loyal to the faith of his missionaries, the London Society, to the extent of mounting a veritable persecution of the Anglicans. He also showed a remarkable capacity to enlist support from outside sources, protecting his people from both Rhodes and the Union of South Africa with equal success, without much positive assistance from Britain.

Kgama's successor Tshekedi had to cope with some particularly difficult colonial representatives and near-total neglect. Although only twenty when appointed as Regent for Seretse in 1925, he proved a skilled and determined negotiator, launching legal attacks on the Colonial Service whenever he considered it in the interests of his people to do so. He rarely received the cooperation to which he was entitled.

Two episodes of colonial clumsiness were outstanding. In 1933 Tshekedi, quite correctly, sentenced a young Afrikaner to be flogged for some unpleasant offences. As had happened nearly a hundred years earlier with Adam Kok, this aroused a violent storm of protest. Admiral Evans, who was standing in as High Commissioner, a dashing sailor who had been south with Scott, rushed up an expedition, complete with naval guns, to depose Tshekedi; seeing sense, and as embarrassed as he was ever likely to be, the Admiral restored the Regent a few weeks later.

More seriously, after the war the Regent's nephew and heir-apparent, Seretse, married an English woman, Ruth Williams, much to the consternation of Tshekedi and the more conservative Tswana leaders. The Labour government then in power handled the affair badly. Prime Minister Attlee wrote disgustedly: 'We are invited to go contrary to the desires of the great majority of the Bamangwato tribe, solely because of the attitude of the Union of South Africa and Southern Rhodesia. It is as if we had been obliged to agree to Edward VIII's abdication so as not to annoy the Irish Free State and the USA.' Nevertheless, it was done, although tranquillity and good relations were later restored between Tshekedi and Seretse. Churchill, with undiminished flair, deflated the reports of discontent: 'Indeed a terrible occurrence. An angry mob armed with stones and staves, inflamed with alcohol, and inspired by Liberal principles.'[21]

When the protectorate became the independent republic of Botswana in 1966, with Sir Seretse as President, 131 years after his great-grandfather Segkoma became chief, it was one of the poorest countries in the world. There were only forty graduates, one doctor to every twenty-two thousand people, and the country was run from a South African town, Mafeking. Within twenty years the situation had changed almost unrecognizably, thanks to a growth rate averaging 8.3 per cent per annum, the most consistently rapid in the world. In part this was due to international donors being much more generous than Britain had been – although grants from that source rose considerably – and the development of minerals (diamonds are a great help to a developing country), but these would have been useless without good internal management. The *per capita* GDP of Botswana became more than twice that of Lesotho and one of the highest in sub-Saharan Africa, considerably greater than those of naturally richer countries such as Zaire and Zambia, both of which had great mineral wealth, Uganda, and even Zimbabwe, well-endowed with fertile land. Almost alone among the countries of Africa, Botswana has continued to have democratic elections 'conducted with scrupulous fairness', an independent judiciary, and a free press. In the first elections of 1965 Seretse's Botswana Democratic Party, uniting the various communities, won twenty-eight of the thirty-one Assembly seats. The Organization of African Unity was not impressed, insisting on recognizing only the well-defeated opposition party, but the OAU has little experience of democracies. Seretse's sense of humour also baffled many critics, as when he declared that the new presidential palace should be known as 'The Woodpile'. Nor did the ANC help when, almost immediately after independence, they despatched a guerrilla force in the hope of destabilizing the new government, only to have them arrested, sitting under a tree, smoking cannabis. Two years later another band, led by Chris Hani, was also quickly picked up. Aggression from the opposite side, Rhodesia and South Africa, was a good deal more violent – seventeen killed in a 1978 invasion – but equally unsuccessful in disturbing Botswana's democratic processes. Britain as a colonial power may have been parsimonious, but it had allowed the Tswana people themselves to develop their own political skills, and left a nucleus of enthusiastic and talented expatriate staff. Although there is still criticism of the poverty and low status accorded to the San/Sarwa, Botswana remains one of the few African countries with a steady record of progress towards independence and democracy.

The third High Commission territory, Swaziland, was not strictly a protectorate, having come under British rule as a result of the Boer War, but it was treated in a similar fashion. Under the Transvaal's nineteenth-century rule, abetted by British neglect of the kingdom except when it needed the Swazi to fight some colonial war, economic aggression had made huge inroads on Swazi lands, with two-thirds of the country being held by Europeans, and only modest improvement was effected under British rule. When Colonial Secretary Leo Amery, who knew South Africa well, visited the country in 1927, he was shocked to see how little had been done to improve conditions. Nor was much done thereafter, in spite of delegations and appeals sent to London; even forty years later nearly 70 per cent of the people were undernourished and less than one-third were literate.

As in Botswana, the country's own leaders provided the initiatives, although of a very different character. The Khamas relied on their personal qualities – Seretse was succeeded by the Vice President, Dr Quett Masire, who came from one of the junior tribes – carrying no prestige of the quasi-mystical quality that surrounded the Swazi royal family, the Dlamini.

Alone among the dynasties of Southern Africa, the Dlamini are the only one in which royal titles have real meaning. The Zulu hereditary monarch 'King' Goodwill Zweletini Ka-Cyprian Bhekezulu, a feeble character, is little more than an obedient junior colleague of Chief Buthelezi, but the Swazi royals have retained considerable power. From 1899 to 1982, an unprecedented period, the country was led first by a queen-regent, Gwamile, and then by her son, King Sobhuza II, who reigned from 1921 to 1982. Between them mother and son consolidated the political and financial hegemony of their clan, retaining the *amabutho* system of their Zulu forebears, assembling every year for the first-fruits ceremonies. Displaying considerable ingenuity over devising new taxes, a large Development and Investment Corporation was established with the purpose of land repurchase. Even though a handsome proportion of this was used to provide a luxurious standard of living for the rulers, the Swazi people displayed no great reluctance to pay, and in the first election after independence was granted in 1967 the King's supporters won all the seats allocated to the Swazis. After the old King's death some diminution in enthusiasm was perceived, as inter-family squabbles and under-the-table agreements with South Africa robbed the Dlamini of some of their former prestige, but King Mswati III was duly crowned in 1986. When South Africa talked of transferring the little homeland of KaNgwane to the Swazis its people firmly rejected the proposal, declaring that they had no wish to be part of a 'medieval monarchy'.

King Mswati, educated at Sherborne school in Dorset, has shown signs of being willing to advance the modest democracy which Swazis have allowed themselves. Objections to the ban on political parties, and the fact that in 1996 the appointed cabinet included three princes and three other members of the Dlamini clan, have gone as far as strikes and the fire bombing of parliament, but the predominantly rural population remains apparently content with their traditional lot.

Taking the three protectorates together, while it is true that only Botswana has contrived to develop into a stable democracy, in all of them the people have on the whole had the governments most of them wanted, have been free to move around without restriction, have not usually been subject to arbitrary arrest and persecution, and have been able to rely upon a legal system to protect their interests – all rare achievements in twentieth-century Africa. Colonial rule might be accorded at least a single cheer.

SEVENTEEN

The Era of Show Trials

Only temporary residents

Dr Malan retired, at the age of eighty, in November 1954. He was succeeded, not as he had hoped by the faithful workhorse Havenga but by the younger Transvaal leader Hans Strydom, a man he detested. Strydom was, Malan argued, intellectually second-rate, domineering, devoted to straightforward *baaskap* rather than his own convoluted idea of apartheid, and divorced to boot, a state certainly unsuited to the leader of a Christian Nationalist party. All this was true: Strydom himself defined his intention that 'the Europeans must stand their ground and remain Baas in South Africa. If we reject the Herrenvolk idea ... how can the Europeans remain Baas? ... in every sphere the Europeans must retain the right to rule the country and to keep it a white man's country.'[1]

Lacking Malan's somewhat strained conception of parliamentary propriety, the new Prime Minister was able to steamroller through the abolition of the Coloured vote that had eluded his predecessor. His method of evading the 1910 Act of Union protection and the courts' objections was simply to pack the Appeal Court, enlarged for the purpose, with acquiescent judges and to treat the Senate in a similar way, so assuring the necessary two-thirds majority of both Houses, and the validation of this dubiously legal measure by the Appeal Court, where there was only one dissident, Oliver Schreiner, son of the Cape Prime Minister who had fought unsuccessfully for black rights.[2] It was thoroughly unprincipled, and entirely effective, proving, if proof were needed, the ruthlessness of Nationalist policies.

Not much could be expected from the divided opposition, although the United Party did its unavailing best to stop so blatant an act; but the only result was the defection to the Nationalists of five of the most right-wing of its MPs, led by the 'evil old liar' Arthur Barlow,[3] and the foundation of the well-meaning but ineffective Liberal Party, with Margaret Ballinger in parliament and inspired by the influential writer Alan Paton, a beacon of decency for many years. J.G.N. Strauss, who was no reformer, supporting as he did the 1936 Hertzog Acts and believing all communist activities to be treason, was replaced as leader of the dispirited United Party in November 1956 by Sir de Villiers Graaf, equally conservative by inclination, 'committed to European leadership and implacably opposed to equality', as he insisted, but a persistent trimmer.

Among the most useful items of Malan's repressive legislation was the 1950 'Suppression of Communism Act'. Conveniently describing communism as 'any effort to bring about any political, industrial, social or economic change . . . by the promotion of disturbances or disorder', and classing as a communist anyone who had ever so professed themselves, this gave the Nationalists an excuse to suppress almost any activity of which they disapproved. 'Named' victims had no right of appeal and were subject to numerous restrictions, including house arrest and a bar on any political participation. Walter Sisulu and Nelson Mandela were among those declared 'communist', as were all veritable communists, and therefore forced out of political life. Albert Lutuli was confined to the area of his home, and James Calata forbidden to celebrate marriages. Official endeavours were made to have Joe Matthews and Nelson Mandela disbarred, but both attempts were quashed by the Appeal Court. Dedicated communists continued their work in a well-organized underground, working parallel to, rather than integrated with, the ANC. Moses Kotane, however, combined the posts of Treasurer General of the ANC and General Secretary of the Communist Party, and Walter Sisulu worked closely with the communists.

Hampered in this way, the enthusiasm raised by the 1952 Defiance Campaign soon waned as the organizational defects of the ANC showed through. The veteran Dr Silas Molema, who had subsidized the empty treasury himself, was forced out of politics by the government, and the burden of exercising discipline fell on the rising star, Nelson Mandela, who instigated a full-scale development strategy, the M-plan, based upon a cellular organization but never put into effect. Stumbling along and allowing rhetoric to run far ahead of realism, the ANC was ineffective in resisting the implementation of the notorious Group Areas Act. Under the pretext of slum-clearance (and in justice some effort was made to provide decent basic accommodation in some of the new locations – 'nigger heavens' – as Z.K.

445

Matthews sardonically termed them) the government displaced established non-European communities: 'black spots' which had the misfortune to find themselves in an area now designated 'white'.[4] Such places, shabby and substandard though they might be, had a lively communal life, public facilities, and provided the security of freehold land for the inhabitants.

While many went willingly, others were compulsorily ejected from Sophiatown, near Johannesburg – resistance to which Lutuli hoped to make 'the Waterloo of apartheid' – and District 6, the lively Coloured quarter of Cape Town, followed by the Johannesburg Indians' deportation to the bleak wastes of Lenasia, twenty miles from the city centre. Once again repression served to encourage unity and bring blacks, Indians and Coloureds together, with some white supporters, of whom Father Trevor Huddleston was the most prominent, in the Congress of the People.

Sponsored by the African and Indian Congresses, the South African People's Coloured Organization and the new non-racial South African Congress of Trades Unions, COSATU, this event, held in June 1955, was the best achievement of racial unity for many years, and the Freedom Charter which emerged the most authoritative statement of reformist aims. Although some speakers, notably the young hothead Benjamin Turok, called for red-blooded worker control, the Charter, as might have been expected of any set of policies conceived by so disparate a group, attempted to be all things to all men; one reflection of a constant concern was the provision that no man's cattle should be taken from him. Even so, there were reservations. Albert Lutuli, dedicated to traditional liberal values, was concerned about the insistence on public ownership of minerals, banking and monopoly industries, although this did not go nearly as far as the policy of the British Labour Party, never a revolutionary organization, while extreme Africanists objected to the fact that many of the most prominent Congress supporters were non-black. For the rest the Charter advanced nothing more than demands for the freedoms commonly accepted in any normal state, but even these modest aims were enough to prevent its being accepted by any parliamentarians as a realistic programme, and the ever-diminishing United Party opposition continued its feeble struggle.

One of the most damaging of the Strydom government's proposals was the 1953 Bantu Education Bill, drafted by the Minister for Native Affairs, Dr Hendrik Verwoerd, the Prime Minister's right-hand man. This was intended to be the knockout blow against the Afrikaner's great enemy, the missionaries. Ever since van der Kemp and James Read had begun their work among the Hottentots, and John Philip circulated his bitter criticism of the Boers, animosities against English-speaking missionaries, who had established a black education system right up to university level which had produced dozens of worryingly talented, mature and impressive black leaders, had permeated Afrikaner society. Ninety per cent of all schools were state-aided mission institutions, and they were given the options of handing over to the government or facing financial extinction. Only the Roman Catholics and Seventh-Day Adventists (an unlikely combination) together with the Anglican Johannesburg diocese were able to resist.

Under the new system there was to be an end to this education for leadership and professional studies, and its replacement with a strictly-controlled curriculum more suitable to the requirements of a permanent underclass. Elementary education was to be in whatever Bantu language was spoken by the pupils, and was to be aimed at producing useful hands: there was to be 'no place for [the black] in the European community above the level of certain forms of labour'. Wherever possible expenditure was curtailed, hours reduced and parents expected to clean the classrooms, but the number of pupils was indeed increased and nominated school boards were introduced. The education system 'lost its best and most competent white teachers, and for the next decade the quality of education deteriorated considerably'.[5] Of all campaigns conducted by the ANC, that against Bantu education was the most poorly-planned, the most confused and, for Africans generally, the most confusing. Once again, the ANC reaction only exposed its old deficiencies. The Executive Committee refused to authorize a stay-away from schools, and when this was begun in the Transvaal it soon petered out, the only victims being pupils and teachers. The result was described as 'bitterness and recrimination'.

The Act was followed by the Extension of University Education Bill (double-speak again), which attempted to ban non-whites from multi-racial white universities (the English-speaking ones – the Afrikaner institutions always having been racially segregated) and to direct them to new tribal colleges. Fort Hare was now to be only for Xhosa, with other colleges serving Coloureds, Indians, Zulu and Sotho. In spite of sustained indignation and protests all over the country, with even the United Party aroused, the Bill became law in 1959.

As well as cutting off blacks from the best higher education, Nationalist governments pushed ahead with 'Christian National Education' – Christian in a decidedly peculiar sense, and National only as appertaining to

Afrikaners. From the first post-Boer War years the demand for Dutch schools in which children would be taught Calvinist doctrines in their own language had been strong, but the Christian National Education propounded by the University of Potchefstroom in 1948 went much further: 'extreme fundamentalist doctrines were put forward as principles on which to base education. The theory of evolution was condemned as opposed to predestination; history and geography were to be taught as divinely inspired in the narrowest sense of the word – God had given to each people a country and a task, and it was the Afrikaner task to rule South Africa, and no one had the right to question what was divinely ordained. Teachers who were not prepared to subscribe to these doctrines would not be appointed.'

In all these measures Malan's government displayed a simple-minded faith that a complex society could be changed by legislation into something better according with the Nationalist world-picture – a picture which grew year by year increasingly remote from reality. Far from producing industrious and obedient labourers and artisans free of any grand ideas of democracy and the rights of man, the legislation changed black distaste for the 'Boer' oppressors into something near detestation, while whites who could not stomach 'Christian Nationalism' began what was to be a steady stream of emigration. Not only liberal intellectuals who found the climate stifling, but many well-trained doctors and dentists were eagerly welcomed in Britain, as were a number of other varied talents – the Channel Tunnel owes its existence to the energy of one such expatriate.

Strydom died within three years of taking office, and was succeeded in September 1958 by the equally adamant but much more talented Hendrik Verwoerd. Born in Holland, Verwoerd had a sparkling academic career (typically, he declined an Abe Bailey Scholarship to decadent Oxford, preferring to study in Germany) before becoming editor of *Die Transvaler,* where he proved too extreme for Malan and his Cape 'liberals' by using his newspaper as a vehicle for German propaganda. A man of terrifying energy and commanding presence – the 'most granite-like man' Harold Macmillan had ever met, the only man who 'scared stiff' the otherwise unscareable Helen Suzman – Verwoerd had been appointed to the Senate in order to become Minister for Native Affairs between 1950 and 1958. In this period he was allowed a free hand to develop his scheme for 'grand apartheid', which would provide the final solution to the native problem and provide a political and theoretical framework on which permanent white, particularly Afrikaner, supremacy could be constructed. More than any other person Verwoerd was the architect of the grandiose and complex system which made South Africa 'the skunk among nations'. During his period of office, altogether sixteen years, ceaseless legislation imposed a virtual police state on black South Africans and, increasingly, on all other communities. There was to be segregation not only in housing and education but in every part of life, public or private; even lifts and beaches were designated '*Blanke*' or '*Nie-Blanke*'. The races were to be kept apart at all public events, and black attendance prohibited at any functions held in 'white' areas. Since this last prohibition included church services even some Nationalists objected, and that Bill was modified slightly.

Given the absurdity of the racial divisions already embedded in South African society and institutionalized by Malan, apartheid – or '*aparte ontwikkeling*', separate development, as Verwoerd preferred to call it – was not as stupid and unjust in theory as it became in practice. Verwoerd's plan of quasi-independent 'Bantustans', which he developed during his eight years in charge of the Department of Native Affairs, could be presented as the creation of 'ethno-national' states and described as the Promotion of Bantu Self-Government Act in 1959. Lesotho was about to be independent; why should the Xhosa not have similar rights? The Transkei, for example, had its own system of (very) limited self-government developed since the Glen Grey Acts of 1896 in the Bunga, a coherent population with a single language, and well-defined boundaries. It was, however, the only example, the other eventually-delineated black self-governing areas being little more than scattered parcels of indifferent land that no whites wanted. Nor was there any possibility of including prosperous towns within a Bantustan; all were to be farming communities, providing sustenance and acting as dormitories and retirement homes for the black men whose labour was needed in the towns. The objectives were bluntly stated:

> It is accepted government policy that the Bantu are only temporarily resident in the European areas of the Republic for as long as they offer their labour there. As soon as they become, for one reason or another, no longer fit to work or superfluous in the labour market, they are expected to return to their country of origin or the territory of the national unit where they fit ethnically . . .
> The Bantu who . . . have to be resettled in the homelands are:
>
> 1 The aged, the unfit, widows, women with dependent children and families who do not qualify for accommodation in European urban areas;

2 Bantu on European farms who become superfluous as a
result of age [or] disability . . . or Bantu squatters from
mission stations and black spots which are being cleared up;

3 Doctors, attorneys, agents, traders, industrialists, etc. [who]
are not regarded as essential for the European labour
market.

Since madam could not be deprived of her maids, black women were
allowed to live with their employers, but otherwise towns were to become
purely white. In principle, there was not too much difference between these
proposals and those of the 1922 Stallard Committee, but now the number
of black residents had very much increased, and the government had no
intention of being as lax as its predecessors. Suburban locations, virtually
a native group area, would be established at a safe distance from towns
where basic housing was provided. More often, nothing more than plots
were made available for blacks to erect whatever they pleased from the old
sacks and oildrums which were usually the only building materials they
could afford.

At the heart of the Bantustan policy lay the convenient assumption that
all South African blacks were members of a 'nation' – Xhosa, Zulu, Tswana,
Sotho, Venda, Swazi or Tsonga. The idea fitted neatly into current anthropological interest in non-European cultures and the desirability of these
developing along their own lines, concepts not without attraction to blacks
enthusiastic about preserving their own history and traditions. If separate
'homelands' could be established for each 'nation', then blacks would have
the opportunity to develop along their own lines, as a citizens of their own
homelands. They could also, and most conveniently, be stripped of South
African citizenship, able to work, if required, as foreigners in South Africa,
and shipped back to their homelands when no longer needed. The 80 per
cent plus of the rest of the country was to be a vast reservation for the
whites, together with, unfortunately, the Coloureds and Indians for who a
'homeland' could not readily be identified. Since black Africans would no
longer be South African citizens, their representation (by whites) in the
Houses of Parliament would no longer be justified, so removing another
irritant to Nationalists.

The Tomlinson Commission, on which the Bantustan concept was based,
had pointed out that the then-existing reserves only contained enough land
to support half the 1951 population, and that even after the remaining seven
million acres still to be purchased under the 1916 recommendations, and

all the improvements, including individual ownership of land, were effected, there would still be a considerable deficiency of land for black occupation. This unwelcome fact was glossed over by assuming that a new generation of black entrepreneurs could develop industrial estates which over ten years would provide some half a million new jobs. As for the resources needed, £100 million would suffice, necessitating a more-than-doubled Native Affairs Department budget. It did not take many years for the economic impossibility of the whole scheme to become apparent, but the homelands began to proliferate, and M.C. De Wet Nel, the Minister of Bantu affairs, triumphantly announced that 'everywhere the Bantu have acclaimed this a new day and a new era.'[6]

Bantustans were opposed with great vigour by the well-attended People's Congress, which united all strands of the ANC, but to others they had their attractions. Blacks prepared to cooperate could expect influential posts, substantial rewards and the possibility of developing their own power-base. Bophuthatswana, Ciskei, Lebowa in 1972, Venda and Gazank-ulu the following year and tiny Qwaqwa in 1974, joined later by Kangwane and KwaNdebele, emerged on the scene equipped with flags, national anthems, an elected assembly, and all the paraphernalia of a real state, which none of them were. Only the Transkei had any pretensions ever to be more than a mythical polity; Bophuthatswana, the next to become independent, was a ludicrous collection of areas scattered over the former Transvaal, Cape and Orange Free State with its southernmost component, Thaba Nchu, three hundred miles away; KwaZulu, the most populous, had some sixty parcels of land, but something that the others lacked – a unifying concept of Zulu identity amounting to nationhood which was to be carefully nurtured by the most outstanding Bantustan leader, Mangosuthu Buthelezi.

It was ultimately decided that Bantustans should become independent, although only four ever availed themselves of the opportunity, and in the meantime were to be self-governing. In keeping with the concept of black 'nations', administration would be through the chiefs, selected for being reliably conservative and obedient to Pretoria's instructions. Not much different, it would seem, from the Shepstone system that had assured peace and some prosperity to Natal; but that had been a century before. Quite apart from the altered expectations of human rights, two factors were important: the Shepstone system had been backed, in the final account, by an overwhelming military force, capable of imposing order, and had been accompanied, although to a much greater extent in the Cape than in Natal, by the example of black political activity and freedom of expression. By the 1960s and seventies the Nationalist government was having to resort to increasingly drastic measures to ensure public order, and had destroyed every freedom of association and expression that had previously been established.

As Prime Minister, Verwoerd continued the repressive measures he had initiated during his time as Minister of Native Affairs. In resisting these, women became, and remained, prominent. The Black Sash, worn by demonstrators – all white – from the Women's Defence of the Constitution League gave its name to their movement, cautious and painstaking but effective over a long term. Much more dramatic was the great demonstration peacefully – and humorously – arranged by the Federation of South African Women to protest against the extension of the pass system to women. In August 1956 twenty thousand women, led by Lilian Ngoyi, President of the ANC Women's League, Helen Joseph, an English social worker, and Rahima Moosa, representing the Indians, gathered silently outside the Union buildings in Pretoria, sang 'Nkosi Sikelel'i Afrika', and quietly dispersed.

Women were increasingly active in confronting official repression. However brutal police and other state servants might be, they acted within their own traditions, which held women in great respect (and generally underestimated them). Widespread and sometimes violent opposition in the black rural areas, especially in Pondoland, continuing for five years after 1957, was often orchestrated by women, who destroyed cattle-dipping tanks and picketed the municipal beer-halls – a move resisted by many men, and which led to one serious riot in the Cato Manor location in which nine policeman were killed. Although it took great courage and even more discipline to face abuse and rough handling, women were less likely to be beaten or imprisoned than men, and were able to take advantage of this. By contrast the Afrikaner women's organization, the Kappie Kommando, commemorating the trek in their Mother Hubbards were mildly ludicrous.

Women of different races often showed a better capacity for cooperation than did their men. When the 1957 Nursing Amendment Act established differential training, in a previously non-racial profession, for non-white nurses and their ejection from white hospitals, Black Sash, the Women's Federation and the Mothers' Union joined together in protest; but the feelings of those Afrikaner parents who 'would be shocked if they knew that the names of their children appear on the same register with non-Europeans and that they wear the same uniforms and insignia' prevailed.

(Within fifteen years reality asserted itself, and the Act was quietly ignored.)

The Pondoland revolt was particularly significant, since this part of the country was well-known for its past respectful allegiance to British authority. Govan Mbeki, a fervent communist with little admiration for colonialism, attributed this to the beneficent influence of the Methodist missionaries on the Mpondo chiefs, who 'trained at the homes of white missionaries, many living with them as members of their families. On the completion of their apprenticeship, they returned to their people, bringing vigour and a new approach to the conduct of chieftainship . . . They exercised real power [which] they used to entrench their chieftainship . . . the people contributed to the chief's treasury with little complaint.'[7] When such orderly and peaceable folk turned to violence it was a symptom of grievous discontent. The reasons for trouble were well-intentioned government proposals to combat soil erosion and disease by culling and dipping livestock, but the demonstrations were countered by police violence judged by one court in 1960 to be 'unjustified, reckless and even excessive'.

The Nationalist government hoped to seal its authority in a spectacular mass trial which began in December 1956 with the arrest of 150 prominent resisters of all races and communities. Originated by the former Nazi, now Minister of Justice, the usually competent Oswald Pirow, the hearing should have been an expertly-arranged show trial, along the lines of those in Nazi Germany or communist Russia, demonstrating the abominable intentions of the vile accused. As it turned out, the five-year trial was indeed a long-running public show, but one in which the advantage was entirely with the accused. The prosecution degenerated into farce, as first one group and then others were discharged for want of evidence, the original accusation of high treason was dropped, and the accused given bail. The high standards of the South African judicial system were again seen to have survived when in March 1961 the solemn Mr Justice Rumpff, who had tried Sisulu and Mandela nine years before, gave a thoughtful summing-up which concluded with finding all the accused not guilty.

Wind of change

Much worldwide attention was focused on the trial, to the considerable irritation of the South African government, and the conduct of two men especially, Albert Lutuli, considerate and courteous, who bore the main burden of the defence for the whole period, and Nelson Mandela, clearly a match for any government lawyer, was much admired. The irritation was considerably aggravated when in December 1961 Lutuli was awarded the Nobel Peace Prize, having to be released from the restriction order placed on him to allow the journey to Stockholm.

In the period covered by the trial the internal unity of the ANC had suffered. Mandela, Tambo and Sisulu, the leaders, were seen as too conventional, too sympathetic to capitalism and insufficiently devoted to Africanism by some members. The subsequent Pan-African Congress (PAC) secession, led by Robert Sobukwe, a Witwatersrand University professor, himself the most decent of men, shaded off into racialism (particularly against 'coolies') and terrorism (by its armed wing, Poqo – 'independent', or 'standing alone'). There was no love lost between the ANC and PAC, and the prospects for united action looked bleak.

They were saved, however, by the tragic shootings at Sharpeville, the 'township' outside Veereniging, where on 21 March 1960 the PAC launched an anti-pass demonstration (getting in before the ANC's own action planned for ten days later). A panic among the poorly-trained and badly-disciplined police – it was only a few weeks since the nine policemen had been killed in Cato Manor – caused them to open fire on the crowd, killing sixty-nine, mostly shot in the back while attempting to escape. Coming in the middle of the 'treason' trial, Sharpeville began to establish South Africa as internationally untouchable; although the USA, with Eisenhower heading a Republican administration, insisted on muting criticism, the President saying he felt that 'we should not sit in judgement on a difficult social and political problem six thousand miles away' – especially since America had 'similar difficulties'.[8] Some of the foreign condemnation was perhaps unjust, insofar as the single incident was concerned: Sharpeville was no different in kind from the shooting of Indians in Amritsar by Brigadier Dyer in 1919, or Irish civilians in Londonderry on 'Bloody Sunday' in January 1972, or Kent State University students in Ohio in 1970. It was the Nationalist government reaction that aroused particular indignation, since they assumed that it was the dead and injured who were to blame, and that no change in their policies needed to be considered (after the Amritsar massacre Dyer was sacked, the Viceroy Lord Chelmsford – son of the Zulu War General – banished to the political wilderness, and government strategy revised).

It had now become clear that Britain could no longer be relied upon to support black aspirations. The Anglo–French invasion of Suez and the suppression of the Mau Mau uprising in Kenya were widely regarded as unacceptable manifestations of old-fashioned colonialism. When South Africa was criticized at the United Nations, Britain often interposed a veto; with the Cold War between the West and Russia at its height, South Africa was perceived as a bulwark against communism and an island of stability in a rapidly disintegrating Africa. Although encouragement from English sympathizers was constant – Canon John Collins of St Paul's was a firm friend – the best that could be expected of any government seemed to be the friendly warning famously given by Prime Minister Harold Macmillan on 3 February 1960 in his 'wind of change' speech, in which he said that political power must be evenly distributed regardless of race, as was happening in so much of the rest of Africa.

By that time all the French colonies and those British colonies which did not already have some form of representative government were independent, including Togo, Cameroon, Malagasy Republic, Independent Congo Republic, Somalia, Ghana, Dahomey, Upper Volta, Ivory Coast, Chad, Central African Republic, Gabon, Mali, Niger, Senegal, Nigeria and Mauritania. With the liberal Iain Macleod in charge of the Colonial Office, arrangements for the independence of Uganda, Kenya, Zambia (Northern Rhodesia) and Malawi were in hand following the collapse of the Central African Federation. Although South Africans saw the worrying spectre of free black nations closing in on them, protection was still afforded by the Portuguese colonies of Angola and Mozambique, and by the intransigent white minority government in Southern Rhodesia.

Prime Minister Verwoerd stoutly asserted that South African policies were 'in the fullest accord' with 'the new direction in Africa'. He displayed with great clarity the Afrikaner misconception of history: 'We settled in a country which was bare. The Bantu, too, came to this country and settled certain portions for themselves.' On such a perversion of the facts, and disregarding the Khoi-San, the only area the Afrikaners could claim would be the Western Cape; but the Prime Minister came to the heart of the matter when he said, 'We have nowhere else to go.' Until the Nationalists could accept that they could only remain with the consent of the majority, South Africa was doomed to constant turmoil.

1960 was a key year. At the time of the 'wind of change' speech Sharpeville was only a month away, and the world's shocked reaction to the massacre seemed to justify Macmillan's warning. The General Assembly of the United

Nations condemned South African policies in April 1960, the only contrary vote being that of South Africa itself. Criticism, and lectures on the need for improvement, gave way to an expressed readiness 'to consider taking such separate and collective action' as might put an end to apartheid. There was little likelihood that South Africa would be moved either by exhortation or threats; a black strike was countered by a State of Emergency proclaimed on 30 March, and eighteen thousand people detained; on 8 April the Unlawful Organizations Act declared both the ANC and the PAC illegal, and the following day saw the attempted assassination of Dr Verwoerd by a disgruntled farmer, David Pratt, later found, oddly enough, to be mentally ill.

Verwoerd's government began to unite the *volk* in their laager after the fashion of their forefathers. The pound sterling was replaced by a new currency, the rand, originally at the rate of two rand to the pound, and backed by considerable gold reserves. A referendum in October 1960 opted for a republican form of government, the voting (52 per cent to 47 per cent) precisely reflecting the division between Afrikaans- and English-speakers. There was no reason why Commonwealth members should not have a republican form of government, as did its largest member, India, but during the Commonwealth leaders' meeting of February 1961 Verwoerd was attacked so sharply that he withdrew South Africa's application to continue its membership. On 31 May 1961 the country therefore became a republic, outside the Commonwealth, and now beyond a peradventure independent, free from any old colonial ties; the treaty of Veereniging and the restrictions of the Act of Union could be forgotten, the Union Flag and 'God Save the Queen' put aside. White South Africa accepted the new regime with varying degrees of enthusiasm; the impotent majority, living in anxiety and under pressure, could see no reason to bother with such academic issues, but refused to join in the celebrations.

One thing that might well have given pause to the advance of apartheid was a flight of investors, which did take place in the months after Sharpeville, when capital was withdrawn at a rate that halved the country's reserves and shook the rand. This nervous state continued until 1964, but had little effect on the economy, which grew at a real rate of 7 per cent in the same period. Nor did international disapproval inhibit exports increasing: in the six years after 1958, in spite of some decrease in South African exports to other African countries, exports to Europe increased by 50 per cent, to America by 65 per cent, and to Asia by more than 300 per cent.

To many South Africans the United Nations possessed little moral authority: the 'young and duck-tailed nations' were displaying 'juvenile aggressiveness and their inferiority complexes ... the grand adventure of the nations has become a sordid struggle for the microphone'. It was not South Africa that was at fault: 'the world is sick', and South Africa must not 'allow herself to be dragged into that sickbed'. At any given time it was easy for South African government spokesmen to find examples of corruption, poverty, inefficiency and sheer horror elsewhere in the continent, by comparison with which the lot of South African blacks was idyllic. There was no need to build frontier defences to prevent hordes of oppressed South African blacks seeking liberty in the newly-independent Zambia and Malawi; the boot was on the other foot, as South African wages and living conditions were consistently better than those of its neighbours. In the worst months after Sharpeville, when an incompetent and often brutal police force was shooting at demonstrators, some seven hundred people were killed; in Nigeria two million died in the Biafran civil war, and a million in Idi Amin's Uganda; while outside ex-British colonies conditions were often even worse. Individual Nationalists might be simple-minded thugs, but the South African government was, in its own peculiar way, always trying to find reasonable answers which would satisfy the majority while assuring white supremacy; which was impossible.

In 1963 Indians were recognized as citizens – second-class, of course, but still with the right to live in (selected bits of) South Africa. The same year saw the establishment of the Transkei as 'a self-governing territory within the Republic of South Africa', with a part-elected assembly and some powers of government, rather greater than those of an English county council, and more akin to those allowed in Northern Ireland until 1972. Chief Kaiser Matanzima – who was, ironically, Nelson Mandela's kinsman and childhood friend – could be relied upon usually to toe Pretoria's line, but an opposition Democratic People's Party emerged, headed by Chiefs Sabata Dalindyebo of the Thembu, also a kinsman of Mandela's, and Victor Poto of the Mpondo, who had been a member of the Native Representative Council at its dramatic meeting with Hofmeyr; both chiefs had also worked closely with the ANC, and were committed to black political rights. Their party won almost all the elected seats, but the nominated majority of biddable chiefs ensured that Matanzima was able to form the government.

For the remainder of the non-European population the outlook was gloomy. Existing restrictions were reinforced in 1962 by adding the imposition of house arrest to police powers, and in the following year by the imposition of ninety-day imprisonment (later extended to 180 days) without trial, in solitary confinement, and without giving reasons. With the Habeas Corpus Act, that cornerstone of civil liberty, abolished, the autocratic powers of the state were perfected. No more extensive armoury of coercive laws existed in any Western state; few anywhere could use legislation retrospectively going back ten years, as did the Unlawful Organizations Act, under which a person who had committed such a crime as defending 'a scheme for United Nations intervention to alleviate non-white grievances [was] liable to be hanged for his proposal'.[9] In fact no such case was ever tested in the courts, where it would probably have been thrown out; even at the worst moments the South African judiciary never wholly abandoned its original principles, and could usually be relied upon to deliver verdicts which were in accordance with the law; but the law was frequently oppressive.

Following much self-examination the ANC decided that the time had come to end its policy of reasonable gradualism and passive resistance, and to accept that some degree of violence was the only route forward. After eighty years of principled political action organized by leaders for the most part committed Christians bred in parliamentary traditions, it took half a century of increasing pressure, culminating in the battery of discriminatory legislation unveiled by the Nationalists, to exhaust their patience. Only when it became painfully clear that there was to be no hope of the smallest advances towards social justice was the ANC brought to the brink. Passive resistance had worked against British rule in India, and had not been ineffective in South Africa when backed by pressure from another Commonwealth country, but after 1961 the susceptibility of South Africa to external influence was much diminished. Even when presented with the clearest evidence the executive committee of the ANC was not convinced by the arguments in favour of a limited degree of sabotage, advanced by Mandela and Sisulu; Lutuli had been an apostle of peace all his life, and was supported by the Indian Congress leaders, Dr Naicker and Mandela's old friend J.D. Singh, who protested: 'Non-violence has not failed us; we have failed non-violence.' The most that could be agreed was that no opposition would be offered to the creation of an independent body engaging in strictly-controlled violence, centring around the sabotage of vital installations; any injury to the person was absolutely forbidden.[10] This group was to be Umkhonto we Sizwe – the Spear of the Nation – usually known as MK, and directed by Mandela and Joe Slovo. Under an affable exterior Slovo was, and remained throughout all the exposures of Soviet tyranny and communist inefficiency, a hard-line Stalinist.

MK's headquarters in the Johannesburg suburb of Rivonia was used as a bomb factory, and the first minor explosions were duly arranged for 16 December 1961, the date of the Afrikaner festival of Dingane's Day. Shortly afterwards Nelson Mandela left on a journey abroad as a delegate of the ANC, which confirmed him as the leading figure in the resistance movement, a position previously adumbrated by a March 1961 conference in Pietermaritzburg which had elected him as head of a new National Action Council.

Mandela was in process of developing from something of a playboy, given to smart suits and large cars, with many sexual involvements, charming, quick in argument but lacking in 'bottom'. Prone to enthusiasms, and an unsteady judge of character (the worst example being his second marriage in 1958 to Winnie Madikizela, devastatingly attractive but unprincipled and ambitious), Mandela was unswervingly loyal to his friends, who fortunately included the irreproachable Oliver Tambo, his previous legal partner, now running the ANC in exile, Walter Sisulu, a man of much wisdom, and the stately Lutuli. Under their influence, and stimulated by the persecution of clearly inferior government representatives, Nelson Mandela was beginning in 1961 to achieve that stature he was to exhibit so clearly thirty years later.

Making an impression wherever he went, which included meetings with the Labour and Liberal leaders in England, and representing South Africa at the Addis Ababa Pan-African Freedom Conference, Mandela was welcomed by leaders of the independent African states. Julius Nyerere of Tanzania, Habib Bourguiba of Tunisia, Sékou Touré of Guinea and the philosopher-President of Senegal, Léopold Senghor, all men of acknowledged eminence (and a sad contrast to many later African leaders), welcomed Mandela as one coming from Albert Lutuli, whose status as an equal they now willingly acknowledged. Before returning to South Africa Mandela spent three weeks in Ethiopia learning something of firearms and the practice of guerrilla war, skills he was never to have the opportunity to use. On his return, enjoying the risky adventure of going about the country in khaki fatigues and carrying a pistol, Mandela lasted for only a few days before being arrested on 5 August 1962.

In his absence, the MK conspirators had been uncommonly careless. Their activity at what was meant to be their secret Rivonia headquarters had been so blatant that it did not need the new Police Special Branch, or the CIA informer who had infiltrated them, to raid the house and find enough evidence to convict any of the resistance leaders who had not already fled abroad. Mandela and Sisulu found themselves once again the leading defendants in what was intended to be another show trial, a more successful repeat of the 1956–61 Treason Trial.

In this case, which was heard in July 1964, the charges of sabotage were not all disputed, but the defendants strenuously denied any intention to provoke an armed rebellion. The ineptness of the prosecution, led by a Dr Yupar, was up to the expected standard, and Mandela was able to turn the occasion into a statement of black ideals with an authority and nobility that attracted worldwide attention and sympathy. Quoting Albert Lutuli, who had said:

> Who will deny that thirty years of my life have been spent knocking in vain, patiently, moderately and modestly at a closed and barred door? What have been the fruits of moderation? The past thirty years have seen the greatest number of laws restricting our rights and progress, until today we have reached a stage where we have almost no rights at all

and denying that he had ever been a communist – of which there could hardly be any doubt – Mandela ended his major four-hour speech by encapsulating African ambitions in the most direct way:

> Africans want to be paid a living wage. Africans want to perform work which they are capable of doing, and not work which the government declares them to be capable of. Africans want to live where they obtain work, and not be chased out of an area because they were not born there. Africans want to own land in places where they work, and not be obliged to live in rented houses which they can never call their own. We want to be part of the general population, and not confined to living in ghettos.
>
> African men want to have their wives and children to live with them where they work, and not be forced into an unnatural exist-ence in men's hostels. African women want to be with their menfolk and not be left permanently widowed in the reserves. We want to travel in our own country and to seek work where we want to and not where the Labour Bureau tells us to. We want a just share in the whole of South Africa; we want security and a stake in society.
>
> Above all we want equal political rights, because without them our disabilities will be permanent.

Ending with a peroration which reduced the court to silence, Nelson Mandela emerged from the trial not only the clear leader of blacks in South Africa, but one capable of transcending racial boundaries.

> During my lifetime I have dedicated myself to this struggle of the African people. I have fought against white domination, and I have fought against black domination. I have cherished the ideal of a democratic and free society in which all persons live together in harmony and with equal opportunities. It is an ideal which I hope to live for and to achieve. But if needs be it is an ideal for which I am prepared to die.

But a leader sentenced to prison for the rest of his natural life.

A nation mourns

The dichotomy between the unsparing use of police powers over four-fifths of the community to create a virtual autocracy, combined with the exercise of normal democratic processes in the remainder, was becoming more marked. As a Prime Minister depending on the continuance of a parliamentary majority, Verwoerd took pains to conciliate English-speaking South Africans, correctly judging that most had as little enthusiasm for majority rule as any Afrikaner. Indeed, as late as 1991, when the ANC was clearly going to be a major force in any government, only 7 per cent of English-speakers (as against 5 per cent of Afrikaners; hardly a major difference) wanted a normal parliamentary system in which blacks had full rights. The wilder ideas of Broederbond chairman Piet Meyer that English South Africans should be forced to accept Afrikaner values were dropped. Verwoerd hoped that residual jingoism would disappear in the new republic, and looked forward 'above everything . . . to the happy day when all of us will be so joined together by a common patriotism into one people . . . that the political differences that might exist will no longer be based on [ethnic/linguistic] sentiment'. But Dr Verwoerd was talking, of course, only of whites.[11]

Two undistinguished former United Party ministers, Alf Trollip and Frank Waring, were even appointed to Verwoerd's cabinet in 1961. That year's election confirmed the Nationalists' popularity: they obtained 105 seats, winning more than 63 per cent of the votes, reducing the United Party to forty-nine seats and the Progressive Party to a single member, the indomitable Helen Suzman.[12] Such an opposition gave little trouble, what liberal resistance as existed being extra-parliamentary. In this the Churches played an active part – at least the English-speaking Churches. For a short time after April 1961 it seemed that the Dutch Churches might join the resistance when a conference at Cottesloe in Johannesburg concluded that almost every aspect of apartheid was un-scriptural and un-Christian. The Dutch Churches added their own glosses, but offered little fundamental objections. *Die Burger*, the influential Nationalist organ, appeared to agree, asking whether Afrikaners were 'prepared to listen again to whether God, perhaps, has something to say to us? Or do we run the risk of our informing God that the route we are following is, in every detail beyond question, also his way for us?'

Such heresies could not be allowed, and the moral authority of apartheid must be above question. Verwoerd called his ecclesiastics to order, and the Dutch Churches duly recanted. Opposition was left to the English-speaking Churches, the French and German denominations and such figures as Archbishops de Blanke and Tutu, with Father Trevor Huddleston providing a power-base for liberal resistance. But the Dutch Churches' attitude was too much for at least one dominee, Dr Beyers Naudé, a 'Broeder' himself, who stubbornly stuck to the Cottesloe conclusions and became an outspoken and influential opponent of apartheid.

Much more violent white reaction to apartheid was initiated by the African Resistance Movement (ARM), mostly composed of young communists, who almost by definition six years after the brutal Soviet actions in Hungary tended to be either hard-liners or confused. John Harris, the ARM member who planted a bomb in Johannesburg Central Station in July 1964, was in fact a member of the Liberal Party; his act led to the death of one old woman and the mutilation of a small girl, and played into the hands of the government as a reason for ever-stricter suppression.

From the right, Verwoerd had no compelling reason to fear Albert Hertzog's supporters, who were keeping their powder dry and awaiting Verwoerd's retirement, due in 1970. However much indignation was aroused by a deal – in fact a very good deal – whereby Harry Oppenheimer's Anglo-American group reversed the General Mining Company into the FVB-owned Federale Mynbou. Although advantageous, this was supping with the cherished devil of reactionary Afrikaners, but such objections mattered little as long as the *volk* were prospering; and that they were certainly doing. Afrikaners had always been dominant in farming, controlling over 80 per cent of the industry, but between 1948 and 1964 Afrikaner ownership in other sectors had increased as follows:

% ownership	1948	1964
Mining	1	10
Manufacturing/construction	6	10
Professional	16	27
Finance	6	21

This success, at the expense of English owners, was parallelled by the expansion of management posts. In the same period the number of Afrikaners in these categories increased.

Afrikaner employment per thousand

Category	1946	1960	Median income (Rand)
Professional & technical	43.2	68.1	2,675
Administrative, managerial & executive	30.7	42.4	3,308
Sales	19.3	26.1	2,168

Again, the increase in numbers was at the expense of English-speakers.[12]

Black African constitutional leaders having been either exiled, imprisoned or silenced, only the alternative of violence seemed to be left. Poqo, the anti-constitutional wing of the Pan-African Congress, began a campaign led by Potlako Leballo, an unequivocal terrorist. This went well beyond the ANC's policy of confining violence to the sabotage of physical plant. After many fatal urban riots, political assassinations in the Transkei, the murder of five whites – including two girls and a woman camping by the Bashee Bridge near Umtata – and a promise of 'shocking determination ... to free the African people in 1963 by Positive Action', Leballo was ejected from his refuge in Basutoland and a ferocious reaction in South Africa provoked. Already-severe penal laws were made stricter: suspects could be 'detained without charge or evidence, to this side of eternity' in solitary confinement. Leballo had drawn down on all blacks the wrath of the government, and forfeited the support of almost all whites and many blacks, who felt 'dismay and anger' at his actions.

With blacks subdued and the government enjoying the enthusiastic support of most Afrikaners and the increasingly general accord of English-speakers, and with the economy having recovered from the Sharpeville shock, it seemed that the iron will of Verwoerd would continue to prevail. The March 1966 election brought National Party representation to the overwhelming total of 126 seats, with thirty-nine left for the United Party, now more divided, and Helen Suzman remaining the only Progressive. Although, with the exception of the well-rewarded Trollip and Waring, all ministers were Afrikaners, many English-speakers had voted for National-ists. Even in Natal, that last fortification of imperialism, over 40 per cent of the votes went to Nationalist candidates. Maintaining white supremacy and the comforts that went with it, English South Africans had opted either for open support of apartheid or unhappy acquiescence. The Nationalists had a clear field in what was for the moment effectively a single-party state.

By 6 September 1966 there was not much of Verwoerd's programme unfulfilled. Five years of the republican constitution had been celebrated, the apparatus of apartheid was in place, the official opposition reduced to mutterings of discontent, foreign exchange and gold reserves at a record high, the GDP growing at an annual rate of 7 per cent and the capital outflow reversed. Then, on that day, a second assassination attempt succeeded when the Prime Minister was stabbed to death on the floor of Parliament by a deranged parliamentary messenger. The British magazine *Private Eye* carried on its cover a group of beaming Zulu warriors leaping with joy, and the caption 'Verwoerd: A Nation Mourns'.

Verwoerd's successor was the Justice Minister, Balthazar Johannes Vorster, junior in rank, but basking in the glory of his six years' successful suppression of the black opposition. There was little likelihood that the new Prime Minister would be more liberal than Verwoerd had been. During the war Vorster had been a leader of the Ossewa Brandwag, and been interned as a Nazi: 'We stand,' he claimed in 1942, 'for Christian National-ism which is an ally of National Socialism. You can call such an anti-democratic system a dictatorship if you like. In Italy it is called fascism, in

Germany National Socialism and in South Africa Christian Nationalism.' But Vorster had not reached the political summit at the age of fifty-one without developing flexibility. Recognizing that the Nationalists could now rely on considerable support from the English-speakers, he foresaw his party becoming what the old Generals had always wanted the United Party to be, a solid alliance of Afrikaners and English bolstering white rule. This was a position guaranteed to alienate such guardians of Afrikaner purity as Albert Hertzog and the Broederbond chairman Piet Meyer. Vorster moved quickly, sacking Hertzog and calling Meyer to heel, forcing Hertzog out of the National Party to form his own Herstige [Reconstituted] Nasionale Party (HNP).

Less of an overpowering personality than Verwoerd, Vorster relied on his qualities as chairman, on selecting and directing a team, and his knowledge of the police. The security services, which had as always proliferated, were united into a new Bureau of State Security, the notorious BOSS, the head of which reported directly to the Prime Minister and to which a rapidly-growing unaccountable budget was allocated. BOSS was given an opportunity to extend its operatives' various talents by the external challenges to the South African state, which became ever more perturbing during Vorster's ten years of office.

Botswana, Lesotho and Swaziland, now independent, formed potential centres for resistance movements, while Ian Smith's white-minority regime in Rhodesia was subject to increased external pressure and was becoming a liability to Pretoria. The major threat from abroad appeared to be the ANC and the PAC, but the latter, angrily opposed to the Congress and all its works, never developed a comparable international status. Even before the ANC was banned in 1960 it had been accepted by them that foreign support was essential, and Oliver Tambo with Joe Slovo and many of the most active ANC members had established a London office, from which international affairs were handled. There was also a headquarters nearer home, at first in Tanzania, moved to Lusaka in 1964 after Northern Rhodesia became independent as Zambia under the guidance of the usually prudent and principled Kenneth Kaunda.

The ANC 'external mission' there soon found itself in an uncomfortable position. In the euphoric days of Nelson Mandela's mission to African heads of state, the ANC had expected massive support for its struggle; this never materialized. As so many of the new states dissolved into dictatorship, corruption and civil war, others found themselves torn between emotional support for black liberation movements and the pragmatic necessity of accommodating themselves to the reality of overwhelming South African power; and the PAC, at daggers drawn, competed for what help was available. Some spectacular success was essential, but none was forthcoming. Attempts to infiltrate fighters into the Republic were easily countered by the security forces, who deployed ever-more ruthless methods of dealing with suspects. The ambitious idea of launching a full-scale guerrilla war was given a rehearsal in 1967 when a combined operation with the Rhodesian Liberation movement, ZAPU, in the Wankie Game Park was crushed with contemptuous ease. More than seventy insurgents were killed and hundreds left in Rhodesian prisons. Intensive self-examination at the 1969 ANC conference led to a decision to embark on a 'People's War' under a 'Revolutionary Council' subject to increasing communist influence – a movement which the patient Christian Tambo was poorly qualified to lead. Africanists, Trotskyites and plain disillusioned followers, among them Joe Matthews, took themselves off. Although the 'People's War' caused only minor concern to South Africa, a much more disturbing situation was arising in South-West Africa.

Malan's unilateral assertion of sovereignty in South-West Africa had been criticized by the United Nations, the International Court of Justice, and much of world opinion, but for the immediate post-war years South Africa was protected by its friends with permanent seats on the UN Security Council. France and Britain, as old colonial powers, were sympathetic, whilst the United States chose to disregard the objectionable features of the South African regime in favour of its value as a staunch anti-communist ally. However many critical resolutions were passed in the General Assembly, increasingly dominated by Afro-Asian countries – seventy-three out of 125 by 1965 – the Security Council could be trusted, until Sharpeville, to squash them. Apart from passing resolutions, there was not much the United Nations could do. The only potentially effective weapon was the use of economic sanctions, and these would work only if South Africa's major trading partners joined in. Since these were, overwhelmingly, Britain, the USA and Western Europe, sanctions had little chance of being implemented in the near future.

Eight years of Republican government in the United States, often hysterically anti-communist and believing South Africa to be a reliable ally in the struggle against the 'evil empire', ended with the election of John Kennedy as President in 1960. There was no immediate change in policy: Robert

McNamara, the Secretary of Defense, insisted on the importance of South Africa's support, and the supply of arms, including three submarines, continued. But attitudes stiffened, and in December 1963 the US concurred with Britain in banning arms sales to South Africa. More international indignation was aroused by the Odendaal Commission's report in January 1964, recommending the imposition of apartheid 'in an extreme degree' in South-West Africa. A US Congress hearing in March 1966 received much adverse testimony, among the most interesting being that of the ANC member Gladstone Ntlabati, who stated that 'my concern is what will happen to that white minority in the future because . . . with all our suffering, we are being hardened. The government claims that it would be committing suicide by giving us political rights . . . the government is in fact committing suicide by not giving us political rights.'[13]

The defence, first advanced by Prime Minister Smuts, that the United Nations could not interfere with any member's domestic concerns (a sentiment with which all UN members concurred, all having something to hide) could not be applied to South-West Africa, which was held by South Africa on the authority of the United Nations itself. It was no surprise therefore that in July 1970 the Security Council – the USA, France and Britain abstaining – finally terminated South Africa's mandate in South-West Africa; from that time onwards South Africa was illegally occupying the territory. Vorster's government was however open to discussion and skilled at procrastination, and the US government, Republican again from 1968, relaxed its pressure. After negotiations with the Secretary General (Dr Kurt Waldheim, another former Nazi), modest progress was made, but too slowly for the United Nations. In December 1974 the Security Council demanded that South Africa should leave South-West Africa, which was now more frequently called Namibia, and mend its ways at home.

Strategically speaking, there was no good reason to hold on in Namibia: its six seats were no longer needed to ensure a Nationalist majority in parliament, and a better policy would have been to continue cooperation with the UN. Instead, the decision was taken to retain control of Namibia as a passage to Angola, where a Russian-backed government emerged in 1975 after the Portuguese unceremoniously left their old colony. It was a decision that was to prove vastly damaging to South Africa's prospects. Dr Salazar's quasi-fascist Portuguese government, admired by many Afrikaners, had continued its authoritarian ways under Caetano Marcello until April 1974, when a *coup d'état* brought in a new government. Realizing that it was impossible to hold on to its embarrassing and expensive African colonies, the decision was taken to disengage as quickly as possible, leaving whatever chaos ensued for someone else to sort out. As a result South Africa was faced with violent upheaval beyond its border with Mozambique and on South-West Africa's frontier with Angola.

South Africa had been given the final date of 30 May 1975 to end all discriminatory practices in what was to be Namibia, and to transfer power, in some way, to the Namibian people; but by then Vorster's government had become thoroughly embroiled in tumults beyond its borders. Had the United Nations resolution been complied with, South Africa, whose own frontiers were several hundred miles away, would never have been sucked into the disastrous Angolan war. The South-West African People's Organization (SWAPO), a movement mainly of the northern Ovambo people and closely allied with the ANC, had been making its presence felt since 1966, with some assistance from Northern Rhodesia, especially after that country's independence as Zambia in 1964. Sporadic SWAPO insurgency had been countered by the South African army when they moved into Namibia in 1973, progressively increasing their strength until 1976, when a 'free-fire zone' was enforced along the entire length of the Angolan frontier. Within the zone, following the example of the German owners seventy years before, soldiers shot to kill, with no questions asked.

Inside Angola, three rival liberation groups were fighting for power. José dos Santos' MPLA had Russian backing, inevitably assuring that the rival parties – FNLA, based in Zaire, with the support of the corrupt Mobuto regime; and UNITA, Dr Jonas Savimbi's personal group – both attracted American support. In July 1975 South Africa, acting in concert with a secret CIA initiative, began to channel arms to FNLA and UNITA. In April of that year the US had been humiliatingly bundled out of Saigon, defeated by a Third World army, leaving the hawks desperate for some sort of success elsewhere, and feeling that South Africa – who had joined the United Nations action in Korea, and frequently reminded the USA of the fact – would be a reliable proxy. When Cuban 'advisers' acting as *Russian* proxies arrived in Angola in April 1975, followed later by ground troops, to support the MPLA, and since this move was viewed apprehensively by Angola's neighbours, including the reliable Kaunda, it seemed that a wonderful excuse had been vouchsafed to strike a blow against communism – and this time without risking American lives.

This particular Henry Kissinger conspiracy brought about the speedy resignation of Nathaniel Davis, the US Assistant Secretary of State for African Affairs, but the action went ahead. Without telling the public, on the basis of an agreement between BOSS and the CIA, South African troops invaded Angola, rapidly moving almost to the suburbs of the capital Luanda, more than three hundred miles north of the Namibian border and some eight hundred miles from the nearest part of South Africa. The invasion was supported not only by the USA, but, following a secret agreement in August, by Zambia. It would probably, whatever had happened, have been defeated by the Cubans, whose artillery and aircraft were more than a match for the South Africans', but defeat was made certain when the Americans – the CIA intervention having been disowned by Congress – backed out.[14] All this had been done secretly, the South African people only being informed when their battered troops had safely withdrawn. The MPLA was widely recognized as the legitimate government and American Senator Dick Clark procured a resolution prohibiting assistance of any kind to Angolan factions unless the President so decided and gave full details to Congress. But the civil war continued.

After the Nixon/Ford administrations between 1968 and 1976, during which Kissinger's unscrupulous plotting had been supportive of the South African government, Jimmy Carter's decent instincts dictated a reverse. On a visit to the United States in 1979 Vorster assured the press: 'South Africa has accepted that it [Namibia] will be independent on 31 December 1978, as they themselves decided.' Elections, well supported and conducted, were indeed held, but were boycotted by SWAPO; independence had to wait for another twelve years, and a very different political climate; meanwhile SWAPO guerrilla violence was countered by South African military retaliation, sometimes unscrupulously massive.

Matters were simpler in Mozambique, where the only real nationalist movement, FRELIMO, took over from the Portuguese in 1975, and a revolutionary black government was installed only two hundred miles from Pretoria, with Joe Slovo running the ANC office in its capital, Maputo. Since Mozambique also had a long border with Rhodesia, where the Smith white-supremacist regime had been installed since 1965, a joint South African/Rhodesian-backed force, the MNR (Moçambique National Resistance – its name later changed, for the sake of lending legitimacy as a supposedly indigenous organization, to the Resistencia Nacional Mozambicana – RENAMO), was able to sustain an unscrupulous terror campaign, without American assistance.

Military adventures of this sort taxed South Africa's limited manpower. Conscription of all young whites for one year had been introduced in 1967, and increased to two years in 1977, as the defence budget quadrupled. Conscripts were going to be needed, not outside South Africa's borders, but in the heart of the country itself.

Elsewhere, South Africa managed things more sensibly. Vorster realized that the Smith regime could not hope to survive, and in a stark reversal of his previous policy of armed support, began working with the governments of Zambia, Malawi, Botswana and Mozambique to pressure Smith towards a settlement of Rhodesia's anomalous position. Vorster had amicable meetings with Chief Jonathan of Lesotho, Sir Seretse Khama of Botswana and Prince Dlamini of Swaziland, good relations with the now independent protectorates being a precondition for success in the Bantustan policy. Dr Hastings Banda's Malawi, the most accommodating of the newly-independent states, was recognized as a reliable ally, and Banda was welcomed on a state visit in 1971. Blacks, as long as they were foreign, could now be dealt with on equal terms, and some relaxation of petty apartheid rules was permitted domestically. The more egregious rules on access to beaches, park benches and some places of entertainment slid into oblivion, but the rigid substructure of white political supremacy was reinforced.

The key to apartheid remained the expulsion of black residents from the towns, and their admittance there only as temporary labourers. Some real improvements in black living conditions were effected: new towns and villages were developed, not entirely unsatisfactorily. One study made between 1960 and 1972 concerned the new town of Mdantsane.[15] It housed eighty-two thousand former residents of East London, for the most part in decent, if dull, four-roomed houses, with some amenities, including sports fields and a hospital. Compensation to those displaced had been reasonable, and the new Township Council, with an elected majority, was working satisfactorily, with between 25 and 35 per cent of voters turning out, a figure comparable with some local elections in Britain. Criticism of the central government continued freely, with the local press fulminating against the Afrikaners, still considered as *the* enemy (there was even nostalgic support for a British protectorate), and their 'quisling chiefs' in the neighbouring Ciskei government. But even such well-intentioned developments ran up against the brick wall of population expansion. In the twenty years between 1951 and 1970 black numbers increased from 8.5 to fifteen million. In spite of the removal of over eighty thousand people to

Mdantsane, East London's black population remained stable at about fifty-seven thousand. Elsewhere the situation was less agreeable. In much of the Transkei, where the people had no access to such centres of employment as East London, rural conditions were regressing towards the intolerable, but political unrest remained more subdued than in the satellite townships surrounding the white urban areas.

Although the Vorster government, with the pervasive assistance of BOSS, was able to stifle most opposition, it did come up against some restraints. An attempt in 1966 to stop possible Progressive Party gains by making it illegal for anyone to belong to any kind of mixed-race association with political overtones had met opposition even from some Nationalists. In 1972 another effort was made to restrict even further the jobs available to blacks – no more black receptionists, telephonists, shop assistants or telephone operators were to be employed in white areas. So absurd a restriction aroused universal indignation (the inconveniences to urban whites would have been unthinkable), and was quietly allowed to drop.

Two new sources of opposition emerged during the Vorster years. In May 1964 the Hertzog Prize for Prose was given to a controversial novel, *Sewe Dae by die Silbersteins* (*Seven Days with the Silbersteins*), by Etienne Leroux, a highly respected Afrikaner writer, which parodied both the Creation and contemporary politics. In the same way that the *Lady Chatterley's Lover* case divided England between ancient reactionaries and reasonable persons, South Africa was divided between the '*verkramptes*' and '*verligtes*'. (And, as with *Lady Chatterley*, it was hardly necessary to read the book to decide on its merits.) Not quite a distinction between conservatives and liberals, the *verkramptes* were those who clung to the pure doctrine of Afrikaner identity, Christian National education and white supremacy, while the *verligtes*, although not necessarily renouncing any of these, recognized the need to make some adjustment to the economic and social facts of life. The controversy was exacerbated by the fact that Leroux was an Afrikaner, known as a staunch Nationalist, and writing in Afrikaans, a sacred symbol of Nationalism. Outraged exponents of 'authentic Afrikaner culture' were insulted further when the acknowledged leader of Afrikaner literature, N.P. van Wyk Louw, seemed to support the liberals. Attacks from such wild young Afrikaners as André Brink or Breyten Breytenbach might be shrugged off, but when van Wyk Louw, a 1930s Nazi sympathizer and ardent patriot, rounded on the *verkramptes*, something, it was clear, was up. English writers might be disregarded by the *verkramptes*, but were more internationally damaging. Alan Paton's *Cry, the Beloved Country*, published in 1948, gained a wide readership in both Britain and America. Paton's work was not banned, but the young André Brink's *Kennis van die Aand* was, and Laurence Gandar, editor of the liberal *Rand Daily Mail*, owned by Jim Bailey until 1984, was found guilty of publishing the truth about prison conditions.

The other new challenge was arising in the new Bantustan of KwaZulu, a polkadot state formed from the remnants of Shepstone's reservations and other odd pockets scattered over an extensive area from the Cape border to Mozambique. Mangosuthu (Gatsha) Buthelezi, twenty years younger than Mandela, a great-grandson of Cetshwayo himself, had become chief of the powerful Buthelezi clan in 1953. Buthelezi, extremely ambitious and an able propagandist, had adopted a different strategy from the ANC, although always anxious to claim apostolic succession from his fellow-Zulu Albert Lutuli. Prepared to operate within the system of apartheid, and well capable of holding his own in argument with Pretoria, Buthelezi worked consistently towards consolidating the dispersed Zulu community, the largest linguistic bloc in South Africa, into a largely personal power-base centred in Natal.

Emphasizing his own hereditary dignity as 'traditional Prime Minister', not owing his power to 'the KwaZulu Legislative Assembly or to Pretoria' – both doubtful *de jure* claims, but *de facto* indisputable – Buthelezi refused on behalf of KwaZulu to accept independence from the government. In what has proved to be a most effective, if not necessarily the most productive, innovation, Buthelezi revived the Inkatha movement of the 1920s. The new organization was to be co-extensive with the Zulu population: 'no one escapes being a member as long as he or she is a member of the Zulu nation.' Having no distaste for expensive cars or houses, and accepting good salaries, the Inkatha leaders were consistent supporters of enterprise, firmly against economic sanctions (though favouring bans on arms), resistant to strike calls and condemning any form of violence. With such ideas Buthelezi became in many Western eyes the ideal black leader, and he was warmly received by President Reagan and Prime Minister Margaret Thatcher, and by many industrialists. Invited to address the Foreign Affairs Committee of the House of Commons, Buthelezi said: 'the blunt truth of the matter is those who reject the free enterprise system, reject the principles of non-violence and the politics of negotiation.' Words which were music to many ears, but very much opposed to the principles of all other black organizations, especially the ANC, always referred to by Chief Buthelezi as 'the ANC's Mission in Exile', with the implication that the true successor of Lutuli's and Dube's movement was the professedly non-violent Inkatha. The ANC's 'method of dealing with black opposition in South Africa', he said, 'is gross; it is indecent and offensive to every democratic norm in the Western civilized world'.[16] Such claims, however much subsequent events proved them to be false, established Buthelezi as a peace-loving democratic anti-communist and encouraged the South African government to welcome Inkatha as an ally in suppressing the ANC.

Inkatha did not encourage dissent, and was so consistently successful in local elections as to be able to press for a one-party state in KwaZulu; it was also accepted as being synonymous with Chief Buthelezi. Claims of a million members may have been exaggerated, but there is no doubt that Inkatha was by far the largest and most powerful black organization in South Africa; hardly surprisingly, since all the others were banned, but this does not detract from its solid and extensive support. But support stemming only from the Zulu and those whites who saw it as a barrier against more frightening oponents. It was true that the ANC leadership was strongly Xhosa – Mandela, Tambo, Susuli – but Congress had always been multi-racial, depending to a great extent on such white communists as the energetic Slovo, and including many Sotho/Tswana, as well as Zulu.

One unsuccessful attempt was made in 1979 to settle ANC/Inkatha differences by a conference in London, after which relations became more and more acerbic. When the United Democratic Front was formed in 1983, following the lead of the World Council of Churches and initially headed by Dr Allan Boesak, a Coloured clergyman, its adherents became targets for Inkatha wrath. 'Xhosa lawyers, foreign representatives, political opportunists' and other 'evil political forces' were accused of a total onslaught against Inkatha. Buthelezi took over the portfolio of the KwaZulu Minister of Police, and became himself directly responsible for policing most of the state. Acting closely with Pretoria the KwaZulu authorities either turned a collectively blind eye to, or cooperated actively in, many acts of violence against ANC supporters.

A man of considerable imagination and more ambition, Buthelezi developed the concept of a federation of black homelands – the 'Autonomous States of Southern Africa' – which could interact with the Republic's government on a basis of equality in a federal system. Vorster took the idea seriously enough to hold discussions with the Bantustan leadership, but more pressing concerns aborted the idea.

EIGHTEEN

Disintegration

We hate the language and we hate the owners of it

The police massacre (and no other word is appropriate) that took place on 13 June 1976 in Soweto, a black township on the outskirts of Johannesburg, was 'like Munich or Suez . . . one of those rare historical catalysts which irreversibly transform the political landscape', beginning a near-continuous cycle of violence. It was that old bugbear, the insistence on the Afrikaans language, that was the immediate cause. Dr Andries Treurnicht, an extreme right-wing minister, former Chairman of the Broederbond, decided to require that black pupils not only learn Afrikaans, but accept the use of it as the teaching medium for all other subjects. Although the policy of 'Bantu education' had increased the numbers of pupils considerably, school conditions for blacks were miserable, classes of sixty being the norm. Most teachers at advanced levels preferred to use English, and the requirement that the language of the oppressors, the 'Boers', become universal provoked demonstrations throughout the country.

Allied to the blacks' appalling conditions in both town and country, the constant harassment by police and the consciousness of political and social paralysis, the inevitability of violence was stark. Three weeks before the massacre the Anglican Bishop of Johannesburg, Desmond Tutu, who was emerging as one of the most influential black leaders, had written an open letter to Vorster expressing his 'nightmarish fear that unless something drastic is done very soon, then bloodshed and violence are going to happen . . . almost inevitably . . . A people made desperate by despair and injustice and oppression will use desperate means.'

When police, using machine pistols, fired on a crowd of demonstrating schoolchildren, over twenty were killed. Photographs of the dead thirteen-year-old Hector Petersen being carried from the scene accompanied by his screaming sister were flashed round the world, arousing universal denunciation; within a few days the UN Security Council had condemned the South African government and demanded the end of apartheid. In the following three months uncontrollable riots in Soweto and elsewhere in the Transvaal, in Cape Town and Port Elizabeth claimed hundreds of lives. Most of the dead were shot by the police; 'Natives,' said Jimmy Kruger, the appalling Minister of Justice, in a revealing statement that added to his monstrous reputation, 'had to be made tame to the gun'; but among those killed were inoffensive civilians beaten to death by rioters.[1]

So violent an outcome would not have resulted merely from the language question, but it acted as a detonator for a multitude of grievances. Any embarrassed government finds the appointment of an investigatory commission useful, and this device was popular with the now often-embarrassed Nationalist administrations. However despicably individuals may have behaved, the Afrikaner conscience was deeply troubled by such events and by the world's reaction to them. The inquiry headed by Mr Justice Cillié forthrightly identified the 'great hatred' engendered by the whole apartheid system as a prime cause of the demonstrations, and thereby did something to preserve the reputation of the judiciary. Although Soweto was a relatively recent community, dating from 1954, living conditions there were already deplorable, between seventeen and twenty people packed into a four-roomed house, with minimal provision of sanitation. Wages, which had been rising, levelled out from about 1974, removing the possibility for economic advancement that had to some extent mollified discontent. And a new prophet had arisen in the land in the shape of a talented young medical student, Steve Biko, the articulate founder of the 'Black Consciousness' movement.[2]

The first president of the South African Students' Organization (SASO), an exclusively black body opposed to the non-racial National Union of South African Students (NUSAS), Biko identified the white liberal dilemma with painful accuracy: 'the liberal is in fact appeasing his own conscience . . . Being white, he possesses the natural passport to the exclusive pool of white privilege . . . Yet, since he identifies with the blacks, he moves around his white circles . . . with a lighter load, feeling he is not like the rest. However, at the back of his mind is the constant reminder that he is quite comfortable as things stand . . . Although he does not vote for the Nationalists . . . he feels secure under the protection offered by the Nationalists and subconsciously shuns the idea of change.' Two centuries earlier,

Coleridge had identified a similar phenomenon among 'professed friends of liberty ... who unaccustomed to the labour of thorough investigation, are yet impelled by their feelings to disapprove of its grosser depravities, and prepared to give an indolent vote in favour of reform'.

Biko insisted on the absolute necessity for black South Africans to act for themselves, not relying on any support from white sympathizers who had proved ineffective allies, and to develop society on the basis of their own African traditions:

> Our belief is that white society will not listen to preaching. They will not listen to their liberals. Liberalism has not grown within white society, and we blacks cannot stand idly by watching the situation. We can only generate a response from white society when we, as blacks, speak with a black voice and say what we want. The age of the liberal was such that the black voice was not very much heard except in echoing what was said by liberals. Now has come the time when we, as blacks, must articulate what we want, and put it across to the white man, and from a position of strength.[3]

Such dangerous ideas immediately attracted attention, and nine of Biko's supporters were sentenced in 1976 to eight years' imprisonment. Had the authorities tried Biko at the same time, and kept him safely on Robben Island, South Africa's history might have been changed, but the following year he was arrested for the infringement of his banning order and so badly knocked about that he died in the back of a police Land Rover. Biko was not the first, and would not be the last, to be murdered by brutal police; such things are nowhere unknown, although the South African police did seem particularly careless in allowing their suspects to fall out of windows or tumble down stairs.

It was again partly the reaction of Jimmy Kruger, who said 'Biko's death leaves me cold,' and of such Nationalist MPs as Frank le Roux, who said that he himself 'would have killed Biko', that, once more, established the credentials of South Africa as the 'skunk among nations', and the Afrikaners as the villains. The insistence on the Afrikanerization of all facets of life had resulted in almost all police officers being Afrikaners, and therefore the visible enforcers of a tyrannical rule; combined with the aggressive and unskilful public relations of government ministers, this was enough to accord the dark pre-eminence to Afrikaners. There was an element of unfairness here, in that as the elections continued to prove, many English-speakers sided with the Nationalists, content with the privileged prosperity that they enjoyed under apartheid; and Kruger himself, in spite of his name, was of Welsh parentage. As the writer Willem (Wim) de Klerk wryly observed, 'When the Bible rains judgement on the Pharisees, only the Afrikaners get wet.'[4] But one survey in 1977, after Soweto, showed that 78 per cent of Afrikaners supported a 'consensus policy of apartheid', a view shared by only 25 per cent of English-speakers, although it has to be said that a much higher proportion consistently took advantage of the benefits of such a policy.

Another decisive Nationalist election victory in 1977 – 134 seats out of 164 – eliminated the Unionists and elevated the Progressives, now the Progressive Federal Party, to the status of the official opposition, with Helen Suzman joined by sixteen others. Albert Hertzog had been replaced at the head of the HNP by Jaap Marais; their party, although not represented in parliament, was amassing a fair amount of support in the rural areas. The United Party had finally disintegrated in July 1975 when its more liberal MPs had joined the Progressives, while those who had not moved to the left shifted their allegiance to the Nationalists.

It was neither internal violence nor foreign aggression that brought ten years of Vorster's leadership to an end, but banal politics. Soweto and the continuing violence of its aftermath, exacerbated by Biko's killing, had convinced the *verkramptes* that concessions to the liberals produced only disaster. Naturally enough the *verligtes* were persuaded that reforms had not gone far enough, and some gestures were made in that direction. The Afrikanerization of education was dropped; Buthelezi's idea of Bantustan federations was discussed, reinforced by one minister, Piet Koornhof, who suggested a move towards a coalition of plural democracies; fictitious 'cabinet status' was offered to Coloureds and Indians – and promptly declined; and commissions of investigation into potential constitutional reforms were set in train. New nomenclature, the most economical of reforms, flourished. The department that had originally been of 'Native Affairs', and had then become 'Bantu Affairs', was now metamorphosed into 'Plural Relations', and thence to 'Cooperative Development'; 'discrimination' became 'differentiation'. The net result was to paper over cracks sufficiently well to allow the 1977 elections to be an unqualified success in establishing a united white front.

Vorster's nemesis eventually came, like Baron Frankenstein's, at the hands of his own monstrous creation (BOSS, in Vorster's case), but this was not until after his resignation as Prime Minister in November 1978, and his elevation to State President. Vorster had been ill for some time, as was revealed by his hesitancy after the Angola fiasco and the Soweto and Biko troubles. His heir apparent was Dr Connie Mulder, an ambitious and unscrupulous politician who, as Minister for Information and the Interior, had worked closely with the sinister General Hendrick van den Bergh, head of BOSS, and Dr Escher Rhoodie, the flamboyant Secretary for Information. Between them, with Vorster's consent, they had set up a secret sixty-four-million-rand clandestine propaganda fund. This amount, and more, was scattered to the winds in 'Operation Senekal', funding dozens of initiatives, few of them legitimate, which enabled Mulder's clique to manipulate practically all South African foreign policy in a conspiracy of 'moral hypocrisy in which absolute power acted as an aphrodisiac to men who used their influence to seduce women both in South Africa and abroad', and which permitted Mulder and his associates 'to seize control of South African foreign policy'.

Mulder's chief rival for the succession to Vorster as leader of the Nationalist Party and therefore as Prime Minister was the violently irascible Defence Minister P.W. Botha, 'the Great Crocodile'. Another Botha, R.F. (Pik), a smoother character, Foreign Minister from 1977, had his hat in the ring, but could muster only limited support.

The Operation Senekal scandal, which became famous as 'Muldergate', began to be investigated by the Auditor General in April 1977.[5] Rumours multiplied before the first public report in February 1978 was followed by a formal investigation. Rhoodie was sacked and the Department of Information disbanded, but Mulder clung to office, lying desperately in an attempt to preserve his bid for the leadership. Vorster's opportunity to evade personal responsibility came in August 1978 when State President Nico Diederichs – who had himself been involved in the establishment of the initial secret fund – obligingly died. In spite of his evasions and lies, Mulder's chances of succession had been severely damaged by the questions raised over the Department of Information, and in September the party caucus chose P.W. Botha as its new leader. Vorster was elevated to the position of President where, as head of state, he would be to some extent insulated from the consequences of what was looking to be a very damaging scandal.

Judge Erasmus' investigatory commission reported in two stages, the first in December 1978 proving the guilt of Mulder, van den Bergh and Rhoodie, but exonerating Vorster. It was the second, in the following June, that recognized Vorster's complicity and forced his resignation in disgrace, after a presidency of less than eight months.

The Great Crocodile

The new broom, P.W. Botha, had every intention of sweeping clean. Apartheid as envisaged by Malan and implemented by Verwoerd was not going to work. Afrikaners, he announced, 'must adapt or die'. The essential was change, 'rapid, visible change: the replacing of outdated political principles, the restructuring of race relations, the rejection of racial domination [*baaskap*], the removal of humiliating discrimination and injustice, equal opportunity and rights, fewer restrictions – and a new disposition'.[6]

But there was no question of merely acceding to the reformers' demands. South Africa, the new Prime Minister believed, was 'experiencing the full onslaught of Marxism', and also 'experiencing double standards on the part of certain Western bodies ... in an attempt to pay a ransom to the Bear whose hunger must be satisfied'. The battle was one between 'the powers of chaos, Marxism and destruction ... and the powers of order, Christian civilization and the upliftment of the people'. Botha was hampered by much of the ideological baggage of traditional Afrikanerdom – a mother in the British concentration camps, a religious conviction in the rectitude of his own views, as well as a violent temper and an inability to work with colleagues as equals; Chester Crocker, the American Assistant Secretary of State, spoke of Botha's 'boundless arrogance'. His pragmatic sense of the possible was limited by his capacity for sullen anger and lack of any facility of expression, which transformed many of his public announcements into confused ranting, which in turn could lead to dangerous actions.

The idea of a battle with 'the powers of chaos' was a poor foundation for any prudent policy, but it was used to justify the doctrine of a 'total strategy' of which General Magnus Malan, the head of the Defence Force, was the chief proponent, and to which Botha had previously, as Minister of Defence, committed himself. Inspired by the French experience in Algeria as described by General André Beaufre, 'total strategy' was the coordination of military activity, foreign policy and domestic social and political administration in order to ensure security and internal unity. Unbridled force was necessary, but this need not necessarily be overt, and must indeed take second place to the overall policy. It might have been thought that since the strategy had failed miserably in Algeria, it could hardly be expected to work in South Africa. The economic penalties were clear. Large numbers of young men – and older ones, since the reserve service was extended to sixty-year-olds – were withdrawn from productive employment, and the expense involved was enormous. Less obvious was the rapid degeneration into the secret terrorism and open violence that eroded the rule of law which had always been the main claim to decency in the South African government.

General Malan was open about his objectives. 'There is,' he admitted, 'a conflicting requirement between that of Total Strategy and the democratic system of government,' to be justified if South Africa was in fact facing a 'total onslaught' which had to be met by 'total counter-measures'. Repression was essential, but not enough: 'Bullets kill bodies not beliefs.'

From 1984, when Ronald Reagan succeeded Jimmy Carter as President, such a policy could count again on support, albeit somewhat patchy, from the United States. President Reagan's sympathy was quickly made clear when on 3 March he described South Africa as 'a friendly country, a wartime ally, and a country of strategic importance to the free world'. Within two weeks the South African Air Force attacked the SWAPO base in Angola, and President Reagan had asked for Senator Dick Clark's restrictions on military aid to be lifted. A prolonged struggle ensued between the CIA, the National Security Council and the President on the one hand, and both Houses of Congress on the other, with the industrious Chester Crocker attempting to bring an end to the violence in Namibian and Angolan territories. The Reagan policy, if that is not too dignified a name, was termed 'constructive engagement', and was in fact nothing more than an undignified compromise between black pressure in America and the interests of American industry. Something very similar was going on in England where, after the Conservatives came to power in 1979 under Margaret Thatcher, policy was pulled both ways by Mrs Thatcher's prejudices – including, after the IRA murders of some of her closest allies, a loathing of any organization committed to violence – and by the growing public indignation at South African state terrorism.

Total strategy demanded that neighbouring states, which were becoming known as 'front-line' states, must either cooperate or knuckle under. In order to encourage them, international law could be set to one side in the interests of national security. One immediate example was an air raid on a Namibian refugee camp in Angola which killed over six hundred people, half of whom were children. ANC bases in Lesotho and Botswana were raided by ground forces and more selective assassinations were arranged, including that of Ruth First, Joe Slovo's wife. In Mozambique RENAMO, an unsavoury collection of avaricious terrorists, responsible, according to the US State Department, for 'one of the most brutal holocausts against ordinary human beings since the Second World War', acted in obedience to and in close cooperation with the South African Defence Force in opposing the legitimate government of Samora Machel.

Internally the total strategy demanded both stick and carrot. The misshapen and wholly unappetizing carrot was an entirely new constitution intended to empower Indians and Coloureds. Much thought was given to this after 1977, resulting in changes which began three years later when the 1910 constitution, and its subsequent amendments, was reconstructed. With the evidence that the parliamentary conventions inherited from Westminster simply had never worked in South African governments, especially in one as entrenched and unchallengeable as that of the Nationalists, the British style of democracy was abandoned for a constitution that would meet, it was believed, the very peculiar circumstances of South Africa. The State Security Council, first formed in 1972, was elevated to an inner cabinet, often acting independently of the constitutional cabinet through a network of local offices, rather as a French government can do through its control of prefectures. At a stroke the Senate was abolished, to be replaced by a President's Council open to all races except blacks, the fiction still being that blacks enjoyed their own political rights as citizens of the homelands. The Council would be expected to recommend further constitutional changes, which were later – much adulterated by political considerations – put to a referendum, of course for whites only, in November 1983. A search for some such constitutional solution had provoked much concerned discussion over the years. One suggestion, based on Indian and Palestinian experience, was of a straightforward partition into a white state approximating to the Cape and the Free State, with most of the Transvaal and Natal, together with Swaziland and Lesotho, becoming a black confederation. Rather less insubstantial ideas had developed into the not impractical plan of a 'consociational polity', of which the most influential protagonist was Dr Denis Worrall, one of the growing band of *verligte* English-speaking Nationalist MPs.

As eventually approved in the new constitution the legislature contained three separate assemblies: a white House of Assembly, a Coloured House of Representatives, and an Indian House of Delegates, each charged with dealing with 'the "own affairs" [sic] of its community'. A Nationalist administration was often government by shaky semantics. One Indian and one Coloured representative were allowed in the cabinet, without specific responsibilities, and the two junior houses were allowed a say in the appointment of the President and his council, but real power was kept firmly in white hands. The two minor assemblies were able to push through the repeal of the Mixed Marriages Act, but the whole structure of the new constitution was fully embedded in the foundation of apartheid.

The 1984 constitution was a development of P.W. Botha's own suggestions first made seven years earlier. The State President, elected by a parliamentary college, would be an executive, rather than a ceremonial, leader, very much on the Gaullist French model, but whereas in France the President appointed the Prime Minister, the new South African constitution merged the two offices. When Worrall, in an unguarded moment, suggested that the new parliamentary system might, just possibly, at some future date, be extended to the blacks, he was banished as Ambassador to Australia. The unrepresented three-quarters of the population were entrusted to the care of the State President, and allowed some further participation in local government.

It was constitutional madness, born of the absurd fantasy that South Africa was a congeries of different races condemned to separate existences, and that by some sleight of hand the white minority had to maintain absolute power while conceding the appearance of equality. The fiction that blacks could be regarded as visiting foreigners, citizens of their own homelands, was every day more clearly seen to be a fiction. In spite of the forced removal of millions into the overcrowded homelands the proportion of blacks in urban areas grew from 38 per cent in 1960 to nearly 60 per cent twenty years later – and these were percentages of increasingly higher figures. Pass laws, imprisonment, and squalid living conditions in shanty towns were little discouragement when a man from Bophuthatswana could work illegally for three months in the Republic, spend another nine in prison for his offence, and still earn five times as much in the year as he could in his 'homeland', where conditions were commonly awful. By 1984 there were nearly nine million blacks attempting to live in the homelands on incomes below the minimum subsistence level, with one doctor to 175,000 patients; in the Ciskei two-thirds of the children were stunted and malnourished. The administration's muddled thinking was reflected in official verbiage: 'The alternative was the purposive development of political practices fashioned by three centuries of experience in Africa so that parallel institutions of government and administration could materialize for the black peoples through which they could reach autonomy and assume full responsibility for their own affairs.'

The new constitution was too little and much too late. Twenty-four years previously Nelson Mandela had suggested a plan that would work. Asked by the prosecutor in the Treason Trial if the black community would accept a qualified franchise on the Cape model which, by degrees, might lead to full participation, perhaps over ten to twenty years, Mandela replied:

> In my own view I would say, yes, let us talk, and the government would say, 'We think that the Europeans at present are not ready for a type of government where there might be domination by non-Europeans. We think we should give you sixty seats. The African population to elect sixty Africans to represent them in parliament. We will leave the matter over for five years and we will review it at the end of five years.' In my view, that would be a victory, my Lords; we would have taken a significant step towards the attainment of universal adult suffrage for Africans, and we would then, for the five years say, 'We will suspend civil disobedience; we won't have any stay-at-homes, and we will then devote the intervening period for the purposes of educating the country, the Europeans, to see that these changes can be brought about and that it would bring about better racial understanding, better harmony in the country.' I'd say we should accept it, but, of course, I would not abandon the demands for the extension of the franchise to all Africans. That's how I see it, my Lords.
>
> Then, at the end of the five-year period, we will have discussions, and if the government says, 'We will give you again forty more seats,' I might say that that is quite sufficient. 'Let's accept it, and still demand that the franchise should be extended, but for the agreed period we should suspend civil disobedience, no stay-at-homes.' In that way we would eventually be able to get everything we want; we shall have our people's democracy, my Lords.[7]

Such practical proposals might have worked in the 1950s, but after a quarter of a century of hopelessness and repression much more was essential. Unsurprisingly, Coloureds and Indians evinced little enthusiasm for their new privileges: only 14 per cent of the former and 16.6 per cent of the latter voted in the first elections; and of course the black communities were, once more, left in the cold, their essential inferiority underlined.

Reactions to the 1984 constitution reflected the confusion in which all South Africa found itself. The Botha 'reforms' were the last straw for many *verkrampte* Afrikaners. Albert Hertzog's HNP, now led by Jaap Marais, was already in the wilderness, supported by a fair number of shell-backed Afrikaner workers, but had no parliamentary representation. A more important division in the National Party now took place as the *verkramptes* within the party rallied round the egregious Andries Treurnicht. After a ferocious power struggle eighteen Nationalist MPs left to form the new Conservative Party, where they were joined by an unrepentant Connie Mulder, a Broederbond faction, 'Aksie Eie Toekoms' (Action for Our Future), and the neo-Nazi 'Afrikaner Weerstands Beweging' (Afrikaner Resistance Movement), led by an unsavoury white supremacist, Eugene Terreblanche. Neither the HNP nor the Conservatives were in a position to challenge the National Party in parliament, but they were backed by some 20 per cent of all the white electorate. The disintegration of Afrikanerdom had begun.

It soon unravelled further. That bastion of Nationalist power, the Broederbond, split, throwing up a new 'Afrikaner Volkswag' – an Afrikaner National Guard. An extremist fringe organized an even more violent faction, the 'Blanke Bevrydigings Beweging', the White Liberation Movement, attacking such enemies of culture as the Jews and the 'mud races'.

More moderate Afrikaners, increasingly loath to be associated with such people, moved towards the liberals. One of the most interesting of these was Wim de Klerk, sacked as editor of the Nationalist newspaper *Die Transvaler* in 1982, inventor of the '*verkrampte*' and '*verligte*' concepts, and author of an illuminating analysis of Afrikanerdom, *The Puritans in Africa*. Willem's younger brother, Frederick (F.W.) de Klerk, was working his way up the National Party ranks, to his final post of State President. Perhaps more significantly Anton Rupert, whose efforts in establishing Afrikaner industries had been immensely successful – his Rembrandt Tobacco Corporation had become a global business – and who had earlier worked closely with such extreme Nationalists as Dirk Hertzog and Nic Diederichs, had changed sides, and in October 1981 advocated a 'Third Trek . . . away from discrimination – towards participation in freedom by all population groups'.

Even those devoted and ingenious supporters of apartheid, the Dutch Churches, were abandoning the cause. The more extreme denominations,

Balthazar Johannes Vorster, Prime Minister 1966-78, State President 1978-79.

Right Steve Biko's death at the hands of South African police robbed the country of a great man.

Below Nobel Peace Prize-winner Albert Lutuli, a pillar of rectitude, banished by the Nationalist government to his home in Stanger, Natal.

Above These corrugated-iron pens, isolated on the veld, were regarded by Nationalists as good examples of 'Bantu rehousing'.

Left and below Two forms of protest. The quiet power of middle-class women: Black Sash members demonstrate. Black protesters take over whites-only railway carriages in September 1982.

Alleged SWAPO guerrillas killed by the Koevoet (irregular South African police) in Namibian fighting. The Koevoet gained a reputation for brutality and indiscipline.

Above The last Afrikaner Presidents: P.W. Botha and F.W. de Klerk.

Left Nelson Mandela voting in the April 1994 election. In the British Cape Colony, blacks had been able to vote since the 1850s, but all non-white franchises were ended by Afrikaner governments.

April 1994: the first election for sixty years in which the franchise was not restricted to whites, and the first non-racial election ever.

Zulu Inkatha leader Chief Mangosuthu Buthelezi and Winnie Mandela both retain considerable support in spite of their implication in violence and fraud.

Left The ebullient Archbishop Desmond Tutu.

Below Thabo Mbeki, South African Deputy President and President of the ANC in succession to Nelson Mandela.

President Nelson Mandela and Second Deputy President F.W. de Klerk after the inauguration of the new government, 10 May 1994.

the GK and the NHK, remained true to Malan's doctrine, but the original and largest Church, the NGK, 'the National Party at prayer', was restive. Its Western Synod, representing the mother Church in the Cape, and the theological powerhouse of Stellenbosch University decided in April 1984 that there was no biblical justification for apartheid, urged its members 'to confess their participation in apartheid with humility and sorrow', and the moderator Johan Heyns proclaimed:

> there is no such thing as white superiority or black inferiority . . .
> all people are equal before God . . . there may not be under any
> circumstances a political policy based on oppression, discrimi-
> nation and exploitation . . . the task of the Church is to protest
> against unjust laws.[8]

With such a rebuttal coming from the mother Church itself, the end of the *volk* was in sight. Reverting to the fissiparious Boer customs of a hundred years before, new Churches and groups sprang up to perpetuate justifications for apartheid.

By 1985 the ANC was also disintegrating. Although funds continued to reach Lusaka, opportunities to carry forward the armed struggle were limited. Operating quite without scruples, the South African security services had infiltrated the camps and were even able to mount an unknown number of murders of sympathizers within the Republic. Ruthless and efficient action by the security services ensured that the few incursions were unsuccessful. Arms, which flowed to the ANC in great quantities, were sent over the borders into the Republic, where they were quietly seized by the forewarned security forces and passed on to RENAMO. The ANC's organized acts of violence were often badly targeted and ineffectively carried through, as in Pretoria's 'Bloody Friday' on 20 May 1983 when two young men exploded a bomb which killed them and seventeen other, innocent, people – a far cry from MK's original intentions. The 'People's War' remained a small-scale and sporadic affair, which never developed into anything to match the continued violence of the SWAPO guerrillas.

Something of a revival had, even so, taken place from 1978 when, after a visit to Vietnam by Slovo, Tambo and other ANC leaders, a three-year strategic plan of joint propaganda and direct action was initiated, resulting in some successful strikes against specific targets – police stations, the Defence Force headquarters and, most spectacularly, an attack on the energy monopoly SASOL's refinery and storage tanks. This was not enough to satisfy the eager recruits who were herded into northern Angolan camps. Doubtful training methods, harsh living conditions and incompetent leaders inevitably led to boredom, disillusion and discontent. Attempts to quit were punished by imprisonment in one of a number of detention centres. Members of 'Mbokodo', the security department, were allowed to beat and torture suspects. Tambo, a gentle soul, was unable to cope with the discontent, or to control the security thugs. In an attempt to provide some action the decision was taken to mount, in conjunction with Angolan government troops, an offensive against UNITA forces in August 1983. After some initial success defective training and administration led to defeats and soon to open mutiny, eventually suppressed only after a pitched battle, followed by the usual beatings and executions. The ANC in exile was beginning to reflect with unhappy accuracy the methods of the security forces in South Africa.

Although Tambo had earned little credit from the latest activities of the ANC in exile, two young communists had identified themselves as potential leaders. Chris Hani, yet another Fort Hare and Lovedale student, had already been conspicuous for his courage in action, his administrative ability and his capacity for leadership. Thabo Mbeki, son of the prominent communist Govan Mbeki who had been sentenced to Robben Island with Mandela (the two did not get on), also from Lovedale, had taken a degree at the new University of Sussex and studied in Moscow. A young man of outstanding ability, Thabo was elected to the Politburo of the South African party while still in his thirties, but was too much of a liberal for such communist stalwarts as Slovo.

More damaging to the ANC even than defeats and mutiny was the outcome of a meeting held on 16 March 1984 between the Mozambique President, Samora Machel, and P.W. Botha. The resulting Nkomati Accord was a formal treaty by which South Africa and Mozambique undertook to respect each other's borders and to ban hostile parties, individuals, and propaganda. Pik Botha, the experienced Minister for Foreign Affairs, had also, with skill rarely shown in South African foreign policy, arranged other détentes to reinforce the accord. Discussions with both Russia and the USA had clarified those countries' intentions, and by an agreement in Lusaka the Angolan MPLA government undertook to remove SWAPO bases, in return for South Africa withdrawing its troops from Angola. Zimbabwe, formerly Rhodesia, now independent after the protracted 1980 Lancaster House Conference, which might have been expected to be sympathetic to the ANC after their joint armed actions, ended its support when Robert Mugabe's new government launched a particularly bloody purge of Bishop Abel Muzorewa's ZAPU followers in a revival of the old Shona/Ndebele hostilities dating from more than a century previously.

Expelled from so many of their bases, the alternative policy of concentrating effort within South Africa was forced upon the ANC leadership. There they found ready to hand the support of the UDF, represented by the personable Dr Allan Boesak and eventually claiming two million adherents, including some six hundred organizations and well-known individuals, among them the splendid Albertina Sisulu, Walter's wife; Archie Gumede, the veteran communist Josiah's son; and an admirable young footballer, Patrick 'Terror' Lekota. The most important components of the UDF were the Indian Congresses and the newly-legal Congress of black trades unions, COSATU.

When 70 per cent of the white electorate ratified the 1984 constitution, black indignation at what was seen as yet another betrayal was expressed by Patrick Lekota:

> My father's contemporaries, the white ones . . . had made laws that he must carry a reference book. They also made a law that an Alsatian dog must have a certain ticket on his neck [a dog licence], and he must also carry a 'reference book'. That Alsatian dog was going to die without ever deciding a law that governs his life. So was my father . . .
>
> The discomfort of prison cells is better than the emptiness of walking in the streets as if you were free when you are a dog in the land of your birth.[9]

When the new constitution was actually enforced the townships exploded once more, beginning in September 1984. Members of the UDF were active, but into the vacuum left by the excision of responsible organized black leadership had been drawn a motley collection of enthusiasts, activists and plain criminals. The effort to provide some element of self-government in black areas collapsed as elected councillors, seen as collaborators with the oppressors, were set upon and killed, including the respected Esau Mahlatsi and Sam Dlamini of Lehoa, whose only offence had been to do their best for their fellows. Efforts were made to establish 'people's courts', which had some success, but too often degenerated into mob rule. Violent youngsters, able to claim absence from school as a patriotic duty, invented the notorious murder method of 'necklacing', in which a tyre filled with petrol was placed around the victim's neck and ignited. One victim among hundreds was a young girl, Maki Skhosana, who was beaten, stoned and stripped before being necklaced with a broken bottle in her vagina.

Another new grouping, AZAPO, the Azanian People's Organization, with its affiliate 'Students'' movement took the opportunity to assert itself against the ANC. Port Elizabeth and Soweto both experienced particularly vicious fighting between the two, but the shanty town of Crossroads, outside Cape Town, was the scene of the most protracted violence, as vigilante *'wit doekes'* – white scarves – imposed their own brand of 'order'. The reviving Pan African Congress (PAC) turned to Iran for help and produced a muddled combination of terrorism and Islamic fundamentalism, exemplified in the erratic career of Patrick Duncan, son of the former Governor General. Older antagonisms between ANC, often perceived as a Xhosa organization, and Buthelezi's Zulu Inkatha supporters began to rekindle, especially in Natal, with Inkatha, usually supported by the police, in the forefront of the violence.[10] None of these activities much helped the cause of African freedom in the outside world. In South Africa itself white liberals were too often shiftily ill-at-ease in condemning, as they certainly should have done, black atrocities as heartily as they had denounced state terrorism. Even the mildest criticism tended to be stifled, and the suppression of Dr Conor Cruise O'Brien's lectures at Cape Town University brought about the resignation of the much-respected Professor of History, David Welsh.

Looking at South Africa from the outside, the issued seemed a simple one of a wickedly perverse, racist government imposing its brutal rule on an oppressed majority. Exaggerated accusations of 'genocide' were flung about by people who ought to have known very much better. Few of South Africa's more vocal opponents were themselves innocent of violent oppression, and some, like the Democratic Republic of Kampuchea, were murdering not hundreds but millions of their own people. Argentina and Mexico, where internal state terrorism was – and in Mexico still is – endemic, contrived to remain nearly respectable members of the international community. Disgust with the United Nations was common not only among *verkrampte* Afrikaners but in the whole white community. Intellectual opposition was gravely damaged in 1975 when the poet Breyten Breytenbach, the most famous of the expatriate Afrikaners, was arrested during a clandestine visit and sentenced to nine years' imprisonment. Breytenbach's writings had been an inspiration to many, but when, hoping for a light sentence, Breytenbach made a grovelling apology – 'my behaviour

was foolish . . . I am sorry for all the stupid thoughtless things I did . . .' –
the disillusion and disappointment was great.

There was also genuine pride in the displays of South African ingenuity
stimulated by the restrictions on arms and energy imports. Atomic energy
was developed, and at least six atomic bombs manufactured; domestic coal
was used to produce petrol products on a large scale; the arms industry
became a successful exporter. The country was, after all, one of the world's
richest sources of minerals, among the first three in alumino-silicates,
chrome, manganese, platinum, titanium, vanadium – and possibly uranium
– together with gold, of which it was still the world's biggest producer.
Although South Africa represented only 6 per cent of the continent's population it generated more than half of its electricity. Compared with the rest
of Africa, even after decades of oppression, South Africa could claim to be
in the lead. Attempting to measure the unmeasurable, the United Nations
Human Development Index placed South Africa at the head of all African
countries, even those of the economically advanced Maghreb: adult literacy
at 85 per cent was well in advance of even Libya and Nigeria, at 56.5 per
cent and 42.7 per cent respectively.[11]

Diplomatically isolated though she was, South Africa could rely on the
support of Israel. Prime Minister Golda Meir had made the analogy with
the Afrikaners clear when she said: 'It was not as though there was a
Palestinian people in Palestine considering itself as a Palestinian people
and we came and threw them out and took their country away. They did
not exist.'[12] More than a thousand South African volunteers assisted Israel
in its 1948 war against its Arab neighbours; Mossad and the South African
intelligence service, together with the arms industries of the two countries,
cooperated closely, and Israel provided instructors in anti-terrorist operations. South Africa's participation with Israel in the development of atomic
weapons was valuable to both countries. Taiwan, another state shunned
by many members of the United Nations opposed to South Africa, was
also a reliable supporter. The Republican Irish were somewhat embarrassed
by their earlier enthusiasm for the Afrikaner cause, exemplified by the
former Irish Foreign Minister Sean MacBride's friendly visit to Malan's
South Africa in 1954, especially when such unsavoury characters as Eugene
Terreblanche sympathized with the IRA; but it was the Protestant paramilit-
aries who enjoyed good relations with BOSS.[13]

The state's ability to crush internal resistance remained intact. It was
another incident of police violence at Langa, near Uitenhage, in March

1985, in which twenty people, mostly women and children, were shot dead by frightened, incompetent (and probably drunk) police, that acted as a turning point. Civil policing being ineffective, seventy thousand troops were sent into the townships, where the provisions of a national state of emergency first imposed in June 1986 enabled them to act almost as if under martial law. Sjamboks and shotguns were replaced by high-velocity bullets and machine-guns. More than twenty-five thousand people were detained in the following twelve months, nearly half of them under the age of eighteen. The Civil Cooperation Bureau – the title is another example of South African doublespeak – arranged covert assassinations, the extent of which only later became apparent. Such drastic actions worked, and by the end of the year the worst of the violence had been suppressed. When Robin Renwick arrived as British Ambassador in July 1987 he asked security chief General van der Merwe why things were so quiet; the General replied: 'This time we have arrested all the right people.'[14]

In keeping with the concept of total strategy, coercion was succeeded by the grant of what might be accepted as reforms. Some of these never got off the ground, such as the proposal, by Botha himself, to have blacks in the cabinet, but many additions were made to the regional and local authorities, producing a state of unparalleled complexity. As well as the central government, the four 'independent' and the six 'self-governing' Bantustans could boast five Presidents, nine Chief Ministers, fourteen cabinets with three hundred members and fifteen hundred members of legislatures. All well rewarded, swallowing over half the national budget – one quarter of the GNP; and all offering eagerly accepted opportunities for corruption.

Business leaders had become increasingly worried about the inadequacy of labour. Modern manufacturing, which had replaced mining as the mainstay of the economy, demanded skilled and flexible workers. The absurd job-reservation regulations, exacerbated by the compulsory long-distance commuting, made this impossible. Far from relaxing controls on labour mobility, the government refused to act, in the face of positive legal judgements and committee recommendations. More attention was paid to another committee report, that of a commission chaired by Professor N.E. Wiehahn, which made the radical recommendation that segregation should be left to individual businesses to decide, and that similar restrictions on trades unions should be abolished.[15] Accepted in the 1979 and 1981 Acts, these reforms were perhaps the most important advance yet secured. Now that a legal outlet for their energies had been secured, non-whites quickly developed negotiating skills and were able to demonstrate that much could be done to improve their conditions by the calculated exercise of their own power.

Hyperoxygenated by the oil crisis of the seventies, the world gold price declined in the eighties, and with it the South African economy. Defence costs, and the real effort to prime the homelands' economies (a high proportion of which funds went on ministerial houses, cars, helicopters and expenses), all ate into the national budget. Foreign investment dried up, and the bold stroke of relaxing exchange controls, which might have revived confidence, merely provided an opportunity for many of the largest foreign companies to take funds amounting to over $1,000 million overseas. American banks, after years of increased lending, had begun to cut back, loans falling by as much as 10 per cent in a single quarter.

The rand's value plummeted, foreign debt soared, and in July 1985 the Chase Manhattan Bank refused to renew $10 million of short-term loans maturing the following year. More than any other incident, this probably marked the beginning of the end of South African self-sufficiency. From that time the country experienced an increasingly serious flight of capital: the Central Bank Governor Gerhard de Kock characterized it as an 'utter disaster', realizing that it was only a matter of time before the capital haemorrhage became fatal. Botha made matters worse a month later by promising to make a speech which would describe how he planned to 'cross the Rubicon' of dismantling apartheid; this turned out to be no more than a confused and convoluted address which did offer some major progress – a commitment to one citizenship and a universal franchise – but was universally adjudged disappointing.[16]

In fact the removal of restrictions continued to progress, and in 1986 the Urban Areas Act, the authority for those pass laws which had caused so much disgust and distress, was finally repealed. With that action the principle of influx control, the foundation of all apartheid, was abandoned. The subsequent repeal of the Mixed Marriages and Immorality Act and the Prohibition of Political Interference Act marked the emergence of a non-racial society, reinforced by the introduction of mixed-race sport; a real change was obvious when the rugby team of the Coloured Paulus Joubert High School at Paarl could play the famous Afrikaner Paarl Gymnasium – and beat them. Conservative Afrikaners were enraged, but the political apparatus of white supremacy was untouched. In October 1986 President Reagan's veto on a comprehensive Anti-Apartheid Act was overridden by sweeping majorities in both Houses of Congress. The most important immediate effects of the Act were the unwilling recruitment into the anti-apartheid movement of both Israel and Japan, South Africa's most willing cooperators, and the flight of American investment; but US opposition to United Nations mandatory sanctions continued.

A similar conflict was taking place within the Commonwealth. While many, perhaps most, Britons had more pressing concerns than the future of South Africa, feelings against the Nationalist regimes were high, and calls for sanctions insistent. Some supermarket chains refused to stock South African fruit, and South African wine vanished from shelves. Sympathetic local authorities named buildings and streets after Nelson Mandela, and the Greater London Council erected a monumental bust of the imprisoned leader outside the Royal Festival Hall; but such demonstrations had little practical effect. Other Commonwealth countries were more vehemently opposed to the South African government, and the conflict came to a head in the Nassau Commonwealth Conference of October 1986. Although Mrs Thatcher had made her own views clear that apartheid must go, Mandela be set free, and forced removals and attacks on other states must cease, her style of argument against the imposition of sanctions was incorrigibly calculated to provoke the rest of the Commonwealth leaders. Arguing against sanctions to the bitter end, she was forced to give way so ungraciously that, according to her own Foreign Secretary Geoffrey Howe, 'she humiliated three dozen other heads of government, devalued the policy which they had just agreed, and demeaned herself . . . even I could scarcely believe my eyes.'[17]

The policy the Commonwealth leaders agreed was the slightly ludicrous one of sending a deputation of 'eminent persons' to South Africa to see for themselves what went on and 'to foster a process of negotiation across the lines of colour, politics and religion with a view to establishing a non-racial and representative government'. Their Eminences were a mixed bag, some with their own agenda to pursue and some present because their own governments could very well spare them, but their conclusion was proved by President Botha's own actions.[18] While in the full flow of discussions in May 1984 Botha, without consulting his dismayed cabinet colleagues, decided to send bombers to attack ANC bases in Zimbabwe, Botswana and Zambia – all Commonwealth countries. The defiance was clear. World opinion, yet again, was horrified.

The beginning of the end

The 'Great Crocodile's' show of force was not enough to avert a setback in the May 1987 general election when the *verkramptes* in the Conservative Party, infuriated by the previous year's liberalization, won twenty-four seats, becoming the official opposition and causing a crisis among the Progressives, who were seemingly ever more irrelevant to political realities. By this time even the cabinet itself was almost an irrelevance as the State President and General Malan lashed out, desperately attempting to find solutions to their insoluble problems.

In August 1987 Cuban and Angolan forces launched a powerful assault on the UNITA headquarters in eastern Angola, which was quickly countered by the South African army. Inflicting a bloody defeat on the enemy at the Lomba River the South African troops, supported by armour, moved on to the isolated town of Cuito Cuanavale; and there they stuck for six painful months, at enormous cost in money and not a little in casualties. It was an expensive way of acquiring wisdom (Chester Crocker disdainfully dismissed the South African military intelligence as 'the stuff of comic books'). Refusing General Malan's pleas for a full-scale assault, President Botha, with the realism he sometimes showed, chose instead the path of retreat and negotiation. The government's public relations machine insisted that the battle had not been a defeat, but a tactical withdrawal in good order – but the results were the same.

It was uncomfortably clear that the Angolan game was up. Eventually Chester Crocker's efforts at mediation bore fruit, helped by the arrival of Neil van Heerden, a reasonable man, as head of the South African Foreign Ministry, and the South African forces withdrew from what was now Namibia at the end of 1988, somewhat consoled by being able to inflict one last incisive defeat on SWAPO. When that organization betrayed its own undertaking to the United Nations and invaded Namibia, the South African army was awarded the opportunity to show what it could do acting for, rather than against, the United Nations. In an operation authorized by the United Nations' man on the spot, Marti Ahtisaari, the invasion was quickly suppressed. The other struggle, inside South Africa, was also drawing to an end as all the tired and dispirited participants accepted that their present strategies had failed. With the pass laws repealed, black trades unions legalized and the 'petty apartheid' restrictions lifted, the only question was when and how a new order would be initiated, at what cost, and most importantly with whom it could be negotiated.

Nationalists were hopelessly split, and the UDF to a great extent discredited by its own adherents' slide into violence (although it was clear enough that most of the violence came from the urban poor and illiterate, who had little knowledge of the issues at stake – one survey showed that only 4 per cent of UDF 'supporters' and 16 per cent of Inkatha followers could name their parties' leaders[19]). The ANC had shot its bolt as far as guerrilla warfare was concerned, and accepted that anything more than urban terrorism, still repellent to the old guard of Christian nationalists, was impossible. International events had continued to deplete its support abroad, and when the collapse of the Berlin Wall in November 1989 marked the end of Russian hegemony in Eastern Europe and the crash of the Soviet economy signalled the end of adventurism, the ANC's main support disintegrated, much to the shock of its Lusaka leadership. It seemed that the new struggle inside South Africa would be one between the ANC and Inkatha, which had been allowed to flourish in the shelter of government approval and support.

Early in 1988 the ANC made its bid to be the prime mover by publishing its 'Constitutional Guidelines for a Democratic Society'. Redefining the Freedom Charter and smoothing out the earlier insistence on state control, the new manifesto accepted the principles of multi-party democracy, a Bill of Rights and a mixed economy. Disavowing their earlier Leninist principles, the ANC communists recognized that with Mikhail Gorbachev at the helm in Russia liberalism had become acceptable; but the ANC continued to be an uneasy marriage of the Lutuli/Tambo reformist traditions and the more radical activism typified by Chris Hani. Even while serious negotiations were continuing between the ANC and the government Joe Slovo despatched Mac Maharaj, another enthusiastic communist, to revive the armed struggle in the Republic without informing the non-communist MK commander, Joe Modise.

A non-socialist ANC made a suitable partner for business interests, which had been drifting into a confirmed opposition to the government. Now not only the traditionally liberal Anglo-American Corporation, but the major Afrikaner businesses saw the writing on the wall; one of the clearest characters was the fact that black purchasing power was now overtaking white, and that the boycotts which a substantial part of the black communities were ready to impose could be fatal. Reconciliation with the ANC began with a September 1985 meeting between a delegation of business leaders and the ANC executive committee, including Tambo and Thabo Mbeki. This was reinforced in 1987 by a group representing both English and Afrikaner business, including Chris Ball of Barclays (now the First National Bank), Chris van Wyk of the Afrikaner Trust Bank, and, rather oddly, the Mr Justice Mostert who had sat in judgement on Muldergate. Developing into a formal organization, the Consultative Business Movement, the liberal business interests went on to support the foundation of a new party, the Democratic Party, which attracted not only former progressives, but such left-wing former Nationalists as Dennis Worrall, now returned from exile and having started his own party, Wim de Klerk and Professor Sampie Terreblanche. Botha's Nationalists were now under particular pressure from both left and right, and the whole economy was suffering from sanctions and disinvestments. By the end of 1988 the historian of Nationalism Dan O'Meara perceived 'a powerful sense of *déja vu*', with Botha 'mired in an impasse remarkably similar to that which finished off Vorster'.[20]

Showing the realism of which he was sometimes capable, but following his policy of not telling his colleagues what he was up to, Botha authorized an officially unofficial approach to the ANC in November 1987. Again it was the friendly, pipe-smoking Mbeki who took the lead in a series of meetings financed by Consolidated Goldfields – Rhodes' own firm – and held at Mells Park House in England. The talks were kept very secret – only Botha and later F.W. de Klerk were in the know, and the ANC delegates were equally nervous of any leakage. Nothing concrete was achieved at these meetings, but the ANC leaders established themselves in the eyes of the Nationalist representatives as reasonable, tolerant – and highly educated – people with whom constructive negotiations could be pursued.[21]

Whether Botha would himself ever have taken the plunge and formalized these negotiations is unsure; realism continued to fight with bred-in-the-bone Afrikaner prejudice in the State President's mind, but in January 1989 Botha was rushed into hospital following a stroke. In a final manifestation of his incapacity for sticking to a single line, he resigned as leader of the National Party but not as State President. Much to everyone's surprise the party caucus elected Wim de Klerk's younger brother as party leader.

Frederick Willem de Klerk was something of an enigma. Commonly regarded as a rather undistinguished, conservatively inclined party politician, he was known to his colleagues as 'the peacemaker'; but at least he was much less frightening than the now permanently angry Botha: 'amiable enough, and he doesn't give anybody the feeling . . . that he actually enjoys stomping on people' was one judgement on the new leader.[22] With Botha hanging on as State President, de Klerk's position was uneasy. However hesitant he may have been in the past, movement now, in February 1989, was possible only in one direction; there could be no return to apartheid, already abandoned, and progress towards an alternative society was inevitable. As yet, however, there was no need to contemplate a straightforward egalitarian democracy. Previous multi-racial constitutions in such countries as Zimbabwe had entrenched minority rights by constitutional devices including reserved seats in parliament, guaranteed ministerial positions, or differential weighting of the franchise – the last abandoned, incidentally, by Britain only in 1950. Some such deal, it was thought by the government, should have been possible in South Africa.

An immediate move was vital. A Defiance Campaign launched by the latest protest group, the Mass Democratic Movement, successors to the now-banned UDF, was gaining momentum, but the Damocles sword engaging everyone's nervous attention was the forthcoming debt repayments scheduled for 1990. Only after much negotiation had the South African Finance Ministry squeezed their way out of a foreign debt crisis in 1986–87 by postponing repayments to 1990, in the hope that economic growth would make that possible. But by the end of 1988 the cash resources available for repayment had fallen to less than 30 per cent of the 1980 level; South Africa's foreign reserves were actually lower than those of Botswana. Within months of de Klerk's succession his government would be obliged to lay its hands on $7,000 million.

But with whom could a political settlement be negotiated? A forlorn hope to promote such acceptable black leaders as Chief Buthelezi as potential negotiating partners collapsed. The parliamentary stalemate was emphasized in a September 1989 election from which the National Party emerged with only a minority of votes cast and a weak majority of parliamentary seats in the face of the Conservatives' thirty-nine – a surprising and significant success – and the new Democratic Party's thirty-three. Nothing could be done in such a parliament, and the essential irrelevance of the constitution was underlined by a strike of three million blacks organized to coincide with the elections. Taking into account the number of potential voters of all races, de Klerk could claim only 6 per cent of the nation's franchise. The inevitable protests in the streets were, once again, suppressed with outrageous brutality. Even the Minister of Law and Order acknowledged, 'Everybody, including the police, the government and country, realizes that the status quo cannot continue.'

In a July 1988 meeting with Hank Cohen, the American Assistant Secretary for African Affairs, de Klerk admitted: 'Unless we bring in blacks as full partners, my country won't be fit for my grandchildren,' and assured Cohen that he was going 'to dismantle apartheid and bring about full democracy through negotiations as soon as possible'. In his inauguration speech after the election he told parliament that he would 'work urgently' to dismantle discriminatory legislation, to continue the release of political prisoners, to give 'urgent attention' to a Bill of Rights, and to open negotiations with black representatives: 'We are determined to turn our words into actions.'[23]

The difficulty remained, however, that of finding an acceptable negotiating partner who could speak on behalf of the disenfranchised blacks with real authority. The government's normally acquiescent Bantustan leaders were little more than a joke, while Chief Buthelezi, although wielding real power in KwaZulu, was regarded with deep suspicion by the ANC and many others. The advice received by de Klerk, State President as well as Prime Minister after Botha's surly resignation in August, was unanimous: Nelson Mandela was the only man of sufficient stature to unite enough of the country behind him.

It might have been thought that by banishing Mandela to Robben Island, that ancient and miserable place of imprisonment, he would be conveniently removed from public gaze. In fact, by 1989, after twenty-six years of imprisonment, Mandela was the best-known and most acclaimed South African in the world. By insulating him from all the errors and misfortunes of the ANC, and the compromises of Buthelezi, successive South African governments had ensured that Mandela's reputation remained spotless. A not inconsiderable additional factor was his freedom from any suspicion of association with his wife Winnie's very dubious activities. During his long years of imprisonment, at first under harsh conditions, Nelson Mandela had developed uncommon personal qualities which marked him as a leader of rare power, unequalled in Africa. Moreover, President Botha had given him a magnificent opportunity to assert the moral ascendancy which he had shown during the Rivonia Trials, but which had increased immeasurably as the man's personal stature had developed through incarceration and suffering. As long ago as January 1981 Botha had formally announced that

Mandela's release would be considered if he gave 'a full commitment that he will not make himself guilty of planning, instigating or committing acts of violence for the furtherance of political objectives, but will conduct himself in such a way that he will not again have to be arrested'. Mandela was able to reject the offer in a splendid reply:

> What freedom am I being offered while the organization of the people remains banned? What freedom am I being offered when I may be arrested on a pass offence? What freedom am I being offered to live my life as a family with my dear wife who remains in banishment in Brandfort? What freedom am I being offered when I need a stamp in my pass to seek work? What freedom am I being offered when my very South African citizenship is not respected?
>
> Only free men can negotiate. Prisoners cannot enter into contracts ... I cannot and will not give any undertaking at a time when I and you, the people, are not free.

In May 1988 Professor Neil Barnard, head of the National Intelligence Service, the successor of BOSS, and a confidant of Botha, made the pilgrimage to Mandela, now more comfortably housed in Pollsmoor prison. Barnard, who was at the same time overseeing the Mells Park House talks in England, hoped to persuade the ANC to disassociate itself from the communists, but Mandela refused, and insisted that only a meeting with President Botha himself could be productive. With superb arrogance the prisoner wrote to the President in March 1989 requiring such a meeting:

> The deepening political crisis in our country has been a matter of grave concern to me for quite some time, and I now consider it necessary in the national interest for the African National Congress and the government to meet urgently to negotiate an effective political settlement.
>
> Two central issues will have to be addressed at such a meeting: firstly, the demand for majority rule in a unitary state; secondly, the concern of white South Africa over this demand, as well as the insistence of whites on structural guarantees that majority rule will not mean domination of the white minority by blacks. The most crucial task which will face the government and the ANC will be to reconcile these two positions.

After some persuasion by Barnard the encounter took place in July, but by then Botha was very much in decline, no longer Prime Minister but only the titular State President, and within weeks not to be even that; de

Klerk had to be the man to take the decision. The ANC had made this easier for him by issuing a policy document in August, the Harare Declaration, adopted in December by the UN General Assembly. Based again on the Freedom Charter, but modified to tone down any references to socialism, the Harare Declaration laid out clearly what action would be needed for sanctions to be ended and South Africa restored to the comity of nations.

When in October de Klerk decided to release all the remaining ANC prisoners, including Walter Sisulu, and began talks with the recalcitrant Mandela, still intent on remaining in gaol until all his conditions had been fulfilled, it was clear what the next step would have to be, but the actual announcement made at the opening of parliament on 20 February 1990 came as a dramatic surprise. All the banned organizations – the MK, the Communist Party and the PAC as well as the ANC – were restored, restrictions on reporting removed, political prisoners released, executions suspended and all remaining apartheid laws repealed. The government would work out a new constitution based on universal suffrage. Finally, as a striking coda to his speech, President de Klerk announced that Nelson Mandela was to be released unconditionally and without delay. The fantasy nightmare of apartheid, that child of delusion and destruction, had taken forty-two years to dispel; and it was not to disappear without protracted and bloody sequelae which are still working themselves out.

NINETEEN

Such a Tumultuous Land

South Africa has had more than its share of prominent figures who, if they have not shaped events, have at least had great events shaped around them. Shaka, Rhodes, Moshoeshoe, Kruger, Milner, John Philips, Piet Retief, Merriman, Frere, Kgama and many others have all tipped the balance of history, as did the contrasted figures of Nelson Mandela and F.W. de Klerk.

When he came to unexpected prominence de Klerk was an undistinguished middle-ranking, middle-aged (fifty-two) politician with a reputation as a conservative.[1] Like Paul Kruger before him, de Klerk was a Dopper, but without Kruger's massive personality: a bald, stout, unimpressive figure, who relied on good humour and a politician's easy style to win supporters. He had breathed a political air from childhood. His grandfather William de Klerk, later a Dopper minister, had been arrested as a rebel while still a student in 1900, and was dedicated to the cause of Christian National Education. His father Jan led the Transvaal National Party and served as Minister of Labour in Strydom's government, where he had insisted on the supremacy of white labour – 'there would be no question of non-white intrusion into the industrial complex of the whites' – and Strydom, a not-very avuncular figure, was married to his aunt. Frederick's own views matched those of his father and uncle. That South Africa might one day have actually a black President, as Anthony Trollope had forecast, and which Pik Botha again rashly suggested in 1986, seemed a heresy to de Klerk, who forced a retraction from the Foreign Minister. Nor did his wife Marike hide her own uncompromisingly racist views.

Jan de Klerk, who died in 1979, had very nearly been elected as State President in 1966, and was badly affected by his failure. At that time F.W. was teaching law at his old university, the Afrikaner stronghold of Potchefstroom. His later experience of National Party politics, beginning with his election to parliament in 1972 and centred on the Transvaal, had given the younger de Klerk a finely tuned sense of what it might be possible to achieve with the consent of the electorate, and how it might be managed – and it should never be forgotten that South African politics were essentially those of a parliamentary democracy, with all the constraints implied by such a system. The percentage of the population not entitled to vote was no higher than that of Victorian England, and governments were similarly dependent on the results of general elections. Certainly the fact that the parliamentary opposition to the Nationalists was permanently enfeebled went some way to modifying this, but conditions in the 1970s and eighties within the government camp were so fraught with contention that de Klerk had many opportunities to develop his skills as a fixer.

In this he was not hampered by too much ideological baggage. Despite his impeccable Afrikaner background, the young de Klerk had taken advantage of an Abe Bailey scholarship[2] to visit England. On his succession to the Transvaal National Party leadership in 1982 he modestly stated: 'I do not want to be a leader with a fanfare, one who is carried on your shoulders and your applause.'

Some, at least, of de Klerk's conservative attitudes had been party political devices. His most threatening opposition in the National Party came not from the *verligtes*, but from the hard-line white supremacists, causing de Klerk 'to make ultra-conservative noises in his attempt to halt the growth of the conservatives'. With the Conservatives under Andries Treurnicht, the Broederbond chairman who had assumed the mantle of Albert Hertzog, doing so well in the September 1989 parliamentary elections by wresting seventeen seats from the National Party, the government had to rely on English-speaking support, which was unlikely to be alienated by de Klerk's invaluable reasonableness. If it came to a choice between a new Mercedes and the preservation of Afrikaner identity, many burghers would join with their English neighbours in choosing the car.

Few people expected decisive action from this essentially emollient denizen of political corridors; even his elder brother Willem wrote that F.W. was 'too strongly convinced that racial grouping is the only truth, way and life'. De Klerk was, however, a pragmatist, who realized that the grand apartheid vision had become unworkable as opposition within South Africa and abroad stiffened, and like many Afrikaners he possessed a strong, and highly individual, sense of justice and fairness. 'The impracticability, unacceptability and unaffordability of apartheid meant that the whole system is falling apart . . . the black revolt is becoming uncontrollable.'

According to Willem, the principal reasons for F.W. de Klerk's dramatic change of policy were the end of the Cold War, which removed both the (largely illusory) Soviet threat and the (rapidly crumbling) US support. If the ANC had indeed been the Soviet arm in South Africa, the carpet had been swiftly pulled from under its feet. The growing cohesion of the European Community also made it essential for South Africa to secure its relations in this, its most important market, but it was the USA that was vital; unless the American banks lifted their sanctions on the provision of capital, the South African economy would certainly seize up. George Bush's administration had not the same sympathy for South African Nationalists that its predecessors had evinced, a fact made obvious when in June 1989 Walter Sisulu's wife Albertina was invited to the White House and de Klerk, very pointedly, was not. He would be received, it was firmly indicated, only after all the opposition parties had been unbanned and the state of emergency lifted. This was finally done in June 1990, and American sanctions were lifted shortly afterwards.[3]

It appeared that there was an element of conversion, if not with Pauline suddenness on the way to Damascus, at least when after a quiet family respite in September 1989 de Klerk prepared the speech in which he announced his proposal. It was at a period of stress, when the Afrikaner banks were quivering on the edge of a crash, supported only by secret state funding, and after an election in that month when his party had been returned on a minority of the votes cast, winning ninety-three of 166 seats, but with 30 per cent of the electorate voting for the Conservatives and 21 per cent for the Democrats. Democratic politicians can shrug off economic crises most of the time, but a threat to their parliamentary majority spells immediate disaster; and de Klerk was a skilled political operator.

His opponent, or rather his vital potential ally, was a man of very different character and appearance from de Klerk.[4] In his own person Nelson Mandela combined much diverse South African history, Khoikhoi, Xhosa and English. A Thembu aristocrat, brought up to accept the obligations and privileges of leadership, he was heir to the Thembu traditions of accommodating oneself to events, reasonable discussion only giving way to action as a last resort. Mandela's great-great-grandfather Ngubengcuka, 'one of the greatest monarchs', had defended his people, who included many refugees from the *mfecane*, with the assistance – largely adventitious – of colonial forces. In 1825 he allowed the Methodist William Shaw to set up a mission station at Clarkebury, and over a century later Mandela attended the school Shaw established there.

Ngubengcuka's heir Mthikrakra cooperated with the British and asked the missionary Joseph Warner to care for his children and his tribe. His son Ngangelizwe ruled from 1863 to 1884, fought Sarhili's Xhosa and got the worst of it, rode with Walter Stanford in the 1877–78 war, the last of the Xhosa frontier wars, and again in the Thembuland rebellion of 1880.[5] Dalindyebo, who succeeded in 1885 and died two years after the birth of Nelson Mandela, carried on the quiet Thembu tradition with considerable efficiency. It was essentially one of compromise, allied with persistence in what, however unpopular – and Ngangelizwe's alliance with the British was fiercely opposed by some of his people – was judged in the best interests of the community.

Saul Bellow once remarked that there had never been a Zulu Tolstoy. Apart from the fact that there has never been an American Tolstoy either, it is pertinent to point out that a Zulu writer would, as Indian writers have done for many years, choose to write in English if he wanted to address a wide audience. Nearly two hundred years of English education has not turned South Africans into black Englishmen, but it has brought all South Africans into the mainstream of Western culture. Aristotle was as much a part of, say, Davidson Don Jabavu's intellectual equipment as it was of his contemporaries – drawing a bow at a venture – Teilhard de Chardin, Gertrude Stein or Carl Gustav Jung. Nelson Mandela was formed in the same traditions as any British social democrat; as he said during the Rivonia trial, 'I have great respect for British political institutions. I regard the British Parliament as the most democratic institution in the world, and the independence and impartiality of its judiciary never fail to arouse my admiration.' Without ever ceasing to be conscious of indigenous African culture, with its own living tradition of democratic debate, and while abominating most manifestations of imperialism (sentiments shared by many Englishmen of his generation – it would be difficult to be less imperialist than George Orwell) Mandela's political values were essentially shaped by the British experience.

Reaching further back in African history, it may not be too fanciful to remark that since the Thembu were one of the Xhosa-speaking peoples with the largest share of Khoikhoi ancestry, the lively charm of that almost vanished race might have lightened the seriousness of the Xhosa aristocrat in Mandela's temperament – and accounted, too, for some of his physical characteristics.

Mandela had, as was the custom of his people, been brought up as a member of the Methodist Church, never a militant communion, and therefore much in accordance with Thembu instincts, but one whose tight system of lay organization had done much to form the British trades union movement. He remained in the Church, and when defending the ANC's decision to abandon its non-violent tactics he insisted that he 'was a Christian, and always had been a Christian', but that 'even Christ used force to expel money lenders from the temple'.

Christian fortitude and that remarkable African patience were very necessary during Mandela's long imprisonment from June 1964 to February 1990. The passing of nearly twenty-seven years does much to alter anyone; when those years have been spent in confinement the effects become more noticeable. In so artificial an environment, the constant necessity to assert prisoners' rights against the administration, the freedom from the need to deliberate, compromise, prevaricate and convince that is part of the common currency of politics, and the dependence on self-instruction for mental stimulation all have a concentrated effect. On Robben Island conditions were always uncomfortable, and often humiliating, but the greatest pain was inflicted by Mandela's forced separation from his family.

There were compensations. Although for much of the time books were censored and newspapers forbidden, prisoners were allowed study facilities, and organized their own classes. They were nevertheless insulated from the outside world, and emerged from their long incarceration, metaphorically blinking, into a society very different from that they had lived in.

In March 1991 Mandela and de Klerk were faced with different agendas. De Klerk, party politician and parliamentarian, had to manoeuvre change through the existing system. He was in no position simply to accept majority rule, as demanded by the ANC, but had to carry his electorate along with him. In so doing he had in mind an agreement such as that which had settled the prolonged Rhodesian crisis in 1980, by which minority rights would be constitutionally safeguarded. Given the failure of unadulterated majority rule in such places as Northern Ireland, there were convincing reasons for seeking some suitable formula in South Africa.

For other reasons, Mandela was in a similar predicament. While de Klerk was hampered by the necessity to work within a well-established constitution, Mandela was constrained by the inchoate, often bitterly opposed, mass of black and liberal supporters united only in their hatred of Nationalist apartheid, and insistent that nothing less than immediate majority rule would suffice. The division between the angry and violent young men of the PAC and the elders of the ANC, burdened by the bitterly-acquired wisdom of a generation of exile and resistance, had been obvious even in the prisons. Just as, thirty-eight years before in 1953, the young Mandela had been rebuked by Chief Lutuli, 'burning with a cold fire' when he criticized the older men's cooperation with white liberals, so now the experienced old leader had to trust that time would calm the young lions.

Oliver Tambo, who had held the centre together for so long, was now old and ill, enabling the more militant activists to make the running. Although Mandela moved quickly, visiting Lusaka only a fortnight after his release in order to come to terms with the exiled ANC command, his authority was by no means unquestioned, but in August 1990 it was agreed that the 'armed struggle' – which by then was so feeble as to be hardly detectable – should be formally suspended. It was a difficult decision for the ANC executive. In the heady atmosphere of the fifties and sixties, amid the dawn of independent Africa, fighters against apartheid could feel themselves part of a noble struggle, and one with every prospect of speedy success. Now, although the battle was officially won, there was precious little to show for it, with the Boers still in power in Pretoria, and the leadership committed to peaceful negotiations.

More immediately pressing was the question of Mangosuthu Buthelezi's Inkatha, resentful of the Xhosa and of the international respect being accorded to the ANC leadership. ANC representatives did little to help. Their Natal organizer was one Harry Gwala, fiercely Stalinist and uncompromisingly anti-Buthelezi, who contrived to sabotage potential reconciliatory meetings with both Walter Sisulu and Mandela himself. Buthelezi, who regarded himself as at least as legitimate a representative of the liberation movement as Mandela, organized the Inkatha Freedom Party (IFP) not only in Natal, but among the Zulu mineworkers in the Witwatersrand. In July 1990 what was in effect a civil war broke out there between Inkatha and the ANC/UDF. Hundreds of people were killed within weeks as armed men ravaged commuter trains, shooting passengers, and mine-hostel dwellers sallied forth armed with spears and clubs to beat and kill any likely ANC/UDF supporters they could find. Pleading the Zulu warrior tradition, largely reinvented for the purpose, Buthelezi argued that his supporters were legally entitled to carry 'traditional weapons'. The Supreme Court exposed this pretence, ruling that the argument was a product of invention and the manipulation of tradition.[6]

It was an opportunity, quickly seized by the state security establishment, to make a dangerous situation very much worse. The securocrats, accustomed to having things very much their own way under P.W. Botha, were profoundly shocked by the prospect of majority rule (which would not be without significant personal risks to many of their number, if their past misdeeds were exposed). A 'third force', directed by General Malan and the Justice Minister Adrian Vlok, had since 1987 been covertly deployed in order to sabotage any negotiations by provoking, and indeed perpetrating, acts of violence.[7] But with a now-free press, the active participation of police and government could not be as effectively hidden as it had previously been. In July 1991 the 'Inkathagate' scandal revealed that government financial support had indeed been given to Buthelezi, that Inkatha volunteers had been secretly trained in violent repression, and that special forces units had been deployed in several massacres, beginning in January 1987 with the killing of thirteen people – eleven of them women and children – the family of an ANC activist, Victor Ntuli. The full story of this particular massacre emerged eight years later, when General Magnus Malan, Minister of Defence in 1987, together with twelve other white officers and seven Zulu Inkatha supporters, was charged with murder. It was proved that in April 1986 some two hundred Inkatha supporters had been trained in Namibia by the South African Defence Force, funded by money deposited in an Inkatha bank account through channels related to Armscor, the government's weapons manufacturer. Buthelezi's own part in this was soft-pedalled by the prosecution, doubtless in the interests of public peace, but even the defence lawyers admitted that 'the only reason for keeping the operation secret was to protect the image of Chief Buthelezi and to prevent a connection being made between the state and the support provided to Inkatha.' In spite of convincing evidence the accused were acquitted, in a much-criticized verdict. But the close links between Inkatha and state terrorism were made abundantly clear.[8]

The Ntuli murders were only the first of thousands of 'third force' outrages, the frequency of which increased as the prospect of majority ANC rule grew nearer. The apparatus of apartheid had indeed been dismantled, but the country seemed mired in chaos and deceit.

De Klerk's protestations that if indeed there were such outrages, his Cabinet knew nothing about it, rang hollow. Although officially it might be true that Malan's men, as they had done even under Botha's much more stringent rule, acted on their own initiative, it was impossible to believe that Cabinet members had no suspicions (and indeed it later appeared that the 'removal' of opponents had been discussed among ministers, who included the jovial, outwardly liberal Pik Botha).

For the time being, however, the Nationalist government and its allies, Inkatha, together with a fair number from the Coloured House of Representatives (the Indian House of Delegates, commonly known as the 'House of Dogs', never commanded any significant support), had achieved international respectability and a remarkable level of parliamentary support, the only dissident being the old Crocodile himself, who splashed off into his lonely swamp in April 1990. The ANC, on the other hand, was still much occupied in dealing with more aggressive black movements and in restoring its own unity. Their task was not helped by the trial of Mandela's wife Winnie on charges of kidnapping and murder, and her estrangement and final divorce from her long-suffering husband.

Mrs Mandela had been one of the many casualties of oppression. Nearly thirty years of separation and harassment had transformed her from a passionate young woman into a frustrated and embittered fury, intoxicated by the uncritical adulation of the world press as the 'mother of the nation' into a conviction of her own central and overweening importance to the 'struggle' – a delusion shared by too many ANC supporters who refused to be convinced by the evidence of her reckless, even criminal behaviour.

Although initially opposed to the idea of an all-comers conference to prepare the ground for a constitutional assembly, rather than moving directly to a new constitution, the ANC accepted de Klerk's proposal for a Convention for a Democratic South Africa (CODESA), which met in September 1991, in an atmosphere of tension and suspicion. Among notable absentees were the Conservative Party and the PAC, which had resorted to chanting the slogan 'one settler, one bullet,' and Buthelezi, who contented himself with the warning that if the Zulu were not satisfied a 'terrible and destructive' conflict would be inevitable. Beginning badly with an angry exchange between Mandela and de Klerk, CODESA did not get far. In the hope of consolidating his support de Klerk held a referendum in March 1992, which produced a convincing vote among the white electorate in favour of his reform programme, on the understanding that there were to be provisions for safeguarding minority rights – power sharing, de Klerk insisted, did not mean majority rule.

Imbued with a new confidence that he had the support of a convincing majority, and believing that the right wing had been marginalized, de Klerk, always looking to the existing parliamentary system in which he had worked, and not addressing the much greater non-voting majority, stiffened his negotiating conditions. The 'CODESA' discussions speedily ground to a halt. Allowing this to happen was a signal misjudgement, de Klerk apparently having failed to realize that he was no longer playing party politics, or dealing with opponents of the calibre of Worrall or Treunicht. In the three years since his release Nelson Mandela had become a formidable figure, an international statesmen of a calibre South Africa had only once before produced. Jan Smuts had been such a one at Versailles, guiding the formation of the League of Nations and, later, drafting the aims of the United Nations. But Smuts had never commanded the confidence of his fellow-countrymen to the extent that Mandela was able to do; nor had the cool and distant Smuts possessed the human warmth and charm that Mandela could not help evincing. De Klerk, the essential fixer and negotiator, tolerated abroad only because he had surrendered to Mandela, was in no position to force any issues.

With the failure of CODESA it seemed that the politicians had shot their bolt, and the street-fighters took over. As had the Terror in revolutionary France two hundred years before, the bloody events that followed the failure shocked the leaders on both sides into a realization that they must act together to prevent the complete disintegration of South African society. In May 1992 the much-admired young leader of the communists, Chris Hani, was murdered by two far-right gunmen, one of whom, Clive Derby-Lewis, had been a Conservative Party MP. Hani had, as Mandela had hoped, abandoned his earlier Stalinist hard line in favour of a democratic socialist attitude, and commanded the allegiance and affection of the young to a degree second only to Mandela himself. His death, and the manner of it, caused an outburst of grief and anger. Only weeks later, in June, Inkatha supporters in Boiphatong, a township south of Johannesburg, attacked a squatter camp, killing forty-five, presumed to be ANC supporters, in fact mostly women and children. The police shot dead another three on their own account a couple of days later. Again there was widespread fury and outrage, as it seemed that the police had not only stood back from the slaughter, but actually supported its perpetrators. In September it was the turn of ANC followers to initiate violence when a crowd, encouraged by the communist Ronnie Kasrils, attempted a charge into Ciskeian territory near Bisho. Fifty of them were killed by Ciskeian police, and Mandela acknowledged that the massacre was the fault of the ANC supporters.

Reinforced by the constant flow of lesser outrages and by a severe lecture from the widely-respected Finance Minister Derek Keys, Cyril Ramaphosa and Roelf Meyer, both reasonable pragmatists, were sent off to prepare a summit meeting between Mandela and de Klerk to be held on 26 September, only three weeks after the Bisho killings. At the summit a Minute of Understanding was signed, which led, after further meetings over the next few months, to a second multi-party convention, this time attended by those who had shunned CODESA.

It was not unlike the National Convention of 1908–9, as arguments about a federal or unitary state were rehearsed. Once again Natal – now KwaZulu Natal and represented by Buthelezi – stood out for provincial independence, joined in the 'Freedom Alliance' by the old right-wing Nationalists and the leaders of the Ciskei and Bophuthatswana homelands. Once again the proponents of the unitary state had their way, and decided that provincial legislatures were again to have only limited powers.

The new constitution, approved on 18 November 1993, provided for universal suffrage and a cabinet constitution, and was – once more in an echo of the Act of Union – only capable of amendment by a two-thirds majority of the popular vote. It was, all things considered, an extraordinary achievement, the voluntary relinquishment of power (with, certainly, internal violence and outside economic pressures acting as potent incentives) by the white minority.

South Africa emerged from the shadow of apartheid badly injured, but alive. The parliamentary system, with the acceptance of elections deciding which government should be in power, had been unbroken. Independent courts had continued to apply the law, not always without prejudice, but without bribery and with not too much improper interference. In spite of the vicious undercover activities of many, at all levels, some decent officers remained in the armed services and police who might perhaps provide the nucleus of a better security force, and to insure against the possibility of an armed coup; all these things were rare enough, not only in Africa, but in most of the world's states.

The economy had survived the impact of sanctions, disturbances and disinvestment; battered but essentially intact, there had been negligible damage to the industrial infrastructure or the functioning of the markets. It was in the deformed labour force that forty years of 'Bantu education'

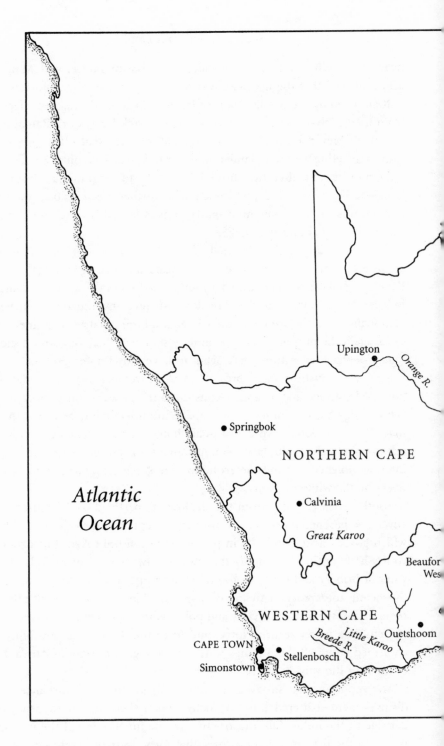

Atlantic
Ocean

Upington

Orange R.

Springbok

NORTHERN CAPE

Calvinia

Great Karoo

Beaufor
Wes

WESTERN CAPE

Little Karoo

Ouetshoom

Breede R.

CAPE TOWN

Stellenbosch

Simonstown

MAP 11   *Present-day South Africa*

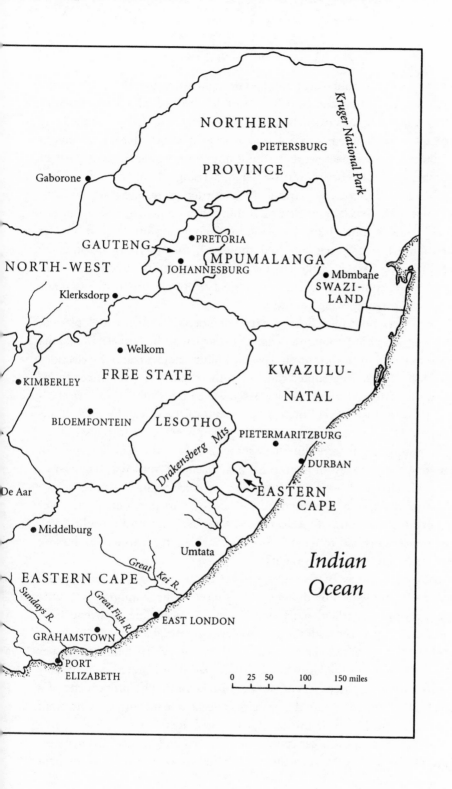

NORTHERN

● PIETERSBURG

PROVINCE

Kruger National Park

Gaborone ●

GAUTENG

● PRETORIA

NORTH-WEST

MPUMALANGA

JOHANNESBURG

● Mbmbane

SWAZI-
LAND

Klerksdorp ●

● Welkom

FREE STATE

KWAZULU-

NATAL

● KIMBERLEY

BLOEMFONTEIN ●

LESOTHO

Drakensberg Mts

PIETERMARITZBURG ●

De Aar

EASTERN
CAPE

● DURBAN

● Middelburg

● Umtata

Indian
Ocean

Great Kei R.

EASTERN CAPE

Sundays R.

Great Fish R.

EAST LONDON

GRAHAMSTOWN ●

● PORT
ELIZABETH

0   25   50   100   150 miles

and ten years of school disruption had brought about that the worst results of job discrimination and apartheid were felt. Skilled labour was in short supply, exacerbated as disenchanted whites emigrated, and a threateningly large number of unemployed – and nearly unemployable in a modern economy – mainly black workers could not be retrained. In some parts of the country social cohesion was shattered. Missing school and withholding rent had been regarded as patriotic duties for ten years, and it was difficult to convince the recalcitrant that such things were now frowned upon: not paying debts is much more agreeable than coughing up. With a murder rate of nearly eighty per hundred thousand, Johannesburg became the world's killing capital. Although the GDP rose steadily after 1992, urban employment continued to fall, and little perceptible progress was made towards improving living conditions.

The first elections to be held on a fully democratic franchise took place in April 1994, after a last-minute agreement to participate by Buthelezi's Inkatha Freedom Party. In the last seven days the killings stopped, and the elections took place in an uninterrupted calm – but there had been over fifteen thousand deaths during the four fallow years. It was a powerfully impressive spectacle, witnessed with keen interest by the rest of the world, to see millions of South Africans of all races queuing patiently together to register their votes. Among them were doubtless some old men who had last voted in May 1933; the youngest of them must have been, by April 1994, eighty-two years old. They had been sixty lost years for black South Africans.

The results gave a substantial majority – over 62 per cent of the votes cast, in a high turnout – to ANC candidates of all races. In KwaZulu Natal, where the results had to be at least questionable, an electoral commission awarded a bare majority to Inkatha.[9]

History has a way of repeating itself, and the new government found itself with problems not dissimilar to those of the Nationalists twenty years previously. Parliamentary opposition was negligible, as it had been in Vorster's day. Faced with the need to develop a new identity, the National Party itself fragmented. The extreme right wing, which had won 30 per cent of the votes in the last white election, had disintegrated, and its only serious national figure, General Viljoen, backed off. The proponents of a racially pure '*Volkstaat*' found themselves relegated to one or two windswept hamlets in the North Transvaal, under the leadership of a few ageing, pot-bellied gunmen, sad caricatures of de Wet's and Smuts' commandos. More liberal former Nationalists also drifted away, the most prominent being Roelf Meyer, who had been responsible with Cyril Ramaphosa for structuring the constitutional settlement. Eventually, in August 1997, de Klerk resigned his leadership of the party.

With the patronage of government at their disposal the ANC had few problems in parliament; but their support in the country suffered as some of their most able leaders, such as 'Terror' Lekota, were forced out of office in party feuds or chose the fleshpots of business, as did Cyril Ramaphosa and Tokyo Sexwale. Their real opposition, as had been that of the Nationalists, was to be found outside Parliament House. The poorer, unemployed third of the population now had the vote, and were able to go where they pleased without a pass, but life continued hard and dangerous. Unless they could be satisfied with the new democratic South Africa the possibility of a peaceful future looked uncertain. Inkatha maintained a sulky, semi-detached attitude in parliament, but its real strength lay in the KwaZulu Natal countryside, where a residual hope for an autonomous state could be sparked into action at an opportune moment. The Western Cape, which regarded its own status in relation to the rest of the country as being 'Belgium to the Congo', was another provincial stronghold where the ANC writ did not run.

One lesson quickly learned by the ANC leaders was that their previous vaguely socialist ideals would have to be modified. By 1994 few informed people believed that a centralized, state-controlled economy could work; the examples of the only surviving Marxist countries, Cuba and North Korea, were enough to prove the point. On the other hand, public expectations had been excited by the 1994 ANC manifesto, which promised better housing and more jobs in abundance, without any indication of how these were to be arrived at. Senior posts were filled, often reasonably successfully, by blacks, Coloureds and Indians, but the levers of economic power remained clutched in white, usually Afrikaner, hands. The Broederbond still exercised much power, and showed little disposition to allow more than cosmetic adjustments. When black business initiatives were made on discriminatory grounds they displayed only moderate success. The most prominent example, the 'black-empowerment' takeover of an Anglo-American subsidiary company, JCI, lost half its value, together with its chairman Mzi Kumalo, in a year.

Even when black economic initiatives are successful, as many are, the immediate benefits are experienced only by the middle classes, rather than percolating down to the levels where unemployment shows no sign of diminishing. Without public investment on a large scale employment prospects will improve only slowly, if at all, but South Africa's capacity to attract investment, and to remain competitive, depends on it remaining a market economy. The dilemma is pointed painfully in neighbouring Zimbabwe, where the Mugabe government, impoverished by widespread corruption and protracted incompetence, is threatening to expropriate white farmers, a move that would certainly inflict grievous damage on an already fragile economy.

While South Africa is unique in that continent, such difficulties are also found in Central and South America. Mexico, Brazil and Argentina are similarly placed economically, with comparable per capita gross national products – Brazil's and South Africa's being the highest. All have experienced distressing breakdowns of social order, those in Mexico and Brazil being especially serious. South Africa, in the comparison, does not come out too badly. Official violence and corruption is punished only tardily, if at all, in the Latin American countries, while in South Africa the imaginative Truth and Reconciliation Commission, before which a full confession can win a pardon for politically induced crimes, has enabled something of a national catharsis to take place. The struggle against apartheid ended with a compromise rather than an outright victory. Economic forces, which included a strong surviving Afrikaner influence on financial institutions, combined with international pressure – discreetly applied, but well understood – to encourage moderation. Something more subtle has also been at work as horrifying stories of brutality and officially-inspired violence have been revealed to the Truth and Reconciliation Commission. In spite of inevitable distress and controversy, and thanks partly to the energy of Archbishop Tutu, this unlikely forum has worked. Vengeance, it is acknowledged, truly is the Lord's.

It was fitting that the healing process was begun by the Archbishop. Eighty per cent of South Africans are Christians: missionary work has been more effective than the van der Kemps or Philips could ever have expected; not only by education, indoctrinating pupils with the ideals (and prejudices) of a mainly Protestant and English-speaking culture, but in less obvious ways. Some eight million Christians follow the Independent African tradition, which has interpreted European and African values to arrive at an impressive synthesis. But it will remain true, as Mary Moffat sighed from Kurnman in 1824, that 'it requires some little fortitude to live at rest in such a tumultuous land.'[10]

NOTES

INTRODUCTION

1 See e.g. J. Bailey, *Sailing to Paradise*.
2 e.g. Hugh Thomas's authoritative *The Slave Trade*.
3 Quoted in B. Davidson, *The African Past*, p. 81.

CHAPTER 1

1 The most convenient collection of early documents is that of R. Raven-Hart, *Before van Riebeeck*. For the early Dutch exploration and empire see Boxer, *Dutch Merchants and Mariners in Asia 1602–1795*, *The Dutch Seaborne Empire 1600–1800*, *The Portuguese Seaborne Empire*, *The Dutch in Brazil* and Hakluyt. J.I. Israel, *Dutch Primacy in World Trade 1585–1740* is the standard work. G.M. Theal, the indefatigable but irretrievably Eurocentric historian, collates Portuguese and Dutch sources in *The Beginnings of South African History*.
2 For the Periplus see L. Casson, *Periplus Maris Erythraei*, the sailing guide prepared by a Greek merchant of about 50 AD. Pharaoh Necho (610–595 BC) despatched an expedition which probably doubled the Cape, in that they reported rowing until the sun rose over their right shoulders. Herodotus (4.4–2), understandably enough, did not believe this, but in fact it indicates the account's likely veracity (see Herm, *The Phoenicians*, Chapter 10).
3 Raven-Hart, op. cit., pp. 3, 5, 7.
4 For Chinese ship design and navigation see J. Needham, *Science and Civilisation in China*, Vol. 4.3, Sec. 29. The standard work on English ships is now N.A.M. Rodger, *The Safeguard of the Sea*.
5 Raven-Hart, op. cit., pp. 10–11. For the identification of the exact spots visited by the early travellers see QBSAL 1991, Vol. 45, nos. 1–3, articles by R.G. Shuttleworth and C.A. Hromnik. Dr Hromnik concludes that D'Almeira met his end not in the bay but in present-day Cape Town's old District Six.
6 Thorne, see Hakluyt Vol. 1, p. 212; Drake, see Hakluyt Vol. 8, p. 74.
7 Hakluyt Vol. 4, pp. 242–4.
8 Raven-Hart and C. de Jong in QBSAL Vol. 49 no. 4, 'The First Dutch Voyage'. The use of alcohol and tobacco as a method of control thus began a long and disgraceful history in South Africa.
9 Raven-Hart, *Before van Riebeeck*, p. 17.
10 Ibid., p. 23.
11 Ibid., p. 107.
12 Dutch guilders are usually taken to equal two English shillings, i.e. 10 guilders = £1. The guilder was used only as a unit of account in the VOC, no actual coins circulating overseas, where the currency was the rixdollar, equal to four shillings at the beginning of the period but thereafter declining to be stabilized in the 1820s at one shilling and sixpence.
13 For the formation of the VOC see Boxer, *The Dutch Seaborne Empire*, Chapter 2.
14 The stones sheltering the mail, with their inscriptions, can be seen in the Cape Town Museum. See also Raven-Hart, *passim*.
15 Particular revulsion was expressed at their eating the intestines of animals, with their half-digested contents – but Italians regard lightly-cooked milk-fed

calves' guts as a delicacy: gastronomic tastes vary greatly.

16 For Coree's story see Raven-Hart, op. cit., pp. 54, 72, 82–4. Coree apparently came to a sad end. In 1627 a Welsh traveller reported that the Capemen 'hated the Dutchmen since they hanged one of the blacks called Cary who was in England and upon refusal of fresh victuals they put him to death'. QBSAL. Vol. 1, 1946–7, p. 81, quoting Historical Manuscripts Commission, 'Report on mss. in the Welsh Language', Vol. 1 part 3, p. 1012.

17 The first major and still the most comprehensive study of Khoikhoi and San is Isaac Schapera's *The Khoisan Peoples*. The recorded history of the Khoikhoi is best dealt with in R. Elphick, *Kraal and Castle*, and summarized in his chapter in Elphick and Giliomee, *The Shaping of South African Society 1652–1820*. Much discussion continues as to the relationship between Khoikhoi pastoralists and San hunter-gatherers, of only peripheral relevance to later history.

18 The more remarkable in view of the inferiority of all other southern African artistic work compared with that of the western African communities. See Johnson and Rabinowitz, *Rock Paintings of the South-Western Cape*. It may be argued that this judgement shows a neglect of the more ephemeral arts, centred around personal adornment, in which the southern Africans certainly excelled.

19 For Dapper see Schapera, *Early Cape Hottentots*, p. 47. Theophilus Hahn's work, published over a century ago, still shows a vivid appreciation of Khoikhoi qualities. He had the advantage of having been born and bred among the Khoikhoi in what is now an almost vanished culture. One striking example of Khoikhoi sensibility is given in *Tsuni-//Goam*: Hahn, calling a girl beautiful – '*isa*' – was reproached by her uncle, who said any girl might be so termed, but his niece was '*anuya*' – 'full of purity' (p. 25).

20 Schapera, op. cit., p. 47.

21 F. Galton, *Narrative of an Explorer in Tropical South Africa*, p. 54; for Copeland see Raven-Hart, op. cit. and 'The Fifteen-Year Journey of David Tappen', in QBSAL.

22 Which is not to say that the Khoi-San were not exploited, wherever this was possible. The Dutch authorities attempted to establish norms of fair dealing, yet lacked either the power or the inclination systematically to enforce their will. Similarly the scattered European stock farmers usually found it better to cooperate with the more powerful of the natives; brandy, guns and horses were appealing incentives.

23 Raven-Hart op. cit., pp. 157–62

24 Ibid., pp. 61, 77, 84.

CHAPTER 2

1 For the reasons for beginning this history with the first records (which happen, even that of Herodotus, to be European) rather than attempting to evaluate the skimpy archaeological and anthropological evidence, see Introduction. For the authenticity of van Riebeeck's portrait see *Jaarboek van Het Centraal Bureau voor Genealogie*, Vol. 38, 1984. The likeness is probably that of one Bartolomeus Vermuyden.

2 Coolhas, *Generale Missiven van Gouverneurs-General en Raden aan Heren XVII der VOC*, Vol. 2, p. 28.

3 The 'Remonstrance' is in D. Moodie, *The Record: A Series of Official Papers*, Vol. 1, p. 1, which is the source of much of what follows, together with van Riebeeck's letters (ed. H.C.V. Leibbrandt, in his seventeen-volume *Précis of the Archives of the Cape of Good Hope*), and *Journal* (ed. H.B. Thom). In order to avoid a multiplicity of notes, it is hoped that quotations may normally be identifiable from the dates. D. Moodie

Notes

and G.M. Theal, whose *Chronicles of the Cape Commanders* are also used, need special mention. Both men were industrious collectors and translators, whose work has saved subsequent writers a great deal of trouble; but both have decided views which make their judgements thoroughly unreliable. Two Dutch historians, H.T. Colenbrander and E.C. Godée-Molsbergen, have produced classic works (but like Theal's and Moodie's, Godée-Molsbergen's judgement is highly questionable).

4 Coolhas, op. cit., Vol. 2, p. 575 for an analysis of the casualties. Leendert was helped in preparing the 'Remonstrance' by one Mathijs Proot, who was several months earlier than van Riebeeck in producing his recommendations for a permanent settlement.

5 P. Geyl, *The Netherlands in the Seventeenth Century*, p. 202.

6 Van Riebeeck's *Journal* is an official record, the work of a number of company servants rather than a personal diary, written in the third person, and very much for head office consumption. For the letters see H.C.V. Leibbrandt, *Précis of the Archives of the Cape of Good Hope*.

7 Boxer, *The Dutch Seaborne Empire 1600–1800*, Chapter 3, *passim*.

8 Ibid., pp. 152–3.

9 More probably Autshumato.

10 Hout Bay does in fact provide a good sheltered anchorage, but has a danger-ous approach, and lacks the abundant fresh water available in Table Bay.

11 And slavery was, indeed, not unknown in Scotland, where miners were held in servitude until late in the eighteenth century.

CHAPTER 3

1 There is a good account of the seventeenth- and eighteenth-century Dutch expeditions in Burman, *Who Really Discovered South Africa?*, from which much of the following is taken, but Godée-Molsbergen's *Reizen in Zuid Afrika in de Hollandse Tijd* is the standard work. Wagenaar continued to have a journal produced, as had van Riebeeck before him, which is printed together with his correspondence (ed. Dr A.J. Böeseken) in *Dagregister en Briewe, Zacharias Wagenaar 1662–66*. Robert Elphick and Hermann Giliomee's *The Shaping of South African Society 1652–1820*, a splendid collection of essays, contrives to be both stimulating and authoritative. The documents are found in G.M. Theal, *Belangrike historische Dokumenten* and *Chronicles of the Cape Commanders*.

2 Van Riebeeck, *Journal*, 12 November 1660.

3 De la Guerre came from Le Havre; the expedition also contained an Englishman, Tobias Smith (*Dagregister en Briewe, Zacharias Wagenaar 1662–66*, pp. 75, 98).

4 It is quite possible that Gonnema was made a scapegoat by his Khoikhoi rivals (Elphick in *The Shaping of South African Society*, p. 14) and *Kraal and Castle*, pp. 127–30.

5 Ten Rhyne, p. 97 in Schapera, *Early Cape Hottentots*.

6 Botma continued to prosper, dying at the age of eighty-two and leaving an estate worth over twenty thousand guilders.

7. M. Yap and D.L. Man, *Colour, Confusion and Concessions*, pp. 5–9.

8 Yussef was a remarkable man, perhaps the most distinguished of all early residents in South Africa, a determined guerilla leader and a venerated philosopher. See A. Tayob, 'Islamic Resurgence', DSAB, and Davids, *The Mosques of Bo-Kaap*, pp. 36–40. Davids is particularly interesting (Bradlow and Cairns and du Plessis being the other works) as being the work of a Muslim scholar. The tomb is on the dunes near Faure.

9 Elphick points out (*The Shaping of South African Society*, p. 15) that 1676 and 1677 marked the start of the

VOC's open control over the Khoikhoi communities, made more absolute after Simon van der Stel's arrival in 1679.

10 In 1707 one Hendrik Biebault of Stellenbosch exulted 'Ik been een Afrikaander' – ironically enough celebrating the downfall of Simon van der Stel's son Willem.

11 The VOC accountants were precise. The colony's expenditure was 1,005,207 guilders, 14 shillings and 10 stuivers, to say nothing of shipping expenses of 451,971.14.9 guilders – a far cry from the estimated fourteen thousand guilders of thirty years previously. Van Goens renewed head office pressure to persuade the Khoikhoi 'to adopt some kind of civilized habits', although he had 'slender hopes' of success. 'Much patient forbearance, discretion, and especially, affability' was needed.

12 For the French see C.G. Botha, *The French Refugees at the Cape*. Their most enduring economic contribution was the foundation of the South African wine industry. Vines had been previously cultivated 'reluctantly' (M.F. Katzen, in Wilson and Thompson, *The Oxford History of South Africa*, Vol. 1, p. 197), but the French brought new expertise and vigour.

13 For 'Franschoek' cigarettes.

14 And Dr Browne, returning from Madras in 1691, was entertained by the Governor to a supper of 'crabfish, strawberries, butter, cheese and tea', QBSA Vol. 5, p. 15; for Ovington see C.G. Botha, 'Voyage', in *Collecteana*, pp. 108–9. Ovington found the Hottentots 'the very reverse of humankind' (p. 102), and van der Stel 'a very kind and knowing person' (p. 109). Dampier is quoted in M.W. Spilhaus, *Early South Africans*, p. 57.

15 See Elphick, *Kraal and Castle*, p. 146. The Governor was censured by Amsterdam, still adhering to their conciliatory policy, and Dorha was released, but the future Cape administrations treated the Khoikhoi as subjects rather than subordinate allies.

16 Simon owned 891 morgen (one morgen approximating to one hectare, or 2.12 acres), Willem 613, and Frans 240, together with extensive grazing lands (see G. Schutte in *The Shaping of South African Society*, Chapter 5, an excellent essay). Adam Tas, with 184 morgen of excellent land, was not far behind.

17 See Adam Tas, *Diary*, pp. 175, 197.

18 See Boxer, *The Dutch Seaborne Empire 1600–1800*, Chapter 10; for the whole of this period, Boxer and Schama are unrivalled sources.

19 For the debate see Chavonnes and van Imhoff, *Reports on the Cape* pp. 87–104. The *Reports* formed the first publication, in 1918, of the Van Riebeeck Society, an admirable institution.

20 Boxer, *The Dutch Seaborne Empire 1600–1800*, p. 305, and Chapter 10 for the decline in Dutch power; also Schama, *Patriots*, p. 25, and J.I. Israel, op. cit.

21 For this and the eighteenth-century VOC generally, see G. Schutte, op. cit.

22 The subject of Cape slavery has inspired a considerable literature. The most recent works are E.A. Eldredge and F. Morton, *Slavery in South Africa* and R. C.-H. Shell's *Children of Bondage*. Eldredge and Morton are particularly good on nineteenth-century quasi-slavery, and have an excellent bibliography. N. Worden, *Slavery in Dutch South Africa*, and R. Ross, *Cape of Torments*, emphasize the violence inflicted on slaves, which should be balanced by the low standards of society in general. By the end of the eighteenth century John Bruce (Brenthurst Library Ms. 061/1) found that slaves were well treated, and that 'there is no farmer's family, nor peasant in England half so well dressed'; but he was probably writing of the handsome slave girls of Cape Town.

23 Mentzel, *Geographical Description*, Vol. 2, p. 125, so described the Buginese. He also marvelled that the

'Bush Chinese' remained 'obstinate and intractable even under a constant rain of blows', ibid., p. 129. See also E.S. de Klerk, *History of the Netherlands East Indies*, Vol. 1, and R. Shell, 'Tower of Babel', in Eldredge and Morton.

24 In 1697 one freeburgher who had beaten his slave to death was blinded and imprisoned for life on Robben Island (J.C. Armstrong in *The Shaping of South African Society*, p. 103). The West Indian atrocities are recorded in painful detail in the Select Committee of the House of Lords Inquiry into West Indian Slavery. (House of Lords Journal, Session 1831–32). For Jeptha and other luckier slaves see J.E. Mason, 'Fortunate Slaves and Artful Masters', in Eldredge and Morton, op. cit., Chapter 4.

25 JSAH Vol. 13 no. 1, S. Marks, 'Khoisan Resistance to the Dutch'.

26 Jan Dideriks was sentenced to twenty-five years' imprisonment for torturing and killing Khoikhoi in 1763 (N. Penn, 'Labour, Land and Livestock', in H.J. and R.E. Simons, *Class and Colour in South Africa*, p. 13, and ibid. section C for Khoikhoi on commando). Valentyn's comments are in *Geographical Description*, Vol. 2, p. 75 and Vol. 1, p. 207.

27 Lichtenstein, *Travels in Africa*, Vol. 2, pp. 281–2.

28 Most of the others were English, but company policy sometimes restricted the services available to them; see SAHJ Vol. 6, M. Boucher, 'The Cape and Foreign Shipping'.

29 Boxer, p. 313; Mentzel, *Life at the Cape in the Mid-Eighteenth Century* and *Geographical Description*; Ross, 'Rise of Afrikaner Capitalism', in *Beyond the Pale*, p. 185.

30 Chavonnes and van Imhoff, *Reports on the Cape*, pp. 136–7. Van Imhoff was an energetic reformer, despatched to clear up the troubles in the Indies, who took the opportunity to invigorate the Cape officials.

31 These figures are from P.J. van der Merwe, in his fine book *The Migrant Farmer in the History of the Cape Colony 1657–1842*, where he lists the geographical expansion: e.g. by 1727 there were settlements as far afield as the Breede River, nearly two hundred miles from Cape Town; within three years these had advanced nearly another hundred miles, to Groot-Brakrivier. The *Oude Wildskutte Boeke* recorded, from 1687, those licences given to hunters permitting them to travel away from the Cape; and the hunters were soon followed by the stockmen. Landdrost Starrenberg of Stellenbosch had unavailingly complained in 1705 that 'the whole country has been spoilt by the recent freedom of bartering and the atrocities committed by the vagabonds [who] have nearly all become Bushmen, hunters and brigands' (Valentyn, *Beschryvinge van Kaap der Goede Hoope*, p. 41). The 'vagabonds' were, of course, the adventurous '*veeboers*'. See also N. Penn, 'Labour, Land and Livestock', in H.J. and R.E. Simons, for Company attempts to retaliate against the vagabonds.

32 Swellengrebel, quoted van der Merwe, op. cit., p. 162. John Bruce (op. cit., n.22) describes the peasantry as 'indolent, ignorant, brutal and pusillanimous in a great degree'.

33 Sparrman *A Voyage to the Cape of Good Hope*, Vol. 1, p. 86. Sparrman made another visit in 1775.

34 Ibid., p. 208.

35 J.A. Templin, *Ideology on a Frontier*, p. 39.

36 Van der Merwe, op. cit., p. 62.

CHAPTER 4

1 The history of South African blacks has been written almost entirely by South African whites; one interesting part-exception is the Afro-Scot John Henderson Soga's work on the Xhosa. But Monica Wilson, born in Africa, a pupil at the famous multi-racial school Lovedale, has produced a compelling

body of work, culminating in her chapters in the *Oxford History of South Africa*. The earlier work of Isaac Schapera is more dated in its social attitudes and its anthropological techniques but is incomparably informative. Among the collections of black African views the James Stuart Archive had no equal, but is restricted to Natal.

2 Or many – up to twenty, according to Monica Wilson's informants (*Oxford History of South Africa*, Vol. 1, p. 116). Her third chapter is drawn upon here, but Winifred Hoernlé's chapters in Schapera, *The Bantu-Speaking Tribes of South Africa*, are worth reading.

3 W.T. Hammond-Tooke, in M.G. Whisson and M. West, *Religion and Social Change in Southern Africa*, p. 36.

4 For 'heaven-herds' and much else of interest, see Whisson and West, op. cit. Only comparatively recently has the part played by traditional African practices in maintaining the balance of society begun to be appreciated and analysed, together with the real utility of herbal therapy, and the nature of psychosomatic illness. Many good babies were thrown out with the bath water of witch-murder. See, *inter alia*, R. Porter, *The Greatest Benefit to Mankind*, Chapter 2, and H.V. Haggard, *Devils, Drugs and Doctors*, *passim*, for a critical excursion.

5 This should be understood only in a South African context. The history of other African peoples is very much a part of world history, but the combination of isolation and disruption is a peculiarity of the region south of the Limpopo. See, e.g. any map of Iron Age remains.

6 Wilson, op. cit., pp. 107, 254–5; but estimates vary considerably.

7 Often 'Tembu' and 'Pondo', especially in references to 'Pondoland'. The nineteenth century also saw Thembu rendered as 'Tambookie'.

8 E.J. Krige, in Schapera, op. cit.,

Chapter 5; but the interfamily compact was presumably blurred when a man had several wives. Lobola is still an important feature of African life. One survey reports that over 75 per cent of modern African 'élite' had combined a Christian marriage with the payment of lobola, and considered it an admirable practice (see Lynette Dreyer's informative *The Modern African Elites of South Africa*).

9 A report in the *Economist* of 9 December 1995 recorded 146 'witch killings' in a single district, and ghastly accounts of the dismemberment of living victims for 'medicine' are not infrequent. On a lighter note a talking goat, previously believed to be one Xolani, a man of poor character, was taken into protective custody by the police (*Daily Despatch*, 28 November 1996).

10 See M. Hall, *Farmers, Kings and Traders*, and Shillington, *History*, a readable overview.

11 Any collection of African art makes, consciously or unconsciously, this point.

12 See M. Wilson in *Oxford History of South Africa*, Vol. 1, Chapter 6, for the northern peoples.

13 President Mandela's people, the Thembu, have a considerable share of Khoikhoi genes, and their culture shows an unusual respect for Khoikhoi. A 'tiny man' features in their praise literature, and the son of a San woman was chosen as a chief (Shack and Skinner, *Strangers in African Societies*, p. 60) – and the Mholo slaughter animals in the Eastern tradition by cutting their throats (ibid., p. 54).

14 Moodie, op. cit., Vol. 1, p. 431. The *Stavenisse*'s crew were not the first sailors to meet Nguni: Portuguese mariners left accounts of wrecks in 1552, 1554, 1589, 1593, 1622, 1635 and 1647. But some of the Dutch survivors lived for three years on friendly terms with the local people and learnt their language (*Oxford History of South Africa*, Vol. 1, Chapter 3.1).

15 About 7 per cent, it is believed, of non-European genes. Since the transmission of cultures is much more important than mere genetic composition, it is interesting to note how many cherished Afrikaner traditions, from the management of oxen to the odd affection for sun-dried meat (biltong), have Khoikhoi roots; to say nothing of the development of Afrikaans from a slave and farmer patois. For references to the literature of miscegenation see Timothy Keegan's excellent book *Colonial South Africa and the Origins of the Racial Order*, p. 300, n.22. Shack and Skinner are also interesting, estimating the 'nuclear stock' in southern African communities as a 'fraction': 10 per cent in the Lobedo, and perhaps 50 per cent in the Xhosa.

16 The Bushmen must have been joined by dispossessed Khoikhoi, and were reported to have killed over a hundred Khoikhoi herdsmen and carried off over twenty-four thousand animals – an unlikely feat for hunter-gatherers.

17 H. Swellengrebel, *Briefwisseling 1778–1792*, p. 358.

18 Phalo is sometimes 'Palo', and might be even more accurate as 'P'halo'. Similarly, Rharhabe is often 'Rarabe'. Noel Mostert's monumental *Frontiers* concentrates on the eastern frontier, and the years of the conflict between whites and Xhosa, while J.B. Peires' *The House of Phalo* is a deeply-researched account of Xhosa history; but Soga's book should not be discounted.

19 There is no better account of the early days of the colonial expansion than van der Merwe's *The Migrant Farmer in the History of the Cape Colony 1657–1842*. 'Kaffirs' – unbelievers – was the uncomplimentary description given to black Africans by the Muslim traders, and adopted by European South Africans. Over the years it has become in South Africa as pejorative a term as 'nigger' in North America, and some historians go to exceptional (in my

view untenable) lengths to avoid it appearing in print. J.B. Peires, for example, in his otherwise admirable *The House of Phalo*, regularly replaces it by 'Xhosa' when quoting, otherwise verbatim, nineteenth-century texts. To do so is to blur the contemporary reality. For van Jaarsveld and what follows see Moodie, op. cit., Vol. 3, p. 74.

20 See van der Merwe, op. cit., p. 243.

21 Swellengrebel, *Briefwisseling*, p. 329. But van Plettenberg regretfully concluded that he had been forced to authorize van Jaarsveld's commando.

22 Moodie, op. cit., Vol. 3, pp. 92–3; van de Merwe, op. cit., p. 220. See also the very helpful extracts in Du Toit and Giliomee, *Afrikaner Political Thought*, many from the Cape Archives. Van Jaarsveld's appeal is in 3.1.

23 As well as Mostert and Peires, see Giliomee's essay, 'The Eastern Frontier', in Elphick and Giliomee, op. cit. For Maynier see J.S. Marais, *Maynier*. The following extracts are taken from du Toit and Giliomee, 4.3a–4.5. De Buys' justification is in ibid., 4.2a.

24 See SAHJ Vol. 4, H. Giliomee, 'Democracy on the Frontier', pp38–44. An extract from the 'Tesamenstemming' is in du Toit and Giliomee, 4.4a.

25 Boxer, op. cit., pp. 323–4 and Chapter 10, *passim*.

26 The Dutch Admiral John Stavorinus made well-informed criticisms in his *Voyages to the East Indies (1768–1778)*; see Boxer, op. cit., pp. 120–2.

27 See Schama, op. cit., for an unequalled description of the period. For the Patriots see also Giliomee, in Elphick and Giliomee Chapter 9, and G. Schutte, ibid., pp. 198–205. Also SAHJ Vol. 7, G. Schutte, 'J.H. Redelinghuys: een Revolutionair Kapenaar'.

28 Thunberg, *Travels at the Cape of Good Hope 1770–5*, p. 152.

29 Swellengrebel, op. cit., p. 321.

30 C. Beyers, *Die Kaapse Patriotte*, p. 29. Extracts from the Petition are

in du Toit and Giliomee 2.1a and
6.1b.
31 Du Toit and Giliomee, 2.1b.

CHAPTER 5

There is an extensive collection of Lord
Macartney's papers concerning South
Africa in the Witwatersrand University
Library, and more in the Brenthurst
Library; G.M. Theal, *Records of the Cape
Colony* (36 volumes); and Eybers, *Select
Constitutional Documents 1875–1910.*
While the first British administration,
from 1795 to 1803, was something of a
temporary patch-up, the second, from
1806 to 1815, took on the character of the
permanent Imperial government it later
became. There follow quantities of printed
evidence in the volumes of 'Blue Books' –
state papers – and the often more
entertaining Colonial Office
correspondence and minutes. For Lord
Caledon's period the Caledon Papers in
the Belfast Public Records Office are a
largely untapped source of great interest.
Herman Giliomee's *Die Kaap* deals with
the first occupation.

1 J.W. Fortescue, *History of the Army*,
Vol. 4, Part 1, pp. 392–3. The accounts
of military action rely upon this same
magisterial, although opinionated,
work.
2 H.C. Bredekamp and H.E.P.
Plüddemann (eds), *Diaries of the
Herrnhut Missionaries*, p. 128.
3 Fortescue, op. cit., p. 402.
4 Letter to Craig, 14 January 1797. Du
Toit and Giliomee, op. cit., 3.3
5 See W.M. Freund, 'The Cape, 1795–
1814' in Elphick and Giliomee, op. cit.,
Chapter 6, *passim.*
6 Theal, *Records of the Cape Colony*,
Vol. 2, p. 6. This was the general
practice in newly-acquired territories.
7 The British forces were helped with
'surprising readiness' by the Cape
burghers; on payment, of course.
Fortescue, op. cit., p. 508.
8 Lady Anne is well documented and
eminently readable; see *South Africa a*

Century Ago, from which the following
extracts are taken.
9 QBSAL Vol. 30, p. 38.
10 Roger Curtis, son of Admiral Sir
Roger, commander-in-chief at the
Cape, left an illustrated journal (R.
Curtis Journal, Brenthurst Library Ms.
053).
11 QBSAL Vol. 19, p. 21.
12 Marais, *Maynier*, pp. 88–9. The
Graaff-Reineters' grievances and
Bresler's comments are in du Toit and
Giliomee, 6.5 and 6.5b.
13 Barrow, *An Account of Travels into the
Interior of Southern Africa*, Vol. 1,
p. 203.
14 CO. 49/9, 27 July 1800.
15 So described by the missionary
Kircherer, *Narrative of his Mission to
the Hottentots*, p. 27.
16 See Marais, op. cit., p. 90, and
Giliomee, 'Democracy on the Frontier'.
17 Marais, op. cit., p. 110.
18 In his copious *Memorandum:
Containing Recommendations for the
Administration of Government at the
Cape of Good Hope*, p. 170. Subsequent
quotations are taken from the English
version of this, pp. 168–254.
19 Letter to Dundas, 24 July 1797, in the
Brenthurst Library. Earl Macartney
Letters, Brenthurst Library Ms. 063f.
Macartney, always the diplomat, later
wrote privately (ibid., 7 May 1798).
20 QBSAL, P. Farmer, 'C.G.K. van
Hagendorp'.
21 De Mist, *Memorandum*, p. 198.
22 '*Mistof*' = fertilizer: the German is even
clearer.
23 All left informative records of their
stays in South Africa: Alberti, *The
Kaffirs*; Paravicini di Capelli, *Reize in
de Binnen-Landen van Zuid Afrika*;
Lichtenstein, *Travels in Africa*; and van
Reenen, *Journal, 1803*. Together they
form a remarkable account of the
frontier districts at that time.
24 Lichtenstein, op. cit., Vol. 1, p. 393.
25 Van Reenen, op. cit., p. 93. The
meetings were arranged by the
colourful character Coenraad de Buys.
A huge man, almost seven feet tall, de

Buys had thrown in his lot with the Xhosa; he became the lover of Ngqika's mother, and after a chequered, adventurous career left a considerable progeny, the Buysvolk. See, *inter alia*, Lichtenstein, op. cit., p. 259. Van Reenen also left a 'Memorandum of Statement Given to the Kaffirs' (pp. 96–113), in which the Xhosa were told that the country was back in the hands of the *'oude Heeren'*.

26 Lichtenstein, op. cit., Vol. 1, pp. 463–4. He found Graaff-Reineters 'in perfect ignorance in short of all social virtues', and regretted the citizens' custom of nurturing all their grievances, committed to paper before witnesses, in the hope that some day they might obtain their revenge.

27 Fortescue, op. cit., Vol. 5, pp. 306–9.

28 Belfast Public Records Office (BPRO), Caledon Papers, D 2431/5/8, 28 June 1807.

29 For Bird see Caledon Papers, 17.5.1–30 and QBSAL Vol. 6, A.F. Hattersley, pp. 117–28. Almost alone among studies of the Caledon administration is Hermann Giliomee's essay in AYB Vol. 29 no.2.

30 Caledon Papers, 30 May 1807.

31 Ibid., 2431/4/2.

32 Collins 'Journal of a Tour', reproduced in the Blue Book *Native Inhabitants of the Cape of Good Hope*, and his reports to Caledon – even franker in many respects – in BPRO, D 2431/5/11–12. The extensive papers included in Blue Books, which were read by most of those influential in public life, were the most important factors in forming educated opinion for most of the nineteenth century.

33 The proclamation is in Eybers, op. cit., pp. 17–18. Being an Irish landowner, Lord Caledon was well aware of labour problems, sympathizing with the colonists to the extent of suggesting that the Khoi Cape Corps, the old Corps of Pandours, be disbanded to supplement the Khoikhoi rural labour force.

34 For South African missions in general see R.H.W. Shepherd, *Lovedale, South Africa*. Recent good accounts are those of Jane Sales and Elizabeth Elbourne (ICS Papers Vol. 18, 1990–91; and 'To Colonize the Mind', D. Phil, Oxford, 1992). T. Keegan, *Colonial South Africa and the Origins of the Racial Order*, has an excellent chapter (4) and a comprehensive bibliography.

35 Shepherd, *Lovedale, South Africa*, p. 5.

36 For van der Kemp's biography see L.H. Enklaar, *The Life and Work of Dr J. Th. van der Kemp*; and for his wife Sara, see QBSAL Vol. 49 no. 4, K. Schoeman, 'Dr van der Kemp's Wife'. Sara married again, to the young son of a Dutch officer.

37 Lichtenstein, op. cit., Vol. 1, p. 297. Van der Kemp, certainly not ignorant, was dismissed as 'a mere enthusiast'.

38 For van der Kemp, Read or Bethelsdorp see Collins, *Report*; J. Sales, *Mission Stations and Coloured Communities of the Eastern Cape 1800–1852*; Kircherer, op. cit.; C. Latrobe, *Journal of a Visit to South Africa 1815 and 1816* (see Chapter 6, n.11, below) – who found that 'nothing can be more miserable and desolate than the situation'.

39 Caledon Papers, 2431/12/3.

40 Quoted J.A. Templin, *Ideology on a Frontier*, p. 33.

41 CO. 48/13 119.

CHAPTER 6

1 And had already been so used, not to any advantage, for an assault on Spanish South America, a tactical and strategic failure (Fortescue, op. cit., Vol. 5).

2 L.C. Duly's *British Land Policy at the Cape 1795–1844* is authoritative, and forms the basis of what follows.

3 Mostert, op. cit., p. 389. This imposingly large book is a good account, with much fascinating detail of the eastern frontier conflicts.

4 Lord Charles has a biographer, sometimes over-generous, in A.K.

Millar, *Plantagenet in South Africa*.

5 Millar, op. cit., p. 38

6 Ibid., p. 37.

7 For the nineteenth-century Colonial Office see particularly D.M. Young, *The Colonial Office*; H.L. Hall, *The Colonial Office*; and the essential W.P. Morrell, *British Colonial Policy* (2 vols).

8 He was sentenced to death by court martial, but reprieved.

9 H.C.V. Leibbrandt, *The Rebellion of 1815*, for what follows.

10 The elder Stockenström, to Colonel Collins in 1809. He wrote that the Zwartbergers were '*de la plus basse classe. Le plus grand nombre sont des bâtards*' – which description, meaning that they were of mixed blood, rather spoils the later elevation of the Bezuidenhouts into Afrikaner heroes.

11 C.I. Latrobe, *Journal of a Visit to South Africa 1815 and 1816*, p. 295. Latrobe was an English Moravian sent to organize the Moravian missions after the peace of 1814 and to persuade Somerset into cooperating. His visit to Uitenhage did not prevent Latrobe from commenting that 'neither the first settlers nor their descendants had the least notion of providing for posterity' (p. 91).

12 To an eminent Afrikaner historian, F.A. van Jaarsveld (who was tarred and feathered for his liberal views!), neither Slagtersnek nor the Black Circuit (see below) remained 'perpetual grievances . . . there was no opposition in principle to the language laws' (*The Awakening of Afrikaner Nationalism*, p. 33). The first, and most violent, expression of the myth came from another Bezuidenhout, C.P., who wrote in 1883 of those who had executed the Slagtersnek 'martyrs': 'Happy shall be he who requites you . . . who takes your little ones and dashes them against the rock.'

13 See also Mostert, op. cit., pp. 448, 452.

14 Williams had been a carpenter, and had failed to qualify for ordination in England. See B. Holt, *Joseph Williams*. There is a good description of the

Cape Corps in Appleyard, *The War of the Axe*, p. 37: 'little men on small active horses . . . armed with a double-barreled carbine . . . excelled in irregular warfare'.

15 Brereton shot himself during his court martial for negligence during the 1837 Bristol riots.

16 Which is not meant to suggest that those who did not opt to join either Europeans or Xhosa were not often forced into poverty and squalor.

17 From, as it happened, Joseph Williams.

18 JICH Vol. 9, J.L. Sturgis, 'The Anglicisation of the Cape of Good Hope'.

19 House of Lords Hansard, 12 July 1819. The Commons was already (10 June 1819) restive about the cost of keeping thirty thousand troops abroad, the Cape garrison costing £229,000, and hoped that the projected settlement would reduce this expense. See also H.J.M. Johnston, *British Emigration Policy 1815–1830*.

20 Which is not to suggest that middle-class Dutch sentiment was uncritically pro-British. Dr Philips and the LMS aroused strong feelings against 'humbug' – '*en vooral . . . de paramount . . . de Philipish-humbug*'. This is 1837, but twenty-five years before Lieutenant de Waal had been thrown out of a party for singing 'Rule Britannia' (S. Trapido in ICS Paper SSA/93/11 and SSA/92/12) For Brand see H.C. Botha, 'Die Rol van Brand' in AYB, 1977.

21 J.C. Chase, *The Cape of Good Hope*, p. 81.

22 See G. Butler, *1820 Settlers*; I.E. Edwards, *The 1820 Settlers in Southern Africa*.

23 The analysis is given in Edwards, op. cit.

24 An unreliable Irishman, not to be confused with the admirable Attorney General of the Cape Colony, also Irish, who shared the same name.

25 Sir Rufane's classical quotations were much appreciated in Cape Town, according to W.W. Bird, the Customs

Notes

Comptroller (Bird, *The State of the Cape of Good Hope in 1822*, p. 151).

26 Moresby has left an interesting unpublished account of the coming of the 1820 settlers (Brenthurst Library, Sir Fairfax Moresby Memorandum, Ms. 305f), from which the following extracts are taken.

27 QBSAL Vol. 6, E.L. Griggs, 'Samuel Taylor Coleridge and Thomas Pringle'.

28 Bodleian Library Mss. Africa S.24.

29 See Pringle's own lively *Narrative of a Residence in South Africa*.

30 Ibid., p. 177.

31 Although Philipps was regarded as the leader of the 'so-called radical' group, he was radical only in his opposition to what was seen as officious interference – a very conservative trait.

32 Scott, journal, quoted W.M. Macmillan, *The Cape Coloured Question*, p. 116. Published seventy years ago, this remains a classic.

33 QBSAL Vol. 39, M.D. Nash.

34 For Bird's controversy see BPRO Caledon Mss. 17/5/1–30; and Duly, op. cit., for examples of corruption and incompetence.

35 See QBSAL Vol. 38, p. 154. The slave Joris was flogged to death, with salt and vinegar being rubbed into his wounds. The lions' meat is recorded in the Accounts of His Majesty's Receiver General for 1825. There were also regular payments of $75 to medical men for administering 'the vaccine virus' – the same payment made to the executioner. The accounts make interesting reading. Among the receipts are proceeds from the sale of commissions in the Cape Corps. In spite of a quarter-million-dollar loan from the HEIC agent there was a negative balance.

36 See JICH Vol. 9, J.L. Sturgis, 'The Anglicanisation of the Cape of Good Hope'.

37 In Hodgson's journal, 30 March 1824. A Hottentot had just been hanged, without arousing much curiosity.

38 See the informative essay by R. Shell,

'Tower of Babel', in Eldredge and Morton, op. cit.

39 QBSAL Vol. 41, F. Bradlow, 'The Revd. John Philip'.

40 The domestic troubles of Read and the irregularities of some of his colleagues are recorded in ICS Papers no. 44, Vol. 18, D. Stuart, 'Wicked Christians and Children of the Mist'. Even though the societies learned the wisdom of sending out married men, the proximity of beautiful naked girls was a constant temptation; but one usually resisted.

41 A huge literature on the Zulu, much of it heavily loaded in one of many directions, flourishes. The most balanced short description is probably still that of Leonard Thompson in Chapter 8 of the *Oxford History of South Africa*, Vol. 1, but this has been supplemented by thirty years of industrious research, of which the most important – apart from the publication of the James Stuart Archives, has been that of J.D. Omer-Cooper, C.A. Hamilton and J. Curry.

42 Historians became excited when an article by Julian Cobbing, 'The Mfecane as Alibi', was published in JSAS Vol. 29 no. 3, pp. 487–519. Much debate followed, culminating (for the moment) in a lively book, C.A. Hamilton's *The Mfecane Aftermath*. The initial article, more concerned with political correctness than credibility, has been in the process much discounted. N.J. van Warmelo, although a historian of a very different persuasion, was more accurate when he wrote (in Schapera, *The Bantu-Speaking Tribes of South Africa*, Chapter 3): 'an almost impenetrable veil was drawn over the past by the mfecane', and that 'research largely consists of the fitting together of fragments'. That was in 1937: the subsequent sixty years have seen more fragments fitted, but the conclusion is still just.

43 See C.A. Hamilton, 'Chaka', in JAH

Vol. 36 no. 1, and a number of similar epithets in the Stuart Archive.

44 For a good analysis see R. Forsyth, *Manipulating the Past*, and D.R. Edgecombe et al, *The Debate on Zulu Origins*.

45 See M. Tew, *People of the Lake Nyasa Region*, pp. 94 ff.; J. Wright and R. Manson, *The Hlubi Chiefdom in Natal*.

46 'Matabele' in the nineteenth century, but to assist the confusion, groups of Nguni had already established themselves north of the escarpment, where they were known as the 'Ndebele'.

CHAPTER 7

There is a vast collection of works on the Great Trek and the Boer republics. It is best to start with the original documents selected by du Toit and Herman Giliomee, with those of Bell and Morrell, Malherbe and Bird's *Annals*. There is an excellent analysis of the reasons for the trek in Chapter 6 of T. Keegan's *Colonial South Africa and the Origins of the Racial Order*.

1 With them died Alwyn Wolfard. The three were members of the Afrikaner Resistance Movement (AWB), who sent a 'commando' which fired indiscriminately into a crowd and were briskly, in turn, shot. Another Fourie, Jopie, was also shot after a court martial for treason in 1914, after which he became a 'martyr' (as Nick doubtless already is, in certain quarters).

2 Cole was a friend of, among others, Lord Palmerston, who became Foreign Secretary in 1830. The two families visited Paris together in 1818, meeting many distinguished personages, including the Tsar (Palmerston, *Letters to Laurence Sulivan*, pp. 141–6).

3 See an excellent essay by Robert Shell in Eldredge and Morton, *Slavery in South Africa*.

4 The sums are in W.M. Macmillan, '*The Cape Coloured Question*, p. 78.

For valuations see an interesting article in QBSAL Vol. 49. no. 3, M.F. van Breda, 'Accounting in Africa 1837'. Mr Mock appears in the Comptroller General's account for 1825. N. Worden's essay, 'Adjusting to Emancipation', in James and Simmons, has examples of slave prices between 1808 and 1826 of £60 to £150.

5 Du Toit and Giliomee, op. cit., 3.8, petition to Burgher Senate, 10 July 1826.

6 Ibid., 2.8b for the Cape Town petition; 3.10 for Christoffel Brand.

7 Bird, *Annals*, Vol. 1, p. 459. For an informative discussion of the reasons for the trek see du Toit and Giliomee, op. cit., pp. 78–89.

8 Du Toit and Giliomee, op. cit., 3.13d and 3.13e. Van der Walt had described the projected 'emigration to foreign countries' as 'to me as a dark valley'. For Zietsman and Pretorius see ibid., 3.15. Zietsman was something of a liberal, in that he eventually chose to remain under British colonial rule rather than joining the former Natalians in the republics: admittedly a very modified liberalism.

9 Surveyor W.B. Rowan's report, 15 May 1828, quoted Duly, op. cit., p. 76. The Colonial Office's drive for economy had spread the whole judicial administrative system very thin, and those colonists away from Cape Town had every reason to complain of neglect. See Keegan, op. cit., p. 186, Chapters 18–21.

10 CO. 49/23, 26 May 1831, for Lord Goderich. Mrs Smuts' explanation is in a letter to Thomas Lamont, American banker and diplomatist, in folder 131–3 of the Lamont Papers.

11 Again, Mostert, *Frontiers*, has a spirited account of the war. Stapleton in *Maqoma* (Chapter 3) makes good use of the sources, and is a useful addition to the sparse library of black biographies.

12 Stockenström left a long apologia for his public life in his *Autobiography*. Essentially in the English liberal-radical

traditions, with a strong authoritarian streak. Stockenström's real worth is best measured by the quality of his enemies, disreputable racists all. For the Kat River Settlement see. J. Sales, *Mission Stations and Coloured Communities of the Eastern Cape 1800–1852*, pp. 101–7, and T. Keegan, op. cit., pp. 117–21.

13 Cape Archives GH 34, 2 July 1836, quoted Galbraith, *Reluctant Empire*, p. 120.

14 The invasion was sparked off by the wounding in one of the frequent cross-border incidents of Macoma's brother (Stapleton, op. cit., pp. 84–6). It may also well be that the extent of the incursion was exaggerated by the frightened colonists.

15 Smith was his own best advocate in his *Autobiography*; to balance the picture see A.L. Harington, *Bungling Hero*.

16 G.J.F. Bunbury, *Goverment of the Caffres 1832*. For Hintsa's killing see Mostert, op. cit., pp. 724–6.

17 See his son Leslie Stephen's *Life* and P. Knaplund, *James Stephen*.

18 For 'cheesemongers' see. F. Welsh, *A History of Hong Kong*, p. 24 For an analysis of British trade see W. Scholte, *British Overseas Trade* and M. Edelstein, *Overseas Investment in the Age of High Imperialism*.

19 Despatch dated 26 December 1835, in Bell and Morrell, *Select Documents*, pp. 463–77. The 'Foolish and Wicked business' is in a private letter, the rest from the despatch itself. For a full account see J.S. Galbraith, *Reluctant Empire*, an admirable book.

20 Retief, something of an adventurer, was perhaps the most sympathetic of the *voortrekker* leaders: enthusiastic, less insistent than others on high standards. (One of his escapades was being charged – apparently correctly – with not paying a slave named Maria 249 rixdollars he owed her for the purchase of 171 sheep and goats, an episode which tells one something of Retief as well as of the economic circumstances of some slaves.) The

Manifesto is in du Toit and Giliomee, 5.5a. For Maria see J.E. Mason, 'Fortunate Slaves', in Eldredge and Mason, op. cit., pp. 81–2.

21 For an example of an increasing and prospering family see ICS Seminar Papers 1994, S. Newton-King, 'In Search of Notability'.

22 For the history of the Griqua see M. Legassick, 'The Northern Frontier', in Elphick and Giliomee, op. cit.; R. Ross, *Adam Kok's Griquas*; K. Schoeman, *Griqua Records*; E.A. Eldredge, 'Slave Raiding', in Eldredge and Morton, op. cit.; and J.S. Marais' classic *The Cape Coloured People*.

23 For Smith's reports and the reactions see P.R. Kirby, *Andrew Smith and Natal*.

24 Both Erasmus and Susanna kept diaries, which together give a remarkable picture of trekker society. Susanna's is particularly interesting as one of the very few accounts by a woman, and a woman of singular abilities, a thinker and something of a mystic. It is instructive if a little exaggerated to contrast Mevrouw Smit with Lady Anne Barnard (H.F. Schoon (ed.), *The Diary of Erasmus Smit* and K. Schoeman (ed.), *Die Wêreld van Susanna Smit 1799–1863*). Jan Bantje's coloured status is indicated by Erasmus in Schoeman, p. 93: a 'bruine jonkman'.

25 There is a good discussion of *trekboer* constitution-making in SAHJ Vol. 1, G.N. van der Bergh, 'Die 33 Artikels'.

26 A.R. Booth, *Lindley*, p. 69.

27 On 25 December 1844; du Toit and Giliomee, op. cit., 4.14c.

28 Napier has an autobiography (1884) edited by his son. The relevant Napier papers are in BL Add. Mss. 49167–8. Napier lost his right arm in action; graphologists would admire his strong, backward-sloping handwriting.

29 Another sizeable body of literature has developed around the events of 1838, attempting to analyse the motives of Dingane and the conduct of the *voortrekkers*. Whatever the truth, it is

clear that Dingane overreached himself, as Mzilikazi had done before, and as Dingane's nephew Cetshwayo was to do later, by inflicting so dramatic a defeat as to provoke a decisive reprisal.

30 J.A. Wahlberg, *Travel Journals*, p. 30.

31 Du Toit and Giliomee, op. cit., 5.5d.

32 See D.J. Kotze (ed.), *Letters of the American Missionaries 1835–1838*.

33 Ibid., p. 215.

34 CO. 48/172, 28 November 1837.

35 Wahlberg, op. cit., p. 45. There are more accounts by this reliable Swedish naturalist of atrocities. He comments of the 'God-fearing' Boers: 'I doubt whether there are more arrant hypocrites anywhere.'

36 CO. 48/91, 8 June 1838, and CO. 48/203, p. 16.

37 Quoted in C.W. de Kiewiet, *British Colonial Policy*, p. 19.

38 CO. 48/163, 18 April 1835, quoted in A.R. Booth, *The US Experience in South Africa 1784–1870*, p. 140.

39 Wahlberg recounts (op. cit., p. 36) that the commando returned with '36,000 head of cattle, and 3–4 children for every man on the commando, by way of plunder'. The fate of the children's parents may be taken for granted.

40 Stephen felt that, unfortunately, it was impracticable to abandon all the Cape: 'worthless except for ports . . . Nations can never recede willingly from any measure of apparent aggrandizement however absurd it may really be' (memo on a despatch from Napier to Lord J. Russell, 1 June 1841, CO. 48/212.

41 Du Toit and Giliomee, op. cit., 5.6c.

42 See Morrell, *British Colonial Policy in the Age of Peel and Russell*, Chapter 6; CO. 49/34, 10 April 1842, Bell and Morrell, op. cit., pp. 490–5. Stanley's decision on annexation in CO. 49/36, 13 December 1842.

43 National Library of Scotland, Minto Mss. 19432, T.F. Elliot, July 1848. In this private memo Elliot, one of the senior Colonial Office staff, discusses 'the unpopularity of the Colonial Office'. The task of 'watching, rebuking and tutoring' Colonial whites, and dealing with 'Speculators, Dreamers and Philanthropists' was bound, he felt, to incur much criticism.

44 For Smellekamp's peregrinations see Natal Volksraad 'Notule', vr. 21/46, 30/47, 51, 52/48.

45 Bird, *Annals*, Vol. 2, p. 259

CHAPTER 8

1 The standard work is Midgely, *The Orange River Sovereignty*, drawn upon here. See also K. Schoeman, *Griqua Records*, pp. 55–6 – essential for an understanding of events north of the Orange River, and Schoeman, *The British Presence in Transorangia, 1845–54*. For Swartkoppies see the latter, pp. 14–19, in a letter from A.H. Bain, who took part in the charge and saw Potgieter's men fleeing 'in scattered parties like herds of springbok, with the Griquas after them like bloodhounds'. Also Buck Adams, who was present at the fight. SAHJ Vol. 1, G.N. van der Bergh, 'Die 33 Artikels', for the trekker constitution. JAH Vol. 16 no. 4, R. Ross, 'The !Kora Wars on the Orange River 1830–80'.

2 The 'ruthless worthless savages' is John Mitford Bowker. It and Porter's reply are both from speeches in the Cape Legislative Council quoted in Mostert, op. cit., pp. 846–77.

3 Institute of Commonwealth Studies, *Structures of Southern African Societies*, no. 3, 1971–72, R.A. Moyer, 'Some Current Manifestations of Early Mfengu History'.

4 B. le Cordeur and C.C. Saunders, *The War of the Axe*, for a full description; Mostert, op. cit., Chapters 23 and 24. There is a short but interesting account of Sarili – usually known as 'Kreli', a more phonetic spelling, in the nineteenth century – and his times in Soga, *Ama-Xosa*. The war began

when a Xhosa, Tsili, stole an axe and was arrested. While being transferred to court the party was ambushed, the Khoikhoi manacled to him killed, and Tsili released. Sandile refused to produce Tsili and the killers. In Stapleton's biography of Macoma, op. cit., the killing is omitted (p. 133). Useful contemporary accounts include Thomas Stubbs' (who raised the Albany Rangers) *Reminiscences*.

5 Lord Grey, *The Colonial Policy of Lord John Russell's Administration*.

6 For Pottinger see G. Pottinger, *The War of the Axe*, and F. Welsh op. cit., Chapters 4 and 5. Pottinger was not, as often stated, a civilian, but an Indian Army officer – a Lieutenant General, no less – although his reputation had been made by his diplomatic work in India and China. For his conditions of employment see SAHJ Vol. 5, J. Benyon, 'The Cape High Commission'. One of the minor mysteries of the period is how Sir Henry achieved his reputation for lechery, an activity for which, at the Cape, he seems to have had little leisure; but see S. Hoe, *The Private Life of Old Hong Kong*. Pottinger's jaundiced views of Cape society were shared by his predecessor: Napier complained of the 'stupid ignorant society composed of all that is vulgar and worthless' (BL Add. Ms. 49168).

7 Le Cordeur and Saunders, op. cit., pp. 106, 108; Mostert, op. cit., Chapter 24; Keegan, op. cit., pp. 217–19. For the Kat River Settlement see Sales, op. cit., p. 145.

8 The Smiths are commemorated in the towns of Harrismith, Ladysmith and Aliwal North.

9 Quoted in le Cordeur and Saunders, op. cit., p. 267.

10 Mostert, op. cit., Chapter 24; Stapleton, op. cit., pp. 144–5.

11 Schoeman, *The British Presence in Transorangia*, p. 105. The interview with Adam Kok showed Sir Harry at his histrionic worst: 'His Excellency exclaimed in a passion, "Treaty is

nonsense. Damn the Treaty." And taking off his glasses, he dashed them on the table. "Southey" (the secretary) His Excellency cried, "tell him I am Governor General, I shall hang the black fellow on this beam . . ." ' For Afrikaner see Galton, *Narrative of an Explorer in Tropical South Africa*, p. 41, and Ross, 'The !Kora Wars'.

12 Schoeman, *The British Presence in Transorangia*, p. 23.

13 Ibid., Chapter 2.

14 The description of Cameron is Major Hogge's, from the Grey Papers – see n.21, below. See also K. Schoeman, *Die Brieweboek van James Cameron*, which has some telling examples of Cameron's permanent state of indignation and Hogge's polished irony. Moshoeshoe's excellent biography is L. Thompson, *Survival in Two Worlds*; see also JAH Vol. 8 no. 1, W.F. Lye, 'The Difaqane: The Mfecane in the Southern Sotho Area (1822–29)'.

15 From I. Staples, 'Narrative' (JPL S.Pam 968.607). Biddulph was one of the least attractive characters of the time, described by his clerk as appearing to 'carry cunning and malignity' in his countenance, together with 'sycophancy, lechery, and ignorance'. (Schoeman, *The British Presence in Transorangia*, p. 25). SAHJ Vol. 1, A.L. Harington, 'The *Graham's Town Journal*', is an informative analysis of the paper's early history; see also AYB, B. le Cordeur, 'Robert Godlonton'.

16 Fortunately, later Roman Catholic missionaries, especially in Natal, did much to repair the damage caused by such as Griffith, who revealed his unpleasant character in a diary (*Cape Diary*, ed. J.B. Brain). His comments are found on pp. 130 and 169. It is interesting to contrast Griffith's ideas with those of Porter and Caledon: all three were Irish.

17 Keegan, op. cit.; Mostert, op. cit., Chapter 26; JAH Vol. 14 no. 3, T. Kirk, 'The Kat River Settlement 1829–54'. The younger John Read gave his own

account in *The Kat River Settlement*. Botha was given a blatantly unfair trial by the disgraceful Chief Justice Wilde, sentenced to death, but reprieved. T.J. Lucas, *The Zulus and the British Frontiers*, has a good account of the war. He spoke highly of the 'Tottys', and said that 'the colonists . . . have never ceased to regret their disappearance' (p. 92). The new Cape Mounted Rifles was a white force. Colonel John Michel of the 91st, who fought alongside the CMR, later lamented that the original regiment had been disbanded, considering that 'one efficient Hottentot of the old stamp would be worth half-a-dozen white faces' (G. French, *Lord Chelmsford and the Zulu War*, p. 10).

18 SAL Ms. A 51. Bell was with the Cape Mounted Rifles, and later served as Resident Magistrate in Basutoland.

19 See J. Mackay, *The Last Kaffir War*, for the fate of Bandmaster Hartung and the colonial volunteers: 'Around the hats of each of these valiant irregulars was written, in flaming letters, the word "Extermination" . . . for they cared not whether it was man, woman or child that they shot down' (p. 219). Mackay was a regular sergeant, with a low opinion of colonial troops. Also Mostert, op. cit., p. 1117.

20 House of Commons Hansard, debate 24 April 1852.

21 The Durham University Library has the original correspondence between Lord Grey and his agents. In particular two long letters from Hogge, of 16 October 1851 and 26 March 1852, are both informative and characteristic of this prejudiced, but perceptive and ironic, officer. The latter was written less than three months before Hogge's death, from pneumonia at Bloemfontein.

22 For the Stellenbosch ladies, etc., see Blue Book Session 1850, Vol. 38. Lord Grey was very much to blame for the fracas, since he had assured the Cape citizens that he would seek their views before despatching the convicts; this he did not do, and although their views

were made vigorously clear, the convicts were still sent. See Elliot memorandum in SNL Ms. 19432, ff.99–103v.

23 See House of Commons debates 27 March 1849 and 15 April 1851. The latter is particularly interesting, exhibiting the wide range of British sentiments, ranging from the need for teaching 'irreclaimable savages' their place, to the radical John Roebuck's 'Is there anything which would justify our aggression [to the Xhosa]?'

24 Blue Book Session 1850, Vol. 38, p. 26

25 For education generally see E.C. Malherbe, *Education in South Africa*. For Herschel see Ferguson and Immelman, *Sir John Herschel and Education at the Cape 1834–40*, E.G. Pell, *Sir John Herschel's Contribution to Educational Development*. The Muslim scholars were those of the Indian Ackmar (Iman Achmed), in evidence given to the Bigge Commission in January 1825.

26 Stanley so wrote on 15 April 1842, recorded in Blue Book Session 1846, Vol. 29; see also J.L. McCracken, *The Cape Parliament*, pp.xxxvii–viii. McCracken remains the authoritative guide to the development of the Cape's parliamentary system. See also JAH Vol. 5 no. 1, S. Trapido, 'Origins of the Cape Franchise', and T. Keegan, *Colonial South Africa and the Origins of the Racial Order*, Chapter 7.

27 Quoted in Ross, *Beyond the Pale*, p. 197.

28 Duke of Newcastle, 14 March 1853, Blue Book Session 1852–3, no. 16, quoted in Morrell, Vol. 2, p. 48.

29 Solomon was an interesting oddity. Born in St Helena, a Jew, a dwarf, he became a leading figure in the colony, his wise and liberal advice being respectfully listened to and often followed. See biography by his grandson, W.E.G. Solomon. For Speaker Brand see AYB 1977, H.C. Botha, 'C.J. Brand'.

30 For Goncharov see QBSAL Vol. 14,

N.W. Wilson and D.H. Varley; for
Jacquelot de Moncets see JPL S. Pam
968 7037, 'La Flotte Française'.

31 For the convention see Bell and
Morrell, op. cit., pp. 526–8; Grey's
letter is in Blue Book Session 1852,
Vol. 33.

32 Clerk's negotiations are recorded in
Morrell, Vol. 2, pp. 51–61 and in
Keegan, op. cit., pp. 276–8. See also
Keegan's article, 'The Making of the
Orange Free State', in JICH Vol. 17
no. 1.

33 Quoted in Schoeman, *The British
Presence in Transorangia*, pp. 120–1.

34 For the Convention see Schoeman,
Griqua Records, pp. 153–6. The *Times*
article is reproduced in Schoeman, *The
British Presence in Transorangia*,
pp. 122–3.

35 Quoted in Morrell, Vol. 2, p. 47.

36 For Clerk and Peel see ibid., p. 57. For
the battle of Berea and Cathcart's
defeat see Schoeman, *The British
Presence in Transorangia*, pp. 92–9.

37 For Lindley see A.R. Booth, *The US
Experience in South Africa 1784–1870*,
E.W. Smith, *Life and Times of Daniel
Lindley*, and D.J. Kotze (ed.), *Letters
of the American Missionaries 1835–
1838*.

38 On 10 July 1848: Blue Book, Session
1850, Vol. 38. The standard work on
the early history of the colony is D.
Welsh, *The Roots of Segregation*; see
also A. Hattersley, *British Settlement in
Natal*.

39 Although, as will be seen, very few
blacks indeed were ever allowed to
become full citizens of Natal, and
those who did in the Cape Colony
were permanently under pressure from
their white compatriots.

40 JSAS 1995 no. 2, J. Lambert,
'Chieftainship in Early Colonial Natal'.
Lambert notes that after 1880 chiefly
power declined.

41 Although exceptions were made for the
application of customary law in civil
cases, when 'not prohibited by law nor
contrary to morality, public policy, or
equity'; see S.M. Seymour, *Bantu Law*

in South Africa, p. 3 and H.J. Simons,
African Women.

42 Simons, op. cit., p. 15.

43 For Buchanan see QBSAL Vol. 18.

44 On 8 July 1854, quoted in Morrell,
Vol. 2, p. 97.

CHAPTER 9

1 Grey has a relatively recent biography:
J. Rutherford, *Sir George Grey*. For a
much more critical – exaggeratedly so
in my opinion – evaluation see J.B.
Peires, *The Dead will Arise*, Chapter 2,
the best account of the cattle-killing
delusion. For the condescension see
NLS Minto Ms. 1423, on the
unpopularity of the Colonial Office.

2 Blue Book Session 1854–55, Vol. 37,
ff.54–5.

3 Lovedale: see R.H.W. Shepherd,
Lovedale, South Africa.

4 Lord John Russell to Grey, 5 June 1855.
Blue Book Session 1854–55, Vol. 37.
The critical debates were on 13 June
1851 and 24 April 1852 in the House of
Commons, and 5 February 1852 in the
Lords.

5 For Brownlee's part see his
Reminiscences of Kaffir Life and History,
and Peires, *The Dead will Arise*,
pp. 156–7.

6 See JSAS Vol. 10 no. 2, J.B. Peires, 'Sir
George Grey v. the Kaffir Relief
Committee', and Peires, *The Dead will
Arise*, pp. 247–67. Peires cites the
remarkable James Hart Junior, 'who
asked for as many Xhosa workers "as
can be procured without limit to
number" '.

7 See Schwaer and Pape, *Die Deutsche in
Kaffraria*. It is still very noticeable that
the old German settlements in the
region are – like those in Texas –
characterized by disciplined cleanliness.

8 The brutality of the filibustering
expeditions, manned by 'deserters,
discharged soldiers and scamps of all
descriptions', is described in Peires,
op. cit., Chapter 9.

9 Mapoch, or more accurately Nyabela

(see SADB), was certainly not peaceful, fighting off both Boers and Pedi until forced to surrender in 1883, after much suffering. For slave raiding and trading in the Transvaal see Eldredge and Morton, *Slavery in South Africa*, Chapters 7 and 8.

10 The assessment of Pretorius is that of the observant but not unprejudiced Marianne Churchill (D. Child, *A Merchant Family in Early Natal*, p. 116). Marianne found the Natalian 'Boors . . . ignorant and intolerant . . . very uncivilized in their manners and habits . . . without books or schools'. The *'Grondwet'* of the South African Republic is in Eybers, op. cit., pp. 363–404. For du Plooy, see J. Chapman, *Travels in the Interior of South Africa 1849–63*.

11 See J.W. de Gruchy, *Liberating Reformed Theology*; R. Ross, *Beyond the Pale*; A.R. Booth, op. cit., p. 77; JSAS Vol. 15 no. 2, R. Grove, 'Scottish Missionaries, Evangelical Discourse, and the Origins of Conservative Thinking'.

12 Merivale and Lytton's minutes of 5 and 6 October 1858, CO. 48/390, quoted Morrell, Vol. 2, p. 113.

13 The Volksraad motion was on 7 December 1858. See Morrell, Vol. 2, p. 117.

14 For the Free State see the illuminating *Memoirs* of Sophie Leviseur, and J. Mackenzie, *Ten Years North of the Orange River*, p. 64. Mackenzie also noticed the high standard of some Griqua houses, waggons and clothes and the quality of good schools. See G. Bauman and E. Bright, *The Lost Republic*, for examples of OFS virtues.

15 Memo to Acting Governor, General R.H. Wynard, 4 February 1860. Quoted Morrell, Vol. 2, p. 121.

16 Zonnenbloem's was the best cricket team on the Cape Peninsula; they also played tennis, croquet, soccer and rugby. ICS Papers no. 4, A. Odendaal, 'South Africa's Black Victorians'.

17 Gladstone memorandum, undated, in BL Add. Ms. 44738. P. Knaplund,

Gladstone and Britain's Imperial Policy, is authoritative on the subject.

18 In a private letter to T.F. Elliot at the Colonial Office, 8 November 1859 – an interesting example of the interdepartmental liaison at official levels. NLS Ms. 19421 ff.31–5.

19 See Morrell, Vol. 2, Chapter 5 for Wodehouse and Kaffraria, on which the following pages rely. The Currie excuse is on p. 140, n.3.

20 Morrell, Vol. 2, p. 143.

21 On 23 November 1868. Blue Book Session 1868–9 Vol. 43, f.92.

22 K. Schoeman, *Griqua Records*, pp. 156–7; see also R. Ross in Saunders and Derricout, *Beyond the Cape Frontier*.

23 J. Shepherd, *In the Shadow of the Drakensberg*, has a contemporary (1857) description of Griqua prosperity (p. 42). For the effectiveness of administration see. K. Schoeman, *Griqua Records*. Natalians were much annoyed to have lost the opportunity of expanding into the area, and never ceased to agitate for its inclusion in their territory. There is a sad, reasoned account by Kok himself of the betrayal of his people given as evidence to a Cape Commission in 1876 reproduced in Schoeman, op. cit., pp. 225–9.

24 The Le Fleur family, claimants to the Kok succession, produced another generation of Griqua leaders, who founded another community at Krantznoek, in Plettenberg Bay, which continues as the main custodian of Griqua tradtions.

CHAPTER 10

1 *Studies in the History of Cape Town*, Vol. 2, J. Hodgson, 'Xhosa Chiefs in Cape Town'; and see J. Hodgson, *Princess Emma*. J. Noble, *South Africa Past and Present*, says (p. 240) that for years afterwards Prince Alfred was a household name. Noble was Clerk to the Cape Assembly, and his account is an informed insider's guide to the period before 1877.

2 See unpublished article by K. Schoeman, 'Some Notes on Blacks' (QBS/OFSB). In the same newspaper that carried the Serfontein episode the shooting of a servant by Field-Cornet Swanepoel was reported.

3 Merriman left some lively accounts of the diggings: see *Selections from the Correspondence of J.X. Merriman* (ed. P. Lewsen), Vol. 1, Chapter 1.

4 For Parker see E.C. Malherbe, *What They Said 1795–1910*, p. 127.

5 The respectful biography is M.A. Macmillan, *Sir Henry Barkly: Mediator and Moderator*. Barkly's papers are in the Marylebone Public Library, ref. NRA 28107.

6 Lord Kimberley took the decision to annex the territory without telling the Prime Minister, '[begging] for confidence in his own discretion in dealing with the South African situation'. Knaplund, op. cit., p. 136. See also Morrell, Vol. 2, Chapter 4.

7 For Brand's very able negotiations see CO. 1631.

8 The official documents on the early days of Griqualand West are in CO. 1342, 6 August 1875 and CO. 1401, February 1876, 'Further Correspondence'.

9 JSAS Vol. 7 no. 2, R.V. Turrell, 'The 1875 Black Flag Revolt'.

10 Ibid.; W. Crossman, CO. 879/9, 1 May 1876, p. 29.

11 For 'swell niggers' see CO. 1342, 6 August 1875. For the Black Flag revolt see Turrell, op. cit., and SAHJ Vol. 7, Jill Smalberger, 'Alfred Aylward'.

12 Lord Carnarvon was chairman of the Committee; see CO. 885/5, 1868. It was found that the Cape's situation would be 'very precarious' in wartime.

13 For Barkly's career in Victoria see McCaughey et al, *Victoria's Colonial Governors*.

14 ICS Papers 1971–72, C. Bundy, 'The Responses of African Peasants'.

15 Merriman's correspondence, edited by Phyllis Lewsen, is an invaluable source, especially for the period between 1870 and 1910, while the same author's

biography of Merriman is essential reading.

16 But many black farmers managed to buy ploughs – more than eight thousand by 1882 – and some of these were provided by the government. The standard history of colonial Natal is D. Welsh, *The Roots of Segregation: Native Policy in Natal, 1845–1910*; for an authoritative analysis of the erosion of black rights and the decline of the Natalian peasantry see J. Lambert, *Betrayed Trust*. The substitution of the plough, 'the missionary's wife', for the hoe enabled a family to cultivate more land, and for the first time men themselves undertook the cultivation of the fields; see N.A. Etherington in B. Guest and J.M. Sellers, *Enterprise and Exploitation in a Victorian Colony*.

17 What Natal Prime Minister John Robinson called 'a life of almost idyllic freedom and repose' (*A Lifetime in South Africa*, pp. 321–2).

18 This was Thomas Phipson (R.N. Currey, *Letters of a Natal Sheriff*, p. 131). Other epithets were 'crafty and cunning, at once indolent and excitable . . . debased and sensual to the last degree'. Behind such caricatures lay not only white settlers' fury at not being able to secure free labour, but envy of black freedoms – and a good deal of suppressed sexuality. See R. Hyam, *Empire and Sexuality*, and D. Welsh, *The Roots of Segregation*.

19 JAH Vol. 16 no. 2, H. Slater, 'Land, Labour and Capital in Natal'; N.A. Etherington in Guest and Sellers, op. cit., p. 267.

20 See D. Williams, *Umfundisi* and *Journal and Selected Writings*.

21 From a sarcastic memo by Fairfield to Lord Carnarvon, CO. 179/114, f.55, 21 July 1884: 'Kafir law – guilty until proved innocent . . . a very popular principle with South African magistrates.'

22 For the organization of Indian passages see CO. 885/5/75, 'Handbook for Surgeons of the Coolie Emigration Service'; JAH Vol. 23 no. 4, P.

Richardson, 'The Natal Sugar Industry'; Vol. 21 no.2, N.A. Etherington, 'Labour Supply and the South African Confederation'; S.A.I. Tirmizi, *Indian Sources for South African History*.

23 The Revd G.W. Stegmann, a Lutheran who acted as Frere's secretary, found Green's views 'rank popery' (QBSAL No. 43, M.A.S. Grundlingh, 'The Diary of G.W. Stegmann'). Green, an opinionated cleric, had been first on the scene, having been rector of Pietermaritzburg before Colenso's arrival.

24 E.M. Stanley (ed. J. Vincent), *Diaries*, 17 November 1874, p. 183.

25 BL Add. Mss. 60792, Queen Victoria to Lord Carnarvon, 28 December 1874. Langalibalele spent a year on Robben Island, followed by twelve years' reasonably comfortable residence near Cape Town, before returning to Natal.

26 The period from 1877 to 1895 is well covered in D.M. Schreuder, *The Scramble for Southern Africa 1877–1985*. Thomas Pakenham's *The Scramble for Africa* puts South Africa in the wider context.

27 A. Ramm, *Political Correspondence*, Vol. 1, p. 273. Grant Duff, House of Commons Hansard, 20 January 1881. Fairfield in CO. 179/555, 21 September 1874.

28 The biography is J.H. Lehmann, *All Sir Garnet*. Wolseley's papers are perhaps the most entertaining of the period. See his *South African Diaries* (ed. A. Preston), and Hove Public Library Wolseley Collection. According to the irascible General, Carnarvon was 'extremely weak'; Lady Barkly 'gauche and sly'; General Cunynghame a mixture of 'funk and insanity'.

29 Lord Carnarvon accepted that it might be thought that he 'was devoured by a single idea and had gone mad over confederation'. BL Add. Mss. 60792, to R. Herbert, 4 January 1875.

30 Stanley, op. cit.

31 BL Add. Mss. 60798, R. Herbert to Lord Carnarvon, 4 March 1874.

32 Carnarvon's despatch is in CO. 1244, 4 May 1875. Merriman *Correspondence*, Vol. 1, p. 67.

33 The slave raiding, then and later indignantly denied by Afrikaners, has been detailed in Eldrege and Morton, *Slavery in South Africa*, Chapters 7 and 8. A contemporary account is in F.W. Chesson, *The Dutch Republics of South Africa*. Chesson, Secretary of the Aborigines Protection Society, was not unprejudiced, but his evidence is striking and has been overlooked. For the Pedi see JAH Vol. 10 no. 2, K.W. Smith, 'The Fall of the Bapedi'.

34 The *Transvaal Argus*. For statistics see F. Jeppe, *The Transvaal Almanac 1877*. By that time there was also one Dutch newspaper, the *Volkstem*. For a highly-coloured picture of the Transvaal government – 'as weak and imbecilic as it is notoriously cruel' – see Chesson, op. cit.

35 JPL, C. Read, 'Diary of the Seccocoeni War 1877'.

36 See K. Schoeman (ed.), *The Free State Mission*, pp. 22–3. The Bishop was Edward Twells.

37 Merriman *Correspondence*, Vol. 1, p. 25. Froude had adopted the Boer views about handling natives, and pressed for the reintroduction of 'apprenticeship', which, as Merriman pointed out, was only a modified form of slavery. Froude's views in BL Add. Mss. 60792, Herbert to Carnarvon, 23 December 1875.

38 BL Add. Mss. 60798, letter to Froude, 7 January 1876.

39 The Act is the South Africa Act 1877, in CO. 1980.

40 For 'heaven born' see Moneypenny and Buckle, *Life*, Vol. 6, p. 420. Lord Salisbury, then a member of Disraeli's cabinet, gave his account later, telling Arthur Balfour that the Transvaal was annexed 'not indeed against the wish of the Cabinet – but actually without its knowledge', R.H. Williams (ed.), *Salisbury–Balfour Correspondence*, pp. 41–3.

41 Rider Haggard observed: 'the

Hollanders abominate the Boers, and call them "les barbares". In fact everyone hates everyone in a manner wholly Christian.' Brenthurst Library Ms. 251, Sir Henry Rider Haggard Memo.

42 There is a good account in C. Read, op. cit.

43 CO. 1961, February 1878, Shepstone to Carnarvon, 24 July 1877.

44 SAHJ Vol. 4, R.L. Cope, 'Shepstone, the Zulus and the Annexation of the Transvaal'. Cope observes that war between the Transvaal and the Zulu appeared inevitable sooner or later, and the annexation meant that the war was between the British and the Zulu. For Transvaal under Shepstone see H.R. Haggard, *The Days of My Life*.

45 The biography is J. Martineau, *The Life and Correspondence of Sir Bartle Frere*. Molteno's letters and P. Lewsen's commentary are illuminating. Contemporary accounts include Sir John Kotze, *Biographical Memories and Reminiscences*. Kotze was appointed as a judge in the Transvaal by Shepstone in 1877 (at the age of twenty-eight), and was confirmed by the succeeding Boer government (see p. 307 below).

46 I was for some years director of a bank with many branches in both Africa and India. It was accepted that expatriate managers who would be effective in India would not be able to function properly in Africa, and vice versa; but Indian clerks were essential in Africa – the whole a paradigm of historical experience.

47 G. Plumtree, *Edward VII*, p. 78.

48 The war, which dragged on until 1878, can hardly be represented entirely as one of black fighters for freedom against colonial oppressors. Almost all the other black tribes joined with the colonial forces in fighting the unpopular Xhosa; Nelson Mandela's collateral ancestor, Paramount Chief Ngangelizwe rode at the side of young Walter Stanford (although the chief prudently removed his trousers before the fight, explaining, 'If we do have to

run it is lighter going without them.' Stanford, *Reminiscences*, Vol. 1, p. 80). The situation, as so often in South Africa, did not lend itself to a simple analysis.

49 So Carrington thought. In fact Sandile's body was respectably buried; the Colonel had been palmed off with someone else's head.

50 SAHJ Vol. 8, C.C. Saunders, 'The Transkeian Rebellion of 1880–81'.

51 Stanford, op. cit., Vol. 1, Chapters 17–20.

52 QBSAL Vol. 47, M.M. Goedhals, 'Peter Masiza'.

53 QBSAL Vol. 34, C.C. Saunders, 'Through an African's Eyes'. Entry for 21 January 1878.

54 From F. Meer, *Higher than Hope*, p. 17; see also JAH Vol. 12 no. 4, S. Marks and A. Atmore, 'Firearms in Southern Africa'. It is in fact arguable that it was not so much white military superiority which broke the back of Xhosa resistance as the other, more subtle, pressures.

55 JAH Vol. 36 no. 2, R.L. Cope, 'Written in Characters of Blood?'; Colenso (ed. W. Rees), *Letters from Natal*, p. 259.

56 Cape Blue Book C.4, 1883; A. Trollope, *South Africa*, p. 313.

57 Bulwer believed that Frere had come 'bent on an immediate war with the Zulus', and continued critical of Sir Bartle. See Cd. 2318, p. 24. T.J. Lucas, *The Zulus and the British Frontiers*, believed (pp. 198, 216) that allegations of Cetshwayo's atrocities were 'mostly gossip'.

58 The correspondence between London and Frere is in Cd. 2000 of April 1878. The letter to Ponsonby is in Queen Victoria's letters, Second Series, dated 23 December 1878.

59 Lord Salisbury believed that Frere's ultimatum should have been the cause of his immediate recall (*Salisbury–Balfour Correspondence*).

60 Writings on the Zulu war proliferate: e.g. S. Clarke, *The Invasion of Zululand 1879* and *Zululand at War 1897*; G. French, *Lord Chelmsford and the Zulu*

War; D.R. Morris, *The Washing of the Spears*; S. Taylor, *Shaka's Children*; J. Laband, *Fight us in the Open* and *Kingdom in Crisis*; JAH Vol. 36. no. 2, R.L. Cope, 'Written in Characters of Blood?'.

61 See Clarke, *The Invasion of Zululand*. The Duke of Cambridge, commander-in-chief, wrote directly to Frere that Lord Chelmsford's account of Isandhlwana 'left us in much perplexity as to what actually happened' (p. 112).

62 There is an interesting account of Cetshwayo after Isandhlwana, 'surrounded by loot', by a captured storekeeper who was impressed by the wonderful order and neatness of Ulundi: 'clean, tidy and well-arranged'. JPL S.Pam 968.303

63 The best account is probably still Monypenny and Buckle, Vol. 6, Chapter 11.

64 JICH Vol. 7 no. 3, C.C. Ballard, 'The Career of John Dunn in Zululand'. SAHJ Vol. 11, C.C. Ballard, 'A Reproach to Civilization: John Dunn and the Missionaries', deals with Dunn's expulsion of the missionaries; the same author's 'John Dunn' in JAH Vol. 23 no. 4 deals with Dunn's family life – forty-nine regularly-married wives – gun trading, and his support for Cetshwayo. As early as 1872 (CO. 179/114/326-) Shepstone had dealt with Dunn as an authorized representative of the Zulu King.

65 Hove Public Library, Wolseley Papers, Private Letter Books, letter to R.G.W. Herbert, 2 July 1877. Wolseley's original proposal, in this letter, was for '3, 4 or 5 independent districts, each with a chief with strong powers and a diplomatic agent'. Such a scheme, if implemented, would have been a great deal more successful.

66 There is a good account by J. Laband and P. Thompson in Duminy and Guest, *Natal and Zululand*.

67 For Cetshwayo's visit to London see J. Guy, *The Destruction of the Zulu Kingdom*, and a summary in S.

Taylor, *Shaka's Children*, Chapter 14.

68 See Laband and Thompson, op. cit., p. 212, and J. Guy, *The Destruction of the Zulu Kingdom*.

69 Brenthurst Library Ms. 251, Sir Henry Rider Haggard Memo.

70 There is a good account of the visit and the annexation's aftermath in Le May, *British Supremacy in South Africa 1899–1907*, Chapter 4. See also W.J. Leyds, *The First Annexation of the Transvaal*.

71 Cmd 1961, February 1878, Jorissen and Kruger to Carnarvon, 28 August 1877.

72 Ibid., Carnarvon to Shepstone, 16 September 1877; and Hove Public Library, Wolseley Papers, letter to Lanyon, 11 November 1879: 'I would strongly recommend your promising Paul Kruger a Government situation of say £6–700 a year' – and Pretorius a seat on the Executive Council, since he was 'so hard up'. A little money might 'square him', but 'in gold, not by any means a cheque'.

73 For the relations between the two men see D.M. Schreuder, *Gladstone and Kruger*. In fact the redoubtable contemporaries never left any record of a meeting.

74 For Chamberlain see P.T. Marsh, *Joseph Chamberlain*, p. 158. For Renan etc. see A.M. Davey, *The British Pro-Boers 1877–1902*.

75 Le May, op. cit., p. 81.

76 With a great deal of Gladstonian wriggling – see House of Commons Hansard, 21 January 1881.

77 Queen Victoria's letters, entries for 19 February and 22 March 1881.

78 In the first draft Gladstone requires Boer 'acceptance of the (Sovereignty) Suzerainty' of Britain. BL Add. Mss. 44226, p. 55, to Lord Kimberley, 17 March 1881.

CHAPTER 11

1 Sir E.W. Hamilton, diary entries for 24 September 1884, 1 September 1883 and 30 September 1884

Notes

2 Hove Public Library, Wolseley Papers, 6 March 1880.

3 Pelissier Ms. in Killie Campbell Library.

4 E.W. Hamilton, diary entry for 26 September 1880.

5 CO. 179/153/68, Herbert's minute of 16 August 1884 on Cabinet telegram to Bulwer of 23 July. See also E.W. Hamilton, diary entry for 30 September 1884.

6 BL Add. Ms. no 44547, Gladstone to Lord Derby, 11 June 1884.

7 BL Add. Ms. 44142, Lord Derby to Gladstone, 26 September 1884.

8 Kruger's address to Volksraad, 29 July 1884, in CO. 48/417/414. Herbert and Derby minutes in CO. 48/417/420.

9 The Hamilton Papers are in BL Add. Mss. 48636 and a selection published by D.W.R. Bahlman. The War Office view is in WO. 33/42 No. 971 of 1 October 1884, reproduced in Schreuder, op. cit., Appendix 3. After Majuba the War Office recommended that Colonial Volunteers be used to fight the freebooters.

10 The standard work on Gladstone is likely to remain that of H.C.G. Matthew. T. Pakenham's *The Scramble for Africa*, Chapter 12, covers the incident, but mistakes Merriman's position (p. 210).

11 G.A. Craig, *Germany*, Chapter 4.3.

12 The evidence produced by B. Morton in Eldredge and Morton, op. cit., Chapter 9, from which this is taken, proves – if proof be needed – that at least one black community was as capable of atrocious conduct towards its slaves as any white society.

13 Quoted Galbraith, *Crown and Charter*, p. 136.

14 CO. 48.417/358, 16 July 1884. Mackenzie's *Papers* (ed. A.J. Dachs) are an essential source. See also Mackenzie's *Autobiography* and W.D. Mackenzie, *John Mackenzie*.

15 BL Add. Ms. 44547, Gladstone to Derby, 17 November 1884. He asks Derby to 'keep a steadfast eye' on Warren.

16 I am indebted to the staff of the Bloemfontein Afrikaner Museum and Library for help with information on the development of the language.

17 For the Bond see T.R.H. Davenport, *The Afrikaner Bond*. The biography is by Hofmeyr's young kinsman, also Jan, with F.W. Reitz, *The Life of Jan Hendrik Hofmeyr*.

18 There is an excellent summary of contemporary reactions to Rhodes in T.R.H. Davenport, *A Modern History of South Africa*, p. 95. For a biography see B. Roberts, *Cecil Rhodes*; R.L. Rotberg, *The Founder*. See also JICH Vol. 10 no. 1, C. Newbury, 'The Capital Accumulation of Cecil Rhodes'; JSAS Vol. 1 no. 1, I.R. Phimister, 'Rhodes, Rhodesia and the Rand'.

19 See JAH Vol. 9, S. Trapido, 'African Divisional Politics in the Cape Colony 1884–1910'. A. Odendaal, 'Vukani Bantu', is essential reading for the early days of black politics. T.G. Karis and G.M. Carter (eds), *From Protest to Challenge*, is a massive four-volume repository of documents with a good text. See also A. Drew, *South Africa's Radical Tradition 1909–1950*.

20 N.A. Etherington, 'Christianity and African Society', in Duminy and Guest, op. cit.; B. Rose and R. Tunmer, *Documents in South African Education*; JAH Vol. 27 no. 1, M. Adhikavi 'Coloured Identity', pp. 109–10; JAH Vol. 27 no. 3, L. Chisholm, 'The Pedagogy of Porter'.

21 J. Bryce, *Impressions of South Africa*, pp. 351–3. Cape attitudes are discussed in JAH Vol. 9 no.1, S. Trapido, 'African Divisions: Politics in the Cape Colony 1884–1910'.

22 CO. 179/114/561, 3 October 1874.

23 See JAH Vol. 36 no. 3, S. Bickford-Smith, 'Black Ethnicities: The Emergence of the "Coloureds" in Late Nineteenth-Century Cape Town'. It should be noted that the Americans were more successful in suppressing black rights. Louisiana had 130,000 black voters in 1897; by 1904 it had succeeded in reducing these to 1,342 – lynching was a powerful disincentive:

see *African Affairs* Vol. 91 no. 364, H.
Giliomee, 'Broedertwis'. The
Registration Act was known by those
affected as 'The Sewing up of the
Mouth' (L. Switzer, *Power and
Resistance in an African Society*).
Jabavu's powerful editorial 'Muzzling
the Natives' appeared on 23 March
1887.

24 Thomas Upington, then Attorney
General, was sharply reprimanded for
his partial handling of the trial, which
was also fiercely attacked by the
admirable Saul Solomon.

25 Trollope, op. cit., pp. 61, 336.

26 For black farming in Natal see C.
Bundy, *The Rise and Fall of the South
African Peasantry*, Chapter 6; D.
Welsh, *The Roots of Segregation*; S.
Marks, *Reluctant Rebellion*, Chapter 3.

27 By 1877 all the fishing and nearly all
the market gardening were in Indian
hands. Dada Abdullah and Co. of
Durban ran a steamship line to
Bombay and Europe. See Guest and
Sellers, *Enterprise and Exploitation in a
Victorian Colony*.

28 The Cape remained, even after the
development of the diamond fields,
primarily an agricultural economy,
with wool the staple. Merriman made
an interesting report to the Royal
Colonial Institute (Proceedings, Vol. 6,
1884–5) on the 'Commercial Resources
and Finances of South Africa', which
he described, regretfully, as 'the ugly
duckling of the British brood'.

CHAPTER 12

1 *Journal of the Society of Arts*, Vol. 29,
1881, H.B. Frere. 'The Industrial
Resources of South Africa'.

2 A. Mabin in James and Simmons,
op. cit., p. 85. The authoritative book
is still R.V. Kubicek, *Economic
Imperialism in Theory and Practice*.

3 For the census see J.S. Marais, *The Fall
of Kruger's Republic*, still the standard
work and relied upon for much of
what follows. For the Jewish influx see,

G. Shimoni, *Jews and Zionism: The
South African Experience*, Chapter 1.

4 Apart from Marais, G.H.L. Le May
should be consulted.

5 J.S. Marais, op. cit., p. 13; Kruger's
Memoirs; J. Meintjes, *President Paul
Kruger*.

6 See C.T. Gordon, *The Growth of Boer
Opposition to Kruger*, for Joubert and
the Progressives.

7 Leyds left a detailed record of his
activities in nine volumes of
correspondence, and two volumes on
the Transvaal annexation.

8 In the 1900 British occupation of
Pretoria the Transvaal Secret Archives
were captured, and extracts
reproduced in CO. 537/59, from which
the Deutsche Bank's views were taken.
For their agent, Adolf Goetz, see JAH
Vol. 19 no. 3, J.J. van-Helten, 'German
Capital in the Transvaal'.

9 Nellmapius had also benefited to the
extent of £30,000 from an unsecured
bank loan; see A. Webb, *The Roots of
the Tree*, p. 154.

10 A.P. Cartwright, *The Dynamite Co.*

11 A. Webb, op. cit., Chapter 8, 'Kruger's
Dream', for a history of the National
Bank's establishment.

12 ICS Papers 104, R. Cornwell, 'Land and
Politics in the Transvaal'.

13 Frere, op. cit.

14 Not only the *uitlanders* but Free State
citizens were so badly treated that
President Steyn had to write seriously
that if this was not improved, it would
be 'all at an end with our dream of
closer union' (on 21 December 1897).
Steyn was also much concerned with
the Transvaal's summary treatment of
Chief Justice Kotzé.

15 S. Marks and S. Trapido, 'Lord Milner
and the South African State', in P.
Bonner, *Working Papers in South
African Studies*, Vol. 2.

16 House of Lords Hansard, 14 February
1895.

17 For his financial manoeuvrings see
JICH Vol. 10 no. 3, R.V. Turrell,
'Rhodes, De Beers, and Monopoly'.

18 J. Rose Innes (ed. H.M. Wright),

Notes

Selected Correspondence 1884–1902, p. 130.

19 The best account of the Matabeleland–Rhodesia adventure is J.S. Galbraith, *Crown and Charter*.

20 CO. 48/417/028, minutes of 5 February 1889; and see Galbraith, *Crown and Charter*, pp. 114–16. 'Dummies and figureheads' is from the diary of Charles Carrington, who went on to foresee 'a great disaster or swindle in which the Royal Family are implicated in South Africa'. Quoted in G. Plumtree, *Edward VII*, p. 132.

21 See C.A. Thomson, 'The Administration of Sir Henry Loch, 1889–1895' (degree dissertation, Duke University, 1973). The Loch papers are in the Scottish Record Office GD 268. See also McCaughey, op. cit.

22 See JICH Vol. 8 no. 3, R. Ovendale, 'Natal, the Transvaal and the Boer War'.

23 For Loch's despatches see Cmd 8159 of 1896.

24 'Rhodes wants nothing,' which H.C.G. Matthew describes as 'one of the most erroneous observations in the history of imperialism', op. cit., p. 347.

25 The story of this disreputable enterprise is in Galbraith, *Crown and Charter*, Chapter 5.

26 The story is told in ibid., Chapter 9. Gifford's bloodthirsty comment on 17 January 1896 quoted in R. Ovendale, op. cit. Jameson's men were helped by the Shona chiefs: see SAHJ Vol. 3, D.N. Beach, 'The Adendorff Trek in Shona History'.

27 For this and the following paragraphs see P.T. Marsh, *Joseph Chamberlain*, pp. 373ff.

28 Ibid., pp. 373–80.

29 Ibid., p. 380.

30 SAHJ Vol. 10, A. Jeeves, 'Aftermath of Rebellion: The Randlords and Kruger's Republic'.

31 Merriman *Correspondence*, Vol. 2, pp. 311–12; *Cape Times* report of Transvaal National Union; Cmd 8159.

32 In addition to the most recent biographies of Rhodes see also J. van der Poel, *The Jameson Raid* (p. 155 for 'just beginning'). Dr Jameson's piles I owe to Mrs Hayward.

33 Molteno (ed. V. Solomon), *Selections from Correspondence 1892–1914*, 4 January 1896: 'What a monstrous and violent act of Jameson's . . . this atrocious attack.' Percy Molteno, Sir John's son, lived in England, and as a Liberal MP between 1906 and 1918 supported Merriman and his fellow South African liberals.

34 Published, to its discredit, in *The Times*, 4 January 1896.

35 Evidence given to a Parliamentary Inquiry, 30 April 1897, quoted Marsh, op. cit., p. 401.

36 Transvaal Secret Archives, CO. 537/59.

37 Unpublished letter, Bower to Merriman, SAL Merriman papers, 28 March 1906; see also Rhodes House Mss. Afr.S. 1737.

38 Olive Schreiner's story of the 1896 war in Rhodesia, 'Trooper Peter Halket' can take its place with Zola's forceful indictments of oppression and injustice.

39 The biography is J.E. Wrench, *Alfred, Lord Milner*. For the documents see C. Headlam, *The Milner Papers: South Africa 1897–8*.

40 The best analyses of the cause of the war are those of I.R. Smith and A. Porter. As with many other South African issues, the question is surrounded by controversy. For Mrs Smuts see Lamont Papers 131.5, letter to T. Lamont, 28 August 1936. Mrs Smuts was objecting to Olive Schreiner's depiction of Tant Sannie in *The Story of an African Farm*.

41 Quoted in J. Wilson, *CB: A Life of Sir Henry Campbell-Bannerman*, p. 300. Milner went on: 'Deep down in the heart of every Dutchman in South Africa is the ideal of a white land-owning aristocracy resting on slave labour.'

42 Chamberlain: meeting with Campbell-Bannerman quoted in J. Wilson, op. cit., p. 301. Grosvenor: G. Ridley, *Bend'Or*, pp. 36–7.

43 The subject is expertly treated in R.
Ally, *Gold and Empire*. See also, *inter
alia*, JAH Vol. 20 no.3, J.J. van-Helten,
'Empire and High Finance'.

44 D. Kynaston, *The City of London*,
Vol. 2, Chapter 11.

45 For June 1897 see Hancock and van
der Poel, *Selections from the Smuts
Papers*, Vol. 1, p. 43. See letter of 30
May 1899 to Leyds: whatever was done
to appease England, that country
'would still seek and find a cause for
hostilities', quoted in W.K. Hancock,
Smuts.

46 Including an attempt to initiate US
mediation on 3 October 1899 (R.B.
Malamay, *The Boer War in American
Politics and Diplomacy*).

47 E. McCourt, *Remember Butler*, p. 225.
See also W.F. Butler, *Sir William
Butler*. Butler later said that he was
'certain he was sent out on purpose to
pick a quarrel with Kruger', which he
refused to do (W.S. Blunt, *My Diaries*,
p. 334). The war eventually needed a
quarter of a million British soldiers to
bring it to a conclusion.

48 See Frazer and Jeeves, *All that
Glittered*, letter of 4 February 1899.

49 From N. J. van der Merwe, *Steyn*,
pp. 186–7, quoted W.A. De Klerk, *The
Puritans in Africa*, p. 21. The detailed
British account of the negotiations is
in Cmd 9345.

50 G. Ridley, op. cit., p. 35.

51 R. Taylor, *Lord Salisbury*, p. 178.

52 E.A. Walker, *The Life of W.P.
Schreiner*, p. 552. Fischer was an
English-speaker, married to a
Scotswoman.

53 Thomas Pakenham's masterly account,
The Boer War, will remain for long the
standard work.

54 J. Fisher, *That Miss Hobhouse*; R.
Roberts, *Those Bloody Women*. Not
only English: other active women
included Louise Maxwell, the
American wife of Sir John Maxwell,
Military Governor of Pretoria, and
Johanna van Warmelo. For Ward see
Cmd 1792, Vol. 4, p. 259. This was
after the war, when the worst was

known. For a more positive defence of
the camps see RCS Mss. 5v. The
illuminated testimonial hangs in the
Johannesburg Rand Club.

55 A.M. Davey (ed.), *Breaker Morant and
the Bushveldt Carbineers*.

56 W.R. Nasson, 'Abraham Esau's War';
also JICH Vol. 11 no. 1, W.R. Nasson,
'Doing Down their Masters'.

57 A. Odendaal, op. cit., Chapter 2: W.R.
Nasson, op. cit., pp. 340–8.

58 T. Pakenham, *The Boer War*, p. 573.

59 Stanford, op. cit., Vol. 2, Chapter 46 –
which also has an account of
commandos killing unarmed blacks.

60 W.R. Nasson, op. cit., Chapter 8.

CHAPTER 13

1 An effort by some Pretoria burghers to
bring about a negotiated peace ended
with their President being shot by
Commandant Viljoen when on his
peace mission (and it is said another
emissary was flogged and shot by
Commandant Froneman: see R.
Kruger, *Goodbye, Dolly Grey*, p. 390).

2 Chartwell Trust CHAR 1/30.

3 There is an interesting account of
Kitchener's move and subsequent
career in India in P. King, *The
Viceroy's Fall*.

4 The original typescript, with Smuts'
manuscript alteration, in the
Brenthurst Library.

5 See R. Hyam, *Britain's Imperial
Century 1815–1914*.

6 *Journal and Letters of Reginald,
Viscount Esher* (ed. M.V. Brett)
pp. 270, 418. Spared, too, would have
been some very bad verse – as the
decaying valetudinarian Algernon
Swinburne exhorting the soldiery:
'To scourge these dogs
Agape with jaws of foam,
Down out of life. Strike,
England, and strike home.'

7 In *Johannesburg Pioneer Journals*,
p. 180.

8 For the Transvaal and Orange Free
State African cultivation see C. Bundy,

op. cit., Chapter 7, and W. Beinart et al, *Putting a Plough to the Ground* (S. Trapido on Veereniging Estates). A contemporary report is G.B. Beak, *Aftermath of War.*

9 For the language controversy see E.C. Malherbe, *Education in South Africa.* On Sargant's list of inspectors and other officials there was 'not a single Dutch name' (Vol. 1, p. 315).

10 *Johannesburg Pioneer Journals,* p. 185.

11 Quoted in Hobart and Dagut, *Source Material in the South African Economy,* Vol. 2, p. 52; and Transvaal Indigency Committee Minutes, TG11 1908.

12 See M. Yap and D.L. Man, *Colour, Confusion and Concessions,* Chapter 5 for a good account of Chinese miners.

13 For Kas Maine see C. van Onselen, *The Seed is Mine,* and JSAS Vol. 5 no. 1, S. Trapido, 'Landlord and Tenant in a Colonial Economy'.

14 Transvaal Indigency Committee Minutes, TG11 1908.

15 See Merriman's comments, *Correspondence,* Vol. 3, Chapter 4.

16 Milner's views are in a letter to H. Asquith, 18 November 1897, Headlam, op. cit., Vol. 1, pp. 177–88, and Merriman, *Correspondence,* Vol. 3, p. 397: 'You have only to sacrifice the "nigger" absolutely and the game is easy. Any attempt to secure fair play for them makes the Dutch fractious and almost unmanageable.' 'Fair play' was far from true equality, which Milner totally rejected. In his view Natal, with its three black electors, had the best native policy.

17 See O.C. Mathurin, *Henry Sylvester Williams,* and M.L. Snail, *The Antecedens* (sic). In his evidence Martin Lutuli agreed that 'native' interests should be represented in Parliament by whites, not blacks.

18 For the Russian correspondence see QBSAL Vol. 49 no. 2, A. Davidson and I. Filatova, 'Africans and Russians in the Nineteenth Century'. For the history of the annexation see Stanford, *Reminiscences,* Vol. 2, Chapters 25–40.

For Pondoland see W. Beinart, *The Political Economy of Pondoland 1860–1930.*

19 D.M. Schreuder, *The Scramble for Southern Africa 1877–1985*: for *Thrush* see A. Preston and J. Major, *Send a Gunboat.*

20 Jeff Guy, *The Destruction of the Zulu Kingdom,* and Shula Marks, *Reluctant Rebellion,* are the best guides to the decline of the Zulu state. For the later period see N. Cope, *Rope of Grass* and *To Bind the Nation.*

21 The James Stuart Archive, five volumes of which have been published, is a rich source of contemporary views and experience.

22 Sir Mancherjee's letter is in the Brenthurst Library, Sir Mancherjee Bhownaggree Papers, Ms. 145. For the Mahatma's racism see also P. French, *Liberty or Death,* pp. 23–9 and A. Odendaal, op. cit., pp. 212–14. Gandhi also objected to Indians being 'muddled together in the same compartment with Natives'. Black Americans visiting Johannesburg objected to being 'placed on a level with the raw, savage totally uneducated aborigines' (SAHJ Vol. 6, C.E. de Waal, 'American Black Residents and Visitors in the SAR Before 1899').

23 P. van Duin, 'Artisans and Trades Unions', in James and Simmons, op. cit.

24 S. Bickford Smith, 'A Special Tradition', in James and Simmons, op. cit. In 1895 Coloureds were banned from the YMCA, in 1903 from the Tivoli Theatre, in 1904 from hotels, in 1905 schools were segregated. For the 'purity legislation' see Merriman, *Correspondence,* Vol. 3, pp. 363–4 (he was for it). For the Liquor Acts see Rose Innes, *Selected Correspondence 1884–1902,* pp. 224–5 (he was also for it). S. Bickford Smith deals with the evolution of the Coloureds in JAH Vol. 36 no. 3, 'Black Ethnicities: The Emergence of the "Coloureds" in Late Nineteenth-Century Cape Town'. See also *The History of Cape Town,* Vol. 7,

M. Adhikavi, 'A Drink-Sodden Race of Bestial Degenerates'.

25 P. Lewsen, *John Xavier Merriman*, p. 269. Merriman, even after thirty years of politics, could be surprised to find a black election committee 'astonishingly business-like and orderly' (*Correspondence*, Vol. 2, p. 417); ICS Societies of Southern Africa 1971–72, R.A. Moyer, 'Some Current Manifestations of Early Mfengu History', pp. 147–8; and 1972–73, W.G. Mills, 'The Rift Within the Lute'.

26 D.M. Balia, *Black Methodists and White Supremacy*, Chapter 5. Bishop Turner found, to his amazement (and to that of later readers): 'No, indeed . . . colour is no bar in Africa'; but he was speaking of Cape Town and not the Transvaal. J.W. Cell, '*The Highest State of White Supremacy*, p. 35. See also A. Odendaal, op. cit., Chapter 1. ICS SSA, Q.N. Parsons, 'Independence and Ethiopianism'; JAH Vol. 11 no. 4, C.C. Saunders, 'Thile and the Thembu Church'; JAH Vol. 11, no. 3, D. Williams, 'African Nationalism in South Africa'. For Mokane see also JICH Vol. 17 no. 1, B. Kennedy, 'Missionaries, Black Converts and Separatists'.

27 JICH Vol. 14 no. 2, R. Hyam, 'Empire and Sexual Opportunity'.

28 The essential work is R. Hyam, *Elgin and Churchill at the Colonial Office*.

29 P. Molteno, *Selections from Correspondence 1892–1914*, pp. 254.

30 Merriman, *Correspondence*, Vol. 4, p. 18 (7 March 1906).

31 R.S. Churchill, *Winston S. Churchill*, Companion Vol. 2, Part 1, pp. 558–65.

32 The classic account is S. Marks, *Reluctant Rebellion*; also B. Sacks, *An Imperial Dilemma*. R. Hyam, *Elgin and Churchill at the Colonial Office* analyses London's reaction, pp. 239–62. For a contemporary account see Col. James Dick, RCS Ms. 58

33 Churchill on 4 December 1907, quoted in Hyam, op. cit. D. Child, *Charles Smythe* – the Natal Premier, who wrote about the executions: 'I am just afraid that we may get into trouble over it, as although they really deserved it, there may be some legal bother about it' (p. 206).

34 R.A. Huttenback, *Racism and Empire*.

CHAPTER 14

1 Merriman showed his teeth over the conference, insisting that the High Commissioner should not be invited to take the chair, an unprecedented event; even Botha had to be persuaded this was possible. See L.M. Thompson, *The Unification of South Africa 1902–10*, the standard work, Chapters 2 and 3. A.P. Newton, *The Unification of South Africa* (2 vols), collates documents from 1858 to 1909.

2 The convention is dealt with in Chapters 3–5 of L.M. Thompson, op. cit. See also SAHJ Vol. 8, G. Martin ,'The Canadian Analogy in South African Union'. A delegation to Canada in 1908 came out firmly in favour of a strong unitary system, with little provincial autonomy.

3 L.M. Thompson, op. cit., p. 115.

4 For Smuts, see SAL Merriman Papers. For Schwikkard, see L.M. Thompson, op. cit., p. 114.

5 The proposal is in a letter from Godée-Molsbergen to Merriman on 18 February 1908, SAL Merriman Papers.

6 'Patently honest, deeply sincere . . . but also painfully slow, thorough and conscientious,' K. Schoeman, *Only an Anguish to Live Here*, p. 56.

7 R.S. Churchill, op. cit., Vol. 2, pp. 203–5. It should be noted that Churchill is quite wrong when on pp. 148–9 he writes: 'No one in South Africa proposed that the coloured man, African or Asian, should have the vote.'

8 In an interview with Hely-Hutchinson on 28 June 1909, SAL Merriman Papers, quoted L.M. Thompson, op. cit., p. 403.

9 In a memorandum by Col. Seely on

Crewe paper concerning the Protectorates. Cab. Priv. Print, 8 November 1909.

10 The biography, a classic, is *Hofmeyr* by Alan Paton.

11 On 7 December 1912, at De Wildt. The previous incendiary speech was in October at Nylstroom.

12 The Plaatje quotation is from B.P. Willan, *Sol Plaatje*, p. 165. In *Imvo*, 24 November 1911.

13 JAH Vol. 21 no. 1, B.P. Willan, 'The Anti-Slavery and Aboriginal Protection Society'. For Mrs Solomon see W.E.G. Solomon, op. cit., pp. 349–50.

14 The documents are in Cambridge University Library, Crewe Papers. Merriman, see *Correspondence*, Vol. 4, p. 197; see also J. Nadoo, *Tracking Down Historical Myths*, and R.A. Huttenback, *Racism and Empire*.

15 W.K. Hancock, *Smuts*, Vol. 1, p. 323.

16 Queens University, Kingston, Canada, John Buchan Papers. From a letter to John Buchan from the editor of the *Transvaal Leader*, 16 January 1914, who also wrote of the strike: 'Practically every trade went on strike simultaneously,' and felicitated the government on its speedy suppression: 'the mobilization of the Defence Force was a record for speed and efficiency, and our syndicalist friends got the biggest surprise of their lives.' For the black strikes see ICS Papers series 4, 1972–73, B. Hierson et al, 'Whatever Happened at Jagersfontein?'

17 For conditions see C. van Onselen in JAH Vol. 14 no. 2, 'Worker Consciousness in Black Miners'. For Philips see Frazer and Jeeves, *All that Glittered*, p. 240.

18 W.K. Hancock and J. van der Peel, *Smuts Papers*, Vol. 1, letter from Major H.C. Hall. JICH Vol 8 no. 1, N.G. Garson, 'South Africa and World War I'.

19 The novelist Francis Brett Young served with Smuts – see his *Marching on Tanga*.

20 S.J. Jingoes, *A Chief is a Chief by the People*; A. Grundlingh, *Fighting Their Own War*, p. 125; N. Clothier, *Black Valour*; JAH Vol. 19 no. 1, B.P. Willan, 'The South African Native Labour Contingent'. D.D.T. Jabavu considered that 'a new sense of [black] racial unity' had been created (paper of July 1920).

21 Merriman, *Correspondence*, Vol. 4, p. 294, letter to Lord Bryce, 23 March 1917.

22 CO. 537/1197–8, quoted in Willan, op. cit., pp. 241–5.

23 Quoted at length in J.C. Smuts, *Smuts*, Chapter 38.

CHAPTER 15

1 For women's protests see ICS Vol. 16, 1988–89, F. Ginwala, 'Women and the ANC'. L. Switzer, *Power and Resistance in an African Society*, p. 269, makes the point that Christian women were particularly well organized in the Anglican and Methodists' '*manyane*', or women's league.

2 B. Bunting, *Letters to Rebecca*, p. 59. For an insider's view of the SACP see E. Roux, *Time Longer than Rope*.

3 See Switzer, *Power and Resistance in an African Society*.

4 And who were betrayed to the Germans by a group led by Maritz seeking refuge after their defeat in 1902. When the German officer heard the news he exclaimed, 'When the Hottentots rebel, we would be glad to have a pretext to exterminate all of them!' QBSAL Vol. 45 no. 3, C. de Jong, 'Manie Maritz and Robert de Kersauson's Secret Meeting with Bondelswart, June 1902'. For the Bondelswarts see A.M. Davey, *The Bondelswarts Affair*, and F. Dewaldt (ed.), *Native Uprisings in South-West Africa*.

5 See C. Kadalie's autobiography, *Life*.

6 M. Lipton, *Capitalism and Apartheid*, p. 18.

7 E.W. Smith, *Aggrey of Africa*. Aggrey was described as rediscovering 'the ancient Christian virtue of hilarity'.

8 The best account of the development of black opposition after 1912 is still P. Walshe, *The Rise of African Nationalism in South Africa,* supplemented by the documents from Karis and Carter, op. cit. H.J. and R.E. Simons' *Class and Colour in South Africa* has to be digested with a handful of salt.

9 The authoritative work is D. O'Meara, *Volkscapitalisme,* on which this section relies. See also H. Giliomee, *Aspects of the Rise of Afrikaner Capitalism,* and James and Simmons, op. cit.

10 Malherbe, op. cit., Vol. 2, p. 12. Young Hofmeyr was caught out by old Hofmeyr in saying '*Ek*' for '*Ik*'.

11 The best accounts of South African industry are D. Yudleman, *The Emergence of Modern South Africa,* and M. Lipton, op. cit.

12 Quoted Le May, op. cit., p. 169

13 See R. Ally, *Gold and Empire,* Chapter 5.

14 There is a revealing autobiography, *South Africa in my Time.*

15 Marwick led seven thousand blacks on foot safely out of the Transvaal into Natal. The story of their epic march is in T. Pakenham, , pp. 120–1 (but Pakenham does not identify Marwick other than as 'a man called Marwick'), and in detail in Cmd 43 of 1899. Stallard's name is perhaps the odd man out, since he was the moving spirit in forcing through the Natives (Urban Areas) Act 1937, in the face of unequivocal civil servants' reports that local authorities generally regarded its provisions as arbitrary and unfair (SAHJ Vol. 2, T.R.H. Davenport, 'The Triumph of Colonel Stallard').

16 See N. Cope, *To Bind the Nation,* for the foundation of Inkatha. The 1928 constitution of Inkatha was drafted by the solicitors J.H. Nicholson and Thorpe.

17 Quoted at length in I. Wilkins and H. Strydom, *The Broederbond,* Chapter 2.

CHAPTER 16

1 Respectively 'a jackal with two arseholes' and 'salt prick' – from having one leg in Africa and one in England.

2 Norval, *Deconstructing Apartheid Discourse,* examines the role of H.G. Stoker in extending Kuyper's 'delicate balance of paradoxes' into a political philosophy akin to, but still recognizably different from, German National Socialism (pp. 68–74). For Verwoerd see W.A. De Klerk, op. cit., p. 246. See also T. Eloff, *Government, Justice and Race Classification,* and W.A. De Klerk, *The Puritans in Africa,* in which he quotes Kuyper as stating that Calvinism is opposed to all hierarchy among men (p. 204).

3 See J.H.P. Sertfontein, *Brotherhood of Power.*

4 See A. Paton, *Hofmeyr,* for his slow conversion.

5 If one excepts Lord Ligonier, who was born French. The Guildhall speech is quoted in J.C. Smuts, *Smuts,* pp. 433–5.

6 *Historical Journal* Vol. 23 no. 3, L. Lloyd, 'A Family Quarrel'.

7 Nelson Mandela found Lembede 'a magnetic personality who thought in original and often startling ways', *A Long Walk to Freedom,* p. 112.

8 Quoted in Z.K. Matthews' autobiography, *Freedom for my People,* pp. 149–50.

9 See Vachter, *Malan's Draft for a Republic,* and Le May, op. cit., p. 188. G.M. Carter, *The Politics of Inequality: South Africa Since 1948,* contains the results of many interviews with Malan and Smuts.

10 It would be a mistake to think of a single apartheid doctrine. Some particularly nasty racialist theories were put about by the Afrikanerbond vir Rassestudies (Racial Studies). Somewhat more respectably, the revered writer 'Totius' (J.D. du Toit) and even such 'liberals' as Hofmeyr and Smuts followed the *voortrekkers* in

protesting against '*gelykstelling*'. See T. Eloff, *Government, Justice and Race Classification*.

11 Between 1940 and 1950 ten of the sixteen most senior officers were English. Ten years later it was three of eleven (P.H. Frankel, *Pretoria's Praetorians*). In 1949 all senior railway officials were English; they had all been replaced by 1955 (T. Cross, *The Afrikaner Takeover*).

12 N. Mandela, op. cit., p. 113.

13 The incident is glossed over in Mandela's autobiography.

14 In particular, Moroka showed a decided lack of nerve during the trial of ANC members after the Defiance Campaign (see N. Mandela, op. cit., pp. 157–9). The papers of Lutuli and Dr Matthews, on microfiche in the ICS, illustrate the different qualities of the two men.

15 By the end of the 1980s the relative populations were approximately: Swaziland 681,000; Lesotho 1,577,000; Botswana 941,000; Transkei 2,876,000. For the protectorates generally see R.P. Stevens, *Lesotho, Bechuanaland and Swaziland*.

16 Stevens, *Lesotho, Bechuanaland and Swaziland*, p. 72. A candid admission of British defects was revealed in 1944 by E.M. Jenkins of the Dominions Office when he warned C.E. Sayers of the Ministry of Information that 'the cards to conceal, play down, over-explain, are our racial arrogance, our former economic exploitation, and our careless laziness' (ICS paper, F. Furedi, November 1996).

17 A letter from Curtis to Abe Bailey (Syfrets ABI Corresponders, S.A. 1938) on 14 February 1938 describes a meeting at the Royal Empire Society in which Thomas had to put up an embarrassed defence of the government's unwillingness to cede the protectorates. There is a good description of the discussions in Wilson and Thompson, op. cit., Vol. 2, pp. 496–501.

18 The standard work is E.A. Eldredge, *A South African Kingdom*. See also: L.B.B.J. Machobane, *Government and Change in Lesotho*; R. Southall and T. Petlane, *Democratisation and Demilitarisation in Lesotho*; S. Gill et al, *Lesotho*; JAH Vol. 36 no. 1, M. Epprecht, 'Women's "Conservatism" in Late Colonial Lesotho'. Lord Selborne's views are in JAH Vol. 10 no. 1, A.R. Booth, 'Lord Selborne and the British Protectorates 1908–10'. He continued: 'they are also more advanced in civilized thought and habit than any other.'

19 Body parts were removed from living victims; the southern equivalent is the euphemism '*muti*'.

20 Botswana's success has aroused much interest. For recent Botswana history see: C. Harvey and S.R. Lewis, *Policy Choice and Development Performance in Botswana* ; P. Granberg and J.R. Parkinson, *Botswana*; P.S. Landau, *The Realm of the Word*; T. Tou, N. Parsons and W. Henderson, *Seretse Kama*; R. Dale, *Botswana's Search for Autonomy*; P.E. Peters, *Dividing the Commons: Politics, Policy and Culture in Botswana*; D. Wylie, *A Little God*; S. Brothers et al, *Botswana in the Twentieth Century*.

21 For the episode see *Historical Journal* Vol. 29 no. 4, R. Hyam, 'The Political Consequences of Seretse Khama'. See also JMAS Vol. 25 no. 1 (1981), M. Crowder, 'Tshekedi Kama, Smuts and South-West Africa'.

CHAPTER 17

1 For Strydom's view see D. O'Meara's invaluable *Forty Lost Years*, pp. 89–91. The quotation is from the *Observer*, December 1952.

2 Paul Sauer, who had constructed the winning manifesto of 1948, had been attacking 'the six old men in Bloemfontein [who] have all the say', and Charles Swart, the Minister of Justice, claimed that the reason was 'to restore Sovereignty of parliament'.

3 See Helen Suzman's description in her autobiography, *In no Uncertain Terms*, p. 33.
4 And others either resisted, or turned blind eyes. ICS Papers Vol. 4, 1972–73, G. Adler, 'Trying Not to be Cruel'.
5 This was E.C. Malherbe's judgement: *Education in South Africa*, Vol. 2, p. 550.
6 D.W. Kruger (ed.), *South African Parties and Policies 1910–60*, p. 451.
7 Govan Mbeki, *The Peasants' Revolt*.
8 Foreign Relations of the United States, Africa 1960, p. 346.
9 A.S. Mathews, *Law, Order and Liberty in South Africa*, p. 102.
10 For the discussion see N. Mandela, op. cit., pp. 321–4.
11 See Suzman, op. cit., *In no Uncertain Terms*.
12 From statistics in Chapter 7 of D. O'Meara, *Forty Lost Years*.
13 House of Representatives Sub-Committee on Africa, Eighty-Ninth Congress, Second Session, pp. 355–7.
14 Botha was furious, claiming: 'We were ruthlessly left in the lurch by an undertaking that was broken' (C. Alden, *Apartheid's Last Stand*, pp. 39–40). See also: D. Spikes, *Angola and the Politics of Intervention*; R.E. Bissell and C.E. Crocker, *South Africa into the 1980s*, which in 1979 described South Africa as 'an outpost of orderliness and well-managed enterprises in a region of disorder and highly uncertain political futures' (p. 227). The National Security Archive publications *South Africa and the United States* and *South Africa: The Making of US Policy* have the whole – or nearly the whole – story in very great detail.
15 See B.A. Pauw, *The Second Generation*.
16 See M.G. Buthelezi, *South Africa: Anatomy of Black–White Power Sharing*, pp. 23, 37.

CHAPTER 18

1 Reports in the *Sunday Times*, 19 February 1977, and much-quoted.
2 The biography is Donald Woods, *Biko*. For a more intimate – and illuminating – account of growing up in apartheid South Africa, see M. Ramphele, *Across Boundaries*.
3 Like many of Biko's ideas (some of which were not well-developed), this is reproduced in Woods, op. cit., pp. 184–5.
4 W.A. De Klerk, *The Second (R)evolution*, p. 54. And it should be noticed that prisoners like Biko or Mandela were prepared to stand up for themselves, engage in legal proceedings and trade blows with their jailers; South Africa had its fair share of thugs, but police maltreatment of prisoners was nearer to that experienced in New York (see e.g. the *Economist*, 23 August 1997) than in Nazi Germany. The real atrocities took place outside the police structure. Often perverted and timid, South African judicial and other investigations could eventually be effective. For the slow exposure of the doctors who lied about Biko's death see M. Rayner, 'Biko', in Manganyi and du Toit (eds), *Political Violence and the Struggles in South Africa*.
5 There is a good account in D. O'Meara, *Forty Lost Years*, Chapter 12.
6 From de Villiers, *PW*. As well as his *Forty Lost Years* see D. O'Meara, 'The New National Party', in D. Innes et al, *Power and Profit*. Patti Waldemeir, *Anatomy of a Miracle*, wrote: 'Botha was deeply religious. Talking to him was like talking to an Old Testament prophet' (p. 40).
7 Quoted in F. Meer, op. cit., pp. 136–7.
8 On 5 May 1986; quoted in D. O'Meara, *Forty Lost Years*, p. 337.
9 R. Moss, *Shouting at the Crocodile*, pp. 26–7.
10 ICS Vol. 4, J. Aitchison, 'Numbering the Dead'. Of the 648 Pietermaritzburg detainees in 1987 *none* was a member

of Inkatha, although 368 of 594 violent incidents were attributed to them: it was clear whose side the police were on. See also the essays by S. Marks and N. Andersson in Manganyi and du Toit, op. cit.

11 T.M. Shaw, *Reformism and Revision in Africa's Political Economy in the 1990s*: the figures are for 1992.

12 Quoted in F.M. Joseph, *Best of Bedfellows*, p. 109. See also K. Osia, *Israel*.

13 ICS Paper, 14 November 1996, D. Lowry, 'The Alliance that Does not Speak its Name: Afrikaner and Irish Nationalists'.

14 R. Renwick, *Unconventional Diplomacy in South Africa*, p. 113. The Langa massacre is described in R. Thornton, 'The Shooting at Uitenhage', in Manganyi and du Toit, op. cit., Chapter 4.

15 P. Waldemeir, *Anatomy of a Miracle*, identifies the formation of Wiehahn's committee as 'one of the most important steps ever taken by a National Party government' (p. 27).

16 R.W. Johnson and L. Schlemmer, *Launching Democracy in South Africa*, p. 3, who point out that the 'Rubicon' speech was abandoned largely through F.W. de Klerk's opposition. G. Leach, *South Africa: No Easy Path to Peace*, p. 178; R. Renwick, op. cit., p. 118.

17 G. Howe, *Conflict of Loyalty*, a revealing book, p. 487.

18 N.A. Mangaliso, *The South African Mosaic*, p. 41.

19 The most solid and admirable figure was that of General Obasanjo, who had brought his country, Nigeria, back to civil rule, and was later (1996) imprisoned there by the military dictatorship. The other co-chairman, Malcom Fraser, ex-Prime Minister of Australia, who had previously supported the South African government, had his views changed by what he experienced there.

20 D.O'Meara, *Forty Lost Years*, p. 380.

21 In particular Lord Barber of the Standard Bank and Sir Timothy Bevan

of Barclays were soundly behind the ANC (see A. Sampson, *Black and Gold*, and S. Thomas, *The Diplomacy of Liberation: Foreign Relations of the ANC Since 1960*).

22 That of journalist Ken Owen, in *These Times*, p. 175.

23 J.A. Baker, *The Politics of Diplomacy*, p. 223.

CHAPTER 19

1 W.A. de Klerk, *F.W. de Klerk*, is a biography by the subject's elder brother on which the next paragraphs rely.

2 Founded by Sir Abe, following the example of Cecil Rhodes, these scholarships, which enabled young South Africans to travel abroad, were regarded with suspicion by some conservative Afrikaners.

3 The discussions surrounding this are in Baker, *The Politics of Diplomacy*, Chapter 13.

4 Mandela's *A Long Walk to Freedom*, although likely to remain a classic autobiography, has little on the events after his release from prison. Anthony Sampson's biography, to be published in 1999, is likely to prove definintive.

5 See pp.??? supra. The facts of Thembu history need underlining since there has been an attempt – somewhat half-hearted – to fabricate yet another myth of heroic Thembu resistance to the colonizers, partly stimulated by Nationalist governments' propaganda intended to exacerbate inter-tribal antagonisms. In the often confused hostilities of the nineteenth century the Thembu were usually to be found as colonial allies rather than militant resisters.

6 D. Golan, *Inventing Shaka*, p. 145.

7 There is an interesting analysis in ICS SSA/96/3, S. Ellis, 'South Africa's Third Force'. The full truth about the activities of the Third Force and the participation in it of the notorious 32nd Battalion of the Defence Force is

only now emerging, and the disgusting character of some earlier Nationalist politicians is being revealed as hitherto secret documents are disclosed. Jimmy Kruger's public accouncements were enough to establish his peculiar nastiness, but in December 1996 (see e.g. *Mail & Guardian*, 29 November–5 December 1996) the Minister of Justice was recorded as having said, after the Soweto massacre in 1976, '*die polisie moet miskien 'n bietjie meer drasties en hardhandig moet optree wat meer sterftes meerbring*' (the police perhaps must be a bit more drastic in roughing people up so as to bring about more deaths).

8 The prosecution was much criticized, and with some weight, for having pulled its punches in order to protect Buthelezi, whose lukewarm adhesion to the government was a source of constant anxiety.

9 Ellis, op.cit., points out that the Security Forces, had they wished, could easily have sabotaged the election; in fact they usually cooperated in preserving order. R.W. Johnson, *Launching Democracy in South Africa*, concludes (p. 348) that the electoral process was largely rescued by white business on the one hand, and the old white-led Defence Force on the other.

10 Mary Moffat was the wife of the formidable pioneer missionary Robert Moffat, and mother-in-law of David Livingstone. I am indebted for the quotation to Diana Madden of the Brenthurst Library.

BIBLIOGRAPHY

The great bibliography is that of Sidney Mendelssohn, revised and continued by the South Africa Library (4 vols, London, 1979; supplement Cape Town, 1991), misleadingly entitled *A South African Bibliography to the Year 1925*, and a tribute to the scholarship of the library staff. Later sources are well covered by the Orange Free State University's Institute for Contemporary History *Bibliographies on South African Political History* (3 vols, Boston, 1979).

A discriminating and lively, although poorly edited, summary is N. M. Stultz, *South Africa: An Annotated Bibliography* (Ann Arbor, 1989). See also R. Musiker, *Standard Encyclopaedia of South Africa*; C. Saunders, *Historical Dictionary of South Africa*; J. McIlwine, *Africa: A Guide to Reference Materials*.

The bibliography in the two-volume *Oxford History of South Africa* is now more than thirty years out of date, and needs to be supplemented by some of the comprehensive bibliographical references given in such authoritative more recent specialized studies such as those of Bundy, Peires, Marks, Welsh, Keegan, Eldredge, Nasson, Walshe, Odendaal, Karis and Carter, to elect only a few from scores of works. The Institute for Contemporary History at Bloemfontein has published a helpful *Register of Private Document Collections* (O. Geyser et al (eds), Boston (USA), 1979).

The *Dictionary of South African Biography* (5 vols, Pretoria, 1968), although often flawed, is particularly useful for its bibliographical references.

ARCHIVAL AND UNPUBLISHED WORKS

Public Records Office

The original 'correspondence' file for the Cape and South Africa is CO 179

Command Papers and Blue Books

Command Papers were initiated as part of the reforming activities of Lord Grey's Whig government in 1833. At first bound in 'Blue Books', they were designated only by the sessional dates and volume numbers. Hence 1826 XXVI contains, *inter alia*, the instructions to the commissions investigating the state of affairs at the Cape. A volume may contain material from several years previously. After 1870, Command Papers were allotted individual numbers, prefaced by C., Cd or Cmd.

Public Records Office Northern Ireland

MICD/221/2431 Caledon papers

Rhodes House, Oxford

Mss Afr. S. 1737, Bowen memo

British National Library (BL)

Gladstone Papers, Add. Ms. 44547, 44738, 44141, 44287
Hamilton Papers, Add. Ms. 49168, 49167
Carnarvon Papers, Add. Ms. 60792, 60798

National Library of Scotland

Minto Papers, Ms. 19420, 19422, 19432

Scottish Record Office

Loch Papers, GD 268

Cambridge University Library

Crewe Papers, Box 1/15
Add 9351.18
Royal Colonial Institute Proceedings, Vol. 6, 1884–5
Journal of the Society of Arts, Vol. 29, 1881
Royal Commonwealth Society, Mss 55
Col. J. Dick, Bambata
Ms. 51, Miss M.A. Wilson

Marylebone Public Library

Barkly Papers, 28107

Johannesburg Public Library (JPL)

Interview with Cetshwayo, S. Pam 968.303
'Escale de l'Armée Française à Cape Town 1860', S. Pam 968.7037
I. Staples, 'Narrative of the War of 1851–53', S. Pam 968.607
C. Read, 'Diary of the Seccocoeni War 1877 (Sights Better Not Recorded)'

South African Library, Cape Town

Methodist Missions, MSC 19.1
Elizabeth Goold's Diary 1863, MSC 39

Bibliography

T.L. Hodgson, 'Sekela Rolong'
C.H. Bell, MSA 51
Merriman Correspondence

Syfrets Correspondence, SA 1938

Queens University, Kingston, Canada

John Buchan Papers, Box 1

Brenthurst Library, Johannesburg

John Bruce MS., MS. 061/1
'Sketches of the Political and Commercial History of the Cape of Good
  Hope'
Sir M. Bhownaggree Papers, Ms. 145
Roger Curtis, journal, Ms. 053
F.T. l'Ons, Stockenstrom Caricatures, ART 343
Earl Macartney Papers, Ms. 061
Sir Fairfax Moresby, memorandum, Ms. 305f

South African Archival Records

Notule van die Volksraad van die Suid-Afrikaanse Republiek

Hove Public Library

Wolseley Papers

Institute of Commonwealth Studies

Z.K. Matthews, 'Proceedings at Tshekedi's Kgotla, September 1935', M932.E
A. Lutuli, M 845/1
Sermon: 'Condemnation of Witchcraft', Autobiography, M8454.22
Report of ANC Natal Executive, M845/148

JOURNALS AND PERIODICALS

African Affairs
African Studies
Archives Yearbook for South African History (AYB)
Historical Journal
Institute of Commonwealth Studies, Structures of Southern African Societies
  (SSA) papers
International Journal of Historical Studies (IJHS)

Journal of African History (JAH)
Journal of Imperial and Commonwealth History (JICH)
Journal of Modern African Studies (JMAS)
Journal of Southern African Studies (JSAS)
South African Historical Journal (SAHJ)
Quarterly Bulletin of the South African Library (QBSAL)
Social Forces
Studies in the History of Cape Town (C. Saunders, ed.)

PUBLISHED WORKS

Abel, R.L., *Politics by Other Means: Law in the Struggle Against Apartheid 1980–1994* (London, 1995)
Abrahams, P., *Return to Goli* (London, 1953)
Abrahams, P., *Tell Freedom* (London, 1954)
Adam, H., *Modernizing Racial Domination* (Berkeley, 1971)
Adams, B., *Narrative 1843–48* (Cape Town, 1941)
Agar-Hamilton, J.A.I., *The Road to the North* (London, 1937)
Ajayi, J.F. and Crowder, M., *Historical Atlas of South Africa* (Cambridge, 1985)
Alden, C., *Apartheid's Last Stand* (London, 1996)
Ally, R., *Gold and Empire* (Johannesburg, 1994)
Amery, L.S. (ed.), *The Times History of the War in South Africa* (7 vols, London, 1900–09)
Amery, L.S., *My Political Life* (3 vols, London, 1953)
Amphlett, G.T., *History of the Standard Bank of South Africa* (Glasgow, 1914)
Anon., *History of the Civilization and Christianization of South Africa* (Edinburgh, 1832)
Anon. ('A Colonial Officer'), *Twenty-Five Years' Soldiering in South Africa* (London, 1909)
Appleyard, J.W., *The War of the Axe and the Xhosa Bible* (Cape Town, 1971)
Arbousset, T. and Daumas, F., *Narrative* (Cape Town, 1846, 1968)
Asquith, M. (Lady Oxford), *Autobiography* (London, 1962)
Atkins, K.E., *The Moon is Dead. Give us our Money!* (London, 1993)
Axelson, E.S.E., *Africa 1488–1530* (London, 1940)
Bach, D.C. (ed.), *La France et l'Afrique du Sud* (Paris, 1990)
Bailey, J., *Sailing to Paradise* (New York, 1994)
Baker, J.A., *The Politics of Diplomacy* (New York, 1995)
Balia, D.M., *Black Methodists and White Supremacy* (Durban, 1991)
Ballinger, M., *From Union to Apartheid* (Cape Town, 1969)
Barber, J. and Barrat, J., *South Africa's Foreign Policy* (Cambridge, 1990)
Bardill, J.E. and Cobbe, J.H., *Lesotho* (Boulder, 1985)

Barnard, A. (ed. Wilkins, W.H.), *South Africa a Century Ago* (London, 1901)

Barrow, J., *An Account of Travels into the Interior of Southern Africa* (London, 1806)

Bauman, G. and Bright, E., *The Lost Republic* (London, 1940)

Beak, G.B., *Aftermath of War* (London, 1906)

Beckman, D., *A Voyage to Borneo in 1714* (London, 1718)

Beer, G.L., *The English-Speaking Peoples* (New York, 1917)

Beer, G.L., *African Questions at the Peace Conference* (New York, 1923, London, 1968)

Becker, P., *Path of Blood* (London, 1962)

Becker, P., *The Pathfinders* (London, 1985)

Beinart, W., *The Political Economy of Pondoland 1860–1930* (Cape Town, 1982)

Beinart, W. (ed.) et al, *Putting a Plough to the Ground* (Johannesburg, 1986)

Beinart, W. and Bundy, C., *Hidden Struggles in Rural South Africa* (London, 1987)

Beinart, W. and Dubow, S. (eds), *Segregation and Apartheid in Twentieth-Century South Africa* (London, 1991)

Belich, J., *The Victorian Interpretation of Racial Conflict* (McGill, 1989)

Bell, K.N. and Morrell, W.P., *Select Documents* (Oxford, 1928)

Benson, M., *Tshekedi Khama* (London, 1960)

Benson, M., *Nelson Mandela* (London, 1986, 1989)

Benyon, J., *Proconsul and Paramountcy in South Africa* (Pietermaritzburg, 1980)

Beyers, C., *Die Kaapse Patriotte* (Cape Town, 1929)

Bezuidenhout, C.P., *De Geschiedenis van het Afrikaansche Geslacht van 1688 tot 1882* (Bloemfontein, 1883)

Bhana, S. and Pachai, B., *A Documentary History of Indian South Africans* (Stanford, 1984)

Bird, W.W., *The State of the Cape of Good Hope in 1822* (London, 1823, Cape Town, 1966)

Bissel, R.E. and Crocker, C.E., *South Africa into the 1980s* (Boulder, 1979)

Blake, R., *Disraeli* (London, 1967)

Blake, R., *A History of Rhodesia* (London, 1977)

Blunt, W.S., *My Diaries* (Cambridge, 1921)

Böeseken, A.J. (ed.), *Dagregister en Briewe, Zacharias Wagenaar 1662–66* (Pretoria, 1973)

Bonner, P. (ed.) et al, *Working Papers in South African Studies*, (2 vols, Johannesburg, 1981)

Bonner, P. (ed.) et al, *Apartheid's Genesis* (Johannesburg, 1993)

Booth, A.R., *The US Experience in South Africa 1784–1870* (Cape Town, 1976)

Botha, C.G., *Collecteana* (Cape Town, 1924)

Botha, C.G., *General History and Social Life of the Cape of Good Hope* (Cape Town, 1962)

Botha, C.G., *The French Refugees at the Cape* (Cape Town, 1970)

Boucher, M. and Penn, N., *Britain at the Cape 1795–1803* (Houghton, 1992)

Bourne, K., *Foreign Policy of Victorian England* (Oxford, 1970)

Boxer, C.R., *Dutch Merchants and Mariners in Asia 1602–1795* (London, 1908)

Boxer, C.R., *The Dutch in Brazil* (Oxford, 1957)

Boxer, C.R., *The Dutch Seaborne Empire 1600–1800* (London, 1965)

Boxer, C.R., *The Portuguese Seaborne Empire* (London, 1969, 1991)

Bozzoli, B. (ed.), *Class, Community and Conflict* (Johannesburg, 1987)

Bradlow, F.R. and Cairns, M., *The Early Cape Muslims* (Cape Town, 1978)

Braun, R.L., *South-West Africa under Mandate* (Salisbury (USA), 1976)

Bredekamp, H.C. and Plüddemann, H.E.P. (eds), *Diaries of the Herrnhut Missionaries* (Belleville, 1992)

Bresler, C.P., *Lineage of Conflict* (Johannesburg, 1952)

Brett, M.V. (ed.), *Journal and Letters of Reginald, Viscount Esher* (London, 1937)

Brink, C.F., *Journal 1761–62* (Cape Town, 1947)

Brookes, E.H. and Webb, C.B., *History of Natal* (Pietermaritzburg, 1963)

Brookes, E.H., *History of the University of Natal* (Pietermaritzburg, 1966)

Brookes, E.H., *Apartheid: A Documentary Study* (London, 1968)

Brookes, E.H., *White Rule in South Africa 1830–1910* (Pietermaritzburg, 1974)

Broster, J., *The Tembu* (Cape Town, 1976)

Brothers, S. et al, *Botswana in the Twentieth Century* (Gaberone, 1994)

Brown, J.A. (ed.) et al, *History from South Africa* (Philadelphia, 1991)

Brown, J.A., *They Fought for King and Kaiser* (Johannesburg, 1991)

Brownlee, C., *Reminiscences of Kaffir Life and History* (Lovedale, 1896)

Bruce, J., *Sketches of the Political and Commercial History of the Cape of Good Hope (Report to Lord Macartney)* (Brenthurst Ms. 061/1)

Bryce, J., *Impressions of South Africa* (London, 1900)

Buchan, J., *The African Colony* (London, 1903)

Bunbury, H., *Narratives of Some Passages in the Great War with France* (London, 1854)

Bundy, C., *The Rise and Fall of the South African Peasantry* (Cape Town, 1988)

Bunting, B., *Letters to Rebecca* (Belleville, 1996)

Burkhardt, F. and Smith, S. (eds), *Correspondence of Charles Darwin* (2 vols, Cambridge, 1985)

Buthelezi, M.G., *South Africa: Anatomy of Black–White Power Sharing* (London, 1986)

Buthelezi, M.G., *South Africa: My Vision of the Future* (London, 1990)

Buthelezi, S. (ed.), *South Africa: The Dynamics and Prospects of Transformation* (Harare, 1995)

Butler, G., *The 1820 Settlers* (Cape Town, 1974)

Butler, J. et al, *The Black Homelands of South Africa* (Berkeley, 1977)

Butler, W.F., *Sir William Butler* (London, 1911)

Butterfield, P.H., *War and Peace in South Africa 1879–81* (Gaberone, 1994)

Carnegie Commission, *The Poor White Problem* (5 vols, Stellenbosch, 1923)

Carnegie Commission Inquiry into Poverty, Conference Papers (1981)

Carter, G.M., *The Politics of Inequality: South Africa Since 1948* (London, 1962)

Cartwright, A.P., *The Dynamite Co.* (London, 1964)

Cartwright, A.P., *The Corner House* (London, 1965)

Cartwright, A.P., *Gold Paved the Way* (London, 1967)

Casson, L., *Periplus Maris Erythraei* (Princeton, 1990)

Cavaliero, R., *Admiral Satan* (London and New York, 1991)

Cecil, G.C., *Life of Robert, Marquis of Salisbury* (London, 1932)

Cell, J.W., *The Highest State of White Supremacy* (Cambridge, 1982)

Chamberlain, J. (ed. Howard, C.H.D.), *Political Memoir* (London, 1953)

Chapman, J., *Account of a Visit to South Africa* (London, 1903)

Chapman, J., *Travels in the Interior of South Africa 1849–63* (Cape Town, 1971)

Chase, J.C., *The Cape of Good Hope* (London, 1843)

Chavonnes, M.P. and van Imhoff, G.W., *Reports on the Cape* (Cape Town, 1918)

Chesson, F.W., *British Rule in South Africa* (Cape Town, 1868)

Chesson, F.W., *The Dutch Republics of South Africa* (London, 1871)

Chichester, D., *Shots in the Streets: Violence and Religion in South Africa* (Boston, 1991)

Child, D., *Charles Smythe* (Cape Town, 1973)

Child, D., *A Merchant Family in Early Natal* (Cape Town, 1979)

Child, D., *Portrait of a Pioneer* (Johannesburg, 1980)

Christopher, A.J., *The Atlas of Apartheid* (Johannesburg, 1994)

Churchill, Lord R., *Men, Mines and Animals in South Africa* (London, 1892)

Churchill, R.S. and Gilbert, M., *Winston S. Churchill* (London, 1966–88)

Churchill, W.S., *London to Ladysmith* (London, 1900)

Clarke, S., *The Invasion of Zululand 1879* (Johannesburg, 1979)

Clarke, S., *Zululand at War 1897* (Johannesburg, 1981)

Cloete, H., *Five Lectures* (Cape Town, 1856)

Clothier, N., *Black Valour* (Pietermaritzburg, 1987)

Cobbett, W. and Cohen, R., *Popular Struggles in South Africa* (Trenton, NJ, 1988)

Cockram, G.M., *South-West Africa Mandate* (Cape Town, 1976)

Cole, M., *South Africa* (London, 1964)

Cole, M.L. and Gwynn, S. (eds), *Memoirs of Sir Lowry Cole* (London, 1934)

Colenso, J.W. (ed. Rees, W.), *Letters from Natal* (Pietermaritzburg, 1958)

Collelo, T., *Angola: A Country Study* (Washington, 1991)

Collins, W.W., *Free Statia* (Cape Town, 1907, 1967)

Colvin, I., *The Life of Jameson* (London, 1922)

Commonwealth Secretariat Mission to South Africa (London, 1986)

Coolhaas, W.P. (ed.), *Generale Missiven van Gouverneurs-General en Raden aan Heren XVII der VOC* (7 vols, The Hague, 1960–79)

Cope, N., *To Bind the Nation* (Pietermaritzburg, 1993)

Corder, H., *Judges at Work* (Cape Town, 1984)

Cory, G.M., *The Rise of South Africa* (London, 1910–30)

Cradock, P., *In Pursuit of British Interests* (London, 1997)

Craig, G.A., *Germany* (Oxford, 1981)

Crais, C.C., *The Making of the Colonial Order* (Cambridge, 1992)

Crealock, J., *Frontier War Journal* (Cape Town, 1989)

Crossley, J. and Blandford, J., *The DCO Story* (London, 1975)

Crowder, M., *The Flogging of Phinehas McIntosh* (New Haven, 1988)

Crwys-Williams, J., *South African Despatches* (Johannesburg, 1989)

Cullman, P.R.J., *Gordon* (Winchester, n.d.)

Currey, R.N., *Letters of a Natal Sheriff* (Cape Town, 1968)

Curtis, L., *With Milner in South Africa* (Oxford, 1951)

Dachs, A.J., *Papers of John Mackenzie* (3 vols, Johannesburg, 1975)

Dadoo, Y.M., *South Africa's Freedom Struggle* (New Delhi, 1990)

Dale, R., *Botswana's Search for Autonomy* (Westport, 1995)

Dampier, W., *A Voyage Round the World* (London, 1703)

Davenport, T.R.H., *The Afrikaner Bond* (London, 1966)

Davenport, T.R.H., *A Modern History of South Africa* (London, 1977, 1991)

Davey, A.M., *The British Pro-Boers 1877–1902* (Cape Town, 1978)

Davey, A.M. (ed.), *Breaker Morant and the Bushveldt Carbineers* (Cape Town, 1987)

Davids, A., *The Mosques of Bo-Kaap* (Cape Town, 1980)

Davidson, B., *The African Past* (London, 1964)

Davidson, B. et al, *Southern Africa* (London, 1976)

Davis, D.B., *Slavery and Human Progress* (Oxford, 1984)

Davis, S.M., *Apartheid's Rebels* (New Haven, 1987)

Dean, E. et al, *History in Black and White* (Paris, 1987)

Debroey, S., *South Africa to the Sources of Apartheid* (London, 1989)

De Gruchy, J.W., *Liberating Reformed Theology* (Grand Rapids, 1991)

De Kiewiet, C.W., *A History of South Africa, Social and Economic* (London, 1941)

De Kiewiet, C.W., *The Imperial Factor in South Africa* (London, 1937, 1965)

De Klerk, E.S., *History of the Netherlands East Indies* (2 vols, Amsterdam, 1975)

De Klerk, M. (ed.), *A Harvest of Discontent* (Cape Town, 1991)

De Klerk, W.A., *The Puritans in Africa* (London, 1975)

De Klerk, W.A., *The Second (R)evolution* (Johannesburg, 1984)

Bibliography

De Klerk, W.A., *F.W. de Klerk* (Johannesburg, 1991)

De Kock, V., *Those in Bondage* (Cape Town, 1950)

De Kock, W.J. et al (eds), *Dictionary of South African Biography* (5 vols, Cape Town/Pretoria, 1968–87)

De Mist, J.A., *Memorandum: Containing Recommendations for the Administration of Government at the Cape of Good Hope* (Stellenbosch, 1920)

Denoon, D., *Southern Africa Since 1800* (London, 1972)

Denoon, D., *A Grand Illusion* (London, 1973)

De Villiers, L., *South Africa: A Skunk Among Nations* (London, 1975)

De Villiers, L., *In Sight of Surrender* (Westport, 1995)

De Villiers, P., *PW* (Cape Town, 1984)

Dewaldt, F. (ed.), *Native Uprisings in South-West Africa* (Salisbury (USA), 1976)

Di Capelli, W.B.E. Paravicini (ed. de Kock, W.J.), *Reize in de Binnen-Landen van Zuid Afrika* (Cape Town, 1965)

Dieterlen, H., *Eugene Casalis* (Paris, 1930)

Doxey, G.V., *The Industrial Colour Bar in South Africa* (Cape Town, 1961)

Dracopoli, *Sir Andries Stockenström* (Cape Town, 1961)

Drew, A. (ed.), *South Africa's Radical Tradition 1909–1950* (Cape Town, 1996)

Dreyer, L., *The Modern African Elites of South Africa* (London, 1989)

Dreyer, P., *Martyrs and Fanatics* (New York, 1980)

Driver, C.J., *Patrick Duncan* (London, 1980)

Dugmore, H.H., *The Reminiscences of an Albany Settler* (Grahamstown, 1871)

Duignan, P. and Gann, L.H. (eds), *Colonialism in Africa 1870–1960* (5 vols, Cambridge, 1969–75)

Duly, L.C., *British Land Policy at the Cape 1795–1844* (Durham, NC, 1968)

Duminy, A. and Guest, B., *Interfering in Politics* (Johannesburg, 1987)

Duminy, A. and Guest, B. (eds) *Natal and Zululand* (Pietermaritzburg, 1989)

Du Plessis, H. and T., *Afrikaans en Taalpolitiek* (Pretoria, 1987)

Du Plessis, I.D., *The Cape Malays* (Cape Town, 1972)

Du Plessis, J., *1,000 Miles in the Heat of Africa* (London, 1905)

Du Pre, R.H., *Separate but Unequal* (Johannesburg, 1994)

Du Toit, A. and Giliomee, H., *Afrikaner Political Thought* (Vol. 1, Berkeley, 1983)

Edelstein, M., *Overseas Investment in the Age of High Imperialism* (New York, 1982)

Edgecombe, D.R. et al (eds), *The Debate on Zulu Origins* (Pietermaritzburg, 1992)

Edwards, I.E., *The 1820 Settlers in Southern Africa* (London, 1934)

Eldredge, E.A., *A South African Kingdom: The Pursuit of Security in Nineteenth-Century Lesotho* (Cape Town, 1993)

Eldredge, E.A. and Morton, F. (eds), *Slavery in South Africa: Captive Labour on the Dutch Frontier* (Pietermaritzburg, 1995)

Ellis, S. and Sechaba, T., *Comrades Against Apartheid* (London, 1992)

Eloff, T., *Government, Justice and Race Classification* (Stellenbosch, 1990)

Elphick, R., *Kraal and Castle: The Khoikhoi and the Founding of White South Africa* (New Haven and London, 1977)

Elphick, R. and Giliomee, H. (eds), *The Shaping of South African Society 1652–1820* (Cape Town and London, 1971)

Emden, P.H., *Randlords* (London, 1935)

Engelenburg, F.V., *General Louis Botha* (London, 1929)

Enklaar, I.H., *The Life and Work of Dr J. Th. van der Kemp* (Cape Town, 1988)

Esterhuyse, W.P., *Anton Rupert: Advocate of Hope* (Cape Town, 1986)

Eybers, G.W. (ed.), *Select Constitutional Documents 1875–1910* (London, 1918)

Fage, J., *Atlas of South African History* (London, 1958)

Favre, E., *Le 25 ans de Coillard au Lessouto* (Paris, 1931)

Feit, E., *African Opposition in South Africa* (Stanford, 1967)

Ferguson, W.T. and Immelman, R.F.M., *Sir John Herschel and Education at the Cape 1834–40* (Cape Town, 1961)

Fisher, J., *The Afrikaners* (London, 1969)

Fisher, J., *That Miss Hobhouse* (London, 1971)

Fisher, J., *Paul Kruger* (London, 1975)

Fitzpatrick, J.P., *The Transvaal from Within* (London, 1900)

Fitzpatrick, J.P., *South African Memoirs* (London, 1932, Johannesburg, 1972)

Fitzpatrick, J.P., *Selected Papers 1888–1906* (Johannesburg, 1970)

Frankel, P.H., *Pretoria's Praetorians* (Cambridge, 1984)

Frazer, M. and Jeeves, A., *All that Glittered* (Cape Town, 1977)

Fredrickson, G., *White Supremacy* (Oxford, 1981)

Fredrickson, G., *The Arrogance of Race* (Middletown, 1988)

French, G., *Lord Chelmsford and the Zulu War* (London, 1939)

French, P., *Younghusband* (London, 1994)

French, P., *Liberty or Death* (London, 1997)

Freund, B., *The Making of Contemporary Africa* (Bloemfontein, 1984)

Fuller, C. (ed.), *Louis Trigardt's Trek across the Drakensberg 1837–8* (Cape Town, 1932)

Furlong, P.J., *Between Crown and Swastika* (Hanover (USA), 1991)

Furnivall, J.S., *Colonial Policy and Practice* (Cambridge, 1948)

Galbraith, J.S., *Reluctant Empire* (Berkeley, 1963)

Galbraith, J.S., *Crown and Charter* (Berkeley, 1974)

Galton, F., *Narrative of an Explorer in Tropical South Africa* (London, 1883)

Geldenhuys, D., *The Diplomacy of Isolation* (Johannesburg, 1984)

Gerhart, G.M., *Black Power in South Africa* (Berkeley and London, 1978)

Geyl, P., *The Netherlands in the Seventeenth Century* (London, 1961)

Bibliography

Gibson, A.G.S., *Eight Years in Kaffraria* (London, 1890)

Gilbey, E., *The Lady* (London, 1993)

Giliomee, H. and Gagiano, J., *The Elusive Search for Peace* (Oxford, 1990)

Giliomee, H. et al (eds), *The Bold Experiment* (Southern, 1994)

Gill, S. et al, *Lesotho* (Bergen Dal, n.d.)

Godée-Molsbergen, E.C., *Reizen in Zuid Afrika in de Hollandse Tijd* (4 vols, The Hague, 1916–32)

Golan, D., *Inventing Shaka* (Boulder, London, 1994)

Golden, R. (ed.), *Petticoat Pioneers* (Pietermaritzburg, 1988)

Goodfellow, C.F., *Great Britain and South African Confederation 1870–1881* (Cape Town, 1966)

Gordon, C.T., *The Growth of Boer Opposition to Kruger* (Cape Town, 1970)

Gordon, Lady Duff, *Letters from the Cape* (London, 1927)

Grafton, A., *The Footnote* (London, 1997)

Granberg, P. and Parkinson, J.R., *Botswana* (London, 1988)

Gregory, J., *Goodbye Bafana* (London, 1995)

Grey, Lord, *The Colonial Policy of Lord John Russell's Administration* (London, 1853)

Griffith, P.R. (ed. Brain, J.B.), *Cape Diary* (Cape Town, 1988)

Grundlingh, A., *Fighting Their Own War* (Johannesburg, 1987)

Guest, B. and Sellers, J.M. (eds), *Enterprise and Exploitation in a Victorian Colony* (Pietermaritzburg, 1985)

Gump, J.O., *The Formation of the Zulu Kingdom* (San Francisco, 1990)

Gutteridge, W. (ed.), *South Africa from Apartheid to National Unity 1984–1994* (Aldershot, 1995)

Guy, J., *The Destruction of the Zulu Kingdom* (London, 1979)

Guy, J., *The Heretic: The Life of John William Colenso* (Pietermaritzburg, 1983)

Haggard, H.R., *The Days of my Life* (London, 1926)

Hahn, T., *Tsuni-//Goam: The Superior Being of the Khoi Khoi* (London, 1881)

Hailey, Lord, *The Republic of South Africa and the High Commission Territories* (London, 1963)

Hall, H.D. and Wrigley, C.C., *Studies of Overseas Shipping* (London, 1956)

Hall, H.L., *The Colonial Office* (London, 1937)

Hall, M., *Farmers, Kings and Traders: The People of South Africa 200–1860* (Chicago, 1987)

Hall, R., *Empires of the Monsoon* (London, 1997)

Hamilton, C.A. (ed.), *The Mfecane Aftermath* (Johannesburg, 1995)

Hamilton, E.W. (ed. Bahlman, D.W.R.), *Sir Edward Walter Hamilton* (London, 1972)

Hancock, W.K., *Smuts* (2 vols, Cambridge, 1962, 1968)

Hancock, W.K. and van der Poel, J. (eds), *Selections from the Smuts Papers* (7 vols, Cape Town, 1966–73)

Harrison, N., *Winnie Mandela: Mother of a Nation* (London, 1985)

Hartshorne, K., *Crisis and Challenge: Black Education 1910–1990* (Oxford, 1992)

Harvey, C. and Lewis, S.R., *Policy Choice and Development Performance in Botswana* (London, 1990)

Hattersley, A., *British Settlement in Natal* (London, 1950)

Headlam, C., *The Milner Papers: South Africa 1897–8* (2 vols, London, 1931)

Hellman, E. and Lever, H. (eds), *Race Relations in South Africa 1929–79* (London, 1979)

Hengeveld, R. and Rodenburg, J., *Embargo* (Amsterdam, 1995)

Herm, G., *The Phoenicians* (London, 1975)

Herrman, L., *A History of the Jews in South Africa* (London, 1950)

Herschel, J.H. (ed. Evans, D.S. and C.), *At the Cape* (Austin, 1969)

Hirson, B., *Revolutions in my Life* (Johannesburg, 1995)

Historical Manuscripts Commission Report on Manuscripts in the Welsh Language (London, 1905)

Hobart, H.D. and Dagut, J. (eds), *Source Material in the South African Economy* (2 vols, London, 1972)

Hobart, H.D., *The South African Economy* (London, 1976)

Hobhouse, E. (ed. van Reenen, R.), *Boer War Letters* (Cape Town, 1984)

Hocking, A., *Oppenheimer and Son* (Johannesburg, 1973)

Hodgson, J., *The God of the Xhosa* (Cape Town, 1962)

Hodgson, J., *Princess Emma* (Cape Town, 1987)

Hodgson, M.L. and Ballinger, W.D., *The Bechuanaland Protectorate* (Alice, 1933)

Hoe, S., *The Private Life of Old Hong Kong* (Hong Kong, 1991)

Hofmeyr, J.H. and Reitz, F.W., *The Life of Jan Hendrik Hofmeyr* (Cape Town, 1913)

Holden, W.C., *A Brief History of Methodism in South Africa* (London, 1987)

Horne, A., *Macmillan* (2 vols, London, 1989)

Howe, G., *Conflict of Loyalty* (London, 1994)

Hublot, E., *Seven Years in South Africa* (London, 1881)

Huttenback, R.A., *Racism and Empire* (Harare and London, 1976)

Huttenback, R.A., *Gandhi in South Africa* (Ithaca (USA), 1971)

Hyam, R., *Elgin and Churchill at the Colonial Office 1905–08* (London, 1968)

Hyam, R., *The Failure of South African Expansion* (London, 1972)

Hyam, R. and Marten, G., *Reappraisals in British Imperial History* (London, 1975)

Hyam, R., *Britain's Imperial Century 1815–1914* (London, 1976)

Hyatt, S.P., *The Northward Trek* (London, 1906)

Immelman, R.F.M., *Men of Good Hope: The Cape Town Chamber of Commerce* (Cape Town, 1955)

Innes, D., *Anglo-American and the Rise of Modern South Africa* (London, 1984)

Innes, D. et al (eds), *Power and Profit* (Cape Town, 1992)

Innes, J.R. (ed. Wright, H.M.) *Selected Correspondence 1884–1902* (Cape Town, 1972)

Israel, J.I., *Dutch Primacy in World Trade 1585–1740* (Oxford, 1987)

Jaarboek van het Central Bureau voor Genealogie (Vol. 38, The Hague, 1984)

Jabavu, D.D.T., *The Life of John Tengo Jabavu* (Lovedale, 1922)

Jabavu, D.D.T., *Findings of the All-African Convention* (Lovedale, 1935)

Jabavu, N., *The Ochre People* (London, 1963)

Jacks, B., *South Africa: An Imperial Dilemma* (Albuquerque, 1967)

James, L., *The Rise and Fall of the British Empire* (London, 1994)

James, W.G. and Simmons, M. (eds), *The Angry Divide* (London, 1989)

James, W.G. and Simmons, M. (eds), *Class, Caste and Colour* (London, 1992)

Jeppe, F., *The Transvaal Almanac 1877*

Jingoes, S.J., *A Chief is a Chief by the People* (London, 1975)

Joffe, J.G. and Koff, M., *The Rivonia Trial* (typescript, n.d)

Johnson, R.W. and Schlemmer, L., *Launching Democracy in South Africa* (London, 1996)

Johnson, T., Rabinowitz, H. et al, *Rock Paintings of the South-Western Cape* (Cape Town, 1959)

Johnston, H.J.M., *British Emigration Policy 1815–1830* (London, 1972)

Johnstone, F., *Class, Race and Gold* (London, 1956)

Joseph, F.M., *Best of Bedfellows* (New York, 1988)

Joseph, H., *Side by Side* (London, 1986)

Juckes, T.J., *Opposition in South Africa* (London and Westport, 1995)

Juta, M., *The Pace of the Ox* (London, 1937)

Kadalie, C., *My Life and the ICU* (London, 1970)

Kance-Berman, J., *Political Violence in South Africa* (Johannesburg, 1993)

Karis, T.G. and Carter, G.M. (eds), *From Protest to Challenge* (4 vols, Stanford, 1972)

Katzen, L., *Gold in the South African Economy* (Cape Town, 1964)

Keegan, T., *Colonial South Africa and the Origins of the Racial Order* (Cape Town, 1996)

Kimble, H.T. (ed.), *Esmeraldo de Situ Orbis of D. Pacheeo Pereira* (London, 1937)

King, P., *The Viceroy's Fall* (London, 1986)

Kirby, P.R., *Andrew Smith and Natal* (Cape Town, 1955)

Kircherer, *Narrative of his Mission to the Hottentots* (London, 1804)

Knaplund, P., *Gladstone and Britain's Imperial Policy* (London, 1927)

Kotze, D.J. (ed.), *Letters of the American Missionaries 1835–1838* (Cape Town, 1958)

Kotze, J.C., *In their Shoes: Understanding Black South Africans Through their Experiences of Life* (Kenwyn (Juta), 1993)

Krige, E.J. and Comaroff, J.L., *Essays on African Marriage in Southern Africa* (Cape Town, 1981)

Krikler, J., *Revolution from Above, Rebellion from Below* (Oxford, 1993)

Kruger, D.W. (ed.), *South African Parties and Policies 1910–60* (Cape Town, 1960)

Kruger, D.W., *Paul Kruger* (2 vols, Johannesburg, 1961, 1963)

Kruger, R., *Goodbye, Dolly Grey* (London, 1959)

Kruger, S.J.P., *Memoirs* (London, 1902)

Kubicek, R.V., *Economic Imperialism in Theory and Practice* (Durham (USA), 1979)

Kuper, L., *An African Bourgeoisie: Race, Class and Politics in South Africa* (New Haven, 1965)

Kynaston, D., *The City of London* (2 vols, London, 1995)

Laband, J., *Fight us in the Open* (Pietermaritzburg, 1985)

Laband, J., *Kingdom in Crisis: The Zulu Response to British Invasion* (Manchester, 1992)

Lagdon, G., *The Basuto* (London, 1909)

Lamb, R., *The Macmillan Years 1957–63* (London, 1995)

Lamar, H. and Thomson, L. (eds), *The Frontier in History* (Yale, 1981)

Lambert, J., *Betrayed Trust* (Scotsville, 1995)

Landau, P.S., *The Realm of the Word* (London, 1995)

Lanning, G. and Mueller, M., *Africa Undermined* (London, 1979)

Lapping, B., *Apartheid: A History* (London, 1986)

Latrobe, C.I., *Journal of a Visit to South Africa 1815 and 1816* (London, 1818)

Laurence, J.C., *Race, Propaganda and South Africa* (London, 1979)

Lazerson, J.L., *Against the Tide: Whites in the Struggle Against Apartheid* (Boulder, 1994)

Leach, G., *South Africa: No Easy Path to Peace* (London, 1986)

Leach, G., *The Afrikaners: Their Last Great Trek* (London, 1989)

Le Cordeur, B. and Saunders, C., *The Kitchinghman Papers* (Johannesburg, 1976)

Le Cordeur, B. and Saunders, C., *The War of the Axe 1847* (Johannesburg, 1981)

Leftwich, A., *South Africa: Economic Growth and Political Change* (London, 1974)

Lehmann, J.H., *All Sir Garnet* (London, 1964)

Lehmann, J.H., *Remember you are an Englishman* (London, 1977)

Leibbrandt, H.C.V. (ed.), *Précis of the Archives of the Cape of Good Hope; Letters Despatched from the Cape; Letters Received by the Cape 1649–62; Journals 1671–74, 1676, 1699–1739*

Leibbrandt, H.C.V., *The Rebellion of 1815* (Cape Town and London, 1902)

Le May, G.H.L., *British Supremacy in South Africa 1899–1907* (Oxford, 1965)

Le May, G.H.L., *The Afrikaners* (Oxford, 1995)

Leviseur, S. (ed. Schoeman, K.), *Memoirs* (Cape Town, 1982)

Lewis, D.L., *W.E.B. du Bois* (New York, 1993)

Lewis, G., *Between the Wire and the Wall* (Cape Town, 1987)

Lewis, J., *Industrialisation and Trade Union Organisation in South Africa, 1924–55* (Cape Town, 1984)

Lewsen, P., *John Xavier Merriman* (New Haven and London, 1982)

Leyds, W.S., *The First Annexation of the Transvaal* (London, 1906)

Lichtenstein, H., *Travels in Africa* (2 vols, London, 1812, Cape Town, 1928–30)

Liebenberg, B.J., *Andries Pretorius in Natal* (Pretoria, 1977)

Liebenberg, B.J. and Spies, S.B., *South Africa in the Twentieth Century* (Pretoria, 1993)

Limb, P., *The ANC and Black Workers: An Annotated Bibliography* (London, 1993)

Lindley, A.F., *Adamantia* (London, 1873)

Lipton, M., *Capitalism and Apartheid* (Aldershot, 1985)

Lobban, M., *White Man's Justice* (Oxford, 1996)

Locke, R., *Blood on the Painted Mountain* (London, 1955)

Lockhard, J.G. and Woodhouse, C.M., *Rhodes* (London, 1963)

Lodge, T., *Black Politics in South Africa Since 1945* (London and New York, 1983)

Lovett, R., *History of the London Missionary Society* (London, 1889)

Lownie, A., *John Buchan* (London, 1995)

Lucas, T.J., *The Zulus and the British Frontiers* (London, 1879)

Luthuli, A., *Let my People Go* (London, 1962)

McCaughey, D. et al, *Victoria's Colonial Governors* (Melbourne, 1993)

McCracken, J.L., *The Cape Parliament* (Oxford, 1967)

McCourt, E., *Remember Butler* (London, 1967)

Machobane, L.B.B.J., *Government and Change in Lesotho* (London, 1990)

McIlwaine, J., *Africa: A Guide to Reference Material* (London, 1993)

Mackay, J., *The Last Kaffir War* (Cape Town, 1978)

Mackenzie, J., *Ten Years North of the Orange River* (London, 1871)

Mackenzie, J. (ed. Dachs, A.J.), *Papers* (Johannesburg, 1975)

Mackenzie, W.D., *John Mackenzie* (London, 1902)

Macmillan, H. and Marks, S. (eds), *Africa and Empire* (London, 1987)

Macmillan, M.A., *Sir Henry Barkly: Mediator and Moderator* (Cape Town, 1978)

Macmillan, W.M., *The Cape Coloured Question* (London, 1928)

Macmillan, W.M., *The Road to Self Rule* (London, 1959)

Madden, F. and Fieldhouse, D. (eds), *Imperial Reconstruction 1763–1840* (Westpoint, 1987)

Maggs, T.M.O.C., *Iron Age Communities of the Southern High Veld* (Pietermaritzburg, 1976)

Makgetia, N. and Seidman, A., *Outposts of Monopoly Capitalism* (Westpoint and London, 1980)

Malamay, R.B., *The Boer War in American Politics and Diplomacy* (New York and London, 1994)

Malan, R., *My Traitor's Heart* (London, 1990)

Malherbe, E.C., *Education in South Africa* (2 vols, Cape Town, 1975, 1977)

Malherbe, V.C., *What They Said 1795–1910* (Cape Town, 1971)

Mandela, N., *Nelson Mandela Speaks* (New York, 1993)

Mandela, N., *A Long Walk to Freedom* (London, 1994)

Mangaliso, N.A., *The South African Mosaic* (London, 1985)

Manganyi, N.C. and du Toit, A. (eds), *Political Violence and the Struggles in South Africa* (London, 1990)

Marais J.S., *The Cape Coloured People* (Johannesburg, 1968)

Marais, J.S., *The Fall of Kruger's Republic* (Oxford, 1961)

Maré, G. and Hamilton, G., *An Appetite for Power* (Bloomington, 1987)

Marizo, K.A., *Dominion, Resistance and Social Change in South Africa* (London, 1992)

Marks, S., *Reluctant Rebellion* (Oxford, 1970)

Marks, S. and Atmore, A., *Economy and Society in Pre-Industrial South Africa* (London, 1980)

Marks, S. (ed.), *Not Either an Experimental Doll* (Pietermaritzburg, 1987)

Marks, S. and Trapido, S. (eds), *Politics of Race, Class and Nationalism in Twentieth-Century South Africa* (London, 1987)

Marquand, L., *People and Policies of South Africa* (Cape Town, 1960)

Marsh, P.T., *Joseph Chamberlain: Entrepreneur in Politics* (New Haven and London, 1994)

Martin, M., *Time of Agony, Time of Destiny* (London, 1987)

Martineau J., *The Life and Correspondence of Sir Bartle Frere* (London, 1985)

Marwick, B.A., *The Swazi* (Cambridge, 1940)

Mathabane, M., *Kaffir Boy* (London, 1986)

Mathews, A.S., *Law, Order and Liberty in South Africa* (Cape Town, 1971)

Mathurin, O.C., *Henry Sylvester Williams* (London, 1976)

Matthew, H.C.G., *Gladstone 1875–98* (Oxford, 1995)

Matthews, Z.K., *Freedom for my People* (Cape Town, 1981)

Mauch, C. (ed. Burke, E.), *Journals 1869–72* (Salisbury, 1969)

Maylam, P., *History of the African People of South Africa* (Cape Town, 1986)

Maynier, H., *The Cape Coloured People* (Cape Town, 1937)

Maynier, H., *The First Boer Republic* (Cape Town, 1944)

Mazrui, A.A. (ed.), *The Warrior Tradition in Modern Africa* (Leiden, 1977)

Mbeki, G., *The Peasants' Revolt* (London, 1964)

Meer, F., *Race and Suicide in South Africa* (London, 1976)

Meer, F., *Higher than Hope* (Johannesburg, 1988, London, 1990)

Meintjes, J., *Sandile: The Fall of the Xhosa Nation* (Cape Town, 1971)

Meintjes, J., *President Paul Kruger* (London, 1974)

Meli, F., *South Africa Belongs to Us: A History of the ANC* (Harare and London, 1988)

Mendelsohn, R., *Sammy Marks* (Cape Town, 1991)

Mentzel, O.F., *Life at the Cape in the Mid-Eighteenth Century* (Cape Town, 1919)

Meredith, M., *Nelson Mandela* (London, 1997)

Merriman, J.X. (ed. Lewsen, P.), *Selections from the Correspondence of J.X. Merriman* (4 vols, Cape Town, 1960–69)

Merriman, N.J., *Passages of Missionary Life* (London, 1853)

Michelman, C., *The Black Sash of South Africa* (Oxford, 1975)

Millar, A.K., *Plantagenet in South Africa: Lord Charles Somerset* (Cape Town and London, 1965)

Minter, W., *Apartheid's Contras* (Johannesburg, 1994)

Modisane, B., *Blame me on History* (London, 1963)

Moffat, R. (ed. Wallis, J.R.R.), *Matabele Journals* (2 vols, London, 1945)

Mokgatle, N., *Autobiography of an Unknown South African* (London, 1971)

Mokoena, K., *South Africa and the United States: The Declassified History* (New York, 1993)

Molema, S.M., *The Bantu Past* (Edinburgh, 1920)

Molema, S.M., *Chief Moroka* (Cape Town, 1951)

Molteno, J.T., *Further South African Reflections* (London, 1928)

Molteno, P. (ed. Solomon, V.), *Selections from Correspondence 1892–1914* (Cape Town, 1981)

Moneypenny, W.F. and Buckle, G., *Life of Disraeli* (London, 1910–20)

Moodie, D. and Philip, J., *Correspondence* (Cape Town and London, 1849)

Moodie, D., *The Record: A Series of Official Papers* (Amsterdam, 1960)

Moodie, D.C.F., *History of the Battles and cetera in Southern Africa* (2 vols, London, 1888, 1968)

Moodie, T.D., *The Rise of Afrikanerdom* (Berkeley, 1975)

Moodie, T.D with Ndatshe, V., *Going for Gold* (Berkeley, 1994)

Morrell, W.P., *British Colonial Policy in the Age of Peel and Russell* (Oxford, 1930)

Morrell, W.P., *British Colonial Policy in the Mid-Victorian Age* (Oxford, 1969)

Morris, D.R., *The Washing of the Spears* (London, 1990)

Moss, R., *Shouting at the Crocodile* (Boston, 1990)

Mostert, N., *Frontiers* (London, 1992)

Muller, C.F.J., *Die Britse Owerheid en die Groot Trek* (Pretoria, 1969)

Murray, M.J., *Revolution Deferred* (London, 1994)

Muthien, Y., *State and Resistance in South Africa 1939–65* (Aldershot, 1994)

Mzala, *Gatsha Buthelezi* (London, 1988)

Nadoo, J., *Tracking Down Historical Myths* (Johannesburg, 1989)

Nasson, W.R., *Abraham Esau's War* (Cambridge, 1991)

Neame, L.E., *The History of Apartheid* (London, 1962)

Needham, J., *Science and Civilisation in China* (Cambridge, 1954)

Neill, S., *Colonialism and Christian Missions* (London, 1966)

Newton, A.P., *The Unification of South Africa* (2 vols, London, 1924)

Ngubo, A., 'The Development of African Political Protest in Southern African 1882–1910' (unpublished thesis, UCAL, 1973)

Nicholls, D., *The Lost Prime Minister* (London, 1995)

Nicol, M., *A Good-Looking Corpse* (London, 1991)

Nienabar, G.S. and Raven-Hart, R. (eds), *Johan Danie Buttner's Account* (Cape Town, 1970)

Nimocks, W., *Milner's Young Men: The 'Kindergarten' in Edwardian Imperial Affairs* (London, 1970)

Noble, J., *South Africa Past and Present* (London and Cape Town, 1877)

Norval, A.J., *Deconstructing Apartheid Discourse* (London and New York, 1996)

Odendaal, A., *Vukani Bantu!* (Cape Town, 1984)

Oliver, R., *The African Experience* (London, 1991)

O'Meara, D., *Volkskapitalisme* (Cambridge, 1983)

O'Meara, D., *Forty Lost Years* (Randburg and Athens (USA), 1996)

Omer-Cooper, J.D., *The Zulu Aftermath* (London, 1966)

Osia, K., *Israel, South Africa and Black Africa* (Washington, 1981)

Owen, K., *These Times* (Johannesburg, 1992)

Pachai, B., *The International Aspects of the South African Indian Question* (Cape Town, 1971)

Pachai, B., *Mahatma Gandhi in South Africa* (Johannesburg, n.d.)

Pakenham, T., *The Boer War* (London, 1979)

Pakenham, T., *The Scramble for Africa* (London, 1991)

Palmer, R., *The Age of Democratic Revolution* (Princetown, 1964)

Palmerston, Lord, *Letters to Laurence Sulivan* (London, 1979)

Parsons, N., *A New History of Southern Africa* (Zimbabwe, 1982, 1991)

Paton, A., *Hofmeyr* (Cape Town, 1964)

Pauw, B.A., *The Second Generation* (Cape Town, 1962)

Peires, J.B., *The House of Phalo: A History of the Xhosa People* (Berkeley and London, 1981)

Peires, J.B., *The Dead will Arise* (Johannesburg, 1989)

Pelzer, A.N., *Verwoerd Speaks* (Johannesburg, 1966)

Perham, M. and Curtis, L., *The Protectorates and South Africa* (London, 1935)

Perham, P., *The Colonial Reckoning* (London, 1961)

Peters, P.E., *Dividing the Commons: Politics, Policy and Culture in Botswana* (Charlottesville, 1994)

Peterson, R.W. (ed.), *South Africa and Apartheid* (New York, 1971)

Bibliography

Philips, L., *Some South African Recollections* (London, 1899)

Pim, A., *The Financial and Economic Position of Swaziland* (London, 1932)

Pim, A., *The Financial and Economic Position of the Bechuanaland Protectorate* (London, 1934)

Pirow, O., *J.B.M. Herzog* (Cape Town, 1957)

Plaatjes, S., *Native Life in South Africa* (Cape Town, 1957)

Plumtre, G.E., *Edward VII* (London, 1995)

Pollock, J., *Gordon* (London, 1993)

Pogrund, B., *Sobukwe and Apartheid* (London and Johannesburg, 1990)

Porter, A.N., *The Press as Opposition* (London, 1975)

Porter, A.N., *Origins of the South African War: Joseph Chamberlain and the Diplomacy of Imperialism* (Manchester, 1980)

Porter, R., *The Greatest Benefit to Mankind* (London, 1997)

Pottinger, E., *The War of the Axe* (Johannesburg, 1980)

Pottinger, E., *The Imperial Presidency* (Johannesburg, 1988)

Preston, A. and Major, J., *Send a Gunboat* (London, 1967)

Pringle, J.A., *The Conservationists and the Killers* (Cape Town, 1982)

Pringle, T., *Narrative of a Residence in South Africa* (Cape Town, 1966)

Rae, I., *J. Barry* (London, 1958)

Ramphele, M., *Across Boundaries* (New York, 1996)

Randall, V.J., *The Theory of the Dutch Disease and the Economics of Gold Mining in South Africa 1970–1989* (Munich, 1991)

Raven-Hart, R., *Before van Riebeeck* (Cape Town, 1967)

Read, J., *The Kat River Settlement* (Cape Town, 1852)

Reader, D.H., *The Black Man's Portion* (Cape Town, 1961)

Renwick, R., *Unconventional Diplomacy in South Africa* (London, 1997)

Rhoodie, E., *P.W. Botha: The Last Betrayal* (Melville, 1989)

Rich, P.B., *Hope and Despair* (London, 1993)

Richardson, L. (ed. Davey, A.M.), *Selected Correspondence* (Cape Town, 1977)

Ridley, G., *Bend'Or* (London, 1985)

Roberts, B., *Cecil Rhodes* (London, 1987)

Roberts, B., *Those Bloody Women* (London, 1991)

Robertson, A.S., *Itinerary of the Colony of the Cape of Good Hope* (Cape Town, 1835)

Robinson, A.M.L. (ed.), *Letters of Lady Anne Barnard* (Cape Town, 1973)

Robinson, J., *A Lifetime in South Africa* (London, 1900)

Rodger, N.A.M., *The Safeguard of the Sea* (London, 1997)

Rorke, M., *Her Amazing Experiences* (London, 1939)

Rose, B. and Tunmer, R., *Documents in South African Education* (Johannesburg, 1975)

Rosenthal, E., *Gold! Gold! Gold!* (London and Johannesburg, 1970)

Ross, A., *John Philip* (Aberdeen, 1986)

Ross, R., *Adam Kok's Griquas* (Cambridge, 1976)

Ross, R., *Cape of Torments: Slavery and Resistance in South Africa* (London, 1983)

Ross, R., *Beyond the Pale* (London and Hanover (USA), 1993)

Rotberg, R.L., *The Founder: Cecil Rhodes and the Pursuit of Power* (New York and Oxford, 1988)

Roux, E., *Time Longer than Rope* (London, 1964)

Royle, T., *The Kitchener Enigma* (London, 1985)

Rutherford, J., *Sir George Grey* (London, 1961)

Sachs, A., *Justice in South Africa* (Berkeley, 1973)

Sacks, B., *South Africa: An Imperial Dilemma* (Albuquerque, 1967)

Salaman, R., *The History and Social Influence of the Potato* (Cambridge, 1949)

Sales, J., *Mission Stations and Coloured Communities of the Eastern Cape 1800–1852* (Cape Town, 1975)

Sampson, A., *Black and Gold* (London, 1987)

Sander, I.F., *Rand Club Centenary* (Johannesburg, 1987)

Saunders, C. and Derricout, R. (eds), *Beyond the Cape Frontier* (London, 1974)

Saunders, C., *Historical Dictionary of South Africa* (New Jersey, 1982)

Saunders, C., *The Making of the South African Past* (Cape Town, 1988)

Schama, S., *Patriots and Liberators* (London, 1977)

Schama, S., *The Embarrassment of Riches* (London, 1988)

Schapera, I. (ed.), *Western Civilization and the Natives of South Africa* (London, 1934)

Schapera, I. (ed.), *The Bantu-Speaking Tribes of South Africa* (London, 1937)

Schapera, I. (ed.), *Early Cape Hottentots* (Cape Town, 1938)

Schapera, I., *Apprenticeship at Kuruman* (London, 1951)

Schoeman, K. (ed.), *The Free State Mission* (Cape Town, 1986)

Schoeman, K. (ed.), *The British Presence in Transorangia, 1845–54* (Cape Town, 1992)

Schoeman, K., *Griqua Records* (Cape Town, 1996)

Schoeman, K., *Only an Anguish to Live Here: Olive Schreiner and the Anglo–Boer War* (Cape Town, 1992)

Schoeman, K., *Die Wêreld van Susanna Smit 1799–1863* (Cape Town, 1995)

Schoeman, K., *Die Brieweboek van James Cameron* (Cape Town)

Scholte, W., *British Overseas Trade* (Oxford, 1952)

Schoon, H.F. (ed.), *The Diary of Erasmus Smit* (Cape Town, 1972)

Schreuder, D.M., *Gladstone and Kruger: Liberal Government and Colonial Home Rule 1880–85* (London, 1969)

Schreuder, D.M., *The Scramble for Southern Africa 1877–1985* (Cambridge, 1980)

Schrire, E. (ed.), *Malan to De Klerk* (London, 1994)

Schrive, R. (ed.), *Wealth or Poverty* (Cape Town, 1992)

Schwaer, J.F. and Pape, B., *Die Deutsche in Kaffraria* (Pinetown)

Sertfontein, J.H.P., *Brotherhood of Power* (London, 1979)

Seymour, S.M., *Bantu Law in South Africa* (Cape Town, 1970)

Shack, W.A. and Skinner, E.P., *Strangers in African Societies* (Berkeley and London, 1979)

Shaw, B., *Memorials of South Africa* (London, 1840)

Shaw, T.M., *Reformism and Revision in Africa's Political Economy in the 1990s* (London, 1993)

Shepherd, J., *In the Shadow of the Drakensberg* (Durban, 1976)

Shepherd, R.H.W., *Lovedale, South Africa* (Lovedale, 1946)

Shimoni, G., *Jews and Zionism: The South African Experience* (Oxford, 1980)

Shorten, J.R., *The Johannesburg Saga* (Johannesburg, 1970)

Simons, H.J., *African Women: Their Legal Status in South Africa* (London, 1968)

Simons, H.J. and R.E. (eds), *Class and Colour in South Africa* (London, 1969)

Skotnes, P. (ed.), *Miscast and Negotiating the Presence of the Bushmen* (Cape Town, 1996)

Slovo, G., *Every Secret Thing* (London, 1983)

Smith A.B. (ed.), *Einiqualand: Studies of the Orange River Frontier* (Cape Town, 1995)

Smith, E.W., *Life and Times of Daniel Lindley* (London, 1949)

Smith, E.W., *Aggrey of Africa* (London, 1929)

Smith, I.R., *Origins of the South African War* (London, 1996)

Smith, J.S., *Buthelezi* (Melville, 1988)

Smith, R., *The Changing Past* (Johannesburg, 1985)

Smuts, J.C., *A Century of Wrong* (1900)

Smuts, J.C., *Jan Christiaan Smuts* (London, 1952)

Smythe, B.L. (ed.), *The Nazis in Africa* (Salisbury (USA), 1978)

Snail, M.L., *The Antecedens* (Munich, 1933)

Soga, Tiyo (ed. Williams, D.) *Journal and Selected Writings* (Cape Town, 1983)

Solomon, W.E.G., *Saul Solomon* (Cape Town, 1948)

South African Government, 'The Republic of Venda' (1979)

South African Government Department of Information, 'Progress of the Bantu Peoples towards Nationhood' (n.d)

Southall, R. and Petlane, T., *Democratisation and Demilitarisation in Lesotho* (Pretoria, 1995)

Sparks, A., *The Mind of South Africa* (London, 1990)

Sparrman, A., *A Voyage to the Cape of Good Hope* (Cape Town, 1971, 1977)

Spear, P., *History of India* (2 vols, London, 1973)

Spence, J.E., *Lesotho: The Politics of Dependence* (London, 1968)

Spikes, D., *Angola and the Politics of Intervention* (London, 1993)

Spilhaus, M.W., *South Africa in the Making 1652–1806* (Cape Town, 1966)

Spoelstra, C., *Are the Boers Hostile to Mission Work?* (London, 1902)

Stanford, W. (ed. Maquarrie, J.W.) *Reminiscences* (2 vols, Cape Town, 1958, 1962)

Stanley, E.M. (ed. Vincent, J.), *Diaries* (London, 1994)

Stapleton, T.J., *Maqoma: Xhosa Resistance to Colonial Advance* (Johannesburg, 1994)

Stephen, L., *Life of Sir James Stephen* (London, 1895)

Stevens, R.P., *Lesotho, Bechuanaland and Swaziland* (London, 1967)

Stockenström, A. (ed. Hutton, C.W.), *Autobiography* (Cape Town, 1887, 1964)

Stone, J., *Colonist or Uitlander: A Study of the British Immigrant in South Africa* (Oxford, 1973)

Strangeways-Booth, J., *Cricket in the Thorn Tree* (London, 1976)

Strassberger, E., *The Rhenish Mission Society in Southern Africa* (Cape Town, 1969)

Streak, M., *The Afrikaner as Viewed by the English* (Cape Town, 1974)

Streek, B. and Wicksteed, R., *Render unto Kaiser: A Transkei Dossier* (Johannesburg, 1981)

Strydom, H., *For Volk and Führer* (Johannesburg, 1984)

Stuart, J., *A History of the Zulu Rebellion 1906* (London, 1913)

Stubbs, T. (ed. Maxwell, W.A and McGeogh, R.T.), *Reminiscences* (Cape Town, 1978)

Sturgis, J.L., *John Bright and the Empire* (London, 1969)

Sundkler, B.G.M., *Bantu Prophets in South Africa* (2nd edn, London, 1961)

Surplus People Project, *Forced Removals in South Africa* (5 vols, Cape Town, 1983)

Suzman, H., *In no Uncertain Terms* (London and Johannesburg, 1993)

Swellengrebel, H. Jr (ed. Schutte, G.J.), *Briefwisseling 1778–1792* (Cape Town, 1982)

Switzer, L., *Power and Resistance in an African Society* (Madison and London, 1993)

Tas, A. (ed. Fouché, L.), *Diary* (Cape Town, 1970)

Taylor, A., *Islamic Resurgence in South Africa* (Cape Town, 1995)

Taylor, R., *Lord Salisbury* (London, 1975)

Taylor, S., *Shaka's Children* (London, 1994)

Temperley, H. and Pinson, L.M., *Foundations of British Foreign Policy* (London, 1962)

Templin, J.A., *Ideology on a Frontier: The Theological Foundation of African Nationalism* (London, 1984)

Tew, M., *People of the Lake Nyasa Region* (Oxford, 1950)

Theal, G.M., *Chronicles of the Cape Commanders* (Cape Town, 1882)

Theal, G.M., *History of the Boers in South Africa* (London, 1887)

Theal, G.M., *The Beginnings of South African History* (London, 1902)

Theal, G.M., *History and Geography of Africa South of the Zambezi* (London, 1909)

Theal, G.M., *History and Ethnography of South Africa before 1795* (3 vols, London, 1907–10)

Theal, G.M., *History of South Africa* (11 vols, London, 1892–1919)

Thomas, H., *The Slave Trade* (London, 1997)

Thomas, S., *The Diplomacy of Liberation: Foreign Relations of the ANC Since 1960* (London, 1996)

Thompson, L., *Survival in Two Worlds: Mosheshoe of Lesotho 1786–1870* (Oxford, 1975)

Thompson, L.M., *The Unification of South Africa 1902–10* (Oxford, 1960)

Thompson, L.M. and Prior, A., *South African Politics* (New Haven and London, 1985)

Thompson, L.M., *A History of South Africa* (New Haven and London, 1990)

Thomson, C.A., 'The Administration of Sir Henry Loch, 1889–1895' (degree dissertation, Duke University, 1973)

Thornton, S., *Africa and the Africans in the Making of the Atlantic World 1400–1680* (Cape Town, 1992)

Thorpe, D.R., *Alec Douglas-Home* (London, 1990)

Thunberg, C.B., *Travels at the Cape of Good Hope 1770–5* (London, 1793, Cape Town, 1986)

Tirmizi, S.A.I., *Indian Sources for South African History* (New Delhi, 1988)

Tou, T., Parsons, N. and Henderson, W., *Seretse Kama* (Gaberone 1995)

Transvaal Indigency Committee, Report TG 11 (Pretoria, 1908)

Trollope, A., *South Africa* (London, 1878)

Trun, M.L. (ed.), *Public Policy and the South African Economy* (Cape Town, 1976)

Turner, V. (ed.), Colonialism in Africa (Vol. 3, Cambridge, 1971)

Turrell, R.V., *Capital and Labour in the Kimberley Diamond Fields* (Cambridge, 1987)

Tutu, D., *The Rainbow People of God* (London, 1994)

Tyler, J., *Forty Years Among the Zulus* (Boston, 1891)

US Government House of Representatives Committee on Foreign Affairs, Sub-Committee on Africa (Washington, 1966)

Vail, L. (ed.), *The Creation of Tribalism in Southern Africa* (London, 1989)

Valentyn, F., *Beschryvinge van Kaap der Goede Hoope* (2 vols, Cape Town, 1971–73)

Van Aswegen, H.J., *History of South Africa to 1854* (Pretoria, 1990)

Van der Merwe, H.W. et al, *White South African Elites* (Cape Town, 1973)

Van der Merwe, H.W. et al (eds), *Perspectives in South Africa* (Cape Town, 1978)

Van der Merwe, P.J., *The Migrant Farmer in the History of the Cape Colony*

1657–1842 (originally *Trekboer in die geskiendenis van die kaapkolonie*) (Athens (USA), 1995)

Van der Poel, J., *The Jameson Raid* (Oxford, 1951)

Van der Ross, R., *Myths and Attitudes* (Cape Town, 1979)

Van der Ross, R., *The Rise and Decline of Apartheid* (Cape Town, 1986)

Van Hengingen, E. (ed.), *Studies in the History of Cape Town* (Vol. 7, Cape Town, 1994)

Van Jaarsveld, F.A., *The Awakening of Afrikaner Nationalism* (originally *Die Eenheidstrewe van die Republikeinse Afrikaners*) (Cape Town, 1961)

Van Jaarsveld, F.A., *The Afrikaner's Interpretation of History* (Cape Town, 1964)

Van Niekerk, L.E., *Kruger se Regterhand* (Pretoria, 1985)

Van Onselen, C., *Chibaro* (London, 1976)

Van Onselen, C., *Studies in the Social and Economic History of the Witwatersrand* (2 vols, London and New York, 1982)

Van Onselen, C., *The Seed is Mine* (London and New York, 1996)

Van Reenen, D.D., *Journal, 1803* (Cape Town, 1937)

Van Reenen, R. (ed.), *Emily Hobhouse: Boer War Letters* (Cape Town, 1984)

Van Riebeeck, J., *Journal* (17 vols, Cape Town, 1896–1906)

Van Riebeeck, J. (ed. Thom, H.B.), *Journal* (3 vols, Cape Town, 1951–58)

Van Rooyen, J., *Hard Right: The New White Power in South Africa* (London and New York, 1994)

Van Ryneveld, W.S., *Aanmerkingen* (Cape Town, 1942)

Van Zyl Slabbert, F. and Welsh, D., *South Africa's Options* (Cape Town, 1979)

Van Zyl Slabbert, F., *The Last White Parliament* (London, 1985)

Venter, A.J. (ed.), *Southern Africa Within the African Revolutionary Context* (Gibraltar, 1987)

Venter, C., *The Great Trek* (Cape Town, 1985)

Vincent, J., *The Formation of the British Liberal Party* (London, 1966)

Viney, G. and Simons, P.B., *The Cape of Good Hope 1806–1872* (Houghton (SA), 1981)

Vorster, B.J. (Ogeyser, ed.), *Selected Speeches* (Bloemfontein, 1977)

Wahlberg, J.A. (ed. Craig, A. and Hummel, C.), *Travel Journals* (Cape Town, 1994)

Waldemeir, P., *Anatomy of a Miracle* (London, 1997)

Walker, C., *Women and Resistance in South Africa* (London, 1982)

Walker, E.A., *Historical Atlas of South Africa* (Oxford, 1922)

Walker, E.A., *The Life of W.P. Schreiner* (London, 1937)

Walker, E.A., *The Great Trek* (London, 1948)

Walker, E.A., *A History of Southern Africa* (3rd edn, London, 1957)

Wallace, E., *Unofficial Dispatches* (London, 1908)

Walshe, P., *The Rise of African Nationalism in South Africa* (London, 1970)

Walshe, P., *Church and State in South Africa* (London, 1983)

Bibliography

Warren, C., *On the Veldt in the '70s* (London, 1902)

Waterston, J.E. (ed. Bean, L. and Heyningen, V.), *Letters* (Cape Town, 1983)

Webb, C. de B. and Wright, J.B., *The James Stuart Archive* (3 vols, Pietermaritzburg, 1976)

Welch, S.R., *Europe's Discovery of South Africa* (Cape Town, 1935)

Wellington, J.H., *South-West Africa and its Human Issues* (Oxford, 1967)

Wells, J.C., *We Now Demand: The History of Women's Resistance to Pass Laws in South Africa* (Johannesburg, 1997)

Welsh, D., *The Roots of Segregation: Native Policy in Natal, 1845–1910* (Oxford, 1971)

Welsh, F., *A History of Hong Kong* (London and New York, 1994, 1997)

Wentzel, J., *The Liberal Slideaway* (Johannesburg, 1995)

Wheatcroft, G., *The Randlords* (London, 1985)

Whibley, P.M., *Merriman of Grahamstown* (Cape Town, 1982)

Whisson, M.G. and West, M., *Religion and Social Change in Southern Africa* (London and Cape Town, 1975)

Whitall, W., *Wm. Botha and Smuts in Africa* (London, 1917)

Wilkins, I. and Strydom, H., *The Broederbond* (Johannesburg, 1978)

Willan, B.P., *Sol Plaatje* (London, 1984)

Williams, D., *Journal and Selected Writings* (Lovedale, 1978)

Williams, R.H. (ed.), *Salisbury–Balfour Correspondence* (Hertfordshire, 1988)

Wilson, F., *Labour in South African Gold Mines* (Cambridge, 1972)

Wilson, J., *CB: A Life of Sir Henry Campbell-Bannerman* (London, 1973)

Wilson, M. (ed.), *Freedom for my People* (London, 1981)

Wilson, M. and Thompson, L., *The Oxford History of South Africa* (2 vols, Oxford, 1968, 1971)

Wolf, L., *Life of the First Marquess of Ripon* (London, 1921)

Wolseley, G. (ed. Preston, A.), *South African Diaries* (Cape Town, 1971)

Wolseley, G. (ed. Preston, A.), *South African Journal* (Cape Town, 1973)

Woods, D., *Biko* (London, 1978)

Woods, D., *Asking for Trouble* (London, 1980)

Worden, N., *Slavery in Dutch South Africa* (Cape Town, 1985)

Worsford, W.B., *Lord Methuen's Work in South Africa* (London, 1906)

Wrench, J.E., *Alfred, Lord Milner* (London, 1958)

Wright, J. and Manson, R., *The Hlubi Chiefdom in Natal* (Ladysmith, 1983)

Wright, J.B., *Bushman Raiders of the Drakensberg* (Pietermaritzburg, 1971)

Wylie, D., *A Little God* (Hanover (USA) and London, 1995)

Young, D.M., *The Colonial Office in the Early Nineteenth Century* (London, 1961)

Young, F.B., *Marching on Tanga* (London, 1917)

Young, P., *A Missionary Narrative* (London, 1860)

Younghusband, F.E., *South Africa Today* (London, 1898)

Yudleman, D., *The Emergence of Modern South Africa* (Cape Town, 1984)

INDEX

Abdurahman, Dr Abdullah 416;
background 356; on British 376; death
of 423; leader of Coloureds 337, 348, 355,
368; in London delegation 371; Malan
and 402
Abolition of Passes Act 430
Aboriginals Protection Association 181,
377
Achmed, Imam 101
Adam (slave) 60
Adderley, Sir Charles 190, 197
Addington, Henry (Lord Sidmouth) 96–7,
103
Affonso, King of Portugal 5
Africa, William 246
African Democratic Party 423
African National Congress (ANC) xxi, 368;
accepts segregation 414; armed struggle
458–9, 485, 505; attitude to whites 424,
426–7; and AZAPO 488; banned 456;
bases attacked 492; Bill of Rights 431;
and Botswana 441; and business leaders
494–5; and communism 402–3, 423–4,
425, 445, 473, 498, 513; in decline 407–8;
Defiance Campaigns 432–3, 434, 445,
447, 496; division in 404, 454, 507;
electoral success 512; in exile 465, 469,
481, 485–6, 487, 505; and German
South-West Africa 422; in government
512–13; guerrilla warfare 441, 494;
Harare Declaration 499; ideology
424–5; and Indians 423, 431–2;
ineffectiveness 485–6; and Inkatha
472–3, 488, 494, 505; Mandela and 505;
manifesto 494, 513; Mells Park House
talks 495; membership 433; MK 458–60,
485, 499; and multi-party convention
507; mutiny in 486; National Executive
424, 431; and Native Franchise Bill 409;
negotiations 494; and PAC 465–6;
People's War 466; prisoners released
499; security department 486; UNITA
offensive 486; violence 508–9; Women's

League 452; Youth League 424–5, 426,
431–2; Xhosa in 473, 488; see also South
African Native National Congress
African Native Congress 376
African People's Organization 348, 355,
370, 423
African Resistance Movement (ARM)
462
Afrikaner, Jager 95, 164
Afrikaner, Jonker 192
Afrikaner Bond 288–9, 291, 309, 348, 365,
373
Afrikaner Broederbond 400–1, 411–12, 418,
428–9, 461, 484, 513
Afrikaner Party 421, 427
Afrikaner Resistance Movement (Afrikaner
Weerstands Beweging) 484
Afrikaners xix, xx, xxii, 21, 222, 380–2; in
administration 409, 429; and apartheid
414–17, 477; attitude to British 115,
121–3, 133, 148, 183, 199, 202, 326, 379,
383; attitude to missionaries 108–9, 135,
153, 175–6, 446–7; attitude to non-
whites 369, 374, 382; and Boer War 322,
336, 338, 341, 347–8, 379; at British
takeover 105; business sector 400, 418,
462–3, 484, 494; Chamberlain and 348;
discrimination against 151–2; dissidents
374; divisions in 223–4, 428, 471, 477,
484; of Eastern Cape 129; economic
power of 417, 513, 514; education 447–8;
employment 463; fascism of 418, 420,
421, 426–7, 464; favour Union 365; first
50–5, 64, 222; Freedom Delegation
385–6, 387; and Germany 379, 418–19;
in government 374, 428–9; Great Trek
xxii, xxiii, 139, 146–8, 150–2, 162, 165–9,
177, 261, 413, 414; hardening attitudes
413; intermarriage 199, 288; Khoikhoi
contribution to 77; language of 105, 125,
287–8, 415, 474; in multi-racial state 512;
myths xxiii, 83, 146–7, 173, 183, 261, 341,
380, 396, 401, 414, 455; of Natal 212;

575

Afrikaners – *cont.*
  national identity of 95, 414–15, 417;
  nationalists 346, 375; organizations 288,
  382, 400–1, 411–12, 417–18; in police
  409, 476; political activity 244, 288–9,
  388–9; poverty 359–60, 401–2, 411,
  417; press 400; racism 109, 110, 115,
  135, 150, 179, 183, 309; rebellions 82–3,
  86–7, 92–3, 95, 122, 379–82, 415;
  relations with English-speakers 461,
  464–5, 476; religion 109, 121, 223–4, 415;
  and slavery 135, 179–80, 238; supremacy
  of 399–400; *trekboers* 18, 64, 77–8, 79,
  115, 140, 184; *veeboers* 64–5, 76; white
  supremacists 382, 404, 501; women 452;
  see also Boer Republics
Aggrey, Revd James 394
agriculture xix, 162; Afrikaners in 462–3;
  black farmers 245–6, 296–7, 345–6, 353,
  376; in Dutch Cape 30, 33, 34, 51, 63–4;
  Indian settlers in 297; labour 410; land
  tenure laws 117–18; landed gentry 345;
  livestock 71, 124, 217–18, 353, 381, 453; in
  Natal 245–6, 247–8, 296–7; post-Boer
  War 343, 345–6; poverty in 380–1;
  sheep-farming 186, 199, 229, 234; sugar
  247
Agter Bruintjes Hoogte 78, 80
Ahtisaari, Marti 493
Akembie, Chief 41
Aksie Eie Toekoms 484
Albany 119, 123, 125, 130, 151, 244
Alberti, Captain Ludwig 101
Aldworth, Thomas 19
Alexander, Morris 408
Alexander VI, Pope 5
Alfred, Prince (Affie) 234
Algeria 479–80
Algoa Bay 68, 126, 128
Aliwal North, Convention of 232
All-Africa Convention (AAC) 408, 409,
  423, 430
Allie, Mohamed 337
Almeida, Bernardo d' 9, 14
Amalinde, battle of 124
Amboina 10, 13, 30
American Board of Commissioners for
  Foreign Missions 175
American Church 357
American Mission Society 111
Amery, Leo 386, 441
Amiens, Treaty of 97

Ampthill, Lord 378
Amsterdam 11–12, 25, 26, 35, 39, 62
Andrews, Bill 404–5
Andries-Ohrigstadt 184
Anglican Church 110–11, 200, 248;
  Missionary Society 111, 170; South
  African 357
Anglo-American Corporation 494
Anglo-Boer War, see Boer War
Angola 8, 35, 286, 311, 455, 467–9, 480–1,
  486, 493
Angra Pequena Bay 283
anthropology 18
Anti-Slavery Society 372
apartheid xxvi–xxvii, 54, 66, 360, 385;
  dismantling of 496, 497, 501, 506, 514;
  Dutch Churches and 415, 416, 462,
  484–5; in education 447–8; English-
  speakers and 464, 477; Group Areas Act
  430, 445–6; laws repealed 499; National
  Party and 427–30, 464; under new
  constitution 482; opponents of 432–4,
  444, 452, 462, 463; origins of 414–17;
  relaxation of 470, 479, 491, 493; rioting
  over 475; in South-West Africa 467;
  Verwoerd and 448–50
Arabs xxiv, 2, 4, 7, 8, 9, 35, 424
Arbousset, Thomas 164
Archbell, James 164, 167, 168, 212
Arckel, Ds Johan van 54
Armed Neutrality, war of 84, 88
Arnold-Foster, War Minister 341
Arnot, David 238
Artoys, Barend Jacob 85–6
Asiatic Land Tenure and Indian
  Representation Bill (1946) 422–3
Asquith, Herbert 321
Assenburgh, Governor van 56
Atlante 103
Attlee, Clement 440
Auret, Johannes 122
Austin, Alfred 318
Australia 198, 200, 216, 239, 299, 405
Axe, War of the 187, 196
Aylward, Alfred 242
Azanian People's Organization (AZAPO)
  488

Baartman, Saartje 114
Baccum, Nicolas van 10
Baden-Powell, Robert, Lord 336
Bailey, Sir Abe 324, 345, 347, 364, 383–4

Bailey, Jim 420, 432, 472
Baines, Andrew Geddes 287
Baines, Thomas 382
Baird, Gen. David 103
Balfour, Arthur 322, 373, 399, 435
Ball, Chris 495
Ballinger, Margaret 404, 412, 445
Ballinger, William 404
Bambatha, Chief 362, 363, 376, 410
Banda, Dr Hastings 470
Banjailand trek 312
Bank of England 324, 325, 405
Bank of Natal 210
Bantjes, Jan 165, 173
Bantu xix, xx, 1, 16, 69–70, 73, 74, 137, 417
Bantu Education Bill (1953) 446–7
Bantustans 449–51, 470, 471, 477, 490, 497
Barberton 301
Baring, Evelyn 275
Baring, Sir Francis 88
Barkly, Sir Henry 238–9, 243, 244, 253, 255, 258
Barlow, Arthur 445
Barnard, Andrew 91, 105
Barnard, Lady Anne 91, 93, 199
Barnard, Prof. Neil 498
Barnato, Barney 308, 324
Barnes, Thomas 182
Barrow, John 93–4, 132
Barry, Surgeon Major James 182
Bartolemi, P. 48
Basle Society 111
Bastaards 18, 62, 77, 95, 105, 107, 147, 163; see also Griquas
Basuto 136, 208, 232, 236, 248, 252, 274, 279, 377, 436
Basuto National Party (BNP) 438
Basutoland 255, 298, 299; administration of 436; and Boer War 335; borders 208, 231, 436; British Protectorate 140, 231–2, 278–9, 298, 355, 435–8; budget 436–7, 438; Cape dependency 239, 274, 277–8; chiefs 436; constitution 438; economy 437; education in 437; Gun War 241, 277–8, 279; independence 437–8; Legislative Council 438; map 141; National Council 436, 437–8; political parties 438; Sotho in 435; and South Africa 435–6; see also Lesotho
Basutoland National Congress (BNC) 438, 439

Batavia 13, 22, 26, 35, 39, 49, 62, 86, 87
Batavian Republic 97, 100, 101–2
Bathurst, Earl 120–1, 125, 131, 151, 182
Batlokwa tribe 259
Bax van Herentals, Johann 50
Beaufort West 200
Beaufre, Gen. André 479
Beaumont Commission 376, 385
Beaverbrook, Lord 358
Bechuana 283, 285, 377
Bechuanaland: British Protectorate 284, 285–6, 314, 355, 439–41; chiefs 439–40; independence 440; missionaries in 283, 439; peoples of 73, 283–4, 435, 436; Rhodes and 284–5, 308, 310, 315–16; see also Botswana
Beit, Alfred 308, 324
Bekri, Abdullah al xxv
Belgium 311, 372
Bell, Charles 196
Bellow, Saul 503
Bereng 438
Bergenaars 163
Berkeley, Gen. Sir George 191
Berlin Missionary Society 222, 237
Bethelsdorp 112, 113
Beutler, Friedrich 78
Beyers, Gen. 380, 381
Bezuidenhout, Freek 122
Bezuidenhout, Hans Jan 122
Bhaca 136, 144, 145, 180, 187, 350
Bhekezulu, King Goodwill Zweletini Ka-Cyprian 442
Bhownaggree, Sir Mancherjee 354
Bhulose, William 411
Bhunu, King 351
Biddulph, Thomas 195, 196
Bigge, John 132
Biko, Steve 432, 475–6, 477
Bird, Christopher 130
Bird, Col. Richard 104, 132
Bisho 509
Bismarck, Count Herbert von 283
Bismarck, Chancellor Otto von 282–3
Black Circuit 115, 123, 341, 414
Black Flag revolt 242
Black Sash 452
blacks xix, xx; aboriginals 1, 16, 67, 68–74; Africanists 424–5; *amalala* 212; under apartheid xxvii, 427, 429–30, 445–6, 449–50, 481–3; atrocities 487–8; and Boer War 322, 334–6, 353–4; Boers

blacks – *cont.*
and 146, 177–8, 179, 184, 292; British
attitude towards 104, 133, 150, 201, 206,
220, 231; businesses 512; of Cape 108,
195, 201, 202, 228, 231, 252, 260, 292–5,
309, 322, 348–9, 355–7, 360, 363,
368; colonial 227–8, 259, 292; culture
of 503; of diamond fields 235;
disenfranchisement 294, 309–10, 397,
407–9, 481, 482, 483–4; education 217,
220, 228, 292–3, 398, 429, 447, 474;
farmers 245–6, 296–7, 345–6, 353, 376;
franchise 202, 244, 245, 288, 292, 295,
348, 349, 367–8, 403, 406, 483, 512; in
Great War 384–5; homelands 210, 230,
450–1, 473, 482, 487, 491; immigration
235; and Khoikhoi 17; labour 235, 241,
245–6, 290–1, 297, 302, 344, 358, 376,
401–2, 410, 411, 447, 450, 471; land
tenure 246, 296, 309, 353, 376; living
conditions 470–1, 475, 482, 513; mass
action by 432; middle class 296, 382;
miscarriages of justice 404; and
missionaries 108; of Natal 210–15,
245–6, 249–50, 256, 262–3, 292, 296–8,
352–4, 362–3, 367, 369; and National
Convention 368; native states 227, 252,
481; of Orange Free State 73, 208–9,
226, 231–2, 236, 242, 298–9, 334–5, 346;
organizations 348–9, 356, 370, 398, 404,
407; political activity xxvi–xxvii, 292,
293, 294–5, 298, 355–7; population
numbers 470; poverty 411; press 293,
295, 349, 432–3; religion 108, 109, 357;
reserves 158, 210–14, 230, 267, 296, 298,
376, 385, 411, 427, 430; ritual 72, 73, 249;
schoolmen 292; segregation 377, 385,
391, 394, 398, 409, 414, 430, 445–6,
449, 470, 490; slaves 100; of South
Africa 369–70, 374–6, 385–6, 388,
390–5, 397–8, 406, 417; strikes 383,
496; subordination of 100, 235, 292,
294; townships 470–1, 487, 490; trades
unions 425, 487; of Transvaal xxi, 73,
221, 222, 254, 255, 335, 345, 359–60,
367; uniting of xx, 377, 398; wages
390; see also specific peoples
Blanke Bevrydigings Beweging, see White
Liberation Movement
Blinkwater 188
Bloemfontein 186, 192, 193, 224, 226,
328–9, 331, 366, 377

Bloemfontein Convention 207, 221, 232,
239
Blokland, Gerard van 103
Blood River 210; battle of 173, 178, 414,
417
Boer Republics xxv, 92, 140, 221–33;
alliances 221, 225; annexation 331; blacks
in 177, 178, 195, 292; Boer defined 151–2,
321–2; in Boer War 321–37; boundaries
176; civil war 147, 196, 224, 226; and
confederation proposal 254;
constitutions 168, 174, 176, 184; divisions
in 185, 223–4; expansion 280–1, 285,
312; franchise in 307–8, 328–30,
339–40; government of 167, 168, 174,
176; and Griquas 185–6; labour in 177;
land in 176–7; land-locked 286; non-
whites excluded 184; peace negotiations
338–40; racism in 177–80;
reconstruction 342–4; relations with
British colonies 167, 170, 174, 177–83,
186, 192–3, 206, 207, 224–5, 226, 232,
320, 364; and Union proposals 254, 365;
Zulu threat to 169–74; see also specific
states
Boer War (1899–1902) xxvi, 321–37, 384,
415, 441; avoidance measures 327–9;
British shame over 372; causes of 168,
323–6; concentration camps 334–5, 339,
341, 415; effects in Britain 341–2; Gandhi
in 354; map 332; peace negotiations
338–41; post-war reconstruction 342–4;
Royal Commission on 342
Boeren Beschermings Verneeniging 288
Boers, see Afrikaners
Boers, Fiskaal Willem Cornelis 85
Boesak, Dr Allan 473, 487
Boiphatong 508
Bok, Edward 268, 269
Bok, Willem 304
Bonaparte, Napoleon 102, 116, 117
Bondelswarts 393
Boniface, Charles Etienne 287
Boom, Hendrik 27, 33, 34
Boom, Mevrouw 31
Boomplats 193, 414
Bophuthatswana 147, 451, 509
Borghorst, Jacob 43
Boshof, Jacobus 174, 175, 181, 182–3, 224,
225, 236
Boswell, James 58
Botha, Andries 196

Botha, Hendrina 166

Botha, Louis: in Boer War 325, 331, 335, 341; cabinet of 374; death 387; heads temporary government 373; as imperialist 346, 379; and Indian rights 378; peace negotiator 338–9, 342; personal popularity of 395; political career 306, 346–7; as Prime Minister 359, 361, 374, 430; and strikers 382; supporters of 373, 374; and Union 368, 369, 370, 371, 372; war in South-West Africa 383; withdraws from customs agreement 365; on Zulu war 279–80

Botha, P.W.: and ANC 492, 495; and Angolan campaign 493; and apartheid 491; and constitution 482; and Mandela 497–8; and Mozambique 486; personality of 479; President 492, 493, 496; Prime Minister 478–9; reformer 484, 490; resignation 495, 497

Botha, R.F. (Pik) 478, 486, 500, 507

Botma, Steven 32, 33, 34, 47

Botswana xxv, 71, 286; ANC bases in 481, 492; as democracy 441, 442–3; economy 440–1; Khama family in xxi; relations with South Africa 465, 470; see also Bechuanaland

Botswana Democratic Party 441

Bourguiba, Habib 459

Bourke, Gen. Sir Richard 134

Bovambaland 227

Bower, Sir Graham 319

Bower, Maude 319

Bowker, Holden 195, 196, 202, 216

Bowker, Robert 202

Bowker, Thomas 238

Bowker family 129

Brand, Sir Christoffel xxii, 127, 150, 177, 202, 243

Brand, Sir John Henry: diamond fields claim 238, 239, 254, 255; as President xxii, 226, 231, 236, 272, 298, 302

Brazil 6, 24, 57

Breda, Michiel van 149

Breda, Treaty of 44, 49

Brenton, Captain Sir Jahleel, RN 128

Brereton, Col. Thomas 124

Bresler, F.R. 92, 93, 94

Breytenbach, Breyten 471, 488

Brickman, Casper 36

Bright, Edmund 343, 344

Bright, John 270

Brill, Dr Johannes 287

Brink, André 471–2

Brink, Gen. 432

Britain, see Great Britain

British Army 46, 117, 193, 243, 260, 264, 271, 341–2

British Commonwealth 399, 456, 492

British Empire xxii, xxvii, xxv, xxvi, 200; administration of 158; African members 126–7, 193, 207, 239–40, 433, 438, 455; dominions of 399; financial arrangements 229; Natal in 209–15; self-government in 433, 438, 455; settlement colonies 134, 158; slavery in 59, 148–9; trade in 159; white supremacy in 19

British Kaffraria, Crown Colony of 239; abandonment proposal 198; annexation of 229–31; cattle-killing in 218; expansion 230, 232; foundation of 191, 227; franchise in 201; military settlements in 220; population of 144, 230–1; subsidies to 217, 229

British Protectorates 372, 388, 414, 434–43; see also Basutoland; Bechuanaland; Swaziland

British South Africa Company 311, 313, 314–16, 320, 355

Brits, J.N. 186

Broderick, St John (Lord Midleton) 341

Brookes, Edgar 412, 424

Brownlee, Charles 191, 219, 230, 245

Bryant, Arthur 138

Bryce, James 293

Buchan, John (Lord Tweedsmuir) 343

Buchanan, David Dale 214

Buckingham, Duke of 232

Bud-M'belle, Isaiah 385

Buijtendag, Carel 85–6, 87

Bulawayo 310, 315

Bulhoek 393

Buller, Gen. Sir Redvers 330

Bultfontein 240, 242

Bulwer, Sir Henry 258, 262–3, 266, 280, 296

Bulwer-Lytton, Edward (Lord Lytton) 225, 251

Bunbury, Sir Charles 158, 160

Bunga 394, 449

Bunting, Sidney 392, 404

Burdett, Francis 104

Bureau of State Security (BOSS) 465, 469, 471, 477, 489

Burger, De (Die) 375, 381, 400, 412, 428, 462
Burger, Jacobus (Kootjie) 174, 185
Burger, Schalk 303, 340
Burgers, Thomas François 254–5, 257, 258, 303, 305
Burt, Thomas 292
Burton, Henry 295, 396, 409
Bush, President George 502
Bushmen xix, xx, xxiii, 27, 46, 68, 79, 82, 249; and British 105, 192; culture 16–17; and Dutch settlers xvi, 18, 40, 76–7, 95; as hunter-gatherers 16; land sales by 163; physical characteristics 17; social structure 17–18
Buthelezi, Chief Mangosuthu: ANC distrust of 497; background of 472; Bantustan proposals 477; and Inkatha revival 411, 472; and multi-party conventions 507, 509; as potential negotiator 496; and violence 505–6; and Zulu king 442; and Zulu nationhood 451
Buthelezi, Wellington 392
Butler, Gen. Sir William 327–8
Buxton, Thomas Fowell 135, 160
bywoners 122, 381

Cachet, Ds F. Lion 226
Caepmen 31, 45
Cairns, Lord Chancellor 272
Calas, Jean 66
Calata, Revd James 408, 431, 445
Caledon, Earl of 103, 104–5, 106–7, 113–15, 117, 126, 132
Caledon Valley 194, 231
Calvin, John 109, 416
Cam, Diego 5
Cameron, Revd 194
Campbell, Admiral 179
Campbell, John 163
Campbell, Magistrate 239
Campbell-Bannerman, Sir Henry 349, 358–9, 373
Canada 251, 252–3
Canning, George 126
Cape Colony 116–17, 252, 355; blacks in 108, 195, 201, 202, 219–20, 228, 231, 235, 252, 260, 292–5, 309, 348–9, 355–7, 360, 363, 368; and Boer Republics 167, 170, 172, 174, 177–83, 185–6, 224–5, 226; in Boer War 336; Boers in 115, 121–2,

151–2; boundaries 105, 106, 118, 144, 163, 178, 192, 204–5, 227, 231; in British Empire 126–7, 158, 200; Burgher Senate 90, 103, 133, 150; Cape Franchise 201–3, 207, 322, 355, 367, 368, 369, 427; as coaling station 253; Commissioners sent to 132, 197; confederation policy 252–6, 275, 355; constitution 200, 201; dependencies 239, 256, 277–9, 290, 294; Dutch population, see Afrikaners; East/West split 201, 227, 229, 230, 243; economy 117, 132, 149, 199, 229–30, 234, 252, 347, 364–5; elections 202, 320, 348, 356, 364; expansion of 158, 161, 163, 178, 191–2, 209, 227, 231, 238–9, 240, 256, 315; garrison 117, 193, 243; government of 116, 132, 189, 200–2, 216, 229, 243–7, 252, 274, 309, 355; High Commissioners 132, 189; immigration 126, 127–30, 234; judicial system 113–15, 118, 132–3; Khoikhoi in 107–8, 134, 152, 153–6, 196; land tenure in 117–18, 150–1; language of 133; Legislative Assembly 202; Legislative Council 200, 243; map 204–5; middle class 199; militia 190; Natal annexation 183, 185; population of 105, 210, 252, 366–7; press in 129, 130–1; rioting in 197; self-government 134; as settlement colony 134; slavery in 59, 105, 118, 134–5, 148–50, 151; taxation 117, 230, 360; trade and commerce 199; and Transvaal customs union proposal 305; Xhosa and 79, 93–4, 96, 105, 118–19, 123–5, 156–8, 187–8, 190, 191, 195–6; see also Eastern Cape; Northern Cape; Western Cape
Cape Council of Justice 53–4, 87, 101
Cape Council of Policy 25–6, 33, 34, 47, 50, 53, 57, 64, 82
Cape Court of Justice 26, 90
Cape Federation of Labour Unions 356
Cape Inquiry on Native Laws and Customs 262
Cape Mounted Rifles 77, 157, 181, 183, 186, 193, 196
Cape of Good Hope 6; convict settlements 19–20; Defence Commission 243; European landings xxv, 9–10, 14–15; naming of 2, 5; travellers in 14, 17; as watering place 13–14, 19; see also Cape Colony; Dutch Cape
Cape of Good Hope Bank 199

Cape Patriots 86–7, 107
Cape Provincial Council 355, 356
Cape Town xxvi, 41, 59, 63, 77, 78, 95, 97, 203; British in 89, 102, 105; Burgher Council 47; City Council 200, 355; docks 234, 243; government in 82, 83, 90, 177, 202; immigration 129; Parliament 286, 366; press 131; rioting in 475; slaves in 148, 149
Cape Verde islands 4
Cardwell, Edward 228–9, 230, 243, 251
Carnarvon, Lord: on Boer Republics 225; and Cape laws 294; at Colonial Office 250–1; confederation policy of 252–3, 355; discredited 269; and Frere 259; on Natal 296; and Orange Free State 239–40; resignation 270, 275; and Transvaal 256, 258, 267–8
Carrington, Col. Frederick 259
Carter, President Jimmy 469
Casalis, Jean-Eugene 164
Caspersen, Lucas 38
Cathcart, Sir George 198, 206, 208
Catherine of Braganza, Queen 44, 45
Cato Manor 452, 454
cattle-killing xx, xxi, 218–19, 220–1, 228, 261–2
Cavendish, Lord Frederick 276
Cecile, Mother 293
Ceded Territory 125, 144, 151, 156, 161, 191
Central Bank 491
Cetshwayo, King 215, 252, 262–3, 265–7, 314, 354, 472
Ceuta 2
Ceylon 44, 50, 110, 116, 158
Chalmers, J.M. 408
Chamberlain, Joseph 322, 323; and blacks 349; and Boer Republics 329, 339; and Boer War 270, 323, 327, 330; as Colonial Secretary 314; and Home Rule Bill 276; as imperialist 308, 327; and Jameson Raid 318, 320–1; and Milner 328, 347–8; resignation 357–8; and Rhodes 314, 315–17; South African visit 347–8; and tariff reform 358
Champion, George 175, 393, 404, 410, 431
Chaneni, battle of 279
Charles II, King of England 44, 50
Charters, Major 172–3
Chavonnes, Capt. Dominique de 57
Chavonnes, Mauritius de 57, 121
Chelmsford, Lord 264, 454

China 2, 43, 189, 289; navigators xxiv, 4, 8; settlers 301, 345, 358
Christian Nationalism 416–17, 448–9, 464–5, 471, 500
Christopher, R.M. 408
Chungwa 94
Chunu tribe 212
Churches xxi, xxii, 4, 48, 61; American 357; Anglican 110, 111, 200, 357; black 357; Calvinist 109, 111, 166, 224; Dutch 54, 66, 109, 110, 111, 112, 121, 165, 166, 223–4, 415, 416, 462, 484–5, 500; Ethiopian 108, 357; opposition to apartheid 462; Presbyterian 111, 121, 223; Protestant 18, 52, 108; review of beliefs 223; Roman Catholic 54, 96, 104, 195; white supremacist beliefs 109, 110, 415–16; World Council of 473; see also missionaries
Churchill, Lord Randolph 280
Churchill, Sir Winston 371; on Bechuanaland 440; in Boer War 320; in Colonial Office 358, 361, 362; and former republics 359; and Smuts 420; supports Cape rebels 338–9
CIA 468–9, 480
Cillié, Mr Justice 475
Cilliers, Sarel 167, 169
Ciskei 187, 227, 244, 293, 411, 451, 470, 482, 508–9
Citizen's Defence Force 375
Citizenship Bill (1949) 429
Civil Cooperation Bureau 490
Claas, Burgert 48
Claes, David 30–1
Clark, Senator Dick 469, 480
Clark family 346, 395
Clerk, Sir George 206–7, 208, 232–3
Cloete, Sir Henry 182, 183, 199, 209, 212
Cloete, Gen. Sir Josias 182, 199
Cock, William 129
Cohen, Hank 497
Cole, Sir Lowry 148, 152, 153
Colenso, battle of 331
Colenso, Harriet 348
Colenso, Bishop John W. 215, 248–9, 250, 263, 264, 266
Coleridge, Samuel Taylor 476
Colesberg 80, 151, 164
Colley, Sir George 221, 251, 271–2
Collins, Canon John 455
Collins, Col. Richard 76, 106, 113, 118–19

Colombo, Cristofero 5, 6
Colonial Conferences 311, 347, 361, 371
Colonial League 311
Colonial Office (British) 113, 125, 131, 152,
    158–61, 189, 214, 355; anti-expansionism
    192, 193, 198, 230, 238; and
    Bechuanaland 285; and Boer Republics
    170, 178–9, 180, 181–2, 206; and BSAC
    314; and Cape finances 229; Carnarvon
    in 251; Chamberlain in 314;
    confederation policy 252–6, 259, 275;
    deputations to 371–2, 385–6; and
    Griqua lands 238; instability in 308; and
    language 133; petitioned 295; protection
    of non-whites 134, 148, 294; and
    Protectorates 437; Secretaries 276–7;
    supports transportation 197; and
    Transvaal 256, 281
Colonial Union (Kolonialverein,
    Germany) 282
Coloured Advisory Council 423
Coloured Men's Protectorate and Political
    Association 349
Coloured Persons Rights Bill 397
Coloured Political Association 337
Coloureds xix, xx, 51, 202, 212; under
    apartheid 427, 446, 450, 477; in Boer
    Republics 367; and Boer War 322,
    334–7; in Cape 369; franchise 202–3,
    288, 292, 322, 355, 367, 368, 397, 433–4,
    481; House of Representatives 482, 507;
    labour 356; and National Convention
    368; under 1984 Constitution 481, 482,
    483; organizations 348–9, 355, 370, 423;
    political activity 337, 355–6; relations
    with Nationalists 423; slave origins of
    35, 148–9; social status 356; South
    African 397, 409; wages 356
Communist Party of South Africa 409;
    and ANC 403, 423–4, 425, 445, 473, 486;
    founded 392; fractionalism in 404; ICU
    and 403; restored 499; suppressed
    430–1, 445
Congo xix, 372
Congress of South African Trades Unions
    (COSATU) 446, 487
Congress of the People 446, 451
Conservative Party (British) 358
Conservative Party (South African) 484,
    493, 496, 501, 502, 507
Consolidated Goldfields Company 308,
    313, 324, 495

Constantia 51, 55, 203
Constitution Act 372–3
Constitutional Convention 370
Consultative Business Movement 495
Convention for a Democratic South Africa
    (CODESA) 507–8, 509
Copland, Revd Patrick 17
Coree 14–15
Cornelia (Khoikhoi girl) 32
Corps of Pandours 77, 103, 107, 157
Cotterell, Bishop 219
Cottesloe Conference 462
Coulter, C.W. 408
Council of Non-European Trade Unions
    425
Courtney, Clara 120
Courtney, Leonard 267, 269
Cradock, Sir John 117–18, 119, 123
Craig, Sir James 89, 90, 92, 93, 101, 102
Cranendonk, Secunde 57
Crause, Dr 325
Creighton, Bishop Mandell 349
Creswell, Col. F.H.P. 373, 383, 401, 403
Crewe, Lord 371, 372, 378
Crimean War 218, 220, 323
Crocker, Chester 479, 480, 493
Croker, John Wilson 131
Cronje, Andries 334
Cronje, Gen. 334, 342
Crosse, James 20
Crossroads 488
Cruijthoff, Corporal Pieter 41
Cruse, Hieronymus 64
Cuba 469, 493
Currie, Sir Donald 269
Currie, Lt Walter 129
Currie, Sir Walter 129, 230
Curtis, Lionel 364, 435
Curtis, Roger 91
Cuvier, Georges 114
Cuyler, Jacob 106, 113, 122, 123, 128

Dadoo, Dr Yusuf 423, 432
Dale, Langham 293
Dalindyebo, Chief 357, 457, 503
Dampier, Capt. William 54
Dapper, Olfert 16
Dassen Island 36, 42, 51
David Masupa, Chief 436
Davis, Nathaniel 469
De Beers 290, 308, 313
De Blanke, Archbishop 462

De Buys, Coenraad 81, 94
De Hase, Martinus 28
De Houtman, Cornelis 10
De Jong, Cornelius 84
De Klerk, Frederick Willem 484;
  background 500–1; dismantles
  apartheid 497, 501–2; and Mandela 504,
  507, 509; at multi-party convention
  507–8; Nationalist leader 495;
  personality of 496, 500; President 497;
  releases ANC prisoners 499; resignation
  513; and third force 506–7
De Klerk, Jan 500
De Klerk, Marike 500
De Klerk, Willem (Wim) 477, 484, 495,
  501–2
De Klerk, William 500
De Kock, Gerhard 491
Delagoa Bay 136, 139, 255, 305, 319
De la Guerre, Sgt 42
Delane, John 182
De la Quellière, Maria 27
De la Rey, Gen. Koos 306, 342, 365, 368,
  379, 382
De Mist, Augusta 102
De Mist, Jacob Abraham Uitenhage
  97–102, 115
De Mock, Mr 149
Democratic League 418
Democratic Party 495, 496, 502
Democratic People's Party (Transkei)
  457
Derby, Lord 250, 251, 253, 270, 275, 278,
  280–2, 308
Derby-Lewis, Clive 508
Derbyshire, J.G. 408
Derdepoort 335
D'Escury, Charles 118, 150, 151
Deutsche Bank 304
De Villiers, Sir Henry 368, 370, 371
De Villiers, J.H. 244, 245, 294
De Wet, Gen. Christiaan 331, 342, 368, 375,
  380
De Wet, Olof 83, 90
De Wet, Piet 334
De Wet Nel, M.C. 451
De Witt brothers 45
Diamond Trade Act (1882) 290
Dias, Bartolomeu 1, 2, 5
Diederichs, Nicolaas 416, 478, 484
Diemer, Lt Elbert Dirksen 46
difaqane, see mfecane

Diggers' Protection Association 242
Dilke, Sir Charles 238, 270, 373
Dingane 164, 169–71, 173–4, 175, 176, 177,
  184
Dingane's Day 173, 459
Dingiswayo, Chief 137
Dinizulu, King 279, 352, 365, 377
Disraeli, Benjamin 272; on Carnarvon 269;
  foreign policy 280; and Frere 259;
  governments of 238, 239, 253, 270; and
  Transvaal annexation 256; and Zulu war
  265
Dlamini, Prince 442, 470
Dlamini, Sam 487
Doman 36, 37, 41
Dominion Party 407, 408
Don, Revd John Davidson 294
Donkin, Sir Rufane 128, 129, 130–1
Doornkop 317
Dorha, Chief 45, 55
Doyle, Sir Arthur Conan 341
Drake, Sir Francis 9
Drakensberg xxv, 136, 140, 249, 330
Drakenstein 51, 52, 59, 64
Drum 432–3
Drury, Robert 75
Dube, Revd John 363; founder of
  newspaper 349; ICU leader 409; Inkatha
  chairman 411; on native councils 395;
  President of SANNC 377, 385; as teacher
  376; as Zulu 410
Du Bois, W.E.B. 402
Duff, Grant 251
Duncan, Sir Patrick 488
Duncan, Patrick Snr 400
Dundas, Gen. Francis 91, 96, 106
Dundas, Henry 88, 90, 91, 95
Dunn, John 265–6, 267
Du Plessis, L.J. 400, 411
Du Plessis, Louwrens 178, 286
Du Plooy, Rudolf 223
Durban 170, 172, 312, 330, 331, 353, 404,
  422, 423, 431
D'Urban, Sir Benjamin 148, 152, 156, 157,
  158, 160–1, 172
Durban Mounted Volunteers 260
Durnford, Col. Anthony 250, 264
Dutch Cape 50–88: Afrikaner rebellions
  82–3, 86–7, 92–3, 95; under Batavian
  Republic 97–103, 107; boundaries 68,
  80, 81, 94; British occupation 88–97;
  colonial project 30–1, 33, 43, 50;

Dutch Cape – *cont.*
  Company victualling station 20, 21–5, 27, 30, 32, 36, 37, 39, 63, 88; established 24, 26–7; expansion xxvi, 38, 43, 46, 51, 53, 63, 78; foreign influences in 84–5; free burghers 31–2, 34, 47, 50, 54, 86–7, 90–1; government 25–6, 33, 47, 53–4, 85–7, 90–1, 97–100, 103; immigration 57–8; law 53; legal standing of 45; map 98–9; militia 37, 47, 57, 61, 76, 77, 103; restored to Holland 97; slavery 35–6, 43, 47, 48–9, 54, 57–8, 59–61, 63, 66, 78, 100, 105; society 46–9; stagnation 83–4
Dutch Cape Church 54, 121, 165, 166; see also Dutch Reformed Church
Dutch East India Company (VOC) 53, 67, 170; bankruptcy 85, 87; Cape station 20, 21–5, 27, 30, 32, 36, 37, 39, 63, 88, 94; in Ceylon 44; Church ministers in 109; Council, see Cape Council of Policy; Council of India 34, 39, 45; despotism of 85–7, 90, 97; and English East India Company 13–14; formation of 12; institutions of 133; journal 26; and Khoikhoi 61; shipping 84; shipwrecks 19; and slavery 35–6; Statutes of India 26
Dutch Reformed Church 66, 109, 110, 111, 112, 288
Du Toit, Daniel Francis 288
Du Toit, R.J. 408
Du Toit, Ds Stephanus 281–2, 285, 288, 305
Dwane, Bishop James 357

East India Company, see Dutch East India Company; English East India Company
East Indies 8, 9, 10–11, 12–13, 88, 109
East London 432, 470–1
Eastern Cape: blacks of 356, 367; and British takeover 105, 106; Defiance Campaign in 432; English immigration 126–9; frontier policy 161–2, 177, 216–17; split with West 227, 229, 230; Thembu of 309, 356; voters of 202–3; wool production 186, 199; Xhosa of 119, 123–5, 156–8, 161, 186, 195–6, 356
Eastern Province Bank 199
Ebden, John 199
Eckstein, Hendrick 93
Economic Institute 418
economy: Afrikaner 417–18; of Cape 149, 199, 229–30, 234, 252, 347; debt crisis 496; devaluation 405; exports xix, 51,

186, 199, 456, 489; gold standard 405; of Natal 347; of Orange Free State 255, 347; of Protectorates 437; and sanctions 491, 495, 502; of South Africa xix, 405, 411, 456, 464, 509, 514; of Transvaal 226, 255, 257, 258, 347
Edendale 246
Edgar, Tom 328
education 63, 100–1; Afrikaner 400, 447–8, 500; Afrikanerization of 474, 477; black 217, 220, 228, 292–3, 398, 429, 446–7, 474; church schools 255, 293; higher 200, 398, 400, 413, 447; missionary 108, 217, 357, 427, 437, 446–7; in Natal 254; in Orange Free State 255; in Protectorates 437; state 109, 199–200, 203; in Transvaal 257, 343; white 293
Edward VII, King 342, 361, 378
Effendi, Ahmed Ataoullah 370
Egypt xxiv, 275, 281, 283
Eisenhower, President Dwight D. 454
Eldon, Lord 104, 126
elections 200, 501; British (1900) 334, (1906) 358; Cape (1854) 202, (1898) 320, (1904) 348, 356, (1908) 364; South African (1910) 373, (1915) 380, (1920) 388, (1924) 396, (1929) 403, (1933) 406, (1938) 412, 418, (1943) 422, 428, (1948) 427, 428, 436, (1961) 461, (1966) 464, (1977) 477, (1987) 493, (1989) 496, 501, 502, (1994) xxi, xxvii, 512; Transvaal (1893) 306, (1907) 361; see also franchise
Elgin, Lord 358
Elliot, Capt. Charles, RN 197
Emigrant Thembuland 221, 227
England, see Great Britain
English East India Company 10, 13, 14, 19, 30, 88, 106, 132, 159, 345
Erasmus, Judge 478
Esau, Abraham 335
Esher, Lord 342
Evans, Admiral (Lord Mountevans) 440
Executive Council 200
exploration 1–10, 18, 33, 40–2
Extension of University Education Bill (1959) 447
External Affairs, Department of 399
Eykamma 37

Fadana, Chief 221
Fairbairn, John 131, 135, 200, 202
Fairfield, Edward 251, 274, 319

Index

Faku, Chief 144, 180, 198, 210, 233, 350
False Bay 6, 89, 117, 420
Farewell, Francis 170
Farquhar, Sir Horace 311
'Fat Captain' 31
Fauré, Revd Abraham 121, 131
Faure, D.P. 223
Fauré, Pieter 318
Federale Mynbou 462
Federale Volksbeleggings (FVB) 417
Federasie van Afrikaanse
   Kultuurverenigings 401
Federation of South African Women 452
financial institutions: Afrikaner 463, 514;
   banks 105, 199, 210, 229, 234, 236, 305–6,
   491, 495, 502; insurance companies 199;
   stock exchange xix, 290, 301
Fingoes, see Mfengu
Fingoland 227
First, Ruth 481
Fischer, Abraham 328, 330, 374
Fish River 80, 82, 94, 106, 118, 144
Fitzgerald, Dr J.P. 217, 219
Fitzpatrick, Percy 312, 324, 328, 367, 373
FNLA 468
Foreign Office (British) 160, 183
Fort Beaufort 109, 196
Fort Cox 196
Fort Hare 196
Fort Hare University xxi, 398–9, 447
Fort Wiltshire 144
Fourie, Capt. Jopie 380, 382
Fourie, Nick 147
France 6, 10, 45, 116, 289, 319; colonies 311,
   455; and Egypt 275; Huguenots 51, 52;
   and Natal 180; and Netherlands 88, 97,
   102; occupation of Cape 84–5;
   Revolution 88; and Transvaal 323; in
   United Nations 433, 466; wars 56, 97,
   117, 322, 326
franchise 501; black 202, 244, 245, 288, 292,
   294, 295, 322, 348, 349, 355, 359–62, 438,
   483, 512; British 104; Cape Franchise
   201–3, 207, 369, 397, 407, 427; Coloured
   202, 288, 292, 322, 355, 367, 368, 397,
   433–4; disenfranchisement 294, 309–10,
   397, 407, 444; Franchise Bill (1892) 309;
   Indian 354, 416, 422; Native Franchise
   Bills 397, 403, 406, 407–9; in
   Protectorates 438; South African 366,
   368–9, 371; in Transvaal 307–8, 359–61;
   universal 491, 499, 509; white 406

Franschhoek 52
Fraser, Dr A.J. 206, 207
Free Diamond Republic 237
Freedom Charter 446, 494, 499
Freeman, John 195
FRELIMO 469
French, Gen. 342
Frere, Sir H.E.Bartle: and Basuto 277–8;
   and Boers 269; colonial career 258–9;
   dismisses Cape ministry 259–60, 286;
   on goldfields 306; on Kruger 300;
   recalled 275; and Xhosa wars 259; and
   Zulu war 262–5
Friend of the Free State 226
Frontier Mounted Police 129
Frontier Wars, see Xhosa: wars
Froude, James Anthony 253, 255–6
Fullarton, Alexander 237

Gaauex, Gaaner 284
Gallwey, Michael 298
Galton, Francis 17, 192
Gama, Vasco da 6, 8, 73, 170
Gamtoos River 67, 68, 69
Gandar, Laurence 472
Gandhi, Mohandas Karamchand
   ('Mahatma') 423; ambulance corps of
   354, 363; arrival of 298; and Natal
   Indians 354; passive resistance of 378,
   390; racism of 379, 394; supports South
   African Indians 377–8
Garvey, Marcus 402; Garveyism 424
Gazankulu 451
Gcaleka Xhosa 79, 145, 157, 187, 221, 231
Gcalekaland 227
Gebhart, Wilhelm 132
Genadendal 112–13
Genoodskap van Regte Afrikaans 287,
   288–9
George VI, King 428
Gereformeerde Kerk (Doppers) 166, 224,
   485
German East Africa 384, 387, 388
German Land and Colonization Company
   350
German South-West Africa 282–3, 286,
   379, 388; revolt in 393; South African
   mandate 388, 422; war in 383–4
Germany 56; Afrikaners and 379, 418–19;
   colonies 282–3, 289, 311, 350, 355, 372,
   379, 383–4, 387; emigrants 18, 58, 220;
   relations with Britain 326; relations with

Germany – *cont.*
Transvaal 304, 316, 319, 323; in World War II 419
Gesellschaft für Deutsche Kolonisation 282–3
Ghana xxv, 433, 438
Gibraltar 2, 11, 56
Gideon, Commandant 166
Giliomee, Hermann 95
Gingindlovu 265
Gladstone, Herbert, Lord 373, 378
Gladstone, William Ewart 268, 276, 321; and Basutoland 279; and Boers 280; on Carnarvon 251; as Chancellor of Exchequer 228; and confederation policy 252; on expansion 349; governments of 236, 243, 266, 275, 285; and Ireland 308; retirement 313; on Rhodes 313; and Transvaal 270, 272, 282; on Xhosa wars 197, 198
Glasgow Missionary Society 111
Glen Grey Act (1894) 309–10, 449
Glenelg, Lord 110, 160, 177, 178, 180
Goa 8, 9
Godée-Molsbergen, Dr E.C. 368
Goderich, Lord 151–2
Godley, J.R. 229
Godlonton, Robert 129, 156, 187, 195, 202, 203, 229, 244
Goens, Rykloff van 33–4, 51
Gokhale, G.K. 378
Gold Coast, see Ghana
Goldie, Sir George 311
goldmines xxiv, 4, 33, 235, 270, 291, 301–2, 306, 489; and Boer War 324–5, 343; and decline in gold price 491; labour 345, 353, 358
Gomes, Fernando 5
Goncharov, Ivan A. 203
Gonnema (Black Captain) 46, 50
Gool, Dr Goolam 423
Gorbachev, Mikhail 494
Gordon, Gen. Charles 275–6, 278, 282, 320
Gordon, Lady Duff 203
Gordon, Col. Robert 80, 89
Goschen, G.J. (Lord Goschen) 324
Goshen, Republic of 147, 279, 280–2
Goske, Isbrande 45, 46, 49
Goulburn, Henry 131
Govan, William 217
government: apartheid 385; under Batavian Republic 97–100; under British

occupation 90–1; Burgher Council/Senate 47, 90, 103, 133, 150; colonial 200; by Council of Policy 25–6, 33, 34, 47, 50, 53–4, 57, 64, 82; dismissal of 260, 274; Executive Council 200; Governors 116, 132, 200, 229; High Commissioners 189, 216, 229; majority rule 215; Legislative Council 200; local 200, 409–10, 490; of Natal 214, 227, 229, 245; Nationalist 210, 231; Patriots and 85–7; reforms 477, 484, 490; representative 200; responsible 200–1, 243–5, 252; of South Africa 355, 365–6, 399–400, 481–2, 490; see also Parliament
Gqishela, Zachariah 294
Gqunukhwebe 80, 81, 94, 124, 188, 228
Graaf, Sir de Villiers 445
Graaff-Reinet 81–3, 87, 92–5, 102, 109, 121–2, 149, 168
Graham, Col. John 119, 183
Graham, Robert 290
Graham's Town Journal 129, 156, 177, 195
Grahamstown 119, 125–6, 128, 144, 156–7, 161, 166, 230
Grand Committee on Native Affairs 406, 407
Granville, Lord 283, 308
Gray, Archbishop Robert 200, 228, 248
Great Britain: abandons gold standard 405; Anglo-Dutch relations 10–11, 13–14, 30, 38, 44–5, 49–50, 84–5, 88–9, 116, 121; annexation of Cape 10; attitude to non-whites 104, 133, 454–5; and Boer Republics 207, 232; and Boer War 321–37, 341–2; chartered companies 311; colonial policy 126, 159–60, 200, 228–9, 252–3, 275–6, 285, 311–12, 326, 435, 441, 455; emigration 126, 127, 200, 344, 429; explorers 6, 9; franchise 104; and gold rush 302; immigration 448; international finance 302, 306, 324–5; and Ireland 276; and Jameson Raid 318; missionaries 19, 108–9; occupation of Dutch Cape 88–97; peace negotiations 338–9; public opinion in 181, 182, 229, 372, 492; reformism in 84, 104, 126, 134; relations with South Africa 455, 466–7, 480; Secret Service 88; shipping 9–10, 30; social unrest in 308; South Africa policy 274–5, 325, 327, 329, 359, 361, 386; and Union 225, 371–2; in United

Nations 433; and Xhosa wars 188–9,
197, 198; wars 56, 271–2, 274, 322, 326,
419; see also Scotland
Great Reform Act (1832) 134, 148
Great Trek xxii, xxiii, 139, 146–8, 150–2,
162, 165–9, 177, 261; centenary
celebrations 413, 414, 417
Great Zimbabwe xxiv, 1, 41
Greater London Council 492
Green, James 248
Greenwood, Sir Hamar 386
Gregorowski, Judge 320
Greig, George 131
Greville, Charles 120
Grey, Albert, 4th Earl 315–16, 319
Grey, Charles, 2nd Earl 134,
Grey, Lord, 3rd Earl: as Colonial Secretary
189, 206; and democracy 200; and
expansion of Cape 191, 193; and Natal
Land Commission 213; and Orange
River Sovereignty 203; and site of Cape
capital 201; and Smith 190, 196–7; and
transportation proposal 197–8
Grey, Gen. George 104
Grey, Sir George: arrival of 216; colonial
career 216; and confederation proposal
252; frontier policy of 216–17, 227; and
Griqua 233; as High Commissioner 216,
234; and support for union 224–5;
Xhosa 219–21, 228, 230
Greyshirts 412
Griffith, Chief 436, 438
Griffith, Bishop Patrick 195
Griquas: Barends 163; and Boers 185–6,
207; British betrayal of 232–3;
constitution 184; diamond fields claim
238, 240; groupings 163–4; Khoikhoi in
153; Kok's 163, 185–6, 192, 196, 208, 227,
232–3, 236; in militias 168, 193; of
Orange Free State 208, 209, 227, 232–3,
236; raids on Matabele 139, 168; Smith
and 192; Trek of 233; Waterboer's 163,
192, 227, 236, 237–8
Griqualand East 233, 236
Griqualand West 239–43, 253–4, 256, 290,
295, 298, 414
Griquatown 164
Grobler, J.H. 224
Groenendaal, Jacob 209
Grosvenor, Bend'Or (Duke of
Westminster) 323
Group Areas Act 430, 445–6

Gubbins, Dr Sir Charles Decimus O'Grady
374
Guinea 4, 36
Gumede, Archie 487
Gumede, Josiah 402–3, 404, 409
Gun War 241, 277–8, 279
Gwala, Harry 505
Gwamile, Queen Regent, see Lomawa

Haarlem 19, 22, 24
Hackius, Pieter 43–4, 46
Haewarden, Mevrouw 31
Haggard, Sir Henry Rider 257, 258, 267–8
Haldane, R.B. 341
Haldane, Robert 111
Hall, William 307
Hamilton, Edward 278, 282
Hamu 266, 267
Handhawersbond 420
Hani, Chris 441, 486, 494, 508
Harare Declaration 499
Harcourt, Sir William 321, 378
Harding, J.A. 173
Hardinge, Lord 377, 378
Hare, Col. John 185
Harlech, Lord 437
Harn, Gerrit van 39
Harris, J.H. 377
Harris, John 462
Harry (Hadah) 28–9, 30–1, 32, 36, 37
Havenga, Nicholas 401, 405, 421, 427, 444
Heemskerk, Admiral 11
Heerden, Neil van 493
Helpmekaar 382
Hendricks, Thilman 48
Hendriks, Hendrik 185
Henry the Navigator, Prince 2, 4–5
Herbert, Robert 250, 253, 269, 281
Herbert, Thomas 14
Herenigde Nasionale Party (HNP) 420
Herold, Tobias 165
Herschel, Sir John 199, 203
Herstige Nasionale Party (HNP) 465, 477,
484
Hertzog, Albert 462, 465, 477
Hertzog, Dirk 484
Hertzog, James Barry Munik 393; and
Afrikaners 396–7, 415, 421; and British
Protectorates 435–6; and Broederbond
412; and Commonwealth 407; death of
421; and dominion 399–400; forms
Afrikaner Party 421; Freedom

A History of South Africa

Hertzog, James Barry Munik – *cont.*
Delegation of 385–6, 387; and gold
standard 405; and Nationalists 346, 375,
380, 421; Native Franchise Bills of 397,
403, 406, 407–9; Pact Government of
396, 401, 403; peace negotiator 339;
personality of 396; political career 347,
374; as Prime Minister 396, 406, 417,
430; rebels and 381, resignation 419; and
Second World War 419
Hertzog Prize for Prose 471
Het Volk 347, 359, 361, 373
Heyns, Johan 485
Hicks Beach, Sir Michael 269
Hintsa, Chief xxiii, 123, 125, 157–8, 165,
259, 424
Hlobane 264
Hlubi 169, 249–50
Hobbes, Thomas 16
Hobhouse, Emily 343
Hobsbawm, Dr Eric 325
Hodgson, Thomas 133
Hoffman, Johannes 207
Hofmeyr, G.R. 393
Hofmeyr, Jan 398, 401; attacked by
Nationalists 427; in Cabinet 406, 421;
death 428, 434; liberal leader 394, 418;
and non-whites 375, 413, 422; opponent
of apartheid 408, 415, 418; on racial
discrimination 426
Hofmeyr, Jan ('Onze Jan') 288–9, 290,
291, 309, 319, 328, 356
Hofmeyr, Willie 400
Hogge, Major 197, 203–6
Holland, see Netherlands
Holland, Sir Henry 276, 295
Hong Kong 189, 190, 197
Hong Xiuqan 125
Hoogenvoet, C.P. 287
Hooper, James 106
Hopetown 235
'Hottentot Proclamation' 107
'Hottentot Venus' see Baartman, Saartje
Hottentots, see Khoikhoi
Hottentots Holland xxvi, 23, 42, 43, 45, 50,
51, 199
House of Commons (British) 160–1, 166,
280; Bondelswart protest 393; Buthelezi
in 472; Jameson Raid inquiry 319; South
African Unification Bill 256; Union Bill
debate 373
Hout Bay 30

Howe, Geoffrey (Lord Howe) 492
Huddleston, Archbishop Trevor 108, 446,
462
Hugo, Victor 270
Huguenots 52, 133
Huising, Henning 56
Hundred Years of Wrong, A (Smuts) 341
Huskisson, William 126, 134

Ilanga lase Natal 349
Illegal Squatters Act (1951) 430
Illustrated London News 199
Imhoff, Baron van 63, 64
immigration 57–8, 234; black 235; British
126, 127–30, 344, 429; Indian 247; labour
345; *uitlanders* 301, 306–7
Immorality Act (1927) 397; (1950) 430, 491
Imperial British East Africa Company 311
Imperial Conference (1926) 399
Imvo Zabantsunu 293, 295, 335, 349, 376
India: British 13, 111, 116, 152, 158, 188–9,
190, 258–9, 263, 339, 454; emigrant
labour 247, 345; Indian Mutiny 196, 220,
258; relations with South Africa 422–3,
433; as republic 456; self-government
416
India Office (British) 160
Indian Congresses 354, 423, 431–2, 446,
458, 487
Indians xix, xx; ANC and 423, 431–2;
under apartheid 427, 446, 450, 457. 477;
attacks on 423, 431; in Boer Republics
378; Cape 355; discrimination against
377–9, 402, 418; empowerment of 481;
franchise 354, 416, 422; House of
Delegates 482, 507; land tenure 422;
Legislative Council 402; militancy 422;
Natalian 247, 292, 297, 354, 367, 377–8,
422–3; under 1984 Constitution 481,
482, 483; opposition movements 354;
racism of 379; South African 377–9,
409; of Transvaal 378, 423; and white
supremacy 355
Indura River 221
Industrial and Commercial Workers'
Union (ICU) 393, 402–3, 404,
409
Industrial Conciliation Act 401
industry 509; Afrikaner ownership 463;
building 356; colour bar in 291, 391, 397,
406; expansion of 345, 390, 401, 411,
420, 425; manufacturing xix, 401, 425,

463, 490; nuclear xix, 489; and sanctions 489; see also mining
Inkatha 411, 472–3, 488, 494, 505–6, 508, 512, 513
Institute for Race Relations 395, 412, 418
Insuzi Valley massacres 362
Inter-Imperial Relations Committee 399
International Court of Justice 466
International Socialist League 392
Ipepa lo Hlanga 349
Iran 488
Ireland 96, 104, 197, 276, 281, 308, 389, 419, 489
Iron and Steel Corporation of South Africa (Iscor) 401, 411
Isandhlwana 253, 264, 265, 275
Islam 101, 202, 488
Israel 489, 492
izwekufa 169
Izwi Labantu 261, 349, 356

Jaarsveld, Adriaan van 80–3, 93, 95, 96
Jabavu, John Davidson Don xxi, xxii, 398, 402, 408, 409
Jabavu, John Tengo xxi, 292–5, 335, 348–9, 356, 370–1, 377
Jacobsen, Pieter 36
Jacquelot de Moncets, Capt. Charles 203
Jamaica 149, 158, 251
James, Duke of York (King James II) 44, 50
Jameson, Dr Leander Starr: Jameson Raid 317–18, 320, 323–4, 329, 382, 415; Mashonaland massacre 314–15; political career 347–8; as Prime Minister 348; supporters of 373
Jans, J. 48
Janssens, Willem 97, 100–3, 110, 113, 115
Japan 492
Jervis, Capt. 173
Jews 412, 420
Jingoes, Jason 384, 404
João II, King of Portugal 5
Johannesburg 301, 302, 312, 317, 331, 383, 390, 423, 446, 512
John Maurice, Count of Nassau 24
Joint Councils of Africans and Europeans 394–5
Jonathan, Chief 438–9, 470
Jones, J.D. Rheinallt 412
Jordan, W.W. 286
Jorissen, E.J.P. 257, 258, 267, 268

Joseph, Helen 452
Joubert, Gideon 172
Joubert, Joshua 166
Joubert, Piet 305; and Bechuanaland 285; and Kruger 306, 312; in London delegation 269; President of New Republic 280; as progressive 303; on Transvaal self-government 273; in triumvirate 271, 300
Joyi 221
judicial system: Advisory Council 132; Cape 90–1, 132–3, 294–5; Charters of Justice 132; Council of Justice 53–4, 87, 101; Court of Justice 26, 90; circuit courts 113, 114–15; in frontier districts 113, 114–15; in homelands 487; Nationalist 433–4, 444; in Orange Free State 255; reform of 132–3; show trials 453–4, 460; South African 376, 409, 433–4, 444, 448, 509; Supreme Court 434; Treason Trial 453–4
Juta, Coenraad 257

Kaapstad, see Cape Town
Kadalie, Clements 393, 402–3, 404, 409, 431
Kaffraria, see British Kaffraria
Kalahari 236, 284, 286
Kalmaga tribe 139
Kama 188, 228
Kambula 265
Kangwane 442, 451
Kappie Kommando 452
Karoo xxvi, 66–7, 76, 78, 81, 84
Kasrils, Ronnie 508
Kat River Settlement 153–6, 187, 190, 195–6
Kaunda, Kenneth 465, 468
Keate, Robert 239
Keate Line 280
Kei River 198, 221, 230, 231
Kelly, Michael 106
Kemp, Major J.C.G. 380
Kennedy, President John F. 466
Kentari, battle of 259
Kenya 433, 455
Kestell, Father 417
Keys, Derek 509
Kgama (Khama), Chief xxi, 284, 293, 310, 314–15, 385, 424
Kgama III, Chief 439
Khaile, E.J. 403

Khama, Sir Seretse xxi, 439–41, 442, 470
Khama, Tshekedi 439–40
Khoikhoi xix, 68, 105; apprenticeships 118; British and 107, 152, 195–6; cattle breeders 14, 15–16; Company and 61; conversion of 66; cruelty towards 100; described 14, 17; de-tribalization of 58, 76–7, 107, 153; disintegration of xx, 38, 62, 76–7; and Europeans xxvi, 1, 6, 10, 14–15, 18, 21, 25, 28–9, 31–2, 34, 37–8, 39, 55, 61–5, 92; and Great Trek 147, 162, 165; 'Hottentot Proclamation' 107; 'Hottentot Venus' 114; Kat River Settlement 153–6, 187, 190, 195–6; land grants 152; legal status of 107, 114, 133, 148; as minority 134; missions to 66, 112–13; rebellion 195, 197; revival 153; and slaves 35, 59–60; society 16–18; of Suurveld 106; trade with 45; troops 76, 77, 103, 119, 122, 123, 157, 181, 183, 188; violence by 46, 95–6, 195; and Xhosa 74, 79, 124, 186
Khoikhoi Cape Regiment 119, 123
Khoikhoi Corps of Pandours 77, 103, 107
Kimberley 235, 240–1, 243, 290, 299, 302, 304, 330, 432
Kimberley, Earl 275; on Boer expansion 281; as Colonial Secretary 238, 277; and confederation policy 252; as Foreign Secretary 351; and London Convention 327; on South Africa 239; and Transvaal 267, 270, 272; and Zululand 266
Kinde, Africa 241
King, Dick 181
King, William McKenzie 399
Kipling, Rudyard 327
Kissinger, Henry 468, 469
Kitchener, Lord 320, 322, 331, 334, 338–9, 358
Klaas, Captain, see Dorha
Knutsford, Lord 308, 310
Kock, Judge 325, 328
Koegas atrocities 294
Koestler, Arthur 396
Kok, Adam 62, 172, 185, 192, 208, 232–3, 236, 440; Griquas of 163, 186, 192, 196, 208, 227
Koornhof, Piet 477
Koosibai 351
Kora 164
Koranna 184, 192, 254, 284
Kotane, Moses 407, 423, 445

Kotze, J.J. 223
Kotzé, John Gilbert 267, 307
Kruger, Caspar 166, 184
Kruger, Jimmy 475, 476–7
Kruger, Paul 184, 500; and Boer War 327, 329; customs union proposal 305; and drift crisis 316; flees abroad 331; Gladstone and 270; in London 258, 267–9, 281; and Jameson Raid 319; as military commander 226, 264; and national bank 306; personality 300, 302–3; as President 176, 279, 285, 300, 302–4, 320; and railways 286, 299, 304–5, 316; and 'Reformers' 317; and Royal Commission 272–3; and Swaziland 352; and trekkers 312; in triumvirate 271, 300; and *uitlanders* 308, 313; as Vice-President 258; and Volksraad 303–4
Kruger National Park 222
Kumalo, Mzi 513
Kuruman 141, 283
Kuyper, Abraham 416
Kuzwayo, Elias 410
KwaNdebele 451
KwaZulu 136, 451, 472–3
KwaZulu Natal 509, 512, 513

Labouchere, Henry 225
labour 390, 509–12; black 235, 241, 245–6, 290, 297, 302, 358, 376, 401–2, 410, 411, 425, 447, 450, 471; Chinese 345, 358; Coloured 356; inadequacy of 490; Indian 247; Khoikhoi 118; labour tax 309; miners 290–1, 301, 344–5; strikes 235, 291, 382–3, 390, 425–6, 496; unemployment 512, 514; wages 356, 390, 401, 475; white 382
Labour Party (British) 373, 377, 438, 440, 446
Labour Party (South African) 373; alliance with Nationalists 392, 399; and colour bar 397, 406; election results 388–9, 396, 403, 428; in Pact Government 396, 403; and trades unions 383, 391
Ladysmith 330
La Guma, James 402
Lancaster, James 10, 23
land tenure: anti-Boer prejudice in 152; Crown lands 117–18, 246, 296, 353; diamond field claims 240; under Glen Grey Act 309; government

incompetence in 150; Indian 422; in Natal 176–7, 213, 246, 296–7, 422; native 246, 296, 309, 353, 376, 377, 407
Landsdown, Justice 437
Langa 489
Langalibalele, Chief 248, 249–50, 252
language xix, xx, 2, 61, 108, 287–8; Afrikaans 61, 222, 287–8, 347, 396–7, 401, 415, 474; English xix, 108, 125, 127, 133, 202, 288, 344, 417; equal rights of 406; under peace agreement 340, 344; taal 105, 108, 134, 163, 222, 287; of South Africa 366
Lansdowne, Lord 322, 329
Lanyon, Owen 267
Latrobe, Christian 122
law xxv; of Batavian Republic 101; blacks under 100, 294–5; British 90, 104, 133, 212; diggers 237; equality before 104, 133, 134–5, 148, 150, 235; Habeus Corpus Act abolished 458; international 480; Khoikhoi under 107, 114, 133, 148; of Rand 307; slaves under 90; traditional black 69, 72, 212–13, 214, 437; trekker 168; whites under 294, 404; see also judicial system
Lawrence, Harry 434
Lazarus family 345
League of Nations 388, 393, 419
Leballo, Potlako 463–4
Lebowa 451
Leendert Janzoon 22–4, 25, 35
Lekhanya, Gen. 439
Lekota, Patrick 'Terror' 487, 513
Lembede, Anton 424–5
Lembotho Mountains 222
Lendy, Capt. 314
Leonard, Charles 317
Lerotholi 277
Leroux, Etienne 471
Le Roux, Frank 476
Lesotho xxv, 71, 255, 279, 435, 439, 465, 470, 480; see also Basutoland
Lesotho Liberation Army 438
Letsie, Chief 277, 436
Letsie II, Chief 437
Letsie III, King 439
Lettow-Vorbeck, Gen. von 387
Leviseur, Sophie 226
Leyds, Dr Willem 304, 319, 323
Liberal Party (British) 308, 313–14, 349, 358–9, 373

Liberal Party (South African) 418, 445
Libertas Bon 418
Libertas League of Action 418
Lichtenstein, Dr Henry 101, 112, 113
Limpopo River 1, 167, 222
Linchwe, Chief 335
Lindley, Daniel 170, 175–6, 185, 209, 212, 213, 223
Lippert 328
Liquor Act (1898) 294, 356
literature 471–2
Liverpool, Lord 121
Livingstone, David 109, 135, 141, 283
Lloyd George, David 386–7, 389
Loan Bank 105
Lobengula 140, 310–11, 314–15
Loch, Sir Henry 312–13, 314, 316
Lomawa (Gwamile), Queen Regent 352, 442
London Convention 281, 282, 286, 313, 316, 324, 327, 351
London Missionary Society 109–10, 112–13, 135, 140–1, 163, 195, 439
Louis (slave) 105–6
Louis XIV, King of France 52, 56
Lourenço Marques 73, 75, 165, 170, 305
Loreburn, Lord 360
Lovedale 217, 246, 261, 292–3, 357, 390, 398
Lovedu 222
Lowther, James 267
Luderitz Bay 5
Lukin, General Sir Henry 384
Luneville, Treaty of 97
Lungu 74
Lutuli, Albert 247, 460, 472: advocates non-violence 458; ANC leader 431, 433; as liberal 446; and Mandela 459, 505; Nobel Peace Prize 348, 454; restriction order on 445, 454; stature of 459; as teacher 424; and Treason Trial 453–4
Lutuli, Martin 348, 354, 363
Lydenburg 147, 224, 226, 254, 257–8, 301
Lyttelton, Alfred, Lord 354, 359, 373

Maatschappij Tot Nut van t'Algemeen 101
Macartney, George, Earl 91, 93, 96, 100
Macaulay, Zachary 114
MacBride, Sean 489
MacCullum, A.J. 408
MacCullum, Sir Henry 362
Machel, Samora 481, 486
Mackenzie, John 226, 233, 285

MacKinnon, Sir William 311
Maclean, John 191, 227
Macleod, Iain 455
Macmillan, Harold 438, 448, 455
McNamara, Robert 467
Macoma, Chief 156–8, 186–7, 191, 196, 198, 227–8, 424
Macrorie, Bishop William 248
Madagascar 43
Madzikane, Chief 144
Mafeking 280, 330, 336, 341, 440
Magena, Alfred 376
Magersfontein, battle of 331
Maguire, Rochfort 310
Mahabane, Revd Zaccheus 395, 403, 408
Maharaj, Mac 494
Mahlatsi, Esau 487
Mahura, Chief 237
Maine, Kas 346
Maintenon, Françoise de 52
Maitland, Sir Peregrine 185, 186, 188, 189
Majuba Hill 271–2, 275, 331, 415
Makana, see Nxele
Makgatho, Sefako 385, 391, 431
Mako, Chief 222
Malan, Dr Daniel François: and apartheid 427–8, 449; and British Protectorates 436; Christian Nationalism of 448; as journalist 375, 381, 400; leads Purified Nationalists 412, 417–18, 421, 427; and non-whites 402, 403, 433–4; as Prime Minister 429–30, 433–4; as republican 399, 406–7; retirement 444; and South-West Africa 429, 466
Malan, F.S. 374, 386, 396, 408
Malan, Gen. Magnus 479–80, 493, 506
Malan, 'Sailor' 420, 432
Malawi 139, 455, 457, 470
Mambe 337
Manchester, Duke of 256
Manchester Guardian 372
Mandela, Nelson 108, 144, 295; as Africanist 425; ANC leader 445, 454, 459, 461, 465; ancestry xx, 75, 425, 502–3; arrest 459; background 504; and Botha 497–8; British influences on 503; as communist 445; in Defiance Campaign 432; and de Klerk 499, 504–5, 507, 509; on democracy 483; divorce 507; imprisonment 461, 497–9, 504; and MK 458–9; personality 459, 503; release 499; stature of 459, 492, 497,

508; trials 454, 460–1, 483; violence advocated by 458; and Xhosa mythology 261
Mandela, Winnie 459, 497, 507
Maphasa, Chief 188, 195
Mapoch, Chief 222
Marais, J.S. 95
Marais, Jannie 400
Marais, Jaap 477, 484
Marcello, Caetano 467
Maritz, Gert 147, 165, 166, 168, 172, 174–5
Maritz, Col. Manie 379–80
Maritz, Stephanus 174, 183, 184
Marks, J.B. 423, 425
Marks, Sammy 345
Marmaree 241
marriage: in black societies 71; intermarriage 74, 112, 199, 246, 412–13; legislation 413, 430; polygamy 72, 74
Marwick, J.S. 408, 411
Maseru 439
Mashonaland 310, 314
Masire, Dr Quett 442
Masiza, Revd Peter 260–1
Mass Democratic Movement 496
Massouw, David 284
Masters and Servants Acts 390, 397–8
Masupha, Chief 278
Matabele, see Ndebele
Matabeleland 284, 309, 310, 315
Matanzima, Chief Kaiser 457
Matiwane 144
Matrimonial Chamber 47
Matroos, Hermanus 196
Matthews, Joe 426, 445
Matthews, Z.K. 398, 408, 416, 424, 425, 431, 432, 445–6
Mauritius 43, 48, 49, 51, 158
Mauritius Eiland 19
Maxeke, Charlotte 390
Maynier, Honoratus 82, 83, 94, 96
Mazeppa 165
Mbalu 81
Mbandzeni, King 351
Mbeki, Govan 453, 486
Mbeki, Thabo 486, 495
Mbeki, Thomas 404
Mboyazi 262
Mdange tribe 80, 81
Mdantsane 470–1
Meade, Sir Robert 275, 319
Meer, Fatima 261

Mehlokazulu 362
Meij brothers 60
Meir, Golda 489
Mells Park House talks 495, 498
Mentzel, O.F. 63
Merriman, John Xavier 379; and Boer
  Republics 328; and Cape rebels 347; and
  dependencies 238, 256, 279, 283, 294;
  and federation proposal 253, 259; on
  Froude 255; on German war 387; on
  Gladstone 378; on Hertzog 396; on
  Hofmeyr 288; on Lerotholi 277; as
  liberal 292, 348, 356; in London 278;
  loses seat 348, 356; Member of
  Parliament 244, 374; and Milner 342,
  347; as Minister 259, 291, 309, 320; and
  non-whites 293, 359, 385, 392, 394;
  opposes franchise restrictions 310; as
  Prime Minister 364; and railways 299,
  305; retirement 394; and Rhodes 236–7,
  318, 319; and South African Union 364,
  371; and *uitlanders* 317
Merriman, Archdeacon Nathaniel 218
Methodism 110, 111, 144, 357, 453, 504
Meurant, Louis 287
Meyer, Dr Piet 418, 461, 465
Meyer, Roelf 509, 513
mfecane xxvi, 136, 137, 141–4, 146, 167, 194;
  map 142–3; dispossessed 292; refugees
  156, 163, 187
Mfengu xxi, 145; black attitude towards
  144; British citizenship 231; of Cape 157,
  212; and disarmament 260; loss of
  traditions 136, 144; in militias 188;
  political activity 356–7; schoolmen 292;
  of Victoria 191, 202; as voters 202, 244;
  and Xhosa 153, 157, 187, 196, 221, 228,
  259
Mhala 195, 261
Mhlangaso 350
Mholo 74
Michell, Charles 151
Middleburg 339, 340
Mierhoff, Eva van 32, 37, 48, 49, 112
Mierhoff, Pieter van 27, 32, 41–2, 48, 112
Militz, Hermann 306
Milner, Sir Alfred (Lord Milner): and
  Anglo-Saxon superiority 289; attempts
  to suspend constitution 347;
  background 321; and Boer War 324, 325,
  327–30, 338; and Cape rebels 322, 338;
  and English-speaking state 344, 347; and

former republics 359; as High
  Commissioner 321; and liberals 347; and
  peace negotiations 338–40; post-war
  342; and Progressives 348; refuses
  Colonial Secretaryship 344; resignation
  358; in war cabinet 386
Mines and Works Amendment Act 397
mining 297; Afrikaner ownership 462–3;
  black conditions 383, 425; and Boer War
  325, 343; Chamber of Mines 302, 307,
  343, 395–6; diamonds 235–43, 274,
  290–1, 302, 383; labour 290–1, 301,
  344–5, 391; strikes 390, 391; see also
  goldmines
missionaries 108–14, 130, 170, 187; aims of
  290; American 168, 175; in
  Bechuanaland 283, 439; evangelical 121;
  expulsions 236; first 19, 110; and Griquas
  163; and Indians 247; and language 108;
  Methodist 453; and *mfecane* survivors
  140–1, 144; missionary road 240, 281,
  284; murders of 228; in Natal 214;
  racism amongst 195; relations with
  Afrikaners 108–9, 113, 135, 195, 207,
  446–7; relations with British 153;
  schools 108–9, 217, 293, 427, 437;
  stations 246; Zulus and 263
Mitchell, C.B.H. 296
Mixed Marriages Act 413, 430, 482, 491
Mlanjeni 195
Mmanthatisi, Queen 165
MNR (Moçambique National Resistance)
  469
Mocke, Jan 185
Modderfontein 335
Modise, Joe 494
Moffat, John 310
Moffat, Mary 514
Moffat, Robert 109, 135, 140–1, 167, 238,
  283, 284
Mohlomi, Chief 194
Mokone, Mangena 357
Molapo 436
Molema, Dr Joshua 382, 408
Molema, Dr Silas 382, 445
Molesworth, Sir William 197, 217
Molitsani, Chief 192
Molteno, Donald 412
Molteno, Sir John 202, 216, 229, 243, 245,
  253, 256, 259–60
Molteno, Percy 318, 360
Montagu, John 200

Montsioa, George 376
Moodie, Benjamin 127
Moodie, Donald 127, 161
Moor, Frederick 368
Moosa, Rahima 452
Morality Act (1902) 356, 360
Morant, 'Breaker' 334
Moravian Brethren 66, 112–13
Moresby, Captain Fairfax, RN 128
Mormons 148
Moroka, Chief 147, 164, 167, 192, 194, 208, 209, 226
Moroka II 299
Moroka, Dr James 408, 431, 432, 433
Moroosi 277
Mosako, Paul 426
Moshoeshoe, Chief 227, 424; and Boers 207, 221, 225, 236; and British 192, 232, 277; founder of Basutoland 140, 208, 219, 231, 436; greatness of 193–4; in old age 231, 277; successors 436; treaties 164, 186; unity of 260
Moshoeshoe II, King 435, 438–9
Moss, Joseph 241
Mossel Bay 1, 2, 5, 6
Mostert, Mr Justice 495
Mothers' Union 452
Moustert, Wouter Cornelis 47
Mozambique: FRELIMO 469; independence 468; native peoples of 71; Nkomati Accord 486; Portuguese 8, 222, 311, 388, 455; relations with South Africa 470, 486; RENAMO 481; as slave market 35, 59; as source of labour 344
Mpande 174, 176, 180, 210, 227, 262
MPLA 468–9, 486
Mpondo 71, 73, 144–5, 180, 210, 230, 259, 350, 377, 453
Mpondomise 230
Mqikela 350
Msane, Saul 385
Msimang, Richard 376, 410
Msimang, Selby 409
Mswati, King 350
Mswati III, King 442
Mthethwa tribe 136–7
Mthikrakra, Chief 188, 503
Mthonga 262
Mugabe, Robert 487, 514
Muizenberg 89
Mulder, Dr Connie 478, 484
Mundy, Peter 14

Murray, Andrew 121
Murray, Ds Andrew Jr 207, 223
Murray, Sir George 134
Mushet, James 410
Muzorewa, Bishop Abel 487
Mzilikazi 139–41, 167, 169, 171, 175–6, 178, 240, 284, 310

Naicker, Dr G.M. 423, 458
Namaqua 41, 164
Namibia xxvi, 1, 5, 15, 467–9, 480, 493, 506; see also South-West Africa
Napier, Gen. Sir George 172, 177, 178, 180–2, 185, 331
Nasionale Pers 400, 428
Natal 192, 209–15, 225, 286, 364; annexation 208–9, 414; blacks in 75, 76, 210–1, 232, 245–6, 249–50, 256, 262–3, 292, 296–8, 352–4, 362–3, 367, 369; Boer War in 330, 335; boundaries 231; British colony 210–14, 355, 369, 451; and confederation proposal 253–4; constitution 251; depopulated 144, 145; downgrading of 251–2, 274; economy 347; education 254; expansionism 349–52; farming 245–6, 247–8; founding of 127; franchise 245, 349, 354, 367; government 214, 227, 229, 251, 355, 362; Home Rulers 406; Indians 247, 292, 297, 354, 367, 377–8, 422–3; as KwaZulu Natal 509, 512, 513; land tenure 213–14, 296–7; law in 250; Legislative Council 250; map 211; Nationalists in 464; opposition movements 348–9, 354; Parliament 245, 250; political parties 389; population 212, 214, 367; presses for increased independence 434; racism 245; railway 312; rebellion in 362–3; responsible government 298; revenues 254; segregation in 414; sugar industry 247; taxation 377; and Transvaal 312; as trekker destination 164, 167; and Union proposals 254, 365–8; and Zululand 266; Zulus in 472, 488, 505
Natal Farmers' Congress 367
Natal Independent 212
Natal Native Congress 348
Natal Witness 214, 315
Natalia, Republic of 147, 169–76, 179–84, 209, 213
National Action Council 459
National Association (Transvaal) 361

National Convention 365–71
National Institute for Christian Education and Instruction 418
National Intelligence Service 498
National Party (Nationalists): and Afrikaners 430; and ANC 495; apartheid of 427–30, 448–50, 464; Christian Nationalism of 447–8, 464–5; coalitions 392, 395, 399, 405–7; congresses 421; divisions 406–7, 428, 484, 494, 512–13; education policy 446–8; election results 380, 388–9, 396, 403, 406, 427, 435, 461, 464, 477, 491, 501, 502; founded 375; governments 210, 231; and Great War 384; Hertzog Freedom Deputation of 385–6; Hertzog leaves 421; and Inkatha 506–7; legal challenges to 433; and liberals 395; opposition to 432–4, 444, 452, 462, 471, 501, 507; in Pact Government 396; Purified Nationalists 412, 418, 421, 422; relations with Coloureds 423, 444; repressive measures of 452–4, 457–8, 464; Strydom governments 444, 446; supports striking miners 391; Transvaal 500, 501; and United Party 407, 434
National Scouts 334
National Union of South African Students 475
Native Administration Act 385, 398
Native Affairs, Department of 410, 429, 477
Native Affairs Act (1920) 394
Native Affairs Commission 394
Native Affairs Council 395
Native Franchise Bills 397, 403, 406, 407–8
Native Land (Amendment) Bill 397
Native Laws Amendment Bill (1937) 409
Native Representative Council 407, 425–6, 457
Natives' Land Act (1913) 375–6, 377
Natives Urban Areas Act (1923) 394
Naudé, Dr Beyers 462
Naudé, Ds J.F. 382
Ncaphayi 144, 180
Ndamese 350
Ndebele (Matabele) 184, 240; and BSAC 310–11, 315, 320; relations with Boers 167–9, 172, 222; trek to Zimbabwe 139–40, 283

Ndlambe 79, 80, 81, 82, 94, 101, 102, 123–5, 156, 227
Ndongeni 181
Ndwande tribe 136–7, 140
Nederduitsch Zuid-Afrikaansche Tijdschrift 131
Nederduitse Gereformeede Kerk (NGK) 223–4, 485
Nederduitse Hervormde Kerk (NHK) 224, 485
Nellmapius, Alois 304
Nelson, Admiral Horatio, Lord 97, 116
Netherlands 6; Anglo-Dutch relations 10–11, 13–14, 30, 38, 44–5, 49–50, 84–5, 88–9, 116, 121; Batavian Republic 97, 101; colonies 24, 30–1, 43, 44, 45; divisions in 88; economic decline 56–7, 58, 83; as French satellite 102, 116; Patriot revolt 85, 88; relations with Portugal 44; relief expedition to Cape 91; shipping 10, 84; Spanish 11; trade 11–12; wars 56; see also Dutch Cape; Dutch East India Company
New Netherlands 44
New Order Group 421
New Republic 147, 279–80, 352
Newcastle, Duke of 206, 225, 227, 228, 230
Ngangelizwe 503
Ngoni 139
Ngoyi, Lilian 452
Ngqika 79, 81, 93, 94, 101–2, 122, 123–5, 156, 227
Ngubengcuka 502
Nguni xv, 71–5, 136–8, 141, 145, 162, 187, 227
Ngwane clan 145
Ngwato tribe xxi, 284, 439
Nicholls, Heaton 406, 411
Nigeria xix, 18, 457
Nkomati Accord 486
Nomansland 227, 233
Nomantshali 262
Nonensi, Queen 198
Non-European Unity Front 423
Nongqawuse 218, 219
Non-Racial Franchise Association 409
Norman, Montagu 405
Normanby, Lord (Constantine Phipps) 180
Northern Cape 105, 330
Northern Ireland 454, 504
Nqiliso 350
Ntlabati, Gladstone 467

Ntuli, Victor 506
Nursing Amendment Act (1957) 452
Nxele 124–5
Nyasaland 410, 433
Nyerere, Julius 459

Oberholster, Michiel 163, 185
O'Brien, Dr Conor Cruise 488
Odendaal Commission 467
Odessen, Commissioner van 43
Oedasoa, Chief 37
Ohrigstadt 184–5
Oldebarnveldt, Jan van 12
Omdurman 320, 331
O'Meara, Dan 429, 495
Ondini 267
Onselen, Charles van 346
Operation Senekal 478
Oppenheimer, Sir Ernest 395
Oppenheimer, Harry 427, 434, 462
Opperman, Gotlieb 77
Orange, House of 85, 88, 89, 97, 116, 121
Orange Free State 147, 298–9; annexation
  331; Basuto troubles 231–2, 236; blacks
  in 73, 208–9, 226, 231–2, 236, 242,
  298–9, 334–5, 346; and Boer War 327,
  330, 331, 339; British and 312;
  constitution 209; Crown Colony, see
  Orange River Colony; diamond field
  claim 235–7, 239–40, 255, 274; economy
  255, 347; education 255; elections 361;
  franchise 339–40, 359, 366; government
  346, 359, 361; and Griquas 232–3;
  independence 207–8; Indians 378; land
  tenure in 376; landlocked 286;
  missionaries expelled 236; National
  Bank 240; Nationalists in 375, 380,
  420–1; peace terms 339–40; political
  parties 347; population 366; Presidents
  of xxii, 202, 207, 225–6; racism in 236,
  242; reconstruction 343; relations with
  Cape 286, 320; relations with Transvaal
  256, 365; society 226; and Union
  proposals 221, 224–5, 227, 236, 365–6,
  368; wars 232
Orange River 163, 164, 167, 185, 192, 227
Orange River Colony 342, 347, 355, 359,
  361, 374
Orange River Sovereignty 192–3, 197, 198,
  203–7, 237
Orangia Unie 347, 361, 373
Order of True Templars 410

Ordinance Fifty 133, 148
Organization of African Unity 441
Orpen, Joseph 209, 278
Orphan Chamber 47, 133, 174
Osborn, Melmoth 265
Ossewa Brandwag (OB) 146, 418, 420, 421,
  427, 429, 464
Otto, P.A.R. 210
Overbeke, Arnout van 45
Overbergers 64
Ovington, Revd John 55
Owen, Francis 170, 171
Owen, Mostyn 197, 203–6

Paardeberg 342
Paarl 203, 287
Paddon, Albury 242
Pakenham, Thomas 335
Pakington, Sir John 198
Palestine 389
Palmerston, Lord 228
Pan-African Conference 349
Pan African Congress (PAC) 454, 456, 463,
  465–6, 488, 499, 505, 507
Pan-African Freedom Conference 459
Pandit, Vijaya Lakshmi 423, 433
Pannevis, Arnold 287
Paravicini di Capelli, Capt. Willem 101
Pardekraal, Proclamation of 271
Paris Mission Society 111, 207
Parker, Stafford 237, 239
Parliament xxii, 216, 217, 225, 234, 286,
  429, 481, 509; Afrikaners in 288–9, 429;
  ANC in 512; and Boer War 322; under
  constitution 200; and diamond fields
  235, 238, 290; and expansion 229, 231,
  238; and federation proposal 253;
  Grahamstown session 230; House of
  Assembly 202, 219; Legislative Assembly
  202; liberals 292, 347; and National
  Convention 368; under 1984
  constitution 482; non-white members
  244, 356; non-white representation 412,
  423; political groupings 292–3;
  responsible government 243–5; Select
  Committee on Native Bills 406
Parnell, Charles Stuart 256, 276
pass laws 107, 235, 242, 295, 390–1,
  409–10, 430, 452, 454, 491
Paterson, Jock 253
Paton, Alan 433, 445, 472
Patriots' Free Corps 85, 88

Pattle, Pat 420
Paulus, Pieter 84, 86
Pedi xx, xxiii, 73, 222, 241, 254, 257, 350–1, 352
Pedi War 241
Peel, Frederick 208–9
Peel, Sir Robert 182
Pegging Act 422
Pelissier, Jacques 207, 277
Pelser, William 294
Penguijn 42
People's Party, see Herenigde Nasionale Party
Perceval, Spencer 110
Peregrino, F.Z.S. 337, 349
Peters, Carl 283
Petersen, Hector 474
Phakadet, Chief 212
Phalo, Chief 79
Phato, Chief 188, 195, 218, 228
Philip, John 109, 135, 157, 160, 201, 447
Philip II, King of Spain 11
Philipolis 164, 185, 192
Philipps, Thomas 128, 131, 166
Philips, Lionel 328, 383
Philipton 195
Phuti 277
Pickering, Neville 308
Pietermaritzburg 173, 174, 183
Piketberg 61
Pim, Sir Alan 437
Pine, Sir Benjamin 213, 214, 248, 250, 251
Pirow, Oswald 403–4, 406, 421, 453
Pitsani 317
Pitt, William 96, 120
Plaatje, Sol 349, 376–7, 385–7, 395, 398, 410, 427
Plettenberg, Joachim van 79–80, 81, 85, 86, 89
Plettius, van 281
Pniel 237, 239
Pole-Carew, Gen. 383
police 409, 429, 454, 457, 465, 474–6, 489–90, 506, 508, 509
Pondoland 227, 230, 231, 262, 298, 349, 452–3
Pondomisi 145, 260
Ponsonby, Col. 263
Population Registration Act (1950) 430
Port Alfred 129
Port Edward 231
Port Elizabeth 128, 186, 192, 390, 475, 488

Port Natal 170, 171, 176, 180, 181, 182–3
Port St Johns 350
Porter, William 128, 186, 198, 200, 201, 231, 243, 244
Portugal: colonies 8, 41, 179, 255, 311, 355, 455, 467–8; explorers 4–6, 8, 18; in Indies 8, 9, 13; landings xxiv, 1–2, 6; railways 305; relations with Britain 326; relations with Dutch 44; slavers 35
Postma, Ds Dirk 224
Potchefstroom 184–5, 224, 226, 254, 404; University of 448, 500
Potgieter, Hendrik: clashes with Ndebele 167, 171; clashes with Zulus 172; coup attempt 185; death 222; as Dopper 166; leaves Natal 184; relations with Maritz 168; treatment of natives 178; as Trek leader 147, 165, 176
Potgieter, Herman 44
Potgieter, Pieter Johannes 222
Poto, Victor 457
Pottinger, Sir Henry 189–90, 191, 192, 195
Pratt, David 456
press 506; Afrikaner 400; black 293, 295, 349, 432–3; British 372; Cape 129–31, 177; war reporting 331
Pretoria 254, 257–8, 302, 316, 323, 366, 485
Pretoria Convention 272–3, 279, 281, 300
Pretorius, Andries; and black neighbours 173–4, 179–80, 184; Boer leader 147, 185; and British 182–3, 192–3, 203; and religion 224; treatment of blacks 150; in triumvirate 271, 300
Pretorius, Martinus Wessel 222–6, 237, 239, 254
Price, Robert 84
Pringle, Thomas 129–30, 131, 156
Prinsloo, Martinus 95
Prinsloo, Willem 78, 80, 81
Private Eye 464
Progressive Federal Party 477
Progressive Party 307, 356; in government 348; Hollander support for 303; irrelevance of 493; Jameson and 348; Joubert and 306; as mine-owners' party 359; in opposition 306, 361; Suzman as sole representative 461, 464; Vorster and 471
Prohibition of Political Interference Act 491

Promotion of Bantu Self-Government Act (1959) 449
Punch 327, 329

Quaelberg, Cornelis van 43
Queen Adelaide's Land 158, 161, 227
Quigley, Michael 193
Qumbu 260
Qwaqwa 451

racial equality 104, 201, 203
racism 293–4; Afrikaner 109, 110, 135, 150, 177–80, 416; British 206; colour bar 291, 356, 373, 391, 397, 406; in Free State 236; immigrant 241–2; Indian 354; missionary 195; in Natal 245; segregation 377, 385, 391, 394, 398, 402, 409, 414, 430, 445–6, 449, 490
railways 299, 315; Cape 234, 240, 316, 365; expansion 344; Natal 299; segregation 391; strikes 382; Transvaal 255, 257, 286, 304–5, 312, 316
Ramagaga family 345
Ramanbe, Seth 345
Ramaphosa, Cyril 509, 513
Rand 301–2, 316, 358, 359
Rand Daily Mail 472
Rautenbach Gert 93
Rawlinson, Col. Henry 335
Raymond, George 9–10
Read, James 112, 113, 115, 135, 161, 196, 446
Reagan, President Ronald 472, 480, 491
Reddingsdaadbond 418
Redelinghuys, J.H. 86
Reede, Hendrik Adriaan van 21, 52–4, 55, 287
Reenen, Dirk van 101
Registration Act (1887) 294, 295
Reitz, Deneys 380, 388
Reitz, Francis William xxii, 199, 202
Reitz, Francis William Jr 244, 255, 327, 329, 330
Remagen, Harman 32
RENAMO (Resistencia Nacional Mozambicana) 469, 481, 485
Renan, Ernest 270
Rensburg, Hans van 418, 420
Rensburg, 'Lang Hans' van 147, 165
Rensselaer, Kiliaen van 24
Renwick, Robin 490
Representation of Natives Bill 408

Retief, Pieter 147, 161–2, 168–9, 170–1, 174–5, 178
Re-United National Party, see Herenigde Nasionale Party
Revolutionary Miners' Council of Action 391
Reyneveldt, C.J. 107
Reynier, Jan 35
Reynierz, Jacob 25
Rharhabe Xhosa 79, 124, 145, 156, 191
Rheede, Hendryk van, see Reede
Rhenius, Johan 90
Rhodes, Cecil John xxi, 285; achievements of 289; attitude to blacks 294; and Bechuanaland 308, 310, 316; and Chamberlain 319; death of 348; diamond interests 235, 236–7, 308, 313; gold interests 308, 313; as imperialist 289–90, 308, 310–11, 313; influence of 316; and Jameson Raid 318, 319; Kgama and 284; and Milner 347; as Minister 291; as politician 284–5, 290, 291; as Prime Minister 308–9, 313, 317; Privy Councillor 314; and Progressives 356; resignation 317; and Thembu 309; and Transvaal 306, 313, 317, 324; and Xhosa 350
Rhodesia: BSAC in 314, 315, 320, 355; emigrants 410; national movement in 433; relations with neighbours 441; political settlement in 504; and Union 364, 388; white minority regime 455, 465, 469–70; ZAPU 466
Rhoodie, Dr Escher 478
Richart, Louis 38
Riebeeck, Jan van 21–30, 33–5, 38–41, 43, 46–7, 52, 68, 112, 431
Riebeeck, Mevrouw van 31
Rimsky-Korsakoff, Lt 203
Riotous Assembly Act (1929) 403
Ripon, Lord 313, 327
Robben Island 20, 32, 36, 42, 48, 227, 228, 252, 476, 497, 504
Roberts, Lord 272, 331, 342
Robertson, William 38
Robinson, Sir Hercules (Lord Rosmead) 278, 285, 310, 312, 316, 317, 319
Robinson, Joseph 324
Roe, Sir Thomas 10
Rolong tribe 164, 168, 208, 209, 336, 377
Romilly, Samuel 104
Roos, Thielman 398, 403, 405

Roosevelt, President Theodore 289–90, 372
Rooy, Prof. J.C. van 412, 418
Rorke's Drift 212, 263, 264
Rose Innes, Sir James 291, 293, 294, 309, 409
Rosebury, Lord 313
Ross, Hamilton 199
Rouliot, François 324
Royal Commissions 272, 342
Royal Institute of International Affairs 364
Royal Niger Company 311
Rubusana, Revd Walter 356, 370, 377
Rudd, Charles 308, 310
Rudolph, Gert 176
Rumpff, Mr Justice 434, 453
Rupert, Anton 484
Russell, Lord John 180, 181, 189, 203, 206, 217
Russell, William H. 266
Russia 319, 350, 402–3, 494
Rustenberg 226
Ryneveld, Willem van 90, 91, 97, 100, 103, 105, 114

Sachs, Solly 405
St Helena 30, 38, 44, 116, 352
St Helena Bay 6
St Lucia Bay 286
Salazar, António de Oliveira 467
Saldanha, Antonio de 9
Saldanha Bay 9, 10, 42, 51
Salisbury 314, 315
Salisbury, Lord 276, 307, 311, 314, 322–3, 327, 334
Sampson, Anthony 432
Samuelson, Robert 266
San, see Bushmen
Sand River Convention 206, 208, 221, 232
Sandile, Chief xx, 187, 190, 195, 198, 219, 227, 230, 234, 262
Santos, José dos 468
Sargant, Edmund 343
Sarili (Sarhili), Chief 72, 158, 187–8, 219, 221, 227–8, 230–1, 259, 261–2, 503
Sarwa 283
Sastri, V.S.S. 402
Sauer, Jacobus W. 291, 309, 320, 348, 374, 375, 427
Sauer, Paul 427–8
Savimbi, Dr Jonas 468
Scanlen, Thomas 289, 291, 294

Schacher, Prince 45
Schayk, Hendrick 37
Scheepers, Gideon 334, 341
Schmidt, Georg 66, 112
Schoeman, Stephanus 223, 224
Schreiner, Olive 291, 320, 427
Schreiner, Oliver 394, 444
Schreiner, William 202, 291, 320, 328, 347, 371–2, 376
Schroders 306
Schwikkard, E.A.O. 367
Scotland xix, xxii, 17, 48, 70; Church of 111, 121, 223; emigration 127, 128
Scott, John 214, 215
Scott, Revd Michael 423
Scott, Sir Walter 131
Sechele, Chief 283
Seely, Col. 373
Sekhukhune, Chief 222, 241, 254, 257, 269
Sekonyela (Sinkonyala), Chief 165, 192, 208
Sekwati, Chief 222, 241
Selborne, Lord 329, 358, 364, 365, 368, 373, 437
Selous, F.C. 349
Seme, Pixley 376–7, 404, 407, 410, 431
Senghor, President Léopold 459
Sexwale, Tokyo 513
Shaka 137–41, 145, 146, 169–71, 179, 187, 212, 219; myth of 261, 424
Shangaans 139
Sharpeville 454, 455, 456, 457, 466
Shaw, Flora (Lady Lugard) 316
Shaw, Revd William 179–80, 228, 502
Shepstone, Henrique 298
Shepstone, John 298
Shepstone, 'Offy' 351
Shepstone, Sir Theophilus 451; Carnarvon on 256; and Cetshwayo 262; and Colenso 250; Haggard on 257; as Land Commissioner 213, 214–15; maladministration of 269, 275; as Secretary for Native Affairs 249; on traditional law 213; and Transvaal annexation 258, 263, 267–8
Shilling, Andrew 10
Shona 139, 140, 240, 310, 320
Sidmouth, Lord 126
Siganande 362
Sigcawu 350
Sigidimi Sama Xosa 292–3
Simons, Cornelis Johan 56
Simonstown 89, 243, 420

Singh, J.D. 458
Sisulu, Albertina 425, 487, 502
Sisulu, Walter 425, 431, 445, 454, 458, 459, 499, 505
Sivewright, James 309
Sixolo 195, 196
Skhosana 488
Slagtersnek 122–3, 129, 341, 414
slavery xxiv, 4, 8–9, 18, 69; abolition of trade 104, 106, 134, 159, 162, 181; Boers and 179–80, 206, 238; in British colony 105, 118, 134–5, 148, 151; compensation payments 149, 199; in Dutch Cape 35–6, 43, 47–9, 54, 57–61, 63, 66, 78, 90, 100; emancipation 121, 134, 135, 148–50, 172; Protectors 134, 148, 150; raids 238, 245; amongst Tswana 75, 237, 283–4; Xhosa attitude towards 75–6
Sloley, Sir Herbert 436
Slovo, Joe 458–9, 465, 469, 473, 481, 485, 486, 494
Sluysken, Commissioner General 89
Smellekamp, Johann Arnold 183
Smit, Erasmus 166, 168–9, 175, 183, 209
Smit, Gen. Nicolas J. 281, 306
Smit, Susanna 166, 175, 176, 183, 209
Smith, Dr Andrew 164, 170
Smith, Sir Harry 75, 156–8, 190–4, 196–8, 203, 213
Smith, Ian 465, 469
Smith, Capt. Thomas 180, 181
Smuts, Isie 152
Smuts, Jan Christiaan 303, 359, 387, 415, 417; and ANC 422; as Attorney General 327; and Boer War 325, 326–7, 328–30, 331, 335, 340–1; and British 318, 346, 435; death 434; as Deputy Prime Minister 417; on dominion status 399; electoral defeats 396, 428; as English-speaker 381, 397, 415; and fascism 419; on franchise 360, 406; and Gandhi 379; on Hertzog 421; as imperialist 379, 407, 430; as international statesman 388–9, 508; and League of Nations 388, 393; as military leader 384; Nationalists and 395, 405; and native problem 367–8, 392, 394, 403, 414, 418; in peace negotiations 339–40; political leader 346–7; and post-war settlement 388; as Prime Minister 387, 419–22; and race 394, 420; and rebel Afrikaners 380; in South African government 374, 384, 406; and

South African Union 364, 367, 369, 371, 372; and strikes 382, 391–2, 425; as turncoat 375; and United Nations 422, 467; on Versailles Treaty 387–8; writings 341, 396
Smythe, Sir Thomas 14, 19–20
Sneeuwberg 80, 81
Sobhuza I, King 140, 350
Sobhuza II, King 352, 442
Sobukwe, Robert 454
Social Darwinism 372
Society for the Expansion of Christ's Kingdom 110
Soga, Alan 349, 356
Soga, Old xx, xxi, xxii, 246
Soga, Tiyo xx, xxi, 108, 246–7
Solomon, Chief 410
Solomon, Georgiana 377
Solomon, Richard 320, 339, 394
Solomon, Saul 202, 229, 231, 244
Somerset 151
Somerset, Lord Charles 119–23, 125, 128, 130–4, 187, 227
Somerset, Colonel Henry 130, 145, 156
Sophiatown 446
Soshangane 139, 140, 169
Sotho xx, xxiii, 139, 250; assembly 70; Bastaard attacks 163; Boers and 222, 231–2; British protection sought 232, 277; colonial war 260; Moshoeshoe and 140, 164, 194, 231; ritual 73; social structure 74; in South Africa 417; Swazi and 352; territory xxv, 71, 435; see also Basuto
South Africa: Afrikaner rebellion 379–82; and British Protectorates 434, 439, 441; civil service 385, 429; Constitution of 364, 370, 377, 477, 481–4, 487, 499, 507, 509; as democracy 369, 430, 480, 481, 483, 494, 496–7, 501; dominion status 399, 407; economy 405, 411, 456, 464; elections 373, 380, 388, 396, 403, 406, 412, 418, 422, 427, 428, 436, 461, 464, 477, 483, 493, 496, 501, 502, 512; emigration 448; established 189, 207; expansion of 388; federation proposal 252–6, 275, 355; first government 373–5; flag of 399, 406; foreign relations 470, 486–7, 489; franchise 366–9, 371, 397, 403, 406–9, 416, 422, 427, 433–4, 444; government in 355, 365–6, 399–400, 481–2; international standing of 422,

Index

455–7, 466–7, 488, 491–2, 494, 502, 507; labour relations in 382–3, 390, 391; land tenure in 375–7; map 510–11; martial law 391; National Convention on 365–70; non-racial society in 491; Parliament 370, 423; political parties 388–9; post-war 388, 390; racial discrimination in 375–9; reforms 477, 484, 490, 491, 507; Republic of 434, 456; royal visit 428; sanctions 466–7, 489, 492, 499, 502; and South-West Africa 383–4, 422, 429; State of Emergency 456, 490, 502; state terrorism 480, 488, 506; Total Strategy concept 479–81, 490; UN and 422, 455–6; Union of 373; violence in 474–7, 487–8, 506, 508–9, 512; wars 468–70; withdrawal from Commonwealth 456; in World War II 419–21; see also Cape Colony; Dutch Cape
South Africa Bank 199
South Africa Company 140
South Africa League 318
South Africa Spectator 337, 349
South African Air Force 480
South African Brigade 384
South African College 200
South African Commercial Advertiser 131, 177
South African Defence Force 379–80, 382, 429, 470, 479, 481, 493, 506, 509
South African Group for Good Government 418
South African Journal 131
South African Missionary Society 110
South African Mutual Insurance Company 199
South African National Native Congress 356
South African National Party 373
South African Native Affairs Commission 348
South African Native Convention 370
South African Native Labour Contingent 384–5
South African Native National Congress (SANNC) 393; deputation to London 385–7; divisions in 395; first meeting 377; protests 390–1; reorganization 395; Women's League 390; see also African National Congress
South African Party (SAP): Afrikaners in

388–9; alliances 348, 405–6; and black vote 395, 406; election results 396, 406; forms United Party 407; Hofmeyr leaves 418; and native problem 414
South African People's Coloured Organization 446
South African Races Congress 377
South African Republic, see Transvaal
South African Students' Organization 475
South African Templars 410
South-West Africa 429, 466, 467; see also German South-West Africa; Namibia
South-West African People's Organization (SWAPO) 468–9, 480, 485, 486, 493
Southampton, HMS 181
Southey, George 158
Southey, Sir Richard 235, 238, 240
Soweto 474–5, 477, 488
Spain 5, 334
Sparrman, Anders 66
Spoor law 124
sport 491
Sprigg, Gordon 244, 260, 277, 289, 294, 318–19, 347–8
Stallard, Col. 394, 407, 408, 450
Standard Bank 234, 236, 290, 305
Stanford, Walter 365, 368, 371, 503
Stanhope, Edward 276, 308
Stanley, Col. 274
Stanley, Sir F.A. 308
Stanley, Lord 152, 156, 160, 182, 200, 201, 275
State Security Council 481
Stavenisse 75
Stead, W.J. 349
Steenkamp, Anna 150
Stegmann, Maria 121
Stellaland 147, 279, 280, 281
Stellenbosch 51, 53, 64, 81, 198, 203; Landdrost 67, 77; slavery in 59, 149; University of 400
Stephen, James 159, 160, 180, 182, 198
Sterthemius, Peter 38
Stewart, Dr James 293
Steyn, Hermanus 92
Steyn, Martinus: in Boer War 331; on native rights 360; as negotiator 328–30, 339–40; personality of 326–7; President of Orange Free State 320; and South African Union 364
Stockenström, Anders 102, 106, 119, 122
Stockenström, Judge Andries 240

Stockenström, Sir Andries 168; advocate of black rights 150, 161, 178; baronetcy 188; Council member 202; Governor of Eastern Cape 161–2, 185; and Khoikhoi settlement 153, 190; resignation 188; and self-rule 200; and Xhosa 123, 125, 186, 188, 191

Stormberg 192, 331

Strauss, J.G.N. 434, 445

Strop Bill 309

Strydom, Hans 418, 444, 448, 500

Sturrock, Claude 421

Stuttaford, Robert 418

Stutterheim, Baron von 220

Stuurman, David 254

Stuyvesant, Peter xxii, 38

Suez 455

Suffren de St Tropez, Admiral de 84, 88

Suppression of Communism Act (1950) 431, 445

Suurveld: attached to Cape 119; settlement of 126, 129; verbal treaty on 125; war in 82; as Xhosa territory 78, 80, 94, 102, 105, 106

Suzman, Helen 430, 434, 448, 462, 464, 477

SWAPO, see South-West African People's Organization

Swart, N.J.R. 257

Swartkoppies 186

Swazi 136, 139, 350–2, 435, 441–2

Swaziland xxv, 71; ANC in 465; as British protectorate 351–2, 355, 441–2; independence 442; peoples of 140, 435; relations with South Africa 470; as Transvaal protectorate 312, 350–1, 436

Swellendam 64, 66, 77, 81, 92, 102, 107

Swellengrebel, Governor 64, 65, 83

Swellengrebel, Hendrik 78, 85, 86

Taaibosch, Gert 192, 208

Table Bay 9, 10, 13–14, 19, 20, 21, 26, 32

Taiwan 489

Tambo, Oliver 247; ANC leader 425, 431, 454, 495; establishes London office 465; gentleness of 425, 466, 486; illness of 505; and Mandela 459; visits Vietnam 485

Tanzania 139, 459, 465

Tas, Adam 55–6

Tati 237, 280

Ten Rhyne, Dr William 46–7

Tennant, Margot 321

Terreblanche, Eugene 484, 489

Terreblanche, Prof. Sampie 495

Te Water, Dr Thomas 320

Thaba Nchu 164, 167–8, 209, 226, 299, 451

Thaele, Prof. James 402

Thatcher, Margaret 472, 480, 492

Thema, Selope 385, 386

Thembu xx, 71, 145, 186, 230; in Boer War 335; chiefs 377, 502–3; colonial cooperation 145, 188, 228; and Glen Grey Act 309; political activity 356–7; religion 357; and Xhosa wars 187, 195, 198, 259, 260

Thembuland 227, 256, 349, 503

Thesiger, Gen. Frederick 263–4, 265

Theumissen, Tryntje 48

Thirstland Treks 286, 312

Thlaping 236, 237, 239

Thomas, J.H. 435

Thorne, Robert 9

Thrush, HMS 351

Thunberg, Carl 85

Tile, Nehemiah 357

Times, The 181, 182, 197, 208, 266, 316, 319

Tlokwe tribe 164

Tobin, John 337

Tomlinson Commission 450

Tonga tribe 139

Tonjeni, Elliot 402

Torch Commando 432

Tordesillas, Treaty of 5

Tot Nut en Vermaak 97

Touré, Sékou 459

Touwfontein 186

trade xix, xxv, 1, 199; customs unions 305, 365; free trade zone 344; Hertzog and 401; tariffs 358 ; war 364

Trade, Board of (British) 117–18

Trades Union Congress (British) 345

trades unions: Afrikaners and 418; black 425; Cape 356; COSATU 446, 487; in diamond fields 291; Labour Party and 383; miners' 391; restrictions on 429, 490; South African 382, 383, 390, 393, 402–3, 404; 348, 355, 370, 423

Transkei 393, 449, 451; annexation 294; as black homeland 230, 451; cattle-killing in 218; General Council 309; living conditions in 471; peoples of 74, 145, 435; Protectorate proposal 279; as reserve 230; self-government 371, 394, 449, 457

Transorangia, see Orange Free State

Transvaal 147; Afrikaners in 512; apartheid in 360; army 271, 323; black organizations 349; blacks of xxi, 73, 221, 222, 254, 255, 335, 345, 359–60, 367; Boer War 322, 325–6, 328, 330, 331, 339; Boers of 257–8, 269, 271–2, 361–2; boundaries 222, 237, 239, 240, 263, 279, 281–2, 300, 312; British and 256–7, 258, 267–71, 274, 312–13, 318–19, 325, 414; BSAC and 316; civil wars 224, 226, 227; and confederation proposal 254; constitution 209, 223, 224, 307, 342, 361; corruption in 304; as Crown Colony 331, 342, 346, 355, 359–61; and customs unions 305, 365; diamond fields claim 237; Dutch Church in 224; economy 226, 255, 257, 258, 347; education in 257, 343; elections 306, 361; European support 323; expansionism 279–81, 285, 310, 312; franchise 307–8, 328–30, 339–40, 359–61; goldfields 270, 291, 301–2, 343; government 304, 346, 359–61; Hollanders in 303–4; immigrant labour 345; importance of 365; independence 206, 268–71, 281; Indians 378, 423; Jameson Raid on 317–19, 320; London Convention 281, 313, 316, 327; martial law in 271; military spending 323; multi-racial 509–14; national bank 305–6; Nationalists in 375, 421, 428; opposition in 303, 306, 307; peace terms 339–40; political parties 347, 359; population 367; Presidents 176, 222–3, 224, 225, 226, 254–5, 300, 303–4, 306; Pretoria Convention 272–3, 279, 281, 300; railways 255, 257, 286, 304–5, 312, 316; reconstruction 342–3; Reformers 317; religious fundamentalism in 303; rioting 475; Royal Commission on 272; slave-raiding 238, 245; society 226, 303–4; as South African Republic 176, 226, 279, 281–2, 286, 300, 303, 304, 340; Swaziland dependency 351–2; taxation 360; trekker settlement 165; *uitlanders* 301, 307–8, 312–13, 316–17, 324, 328; and Union proposals 221, 224, 225, 254, 365, 367–8; Volksraad 268, 271, 273, 303, 307; wars 207, 241, 271, 274, 303

Transvaal Federation of Trades 382

Transvaal Indigency Committee 344

Transvaal Natives' Union 368

Transvaalsche Bank 306

Transvaler, Die 448, 484

Tregardt, Louis 147, 165, 167

Treurnicht, Andries 416, 474, 484, 501

Trollip, Alf 461, 464

Trollope, Anthony 257, 263, 295, 346, 500

Tromp, Admiral van 44

Truter, Sir John 105, 114, 132

Truter, Oloff 237, 239

Truth 313

Truth and Reconciliation Commission 514

Tshatsu, Dyani (Jan) 123, 161

Tsonga 71, 73, 139, 222, 241, 351

Tswana xx, xxi; assembly 70; Bastaards and 163; in Boer War 335; in British Protectorate 280, 284, 310, 314, 441; divisions in 284; and Griqua 236; newspaper 349; slavery practised by 75, 237, 283–4; society 73–4; territory xxv, 71, 240, 435

Tukela River 171, 174, 176, 192, 264, 331

Tulbagh 100

Tulbagh, Ryk 65–6, 78, 83

Turkey 2

Turner, Bishop Henry 357

Turner, Captain Sidney 260

Turok, Benjamin 446

Tutu, Archbishop Desmond 439, 462, 474, 514

Tyumi River 220

Uitenhage 100, 101, 106, 113, 122, 128, 149, 201

Ulundi 265

Umhala, Nathaniel 260–1

Umtata 394

Umteteli wa bantu 395

Union, Act of (1910) 373, 397, 416, 434–6, 444, 456, 509

Union Native Council 397

Unionist Party of South Africa 373, 388–9, 395, 477

UNITA 468, 486, 493

United Democratic Front (UDF) 473, 487, 494, 496, 505

United Front 392

United Nations xxvii; condemnation of South Africa 423, 455–6, 466, 476; former colonies in 433; Human Development Index 489; sanctions 492,

United Nations – *cont.*
   499; South African attitude towards 457,
   488; and South-West Africa/Namibia
   422, 467–8, 493; support for South
   Africa in 423, 466
United Party 427; defections 419; election
   results 422, 428, 461, 464; factions in
   434; formed 407; opposes Nationalists
   408, 444–5, 446, 447; racism in 418
United States xxvii, 159, 190, 200; and
   Angolan War 468–9; Anti-Apartheid
   Act 491–2; Civil War 322, 334;
   colonialism 179, 289; missionaries 111,
   175; relations with Britain 319, 326;
   relations with South Africa 454, 466–7,
   468–9, 480, 502; religious influences 357
Unlawful Organizations Act 456, 458
Unwin, Jane 377
Upington, Thomas 289, 305
Upingtonia, Republic of 286
Urban Areas Act 491
Usuthu 279
Utrecht, Republic of 147, 210, 224
Utrecht, Treaty of 56, 62
Uys, Fanie 147
Uys, Piet 169, 170, 172

Vaal River 163, 167, 176, 193, 206, 222, 235,
   316
Valentyn, François 61
Van de Graaff, Cornelius 87
Van den Bergh, Gen. Hendrick 478
Van der Bergh, Marikye 48, 49
Van der Bijl, Dr H.J. 421, 428
Van der Bronke (Broecke), Commissioner
   43
Van der Capellen, Johan 84, 87
Van der Hoff, Dirk 224
Van der Kemp, Dr Theodorus 112, 113, 115,
   135, 446
Van der Merwe, Gen. 490
Van der Plank, Johannes 210
Van der Post, Laurens 17
Van der Stel, Frans 55
Van der Stel, Simon 21, 50–5, 63, 133
Van der Stel, Willem 51, 55–6
Vansittart, Nicholas 117, 126
Venda 73–4, 222, 254, 260, 451
Verburg, Nicolas 50
Vereeniging Estates 343, 346, 376
Vereeniging Treaty 339–41, 347, 348, 361,
   374, 456

Vergelegen 55, 56
Versailles Peace Conference 386, 387–8,
   508
Verwoerd, Dr Hendrik: as Afrikaner 417,
   455; and apartheid 448–9, 462, 464;
   assassination of 464; background 448;
   and Bantu Education Bill 446; and
   English-speakers 461; Minister for
   Native Affairs 446, 448; as Prime
   Minister 448, 452, 461, 464
Victoria (Australia) 191, 195, 202, 237, 243,
   244, 314
Victoria, Queen 250, 265–6, 272, 286,
   319–20, 326, 349
Viervot, battle of 208
Viljoen, Gen. 512
Viljoen, Jan 226
Vissering-Kemmerer Committee 405
Vlok, Adrian 506
Vogelaer, Volunteer 27
Volkskas 411
voortrekkers, see Great Trek
Voortrekkerhoogte 417
Vorster, Balthazar Johannes 474; and
   African governments 470; and Buthelezi
   473; background of 464–5; and Namibia
   467–9; opposition to 471; as Prime
   Minister 464; resignation 479; as State
   President 478–9
Vos, Ds M.C. 110
Vryburg 280

Wagenaar, Zacharias 39, 40, 42–3
Wahlberg, Johan 174, 178
Waldheim, Dr Kurt 467
Walvis Bay 256, 282
Wanckochuuse, Ytchio 49
War Office (British) 282, 328, 330, 354
Ward, Edward 334
Warden, Major 186, 193, 194, 208, 231
Waring, Alf 461, 464
Warner, Joseph 503
Warren, Gen. Sir Charles 285, 308
Washington, Booker T. 357
Waterboer, Andries 163
Waterboer, Capt. Nicholas 236, 238–9
Wavell, Lord 422
Waveren, Land of 63
Wearing, J. 199
Weenen 172, 177, 178, 183
Weizmann, Chaim 389
Wellesley, Lord 91

Welsh, David 488
Wen Kommando 173
Wepener, Louis 236
Wernher, Julius 324, 328
Wernher Beit 306, 383
Wesley, John 110
Wessels, Cornelius 366
West, Martin 213
West India Company 24
West Indies 116, 149
West-Ridgeway Committee 361
Western Cape 15, 202–3, 227, 229, 367, 513
Westminster, Duke of 293
Westminster, Statute of 407
White Liberation Movement (Blanke Bevrydigings Beweging) 484
whites xx, xxii; emigration 448, 512; labour 382; law and 294, 404; liberals 432, 475–6, 488; numbers 134, 366–7; opponents of apartheid 462; poor 291, 346, 359–60, 401–2, 411, 417; and precedence of settlement 68; relations with natives 18–19; and slavery 35; supremacy (*baaskap*) xx, xxvi–xxvii, 65, 110, 115, 206, 215, 235, 355, 382, 396–7, 404, 412, 434, 444, 470, 491, 501; white state proposal 481
Wiehahn, Prof. N.E. 490
Wijk, Field-Cornet van 122
Wilhelm, Kaiser 318–19, 362
William III, King 50, 88, 89, 90, 170
Williams, Joseph 123
Williams, Ruth 440
Wilson, Monica 293
Winburg, Republic of 147, 176, 184, 192, 193
Windham, William 120, 132
Witwatersrand 301, 325, 505; University 413
Wodehouse, Sir Philip 229–30, 232, 234, 243
Woeke, Martinus 81
Wolseley, Gen. Sir Garnet 251–2, 265–6, 269, 270, 275, 277, 331–2, 342, 351
Women's Defence of the Constitution League 452
Wood, Gen. Sir Evelyn 265, 272
Working Men's Association 291
World Council of Churches 473
World War I 379, 383–4, 387, 390

World War II 419–21, 432, 437
Worrall, Dr Denis 481, 482, 495
Wyk, Chris van 495
Wyk Louw, N.P. van 471
Wylant, Willem 27
Wyndham, George 323

Xesibe 350
Xhosa xx–xxi, xxiii, 69, 71, 75–6, 78, 230, 350; as ANC leadership 473, 488; assimilation proposals 216–17, 219, 220; Batavian administration and 101–2; and British 79, 93–4, 96, 105, 118–19, 123–5, 129, 157–8, 187, 189, 191, 221; cattle-killing xx, xxi, 218–19, 220–1, 228, 261–2; charismatic prophets 125; Ciskeian 227, 230; civil war 124; co-existence 94–5, 119; diplomatic approaches 123–4; divisions 79, 81, 219, 260; end to resistance 260; extermination of 119, 123, 160, 219, 350; and Great Trek 162; and Khoikhoi 74, 79, 124, 152; and *mfecane* 144; missions to 112; myths 261–2; of Natal 249; political activity 356; relations with whites 76, 78–83, 106, 156, 228; retreat to traditional areas 292; in South Africa 417; subordination of 189; of Suurveld 78, 80, 94, 102, 105, 106, 119; territories 154–5, 435; treaties 161, 186, 189; uprising 96; wars 153, 157–8, 187–8, 190, 191, 195–6, 198, 259, 260–2, 274, 503; and witchcraft 72–3, 217, 218
Xhosaland 187
Xuma, Dr Alfred 382, 408, 422, 423, 431, 432

Yonge, Sir George 96
Young, Brigham 148
Yupar, Dr 460
Yussuf, Sheikh 49

Zaire 468
Zambia xx, 455, 457, 465, 468, 469, 470, 492
Zanzibar xxiv, 4
ZAPU 466, 487
Zibhebhu 265, 267, 279–80, 352
Zietsman, Paulus 150, 210
Zimbabwe 33, 140, 350, 486–7, 492, 496, 514
Zonnenbloem 228, 261

Zoutpansberg 167, 185, 222, 224, 226

Zuid-Afrikaan 177, 202

Zulu xx, xxiii, 153, 252, 257; assimilation in 74; black homeland of 451; in Boer War 335; divisions 267; Inkatha 472–3, 488, 505; and mfecane 136, 141–5; myths 146, 261; of Natal 71, 210, 248–9, 354; national pride 354; organizations 348, 411; royal house 266, 410–11, 442; Shaka 137–9; in South Africa 410, 417; and trekkers 165, 169–74, 176; wars 212, 262–6, 269, 270, 274

Zululand 164, 227, 277; Boer republics in 169, 173, 174, 179, 210; British and 264, 266, 286, 352; dismemberment of 279, 282, 292; and mfecane 141–4; Natal and 352; Native Reserve 267

Zwangendaba 139

Zwartberge 66–7, 106

Zwide, Chief 137, 140, 144

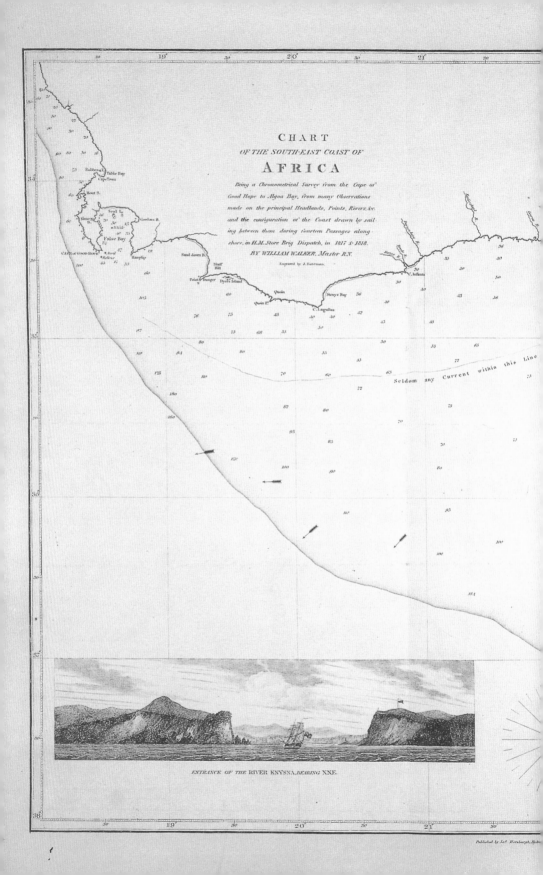

CHART

OF THE SOUTH-EAST COAST OF

AFRICA

Being a Chronometrical Survey from the Cape of
Good Hope to Algoa Bay, from many Observations
made on the principal Headlands, Points, Rivers &c.
and the configuration of the Coast drawn by sail-
ing between them during fourteen Passages along
shore, in H.M. Store Brig Dispatch, in 1817 & 1818.
BY WILLIAM WALKER, Master R.N.

Engraved by J. Bateman.

Seldom any Current within this Line

ENTRANCE OF THE RIVER KNYSNA, BEARING NNE.

Published by Jas. Horsburgh, Hydr.